Tumultuous Times

Tumultuous Times

The Twenty General Councils
of the Catholic Church

and

Vatican II
and
its Aftermath

Fr. Francisco Radecki, CMRI   Fr. Dominic Radecki, CMRI

© 2004 Fr. Francisco Radecki, CMRI

Fr. Dominic Radecki, CMRI

All rights reserved. No part of this book may be used or reproduced or transmitted in any form or by any means, electronic or mechanical, including photocopying, recording or by any information storage or retrieval system, without permission in writing from the authors.

ISBN Number: 0-9715061-0-8

Library of Congress Control Number:
2001 135934

Manufactured in the United States of America.

St. Joseph's Media

P. O. Box 186	P.O. Box 220208
Wayne, Michigan	Newhall, California
48184-0186	91322

Dedicated to
the Sacred Heart of Jesus
and
the Immaculate Heart of Mary

Acknowledgements

We would like to extend special thanks to Bishop Mark Pivarunas, CMRI for his advice and encouragement; Andrew Grimm for his editorial assistance; Barbara Hopkins for her drawings for the front cover and the introduction to Part II; the twins Amanda and Michelle Diehl for their map illustrations, charts and lighthouse drawing; Paula Storm for her assistance in typing and her efforts in locating reference books from around the world for use in this work; Antonio Perrino for his assistance in finding additional books and periodicals. Finally, we express our sincere gratitude to the many others who have assisted in a variety of ways.

Contents

Preface   p. xi

Introduction   p. xiii

Part I Twenty General Councils of the Church

Section I—Eight Councils of the East

Chapter 1   First Council of Nicaea   p. 3

Chapter 2   First Council of Constantinople   p. 13

Chapter 3   Council of Ephesus   p. 31

Chapter 4   Council of Chalcedon   p. 39

Chapter 5   Second Council of Constantinople   p. 47

Chapter 6   Third Council of Constantinople   p. 57

Chapter 7   Second Council of Nicaea   p. 67

Chapter 8   Fourth Council of Constantinople   p. 75

Section II—Twelve Councils of the West

Chapter 9	First Lateran Council	p. 85
Chapter 10	Second Lateran Council	p. 93
Chapter 11	Third Lateran Council	p. 99
Chapter 12	Fourth Lateran Council	p. 105
Chapter 13	First Council of Lyons	p. 117
Chapter 14	Second Council of Lyons	p. 123
Chapter 15	Council of Vienne	p. 127
Chapter 16	Council of Constance	p. 139
Chapter 17	Council of Florence	p. 161
Chapter 18	Fifth Lateran Council	p. 177
Chapter 19	Council of Trent	p. 185
Chapter 20	Vatican Council	p. 229

Part II   Vatican II and its Aftermath

Commentary on the Present Crisis in the Church   p. 282

A. The History and Origin of Vatican II   p. 283

B. The Heresies of Vatican II   p. 343

C. The Tridentine Latin Mass and the New Mass   p. 373

D. The Seven Sacraments and the New Sacraments   p. 423

E. Statistics   p. 481

F. The Third Secret of Fatima   p. 501

G. The Rosary   p. 507

H. How Could This Have Happened?   p. 511

I. Who is Ultimately Responsible?   p. 529

J. Conclusion   p. 569

K. Plan of Action   p. 575

Appendix   p. 579

Bibliography   p. 597

Index   p. 643

Preface

Jesus Christ founded the Catholic Church for the salvation of souls and to faithfully preserve and teach His doctrine to the world until the end of time. To keep these doctrines unchanged and free from error "Our Lord Jesus Christ entrusted the Deposit of Faith to the Church, that under the constant guidance of the Holy Ghost, She might sacredly guard and faithfully explain this divine revelation."[1] The Holy Ghost accomplishes this miracle through the infallible teaching authority of the Church. In this way, Christ has protected the Church's sacred teachings from distortions, erroneous interpretations and blatant heresies promulgated by fallible men throughout the centuries.

The Deposit of Faith is the very foundation of the Catholic Church itself as established by Jesus Christ. It is composed of two immutable elements: Sacred Scripture and Tradition. The *Baltimore Catechism* defines Sacred Scripture (the Bible) as "...the word of God written by men under the inspiration of the Holy Ghost and contained in the books of the Old and the New Testament," and Tradition as "...the unwritten word of God—that body of truths revealed and handed down from Christ to the apostles, and not committed by them to writing, but handed down by word of mouth."[2]

Since God Himself is immutable, neither Scripture nor Tradition can ever be altered to satisfy the fickleness, mores or philosophies of a contemporary world. God's Church can never propose nor initiate new doctrines for our belief since Divine Revelation ended with the death of the last apostle, St. John the Evangelist (c. 100 AD). However, because the customs and philosophies of cultures are always changing and developing, and because of attacks on the Faith, Holy Mother Church has found it necessary to elucidate and expound elements of the Deposit of Faith. Christ's original teachings were defended and more clearly set forth by means of the General Councils of the Church. Doctrines that were previously believed were better understood when bishops from various countries assembled together in council to explain them in greater detail.

---

[1] *Codex Juris Canonici,* Canon 1322.
[2] No. 3, Fr. Francis Connell, C.SS.R., p. 16.

It is the purpose of Part I of this book to show how attacks on the doctrines of the Catholic Faith, whether promulgated by heretics or intentionally proposed in order to destroy the Church, have been overcome through these councils.

The history of the General Councils of the Church vividly portrays how God draws good out of evil. Whenever heretics or other enemies of the Church attempted to alter Catholic teaching, the popes and bishops used the opportunity to expound and clarify Her teachings, thus instilling them deeper into the hearts of the faithful. Every time an attack was made on the Catholic Faith, God raised up champions to defend it. St. Augustine (354-430 AD), a great Father and Doctor of the Church, wrote:

> For while the hot restlessness of heretics stirs questions about many articles of the Catholic Faith, the necessity of defending them forces us both to investigate them more accurately, to understand them more clearly, and to proclaim them more earnestly; and the question mooted by an adversary becomes the occasion of instruction.[3]

By perusing the pages of Part I of this book the reader will discover many interesting facts about the history of the Catholic Church as seen through its 20 General Councils. One will also see how the storms which the Church has survived in the past parallel those of the present day.

Many Catholics are perplexed today as they witness the widespread confusion, dissention and division current in the Church throughout the world. Part II will explore Vatican II and its aftermath. We are indeed living in tumultuous times.

It is the desire of the authors that Catholics gain new hope and a deeper faith as they discover how God's providential care has brought His Church through such turbulent times in the past. In addition, they will realize that the Catholic Church has survived and will continue to survive regardless of its assailants.

---

[3] *The City of God*, p. 16, 2.

Introduction

This book is a concise summary of the history of the General Councils of the Catholic Church with a special section dedicated to the Second Vatican Council. It is divided in the following way:

>Part I—The 20 General Councils of the Catholic Church
>>Section I—Eight General Councils of the East
>>Section II—Twelve General Councils of the West
>
>Part II—Vatican II and its Aftermath

Since it would have been a monumental task to cover every detail of these councils, we have limited ourselves to only the main events and persons behind each council. Our purpose is to call attention to the fact that the Church has gone through difficult times in the past and should expect to experience similar trials in the future.

The 20 General Councils of the Catholic Church

There have been 20 General Councils of the Church. Eastern Emperors convoked the first eight General Councils of the East because from the Fall of Rome in 476 until 800 AD there was no other Roman emperor except the one reigning in Constantinople.[4] Popes convoked the 12 General Councils of the West. In order to be legitimate, general councils must receive papal approbation of their acts, decrees and canons which treat of Catholic doctrine, ecclesiastical discipline and legislation. This guarantees their freedom from error in matters of faith and morals.

A pope does not have to approve all the acts, decrees and canons of a council. At times popes have rejected certain aspects of a council, although the council itself and its general work were not invalidated by this action as at the First Council of Constantinople and the Council of Constance.

> The Western Church recognizes 20 councils as ecumenical, but the acceptance of certain councils as ecumenical was a matter of dispute as late as the Council of Trent [1545-1563]. Cardinal [St.] Robert Bellarmine (1542-1621), who had made special investigations in the history of the councils, was the first to introduce the

---

[4] See Lynn Thorndike, *History of Medieval Europe*, p. 86.

enumeration of the ecumenical councils that has come to be regarded as traditional. The twenty ecumenical councils span nearly sixteen centuries in the history of the Church [325-1870 AD]. They thus reflect the conditions and problems of widely different periods in the life of the Church and in the world in which She carries out Her divine mission.[5]

Plenary councils include bishops from one country. Local councils or synods are comprised of bishops from one region. A general or ecumenical council derives its name from the Greek word, οικουμενε, which translates as, "the entire inhabited world." Catholic bishops from around the globe come together either to clarify existing doctrines of the Church or to condemn heresy.

> Ecumenical councils are extremely useful because, (a) in an ecumenical council, where there are gathered together the lights of the entire Church, there are abundant means for investigating the tradition and mind of the Church and for laying down the disciplinary laws best suited to meet the necessities of the times; (b) the splendor of authority, native to the decrees of an ecumenical council, does a great deal to incline men to obey more easily; (c) decrees of reform, laid down in an ecumenical council are more smoothly and efficaciously put into practice; for it is quite natural that the bishops should with greater zeal urge the fulfillment of those decrees in whose formulation they themselves had a hand.[6]

The General Councils of the Church cannot establish or introduce new teachings. In the year 1871, Fr. Delaporte wrote:

> The twelve Apostles ...and their countless successors, proclaimed everywhere the same creed, and so the testimony of one is strengthened and confirmed by the testimony of all the others. When a priest today teaches Catholic truth two hundred and fifty-nine popes, ninety thousand bishops, millions of priests, doctors, martyrs, saints, the learned, myriads of faithful, the noblest portion of mankind, the most enlightened and virtuous for over eighteen hundred years, in one magnificent concert, teach with him. The distinctive sign of truth shines forth, *Unity!*[7]

---

[5] Msgr. William McDonald, *General Councils*, p. 36.
[6] Msgr. G. Van Noort, *Christ's Church, Vol. II*, p. 337.
[7] *The Devil*, pp. 88-89.

What is truly "Catholic"?

Catholics of today must realize it is an erroneous notion to believe that the Church has survived in relative peace throughout Her history. In fact, it is difficult to find a single, 25-year period during which the Church was at peace. This should make us stand in awe of the fact that God has guarded the Church from dangers throughout Her history and has preserved Her doctrinal integrity in spite of numerous and various attacks both from within and without.

Our modern age witnesses a variety of religious groups, each claiming that it has possession of spiritual truth. The fallacy of the claim of each can be easily seen by Catholics who securely believe that the Catholic Church is the true Church, since it alone traces its foundation directly to Christ.

In the first century AD, this Church was christened with the name "Catholic"[8] by St. Ignatius, bishop of Antioch (d. 107 AD), who declared, "Where Jesus Christ is, there is the Catholic Church."[9] However, since the Church has never been free from the attacks of Satan, who seeks to corrupt what is good and true in order to destroy it, even Her very name has been used to cause confusion and contention.

Truth is absolute. A church is either Catholic or not, though at times it is not easy to distinguish between the two. Many modern Catholics think that if a group calls itself Catholic and in part "looks" somewhat Catholic, it must be a part of the Catholic Church. But what if clerics claim to be Catholic while yet promoting tainted doctrine? Is this possible? Wasn't the Catholic Church promised freedom from error in matters of faith and morals?

The Church indeed has been promised freedom from error in matters of faith and morals, but it has not been promised freedom from struggle and attack. In the very beginning of the Christian Era, even within the lifetime of the Apostles, erroneous teachings were promoted by heretical priests and bishops. These clerics claimed to hold the true message of Christ, while in fact they were heretics.

It is easy for us, in retrospect, to identify the heresies of those early days, but for the Christians living during that time it was much more confusing. Many

---

[8] From the Greek: catholicos (καθολικos) *universal*.
[9] *Ad Smyrnaeos* ch. 8, 2.

pastors worthily bore the sacred trust of leading Christ's flock and preserving His teachings intact, while usurpers taught their corrupt doctrines and led many astray. It was sometimes difficult to identify wolves disguised in sheep's clothing, for all claimed to belong to Christ's true Church. Those who remained Catholic followed the Faith as it had been preserved through the centuries. Sadly though, many of those who were deceived by heretical clergy never realized that through the course of time they gradually adopted beliefs and practices that could eventually lead them outside the Catholic Church.

History indeed repeats itself. As we view modern times in the light of the past history of the Church, we can easily recognize that error and heresy can be taught in the name of Catholicism and by "Catholic" clergy just as easily as in the name of a false god or non-Catholic religion. If Satan was not content to let Catholic clergy preach incorrupt truth in the early ages of the Church, why should we think he would be any less active today?

As you read through this book, ask yourself if there are any parallels between the heresies and false councils of the past, and the heresies and false teachings of today. Previous heresies at the time that they were taught were not labeled as "Arianism," "Lutheranism" or "Protestantism," but were preached as Christ's truth. So too, the heresies that we witness today are enveloping the world in the same way. Multitudes are being led astray as in days of old.

Heresy

Heresy is the denial of one or more teachings of the Catholic Church. Two examples from the past are the Arian heresy and the Nestorian heresy, both of which denied fundamental doctrines of the Church. St. Isidore (d. 636 AD) wrote:

> Therefore, heresy is so-called from the Greek word [αιρεσισ] meaning choice, by which each chooses according to his own will what he pleases to teach or believe. But we are not permitted to believe whatever we choose, nor to choose whatever someone else has believed. We have the apostles of God as authorities, who did not themselves of their own will choose what they would believe, but faithfully transmitted to the nations the teaching received from Christ. So, even if an angel from heaven should preach otherwise, he shall be called anathema.[10]

---

[10] *Etymologies,* 8, 3.

In his book *The Great Heresies,* Hilaire Belloc stripped off the mask of heresy when he wrote, "It is of the essence of heresy that it leaves standing a great part of the structure it attacks. On this account it can appeal to believers and continue to affect their lives."

By the same token, a heretic is "One who after baptism, while remaining nominally a Christian, *pertinaciously* (that is, with conscious and intentional resistance to the authority of God and the Church) denies or doubts any one of the truths which must be believed *de fide divina et catholica* [of divine and Catholic faith]."[11] "A doctrine is *de fide divina et catholica* only when it has been *infallibly declared by the Church to be revealed by God.*"[12]

"If a Christian were unconsciously to hold an error, he would be what is called a *material heretic;* if he were conscious of his error, and still persisted in it, he would be a *formal heretic.* Formal heresy incurs the penalty of excommunication."[13]

Pope Leo XIII[14] wrote in the Encyclical *Satis Cognitum,* "There can be nothing more dangerous than those heretics who admit nearly the whole series of doctrine, and yet by one word, as with a drop of poison, taint the real and simple Faith taught by Our Lord and handed down by Apostolic Tradition."[15]

It is difficult to comprehend how heretics have been, and still can be, so convincing and persuasive in their arguments that they hold great sway, not only over the laity, but even over the clergy. One only needs to remember that Lucifer is the teacher of all heretics and therefore they bear a close resemblance to him. Being proud and arrogant, heretics claim to be more enlightened than others. They haughtily attempt to "improve" the Church by making doctrinal changes.

The devil has also deceived millions by the feigned or apparent "holiness" of heretics. Arius was an ascetic priest, Nestorius a bishop and Eutyches an aged abbot. It was not an easy matter for the faithful to identify them as wolves in sheep's clothing, for they all claimed to belong to the true Church.

---

[11] *Codex Juris Canonici,* Canon 1325, 2.
[12] T. Bouscaren, S.J., Adam Ellis, S.J., *Canon Law: A Text and Commentary,* p. 677.
[13] Fr. John Laux, *Catholic Morality,* p. 56.
[14] June 29, 1896.
[15] Auctor Tract. de Fide Orthodoxa contra Arianos.

Apostasy

Bishop Louis Morrow defines apostasy as "...the total rejection of his Faith by a baptized Christian."[16] This denial of most of the teachings of the Catholic Church usually takes place slowly (a step at a time) through doctrinal deviations and liturgical aberrations. Large numbers of Catholics are unwittingly led into apostasy by heretical priests and bishops who use their parish churches to promulgate erroneous teachings. People who continue to attend what they think are "Catholic Churches" (though in reality they are non-Catholic) are insidiously indoctrinated into a false religion and gradually lose their faith.

This was demonstrated by the fact that followers of Luther were not called Lutherans until many years later. Such former Catholics became apostates and lost their faith because they attended "Catholic" churches run by Lutheran clergy. Other counterfeit churches directed by Cranmer and Calvin led multitudes of Catholics into apostasy (loss of faith) in the same way. Some well-known apostates were Julian the Apostate, Queen Elizabeth I of England and Martin Luther.

St. Paul (d. 65 AD) warned the faithful of a Great Apostasy to come in which many would be led astray by deception and false teaching. In his Second Epistle to the Thessalonians he wrote: "Let no one deceive you in any way, for the day of the Lord [Second Coming of Christ] will not come unless the apostasy come first." (II Thes. 2: 3, 10-12)

Schism

The third category of separation from the Catholic Church is called schism. It is derived from the Greek word σχισμα meaning *division*. The Greek Schism which occurred in the year 1054 and the Western Schism of 1378-1417 are prime examples. The Code of Canon Law defines a schismatic as a baptized person who "rejects the authority of the Supreme Pontiff or refuses communion with members of the Church who are subject to him."[17]

---

[16] *My Catholic Faith*, p. 152.
[17] Canon 1325, 2.

The Papacy

The decrees and canons of a General Council of the Church do not possess infallibility of themselves but must be ratified and approved by the reigning pope or one of his successors.

> Therefore, if the Supreme Pontiff, without holding a General Council of bishops, defines a doctrine of faith or morals to be held by the Church, he is infallible in so doing. If he summons such a council and confirms its decisions in doctrinal matters, such action of his is likewise infallible. And if he convokes a synod or council of part of the bishops, and afterwards extends its decrees to the whole Church, these decrees are then a part of the Christian faith, and the Pope is infallible in promulgating them.[18]

Occasionally during the course of Church history, such as during the Western Schism and during the reign of several antipopes, Catholics have been faced with the dilemma of a doubtful pope. During these turbulent periods, many of the Catholic faithful had serious doubts as to the identity of the true pope. By remaining faithful to the Holy Sacrifice of the Mass, the Seven Sacraments and the infallible teachings of the Church, Catholics were able to weather these storms and preserve their faith. Fr. Francis Doyle, S.J. elucidates this matter:

> The Church is a visible society with a visible Ruler. If there can be any doubt about who that visible Ruler is, he is not visible, and hence, where there is any doubt about whether a person has been legitimately elected Pope, that doubt must be removed before he can become the visible head of Christ's Church. Blessed [St. Robert] Bellarmine, S.J., says: 'A doubtful Pope must be considered as no Pope'; and Suarez, S.J., says: 'At the time of the Council of Constance there were three men claiming to be Pope. ...Hence, it could have been that not one of them was the true Pope, and in that case, there was no Pope at all, because not one of them had been accepted by the sufficient consent of the Church.'[19]

Fr. Doyle further states that there are four ways in which the Supreme Pontiff can lose the papacy: "1. By voluntary resignation, as in the case of (St.) Celestine V (1210-1296); 2. By open heresy, by which he ceases to be a member of Christ's

---

[18] Fr. John Sullivan, *Fundamentals of Catholic Belief*, pp. 123-124.
[19] *Defense of the Catholic Church*, p. 259.

Church, (this, however, while not contradictory to reason, is hardly conceivable); 3. By insanity. 4. By death."[20]

Edmund Campion, a martyr for the Catholic Faith during the Reformation, writes "As, therefore, when converted, Peter confirmed the Apostles his brethren, the Pontiffs also must confirm their brethren, the rest of the Bishops. Under his guidance they cannot err from the right path of the faith."[21]

Antipopes

Throughout the history of the Catholic Church there have been a total of 41 illegitimate popes, or *antipopes*. Several of these men actually marched into Rome with mighty monarchs and forcibly seized the Chair of St. Peter. Other antipopes were more insidious; they were fraudulently elected, adding further to the confusion of the time.

These men were either impostors or were uncanonically elected, making them illegitimate successors of St. Peter. At some periods of history, it was difficult to ascertain who was the true pope.

Not all antipopes died as schismatics. Several resigned their feigned office and became reconciled with the legitimate popes. Hippolytus, who was the first antipope, is now a canonized saint. He unwittingly became involved in the schism of Novatus, but once he realized his mistake, he repented, united himself to the true pope and died as a martyr of the Church. Another antipope named John XXIII (1411-1414) was a former pirate who poisoned his predecessor. However, he too was reconciled with the Church before his death.

Heretical Councils

What designates the differences between legitimate and illegitimate general councils? Just as there have been illegitimate popes throughout the history of the Church, there have also been a number of councils declared illegitimate because they deviated from Church teaching.

If the canons or the acts (teachings) of a council are contrary to the Deposit of Faith, as at the Latrocinium of Ephesus, the council is declared invalid and the

---

[20] *Defense of the Catholic Church*, p. 260.
[21] *Confutatio responsionis G. Whitakeri*, p. 44, Parisus 1582.

proceedings null and void. If a council acts on its own authority, as did the Council of Pisa when it elected another pope, the council is likewise declared invalid and the proceedings are declared null and void. Such councils are called pseudo-councils, from the Greek word ψευδες meaning *false*. Many of these spurious councils were even held within the same time period as legitimate ones.

Council Procedures

The General Councils of the Church followed procedures that closely paralleled those used at Roman Civil Hearings. As in the Roman Senate, each general council had a stenographer recording the minutes and acts. The president of the assembly, who was chosen by the pope or emperor, oversaw the workings of the council.

The Council Fathers consisted of major religious superiors, bishops, archbishops, patriarchs and cardinals who spoke in order of precedence on the topics that were to be discussed. The open discussions of the bishops along with the work of the committees were codified into ecclesiastical laws called *canons*.

Each general council took its rightful place in history and fulfilled a specific need of the time. God's grace was clearly evident at each council as His work proceeded in spite of personal temperament, diversity of language and turbulent world conditions. Through the work of the general councils heresies were vanquished, schisms were healed, Catholic doctrines were clarified and Church discipline was codified.

Theology was shown to be an exact science with no room for doctrinal alteration. The proper choice of words and their precise meanings are always of utmost importance when communicating truth, as the history of error and heresy clearly demonstrate.

God preserved His Church throughout these tumultuous times, raising up great saints to fulfill monumental tasks. God's champions took the field when and where champions were needed. Catholics should take courage from these valiant soldiers of Christ of past ages and follow their example realizing that the Church has weathered stormy seas before, even when all seemed lost. God has never abandoned the Church during its tumultuous past—so too, He will not abandon it today.

May this work give Catholics new hope so they will renew their confidence in God and reflect upon the words of Christ resounding through the ages, "...behold, I am with you all days, even unto the consummation of the world." (Matthew 28: 20)

Part I

Twenty General Councils of the Catholic Church

Eight General Councils of the East

(In Anno Domini 325-870)

The Eight General Councils of the East were convoked by Eastern Roman Emperors, addressed dogmatic topics and condemned contemporary heresies. Almost all the attendees were bishops from the East. The Eastern General Councils were held in cities located in Turkey:

> Chalcedon (Kadiköy)
>
> Constantinople (Istanbul)
>
> Ephesus
>
> Nicaea (Isnik)

The history of the 20 General Councils of the Catholic Church vividly portrays the ceaseless conflict between good and evil, between the City of God and the Kingdom of this World: the ultimate conflict between God and Satan. God has guided and protected His Church through tumultuous times and will continue to do so until the end of time.

Section I

Eight General Councils of the East

First Council of Nicaea	325 AD
First Council of Constantinople	381 AD
Council of Ephesus	431 AD
Council of Chalcedon	451 AD
Second Council of Constantinople	553 AD
Third Council of Constantinople	680-681 AD
Second Council of Nicaea	787 AD
Fourth Council of Constantinople	869-870 AD

CHAPTER ONE

First Council of Nicaea

325 AD

This council was held during the pontificate of Pope St. Sylvester I.

Background of the Roman Empire

Under the Emperor Trajan (98-117 AD) the Roman Empire had reached its greatest extent and by the time of his death, its legions controlled most of the known world. Roman territories rested on the three continents of Europe, Asia and Africa. By 285 AD its tremendous size made it a practical necessity to divide the empire into two major sections, the East and the West. The Eastern Empire centered in Byzantium (later called Constantinople), while the center of the Western Empire was Rome.

Terrible persecutions of the Church raged throughout the Roman Empire from 68 AD (the reign of the Emperor Nero) until the early fourth century. In his book, *The Victories of the Martyrs,* St. Alphonsus Liguori (1696-1787 AD) tells us that during those frightful years 11,000,000 men, women and children died for their faith. The first 31 popes were also martyred.

Emperor Constantine the Great

Emperor Constantius Chlorus was succeeded by his son Constantine the Great (306-337 AD). His opponent was the former Emperor Maximian's son Maxentius who ruled Italy and North Africa and had vastly superior forces. The night before the battle Constantine was given a vision by God in which he was promised victory if he would use the cross as his new standard. Maxentius had 170,000 foot soldiers compared with Constantine's 90,000 and fielded 17,000 cavalry compared with Constantine's 8,000. Yet by the power of the Cross Constantine put an end to the civil war and defeated Maxentius at the Battle of the Milvian Bridge outside Rome in 312 AD. Christian persecutions in the West finally ended with the Edict of Milan in February 313 AD.

The Eastern Roman Emperor Licinius resumed persecution of the Church in the East in 321 AD and threatened the security of the Western Empire. Constantine defeated Licinius who "...was first vanquished near Adrianople [Edirne, Turkey], where he left almost 34,000 dead upon the spot, in July, 324; and in a second battle near Chalcedon, in which, out of 130,000 men, scarce 3,000 escaped."[1]

Constantine's glorious victories brought apparent peace to the Church in the East. Yet this peace was of short duration. The Catholic Church was just emerging from the Roman catacombs, and misunderstanding, prejudice and skepticism still remained in the minds of many of the pagan Romans concerning Catholics and their beliefs.

A World Ripe for Arius

The church in Egypt was sadly divided in 306 AD when Bishop Meletius of Lycopolis, spurning the authority of Bishop Peter of Alexandria, consecrated his own set of bishops and formed a new church called the Church of the Martyrs. Later, a number of schismatic Meletians returned to the Catholic Church.

---

[1] Fr. Alban Butler, *Lives of the Saints, Vol. III,* p. 188.

One of the many followers of Meletius had been the charismatic deacon Arius (250-336 AD). Due to his participation in the Meletian schism, Arius was excommunicated in 310 AD by Bishop Peter of Alexandria but was later ordained by Bishop Achillas in 313 AD and given charge of an important and influential parish. (Excommunication denotes being cut off or formally separated from the Catholic Church.)

In 318 AD Arius denied the central doctrine of Catholicism, the Divinity of Christ, by claiming that Jesus Christ was like God, but was not really God. He thus fashioned a Jesus who would be acceptable to the non-Christian world. Millions were consequently led astray by this dynamic leader.

As Arius persisted in his heretical teachings regarding Christ, he was again excommunicated by 70 bishops from Egypt and Libya during a council convoked by St. Alexander in Alexandria in 320 AD.

Despite his censure and banishment, Arius continued his evil work. He traveled to Palestine and was later given asylum by Eusebius, a trusted advisor of Constantine and bishop of the former imperial capital Nicomedia (Izmit, Turkey). Many bishops from the region who patronized Arius held a synod of their own that condemned Bishop Alexander and exonerated Arius.

In 325 AD, a council was held in Antioch (Antakya, Syria) presided over by Hosius of Cordova where 59 bishops condemned the teachings of Arius. Later that year, 46 of these same bishops attended the First Council of Nicaea.

Even in these early years of the Church the clergy were divided: St. Alexander and faithful bishops opposed Arius, while Eusebius of Nicomedia and heretical bishops supported him. Tragically, the Arian heresy had succeeded in destroying the unity of the Christian East. There are parallels today as we see bishops, priests and laity remaining faithful to the Church while others viciously attack Her teachings. History indeed repeats itself.

The Arian Heresy

The Arian heresy caused one of the greatest rifts in the history of the Catholic Church. It attacked Her very foundation, thereby creating a Christianity devoid of Christ. The Catholic Church believes and teaches that Jesus Christ is the Second Person of the Blessed Trinity, True God and True Man. Belief in the doctrine of the Blessed Trinity is the keystone of the Catholic Faith that supports all other teachings. Fr. Ernest Simmons made the following powerful statement:

> The Arian heresy, which reduced the Second Person of the Blessed Trinity to the status of a demigod, would ultimately have destroyed not only the Trinity, but also the Incarnation and Redemption. Take away the God-Man, and all that lies between Bethlehem and Calvary becomes meaningless. The teaching of the Church is a house of stone where one floor rests upon another. Remove one and the whole house will tumble down.[2]

Belief in the Triune God (One God in Three Divine Persons: Father, Son and Holy Ghost) is the foundation of the Catholic Church. This doctrine is of such paramount importance that Cardinal Newman wrote in his book, *Causes of the Rise and Successes of Arianism*, "…it is impossible to view historical Christianity apart from the doctrine of the Trinity."

Deceiving the Masses

Why was Arius such a charismatic leader? The popularity of his message, the large crowds in attendance and the powerful ecclesiastical and secular leaders who sponsored Arius only added to his "credibility." He was able to teach his false doctrines with unparalleled success and his ideas spread like wildfire.

> His dress and demeanor were those of a rigid ascetic. He always wore a long coat with short sleeves, and a scarf of only half size, such as was the mark of an austere life; and his hair hung in a tangled mass over his head. There was a wild look about him, which at first sight was startling. He was usually silent, but at times broke out into fierce excitement, which gave the impression of madness. Yet with all this there was a sweetness in his voice and a winning, earnest manner which fascinated those who came across him. His reputation for sanctity, learning and eloquence, coupled with his skill in disputation, soon made him the center of religious thought and activity in the second church of Christendom [Alexandria].[3]

---

[2] *Fathers and Doctors of the Church*, p. 5.
[3] Fr. John Laux, *Church History*, pp. 106-107.

The Arian heresy was widely disseminated as excerpts of Arius' writings were set to music and sung in the marketplace, fields and docks. "During his stay in Nicomedia, Arius composed his principal work 'Thaleia' ('Banquet'), of which only fragments are still extant in the writings of St. Athanasius. It was written partly in prose and partly in poetry, and contained all the heretical views of Arius. Among his followers this book had the authority of the Bible."[4]

Working like destructive termites by attacking the Church from within, Arians were far more dangerous than previous heretics. Prior to this time, most heretics who left the Catholic Church founded new churches and separated themselves from Catholics. Unfortunately, the Arian bishops and priests did not physically "leave the Church." They did not build new churches of their own. Arius and the clergy who adopted his errors continued to preach and offer liturgical services in Catholic churches.

These churches were Catholic on the outside but heretical on the inside. Catholics who opposed Arius by remaining faithful to the teachings of the Church were the ones who had the Faith, even though Arians controlled many of the church buildings. "Two-thirds of all priests at that time were heretical, preaching versions of Arianism."[5] Only those who severed themselves completely from Arianism remained Catholic.

Throughout history various heretics have even feigned miracles to prove the veracity of their claims.

> God never permits wonders to be wrought in confirmation of what is not true. At the time when the Arian heresy prevailed, the Arian bishop of Carthage, Cyril, thought to deceive the inhabitants of Carthage, and by a wily stratagem make them believe that God worked miracles to prove the truth of the Arian tenets. He sent for a man who was a stranger in the town and gave him fifty pieces of gold, on condition that he should pretend to be blind, and after the lapse of an appointed time, should beg the Arian bishop to cure him. The man took the bribe, and did as he was desired. Openly upon the market place he solicited the bishop to work his cure. When a great crowd had collected, the bishop said in a

---

[4] Fr. Clement Raab, O.F.M., *Twenty Ecumenical Councils of the Catholic Church,* p. 4.
[5] *USA Today,* December 23, 1997, Comment by Fr. Michael Beers.

loud voice: 'To prove that we Arians hold the true faith, in the name of God I restore sight to this blind man.' He bade that man open his eyes, but alas! to his astonishment and confusion, he found the feigned blindness had become real, the man had actually lost his sight. The poor fellow began to lament bitterly, and told all the bystanders how he had been bribed, and for what end. It need scarcely be said that the bishop took his departure hastily. At a subsequent time the blind man's sight was restored by the prayer and imposition of hands of St. Eugenius, the Catholic bishop of Carthage.[6]

The First Council of Nicaea

Emperor Constantine convoked the first General Council of the Church at Nicaea in order to restore peace to the Church and put an end to the great religious and civil turmoil caused by the Arian heresy. He tried to be a peacemaker and did not interfere with the council proceedings. The First Council of Nicaea began on May 20 and ended nearly a month later on June 19, 325 AD.

The council was held in Nicaea because the emperor's summer residence was located there and its location on the sea made travel convenient for the Council Fathers who came from many nations. This was the first time in history that the majority of Eastern bishops had assembled together from various parts of the world for the purpose of defending and defining Catholic teaching. There were 250 bishops present at the first session of the council and 318 at the last. In addition, Eusebius of Nicomedia and 16 other bishops sided with Arius.

A famous historian of that era, Eusebius of Caesarea, wrote:

> From all the churches which are spread over Europe, Africa and Asia, the most renowned servants of God came together. ...One house of prayer received them all: Syrians and Cilicians, Phoenicians and Arabians, Palestinians and Egyptians, Thebans and Libyans as well as men from Mesopotamia. There also appeared at the Synod a Persian bishop, and a Scythian. ...Pontus and Galatia, Pamphilia and Cappadocia, Asia Minor and Phrygia had sent the flower of their episcopacy. Yea, Thracians also, and Macedonians, Achaeans and Epirotes, and such as lived much farther away still, were present. Even from Spain a world-renowned man (Hosius of Cordova) took his place with the multitude of the others in the assembly. The Supreme Bishop, however of the Imperial City [Pope Sylvester I]

---

[6] Fr. James Spirago, *Anecdotes and Examples,* pp. 107-108.

was prevented by the infirmities of old age from coming; but his priests appeared and represented him.[7]

As the Council Fathers entered the great hall the faithful were moved with compassion as they beheld what many of them had suffered for Christ.

> Many bore the glorious marks of the sufferings they had endured for Christ; others were wasted with long years of prison. There were the hermit bishops of Egypt, Paphnutius and Potamon, who had each lost an eye for the Faith; Paul of Neo-Caesaria, whose muscles had been burned with red hot irons and whose paralyzed hands bore witness to the fact; Cecilian of Carthage, intrepid and faithful guardian of his flock; James of Nisibis, who had lived for years in the desert in caves and mountains; Spyridion, the shepherd bishop of Cyprus, and the great St. Nicholas of Myra [Demre, Turkey], both famed for their miracles.
>
> Among the bishops of the West were Theophilus the Goth, golden haired and ruddy, who had won thousands to the faith; and Hosius the Spaniard, known as 'the holy,' who had been named by the Pope as his representative; together with the two Papal Legates, Vito and Vincent. Among those of the Eastern Church were the venerable St. Macarius, Bishop of Jerusalem, and St. Amphion, who had been put to torture in the reign of Diocletian.[8]

In stark contrast to these champions of Christ were the 17 bishops who sided with Arius. The terminology they adopted during the discussions was often ambiguous and filled with sophistry and equivocation. "The council raged for days. Legend has it that [St.] Nicholas became so angry during the debate that he let fly a roundhouse punch to the jaw of Arius."[9] "Such was St. Nicholas' infuriation with Arius, proponent of the Arian heresy, that it is said that he struck the apostate so severely that 'the bones in his body rattled.' "[10]

The Work of the Council

The heretic Arius, the Libyan bishops Secundus and Theonas and several priests remained obstinate. These ecclesiastics were exiled by order of the Emperor Constantine and Arius' writings were burned. Many believed that the

---

[7] *Life of Constantine* III, 7.
[8] F. Forbes, *St. Athanasius,* p. 19.
[9] *USA Today,* December 23, 1997.
[10] *National Catholic Register,* November 15, 1998.

matter was finally resolved and that peace would be restored. Sadly, this was not to be, for Arianism would resurrect at a later time.

There were a total of 20 canons enacted during the course of the council. Some of these ecclesiastical laws concerned the filling of vacant episcopal sees and the inquiry required in cases of excommunicated persons. Furthermore, the controversy regarding the date of Easter was settled. The Council Fathers also composed the Nicene Creed which definitively proclaims the Divinity of Christ.

Other laws stated:

- Remarriage was allowed after the death of a spouse.
- Converted heretics and apostates were to be received back into the Church after performing public penance and making a public act of faith.
- The ancient Canon Law regarding Holy Viaticum was "...still to be maintained, namely that those who are departing are not to be deprived of their last, most necessary Viaticum."[11]

The council even discussed the topic of indulgences:

> In the early centuries the canons imposed long and painful public penances on certain grievous transgressions. A canon of the General Council of Nicaea, in 325, had given to the bishops a discretionary power to remit the whole or part of those penances, when the penitent manifested special fervor. Other councils made similar enactments. During the Middle Ages the rigor of the ancient penitential system was greatly softened down: and the penances themselves were often commuted into alms or other pious works.[12]

The doxology (the prayer, "Glory be to the Father...") combated the Arian heresy by clearly and concisely manifesting the doctrine of the Blessed Trinity. The first part of the prayer had been composed by the Apostles, while the second part was composed at this First Council of Nicaea. The regional Council of Vaison of 529 AD instructed the clergy to add this doxology after each of the psalms of the Divine Office. The doxology is recited three times during the Holy Sacrifice of the Mass.

---

[11] Norman Tanner, S.J., *Decrees of the Ecumenical Councils, Vol. 1*, p. 12.
[12] Bishop M. Spalding, *History of the Protestant Reformation*, p. 114.

The First Council of Nicaea also condemned the Novatian and Donatist heresies. The Novatian heresy is named after its founder, the rigorist Roman priest Novatus who later became an antipope and reigned from Rome during the years 251-258 AD. Novatus taught that the Church could not absolve certain sins such as apostasy, idolatry, immorality and murder, and claimed that mortal sins committed after baptism could not be forgiven.

This was contrary to the Catholic Church's teaching that all confessed sins are forgiven if the penitent is truly sorry. In his work *De paenitentia* St. Ambrose wrote: "God, however, makes no distinction. He promised mercy to all, and granted to His priests the license of forgiving sins without exception."

The Donatist heresy was started by an African bishop named Donatus the Great who claimed that sinful ministers rendered a sacrament invalid. The Catholic Church teaches that an unworthy minister commits a sacrilege by administering a sacrament while in the state of mortal sin, but that the sacrament is still validly conferred.

Western bishops condemned the Donatist heresy 11 years earlier at the Council of Arles in 314 AD when they declared that the validity of sacraments did not depend on the virtue of the minister (priest or bishop) who conferred them. In the same year, the Eastern bishops assembled at Ancyra (Angora) and condemned the Donatist teaching that certain sins could not be forgiven.

Nearly 100 years later the Donatists were still very powerful in the East. In the year 411 AD, 286 Catholic bishops, including St. Augustine (354-430 AD) and St. Aurelius of Carthage, met with 279 Donatist bishops. "Several Donatist communities with their priests and bishops returned to the Church. Many, however, remained obstinate, and the schism maintained itself in some parts of Northern Africa, until the invasion of that country by the Saracens, when the Donatists disappeared altogether."[13]

---

[13] Bishop M. Spalding, *History of the Protestant Reformation*, pp. 222-223.

Pope St. Sylvester I did not personally attend the proceedings of the council due to his advanced age. However, prior to the council he worked closely with his papal legates and the emperor. Pope St. Sylvester I approved all the council's acts (its decrees and canons) once its work was completed. It seemed that peace had finally been achieved. In reality, the tumultuous times had just begun.

CHAPTER TWO

First Council of Constantinople

381 AD

This council was held during the pontificate of Pope St. Damasus I.

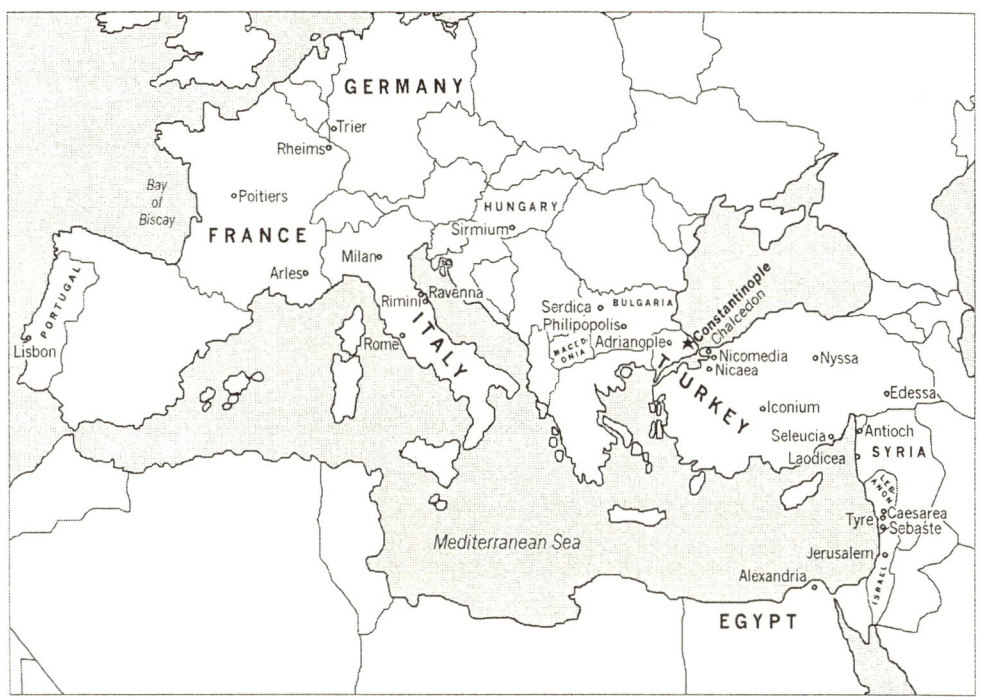

Background

Unfortunately, the First Council of Nicaea was not successful in eradicating Arianism. This was chiefly due to the machinations of the Arian Bishop Eusebius of Nicomedia. He persuaded Constantine's favorite sister Constantia to ask the emperor, as she lay dying, to restore the exiled heretical bishops to their former sees (328 AD). Two years later Constantine became a defender of Arianism after the heretic deceived him with a false Profession of Faith. The Arian heresy, by then a popular religion, spread like wildfire throughout the empire among bishops, priests and laity.

St. Athanasius

St. Athanasius (c. 297-373 AD) was a young deacon from Alexandria who attended the First Council of Nicaea in 325 AD with his bishop St. Alexander. Following the death of the bishop in 328 AD, St. Athanasius was chosen to fill the vacant see. The new bishop refused the imperial command of Constantine to restore Arius to his former position in Alexandria. "As consequence, he aroused the undying hatred of the Arian party and they did all they could, from that time forward to make life as miserable for him as possible."[14]

Protected by the emperor, Arians remained in power and persecuted all who opposed them. St. Athanasius relates in his *History of the Arians* the sufferings endured by those who remained Catholic: clergy and laity were banished, robbed or forced to labor in stone quarries and 26 bishops were exiled or killed. The priests Dioscorus and Hierax together with 16 bishops from Egypt and Libya were apprehended and exiled. Many died on the journey.

Soon afterwards, St. Athanasius had to answer trumped up charges of murder, treason and magic at Tyre and Constantinople. He was easily vindicated. However, because Constantine believed additional slanderous stories about him, St. Athanasius was exiled to Trier, Germany, in 336 AD. The courageous bishop lived in exile in various places for 17 years.

Some voices of the time rose up saying that it was "Athanasius against the world." "Athanasius held the fortress of orthodoxy almost unaided against the world. He held it against heretical bishops, priests, and laymen, and even against the powerful Emperor Constantine."[15] The Arians made numerous attempts on his life "and he only avoided being murdered by hiding himself for five years in a dry well where he was fed by one of his friends, who was the only person that knew the place of his concealment."[16]

> With the Church of both East and West cowed into submission, Constantius attacked Athanasius. The Dux Syrianus was ordered to assemble the legions of Egypt and Syria and remove the bishop from Alexandria. On the night of February 8, 356, imperial troops broke into the Church of Theonas, where Athanasius, surrounded by his clergy and consecrated virgins, was conducting a vigil service. As the arrows flew and the dead and wounded fell, his clergy hurried the reluctant bishop from his throne and Athanasius dropped

---

[14] Fr. George Johnson, *Story of the Church,* p. 89.
[15] Fr. Ernest Simmons, *Fathers and Doctors of the Church,* p. 5.
[16] Dom Gueranger, O.S.B., *The Liturgical Year VII,* p. 408.

completely from sight. In the next year George of Cappadocia ceremoniously entered the sullen city to be enthroned as the new bishop. He soon released a reign of terror against Athanasius' supporters while on the side organizing profitable monopolies in pork, salt, papyrus... In the desert, moving from one hiding place to another, welcomed by the monks, never once betrayed by his people, Athanasius remained the religious leader of Egypt, pouring out a steady flood of well-informed books and pamphlets defending the Nicene faith.[17]

Cardinal Newman relates that during this period Catholic churches were desecrated and cemeteries were ransacked. Furthermore, the Arian Bishop George of Cappadocia "brought out some of the consecrated virgins and threatened them with death by burning, unless they forthwith turned Arians. On perceiving their constancy of purpose, he stripped them of their garments, and beat them so barbarously on the face, that for some time afterwards their features could not be distinguished. Of the men, forty were scourged; some died of the wounds, the rest were banished."[18]

> Not long after, however, he [Athanasius] was again obliged to flee, owing to the persecution he suffered from Julian [the Apostate], who was instigated by the Arians. On one occasion, when he was being pursued by the emperor's satellites, who were ordered to put him to death, the saint ordered the boat, in which he was fleeing from danger, to be turned back. As soon as he met the persecutors, they asked him if Athanasius was anywhere near. He answered, that he was not far off. Whilst they, therefore, went one way, he sailed the other way and got back to Alexandria, where he remained in concealment until Julian's death.
>
> Another storm soon arose in the city, and he was obliged to hide himself, for four months, in his father's sepulchre. Having thus miraculously escaped from all these great dangers, he died peacefully in his own bed at Alexandria [on May 2, 373 AD] during the reign of the Emperor Valens.[19]

The situation was desperate; nevertheless, Christ protected His Church and ultimately triumphed over the heretics. God raised up valiant saints to vigorously oppose the inroads of heresy; the greatest of these was St. Athanasius.

---

[17] Leo Davis, *The First Seven Ecumenical Councils*, pp. 93-94.
[18] Cardinal John Newman, *Arians of the Fourth Century*, p. 332.
[19] Dom Gueranger, O.S.B., *The Liturgical Year VII*, p. 408.

"The feat of Athanasius is astounding. Clear headed, intuitive, and indomitable, he looms across the distance of history like another Abraham, the man in whom the future resided, and who stood alone."[20]

St. Ambrose of Milan

St. Ambrose (c. 340-397 AD) replaced the Arian Bishop Auxentius, who had ruled for 20 years. "At the Council of Sirmium in 378 AD, Ambrose, supported by the young Emperor Gratian, deposed six Arian bishops in a series of laws in 379/380. Gratian, under Ambrose's tutelage, proscribed Arianism in the West."[21]

In his *Exposition of the Gospel* he strongly condemns heresy: "...we are to understand that heretics and schismatics are also severed from the Kingdom of God, and from the Church. And so He [Christ] makes it clearly evident that every assembly of heretics and schismatics belongs, not to God, but to the unclean spirit."[22]

In 385 AD, St. Ambrose was summoned to the imperial palace by the Emperor Valentinian II and his mother, the Empress Justina (who was an Arian) and ordered to give churches to the Arians. St. Ambrose flatly refused and related the events in a letter to his sister:

> If the emperor were asking for anything that belonged to me—lands, money, anything that I possess—I should not refuse him a thing, although all my possessions belong to the poor. But things divine are not the property of the emperor. If you must have my patrimony, take it. If it is my person, here it is. Is it your wish to cast me in irons, to lead me to execution? I accept everything with joy. I will not hide behind the multitude, I will not embrace the altars pleading for my life: I would rather be immolated for the altars.
>
> ...They urge that everything is lawful to the emperor, since everything belongs to him. To this I reply, 'Do not think, O emperor, that you have any imperial right over things divine. Do not advance such pretensions, and if you desire a long reign, submit yourself to God. It is written, To God what is God's, to Caesar what is

---

[20] Jean Guitton, *Great Heresies and Church Councils,* pp. 88-89.
[21] Leo Davis, *The First Seven Ecumenical Councils,* p. 116.
[22] PL 15. Expos. Lucam Lib. VII, 91-5.

Caesar's. To the emperor the palaces, to the priest the churches. The right which is allotted to you extends over the public edifices, not over the sacred ones.'[23]

Peace was eventually restored to the Church. The Ambrosian rite, named after this valiant saint, is still observed in Milan.

St. Hilary of Poitiers

The convert, St. Hilary (c. 315-368 AD) became bishop of Poitiers. He courageously opposed the Arian heresy in Gaul (France) and was subsequently exiled to Phrygia (Turkey) by the Emperor Constantius in 356 AD. Even while in exile, St. Hilary frequently encouraged the bishops of England, France, Germany and Switzerland to remain faithful to the teachings of the Church and "…he proved himself such a thorn in the side of the Arians and semi-Arians of the East that they persuaded the emperor to send him back to Gaul."[24] Though many clergy fell prey to Arianism, most of the laity in the West remained faithful due to the efforts of Christ's champions.

Numerous tracts were written by saintly bishops from both East and West to refute Arianism and defend their flocks from the virulent ravages of heresy. "In spite of prolonged and bitter persecution, the Catholics were marching on to final victory. New champions of the Nicene faith were rising up everywhere. In the East the most renowned of these were St. Basil, his brother St. Gregory of Nyssa, and his intimate friend St. Gregory of Nazianzus."[25]

The Death of Arius

Bishop Alexander of Constantinople, who was commanded to receive Arius into the Church in 336 AD, prayed that either he or Arius die before such a sacrilege occur. Canon Howe describes this event in *Stories from the Catechist:*

> The frightful death of Arius is a terrible example of the just anger of God against the teachers of false doctrine. …He had many followers and powerful support, and even secured that he should be solemnly received again into the Church. On the day appointed, a great procession was formed in Constantinople, and, with songs of triumph, Arius was led toward the Church, boasting of the victory he had gained

---

[23] P. De Labriolle, *St. Ambrose,* pp. 44, 47-48.
[24] Fr. F. Drinkwater, *Catechism Stories,* p. 174.
[25] Fr. John Laux, *Church History,* p. 119.

over the Bishops. Then suddenly he was seized with frightful spasms, which compelled him to retire, till he should be able to resume his journey. Time passed away and he did not reappear; his followers became alarmed, and at length went to his room. There a fearful sight awaited them: Arius lay stretched on the ground, his face pale and livid, his body stiff in death, and the floor covered with his blood and intestines. His body had burst asunder, like that of Judas.

Arian Bishop Eusebius of Nicomedia

Following Arius' death, Bishop Eusebius of Nicomedia became the powerful leader of the Arians who were now called Eusebians. He banished the traditional Catholic bishops of Chalcedon, Nicaea and Nicomedia and worked tirelessly to keep Arianism alive. "All the most powerful churches of Eastern Christendom, by the commencement of the reign of Constantius (AD 337) had been brought under the influence of the Arians; Constantinople, Heraclea, Adrianople, Ephesus, Ancyra, both Caesarias, Antioch, Laodicea and Alexandria."[26] Eustathius of Antioch was exiled to Philippi with many priests and deacons of his church.

Eusebius' plan was threefold: first, to slander and depose St. Athanasius, the fearless opponent of Arianism; second, to deceive the masses by replacing Catholic bishops with Arians; third, to use Catholic theological terms and alter them in such a way that, with very little outward change in wording, they were given a completely different meaning. Thus, unwittingly at times, bishops, priests and laity became engulfed in the Arian heresy. This method is similar to that used today by the new church formed after Vatican II.

M. Cozen's *Handbook of Heresies* describes the turmoil caused by Arius:

> So great was the dispute engendered by Arius and his friends—some bishops adopting his heresy, others excommunicating him and his adherents, while others, deceived by his use of orthodox terms, scarcely knew which party to encourage—that the whole East was in a ferment and it became necessary to convoke a council of the whole Church.

How could so many bishops and priests imbibe these heretical doctrines? Some may have used this controversy as a means for their own material gain and

---

[26] Cardinal John Newman, *Arians of the Fourth Century*, p. 280.

ecclesiastical promotion. Acceptance by their peers and financial security were seemingly more important to such clergy than the salvation of souls and doctrinal integrity. Others may have lacked a deep faith and solid prayer life.

Mutated Forms of Arianism

The First Council of Nicaea used the Greek word *homooúsion* (in Latin, *consubstantialis*) to state that Jesus was of one substance (consubstantial) with God the Father. Arians used the Greek term *homo-ioúsion* to state that Jesus was only like God. By adding the single Greek letter iota to *homooúsion*, the Arians cleverly changed the entire meaning of the word.

Arianism was like a cancer that often mutated in order to survive. Three common variations of Arianism and two similar heresies are listed below:

a) *homo-ioúsion*—Like the Father (Arius) *homoios* (Acacius of Caesarea)

b) *anomoios*—Unlike the Father (Aetius of Antioch)

c) *homoiousios*—Like in substance to the Father (Basil of Ancyra)
Semi-Arianism

d) Macedonianism—Denied the divinity of both Jesus Christ and the Holy Ghost. (Macedonius, bishop of Constantinople)

e) Apollinarianism—Taught that Jesus lacked a rational soul (Apollinaris the Younger, Bishop of Laodicea)

Apollinaris, who developed his heresy about 360 AD, was never reconciled to the Church. Although at one time Apollinarianism had many followers in Constantinople, Phoenicia and Syria, it quickly faded into oblivion by 393 AD.

Persecution is Renewed

Constantine was baptized on his deathbed by the Arian bishop Eusebius of Nicomedia in 337 AD. His vast empire was subsequently divided among his sons. Constans, who was a nominal Catholic, ruled the West from 340-350 AD. Constantius (II), a fervent Arian, ruled the East and later the West also.

Constantius sought to make Arianism the official religion of the empire. He convened numerous pseudo-councils that attacked the Divinity of Christ through ambiguous terminology, thereby deceiving both clergy and laity alike. Other means were employed to insure compliance: the burning of churches and monasteries, defamation, exile, imprisonment, beheading and death.

St. Athanasius, patriarch of Alexandria, Paul, patriarch of Constantinople, and Lucius, bishop of Adrianople were among the exiled. They traveled to Rome and laid the matter before Pope St. Julius I who restored them to their rightful sees. However, their victory would be short lived.

In defiance of the pope's action, Eastern bishops held a council in Antioch in 341 AD that turned violent. St. Athanasius and Paul, the patriarch of Constantinople, fled in fear of their lives. Paul was later strangled and replaced by the heretic Macedonius. Lucius, bishop of Adrianople, died in prison.

Councils at Serdica

In order to settle various doctrinal and juridical disputes between East and West, Pope St. Julius I convoked a council to be held at Serdica (Sofia, Bulgaria), a city within Constans' domain, in the year 343 AD.

> The Easterners, however, withdrew when the Western bishops insisted on seating [St.] Athanasius and other bishops who had been deposed in the East [by the Arians]. Under the presidency of Ossius, the council proceeded without them, reaffirming the validity of Athanasius's claim to the see of Alexandria and ratifying the teaching of the Council of Nicaea by forbidding the use of Arian language. The council also made provisions for bishops condemned or deposed by provincial synods to appeal to Rome, 'in order to honor the memory of blessed Peter.'[27]

The Latin bishops who attended the Council of Serdica drafted a Profession of Faith and approved canons that recognized the papacy as the Supreme Court of Appeal. This action publicly acknowledged the popes' jurisdiction over the Universal Church. These bishops also exonerated St. Athanasius and the other Catholic bishops who defended Nicaea and were "excommunicated" by the Arians. Clergy who previously accused St. Athanasius of various crimes repented and were received into the Church by Pope St. Julius I.

The rift between East and West grew progressively wider during the council as the doctrinal and jurisdictional disputes could not be resolved. The Eusebian

---

[27] Richard McBrien, *Lives of the Popes*, p. 60.

bishops stormed out of the council and held a rival council of their own at Philippopolis (Plovdiv, Bulgaria), a city named after Alexander the Great's father, King Philip of Macedonia.

"The Western group, however, remained at Serdica, excommunicated the Eastern leaders, confirmed the Nicaeanum, [the teachings of the First Council of Nicaea], rejected the anomoios and inserted in their letters addressed to all the Churches the doctrine of consubstantiality."[28] Catholic bishops taught that Christ is the Son of God by nature and that Christians become holy through God's grace.

St. Robert Bellarmine in his work *De Conciliis et Ecclesia* wrote of a later council held at Serdica in 351 AD at which 300 Eastern bishops confirmed the Catholic Faith while 76 Eastern bishops subscribed to the Arian faith.

> What may be surprising in this story is that the Church should have been so vulnerable in what mattered most, its faith. [Cardinal] Newman expressed his astonishment that eminent bishops did not see what was at stake even though the faithful sensed it... Despite the excessive caution of [Pope] Liberius, the Nicene faith was saved by the convergence of the faith of the people with that of a few clear-headed and courageous bishops. It was saved against power and the friends of power, against the clever, the cunning, and the submissive. The like of it has not been seen again on the same scale—though it is not perhaps ruled out of the future of the Church.[29]

Pseudo Councils Subsequent to the First Council of Nicaea

> At some of them [heretical councils] the Arians turned to strong-arm tactics; the decrees issued were simply heretical. Meeting after meeting ended in this fashion. ...The whole question now centered about the Nicean Creed: Should it be accepted or not? At one gathering at Milan the Arian bishops became so enraged that they dragged the pen from the hand of the bishop of Milan as he was about to sign the Creed; a veritable riot resulted. The emperor finally intervened and forced the bishops to condemn Athanasius, to reject Nicaea, and receive the Arians in full union in the Church![30]

---

[28] Leslie Barnard, *Council of Serdica 343 A.D.*, p. 120.
[29] Jean Guitton, *Great Heresies and Church Councils*, p. 88.
[30] Fr. John Murphy, *General Councils of the Church*, p. 39.

"The great episcopal sees were held by semi-Arians: Lisbon, Arles, Ravenna, and Sirmium in the West, Alexandria, Jerusalem, Caesaria, Antioch, Nicomedia, and Constantinople in the East."[31] The situation in the Church was bleak. Some bishops at the Council of Sirmium (Mitrovica, Yugoslavia) spoke of the "eternal emperor" but denied the divinity of Jesus Christ.

> In council after council the bishops gave way wholesale, at Arles (353 AD), Milan (355 AD), Sirmium (357 AD), and, most spectacularly, at the simultaneous councils of Rimini-Seleucia (359 AD) about the morrow of which St. Jerome [329-420 AD] wrote a celebrated phrase, that the whole world woke up one morning, lamenting and marveling to find itself Arian.[32]

The Second Council of Sirmium of 357 AD drafted a creed that absolutely subordinated God the Son to God the Father. St. Hilary of Poitiers called this infamous document "The Blasphemy."

Soon afterwards Bishop Hosius of Cordova, who was 101 years old, was imprisoned, scourged and racked for not accepting the beliefs of the Arians. Under duress he finally capitulated and signed a document that promoted Arianism. Catholic Bishops from Gaul and Africa protested his action and he subsequently recanted on his deathbed two years later. Meanwhile, Arian and Semi-Arian bishops controlled every major diocese in the East.

To further control the clergy Constantius convoked a council for Western bishops at Rimini (Italy) and one for Eastern bishops at Seleucia (Turkey). There were no representatives of the pope invited to these councils and 80 Arian bishops at Rimini held the assembly in an iron grip. There were only 12 Catholics among the 150 bishops who attended the Council of Seleucia.

> Following a complicated series of intrigues on the part of the Arian bishops, and ruthless coercion by Constantius, nearly 400 bishops from the West and 150 of the East gave their consent to the new Arian Creed. ...This heretical Creed stated that the Son of God is, *like* the Father (not of like *substance* with the Father, just '*like*').[33]

---

[31] Jean Guitton, *Great Heresies and Church Councils*, pp. 86-87.
[32] Msgr. Philip Hughes, *Church in Crisis*, p. 42.
[33] Anthony Gilles, *People of the Creed*, p. 70.

"Speaking generally, 'the Catholic people,' says Newman, 'in the length and breadth of Christendom, were the obstinate champions of Catholic truth and the bishops were not.' "[34]

Pope Liberius

Pope Liberius (352-366 AD) was exiled by the emperor for his opposition to the Arian heresy. In response to the imperial sentence the pope replied, "The laws of the Church are more important than residence in Rome."[35]

Constantius installed an antipope in Rome named Felix II (355-356 AD). The populace rejected the usurper and consequently his churches were empty. "With the Roman public clamoring for Liberius' return, the emperor thereupon allowed him to go back to Rome, but on condition that he jointly rule with the antipope Felix."[36] This absurd compromise was not acceptable to the Romans because they recognized Liberius as the legitimate pope. Felix then fled the city.

To further add to the confusion, the antipope Felix II was succeeded by the antipope Ursinus (366-384 AD) whose illegitimate reign paralleled that of Liberius' successor, Pope St. Damasus I.

> The circumstances of Liberius' return are clouded with historical dispute for many authorities have agreed that the harassed man, in the plight of his exile and in the weariness of his advanced age, did eventually sign his name to a document insufficiently explicit against Arian doctrine. Whether he did or not may be the subject of argument but what remains clear is there is no evidence of any kind to prove he ever *taught,* or approved the teachings of any part of the Arian philosophy which differed from the Catholic faith.[37]

Even though opponents of papal infallibility have repeatedly cited the so-called "fall of Pope Liberius" to defend their erroneous position, the "capitulation" of Liberius does not really bear on the question. "Liberius, at the time of his fall, taught nothing and imposed no belief. Besides, if the pope is to teach *ex cathedra*, common sense requires that he be free."[38]

---

[34] Maisie Ward, *Saints Who Made History,* p. 108.
[35] John Farrow, *Pageant of the Popes,* p. 35.
[36] Richard McBrien, *Lives of the Popes,* p. 61.
[37] Farrow, 35.
[38] Addis and Arnold, *Catholic Dictionary, "Liberius."*

Fr. Murphy in *General Councils of the Church* clarifies the Liberius question:

> Liberius continued to insist upon a free council, but his wishes were not heeded. Instead, there came forth from Sirmium (the villa of the imperial court) one formula after another, more or less Arian in tone. The first such formula had passed over the word *homoousion* entirely; the second was an obvious Arian decree, an open denial of Nicaea; and the third was something of a compromise, but, understood in proper fashion, it could be viewed as in agreement with Nicaea.
>
> The signature of Liberius was needed, of course, to give real force to these formulas, and to this day historians debate whether Liberius signed any of the formulas, and if so which one he did sign. Whatever did take place, it is certain enough that Liberius was, in point of fact, a staunch defender of Nicaea (and also of Athanasius, which then meant the same thing). If he signed any, it would seem that it was the third formula, which admits of a proper interpretation; if he signed the second, however, it is clear from his other actions that he was tricked into it. In any event, it raises no special problem in regard to papal infallibility, since Liberius never clearly issued a solemn statement on his own authority.[39]

Liberius is the first pope of the early Church not listed as a saint and although historians and theologians concur that Liberius was a "weak pope," he never taught heresy. Pope St. Anastasius I (399-401 AD) confirms this fact in his letter to Bishop Venerius of Milan, found in *Denzinger* 93. Pope Liberius was also instrumental in receiving many Arians back into the Church.

Julian the Apostate

Emperor Constantius was baptized on his deathbed in 361 AD by an Arian[40] and was succeeded by his cousin, Julian the Apostate, who reigned for 20 months.

---

[39] pp. 39-40.

[40] "At this critical moment Constantius died, when the cause of truth was only not in the lowest state of degradation, because a party was in authority and vigor who could reduce it to a lower still; the Latins committed to an Anti-Catholic Creed [Rimini], the Pope a renegade [Liberius], Hosius fallen and dead, Athanasius wandering in the deserts, Arians in the sees of Christendom, and their doctrine growing in blasphemy, and their profession of it in boldness, everyday. The Emperor had come to the throne when almost a boy, and at this time was but forty-four years old. In the ordinary course of things, he might have reigned till orthodoxy, humanly speaking, was extinct." Ath. Tr. Vol. 1. p. 121.

Julian revived paganism and sought to divide the Church by returning exiled bishops back to their sees, causing Arians and Catholics to battle each other. His efforts backfired as Catholics became stronger and Arians converted. The apostate emperor even attempted to rebuild the temple in Jerusalem but his efforts were thwarted by fire and earthquakes.

He died as a result of an arrow wound he received during a cavalry charge against the Persians. It is claimed by some authors[41] "that Julian collected the blood flowing from his wound in the hollow of his hand and tossed it to the sky with the exclamation: 'Galilean, Thou hast conquered!' "[42]

Emperor Valens

Julian's successor, the Arian Emperor Valens (364-378 AD), persecuted both Catholics and Semi-Arians. As a result of these persecutions, many gave up their Arian or Semi-Arian beliefs and returned to the Catholic Faith. Semi-Arianism disappeared from ecclesiastical history by 367 AD.

Emperor Valens attended Mass in Caesarea offered by St. Basil (329-379 AD) on January 6, 372. "Such was the order and pomp in and about the sanctuary that it looked more like heaven than earth."[43] The emperor was so moved by the majestic ceremonies and the devotion of the people that he not only ceased his persecutions, but even allowed St. Basil to fill vacant sees with bishops loyal to the Catholic Faith.

Emperor Theodosius I

A Catholic general from Spain named Theodosius I, who became the next Eastern Emperor, finally restored liberty to the Church in the year 378 AD. "Yet when Theodosius came to power, the Arians dominated everywhere in the East, especially at Constantinople; the orthodox believers in the city [Catholics] had neither bishop nor church. The new Emperor, however, was a devout Catholic and he wished to change all that. He decided, therefore, to restore the Catholics to power and expel the Arians."[44]

---

[41] See Theodoret, 3.20: c.f. Sozomen, 6.2.
[42] Abbot Giuseppe Ricciotti, *Julian the Apostate: Roman Emperor 361-363*, p. 254.
[43] As described by St. Gregory Nazianzen in Aloysius Horn's *Christmas Chronicle*, p. 20.
[44] Fr. John Murphy, *General Councils of the Church*, p. 40.

On February 28, 380 AD, Emperor Theodosius I (379-395 AD) ordered the populace within his empire to profess the Catholic Faith which "the Apostle Peter had taught in days of old to the Romans, and which was now followed by the Pope Damasus and by Peter, bishop of Alexandria..."[45] This decree contained an explicit act of faith in the Triune God. All churches in Constantinople previously held by Arians were returned to Catholics in May, 381 AD.

> All who failed to adhere to this faith were branded heretics... and had all the assemblies forbidden. The churches of Constantinople were taken from the Arians, and their bishop Demophilus was deposed. Theodosius was himself present at the installation of [St.] Gregory Nazianzen, hailed as bishop [of Constantinople in 379 AD] by the people as the sun triumphantly lit the darkened basilica.[46]

> When Gregory took charge of that see, he found very few Catholics. He made his residence in a small house where he offered the Holy Sacrifice of the Mass and began to teach the people the true doctrine of the Church concerning the Blessed Trinity. Before two years had passed, he had converted more than half the city.[47]

The First Council of Constantinople

It had been 50 years since Emperor Constantine transferred the seat of Roman power from the West to the strategically located ancient Greek City of Byzantium in the East. After being rebuilt and renamed Constantinople (now Istanbul, Turkey), it became a military and economic stronghold on the Bosporus between Europe and Asia. Theodosius I took his stand against Arianism by holding the council in his imperial palace in Constantinople in 381 AD.

"To secure a lasting peace, he finally convoked the free council that had been sought twenty or thirty years before by Pope Liberius. In this way the State officially broke with Arianism, and for the first time in years expressed in a clear fashion its acceptance of the Nicean faith."[48]

---

[45] Leo Davis, *First Seven Ecumenical Councils,* pp. 118-119.
[46] Davis, 119.
[47] Fr. George Johnson, *Story of the Church,* p. 93.
[48] Fr. John Murphy, *General Councils of the Church,* p. 40.

Emperor Theodosius I convened the First Council of Constantinople on his own authority and it is doubtful whether the pope was consulted or even invited. The emperor invited all the bishops of the East to attend. The fact that no Western bishops attended the sessions provides substantial evidence that they too were probably never invited.

St. Damasus I was the first pope to refer to the Papacy as the Apostolic See thereby distinguishing it from all other sees (dioceses). He was fearful of infringements on papal jurisdiction and reluctant to give approval to the council.

The First Council of Constantinople began in May, 381 AD and ended two months later. Among the 150 Catholic bishops who attended the council were saints: Gregory Nazianzen, Meletius of Antioch, Gregory of Nyssa, Peter of Sebaste, Amphilochius of Iconium, Pelagius of Laodicea, Eulogius of Edessa and Cyril of Jerusalem. The 36 heretical Macedonian bishops who attended the first session of the council refused to renounce their errors and departed.

St. Meletius presided over the council, though he died during its sessions. He was succeeded by St. Gregory Nazianzen (330-389 AD), who was elected bishop of Constantinople, but later resigned. Nectarius, who was subsequently elected to fill the vacant office, concluded the council.

Main Accomplishments of the First Council of Constantinople

- The Arian heresy was condemned and the faith of the First Council of Nicaea was reconfirmed.
- The Macedonian heresy was condemned.
- Maximus, the bishop who fraudulently usurped the See of Constantinople, was condemned, deposed and banished.

A summary of Catholic belief called the Nicene-Constantinopolitan Creed was approved during the First Council of Constantinople. In the Latin Church this Creed has been recited during Holy Mass on every Sunday and on major feasts since the sixth century. It clearly expresses the Catholic doctrine of the Blessed Trinity. The last addition to the Nicene-Constantinopolitan Creed took place in the year 1024 AD when Pope Benedict VIII added the word *Filioque* to declare that the Holy Ghost proceeds from the Father and the Son. This word has remained a point of contention in the East up to the present time.

There were seven canons enacted at the council:

a) One reminded bishops to stay in their dioceses and not to meddle in the affairs of other bishops.

b) Another canon delineated the manner of receiving heretics back into the Church.

c) The third canon gave the bishop of Constantinople preeminence over all the other bishops, except the bishop of Rome, since Constantinople was styled the New Rome.

d) Several canons condemned the Macedonian heresy, the Apollinarian heresy and Arianism in all its forms.

Since Constantinople was styled the New Rome, the third canon of the council placed the bishop of Constantinople above all the other bishops, although the pope would continue to be acknowledged as the supreme head of the Church. This novel idea was contrary to the customary practice of the Church, dating back to Apostolic Times, of placing Alexandria and Antioch above Constantinople because of their special relationship with St. Mark and St. Peter.

Canon five of the Fourth Lateran Council of 1215 later accepted this new order of precedence. Michael Walsh, in his book *The Popes*, writes:

…The See of Alexandria had, according to tradition, been founded by St. Mark, Peter's disciple, and because Peter… presided over the See of Antioch for a time before moving on to Rome, these Churches were to rank second and third. And as extra proof of Rome's preeminence, if more were needed, the council [the one Pope St. Damasus I called at Rome in 382 AD] pointed out that a second Apostle, St. Paul, had been associated with Peter in founding the Church in the Empire's capital city [Rome]. Constantinople came nowhere. Ecclesiastical status was not to depend upon civil status as far as the authority of the local Church was concerned.

The First Council of Constantinople differs from all other General Councils of the Church since it was not approved by the reigning pontiff but by subsequent popes and by the Council of Chalcedon in 451 AD.

"In the West, Pope Gregory the Great, following the example of Pope Vigilius and Pope Pelagius II, recognized it as an ecumenical council, but *only in its dogmatic utterances*, by which the true doctrine on the divinity of the Holy Ghost was defined, and heresies denying this article were condemned."[49]

Great Trials for the Church

Unfortunately, the First Council of Constantinople did not deliver the deathblow to Arianism. Toward the end of the fourth century the Burgundians and Lombards became Arians. "The greater part of the Germanic tribes adopted Christianity in its Arian form, and in many places, right up to the sixth century, alongside the Catholic parishes there were Arian parishes with their own churches and baptisteries."[50]

Meanwhile, the Arian Vandals and Visigoths incited great persecutions of the Church. Things looked so bleak that many, unmindful of God's protection of the Catholic Church, predicted its ultimate demise.

> With the coming of the barbarians the Catholic Church fell on evil days, since the Goths and Vandals were Arians, having been converted by the Arian Bishop Ulfilas (d. 383). Wherever they took over, they persecuted the Catholics. Huneric, the Vandal ruler in Africa in 484, summoned the 466 Catholic bishops to a meeting with their Arian colleagues; at its conclusion his edict was read, which prohibited all assemblies of Catholics, confiscated their churches, and drove the bishops out of their sees. The Visigoths in Spain also severely restricted the freedom of the subjugated Gallo-Roman Catholic populace. Everywhere, in fact, the Gallo-Roman Catholic populace was under the sway of persecuting Arian conquerors.[51]
>
> Possidius writes of St. Augustine seeing, in the early years of the Vandal invasion, towns ruined, people murdered and driven to flight, churches without clergy, maidens dedicated to God wandering about homeless or suffering in intolerable servitude, the sacraments disregarded or asked for in vain, refugees pursued into their very hiding-places or dying of want, and the leaders of the churches stretching out their hands for help where there was none *(Life of Augustine, ch. xxviii)*, and to all this was soon added the demand for apostasy to Arianism, in response to which there were many martyrs direct and indirect.[52]

---

[49] Fr. Clement Raab, O.F.M., *Twenty Ecumenical Councils of the Catholic Church*, p. 14.
[50] Leonard Von Matt, *Councils*, p. 6.
[51] Thomas Bokenkotter, *A Concise History of the Catholic Church*, pp. 108-109.
[52] Donald Attwater, *Martyrs*, p. 71.

The Demise of Arianism

St. Clotilda, a Burgundian princess, was instrumental in converting her husband Clovis, King of the Franks. He was baptized by St. Remigius at Rheims, France in 496 AD together with 3,000 of his soldiers. A great miracle occurred during this historical event.

> Hincmar of Rheims, who wrote the Life of St. Remigius in the 9th century, is the first to mention a legend that at the baptism of Clovis the chrism for the anointing was found to be missing, whereupon St. Remigius prayed and a dove appeared from the heavens, bearing in its beak an *ampulla* of chrism.
>
> A phial of oil, fabled to be the same, was preserved at the abbey of Saint-Remi and used in the consecration of the kings of France until Charles X in 1825.
>
> It was broken up at the [French] Revolution, but a piece of *la Sainte Ampoule* and its contents were saved and are kept in Rheims cathedral.[53]

In 507 AD, Clovis defeated the Visigoths and killed Alaric II, King of the Visigoths at the Battle of Vouillé near Tours. Clovis then conquered or pacified the remaining tribes and became the sole ruler of the Franks. "Then taking into account the political views which still animated his Roman subjects, Clovis had the incumbent emperor of the Roman Empire of the East, Anastasius, confer on him the title 'Patricius'; and thus had his rule in Gaul recognized by the highest authority then existing."[54]

Many Arians then converted to Catholicism and the last vestiges of Arianism finally faded into oblivion on the plains of Lombardy in 744 AD. The Arian heresy had persisted for over 400 years "but like all heresies faded in time and disappeared."[55] The Triumph of the Faith envisioned by the First Council of Nicaea and the First Council of Constantinople was at last fulfilled.

---

[53] Editors of Bulfinch Press, *One Hundred Saints,* p. 136.
[54] H. Günter in "Hist. Jahrb." (1934).
[55] M. Toal, *Sunday Sermons of the Great Fathers, Vol. IV,* p. 459.

CHAPTER THREE

Council of Ephesus

431 AD

This council was held during the pontificate of Pope St. Celestine I.

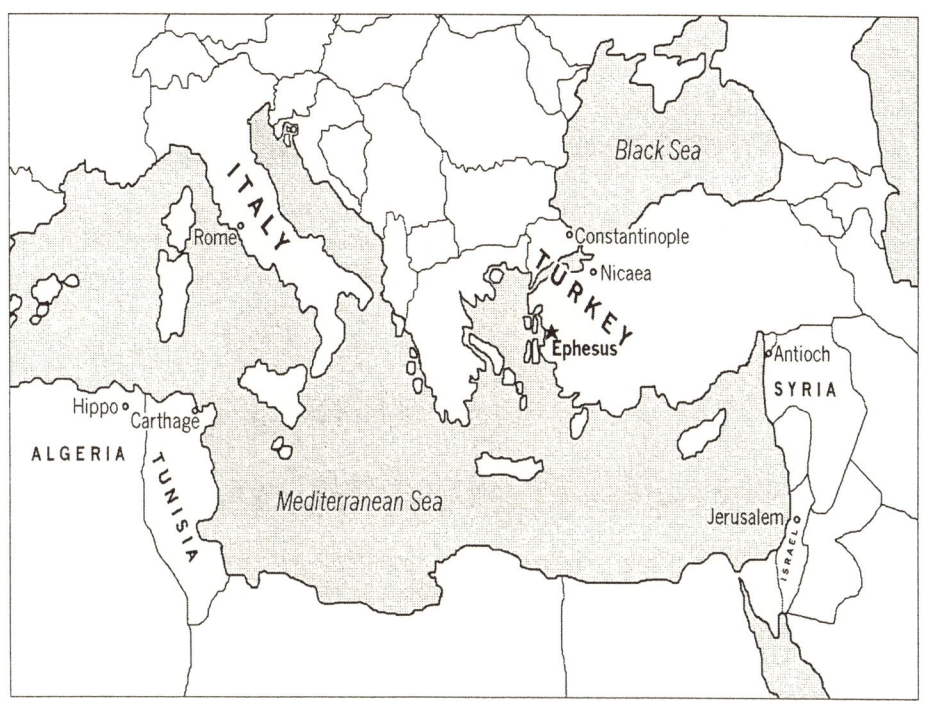

Background

During the fourth and fifth centuries the Huns, Vandals, Visigoths, Ostrogoths and other marauding bands of barbarian tribes ravaged the continent of Europe, causing violent upheaval. The Roman Empire was in shambles and geopolitical and economic stability were nonexistent.

The turmoil increased with new external and internal attacks on the Church. Shortly before the Council of Ephesus began, the antipope Eulalius reigned from the city of Rome until he was forcibly expelled by the imperial troops of the Western emperor. New heresies arose making the anarchy complete.

The Heretics Pelagius & Coelestius

The Council of Ephesus was convoked to condemn the heresies of Pelagius and Nestorius. In the year 400 AD an English monk, Pelagius, led multitudes astray by his heretical teachings concerning grace and justification. Pelagius taught that natural goodness was sufficient for salvation; divine grace was not necessary. Pelagius possessed many traits of the heretic Arius: intelligence, eloquence and craftiness. A Scottish monk named Coelestius assisted him in his diabolical work.

Fr. John Laux in *Church History* states: "In order to deceive their hearers and readers, Pelagius and Coelestius made use of Christian terms, such as baptism, original sin, grace, redemption, but attached entirely different meanings to them." [Much like the Modernists of today.]

> After the sack of Rome by Alaric in 410 AD, Pelagius and Coelestius fled to Carthage where Coelestius remained for some years, whilst Pelagius passed over to Palestine. Coelestius was condemned by a council held at Carthage in 411 AD. Pelagius succeeded in deceiving a number of Eastern bishops and for a time maintained his ground against all opposition. In Jerusalem he won over hundreds of monks who were ready even to use violence to propagate his errors or to quash the arguments of his opponents ...Banished by [Emperor] Honorius from the Western Empire, Pelagius and Coelestius found an asylum with Nestorius, Bishop of Constantinople, and along with him they were condemned by the Council of Ephesus in 431.[56]

Pope St. Innocent I excommunicated Pelagius and Coelestius because of their erroneous teachings. St. Augustine, Bishop of Hippo Regius (Annaba, Algeria) was an eloquent orator and a dauntless fighter against the Pelagian heresy. His writings clearly explained the proper relationship between free will and the grace of God: "Justification takes place not through man alone, as Pelagius taught, nor through man and God as the more moderate amongst his followers (Semi-Pelagians) maintained, but through *God and Man,* as the Catholic Church teaches."[57] St. Augustine also strongly opposed other heresies prevalent at the time including Manicheism and Donatism.

---

[56] p. 150.
[57] Laux, 150.

The Heretic Nestorius

Emperor Theodosius II (d. 450 AD) appointed Nestorius, a conceited monk from Antioch, to serve as bishop of Constantinople in the year 428 AD. Nestorius was born in Syria, though his parents were Persian. Like Arius, he studied theology at Antioch where he became a famous preacher.

The new bishop taught that there were two distinct persons in Jesus Christ: God the Son and, Jesus of Nazareth the man. Nestorius also claimed that God dwelt in Jesus as in a temple and that He became God by degrees. According to Nestorius, the Blessed Virgin Mary was only the Mother of the man Christ, and therefore should not be called the Mother of God.

On the contrary, Catholic theology teaches that Jesus Christ is only one Person with two distinct natures: the divine nature of God and the human nature of man. The Second Person of the Blessed Trinity became incarnate in the womb of the Blessed Virgin Mary at the moment of conception. Our Lady conceived and brought forth the Son of God made man. Therefore, the Blessed Virgin Mary is rightly called the Mother of God because her Son is God.

The whole Nestorian controversy came to a head in the year 428 AD, when Anastasius, a disciple of Nestorius, preached that Mary should not be called the Mother of God. The clergy and laity who heard the sermon were shocked and appalled. "When they complained of it to the bishop, Nestorius not only refused to condemn the teaching, but he made use of the opportunity to set forth the doctrine himself."[58] "When the monks of Constantinople deeply devoted to Mary protested before the patriarch, they were imprisoned and scourged. Nestorius himself extended the controversy by publishing his sermons far and wide."[59]

Fr. John Murphy assures us that the title "Mother of God" was already held dear by the faithful:

> For many years now, the faithful had spoken of the Blessed Mother as the θεοτοκοσ (Theotokos) the 'Mother of God.' There are indications of its use in prayers as early as the third century. Nestorius now claimed that this was a dangerous word. He held that we ought to speak of Mary only as the

---

[58] Fr. John Murphy, *The General Councils of the Church*, p. 47.
[59] Leo Davis, *The First Seven Ecumenical Councils*, p. 140.

Χριστοτοκοσ (Christotokos) the 'Mother of Christ.' Thus the defense of the true doctrine concerning Christ was necessarily linked so intimately to the honor given to Mary as His Mother. One cannot dishonor Mary without dishonoring Christ as well, and those who heard Nestorius preach realized this.[60]

St. Cyril of Alexandria

St. Cyril, Bishop of Alexandria (c. 376-444 AD), soon received news of the controversy in Constantinople. In response, he wrote a number of articles defending the doctrine of the Incarnation. These pastoral letters were sent throughout Egypt and some found their way to Constantinople.

> Cyril's writings were eagerly read in Constantinople to the great discomfiture and chagrin of Nestorius who had won high favor at the imperial court. Cyril, in his clear exposition of the Incarnation, informed the emperor and the imperial family of the new heresy. 'Obligated by the old custom of the Church' Cyril reported the heretical teachings of Nestorius to Pope Celestine I. Nestorius, also, had written to the pope, putting the blame of the whole controversy on Cyril, and he recommended in his letter to the pope that the term 'Mother of Christ' should be the golden mean between 'Mother of God' and 'Mother of man.'[61]

Pope St. Celestine I convoked a synod in Rome in the year 430 AD to examine the writings and teachings of Nestorius. The synod declared that Nestorius was to be excommunicated and deposed unless he renounced his heresy.

The Council of Ephesus

"The grandest of the ancient cities of Turkey is Ephesus. ...St. Paul spent two years in Ephesus, ministering to a small Christian community and later wrote them an epistle from captivity."[62] Shortly after the death of Christ, St. John the Evangelist and the Blessed Virgin Mary had lived in this city. Our Lady always held a special place in the hearts of the Ephesians because she had taught them the rudiments of Christianity.

---

[60] *The General Councils of the Church,* p. 57.
[61] Fr. Clement Raab, O.F.M., *Twenty Ecumenical Councils of the Catholic Church,* p. 17.
[62] *National Catholic Reporter,* April 11, 2003, "Turkey richly rewards search for the sacred," by Len Biallas.

Emperor Theodosius II convoked a general council to be held in the port city of Ephesus in order to resolve the Nestorian problem. It was scheduled to begin on the Feast of Pentecost, 431 AD. Pope St. Celestine I responded to the emperor by sending three legates with specific instructions for the *modus operandi* of the council.

> First of all, they were to attach themselves firmly to Cyril of Alexandria, who would serve as their guide. Second, they were to safeguard the rights of the Bishop of Rome. They were to come as judges, not as parties to a controversy. The Bishop of Rome had already settled the question of Nestorius and his teaching; they were simply to make sure that this was carried out. Owing to this directive the council produced some of the most outstanding testimony of the century to the Roman primacy, since the bishops gave vocal expression to their acceptance of papal authority. Lastly, considering the difficulty of travel in those days, the legates were told that, should they arrive late, they were to investigate carefully everything that had taken place before their arrival. As time would prove, this was a bit of advice well given.[63]

Among the bishops in attendance, 50 came with St. Cyril of Alexandria, 40 came with Memnon, the Bishop of Ephesus, 15 came with the Bishop of Jerusalem, 12 came from Pamphilia and 6 bishops were associated with Nestorius. Nestorius, who had resided at Ephesus since Easter, was not well liked by the local populace. He requested an imperial bodyguard composed of a group of gladiators. St. Cyril brought a contingent of sailors from Alexandria for his own protection.

> When the appointed day arrived, the papal legates had not yet arrived, and the patriarch of Antioch, John (who had been appointed by the emperor to preside), was also absent. In John's case the delay may have been on purpose. He was a friend of Nestorius, and may not have wished to take part in the condemnation; at any rate, he did send word that they ought not to wait too long, should he be delayed.[64]

---

[63] Fr. John Murphy, *General Councils of the Church,* p. 51.
[64] Murphy, 51.

After 16 days of waiting St. Cyril of Alexandria determined it was time to begin. He therefore took it upon himself to preside over the first session of the Council of Ephesus on June 22, 431 AD.

Nestorius was officially summoned to the council three times, but he obstinately refused to attend. Nevertheless, the council proceeded with its important work. Letters written by Pope St. Celestine I and St. Cyril condemning Nestorius were read to the Council Fathers. Cyril's treatise describing the union of two natures in one Person in Christ (also called the *hypostatic union*) was read and approved. Writings of the early Fathers of the Church were also read confirming the teachings of Pope St. Celestine I and St. Cyril. The Nicene Creed was recited and the bishops professed their adherence to the teachings of the First Council of Nicaea. The Council Fathers publicly read 20 extracts from the writings of Nestorius and his heretical teachings were formally condemned. Nestorius was excommunicated and deposed.

Eyewitnesses described the joyful scene that resulted from the council's proclamations:

> The whole population of the city, from earliest dawn until the evening stood around, in expectation of the council's decision. And when they heard that the author of the blasphemies had been stripped of his rank, they all began with one voice to praise and glorify God, as for the overthrow of an enemy of the faith. And as we [the bishops] came forth from the Church, they led us with torches to our lodgings, for it was now evening. Throughout the city there was great rejoicing, and many lighted lanterns, and women who walked before us swinging thuribles.[65]

The Ephesians celebrated the decision of the council with jubilant cries, exclaiming, "Theotokos! Theotokos!" *(Mother of God! Mother of God!)* The following day Nestorius was officially notified of his excommunication and messengers were sent to Constantinople to announce that Nestorius had been deposed. However, the emperor's representative at the council, Candidian, opposed St. Cyril of Alexandria's beginning the council without John of Antioch

---

[65] The text of this letter, Greek and Latin, is printed in Kirch, *Enchiridion Fontium Hist. Ecclesiasticae Antiquae,* pp. 461-462.

and so declared it null and void. He then sent a report to Theodosius II, together with a letter written by Nestorius.

The Counterfeit "Council of Ephesus"

Bishop John of Antioch, accompanied by 42 bishops, finally arrived in Ephesus on June 24, but obstinately refused to attend the council. These bishops held a pseudo-council of their own where they excommunicated St. Cyril and Memnon, and declared the excommunication and deposition of Nestorius null and void. A copy of the minutes was forwarded to Emperor Theodosius II.

Final Sessions of the Legitimate Council of Ephesus

The papal legates of Pope Celestine I arrived on July 10th and reviewed the acts of the council. They approved the legitimate council's proceedings, including the excommunication of Nestorius and the condemnation of the Pelagian heresy. The acts and excommunications issued by the pseudo-council were declared null and void. On July 17th, John of Antioch was summoned three times to appear before the council. He was later excommunicated for his refusal.

The Race to the Emperor

Once the legitimate council concluded on July 31, 431 AD, representatives from each of the factions left for Constantinople to seek imperial approval. Count Irenaeus, a friend of Nestorius, was the first to arrive in Constantinople and was therefore able to turn the emperor against the delegates from the legitimate Council of Ephesus, who arrived some days later.

Emperor Theodosius II sent Count John to settle matters in Ephesus by arresting Nestorius, Cyril and Memnon and imprisoned them until the dispute could be settled. Since St. Cyril came from the wealthy diocese of Alexandria, he sought his release from prison by offering the emperor costly presents, including gold coins, ivory chairs, exotic animals and valuable furnishings. Although the three bishops remained in prison for a time, the gifts were instrumental in obtaining their freedom.

In the meantime, the disciples of Nestorius intercepted correspondence from the Council Fathers to the emperor. The Council Fathers outwitted the Nestorians by executing a clever plan. A courier, posing as a beggar, cleverly concealed letters addressed to the emperor and the clergy of Constantinople inside his hollow walking stick and passed undetected.

> In this epistle the bishops refused firmly to communicate with John of Antioch and his followers, unless they would consent to the condemnation of Nestorius; they demanded also the liberation of Cyril and Memnon. In the hollow of the reed they enclosed also a letter addressed to all the bishops, who were then in the capital, and to the clergy of Constantinople. As Theodosius was so beset with supplications, the consequence of this letter was to decide him to receive a delegation of eight from each side. He met the delegates at Chalcedon. After he had heard their respective arguments, he became convinced of the righteousness of the acts of Cyril.[66]

Nestorius was rightfully deposed and excommunicated, and Maximian was chosen as the new Bishop of Constantinople. Nestorius was first exiled to Antioch, then to Egypt. The heretic died a horrifying death, for his tongue was consumed by worms—a fitting punishment for one who blasphemed not only the Blessed Virgin Mary, but also her Divine Son, Jesus. St. Cyril and Memnon were released from prison and returned to their flocks. Emperor Theodosius II officially ended the council in October, 431 AD.

> A division had resulted from the council, and this had to be healed. Neither the pope nor the emperor accepted the condemnation of John of Antioch and his party. By thus leaving the door open for a peaceful solution, much good resulted. By 433, the followers of Cyril and John of Antioch had discussed the questions and assured one another that they both held to the same doctrine, even though their terminology might differ. All signed the formula of agreement, and the matter rested, for the time being at least. Ephesus had won over all of those concerned.[67]

Members of the Assyrian Orthodox Church of Iraq still adhere to the Nestorian heresy. Iraqis and Kurdistanis who remained faithful to the Council of Ephesus and Catholic teaching belong to the Eastern Rite of the Church known as the Chaldean Catholic Church. They were united with Rome in 1681.

---

[66] Fr. Clement Raab, O.F.M., *Twenty Ecumenical Councils of the Catholic Church*, p. 22.
[67] Fr. John Murphy, *General Councils of the Church*, p. 54.

CHAPTER FOUR

Council of Chalcedon

451 AD

This council was held during the pontificate of Pope St. Leo I.

Background

In order to address a new crisis in the Church that sprang up a mere 20 years after the Council of Ephesus, a general council was held at Chalcedon (Kadiköy, Turkey), a city across the Bosporus from Constantinople. This council was convoked to condemn a 90-year-old abbot named Eutyches who began the Monophysite heresy.

Pope St. Leo I (400-461 AD), one of the truly remarkable men of history, opposed Eutyches and convoked the Council of Chalcedon. The pontiff was a learned theologian and skillful diplomat who persuaded Attila the Hun to spare Rome in 452 AD and succeeded in mitigating the fury of Genseric's Vandal onslaught in 455 AD against the Romans.

Throughout the history of the Church we find that numerous heresies arose when individuals, such as Eutyches, exaggerated a particular article of Church teaching to such a degree that they actually opposed or denied an infallible doctrine. In his letter to Pope Leo the Great in 448 AD, Eutyches defended his heretical teachings by claiming that he was only combating Nestorianism.

Fr. Clement Raab, O.F.M. says in *Twenty General Councils of the Church:* "So weak is human reason that in trying to escape from one error, it rushes headlong into another. Only the infallible Church of God, because it is visibly guided by the Holy Spirit, condemns all errors and is affected by none."[68]

While Nestorius divided Jesus Christ into two persons, human and divine, Eutyches denied the human nature of Christ. His followers were known as Monophysites because they taught that after the Incarnation, Jesus Christ had only one nature. The term *monophysite* is derived from two Greek words which mean *one nature*.

Eutyches, the abbot of the largest monastery in Constantinople, was rather unlearned and terribly stubborn. Pope St. Leo the Great believed that Eutyches went astray through ignorance rather than malice. Eutyches was in close contact with monks in Asia, Syria and Egypt and was also very influential in the religious life of Constantinople; he was second only to the bishop.

Eutyches was the godfather of the emperor's chief minister, Chrysaphios, and was venerated by the Emperor Theodosius II for his long life of asceticism. The façade of feigned holiness caused many to follow his heresy, and this same deception would be used by heretics for years to come. We should be reminded that true holiness must include fidelity to all the teachings of the Church.

The Monophysite Heresy

The Monophysite heresy began when Eutyches misinterpreted the teachings of St. Cyril of Alexandria on the two natures of Christ. Unfortunately, St. Cyril had used terminology that could be misleading. For example, St. Cyril often referred to Christ as the "one incarnate nature of God the Word," indicating that there was only "one divine Person" in Christ. However, others interpreted this to refer to only "one nature" in Christ. "What made matters even worse, men not

---

[68] pp. 24-25.

only used different Greek or Latin words when speaking about 'nature' or 'person,' but they sometimes used the *same* word to mean both things."[69]

Realizing that some of his writings were ambiguous and could be misconstrued, St. Cyril clarified them and adopted a more precise terminology, 'the union of two natures in Christ.' In other words, St. Cyril simply stated the Catholic doctrine that Christ is one Person with two distinct natures: the nature of God and the nature of man. Following St. Cyril's death in 444, Eutyches taught that Christ's humanity was entirely absorbed in His divinity—that there was only one composite nature in Christ after the Incarnation.

The Synod of Constantinople

When Eutyches' heretical teachings became manifest, Theodoret, bishop of Cyrrhus rose up against him and Bishop Eusebius of Dorylaeum denounced him to St. Flavian who was the bishop of Constantinople. A local synod was convoked in 448 AD and Eutyches was summoned to appear before it.

> When Eutyches finally consented to appear, he arrived with a high official of the court, sent by the emperor, as his protector, and with an escort of hundreds of monks. He was heard, there was a vast amount of argument, and even the court dignitary did his best to win the old man over. But he would not agree that there are two *physes* [natures] in God incarnate. The synod proclaimed him a heretic, disposed him from his post in the monastery, forbade him to exercise his priesthood, and ordered that none should have any access to him for the future. Thirty-two bishops put their names to this sentence, and twenty-three heads of monasteries endorsed it.[70]

However, two very influential persons, the Emperor Theodosius II and Dioscorus, bishop of Alexandria, did not accept the council's deposition of Eutyches. Dioscorus convoked a synod and annulled the deposition of Eutyches.

Pope St. Leo the Great asked St. Flavian for a complete report of the proceedings against Eutyches. Once the pope thoroughly understood the situation, he confirmed the actions of St. Flavian and wrote a dogmatic letter

---

[69] Fr. John Murphy, *General Councils of the Church,* p. 56.
[70] Msgr. Philip Hughes, *Church in Crisis,* p. 73.

called the *Tome* in 449 AD which stated, "The One Person of Our Lord possesses two Natures, the Divine and the Human, neither confused nor mixed."[71]

Meanwhile, Dioscorus persuaded Theodosius II to convoke a council at Ephesus in 449 AD. Pope St. Leo the Great sent three legates to this council.

The Robber Council (Latrocinium)

On August 8, 449 AD, 130 bishops attended the illegitimate council at the church of the Mother of God in Ephesus where the previous general council convened 18 years earlier. Unfortunately, Dioscorus and a powerful faction of bishops, with the full support of the state, seized control of the council. They prohibited Pope Leo's *Tome* from being read and banished the papal legates. This illegitimate council reversed the decision of the previous synod by exonerating Eutyches and condemning St. Flavian. The Egyptian bishops, many of whom were Monophysites, sided with Dioscorus and soon violence erupted.

> The name of his [Eutyches'] accuser, [Bishop] Eusebius of Dorylaeum, was greeted by cries of 'Burn him alive,' 'Cut him in two, the man who wants to divide Christ,' 'Anathema,' and so forth, while 114 bishops agreed that Eutyches' theory was good Christian doctrine. By the emperor's orders no bishop who had taken part in the condemnation of Eutyches was allowed to vote.

> ...Dioscorus cried that his life was in danger, and on his appeal the imperial officials threw open the doors of the church, and a mob of soldiers, seamen, monks, and the general rabble poured in. Flavian took refuge in the sanctuary, and clung to the pillars of the altar. In the end, he was dragged away, and taken to prison. The bishops then voted his condemnation, 135 of them signing the decree, many through sheer fear, and unable to escape.[72]

St. Flavian was severely beaten and died several days later as he made his way to Constantinople. Two victims of the terrorism, Stephen of Ephesus and Acacius of Ariarathia, later wrote, "We were kept shut up in the church until night-time, ...but soldiers, with sticks and swords, and monks were placed near us, and thus we were compelled to subscribe."[73]

---

[71] Joseph McSorley, *An Outline of the Church by Centuries*, p. 109.
[72] Msgr. Philip Hughes, *Church in Crisis*, p. 75.
[73] Mansi, t. vi. pp. 623-626; Hardouin, t. ii. p. 94.

The full report, however, finally reached Rome. Before he died, [St.] Flavian had sent an appeal, and Theodoret [of Cyrrus] also wrote to Leo; and when the papal legates returned, Rome understood all. Leo gave to this gathering the name by which it had been known since: 'the Robber Synod of Ephesus.' In these proceedings, said Leo, we see no council but a den of thieves *(Latrocinium)*. He at once declared invalid all that had been done. This was on October 6, 449 AD. With the support of the emperor, however, it did seem at the time as though the Monophysites had triumphed.[74]

The Council of Chalcedon

God's vengeance was not long in coming, for Eutyches' powerful ally, the Emperor Theodosius II, died suddenly the following year. His sister St. Pulcheria (399-453 AD) now took the reins of government and soon afterwards married Marcian, a famous general. Together they helped eradicate the Monophysite heresy by sending Eutyches away, recalling the exiled bishops and bringing back the remains of St. Flavian to Constantinople for honorable interment.

Emperor Marcian (450-457 AD) and St. Pulcheria convoked a council to be held at Nicaea on September 15, 451 AD. However, Marcian transferred the site to Chalcedon, opposite the capital, so he could attend the proceedings. The council officially began at the Church of St. Euphemia on October 8, 451 AD with the four legates of Pope St. Leo I presiding over the proceedings. It concluded on November 1 of the same year. This council took place two years and two months after the "Robber Council." It is generally agreed upon that there were only 16 sessions held and 30 canons formulated.

> Of the first four councils, Chalcedon stands out as by far the most important and glorious. It was attended by more bishops (almost 600) than any of the previous gatherings. They came mostly from the East because of difficulties with the barbarian invasions from the West. ...This council also stands out because of the profundity of the doctrinal decree, which is a superb summary of all that had been clarified concerning Christ and the Trinity during these first centuries; it also established firmly the terminology that has remained with the Church until this very day. In this way, it completed the work of these earlier councils.[75]

---

[74] Fr. John Murphy, *General Councils of the Church,* p. 60.
[75] Murphy, 61.

The Council of Chalcedon deposed Dioscorus of Alexandria, Juvenal of Jerusalem and four other bishops who were the ringleaders of the "Robber Council," declared the innocence of St. Flavian and Eusebius and denounced and exiled Dioscorus and Eutyches. Sadly, Eutyches continued to teach his heretical doctrines while in banishment and died shortly afterwards.

> Among the bishops whose cases were discussed at Chalcedon two are especially important because of the role their writings will play in the next century. One was Ibas, the bishop of Edessa; the other, Theodoret of Cyrrhus. These two had been condemned along with Flavian at the 'Robber Synod.' They were now reinstated by the General Council.[76]

When the *Tome* of Pope St. Leo the Great, which contained the beliefs of the Catholic bishops, was read to the Council Fathers, there arose the cry: "That is the faith of the Fathers; that is the faith of the Apostles! So we all believe. Peter has spoken through Leo."[77] The Creeds of Nicaea and the First Council of Constantinople were publicly reconfirmed by the Council Fathers.

Tragically, however, after the council many monks became Monophysites or joined schismatic churches. What began as a heresy ended in schism.

> The definition of the Council of Chalcedon was not accepted by the whole Church. The Monophysite controversy went on for nearly a hundred years. Finally all those parts of the Eastern Empire in which Greek was not the language of the people severed themselves from the Church and have remained in schism.[78]

The Oriental Orthodox Churches are independent but jointly reject the teachings of the Council of Chalcedon. These include the Armenian Apostolic, Coptic (Egyptian), Ethiopian and Syrian (Jacobite) Churches.

Disciplinary Canons of the Council of Chalcedon

Several canons or disciplinary laws were enacted concerning bishops, priests and monks along with laws regarding the jurisdiction and responsibilities of bishops. Priests were required to work in one diocese and have a means of support while monks were to observe celibacy and remain attached to a monastery. Much of

---

[76] Fr. John Murphy, *General Councils of the Church,* p. 63.
[77] Fr. John Laux, *Church History,* p. 156.
[78] Laux, 156.

this legislation, which could be considered early Canon (Church) Law, is still followed today.

Canon Twenty-Eight

One area of contention in the East that would eventually lead to the Greek Schism was the status of the bishop (patriarch) of Constantinople. Patriarch Acacius of Constantinople was excommunicated by Pope St. Felix III in 484 AD and the East remained in schism for 35 years. The final break between East and West occurred nearly 500 years later in 1054. In order to grasp the causes of contention between East and West, it is necessary to have a basic understanding of the hierarchical structure of the Church.

The First Council of Nicaea (325 AD) gave the following order of precedence: Rome, Alexandria and Antioch. The First Council of Constantinople (381 AD) attempted to give preeminence to the see of Constantinople since it was deemed the "New Rome." On October 31, 451 AD the 15th session of the Council of Chalcedon was held even though the papal legates were absent. Several Eastern bishops tried "an end around" and skillfully composed the controversial 28th canon that attempted to give the see of Constantinople precedence over other more ancient sees.

Even though the papal legates opposed Canon 28, the council nevertheless approved it. Pope Leo refused to accept this canon and responded with a series of letters attempting to persuade the patriarch of Constantinople not to meddle with the established order of ecclesiastical precedence. He explained how Jerusalem, Alexandria and Antioch (all ancient cities existing before Constantinople itself) were considered apostolic sees and as such, preceded Constantinople in rank. Constantinople held primacy in the civil realm as the imperial city but did not hold primacy according to ecclesiastical rank. This issue was addressed many centuries later during the Fourth Lateran Council and this order of precedence was altered.

Pope St. Leo I ordered St. Peter Chrysologus (c. 406-450 AD) to write a refutation of the Monophysite heresy to the Council of Chalcedon. His condemnatory letter to Eutyches was added to the acts of the council.

Papal Primacy

One must realize that the preeminence of the See of Rome was not as clearly delineated at that time as it is today. Pope St. Leo the Great emphasized Papal Primacy as no previous pope had done. This was of paramount importance in order to preserve the unity of the Church and the authority that Jesus Christ had entrusted to St. Peter and his successors, the popes.

Pope St. Leo the Great frequently made reference to the fact that he was the heir of "St. Peter." As defined by Roman law, the heir inherited the rights and authority of the deceased predecessor. Therefore, the pope inherited St. Peter's jurisdiction over the universal Church.

> Leo was the first pope to develop such a clear connection between [St.] Peter and his successors. Previous Bishops of Rome had spoken of their succession to 'Peter's chair'; of the preeminence of Rome as the imperial capital; and of Peter's residence, martyrdom, and burial at Rome. None of these ideas provided a firm foundation for papal power, however. Since ... Peter was at Antioch before he went to Rome, succession to Peter's chair was also claimed by the bishops of Antioch. Rome's preeminence declined with the establishment of the imperial capital at Constantinople and the removal of the Western seat of government first to Milan and then to Ravenna. And while no one disputed Rome's claim to have been the scene of Peter's final years, martyrdom, and burial, this hardly provided a secure basis for the powers claimed by his successors.[79]

Subsequent popes have upheld and validated the first four general councils (Nicaea, Constantinople, Ephesus and Chalcedon) in a special way because of their exposition of Catholic doctrine and their refutation of heresy. This is manifested by these words of Pope St. Gregory the Great (c. 540-604 AD): "Just as the four books of the holy gospel, so also I confess to receive and venerate four councils."[80]

---

[79] John Hughes, *Pontiffs*, pp. 30-31.
[80] Archbishop Peter L'Huillier, *Church of the Ancient Councils*, p. ix.

CHAPTER FIVE

Second Council of Constantinople

553 AD

This council was held during the pontificate of Pope Vigilius.

Background

The Second Council of Constantinople, which began on May 5, 553 AD and concluded on June 2, 553 AD, differed from all previous general councils. Its primary purpose was to scrutinize the writings of three men who had lived nearly a century earlier. The three men involved were: Theodore, the heretical bishop of Mopsuestia in Antioch; Theodoret, bishop of Cyrrhus; and Ibas, bishop of Edessa.

Theodore's *Creed*, a theological work, had been condemned at the Council of Ephesus in 431 AD, but Theodore himself was never personally condemned as a heretic. The infamous heretic, Nestorius, had been one of Theodore's pupils.

Theodoret of Cyrrhus, who had once been a friend of the heretic Nestorius, wrote a letter in favor of Nestorius in opposition to St. Cyril and the Council of Ephesus. He later renounced his heretical beliefs and became the greatest opponent of the heretic Eutyches. Theodoret had attended the Council of Chalcedon and solemnly anathematized Nestorius before the Council Fathers.

> He was the man who, so to speak, had taken over the leadership of the orthodox [traditional] believers when Cyril of Alexandria died in 444. He was not the great mind that Cyril had been but he was a more precise and exact theologian. Thus he was able to clear up some of the misunderstandings caused by the terminology of Cyril.[81]

Ibas of Edessa had written a heretical letter to the Persian bishop Maris; however, he later renounced his heretical beliefs and was subsequently restored to his bishopric by the Council of Chalcedon in 451 AD.

The collection of specific writings of Theodore of Mopsuestia, Theodoret of Cyrrhus and Ibas of Edessa contained a number of heretical passages and came to be known as the *Three Chapters*. The Monophysites attempted to bring about a condemnation of this work and its authors in order to discredit the Councils of Ephesus and Chalcedon.

Emperor Justinian

Emperor Justinian (527-565 AD), who convoked the Second Council of Constantinople, had great administrative qualities, worked for the common good of his people and endeavored to restore order to a fragmented empire. Justinian's priorities included public works, the economy and the security of the empire, even though taxation increased proportionately. Although the emperor's ideals were high, his plans were not always successful.

> From the statements of public documents themselves we learn that the peace continued to be disturbed, the officials continued to steal openly 'in their shameful love of gain'; the soldiers continued to pillage, the financial administration was more oppressive than ever; while justice was slow, venal and corrupt, as it had been before reform.[82]

The Eastern emperors of this era vacillated between defending the Catholic Faith, defending the Monophysite heresy or finding a middle course between the

---

[81] Fr. John Murphy, *General Councils of the Church*, p. 58.
[82] J. Bury, *Cambridge Medieval History, Vol. II*, p. 42.

two. Like the Emperor Constantine, Justinian ruled over a vast empire and frequently meddled in the affairs of the Church.

> Both Justinian's *Code* [529 AD] and the *Novellae* [compendium] abound in laws dealing with the organization of the clergy, the regulation of their moral life, the foundation and administration of religious houses, the government of ecclesiastical property and the control of the jurisdiction to which clerics were liable. During his whole reign Justinian claimed the right to appoint and dispossess bishops, to convoke and direct councils, to sanction their decisions, and to amend or abolish their canons. Since he enjoyed theological controversies, and had a real talent for conducting them, he was not deterred by pope, patriarchs and bishops, from setting himself up as a doctor of the Church, and as an interpreter of the Scriptures. In this capacity he drew up confessions of faith and hurled anathemas.[83]

Since his wife Theodora was a Monophysite at heart, Justinian did not consider them to be heretics. The ruthless empress eliminated all who opposed her designs. Theodora was responsible for the deaths of two popes (St. Agapitus and St. Silverius) and instrumental in installing Monophysite bishops in the sees of Constantinople and Alexandria.

When Justinian's legions threatened Italy, Pope St. Agapitus traveled to Constantinople in 536 AD to seek peace on behalf of the Gothic king Theodehad. Before returning to Rome the pontiff met with the bishop of Constantinople, Anthimius, whom he suspected to be a Monophysite. The Holy Father asked him whether he believed in the two natures of Jesus Christ after the Incarnation. Realizing that St. Agapitus knew he was a Monophysite, and not really wanting to hold such a politically manipulated ecclesiastical office, Anthimius cast off his patriarchal robes and fled.

The emperor and empress were furious at this affront to their authority and tried to intimidate Pope St. Agapitus by threatening him with banishment. The pope boldly replied, "I came to gaze upon a Christian emperor Justinian. In his place I find a Diocletian whose threats, however, terrify me not."[84]

---

[83] J. Bury, *Cambridge Medieval History, Vol. II*, p. 43.
[84] John Farrow, *Pageant of the Popes*, p. 50.

Sadly, Pope St. Agapitus was found dead several days later. Historians believe he was murdered through the collusion of Theodora and Vigilius.

Before returning to Rome, Vigilius [who was in the papal entourage] met with Theodora, and received from her 700 pounds of gold and the promise of the papacy if he would cooperate with her heretical schemes. Though there is no conclusive proof, it seems likely that the two main people behind the death of Pope Agapitus were Vigilius and Theodora.

In June 536 Silverius was elected as successor to Agapitus. He soon received a letter from Theodora demanding the restoration of Anthimius. The pope, of course, refused. Theodora wrote then to Belisarius [the commander of Justinian's armies in Italy]: 'Find some occasion against Silverius and depose him, or at least send him to us. Herewith you have our most dear deacon Vigilius, who has promised to recall the patriarch Anthimius.' Belisarius ordered Silverius seized, stripped of his pallium (symbol of office), and sent off to exile.[85]

Silverius was banished to Patara in Lycia. The bishop of that city received the illustrious exile with all possible marks of honor and respect; and thinking himself bound to undertake his defense, repaired to Constantinople, and spoke boldly to the emperor, terrifying him with the threats of the divine judgments for the expulsion of a bishop of so great a see, telling him, 'there are many kings in the world, but there is only one pope over the Church of the whole world.' It must be observed that these were the words of an Oriental bishop and a clear confession of the supremacy of the Roman See. Justinian appeared startled at the atrocity of the proceedings and gave orders that Silverius should be sent back to Rome, but the enemies of the pope contrived to prevent it and he was intercepted on his road toward Rome and carried to a desert island, where he died on the 20th of June, 538.[86]

…Silverius was dead of starvation on the island of Palmyria, a painful and lingering death arranged by 'our dear deacon': Vigilius. Vigilius was recognized as pope, because the clergy of Rome feared that anyone else would meet the same fate as had Agapitus and Silverius.[87]

---

[85] Anne Carroll, *Christ the King: Lord of History*, pp. 114-115.
[86] Fr. Alban Butler, *Little Pictorial Lives of the Saints*, p. 340.
[87] Carroll, 115.

Vacillating Vigilius

The corrupt Vigilius had the distinction of being personally responsible for the deaths of two of his predecessors, Pope St. Agapitus and Pope St. Silverius. Yet once he became pope he showed no loyalty to the Empress Theodora. His ill-gotten papacy caused him continuous anguish. During his 17-year pontificate he was kidnapped, exiled and suffered persecution for the Faith. His greatest weakness was his vacillation.

Several bishops proposed the convocation of a council at Constantinople to put an end to doctrinal disputes, but Pope Vigilius had other plans. "He had envisaged a council held in Italy or Sicily, with many Western bishops present. This Eastern council, held so close to the emperor's court, would be much too closely under his supervision for Vigilius' taste."[88]

> A stronger man might have avoided a crisis, but Vigilius did not. He issued a *Judicatum* in 548, a decree that condemned the 'Three Chapters'; then, in 550, he revoked this statement, deciding with the emperor to refer the matter to the council.
>
> His moves were not well received, to say the least. Why he acted as he did is difficult to say: weakness, ambition, fear. The West, however, was greatly upset. One group of African bishops met and attempted to excommunicate the pope in 550. About the same time, Vigilius decided to excommunicate the leader of the Monophysite group, Askidas, and found himself in trouble from the East.[89]

Justinian uses Violence to Achieve his Ends

By an imperial edict bearing the date 551 he [Justinian] solemnly condemned the Three Chapters a second time, and set himself to overcome all opposition by the use of force. The most recalcitrant bishops in Africa were deposed, and the rest appeased by means of intrigues; and since Vigilius, alarmed at what he had done, insistently clamored for an oecumenical council to settle the dispute, strong measures were taken against him. In August 551 the church of St. Peter in Hormisda, where he had taken refuge, was entered by a band of soldiers, who dragged the clerics composing the pontifical train from the sanctuary. Vigilius was clinging to the altar pillars; he was seized by the feet and the beard, and the

---

[88] Patrick Gray, *Studies in the History of Christian Thought, Vol. XX*, p. 68.
[89] Fr. John Murphy, *General Councils of the Church*, p. 69.

ensuing struggle was so desperate that the altar was pulled over and fell, crushing the pope beneath it [though not killing him]. At the sight of this dreadful occurrence the assembled crowd cried out in horror, and even the soldiers hesitated. The Praetor decided to retreat; the plan had miscarried. But the pope was nothing more than the emperor's prisoner. Surrounded by spies, fearing for his liberty, even for his life, Vigilius decided to flee. On a dark night (23 Dec. 551) he escaped from the Placidian Palace with a few faithful followers, and sought refuge in the church of St. Euphremia at Chalcedon, the same place where the council had been held for which Vigilius was suffering.[90]

Pope Vigilius remained at Chalcedon for eight months and continued to oppose the emperor's usurpation of Church authority.

The emperor now arrested all those who had joined the pope at Chalcedon. Some of the Italian bishops he put to the torture; Pelagius (the pope's chief intelligence officer, as ever) he threw into prison. Vigilius retorted with strength, by publishing the deposition of Theodore Askidas from his see, and an excommunication of all who had signed the emperor's Declaration of Faith, the patriarch of Constantinople notably. And he contrived to have these sentences posted in various places of the capital. It was a bold act that, once more, rallied the city to his side. Justinian bade his bishops make their submission, and in the basilica at Chalcedon they did so, very fully if something less than sincerely. And the pope returned to Constantinople (August 552).[91]

The Second Council of Constantinople

Emperor Justinian convoked this council in order to settle the controversy of the *Three Chapters*. It was held at the Church of Hagia Sophia from May 5 through June 2, 553 AD and more than 150 bishops attended. Only a few Western bishops came to the council because they mistrusted Justinian. The patriarch of Constantinople presided over the eight sessions of the council and 14 canons were enacted. The council condemned the person and writings of Theodore of Mopsuestia, and the writings of Theodoret of Cyrhhus and Ibas of Edessa which contradicted the teachings of St. Cyril and the Council of Ephesus.

---

[90] J. Bury, *Cambridge Medieval History, Vol. II*, pp. 47-48.
[91] Msgr. Philip Hughes, *Church in Crisis*, p. 110.

The emperor had the council condemn the 'Three Chapters' and then he threw the pope's deacon into jail, deposed and exiled uncooperative Latin bishops, and placed the pope himself under house arrest. After six months, the ill and isolated pope gave in and on December 8, 553, wrote to the new patriarch, revoking his earlier defense of the 'Three Chapters' and admitted they needed to be condemned. But the emperor was still not satisfied. On February 23, 554, Vigilius issued his Second Constitution, which completely endorsed the action of the council in condemning the 'Three Chapters.'[92]

Meanwhile, the Monophysites, ironically enough, declared that the concessions made to them were insufficient, and they behaved with such arrogance that the exasperated Justinian launched a whole-hearted persecution against them! Such was the chaos which resulted from Byzantine Caesaro-Papism.[93]

Pope Vigilius

No serious person would contend, that Vigilius was consistent in his action on the Three Chapters, but no honest critic acquainted with the facts, which we have been investigating, would deny that he constantly admitted the doctrinal errors of the Three Chapters, though in the case of the attacks on Cyril which are found in the letter ascribed to Ibas, Vigilius gently ascribes them to ignorance. He fluctuated only on the opportuneness of the anathema, now that the three were dead, and because Theodoret and Ibas had been received as orthodox at Chalcedon. The pope looked upon the condemnation of the Three Chapters, (i.e., if we take the view set forth in his first constitutum), as the altogether unnecessary digging up of a corpse, and as a slur upon the Fourth Oecumenical Synod. His fluctuation did not concern itself either with a doctrine or a dogmatic fact, but with a question as to the prudence of a certain action. When he came to the right view of the question, he acknowledged his former mistake. 'The question about which Vigilius could not make up his mind,' says Fortesque, with a certain lightness of touch, 'was whether it was expedient to condemn men who had died a century ago, whose names, in the West at any rate, were hardly known.'[94]

---

[92] Richard McBrien, *Lives of the Popes*, p. 93.
[93] H. Daniel-Rops, *The Church in the Dark Ages*, p. 178.
[94] Fortesque, *Orthodox Eastern Church*, viii, p. 83.

Pope Vigilius died in Syracuse, Sicily on June 7, 555 AD and was buried in San Marcello on the Salerian Way. Even after his demise there was great resentment against Vigilius because of his involvement in the deaths of his predecessors.

Tragically, the vacillations of Pope Vigilius created a terrible schism in Northern Italy and Northern Africa that would last for almost 150 years. Many of the Western clergy believed that the pope had compromised the Faith. This was not the fact, but one must keep in mind that telephones, radios, fax machines and the Internet were nonexistent in the sixth century. Global news was often related by couriers whose journeys could take up to six months.

The State of the Eastern Church

In the fifth and sixth centuries numerous countries in the East persisted in error and others have separated from the Catholic Church since that time. Msgr. Philip Hughes gives a detailed description of these tragic occurrences in his book, *The Church in Crisis:*

> ...let it be remembered that in the next eight years after 553 the differences had so undermined the stability of a good half of the empire in the East, as to lose forever to the emperors the loyalty of Egypt and Syria, and reduce the numbers of the Catholics there to a handful, and the jurisdictions of Alexandria, Antioch, and Jerusalem to all but naught. These lands were the original strongholds of the Catholic Faith, Egypt, Syria, and the rest, names which whatever they now bring to mind do not suggest the triumph of the religion of Christ Our Lord. Islam, of course, has for a thousand years and more dominated them. But the break with the Catholic Church, and its destruction in these lands, goes back earlier still, to long before Muhammad was born [570 AD], to the Monophysite reaction following the Council of Chalcedon.[95]

Justinian's Last Years

Emperor Justinian's attempts at religious compromise often were fruitless and frustrating for both sides. The violence used to achieve his ends embittered many against the emperor.

> At the Council of Constantinople he seems to have cheated himself, for what appeared as a triumph for the emperor was nothing of the kind. The Mono-

---

[95] pp. 94-95.

physites persisted in their beliefs, and condemnation of the Antioch school did not in any way impair the creed pronounced at Chalcedon, as Pope Vigilius had realized.[96]

He [Emperor Justinian] had such a great wish to find some common ground with them [Monophysites] that to satisfy them he slipped into heresy on the eve of his death. In an edict of 565 he declared his adherence to the doctrine of the *Incorrupticolae,* the most extreme of all the heretics, and as usual, he used force against the prelates who made any resistance. Thus until the end of his life Justinian had consistently endeavored to realize the ideal of unity which inspired and dominated the whole of his religious policy. But nothing came of his efforts; the Monophysites were never satisfied with the concessions made to them, and upon the whole this great theological undertaking, this display of rigor and arbitrariness, produced no results at all or results of a deplorable nature.[97]

Summary

It would take years before the events of the Second Council of Constantinople could be accurately related to the populace. Few Western bishops attended the council and many of those who did, including Vigilius' successor Pelagius I, suffered torture, imprisonment or exile at the hands of Justinian. These men surely would not be objective in narrating the events of the council. Also, Vigilius was one of the most hated popes in history; years earlier crowds had cheered when he was kidnapped and taken to Constantinople.

Eventually, peace would be restored. In spite of misunderstanding and human weakness the Catholic Church would live on. Popes Vigilius, Pelagius I and Benedict I approved the Second Council of Constantinople, thus giving it legitimacy.

Through the centuries individuals have made reference to the actions of Pope Vigilius to justify their opposition to the doctrine of papal infallibility. However, the case of Vigilius was thoroughly examined during the Vatican Council of 1869-1870 by many of the best intellects in the world. Fr. Wilfred Hurley, C.S.P. states that historians and theologians were unable to prove that Vigilius had erred

---

[96] Anton Henze, *The Pope and the World,* p. 16.
[97] J. Bury, *The Cambridge Medieval History, Vol. II,* p. 49.

when he pronounced judgment upon matters of faith and morals in his official capacity as Head of the Church.

> All that was necessary for them to do was to find a single definition which had been proven wrong. Or to find where one pope contradicted another, or contradicted a general council. ...But with what results? The record was without blemish. Down through the centuries the hand of God never faltered. His promises were kept with Divine, Infinite Perfection. The teachings and the commands of Christ safeguarded and protected. And thus it must always be.[98]

Fr. Clement Raab, O.F.M. clearly summarizes the case of Vigilius:

> It is to be observed that throughout this controversy no doctrine of the faith was at issue. On this both parties agree, pope and bishops, the East and the West alike. The question was whether, in the present state of the Church, it was prudent to condemn those writings which the Council of Chalcedon had not condemned, and to excommunicate a man whom the council had not anathematized. The question, thus, was one of prudence, not of Faith. The pope changed his measures when circumstances were altered. He deemed one mode of action advisable at one time, and when conditions changed, he adopted another. Here, also, we may note the sovereign power claimed and exercised by the Church of examining suspected writings, of condemning errors, and of requiring the faithful to submit to Her judgment. This authority is essentially necessary for the Catholic Church, guardian of truth.[99]

---

[98] *The Pope is Infallible*, pp. 22-23.
[99] *Twenty Ecumenical Councils of the Catholic Church*, p. 40.

CHAPTER SIX

Third Council of Constantinople

680-681 AD

This council was held during the pontificates of Popes St. Agatho and St. Leo II.

World Conditions

Marauding Germanic tribes drastically changed the face of Western Europe from the end of the fifth century until around 600 AD. The popes and the Catholic Church had been a stabilizing factor in the midst of the chaos. Gradually, the barbarian tribes of Western Europe began converting to the Catholic Faith: the Irish in the fifth century, the English and Franks in the sixth century and the Lombards of Northern Italy in the seventh.

By 610 AD, Muhammad (570-632 AD) was latently developing Islam in Arabia. "In 633, the year following the prophet's death, Arab armies, ardent in the Islamic faith, set out on a trail of conquest that was to alter the course of history and redraw the map of the Mediterranean and Middle Eastern worlds."[100]

Thirteen centuries later, by the year 1997, nearly 20% of the world's population would be members of the nearly 100 sects of Islam. "Some 1.3 billion human beings—one person in five—heed Islam's call in the modern world, embracing the religion at a rate that makes it the fastest growing on Earth, with 80% of believers now outside the Arab world."[101]

In the early years of the seventh century, war raged between the Persians and the Eastern Roman Empire. The Persians sacked Jerusalem, captured the True Cross and took Damascus. "During the Persian invasion in 614 over 300 churches, monasteries and hospices were destroyed; 90,000 Jews and 100,000 Christians were murdered, 140,000 people being put to the sword in Jerusalem alone."[102]

By 616 AD Egypt had fallen and by 617 AD the Persians, who had taken positions in the Hellespont, were within a mile of Constantinople itself. Heraclius was finally able to defeat the Persian armies at Nineveh in 627 AD. He rescued the True Cross and returned it to Jerusalem in 629 AD. The new confederation of the lands of the Eastern Roman Empire and the newly acquired lands of the former Persian Empire began to be called the Byzantine Empire.

The Monothelite Heresy

Since many of the inhabitants of the war zone were Monophysites, Emperor Heraclius devised a plan to win their loyalty by theologically compromising with them. Sergius, the patriarch of Constantinople, assisted the emperor in this undertaking. The result was a new heresy called Monotheletism. The name is derived from the Greek words: *mono*, meaning *one* and *thelema*, meaning *will*. In 610 AD, Sergius publicly taught that Christ had only one will; i.e., His human and Divine wills were mixed. The Monothelite heresy was just another form of the old Monophysite heresy. The former denied the human will of Christ, the latter denied the human nature of Christ.

---

[100] Robert Stewart, *Illustrated Almanac of Historical Facts*, p. 47.
[101] (In 2001), National Geographic (edited by Don Belt), *The World of Islam*, p. 16.
[102] *Pope Paul VI in the Holy Land*, p. 134.

The Rise of Islam

The Monophysite and Monothelite heresies were instrumental in facilitating the Islamic conquests of Egypt, Mesopotamia, Palestine and Syria. This point is elucidated by Msgr. Conway in his work, *Times of Decision:*

> The Arabs promised the heretics religious tolerance—and less taxes, too. Many of the peoples of Syria and Palestine share ethnic similarities with the people of the desert; they spoke a Semitic language related to the Arabic. In the cities, Hellenism in language, custom and religion had been forced on the people, but in the little towns and in the country—and in some of the mountain cities—the people remained strongly Syrian in race, language and even in religion. They were glad to be rid of the foreign government of Constantinople and to welcome their Arab cousins. The invaders, in turn, were generally kind to the little people, favoring their religion over the Orthodoxy of the Empire.
>
> The outstanding feature of that era was the transformation which had taken place in the ancient Christian world of the Mediterranean. Moslem Arabs had taken over half of it and were threatening the rest. It had all happened in less than 50 years. Muhammad had captured Mecca in 630 and died two years later. His fervent followers were mostly desert nomads, but they showed no reluctance in taking on the world's two oldest and greatest empires—Roman and Persian—and they met with little effective opposition. The two giants had just finished beating each other into exhaustion in a 27-year war: so that the disciples of the Prophet moved rapidly.

The Spread of Islam

> Syria fell [to Islamic forces] in 635, Iraq in 637, Palestine in 640, Egypt in 642 and in 650 the entire Persian Empire. So swiftly did Islam's onrushing armies advance that in the beginning they had time neither to convert nor govern their new domains. They contented themselves with exacting tribute, granting tolerance to all who paid it. Yet in ever-growing numbers, hordes of their conquered subjects embraced the new dynamic faith that had come to them from the desert wastes. As triumph piled on military triumph, the momentum of conquests carried the Arabs eastward to India, westward to the Atlantic, and across the strait of Gibraltar and to Spain, Portugal and France.[103]

---

[103] Editors of Life Magazine, *The World's Great Religions,* p. 102.

Pope Honorius I

Meanwhile, a monk of Alexandria named St. Sophronius (d. 638 AD) recognized the fact that this new heresy of Monotheletism was more entrenched than ever and warned others of the danger. The newly elected patriarch of Jerusalem used this position of influence to oppose Monotheletism. Sergius, the heretical patriarch of Constantinople, tried to silence his adversary by writing to Pope Honorius I (625-638) and asking that all discussion on the matter cease.

> His [Sergius'] letter was one of artful dissimulation and crafty deceit. Suppressing the role which he really acted, he pretended in all simplicity to consult the pope concerning the doctrinal difficulty which might be the occasion of scandal. He employed theological terms calculated to mislead the pontiff and to obscure the true question at issue.[104]

The misinformed Honorius wrote back to Sergius explaining the "moral union" between the two wills of Christ. The heretic, however, believed in a "physical union" of the two wills, but Pope Honorius did not actually address the questions disputed between Sergius and Sophronius. This gave Sergius apparent papal approbation to his crafty work and left him with the time to promulgate his erroneous teachings.

> In fact, the arguments of Schneeman, who compares the expressions of the pope with passages of St. Augustine, which he had before his eyes,[105] have nowhere yet been refuted; and in the import of their words, these letters, which appear as *epistolae privatae* [private letters], and not *epistolae dogmaticae* [dogmatic letters],[106] are free from heresy.[107]

"Had Honorius been less gullible in relying so fully on Sergius, and had he investigated the matter more carefully, much of the trouble could have been avoided. As it was, he unwittingly helped spread the error."[108]

Honorius, who believed that the opponents of Sergius held that there were two conflicting wills in Christ, responded by asserting that there was only one will in

---

[104] Fr. Clement Raab, O.F.M., *Twenty Ecumenical Councils of the Catholic Church*, p. 42.
[105] *Studies on the Question of Honorius*, especially p. 48 *seq*. Freiburg, 1864.
[106] Natal, Alex. H. E. Saec. vii., Diss. ii., prop. I Hefele Conc. ii., p. 284.
[107] Rump in Rohrbacher's Church Hist., vol. x., p. 134, *seq*. p. 146 (Germ. trans.)
[108] Fr. John Murphy, *General Councils of the Church*, p. 78.

Christ, meaning thereby that there could not be a conflict between the divine will and the human will and agreed with Sergius that the expressions, 'one principle of action' or 'two principles of action' (one will or two wills) were in future to be avoided as grammatical subtleties.[109]

During this controversy Pope Honorius I refused to teach *ex cathedra* on the subject or to issue a decree binding the universal Church.

> There may still be disagreement as to the belief and intent of Honorius and about his grasp of the theological points at issue, but it is entirely clear that his letters to Sergius, patriarch of Constantinople, whatever harm they may have done at the moment, were not *ex cathedra* statements by which the pope sought to impose a doctrinal definition on the whole Church, and consequently were not protected by his infallible teaching authority.[110]

> The Fathers of the Sixth General Council [Third Council of Constantinople] condemned Honorius as a heretic. But, in confirming the decrees of the council—and it must be remembered that no council has any infallibility unless its definitions are confirmed by the pope—Pope Leo II declared that Honorius was guilty of heresy only insofar as he permitted himself to be duped by Sergius and, through his negligence, had been largely responsible for the spread of the heresy. The action of Honorius cannot be used for the argument against papal infallibility. A careful reading of his two letters to Sergius—one is preserved entire, the other in part—leaves the impression on an unprejudiced mind that he was no Monothelite, although he uses expressions that could be easily misinterpreted, especially if torn from their context. He adopts the words of Sergius, but understands them in an orthodox sense. It is true that he forbids the use of the expressions 'one will' and 'two wills,' but he nowhere says that he requires all the faithful to accept this decision under pain of separation from the Church. Hence he did not intend to teach *ex cathedra*.[111]

In a second letter Honorius I again failed to condemn Sergius or Monotheletism. Pope Honorius I should have struck at the root of the problem and condemned Monotheletism at the very beginning as being heretical, or at the

---

[109] Fr. John Laux, *Church History*, pp. 157-158.
[110] Msgr. J. Conway, *Times of Decision*, p. 70.
[111] Laux, 158.

least, ambiguous. His failure to do so could probably be attributed to his lack of courage or to an improper understanding of the issue, which later popes were able to comprehend much better.

Although Pope Honorius I himself did not teach the Monothelite heresy he allowed it to grow and prosper through his inaction. Pope St. Leo II finally condemned the heresy. If Honorius had been diligent, the heresy would never have had such widespread promulgation. Following on the pope's failure to condemn either Sergius or the heresy, in 638 AD the Emperor Heraclius issued a decree called the *Ekthesis* erroneously stating that Monotheletism was the official teaching of the Catholic Church.

Persecution of the Church

Honorius' successors suffered terribly because of his inertia. Pope Severinus, who succeeded Honorius, was elderly and reigned for a mere two months. The emperor's soldiers plundered his cathedral (the Basilica of St. John Lateran) and his residence (the Lateran Palace) because of his refusal to accept Monotheletism. His successor, Pope John IV, personally ordained 28 priests and consecrated 18 bishops to be assured of their doctrinal integrity. There are strong suspicions that his successor, Pope Theodorus I, was poisoned by order of the Emperor Constans II, who had succeeded Heraclius.

Finally in 649 AD, Pope St. Martin I held a Synod for Western bishops at the Lateran in Rome and condemned Sergius and several other Monothelite heretics. Papal legates were sent to the East to depose heretical bishops and fill the vacancies with bishops loyal to the Catholic Faith.

Emperor Constans II retaliated by hiring an assassin to murder the pope as he offered Holy Mass. Miraculously Pope St. Martin I escaped this danger; nevertheless, he was kidnapped, taken to Constantinople and thrown into prison. St. Martin himself tells us of the appalling conditions he endured:

> For forty-seven days I have been given no water, whether hot or cold, in which to wash, and I am wasting away and frozen through with dysentery, which has never left me, on sea or land. At this time of bitter need I have nothing whatever to strengthen my broken and unhappy body, for the food that is given me is disgusting. But God sees all things, and I trust in Him, hoping that when He shall

have taken me out of this world He will enlighten my persecutors, that thus they may be led to repentance and better ways.[112]

On December 15, 654 AD, the pope was brought before the Senate, divested of his insignia of office, dragged half-naked through Constantinople loaded with an iron collar and chains. He was then imprisoned and later exiled to Kherson (Chersona) in the Crimea. He died on September 16, 655 AD.

Pope St. Martin's successor, Pope St. Eugenius I, opposed the Monothelite heresy while the patriarchs of Constantinople still continued to promote it. The Abbot St. Maximus of Constantinople (c. 580-662 AD) and two of his companions who opposed Monotheletism were horribly tortured by order of Constans II. Their hands and tongues were cut off and they died soon afterwards. The hated tyrant Constans II was ultimately driven from Constantinople by an unruly mob and was later murdered in Sicily.

The Third Council of Constantinople

Constans' son, Constantine IV Pogonatus (668-685 AD), became the next emperor and convoked a general council. After numerous delays, the council was held in the domed hall of the emperor's palace in Constantinople and lasted from November 7, 680—September 16, 681 AD. Historians debate about the exact number of sessions but agree there were at least 16. Although only 43 bishops were present at the first session, 174 attended the final session. Eight papal legates presided over the assembly. Pope St. Agatho sent a *Dogmatic Epistle* to the council, expounding on Catholic teaching of the two wills of Christ and defending papal infallibility.

Catholic Theology classifies three distinct actions performed by Christ:
1. Strictly divine: works of creation and providence, which this Second Person of the Trinity performed in union with the Father and the Holy Spirit, and in which the human nature had no part.
2. Miracles, in which the divine nature uses the human nature, but as a complete, rational and responsible human nature—not as a tool.
3. Strictly human: walking, eating and sleeping which are determined by the

---

[112] St. Mart. Ep. 15.

human will of Jesus, which is free, rational and by nature independent, but always subject to and conformant with the divine will.[113]

Forgery

At the council, Macarius, patriarch of Antioch, began to expound on the merits of Monotheletism. Since Macarius claimed that his belief (Monotheletism) was based on previous teachings of the ecumenical councils and the Fathers of the Church, manuscripts of the minutes from the councils of Ephesus, Chalcedon and Second Constantinople were brought to the council and read to the assembly.

Suspicions were aroused when several passages from those manuscripts clearly favored Monotheletism. Experts were therefore brought in to examine the documents. When placed next to the originals, it was found that the heretical passages were of recent composition and were purposely altered to support the new heresy. Emperor Constantine IV commanded that the original documents be locked up and, in order to prevent further tampering, all access was forbidden.

It was during the ninth session of the council that Macarius was removed from office for refusing to renounce his heresy. On March 28, 681 AD the council's 13th session condemned the Monothelite heresy and denounced Pope Honorius I for his negligence. The previous patriarchs of Constantinople (all deceased at the time) who had embraced Monotheletism (Sergius, Cyrus, Pyrrhus, Paul and Peter) were also anathematized.

Raised From the Dead?

A highlight of the council was the supposed miracle that was to be effected by an adherent of the Monothelite faith. On April 26, 681, "Polychronius, a priest and monk, promised to restore a dead man to life as an act of divine confirmation of Monotheletism. The Fathers of the council witnessed the farce from a window; Polychronius failed to work the miracle. He was asked to renounce the heresy. When he refused to do so, he was anathematized."[114]

---

[113] Msgr. J. Conway, *Times of Decision*, p. 79.
[114] Fr. Clement Raab, O.F.M., *Twenty Ecumenical Councils of the Catholic Church*, pp. 47-48.

Final Work of the Council

The Third Council of Constantinople clarified Catholic teaching regarding the two distinct wills of Christ:

> [We] ...likewise proclaim according to the teaching of the holy fathers that Christ has two volitions or wills, and two natural operations without division or change, without partition or co-mingling. And the two natural wills are not opposed (by no means!) as the godless heretics have said; but the human will is compliant, and not opposing or contrary; as a matter of fact it is even obedient to his divine and omnipotent will.[115]

Fr. Murphy masterfully described the Church's position regarding Pope Honorius:

> [Pope St.] Agatho had died before the end of the council, but the next pope, Leo II, approved of its decrees (including the condemnation of Honorius). His approval, in fact, indicates the mind of the council best of all. Leo explained to the bishops of Spain why Honorius had been condemned: '...because instead of extinguishing the incipient flame of heretical doctrine, as befits the holder of the apostolic authority, he rather fanned it *by his negligence.*' Had Honorius been less gullible in relying so fully on Sergius, and had he investigated the matter more carefully, much of the trouble could have been avoided. As it was, he unwittingly helped spread the error.[116]

Fr. Birkhaeuser further explained the condemnation of Honorius by the Third Council of Constantinople: "He rendered himself morally responsible for the spread of heresy, by having neglected to publish decisions against it; and in this sense alone, was his condemnation confirmed by Leo II."[117]

The anathema issued by this council "punished a forgetfulness of duty, rather than a *moral* complicity in the Monothelite errors."[118] "This has been the view hitherto taken by the most distinguished theologians, and among others, by many doctors of the Sorbonne, to wit, that Honorius was not a heretic, but only a

---

[115] Fr. John Murphy, *General Councils of the Church*, p. 77.
[116] pp. 77-78.
[117] *History of the Church From Its First Establishment to Our Own Times*, p. 217.
[118] Rump in Rohrbacher's Church Hist., vol. x., p. 77 (Germ. trans.).

favorer of heresy,[119] or that he was condemned for an error as to fact, *errore facti.*"[120]

According to Habert, the man who presided over this council "Pope Agatho does not name Honorius among the heretics, and that Maximus, the most decided opponent of Monotheletism, regards him and his expressions as perfectly orthodox, knowing as he did the assertions of Pyrrhus, and of his fellow-sectaries."[121]

The Monothelite heresy was finally eradicated except in Lebanon, where the Maronites tenaciously adhered to it until they were finally reconciled with the Church during the Crusades in the year 1182.

---

[119] Petrus Ballerini *loc. cit.,* pp. 306, 307; damnatus a sexto Synodo non ob haeresin, sed quia improvida dispensatione et nonnullis minus cautis locutionibus haeresin favorem impendisse visus est., pp. 306, 307, not. Praescriptum ab eo silentium, not fuit definitio fidei. The Gallican Natalis Alexander (HE. Saec. vii., Diss. ii., prop. 2, 3) says Honorius is acquitted of the charge of heresy *tam vere quam pie,* and appeals against his accusers to Combefis and Garnier. Cf. also Lud. Thomassin., Dissert. In Conc., Diss. xx., n. 18, *seq.* Bennettis *loc. cit.,* vol. vi., pp. 655-686.

[120] L. Cozza Hist. Polem. de Graecorum Schismate. Romae, 1719, P. ii., c. 17, p. 339.

[121] Dr. Hergenröther, *Anti-Janus,* p. 82.

CHAPTER SEVEN

Second Council of Nicaea

787 AD

This council was held during the pontificate of Pope Hadrian I.

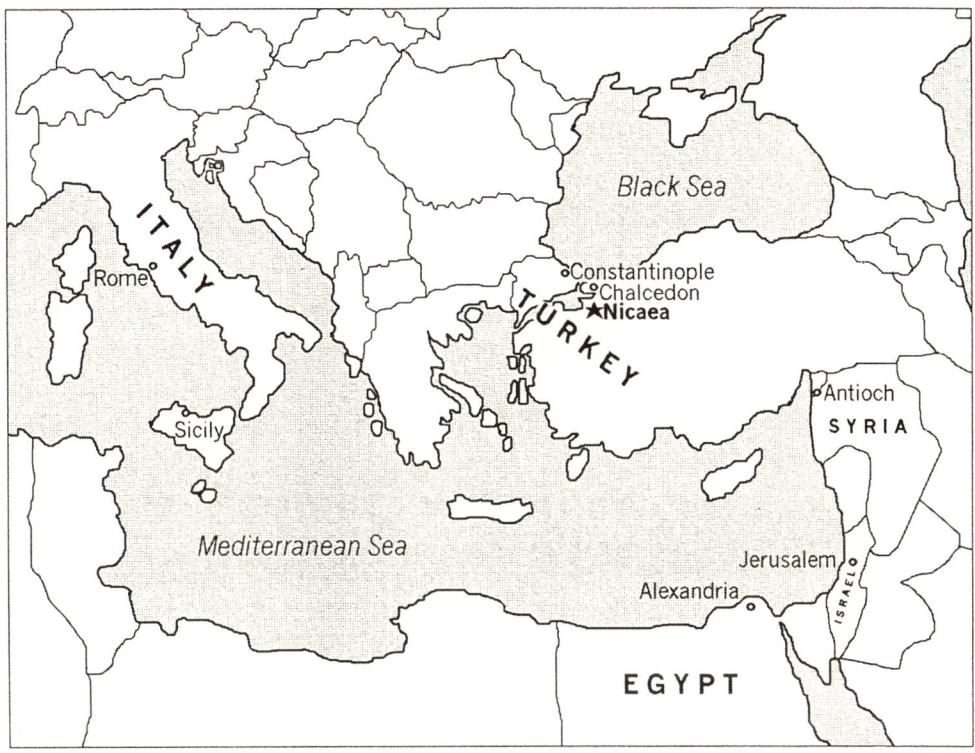

State of the Byzantine Empire

During the 8th century, the Byzantine Empire was in a state of devastation and decay. Leo III the Isaurian (717-740 AD) was a powerful general and skillful administrator who restored stability to the empire, but also began terrible persecutions of the Church.

Six emperors had been dethroned within the space of twenty-one years. Four perished by the hand of the public executioner, one died in obscurity, after having been deprived of sight, and the other was only allowed to end his days peacefully in a monastery, because Leo felt the imperial scepter firmly fixed in his own grasp. Every army assembled to encounter the Saracens [Muslims] had broken out into rebellion. …The Saracens ravaged the whole of Asia Minor to the shores of the Bosporus.[122]

Islam would have enveloped the entire known world had the tide not been turned by two great generals: Leo III in the East (718 AD) and Charles Martel in the West (732 AD). Though both military leaders had similar goals, differences in culture and religious practices between the Byzantine East and the Latin West kept the two regions worlds apart. This separation only increased with time.

> It was now to be one of the greater misfortunes of Christendom that, in the first centuries of this new religious menace [Islam], the long latent antagonism between Latin speaking and Greek speaking Catholics grew steadily more acute, and the obedience of the East to the Roman Primacy was, first of all, seriously weakened and then disappeared altogether.[123]

Iconoclasm

Caliph Yezid II[124] ruled the Islamic Empire of the East from 720-724 AD. He prohibited and destroyed images in the mosques and churches within his domain. "To Muslims, any kind of picture, statue, or representation of the human form is an abominable idol."[125]

Emperor Leo III, inflamed with a misguided zeal, imitated the action of the Caliph and in 726 AD decreed that all statues, icons and images of Our Lord, the Blessed Virgin and the saints be destroyed. He claimed that the people were worshipping images and were committing idolatry by praying before them. This practice of destroying sacred images is called iconoclasm. The name is derived from the Greek words: eikon (εικον) *image* and klao (κλαο) *to break*.

St. Germanus, patriarch of Constantinople, firmly resisted these innovations and explained to the emperor what the Catholic Church taught regarding the proper use of images: "The images of the saints are incentives for virtue in the same way as edifying discourses are; a picture is a compressed history, which

---

[122] Finlay, *The Byzantine Empire* (Everyman's Edition), p. 3.
[123] Msgr. Philip Hughes, *Popular History of the Catholic Church*, p. 93.
[124] A caliph is a successor of Muhammad who is both a spiritual and temporal ruler of Islam. See Henry Suzzallo, *National Encyclopedia, Vol. II*, p. 367.
[125] Charles Herbermann, *Catholic Encyclopedia, Vol. VII*, p. 620.

directs our thoughts towards our Heavenly Father."[126] He also wrote a letter to Pope St. Gregory II who confirmed the devotional use of images to remind the faithful of Jesus, Mary and the saints. However, the hard-hearted emperor refused to accept the consistent practice and teaching of the Church concerning images and began a campaign of brutality and destruction.

Today, many non-Catholics have been misled into thinking that Catholics worship statues of Jesus Christ, the Blessed Virgin Mary and the saints. When the occasion or topic arises, we should simply explain that these are reminders of people we honor as role models for our edification, just as athletes, political figures, presidents and generals, etc. are honored with statues, memorials and coins.

Paintings, statues and icons of the saints are no more objects of worship than are paintings of great national heroes, famous generals or even family photographs. Even memorabilia and decorative pieces in homes can be used to show non-Catholics that these items, even though much admired, are not worshipped.

> The use of images in the Church dates from very remote antiquity. This is sufficiently proved from the monuments of the Apostolic age, and from the numerous symbols and images of Christ, the [Blessed] Virgin, the Apostles, and biblical personages which adorn the Roman Catacombs; many of these symbols belong to the first and second centuries.[127]

"St. Gregory the Great says: 'Paintings are placed in the churches, in order that those who cannot read may at least learn from the pictures what they cannot read in books.' "[128]

Nevertheless, Leo adamantly opposed the appeals of both St. Germanus and the pope. He held a council in Constantinople in 730 AD to condemn the veneration of sacred images. The patriarchs of Alexandria, Antioch and Jerusalem did not attend the council and the reigning patriarch of Constantinople, St. Germanus, who opposed the emperor's plans, was banished.

---

[126] Fr. H. Rolfus, *Explanation of the Commandments,* p. 111.
[127] Fr. J. Birkhaeuser, *History of the Church,* p. 313.
[128] Rolfus, 111.

Iconoclasm caused an eruption of violence throughout the Byzantine Empire as Leo's hatred for sacred images burned uncontrollably.

> The emperor replied in the manner of men who are accustomed to wield force more readily than argument. He burnt all the sacred images in one of the public places of the city, and in the churches he whitewashed the walls, which were covered with precious paintings. He ordered that a large picture of our Lord, which had been erected by Constantine at the entrance of the palace, be smashed. Some women who happened to be on the spot implored the military officer to desist from his impious task, but their prayers were disregarded. The officer mounted a ladder, and with a hatchet hacked away the countenance of Our Lord. The women, beside themselves with grief and indignation, pulled away the ladder; the officer fell down and was killed on the spot.[129]

Violent Persecution Begins

On January 17, 731 AD, Leo III issued a decree which stated that anyone who did not destroy images in their possession or who honored them in any way would be guilty of treason. Thus began a severe persecution of the Church that was to last for over 50 years.

> The icons were broken up; illustrations of Christ and the saints were torn out of manuscripts; relics were cast into the sea. And when people resisted these imperial moves, prison, exile, torture, and death followed. Much of the brutality and savagery associated with the Byzantine Emperors has resulted from their activity in this matter.[130]

In his work entitled *The Pope and the World,* Anton Henze declares that iconoclasm became a vehicle to increase the political power of the emperor:

> In ancient Rome the image of the emperor had had vicarious power. If the emperor was unable himself to be present, he sent his image and that acted for him, as his representative. It had retained this function even after the emperors became Christians and regarded themselves as the representatives of Christ on earth. As the saints became venerated more and more, it was not long before

---

[129] Fr. Clement Raab, O.F.M., *Twenty Ecumenical Councils of the Catholic Church,* pp. 53-54.
[130] Fr. John Murphy, *General Councils of the Church,* p. 85.

their pictures were beginning to compete with the emperor and his image. The question then arose: who represented Christ on earth, the emperor and his image or the saints and theirs? The people of Byzantium decided in favor of the saints, and this seemed dangerous to the emperor.

Popes Fight Back

The pope [Gregory III] published a sentence of excommunication against all who, 'despising the ancient practice of the Church,' set themselves against the veneration of images, destroyed or profaned them. The emperor, on receipt of this news, prepared an expedition to punish the Italian bishops and to arrest the pope. But the fleet was wrecked by storms. Only the remnant of it reached Sicily.[131]

Popes St. Gregory II and St. Gregory III both held councils in Rome to condemn the destruction of sacred images. Patriarch Theodore of Jerusalem and St. John Damascene (c. 675-749 AD) also vigorously opposed iconoclasm.

Iconoclastic Council of Hieria

Emperor Leo III's son, Constantine V Copronymus, who succeeded his father in the year 740 AD, ruled the empire for 35 years and continued to promote iconoclasm. At his imperial palace in Hieria (present day Fanaraki) near Chalcedon, he held a council that began on February 10, 753 AD and lasted nearly seven months. There were 338 bishops in attendance at the council.

> So far as numbers went, this was one of the greatest councils so far. The pope was not invited to it; the see of Constantinople was vacant, Alexandria, Antioch, and Jerusalem were now well and truly sees *in partibus infidelium* [located in the lands of infidels]. The president was that archbishop of Ephesus who, nearly thirty years before, had been one of the first promoters of iconoclasm. What took up the time of so many bishops for so many months was not the proposal to forbid the veneration of images. Here all were agreed. But the bishops resisted the emperor steadfastly when he proposed to go back on the earlier, acknowledged general councils. They refused to endorse his heresies about the nature of Christ, the *Theotokós*, and her role of intercessor for mankind, the practice of prayer to the saints, the veneration due to their relics. So that the

---

[131] Msgr. Philip Hughes, *Church in Crisis*, p. 150.

final summing up of the council does no more than speak of the images as being idolatrous and heretical, a temptation to the faith that originated with the devil. No one is to possess or venerate an image, even in the secrecy of his home. All who disobey are to be excommunicated, and also to be punished by the law of the emperor, for their disobedience is also a crime against the state.[132]

Widescale destruction of images and icons followed, as few bishops had the courage to oppose the emperor. The Iconoclasts became so radical that they turned against the Patriarch Constantine even though he had been an Iconoclast himself. They prepared a special death for him.

> The Patriarch Constantine was required to mount the pulpit of Hagia Sophia and there swear by the wood of the Holy Cross that he was not an image worshipper. He had to renounce his status of a monk and become a secular. Even then rumors ruined him; he was deposed and sent into exile; and then he was brought back for torture and death. He was beaten until he could not walk, and then put on his throne in Hagia Sophia in mockery; then a long list of his crimes was read out and they struck him in the face for each one of them. Next they put him on an ass riding backward and led him to the Hippodrome to be insulted by the mobs. Then they cut off his head.[133]

McSorley gives other gruesome details in *An Outline History of the Church by Centuries:*

> In accord with the declaration of the council, an active persecution was inaugurated; pictures and mosaics in churches were painted over or destroyed; libraries, monasteries, and churches were robbed of art treasures and sacred vessels; and clerics who refused to obey the edict were abused, scourged to death, drowned, or executed in other ways. The abbot St. Stephen, best known of these martyrs, while awaiting his execution in 767, saw nearly 350 prisoners who had been horribly mutilated, many with ears and nose cut off, eyes put out, or hands chopped off. Most of the monks went into hiding or scattered into far regions, some of them migrated to Rome. The persecution lasted for years.

The monks who opposed his renovations and iconoclasm were a special object of Leo's fury. "Their beards were steeped in pitch and set on fire and the

---

[132] Msgr. Philip Hughes, *Church in Crisis,* pp. 150-151.
[133] Msgr. J. Conway, *Times of Decision,* p. 95.

sacred images were broken on their battered heads."[134] "And in the eighth and ninth centuries, according to certain scholars, as many as 50,000 eastern monks and, to a lesser extent, ecclesiastics arrived in Calabria in order to escape the persecutions of the Byzantine Iconoclast Emperors."[135]

No one was excluded from the persecution as 16 royal officials, including members of the imperial guard, were executed for retaining images of Christ, the Blessed Virgin and the saints. Monasteries and convents that failed to destroy icons were converted into barracks, granaries or stables. Artists found creating new icons had their right hands cut off.

The Iconoclasts then forbade prayers to the saints and desecrated their relics. "The vandals tore them out of the sanctuaries; they threw them into rivers and common sewers; they burnt them together with the bones of animals; they deemed no outrage too gross or too revolting to be inflicted on the relics."[136]

Putting an End to Iconoclasm

In 775 AD, the Byzantine Emperor Constantine V was succeeded by his son Leo IV. He persisted in following the Iconoclast heresy during his short reign of five years. After Leo's death, his wife, Empress Irene, became ruler. She consulted with St. Tarasius, patriarch of Constantinople, and Pope Hadrian I about the possibility of convoking a council to formally put an end to iconoclasm. Militant Iconoclasts disrupted the proceedings of a council presided over by the saint that was held at the Church of the Apostles in Constantinople in August 786 AD. In order to prevent further interruptions, the council was transferred to the Church of St. Sophia in Nicaea where the sessions began on September 24, 787 AD.

The Second Council of Nicaea

The council was attended by 368 bishops and two papal legates. The Epistle of Pope Hadrian I was read to the assembled Council Fathers and they proceeded to expound upon Catholic teaching concerning the use of images. Scriptural references and the writings of the Fathers of the Church were used in order to

---

[134] Fr. Clement Raab, O.F.M., *Twenty General Councils of the Catholic Church*, p. 54.
[135] Deno Geanakoplos, *Byzantine East and Latin West*, pp. 14-15.
[136] Raab, 55.

clarify the proper usage of sacred images. This Second Council of Nicaea enacted a total of 22 canons on ecclesiastical discipline. Many Iconoclast bishops were received back into the Church after they renounced their errors and the false Council of Hieria and all its acts were condemned.

The following is an excerpt from the Second Council of Nicaea:

> We define with all certainty and diligence that, as the figure of the precious, and life-giving Cross, so the venerable and holy images, both painted and of stone and of other proper material, should be set up in the holy churches of God, put on the sacred vessels and vestments, on the walls and on table, in houses and along the roads: that is, the image of our Lord God and Savior Jesus Christ, and of our inviolate Lady, the holy Mother of God, and of the honorable angels, and of all holy and distinguished men.[137]

The final session took place on October 23, 787 AD at the Magnaura Palace in Constantinople where Empress Irene and her son, Constantine VI (780-797 AD), signed the council's decree. Pope Hadrian I later approved the council's work.

> After II Nicaea, the heresy of the Iconoclasts lay dormant for the time. It was to arise again in 813 under Emperor Leo V. But in 842 another woman ruled in place of her infant son, this time Theodora. With the help of St. Methodius, who replaced the Iconoclast patriarch of Constantinople, she was able to give the decrees of Nicaea once again the respect due them as a Council of the Holy Spirit.[138]

> The controversy with the Iconoclasts began to have a more far-reaching effect both in Rome and Constantinople. The Eastern bishops had once again been cut off from Rome. ...The popes, on the other hand, became increasingly distrustful of the East, and of the Eastern emperors especially. ...The Byzantine kingdom would continue at least until the fall of Constantinople in 1453, but the close relationship with the papacy ceased after II Nicaea.[139]

The iconoclastic controversy added to the differences that would eventually pull the East and West further apart. There would only be one more general council held in the East, the Fourth Council of Constantinople.

---

[137] Fr. Clement Raab, O.F.M., *Twenty General Councils of the Catholic Church*, pp. 57-58.
[138] Fr. John Murphy, *General Councils of the Church*, p. 89.
[139] Murphy, 91.

CHAPTER EIGHT

Fourth Council of Constantinople

869-870 AD

This council was held during the pontificate of Pope Hadrian II.

Background

Following the heresy of iconoclasm, a number of events caused the rift between the Latin West and the Byzantine East to widen. One of these events was Pope St. Leo III's coronation of Charlemagne as Holy Roman Emperor on Christmas Day, 800 AD. The Byzantines believed they were still Romans even though Eternal Rome had long since fallen to the barbarian tribes. They strongly resented the establishment of the Frankish Kingdom in the West and were infuriated when Charlemagne gave himself the title of Holy Roman Emperor. There were now three world powers: the Arab Empire (Muslim), the Byzantine Empire (Eastern Catholic) and the Frankish Empire (Roman Catholic).

Charlemagne now enjoyed at least equal status to his imperial counterpart in Constantinople and a clearer legal position with regard to Rome and the Papal States. For Leo III the coronation established a secular power in Rome to maintain order, ended the papacy's dependence on the Byzantine Emperors, and added prestige to the papal office itself since it was the pope who bestowed the crown upon the emperor. The coronation, however, also sowed the seeds of eventual conflict between the two powers—a conflict that would endure through much of the Middle Ages.[140]

Ignatius vs. Photius

Ignatius, the son of the former Byzantine Emperor Michael I, became patriarch of Constantinople during the reign of Emperor Michael III, the Drunkard (842-867 AD). On January 6, 857 AD, Patriarch Ignatius refused to give Holy Communion to the emperor's uncle Bardas because of his scandalous life. For this affront, Ignatius was put in chains and exiled for a period of ten years. A brilliant and crafty layman named Photius was quickly consecrated bishop and appointed by the emperor to replace Ignatius.

In order to give his actions some semblance of legitimacy, Photius wrote a letter to Pope St. Nicholas I in which he claimed that the elderly Ignatius voluntarily chose to enter a monastery, and thus Photius reluctantly accepted the vacant office. A letter from the Byzantine Emperor confirmed this tale. Pope St. Nicholas I then sent two papal legates to Constantinople to ascertain the truth. In May 861 AD, a synod of 318 bishops together with the papal legates (under duress) deposed Ignatius and acknowledged that Photius was the legitimate patriarch. Ignatius appealed to Rome. A synod held in Rome in March 862 AD reinstated Ignatius, deposed Photius and suspended the papal legates.

Photius used the differences between the Byzantine East and the Latin West to further expand the devastating rift that remains to this day. These differences are quite apparent. The Greek Catholic Church had the domed Byzantine type of architecture, its liturgy was in Greek, leavened bread was used in the Mass, mosaics and icons were prevalent in the churches and members of the clergy were allowed to marry. In the Latin Rite of the Catholic Church, Romanesque

---

[140] Richard McBrien, *Lives of the Popes*, p. 130.

architecture was used, the liturgy was in Latin, unleavened bread was used in the Mass, statues were dominant in the churches and most of the clergy observed celibacy. In a peculiar synod held in 867 AD, the insolent Photius and 21 other ecclesiastics "excommunicated" and "deposed" Pope St. Nicholas I. They drafted an "official" document that contained their names and over 1,000 forged signatures. Photius further claimed that the West taught heresy by claiming that the Holy Ghost proceeded from the Father and the Son.

"The triumph of the arrogant patriarch was short lived. The drunken and vicious emperor over whom he had held sway so long was murdered in 867 AD. Basil, his murderer and successor [867-886 AD], cast Photius into prison and reinstated Ignatius."[141]

Further Obstacles

The language barrier was one of the greatest obstacles to union between the East and West and ultimately led to serious misunderstandings. The Greeks did not understand Latin and the Latins did not understand Greek.

> The majority of the Western bishops in the age of Constantine were still bilingual, but extremely few Easterners had any appreciable knowledge of Latin. In the second half of the fourth century, and especially in the fifth and sixth centuries, the decline of Greek in the West was very rapid. Pope Leo the Great had to rely on Latin translations of the acts and decrees of the Council of Chalcedon. Pope Gregory the Great (590-604) tells us that he did not know Greek himself and that it was practically impossible to find a competent translator of Greek in Italy, and that at Constantinople no one could be found capable of translating Latin into Greek.[142] This breakdown in linguistic communication between East and West was a major factor in the misunderstandings that so often arose on doctrinal questions, and the resulting cultural cleavage was an underlying cause of the Greek Schism.[143]

Cultural peculiarities also created suspicion and uneasiness between the two peoples. The distance between Constantinople and Rome was considerable.

---

[141] Fr. John Laux, *Church History,* p. 295.
[142] M.R.P. McGuire, "The Decline of the Knowledge of Greek in the West from 150 AD to the Death of Cassiodorus," *Classical Folia,* 13, No. 1, pp. 3-25.
[143] Msgr. William McDonald, *The General Council,* p. 48.

Correspondence was often inaccurate or outdated due to hazardous travel, inclement weather and unfavorable winds.

Hagia Sophia

The Fourth Council of Constantinople, which began on October 5, 869 AD at the Church of Hagia Sophia, definitively settled the struggle between Ignatius and Photius. Hagia Sophia had been built during the reign of the Emperor Justinian between the years 532-537 AD and was the largest church in the world. Procopius, an eyewitness to the imposing beauty of this Church of "Divine Wisdom," wrote in his book, *De Aedificiis:*

> The inside is too magnificent to appear commonplace, too tasteful to be thought flamboyant. The brilliance and sparkle of sunlight fills it. You could almost say that it was not lit from outside by the sun, but that it generated its own light so full of light is this holy place. From the round arch rises a tremendous spherical cupola of unique beauty. It scarcely seems to rest on its solid substructure, but rather to be a golden bowl hanging free above the interior. Up there in its heights everything merges in the most incredible harmony. One thing depends on another, yet takes support only from what is immediately beneath it. Each detail guides the eye further and so over the whole. Entering the church to pray, your soul is thus conducted on high. You ascend into Heaven. You feel that God is not far away and wish to linger in a place that He Himself has chosen.

The structure was so magnificent that the Ottoman Turks could not bring themselves to destroy it when they conquered Constantinople in 1453. Instead, they converted it into a mosque, replaced the cross with a crescent and added four minarets during the 15th and 16th centuries. The mosaics and frescoes that adorned the walls were whitewashed during the 16th century. The building was finally converted into a museum on February 6, 1935.

The Fourth Council of Constantinople

Patriarch Ignatius of Constantinople, the delegates from the patriarchs of Antioch and Jerusalem, the three papal legates and the twelve bishops who attended the opening session of the Fourth Council of Constantinople must have felt very insignificant in such an imposing edifice.

The ten-session Fourth Council of Constantinople condemned both Photius and the false council of 867 AD and enacted a total of 27 canons, many of which defined the duties and rights of metropolitans and bishops. Legislation was also enacted that concerned the various steps toward the priesthood and the time interval between these steps. Pope Hadrian II gave instructions for a new order of ecclesiastical precedence in Canon 21: Rome, Constantinople, Alexandria, Antioch and Jerusalem. The final session took place on February 28, 870 AD with 102 Council Fathers present including 37 metropolitans (archbishops). The True Cross was exposed for public veneration throughout the sessions of the council.

There had been consistent problems with unworthy or heretical bishops filling the see of Constantinople. "Photius was the sixtieth bishop of Constantinople. Of his predecessors, 22 were heretics, 21 were deposed, rightly or wrongly by emperors or councils or popes."[144] In his book *Separated Brethren*, written in 1958, William Whalen states, "Of the 239 Patriarchs of Constantinople, only 31 have died in office; the others have been deposed or murdered. At one time during the past century seven deposed patriarchs were living in the city."

The papal legates of the council had a miserable trip home as they were attacked by pirates, robbed and held prisoner. They were finally released and arrived in Rome in December, 870 AD. After being informed of the council proceedings, Pope Hadrian II formally recognized the Fourth Council of Constantinople the following year.

> After the death of Ignatius in 877 AD Photius again ascended the patriarchal throne, and in order to be approved by Pope John VIII professed in express terms to acknowledge the Roman Primacy. He soon broke his word and was excommunicated once more. He ended ingloriously. In 886 AD, the Emperor Leo the Philosopher deprived him of his office and banished him to a monastery in Armenia. After this, we hear no more of him.[145]

---

[144] Walter Ullmann, *Medieval Papalism*, p. 83.
[145] Fr. John Laux, *Church History*, p. 295.

The Legacy of Photius

Unfortunately, the death of Photius in 891 AD did not bring about an end to his influence. Fr. Murphy explains in his *General Councils of the Church:*

> The entire history of Photius was but an episode; the actual separation between Constantinople and Rome was relatively short. But the case had extremely grave consequences. For one thing, it brought into the open the antagonisms against Rome that had been lurking beneath the surface of the Eastern mind. Even more to the point, however, it marked a change in attitudes. While earlier patriarchs and bishops had been concerned about defending the east against the 'pretensions' of Rome, Photius had now directly attacked the papacy and accused the West of heresy.
>
> Thus it was the 'spirit' of Photius that was to dominate the Eastern Church in later centuries. While at the time of the break in the eleventh century, his name was scarcely mentioned, the seed of discord that he had sown came to full growth. As we may note later, in the discussions concerning the procession of the Holy Spirit at II Lyons and Florence, it was to Photius that the Greek theologians turned for support. His name became a rallying cry for those opposed to reunion.[146]

The Greek Schism

There were three breaks with Rome instigated by various patriarchs of Constantinople: the schism of Acacius in 484 AD, of Photius in 867 AD and the Greek Schism of Michael Cerularius in 1054 AD. These schisms occurred because of a variety of factors including human ambition, politics, economics and differences in language and customs.

Because one of the council's main works was the affirmation of Papal Primacy, the Orthodox rejected the Fourth Council of Constantinople following the Greek Schism of 1054. In its place, they accepted the Synod of Photius of 879-880 AD. Ironically, Ignatius, who was deposed by Photius, is recognized as a saint in both the Eastern and Western Churches.

The third and final split between East and West was precipitated by a man who held the office of patriarch nearly two centuries after Photius.

---

[146] p. 97.

Cerularius was as proud and ambitious as Photius, but with none of his learning and cleverness. It was he who inspired the infamous letter sent by Bishop Leo of Achrida to the West. In this letter the use of unleavened bread in the Holy Eucharist is declared to be invalid, and the Latins are reproached in unmeasured terms for fasting on Saturdays... for omitting the Alleluia during Lent, for shaving their beards, and for other divergencies from Eastern customs. Cerularius himself closed the churches of the Latins in Constantinople and impiously ordered the Blessed Sacrament to be cast out and trodden under foot as invalid. At the request of the Emperor Constantine Monomachus, who earnestly desired peace, Pope St. Leo IX sent three legates to Constantinople, but Cerularius obstinately refused to receive them. Thereupon they laid the document containing his excommunication on the altar of St. Sophia in the presence of the clergy and the people with the words 'Let God be the Judge' and immediately left the city. It was the 16th of July, 1054.[147]

Before long the body of schismatics would include Christians of the Coptic Rite from the Patriarchate of Alexandria who had earlier been infected by the Monophysite heresy, Christians of the Antiochene Rite from the Patriarchates of Antioch and Jerusalem, and, of course, chiefly, Greek Christians of the Byzantine Rite from the Patriarchate of Constantinople.[148]

The new church that was formed was called the Orthodox Church. They have separated themselves from the Catholic Church through schism by formally renouncing the primacy and the supreme authority of the pope.

The antagonism between the Byzantine East and the Latin West remains to this day. "The Greek Orthodox Church looks upon Rome as an enemy, regards the pope as a heretic, and does not recognize the validity of Catholic sacraments."[149] These prejudicial tendencies may be present at some Orthodox churches, though they are not held by all Orthodox. The Postconciliar Church, especially following Vatican II, has made a concerted effort to amalgamate the various religions in order to form a one-world church.

---

[147] Fr. John Laux, *Church History*, p. 296.
[148] Edward Finn, S.J., *A Brief History of the Eastern Rites*, p. 30.
[149] *Catholic World Report*, June 2001.

Since the Greek Schism, the Patriarch of Constantinople has remained a mere figurehead. "The Ecumenical Patriarch of Constantinople is recognized by the Orthodox world as the 'first among equals,' but has no direct authority over the conduct or policies of the Greek Orthodox Church."[150] For obvious reasons, no further General Councils of the Church were held in the East.

---

[150] *Catholic World Report,* June 2001.

Section II

Twelve General Councils of the West

(In Anno Domini 1123-1870)

The Twelve General Councils of the West were convoked by popes and addressed disciplinary and dogmatic matters. The majority of the bishops in attendance came from the West. The Western General Councils were held in: Lyons, Vienne—France, Florence, Rome, Trent—Italy and Constance—Germany / Switzerland.

First Lateran Council	1123 AD
Second Lateran Council	1139 AD
Third Lateran Council	1179 AD
Fourth Lateran Council	1215 AD
First Council of Lyons	1245 AD
Second Council of Lyons	1274 AD
Council of Vienne	1311-1312 AD
Council of Constance	1414-1418 AD
Council of Florence	1438-1443 AD
Fifth Lateran Council	1512-1517 AD
Council of Trent	1545-1563 AD
Vatican Council	1869-1870 AD

Papal States

A basic knowledge of the Papal States is required in order to properly understand some of the political and spiritual problems that faced the Catholic Church in (present day) Italy. This included bitter conflicts between pope and emperor. In some cases, a general council was required to resolve the issue.

During the mid-8th century, Rome was in great peril of being invaded by the Lombards of Northern Italy. Pope Stephen II appealed to the Frankish leader Pepin who quickly responded by conquering the invaders and giving the duchy of Rome, Ravenna and former Lombard territories to the pope in 754 AD. He "established the independence of the papacy from the Byzantine Empire and placed it under the protection of the Frankish kingdom, thereby shifting the sphere of influence over the papacy from the East to Western Europe."[151]

These territories had been held by the popes for over 1,000 years. The Papal States allowed the pope to be free of political influence in the administration of Church affairs. The famous Catholic historian Pastor stated that the pope, "…in order to fulfill his high office must be a monarch and not a subject."[152] Avarious kings have frequently attempted to seize these lands.

"When the Byzantine Emperor [Constantine V] protested the transfer of former imperial possessions to the pope, Pepin replied that he had taken up arms solely out of love for St. Peter and for the forgiveness of his sins and, therefore, could not hand over his conquests to anyone but the pope."[153]

The Papal States, which were a pivotal cause of enmity between popes and emperors during the 12th and 13th centuries, would finally be absorbed by the newly established Italy in the late 19th century during the Vatican Council of 1869-1870.

---

[151] Richard McBrien, *Lives of the Popes*, p. 121.
[152] *History of the Popes I*, p. 20.
[153] McBrien, 122.

CHAPTER NINE

First Lateran Council

1123 AD

This council was held during the pontificate of Pope Calixtus II.

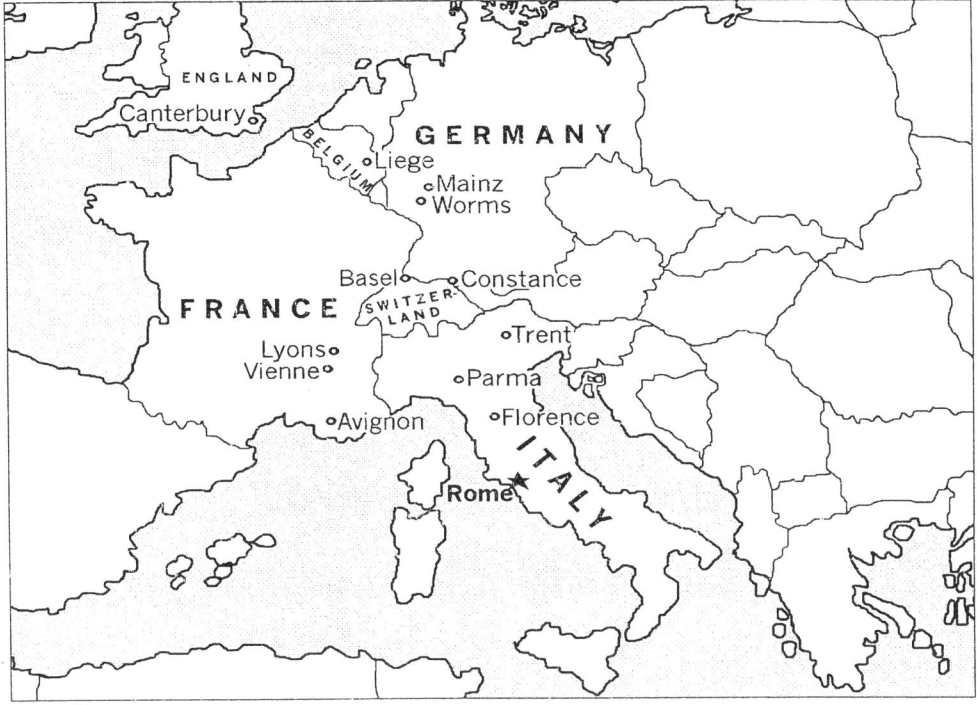

The Papacy During the Early Middle Ages (870–1096 AD)

During this period of history the papacy was in a position that was not only insecure but also dangerous. Due to the conflict of warring factions in Rome many popes were strangled, beaten to death or poisoned by powerful Roman families who wanted their own candidates in office. The average reign of the popes during the early Middle Ages from 896-1096 AD was a mere four to five years. Some popes reigned for years; many reigned for months; some for only weeks; while others held office for only days. Because of such criminal activity the power of electing the popes was taken out of the hands of Roman nobles so that such conditions would never be repeated in the future.

Simony & Clerical Immorality

The practice of selling spiritual offices and benefices is called simony. The word traces its origin from Simon the Magician who attempted to acquire priestly powers by purchasing them from the Apostles. Clerical avarice and immorality plagued the Church in the West because these practices opened the door for selfish and worldly men to procure important ecclesiastical positions. These abuses caused untold havoc in the Church.

Lay Investiture

Lay investiture was a prevalent abuse resulting from the feudal system. The king or feudal lord chose the candidates for the episcopacy and invested abbots of monasteries. Due to political maneuvering by lay authority, sacred offices were often bestowed on unworthy individuals loyal to the Crown or lord, or were sold to the highest bidder in order to increase revenues. Terrible scandals followed, greatly weakening the authority of the Church. Since great tracts of land often accompanied the position, and because many of these men were worldly minded, numerous priests and abbots became avaricious and completely neglected the care of souls.

> The origins of the Investiture Controversy can be traced to the policies of Emperor Otto the Great (ruled 936-973), the patron of Liutprand of Cremona. Otto attempted to bring large areas of Germany and Italy under his control but, his efforts were hindered by the opposition of the great German nobles. These men, under normal circumstances, would have been responsible to the emperor for the maintenance of local order and the collection of taxes. But Otto was reluctant to trust the administration of the empire to the territorial nobility. For Otto's most powerful vassals were also his potential rivals; several of the German lords sought to replace him on the imperial throne.
>
> In choosing his administrators, therefore, Otto turned to the clergy. He endowed bishoprics and monasteries with large grants of land, then made the bishops and abbots directly responsible to him for civil administration in their new territories. Otto likewise appointed his advisers and the chief officers of his court to Church offices: witness the example of Bishop Liutprand. As high ecclesiastical positions throughout the empire fell vacant, Otto filled them with his own men; he required that each new appointee become a royal vassal before

taking office. And Otto himself assumed the privilege of investing each candidate with the outward symbols of ecclesiastical authority—in the case of bishop, the ring and staff.

This 'Ottonian system' had several advantages for the emperor. It freed him from dependence on the hereditary nobility. It hindered the growth of rival families; since clergymen did not marry, they could not pass their offices on to their descendants. And it provided Otto with a reliable means for gathering revenue, administering justice, and supporting an army. For the next hundred years, Otto and his successors continued to rule the empire primarily through their clerical appointees.

As Otto himself recognized, the success of his system of administration depended upon papal sympathy. A hostile pope could bring the considerable authority of the Roman Church to bear against imperial policies or appointments. Thus Otto was careful to reserve to himself and his successors the right of controlling the selection of popes.[154]

On April 13, 1059 a synod held by Pope Nicholas II decreed that subsequent popes were to be elected by a majority of the cardinals with the acquiescence of the Roman clergy and laity. Since this decree of 1059, the protocol for papal elections has been altered several times.

Hildebrand

In 1075 Pope Gregory VII, also known as Hildebrand, held a synod in Rome to abolish lay investiture. The synod decreed: "Lay investiture makes all appointments null and void; whoever receives a spiritual office at the hands of a layman, whether he be baron, duke, king or emperor, is to be deposed, and a layman who dares to confer a spiritual office, is to be excommunicated."[155]

Papal legates (also known as nuncios or apostolic delegates) backed by the authority of the pope, traveled throughout Europe in order to put an end to this evil. Many of these legates later became popes and worked strenuously to reform the Church.

> Gregory VII was the 'marvel of his century' and in some respects the greatest of all the popes. He was not only the instrument of Providence for the reform of the

---

[154] William McNeill, *Medieval Europe*, pp. 165-166.
[155] Sr. Mary Loyola, O.P., *Visualized Church History*, p. 104.

Church, but also the savior of European society. By establishing the supremacy of the spiritual authority over the secular power—the *Sacerdotium* over the *Regnum*—he held in check the passions of the great ones of earth, the violent and lawless feudal aristocracy, who, if given free rein, would have thrust Europe back into barbarism. His death did not compromise his work. His ideals and ideas lived after him and triumphed under his successors. The glories of the twelfth and thirteenth centuries are the direct results of the policy of Hildebrand. 'The victory of the unarmed monk,' says the Protestant historian Gregorovius, 'challenges the admiration of the world with more right than all the conquests of Alexander, Caesar, or Napoleon. The popes of the Middle Ages did not wage their wars with lead and iron, but with moral force alone.'[156]

Emperor Henry IV

Henry IV, who became the Holy Roman Emperor in 1070, was admired for attempting to restore the former glory of the empire and his fastidious care for his subjects. However, the emperor totally disregarded the warnings of the pope and his threat of excommunication and continued to sell ecclesiastical offices at court. Bishops were consequently appointed for the dual role of minister of the Church and minister of the empire. Henry went so far as to assemble his bishops at the pseudo Council of Wörms in 1076 in order to depose the pope.

The situation was desperate and the pope acted quickly. "Gregory at once excommunicated the emperor and proclaimed that his subjects no longer owed him obedience. Europe was stunned. Henry found himself deserted by everyone. The bishops no longer supported him, and those who were opposed to him politically disregarded his authority. The princes of the empire decreed that Henry must stand trial before the pope."[157]

In order to avoid losing his empire, the monarch crossed the Alps with his wife and three-year-old son during the terrible winter of 1077 and arrived in Canossa, Tuscany. Once there he voluntarily performed public penance by divesting himself of his royal robes, donning a woolen cloak and begging for absolution from Pope St. Gregory VII while barefoot in the snow. Though penitent in appearance, Henry soon returned to his evil ways and civil war

---

[156] Fr. John Laux, *Church History,* pp. 308-309.
[157] Fr. George Johnson, *Story of the Church,* p. 210.

ensued. Although the emperor was again excommunicated and deposed in 1080, many nobles and ecclesiastics still supported him.

An Era of Antipopes and Pseudo Councils

Henry IV found a way to circumvent future papal interference; he merely created popes of his own. The creation of antipopes is the logical outgrowth of the practice of lay investiture. If a monarch could appoint bishops, what would prevent an emperor from appointing a pope?

The term *antipope* began to be used about the 11th century. Prior to that time they were called heresiarch, schismatic, intruder or invader. "*Pseudopapa* was often employed by authors of the eleventh and twelfth centuries. Terms such as papa falsa [false pope] were also used."[158] There were four antipopes and six false councils between 1061-1098 and 12 antipopes between 1100-1180.

Six Antipopes created by the Emperors Henry IV and Henry V

Bishop Cadalus of Parma as Honorius	(1061-1064)
Archbishop Wibert of Ravenna as Clement III	(1080-1100)
Bishop Theoderic of Albano as Theoderic	(1100-1102)
Bishop Albert of Silva Candida as Albert	(1102)
Archpriest Maginulfus of S. Angelo as Sylvester IV	(1105-1111)
Bishop Mauritius Burdinus of Braga as Gregory VIII	(1118-1121)[159]

Six Pseudo Councils Presided over by Antipopes between 1061-1098

The Council of Basel	(1061)
The Council of Parma	(1063)
The Councils of Mainz & Brixen	(1080)
Roman Councils	(1084) (1089) (1098)

Emperor Henry IV had the support of a number of bishops and lesser ecclesiastics who owed their appointments to him or who feared prison or other reprisals if they didn't cooperate with his plans. Due to the confusion of the era many well-intentioned clerics and lay people were misled by antipopes.

---

[158] Michael Stoller, *Schism in the Reform Papacy: the Documents and Councils of the Antipopes, 1061-1122*, pp. 379-380.
[159] Stoller, 2.

Concerning the divine protection of the Church, Fr. Murphy makes this remarkable statement in his book *The General Councils of the Church:*

> Had the Church of Christ rested upon the strength of men alone, their human weakness would long ago have sent it toppling to the ground. From a purely human standpoint, there was nothing that could have happened to ruin the Church that did not actually take place. Yet the Church survived because it was sustained not by men but by God.[160]

Reverse of Fortune

In 1093, Henry IV's son Conrad turned against him; in 1094, his wife Praxedis left him; and ten years later his son, Henry V, met him on the field of battle. Peasants endured great hardships due to the conflict between father and son.

> Promising to assist his [Henry IV's] reconciliation with the pope, he [Henry V] persuaded his father to meet him and accompany him to Mayence. Nothing was wanting that hypocrisy could suggest—tears, prostration at his father's feet, solemn and repeated pledges of safe-conduct. By these means he induced him to dismiss his retinue, and, on arriving at Bingen, represented the danger of going to Mayence and enticed him into the castle of Böckelheim, where he kept him a close prisoner.[161]

Henry IV was finally forced to abdicate in 1104 and escaped two years later. He died at Liège in 1108 as he prepared his troops to battle his son. Henry V was crowned Holy Roman Emperor in 1111.

Compromise

> He... [Emperor Henry V] wanted peace with the pope, but he was reluctant to give up his control of Church appointments. Twice he took an army to Rome to intimidate the pope, he set up an antipope, and at one point almost obtained title to all the temporal possessions of the Church.[162]

The bitter dispute concerning lay investiture was resolved on September 23, 1122 by the Concordat of Wörms. Pope Calixtus II and Emperor Henry V signed an agreement that assured the rights of both Church and State. The pope approved the process whereby the elections of bishops and abbots would take

---

[160] p. 105.
[161] J. Bury, *Cambridge Medieval History, Vol. V,* p. 150.
[162] Msgr. J. Conway, *Times of Decision,* p. 117.

place in the presence of the emperor who would not interfere with the election process and would aid in the return of Church properties. The consecrating bishop would henceforth bestow the symbols of spiritual power, the ring and crosier, on the new bishop. The emperor would hand the new prelate the symbol of temporal power, the scepter.

The First Lateran Council

Pope Calixtus II realized that serious problems still remained which could only be resolved by a General Council of the Church. The First Lateran Council was held in Rome at the Lateran Basilica on March 18, March 27 and April 6, 1123.

The Church of St. John Lateran took its name from an adjacent Benedictine abbey carrying the name St. John, and further added the title Lateran in honor of the Laterani family who once lived there. It is one of the four major basilicas of Rome and the pope's cathedral church. Its altar encompasses the altar once used by St. Peter when he offered Mass in Rome. The Lateran Palace itself was the residence of the popes from the time of Constantine until their departure to Avignon in the 14th century.

This site was chosen for the council since the pope resided at the Lateran and there were adequate accommodations for the numerous prelates in attendance. Calixtus II was the first pope to personally attend a general council.

> This general council of 1123 was, beyond a doubt, the grandest spectacle Rome, and the whole West, had seen for hundreds of years. Bishops and Abbots together were reckoned at something like a thousand, there was a host of lesser ecclesiastics, and the vast train of knights, soldiers, and other attendants of these ecclesiastical lords, as well as of the lay notabilities who attended.[163]

The First Lateran Council was conducted in efficient Roman fashion and concluded after only three days of sessions. The 22 canons of the council dealt mainly with matters of Church discipline:

- Simony and clerical immorality were condemned.
- Lay investiture was condemned by confirming the fact that spiritual authority can only come from the Church and by abolishing the claim of

---

[163] Msgr. Philip Hughes, *Church in Crisis,* p. 194.

- the emperors to appoint their own popes.
- Those who counterfeited money, or robbed or kidnapped pilgrims on their way to Rome, were to be excommunicated.
- Those in Holy Orders must not marry.
- "Marriages already contracted by such persons are to be broken, and the parties bound to penance."[164]
- The council sanctioned the terms of the Concordat of Wörms of 1122.

St. Thomas à Becket

Almost 50 years after the First Lateran Council, the courageous Archbishop of Canterbury, St. Thomas à Becket (1118-1170), made the ultimate sacrifice to defend the rights of the Church. Using his additional offices of being Primate and Chancellor of England, he almost single-handedly fought to preserve the liberty of the Catholic Church against the tyrannical King Henry II of England. When knights of the king entered the Canterbury Cathedral with drawn swords in order to murder the saintly archbishop, one of them shouted:

> 'Now you must die!' He ...[Becket] answered, 'I am ready to die for God, for justice and for the liberty of His Church. ...I have defended the Church as far as I was able during my life, when I saw it oppressed, and I shall be happy if, by my death at least, I can restore its peace and liberty.' He then fell on his knees, and spoke these his last words, 'I recommend my soul and the cause of the Church to God, to the Blessed Virgin, to the holy patrons of this place' ...He then prayed for his murderers, and bowing a little his head, presented it to them in silence. ...[thereby] ardently offering himself to God. He died on December 29, 1170 and Pope Alexander III canonized this martyr on February 21, 1173.[165]

The numerous miracles that have occurred at the shrine of the saint gave vivid testimony of God's blessing upon the work of St. Thomas à Becket. If lay investiture, simony and clerical immorality had continued unchecked, the Catholic Church would have ceased to exist. Courageous clergy who defended the rights of God preserved the episcopacy and papacy during these troubled times. A bishop's duty is to lead his flock to God rather than merely to please his king.

---

[164] *Contracta quoque matrimonia ab hujusmodi personis disjungi ...judicamus.*
[165] Fr. Alban Butler, *Butler's Lives of the Saints*, Vol. IV, pp. 398-399.

CHAPTER TEN

Second Lateran Council

1139 AD

This council was held during the pontificate of Pope Innocent II.

Background

Since no official records remain from the Second Lateran Council, much of our information is derived from correspondence and other documents of the time. This council which condemned the antipopes Anacletus II and Victor IV and the radicals Arnold of Brescia and Peter of Bruys was held at the Lateran. It is believed to have begun on April 2, 1139 (Laetare Sunday) and ended on April 16 (Palm Sunday).

Pope Calixtus II died in 1124 and was succeeded by Pope Honorius II. Due to the turbulence of the times, Honorius II was the first pope in nearly 100 years to live his entire pontificate in Rome. This would appear to represent a new period of peace; however, troubles were brewing and would soon erupt.

A Contested Papal Election—Pope vs. Antipope

Two leading Roman families, the Frangipani and the Pierleoni, contended to place one of their own on the Throne of Peter. Both families were strongly represented in the College of Cardinals and both families used intrigue, plots and clandestine measures to achieve their desired ends. This power struggle would eventually result in an eight-year schism with two men claiming to be pope.

Pope Honorius II died during the night of February 13, 1130 and was quickly buried before sunrise. Five cardinals of the Frangipani faction immediately elected Gregory Papareschi as Pope Innocent II.

Once the Pierleoni faction heard what had happened, they denounced the newly elected pope and elected Pietro Pierleoni to the papacy. He is known in history as the antipope Anacletus II. Rome was in a state of anarchy.

> Who knows which one had a better legal right to the office? Neither election had followed even the vague rules laid down by Nicholas II in 1059. The electors had voted when two of their members were absent. The assembled cardinals who accepted their vote and acclaimed Innocent Pope were only a minority of the College. Yet the group which elected Anacletus, while more numerous, did not represent the whole College either, and they were acting contrary to an earlier agreement to delegate the election to a committee of eight. There seemed no way of deciding which was really Pope. It was a pretty mess and lasted eight years.
>
> The legal right could be disputed, but Anacletus had more power in Rome; his family had money and he used it; he got an army together and captured St. Peter's and the Lateran. Innocent had to hide in a monastery, and Anacletus tried to capture him there. But somehow Innocent managed to get to Cardinal Aimeric's church on January 23 to be solemnly consecrated by the Cardinal Bishop of Ostia. But to compound the confusion Anacletus was consecrated the same day in St. Peter's by the Cardinal Bishop of Porto.[166]

King Robert II of Sicily married Anacletus' sister and allied himself to the cause of the antipope. Pope Innocent II fled across the Alps and with the aid of St. Bernard of Clairvaux and St. Norbert, gained the support of the rulers of England, France, Germany and Spain. Pope Innocent II finally returned to Italy

---

[166] Msgr. J. Conway, *Times of Decision*, p. 132.

and there crowned his protector, the Emperor Lothar III (Lothaire) in Rome on June 4, 1133.

Ironically, Anacletus still held St. Peter's, the Lateran and much of Rome until his untimely death on January 25, 1138. The antipope Victor IV was elected soon afterwards, but through the intervention of St. Bernard quietly resigned.

The Second Lateran Council

Pope Innocent II opened the Second Council of the Lateran on April 4, 1139. The three sessions were attended by 500 bishops and nearly 1,000 abbots from Austria, England, France, Germany, Italy, Jerusalem and Switzerland.

The 30 canons enacted by the Council Fathers confirmed the canons of the First Lateran Council and included much of the legislation enacted at the Councils of Clermont (1130), Rheims (1131), Piacenza (1132) and Pisa (1135).

- The Second Lateran Council declared that marriages contracted by monks, subdeacons, deacons, priests and bishops were to be henceforth considered invalid, null and void.
- Clergy were to don clerical attire and not that of the nobility or of the commoner.
- Laws of chivalry and "battle etiquette" were discussed and new regulations were enacted. Battles were to be fought between knights and soldiers. Merchants, farmers and clergy were not to be attacked nor taken prisoner. Deadly tournaments were condemned and those killed during these spectacles were to be denied Christian burial.
- Usury was condemned.
- Those who struck a cleric incurred *ipso facto* (automatic) excommunication reserved to the pope.
- Laity were forbidden from assisting at the Mass of a priest who was married or living in sin.
- The practice of raiding the bishop's palace after the death of the bishop was condemned.
- Canon 22 specifically commanded bishops to instruct their people on the

need for true repentance from the heart, not merely exterior manifestations of penance.

- Canon 23 excommunicated heretics who denied the Sacraments of Baptism, Holy Eucharist, Matrimony and Holy Orders.
- Canon 24 forbids the sale of the Holy Oils and the practice of demanding a specific price to perform a burial.

Clerical Celibacy

- "During Catholicism's first three centuries, no universal law or consensus governed celibacy for the Catholic clergy. All were permitted to marry and many did.
- Celibacy was advocated in the fourth century and preliminary restrictions were introduced. A married priest couldn't remarry upon his wife's death, for instance. Popes ordered celibacy of clergymen in the fourth and fifth centuries, but it was not fully embraced.
- The practice waxed and waned until Pope Gregory VII, in the late 11th century brought about a consistent observance of celibacy. Observant priests consider celibacy a gift that brings them closer to God and church without the distractions and duties of families.[167]

Pope Innocent II

Pope Innocent II was a man of extreme contrasts. On one hand he is said to have been devout, religious and prudent, while on the other, he seems to have been extremely unforgiving and vindictive. St. Bernard of Clairvaux's admonitions had little effect.

> If we can believe some of the stories, the Pope was really rough with the former partisans of Anacletus.... it is claimed that Innocent personally jerked crosses, rings and mitres from the bishops, and when one penitent bishop laid his mitre at the Pope's feet in sign of submission, Innocent kicked it down the aisle.[168]

---

[167] *The Detroit News*, April 21, 2002, "Celibacy Tests Catholic Church," by John Bebow. Source: Encyclopedia of Catholicism.
[168] Msgr. J. Conway, *Times of Decision*, p. 135.

Arnold of Brescia

The Second Council of the Lateran also condemned and exiled from Italy an ascetic named Arnold of Brescia. He was the superior of a community of priests in Brescia who attempted to impose monasticism on all clergymen.

"In flight, he was befriended by Guy, papal legate to Bohemia, who persuaded him to submit and accept penance. Misguidedly, Pope Eugenius III invited him to Rome to keep him under his eye, only to discover that the spectacle of abuses of the curia and the involvement of the papacy in temporal affairs caused a revival of his agitation in a fiercer form."[169]

Lambert describes conditions in his book, *Medieval Heresy:*

The grievances of Rome's citizens offered him a better platform than the communal movement of Brescia, and with their aid he expelled the pope and declared the independence of the city, where he attempted to realize his ideal of the poor clergy—preaching, administering the sacraments, wholly unencumbered by possessions or political power. For a time his views, especially his rejection of the Donation of Constantine and his belief that the emperor should receive his crown from the citizens of Rome rather than the pope, recommended him to the imperial party. The pope, though he returned with the aid of military force, was again expelled in 1150. But Arnold's reform plans of that year revealed what a radical he was, and he could only retain his place through a conspiracy of faithful followers of the inferior class and without further aid from the nobles. The logic of his own radical religious positions led him into an extreme democratic position in politics. It was as a revolutionary holding on to power with limited numerical support that he was finally hunted down under Pope Hadrian IV and executed in 1155.

His eloquence and appeal to the crowds assimilate him to the inspired wandering preachers of France, and he is fully in accord with the ideas of the time in his stress on the overwhelming value of poverty. But he differed from the wandering preachers in his readiness to use political force to gain his ends, and in the fact that he offered a program, not merely for the salvation of the individual, but also for the Church at large—a program he was prepared to enforce with the sword.

---

[169] Malcolm Lambert, *Medieval Heresy,* pp. 52-53.

Its fundamental tenet was that clergy and monks who had possessions could not be saved.

Peter of Bruys

About the year 1120, Peter of Bruys (Bruis) revived the Manichaean heresy in the province of Arles in France and claimed that material things were intrinsically evil. He condemned Friday abstinence, infant baptism, the need for a visible church and the use of religious artifacts.

"He decried churches as places of divine worship, and taught that the crucifix should be broken to pieces and burnt. He denied the Real Presence of Christ in the Holy Eucharist, ridiculed all sacrifices, prayers and alms offered for the dead. He rejected Tradition and the authority of the Fathers."[170]

Peter of Bruys was condemned during the Second Lateran Council. His beliefs would resurface years later in the sect of the neo-Manicheans, better known as the Albigensians. This matter will be treated in greater detail in Chapter 12—The Fourth Lateran Council.

The Second Lateran Council was beneficial in a variety of ways: it helped to end a schism, restored peace and rooted out heresy. The legislation enacted during this council brought about a reform of the clergy and a brief cessation of hostilities.

---

[170] Fr. Clement Raab, O.F.M., *Twenty Ecumenical Councils of the Catholic Church*, p. 78.

CHAPTER ELEVEN

Third Lateran Council

1179 AD

This council was held during the pontificate of Pope Alexander III.

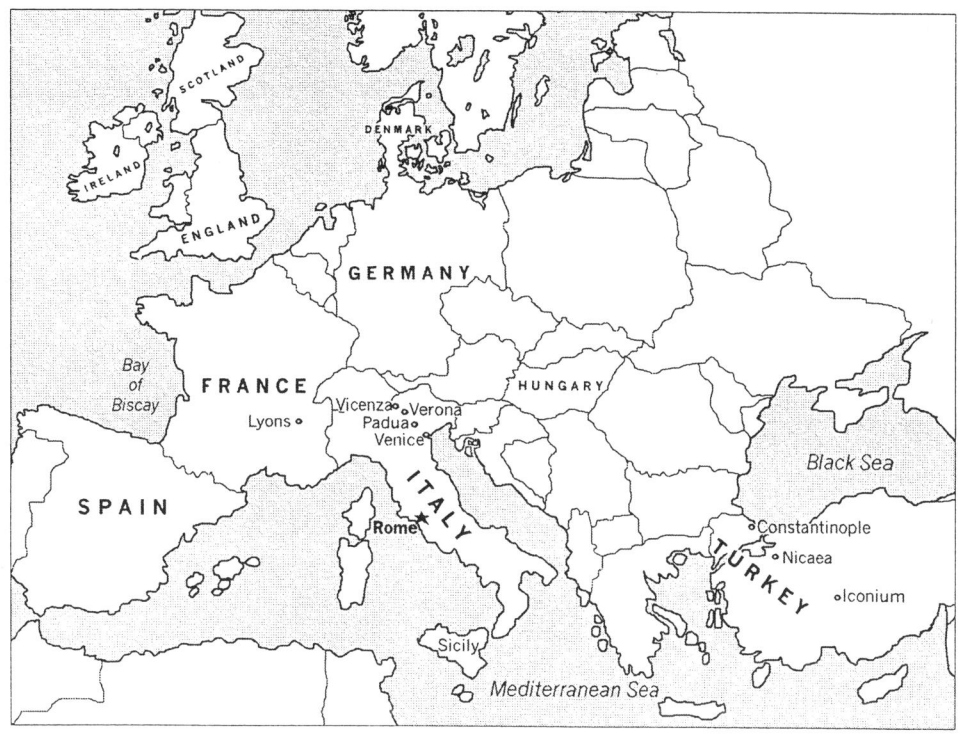

Background

Pope Alexander III, who reigned over the Church at this time, is universally recognized as one of the ten greatest popes in history. Besides being a brilliant scholar, he was an upright and courageous leader who would not be intimidated. Alexander did all in his power to preserve the liberty and unity of the Catholic Church in spite of almost insurmountable obstacles.

Early Canon Law

Pope Alexander had once been taught by Gratian, the monk-lawyer who performed the monumental work of codifying existing Church law. These laws were based on papal pronouncements and the canons enacted during the general councils. This summary of 3,458 canons came to be known as the *Decretals* of Gratian and remained essentially unchanged until a New Code of Canon Law was promulgated in 1918.

In the early 20th century Pope St. Pius X ordered a revision of Canon Law. This was necessary because through the course of time new laws were introduced and those that were obsolete needed to be revoked. To add to the confusion, some moralists wrote commentaries into collections of Canon Law which, though they appeared to be official rulings, were merely personal opinions.

Canon Law acquired tremendous importance in the life of the Church. Pope Julius II declared the divine character of Canon Law during the Fifth Lateran Council. "There this pope avowed the unalterable nature of the canons because 'these decrees were issued as it were by divine inspiration.' "[171] "The decrees of the popes as a legislator were credited with greater authority than the sayings of the saints."[172] "More weight was attached to the canonical enactment than to the *dicta* of St. Augustine or St. Jerome,[173] those who disregarded Canon Law were 'ipso jure' condemned as heretics,[174] for they thereby denied their faith."[175]

Red Beard

Emperor Frederick I, also known as Barbarossa (literally, *red beard*) had aspirations of becoming another Charlemagne or Constantine and holding absolute dominion over Europe. Barbarossa invaded Italy six times between the years 1154 and 1185; cities that opposed him were vanquished and often burned to the ground. He attempted to conquer the Papal States, but Pope Alexander III

---

[171] See Raynaldus, *Annales Ecclesiastici,* AD 1512, No. 100.
[172] See Antonius De Butrio, *Com. In Decretales,* I. IV. 17, No. 49, "Dicunt Doctores, Quod in Opinione Magis Esse Credendum Papae Quam Dictis Sanctorum."
[173] See Huguccio who was usually rather moderate: "In Negotiis Defininis Major Est Auctoritas Canones Sive Apostolici Quam Auctoritas Augustini Vel Hieronymi," *Summa Decretorium,* Dist. XX, Ante Cap., 1, 5, V. "Secundum Post," Fol. 129, p. 72.
[174] Huguccio. Loc. Cit., c.i.s.v. "Indifferenter," Fol. 129 verso: "Ipso Jure Sunt Damnati Tamquam Haeretici." He referred to *Dist.* XIX, c.5, *Dist.* XXII, Cap. 1 & C. XXV, q.i.c.5, 6.
[175] *ID* Ibid., *Qua Statuta Conciliorum et Apostolicorum Contemnit Contra Sedem Apostolicam.*

strenuously resisted his advances. The pope was often "on the run," leaving Barbarossa and his allies to occupy Rome during most of Alexander's reign.

> The popes fought to retain what they had gained—the recognition of the supremacy of the *sacerdotium* over the *regnum*, of the spiritual over the temporal power. The conflict was all the keener because the ablest and most energetic of the European emperors—Barbarossa, Henry VI and Frederick II—were opposed by Popes of no less energy and ability—an Alexander III, an Innocent III, and a Gregory IX.[176]

England, France and Spain, (as well as other allies of the pope lying to the north and south), remained faithful to the legitimate pontiff. Pope Alexander III organized the Lombard League of Sicily, Padua, Vincenza, Verona, Venice and Constantinople in order to prevent Italian cities from meeting the fate of Milan and other municipalities—cities which were razed by Barbarossa's armies.

More Antipopes

Barbarossa set up three successive antipopes in Rome: a second "Victor IV," Paschal III and Calixtus III. Thus began an 18-year conflict between Pope Alexander III and the three antipopes. The struggle between popes and emperors would continue for almost a century. Barbarossa commanded his German subjects to reject the legitimate pope (Alexander III) and give allegiance to the popes he created. Germany went into formal schism for 20 years while antipopes continued to reign for 21 years. "All bishops, abbots, priests, and monks were ordered to take an oath abjuring [renouncing] Alexander and acknowledging the antipope. The penalty for refusal was deposition, loss of goods, mutilation, and exile."[177] This hostility to the papacy would ultimately lead to the formal break from Rome by Martin Luther in 1520.

God is not Mocked

When the antipope Pascal III crowned Barbarossa Holy Roman Emperor at St. Peter's in Rome during the year 1167 it seemed as if the tyrant had ruled the day. However, on the following day a plague ravaged his legions and nearly

---

[176] Fr. John Laux, *Church History*, p. 334.
[177] Msgr. Philip Hughes, *A Popular History of the Catholic Church*, p. 126.

annihilated his entire army. The emperor fled Italy incognito in order to avoid being killed by his own soldiers, for they felt this was God's retribution upon Barbarossa's evil acts. The Lombard League was finally able to defeat Barbarossa at the Battle of Legnano in 1176. The following year the emperor surrendered to the pope in Venice and peace was finally restored. According to Fr. Laux:

> The years following the Peace of Venice were the most brilliant period of Frederick's reign. After the fall of Jerusalem in 1187, though nearly seventy years of age, he put on the cross, and by his ever firm and powerful will collected an army of fifty thousand Crusaders. After defeating the Turks in the desperate battle of Iconium, he was drowned while attempting to swim the rapid mountain stream of the Seleph in Cilicia.[178]

The Third Lateran Council

Pope Alexander III convoked the Third Council of the Lateran in 1179 in order to end the confusion caused by the previous usurpers of the papal throne. All three antipopes were condemned and their acts were declared null and void. The Catholics who followed them were restored to the Church after taking an oath of loyalty to the legitimate pope.

The Third Lateran Council began on March 5, 1179 and lasted about two weeks. In attendance were 300 bishops and nearly 700 other prelates from Dalmatia, Denmark, England, France, Germany, Hungary, Ireland, Italy, Palestine, Scotland and Spain.

Of the 27 canons that were enacted, one stated that a bishop must be at least 30 years of age, of good character and of suitable education. Canon 18 declared that bishops were to assign a member of the cathedral chapter to educate the clergy and poor students. The 23rd canon stated that lepers should have their own churches, priests and cemeteries. The 24th canon excommunicated pirates. Episcopal Visitations were also discussed in the canons.

> One never ceasing complaint is that the bishops' official visitations tend to be ruinously expensive for the places they visit. Their train—officials, guards, servants—is now cut down: archbishops to a maximum of 40 to 50 horses,

---

[178] *Church History*, p. 337.

according to the country and its resources, cardinals 25, bishops 20 to 30, archdeacons 7, deans are told to be content with 2. No hunting dogs, no hawks and falcons. And let them not demand sumptuous feasts, but gratefully take the seemly sufficiency set before them. Bishops are not to burden their subjects with taxes.[179]

One of the major accomplishments of the Third Lateran Council was to change the electoral process for papal elections. A two-thirds majority by the College of Cardinals was now required for validity. An absolute majority or the "morally better part" henceforth became inadequate for election to the papacy. The emperor, the citizens and clergy of Rome were no longer to be active participants in papal elections. The guidelines established by the council have remained in force for nearly 1,000 years.

In spite of the fact that these specific rules had been established to prevent the recurrence of antipopes, the problem continued to plague the Church. Antipope Innocent III ruled from 1179-80 and eight subsequent antipopes reigned during the 14th and 15th centuries. (The legitimate Pope Innocent III convoked the Fourth Lateran Council in 1215.)

The Third Lateran Council issued a decree condemning the Cathars (later called the Albigensians) and those who supported them in order to put an end to the excesses and mass suicides.

Peter Waldo

A wealthy merchant from the city of Lyons named Peter Waldo (Waldes) founded a religious group that came to be known as the "Poor Men of Lyons." (They were later called the Waldenses.) He and a number of his followers renounced worldly possessions and chose to live a life of evangelical poverty. They initially remained loyal to the Catholic Church, sought advice from ecclesiastics and journeyed to Rome in the year 1179 to present their case before Pope Alexander III and the Roman Curia.

The Waldensians arrived at the close of the Third Lateran Council, sought permission to preach and were approved after only a superficial examination.

---

[179] Msgr. Philip Hughes, *The Church in Crisis*, pp. 207-208.

Peter Waldo was later excommunicated (1184) because of his heretical teachings. He "founded still-existing 'Protestant' churches in Italy almost four centuries before the term Protestant was coined."[180] The Fourth Lateran Council would condemn the Waldenses, the oldest sect of Protestantism.

---

[180] *Life Magazine,* December 26, 1955.

CHAPTER TWELVE

Fourth Lateran Council

1215 AD

This council was held during the pontificate of Pope Innocent III.

World Conditions in the Thirteenth Century

Many Catholics have been led to believe that the Catholic Church enjoyed uninterrupted peace during the 13th century. This assumption is based on the fact that Europe was predominantly Catholic and many great saints lived during this era. However, the 13th century was not free from the turmoil caused by heresy and various world events.

Constantinople fell to the Crusader armies of the Fourth Crusade in 1204, thus causing a permanent rift between the Byzantine East and the Latin West. Entire nations were placed under papal interdict due to the actions of immoral and tyrannical kings, while wandering bands of beggars and heretics roamed the countryside preaching radical doctrines.

The Catholic Church survived these trials and dangers, proving once again that Christ is true to His promise; He will continue to preserve His Church until the end of time so that it can fulfill its divine mission of working unceasingly for the salvation of souls.

Age of Confusion

It was difficult to distinguish truth from error during the 12th and early 13th centuries. Misguided preachers conveyed a false gospel of their own making. It was difficult for bishops to keep track of these independent and heretical bands as they traveled from city to city since they lacked efficient methods of communication. On November 4, 1184 Pope Lucius III and Barbarossa jointly opposed the many heresies that were propagated at the time, forbade unlicensed preaching and condemned all those who rejected the sacraments and Catholic teaching.

> If the heresy of the twelfth century had been a 'sect' with a 'founder' and particular dogmatic errors like the heresies of earlier times, the Church would have been able to combat it as it had others before. But heresy in the twelfth century was a religious movement without a 'founder' and hence without a single name, lacking a solid organization and the universal mark of earlier heresies, namely, a particular heretical doctrine defining the nature of the heresy. Instead, there was an emphatic concept of religious life, thought authorized by the gospels and apostolic writings, and it was here where it parted company with the Catholic Church.[181]

The Cathars (Albigensians)

A number of religious groups emerged and spread throughout Europe during the latter Middle Ages. The members of these loosely knit organizations often fell into heresy and fanaticism since they operated outside the Catholic Church and were answerable to no one.

More than mere heretics, the Cathars were actually pagan infidels who revived the ancient Manichean heresy. The founder of the Manichean heresy,

---

[181] Herbert Grundmann, *Religious Movements in the Middle Ages*, p. 22.

Mani (c. 215-277 AD), had combined the ancient religions of Babylon, Zoroaster[182] and Buddhism[183] while adding various facets of Christianity.

The Cathars taught that there were two gods: one good and the other evil. They believed that anything of a spiritual nature was intrinsically good and emanated from a good god and anything material was evil and emanated from an evil god. "In the Manichean view, God and Satan are opposites, and both are absolute. ...This view has been labeled a heresy in Christian history. 'Actually the Christian doctrine is that evil is limited. We profess actually there is only one absolute being—God. Everything else is finite.' "[184]

> This was a peculiar perversion: Manichaeanism (or as we say today, 'Puritan'), in producing a social effect of the worst kind, ruinous to beauty without the goodness within. Yet it rapidly became dominant in the richest and most central part of Catholic Europe, the South of France, during the last half of the twelfth century—that is, in the lifetime before 1200. In the early thirteenth it was spreading everywhere, and it looked as though it might win. It had a very strong organization of its own: its own bishops, priests and councils: it was only conquered after the most desperate fighting and through [the power of the Rosary and] the inspiration of St. Dominic. The struggle was like the difficult stamping out of a raging fire. Great parts of Spain sympathized with the Albigensian lords: a Catalan army of 1,000 men came up in relief of the Albigensians and had it not been for the battle of Muret in 1213, Catholicism and European civilization today might be confined to some isolated corners of Europe; or perhaps it might not have survived at all.[185]

The Cathars fell into one of three classifications: hearers, believers and the "perfect ones." "Perfect ones" took part in a special initiation ceremony where they renounced Catholicism, accepted Catharism and promised to observe chastity, strict diet and isolation from society. The "perfect ones" then believed

---

[182] Zoroastrianism is an ancient dualist Persian religion that was founded by Zoroaster about the year 1000 BC. Its adherents "worship fire, earth, water, air as sacred..." Philip Wilkinson, *DK Illustrated Dictionary of Religions,* p. 21.
[183] "A religion of eastern and central Asia growing out of the teaching of Gautama Buddha that suffering is inherent in life and that one can be liberated from it by mental and moral self-purification." *Merriam-Webster's Collegiate® Dictionary,* 1998, p. 232.
[184] Quote from Fr. Peter Phan, *National Catholic Reporter,* January 11, 2002.
[185] Hilaire Belloc, *How the Reformation Happened,* p. 28.

that they could no longer sin because the Holy Ghost took up residence in them during their initiation ceremony.

Cathars condemned marriage, procreation and the eating of meat. "They also condemned military service, and considered voluntary suicide as the ideal of sanctity. Some of them opened their veins to die in a bath, or took poison. But the most widespread form of suicide consisted in undergoing the endura, or allowing themselves to starve to death."[186]

The Cathars had a clearly delineated type of caste system. Thus Catharism seemed to outsiders as a religion essentially based on pride.

Heinrich Fichtenau, in his book *Heretics and Scholars in the High Middle Ages, 1000-1200*, gives the etymology of the term *Cathar*:

> In the third century the sectarian Novatianists called themselves Katharoi, and a branch of the Manichaeans viewed themselves as *katharistae* purifying ones. It has been proposed that the heretics themselves used the term 'Cathars,' in other words the pure ones (Greek: *katharoi*).

The name *Cathar* may also have been derived from the German word for heretics, "ketzer." The Council of Tours (1163) gave them the name Albigensians, since many Cathars settled in the French city of Albi. Other Albigensians settled near Cambrai, Limoges, Orléans, Poitiers, Tournai, Tours and Toulouse.

State of the Clergy

Pope Innocent III tried to rally the bishops and priests to oppose the inroads of heresy, only to realize that they were often oblivious to the dangers that threatened their flocks. Others contributed to the spread of heresy because of their laxity, ignorance, worldliness or scandalous lives.

"This condition was not universal. Here and there might be found zealous prelates and edifying pastors. Some even shone with the radiance of holiness in the firmament of the Church. Unfortunately they were rare stars in a dark night."[187]

---

[186] Msgr. Léon Cristiani, *Heresies and Heretics*, p. 63.
[187] Pierre Mandonnet, O.P., *St. Dominic and His Work*, p. 16.

Dominicans to the Rescue

Divine intervention was needed to eradicate the evil epidemic of heresy. In 1214 the Blessed Virgin Mary appeared to St. Dominic (1170-1221), the founder of the Order of Preachers, and taught him the devotion of the Rosary. Our Lady promised that by means of this unique combination of vocal and mental prayer peace and order would finally be restored. The results from St. Dominic's preaching the Rosary were nothing short of miraculous. As the Rosary devotion spread throughout the Christian world piety flourished, sinners were converted and many of the Albigensians renounced their errors.

The Dominican St. Peter of Verona (1205-1252) worked with great success among those who fell victim to the Albigensian heresy in Italy. He was hated by the enemies of the Church and later gave his life for the Catholic Faith.

> He possessed splendid talent for instructing the people, and for convincing them of the truths which he preached. More admirable still was his gift of touching hearts and inspiring even the most obdurate with salutary fear. It was this that led his superiors to send him through Italy as an apostolic man. ...Everywhere his labors brought about striking conversions. Persons who had long been public enemies mutually forgave the injuries they had received. Noted sinners gave up their ways of evil. Many heretics abjured their errors, and were received into the fold of the Church....[188]

The Waldenses—Precursors of Protestantism

Peter Waldo, who was mentioned in the previous chapter, organized the "Poor Men of Lyons" about the year 1176. The Waldenses were a diverse group of wandering preachers whose common traits included a love for poverty and a desire to preach. There were two types of Waldenses: those who remained faithful to the Catholic Church and those who were heretics.

Catholic Waldenses: The Waldensian leader Durandus of Huesca together with many of his followers were received back into the Church after making a profession of faith in 1208. Similarly, other groups of Waldenses were reconciled

---

[188] Father Anthony Touron, O.P., *First Disciples of St. Dominic*, p. 11.

with the Church at a later time. Many of the itinerant Waldenses were members of the clergy and were allowed to preach against heretics and to maintain schools.

Heretical Waldenses: Rejected the baptism of infants, the priesthood, Purgatory, praying for the dead, veneration of the saints, vestments, bells, organs and relics. Some Waldenses revived the ancient Donatist heresy and claimed that sinful priests did not validly confect the sacraments.

These heretics opposed the concept of a hierarchical Church, offered a prayer service that was called "the Lord's Supper" and began to confess their sins to one another. They resembled the "Born Again Christians" of today by their memorization of multiple Biblical texts. Heretical Waldenses were excommunicated on numerous occasions.

The Humiliati

The Humiliati, often called the "Catholic Poor," were men and women from the Lombard region of Italy who wished to lead a life of perfection and detachment while yet remaining in the world. They were known for their life of poverty and for their abhorrence of oaths and lies.

Pope Innocent III and the Roman Curia approved the Humiliati in 1201 and allowed them to belong to a religious community, preach against heretics and live in the spirit of poverty. The organization was divided into three categories: canons, monks and a religious society consisting solely of laity.

Franciscans and Dominicans

Pope Innocent III would finally put an end to the confusion arising from all these various groups by holding the Fourth Council of the Lateran and approving the Dominican and Franciscan Orders. St. Dominic (1170-1221) and St. Francis of Assisi (1181-1226) were instrumental in transforming the 13th century into a glorious age for the Catholic Church by their respective orders of priests, friars and religious brothers (First Order), religious sisters (Second Order) and the laity (Third Order). The Third Orders allowed the laity to share in the apostolic works and prayers of the religious. St. Louis IX, King of France, and St. Elizabeth of Hungary were members of the Franciscan Third Order.

There was a stark contrast between the religious who were faithful to the doctrines of the Church and who lived a deeply spiritual life and the various bands of heretical beggars and preachers who taught a gospel based solely on their literal interpretation of Holy Scripture. Dominicans and Franciscans were well versed in theology, led a life of prayer, practiced poverty and assisted the poor. The priests of both these religious institutes worked closely with the bishops to rekindle the faith by offering Holy Mass, preaching dogmatic sermons and being available to hear the confessions of the populace.

St. Francis of Assisi's Crusade

St. Francis of Assisi had a great love for humanity, yet he never condoned dialogue with other religions. History relates that in 1219 he attempted to convert the Muslim leader Sultan Melek-el-Kamil during the Fifth Crusade. When the leader asked him why he had come, St. Francis replied, "I am sent not by men but by the Most High God, to show you and your people the way of salvation, by announcing to you the truth of the gospel."[189] The sultan then said to the saint and his companion, " 'My doctors counsel me to have your heads cut off, but I will never send to his death one who would give his life for my salvation.' He let them go free with a decree permitting Francis and his fellow friars to roam undisturbed through Saracen lands, including Palestine, and go to the Holy Sepulchre without paying tribute."[190]

St. Francis was then escorted to the crusader camp at Damietta and went on to visit the sacred sites of the Holy Land. He returned to thank the sultan and was greeted with these words, "Pray for me, that God may make known to me the true religion, and conduct me to it." Two Franciscan friars journeyed to the palace of Melek-el-Kamil 19 years later and baptized him shortly before he expired. St. Francis' faith and love for God accomplished more than all eight crusades from 1096 to 1291 put together, since he and his friars retain custody of the holy sites of Palestine even to this day.

---

[189] Fr. Alban Butler, *Butler's Lives of the Saints, Vol. III*, p. 454.
[190] Maria Sticco, *Peace of St. Francis*, p. 168.

"A colorful fresco by Giotto in the main Basilica of San Francesco shows Melek-el-Kamil, the Sultan of Cairo under siege by Christians of the Fifth Crusade (1217-1221), offering his hand to Francis, who had crossed battle lines to preach the Gospel to him."[191]

The Fourth Lateran Council

This council was certainly the largest and most splendid the world had known. We are told that there were 412 archbishops and bishops, more than 800 abbots and priors, a multitude of representatives of cathedral and collegiate chapters and of bishops who were not able to attend personally. Just about every king of that day was represented there, along with princes, barons, dukes and counts down to the municipal level. There was no Roman Emperor at the moment, but the western emperor of Constantinople had his ambassador there.[192]

Turbulent times called for serious action. As Pope Innocent III convoked the Fourth Council of the Lateran, he sent a detailed memo to the bishops around the world to adequately prepare them for this important event.

In each province only two bishops shall remain at home to attend to its needs, but they and all others who are prevented from being present, must send representatives. Each prelate may bring with him only a moderate retinue, in accordance with the prescription of the Third Lateran Council (canon 4), rather less than more. Cathedral and collegiate chapters also shall send representatives, for with them the council must also occupy itself. In the meantime bishops must carefully investigate and make note of those things that in their respective dioceses need correction, in order to lay them before the council. They must likewise faithfully support and encourage the papal deputies appointed for the Holy Land, and no one may be negligent in carrying out the above instructions without laying himself open to canonical punishment.[193]

The Fourth Lateran Council is considered by many historians as the most important General Council of the Church prior to the Council of Trent. Canon Law refers to it as the "Great Council" or the "Great Council of the Lateran".

---

[191] *Rome Sentinel*, October 26, 1986.
[192] Msgr. Conway, *Times of Decision*, p. 149.
[193] Fr. H. Schroeder, O.P., *Disciplinary Decrees of the General Councils*, pp. 236-237.

Aragon, Bohemia, Constantinople, Corsica, Cyprus, Dalmatia, England, Estonia, France, Germany, Hungary, Ireland, the various Italian states, Lithuania, Poland, Portugal, Sardinia, Scotland, Sicily, Syria and Jerusalem[194] were represented.

However, the number of German bishops attending was small due to tensions between the pope and Frederick II. This was the first time that bishops from the recently converted Slavic nations attended a General Council of the Church. Pope Innocent III presided over all three sessions of the council which were held at the Lateran Basilica on November 11, 20 and 30, 1215.

Canons of the Fourth Lateran Council

There were 70 canons and decrees formulated at the Fourth Lateran Council and much of this legislation is still in force today. The new canons helped ensure that the lives of bishops, abbots and priests be consistent with their elevated vocation so that clergy could lead their flocks by both word and example.

Clergy were to observe celibacy and delinquents were suspended. Irresponsible bishops who tolerated abuses were permanently deprived of their office. Laws were enacted against bishops and priests who never said Mass and those addicted to alcohol. Clergy were to dress in the attire proper to their rank. Priests who violated the seal of confession were never allowed to hear confessions again and were to spend the remainder of their lives in a monastery.

Several canons of the council forbade the formation of any new religious orders, yet Pope Innocent III invited both St. Dominic and St. Francis of Assisi to attend the Fourth Lateran Council along with the founders of other religious orders. It would be his successor, Pope Honorius III, who would approve both the Dominican and the Franciscan Orders by a papal bull dated December 22, 1216. To circumvent the prohibition, future religious foundations of men and women took the names of Congregations (e.g., C.SS.R.-Congregation of the Most Holy Redeemer) or Societies (e.g., S.J.-the Society of Jesus, i.e., the Jesuits).

Other canons of the council addressed the Sacrament of Matrimony. One specifically declared that the banns of marriage must be announced.

---

[194] It fell to Saladin in 1187.

- Canon 1-Treated of Transubstantiation.
- Canon 2-Defined the traditional belief in the Blessed Trinity.
- Canon 3-Condemned the Albigensian and Waldensian heresies. Monarchs were held personally responsible for the eradication of heresy within their domains.
- Canon 4-Those baptized by Latins were not to be rebaptized by Greeks.
- Canon 5-Order of precedence: Rome, Constantinople, Alexandria, Antioch and Jerusalem.
- Canon 6-Synods were to take place to correct abuses.
- Canon 7-Bishops were to correct abuses in their dioceses.
- Canon 16-Clergy were not to engage in secular pursuits.
- Canon 17-Clergy in Major Orders were commanded to pray the Divine Office daily.
- Canon 18-Clergy were not to pronounce the sentence of death, nor act as judges in extreme criminal cases. Clergy were forbidden to take part in trials involving capital punishment. Further, they were not to act as surgeons nor take an active role in the military save that of chaplain.
- Canon 19-Churches were to be kept clean.
- Canon 20-The Holy Eucharist and chrism were to be kept under lock and key.
- Canon 21-The annual Easter Duty: All Catholics of both sexes who had attained the age of discretion (the use of reason) were to confess their sins at least once a year and receive Holy Communion at least once during the Easter time. This Law of the Church was declared binding under pain of mortal sin and those failing to observe it were to be deprived of ecclesiastical burial.
- Canon 27-Dealt with the serious obligation of bishops to ensure the proper training of candidates for the holy priesthood.
- Canon 46-Clergy were exempt from taxation by secular rulers except with special permission of the Holy See.

Final Work of the Council

Pope Innocent III's agenda of rooting out heresy and carrying out a reform of the Church and clergy were wonderfully fulfilled by the Council Fathers. This council also condemned the erroneous teachings of the Calabrian Abbot Joachim of Floria regarding the Blessed Trinity while at the same time defining the doctrine of the Catholic Church on the matter.

Msgr. Hughes explains the penalty that the council reserved for heretics in his work, *The Church in Crisis:* "Those who supported heretics were excommunicated. Those suspected of heresy are to prove themselves innocent. Should they neglect to do so they are excommunicated; if they continue in the excommunication for twelve months they are to be condemned as heretics."[195]

The Fourth Lateran Council officially taught the doctrine of Transubstantiation of the bread and wine at Holy Sacrifice of the Mass and the Real Presence of Christ in the Holy Eucharist. The term, *Transubstantiation*, is derived from the Latin *transsubstantiare*, which means "changed substantially." The word *Transubstantiation* was first used by Hilbert of Tours in 1079.

In 1062 the heretical archdeacon of Angers, Berengarius of Tours, denied the Real Presence of Christ in the Holy Eucharist. Although it is claimed that he was reconciled to the Church before his death, he greatly feared for his salvation since he had led so many astray. To outwardly manifest belief in the Real Presence of Christ in the Holy Eucharist, Pope St. Gregory X (1271-1276) instituted the practice of elevating the Host and Chalice during the Canon of the Mass.

---

[195] p. 220.

Its reform of the clergy, the combating of heresy and the *Code of Canon Law* remain lasting fruits of this 12th General Council of the Catholic Church. Walter Ullmann in his book, *A Short History of the Papacy in the Middle Ages,* pointed out that "Innocent III was the first pope to publish an official collection of Canon Law. Hitherto all collections, codifications, excerpts and summaries of Canon Law were purely private works, however official the individual papal decretal may have been."

CHAPTER THIRTEEN

First Council of Lyons

1245 AD

This council was held during the pontificate of Pope Innocent IV.

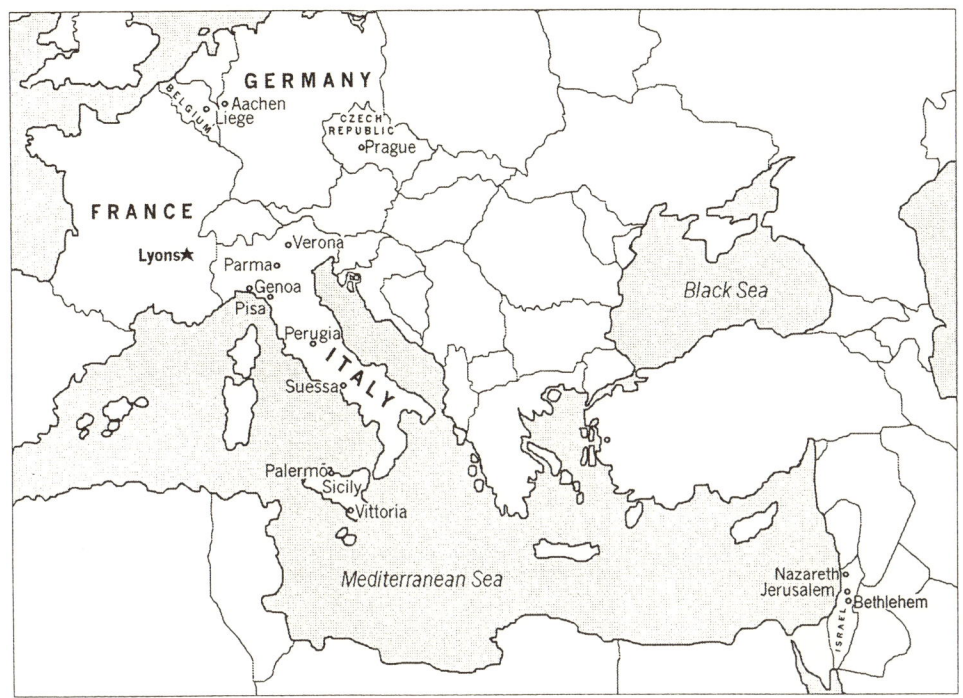

Background

Although the Middle Ages produced great saints and scholars, yet the Church also had to contend many difficulties. The First Council of Lyons, which was called a mere 30 years after the conclusion of the Fourth Lateran Council, witnessed Pope Innocent IV's struggle against Barbarossa's grandson, Emperor Frederick II over Church sovereignty.

Emperor Frederick II

Frederick II was raised in Sicily, an island that was ruled successively by Carthaginians, Greeks, Romans and Byzantines. The Muslims conquered this land in the year 827 AD and Frederick's ancestors, the Normans, ultimately became its masters in the year 1059.

Sicily was a land of diverse peoples and languages. Here the Greek mingled with the Roman and the Muslim with the Christian. Carthaginians, Italians, Normans, North Africans and Palestinians all called this beautiful island their home. Frederick, King of Sicily, was not immune from this diversity of culture and religion and his later dealings with the pope and sultan reflected this.

Frederick II was crowned Holy Roman Emperor by Pope Honorius III in the year 1220. He considered himself to be a divinely christened ruler who would bow to none and hold absolute sway over all: a potentate from the mold of Constantine and Charlemagne whose word was law and whose power was absolute. Frederick II made a vow on Charlemagne's tomb in Aachen, Germany to lead a Crusade to the Holy Land, but for seven years he delayed fulfilling it. When finally executed, his "crusade" of 1227 lasted a mere two days because of an outbreak of the plague on board ship.

The subsequent pope, Gregory IX (a relative of the mighty Pope Innocent III) had borne with enough of Frederick's manipulations. He excommunicated Frederick II for breaking his vow and gave him a personal interdict. This meant that wherever the emperor resided, the churches were to be closed so none could attend Mass or receive the sacraments. However, priests were still allowed to baptize infants and to administer the Last Sacraments to the dying.

The emperor finally embarked on the Sixth Crusade on June 28, 1228. A peace pact was made with the Sultan Kamil of Egypt whereby the cities of Bethlehem, Jerusalem and Nazareth would be held by the Christians on condition that no Western army would attack during a ten-year period. The Muslims in return would remain loyal subjects of the sultan, were free to practice their religion and were given the Mosque of Omar in Jerusalem.

Thus began a 30-year campaign by the emperor against the Church in general and against the pope in particular. To further complicate matters, the Papal States were a perpetual thorn in Frederick's side since they divided his lands of Germany and Lombardy in the north and Sicily in the south.

The emperor not only attacked the popes, but also Catholic teaching. Msgr. Hughes in his book *The Church in Crisis* remarks: "Frederick was a heretic for his denial of the pope's authority, for his mockery of the virgin birth, and his declaring that nothing is to be believed that cannot be proved by the natural reason."[196]

Need for a Council

Pope Gregory IX lifted his excommunication of Frederick II, but the peace between pope and emperor was short-lived. The pope convoked a general council at the Lateran to deal with the emperor and commissioned the Genoese to convey the bishops and cardinals to Rome. On May 4, 1241, Frederick II's allies from Pisa attacked the Genoese fleet and imprisoned over 100 bishops and two cardinals. Pope Gregory IX died three months later and was succeeded by the elderly and sickly Pope Celestine IV, whose reign lasted about two weeks.

Because the cardinals feared the wrath of Frederick II, the Chair of Peter remained vacant *(sede vacante)* for nearly two years. The period between the death of a pope and the election of his legitimate successor is called an *interregnum*.

On June 25, 1243, the cardinals finally elected to the papacy Cardinal Sinibaldo Fieschi who took the name Innocent IV. Frederick II then mobilized his armies to attack Rome. Fearing for his life, Pope Innocent IV fled to Genoa and finally took up residence in the fortified monastery of St. Just in the city of Lyons on December 2, 1244. During this same year the city of Jerusalem, which was held by the Crusaders, fell to the armies of the Egyptian Khwarazmi.

The world was in a terrible state of affairs. Pope Innocent IV lamented the evil lives of the clergy and laity, the fall of Jerusalem, the Greek Schism, the Tartar invasion of Hungary and the affronts accorded the Church by Frederick II. A general council was sorely needed.

Early History of Lyons

M. Guizot explains in his book, *A Popular History of France Vol. I* that Lyons, the location chosen for the council, was an ancient center of Christianity:

> It was not, however from Italy, nor in the Latin tongue and through Latin writers, but from the East and through the Greeks, that it [Christianity] first came and

---

[196] p. 228.

spread. ...As early as the first century there existed there a Christian congregation, regularly organized as a church, and already sufficiently important to be in intimate and frequent communication with the Christian Churches of the East and West. There is a tradition, generally admitted, that St. Pothinus, the first Bishop of Lyons was sent there from the East by the Bishop of Smyrna, St. Polycarp, himself a disciple of St. John. One thing is certain, that the Christian Church of Lyons produced Gaul's [France's] first martyrs, among whom was the Bishop St. Pothinus.

The First Council of Lyons

In order to prevent his condemnation by a general council, the emperor blocked all sea entrances to Lyons. The bishops outfoxed him and came to Lyons by other routes.

The three sessions of the First Council of Lyons were held on June 28, July 5 and July 17, 1245 in the Cathedral of St. John. Its main purpose was to resolve the problems with Emperor Frederick II. About 145 bishops and a number of abbots came from England, France, Italy and Spain. Only two bishops from the Holy Roman Empire attended the council: one bishop from Liege, the other from Prague. This was due to either their loyalty to Frederick or their fear of reprisals for at times Frederick tortured his enemies, and even had some skinned alive.

Frederick was summoned to appear but made no attempt to attend the proceedings, even though he was residing in the nearby city of Verona. The Archbishop of Palermo, Thaddeus of Suessa, represented the monarch at the council. When Frederick failed to appear, he was deposed and excommunicated by Pope Innocent IV on October 10, 1227. The bishops had seen enough. Many recalled the emperor's cruelty which they had witnessed firsthand.

> At the third session of July 17th, the council sanctioned all the measures proposed in the twenty-two canons or 'chapters' and continued the case against the emperor. Frederick was accused of perjury, suspicion of heresy, sacrilege, and cruelty towards both clergy and laymen alike. The pope proposed to excommunicate him afresh and to depose him. The majority of the bishops signed the deposition. Frederick's subjects were released from their allegiance to him and the Prince-Electors were invited to choose a new king and emperor. The

severe measures inaugurated the final downfall of the Hohenstaufen dynasty. It is one of the greatest triumphs of the medieval papacy.[197]

Guelfs and Ghibellines

Europe was subsequently divided between those loyal to the pope (Guelfs) and those who remained faithful to the emperor (Ghibellines). Civil wars, uprisings and violence erupted throughout the continent.

> Scenes of horror were enacted in towns and cities all over Europe as partisans of pope and emperor, opposing parties called Guelf and Ghibelline, fought for control. Frederick saw papal assassins and conspirators in every shadow and treated hapless suspects with the utmost barbarism: He had them blinded with red hot irons, dragged to death by horses over stony ground, sewn up in leather sacks with poisonous snakes, and tossed into the sea. The pope for his part mobilized every resource of the Church and effectively deployed his spiritual artillery for fighting the holy war against Frederick: indulgences, excommunication, interdict. With magnificent concentration he strained every fiber of the Church in order to crush one of the most lethal enemies it ever faced.[198]

At times the pope's cause seemed hopeless. Bloody wars followed for the next five years, though Frederick's unbridled ambition eventually brought about his demise.

> Frederick seemed on the point of victory when he suffered a terrible defeat in 1248 in Parma, which he had under siege for several years. Taking advantage of his absence while he was hunting, the besieged Parmans burst from behind their walls and burned down his camp, an entirely new city called Vittoria. He was able to recover, however, and again seemed near victory when he was struck down by illness and succumbed in 1250.[199]

Parmesean armies defeated the emperor on two separate occasions. Following Frederick's final defeat, the citizens placed the royal crown on the head of a hunchback vagrant and paraded him triumphantly through the town.

---

[197] Francis Dvornik, *Ecumenical Councils*, p. 57.
[198] Thomas Bokenkotter, *A Concise History of the Catholic Church*, p. 183.
[199] Bokenkotter, 183.

Canon Law

Under the direction of the brilliant pope-lawyer Innocent IV, the First Council of Lyons enacted 22 canons dealing mainly with juridical practices to help settle ecclesiastical difficulties. Years earlier, Pope Gregory IX had commissioned a number of clerics, including St. Raymond of Peñafort, to compile a code of ecclesiastical laws under one cover. This six volume series, called the *Decretals,* was completed on September 5, 1234. It would be the framework for the future Code of Canon Law. Henceforth Canon Law began to take on a definitive shape and became the accepted norm in settling ecclesiastical difficulties.

Many of the laws enacted at the First Council of Lyons are still in force today:

> Judges delivering an unjust sentence are, by the fact, suspended from office, and must make good the damage caused. They must not, while suspended say Mass, under pain of censure from which only the pope can absolve them. Plaintiffs who fail to appear in court are to pay the cost of the suit. Excommunications are to be set down in writing, with the reason, and a copy given to the person affected. ...Bishops are not affected by suspensions or interdicts, unless the decree makes special mention of bishops. ...There is a canon about elections, which decides that conditional votes are invalid, and in the count are to be disregarded. And there is a canon about homicide—about the practice of hiring murderers to get rid of an enemy. 'Prominent persons,' says the canon, 'have been reduced through fear of this danger, to pay money to the chief of the gang... not without detriment to their Christian dignity.' So any prince or prelate, or indeed anyone at all, who makes such an arrangement with assassins, incurs by the fact excommunication, and deposition from office—whether the murder takes place or not.[200]

---

[200] Msgr. Philip Hughes, *Church in Crisis,* p. 232.

CHAPTER FOURTEEN

Second Council of Lyons

1274 AD

This council was held during the pontificate of Blessed Pope Gregory X.

Sede Vacante

The papal throne was vacant[201] for nearly three years following the death of Pope Clement IV on November 29, 1268. A vacancy in the Apostolic See occurs every time a pope dies. The vacancy is filled by the election of a successor. A special seal has been created for the occasion depicting the papal keys surmounted by a black umbrella. The liturgy makes provisions for the period of interregnum. In its instructions on the rubrics of the Mass, the *Missale Romanum* indicates that when the chair is vacant the name of the pope is

---

[201] "Interregnum: That period of time between the death of a sovereign and the assumption of rule by a successor. When referring to the time following the death of a Pope and the election of a successor, it is more commonly known as *sede vacante* ('While the See is vacant.')" Fr. Peter Stravinskas, *Catholic Dictionary*, p. 414.

omitted.[202] The Litany of the Saints has a notation printed in red ink[203] that gives an alternative form for several prayers during the *sede vacante* period.[204]

St. Philip Benizi, the Superior General of the Servite Order, chastised the cardinals for their sloth. St. Bonaventure (1221-1274) told the townsfolk to remove the ceiling tiles from the papal palace in Viterbo in order to hasten the election of the pope.

The citizens of Viterbo locked the cardinals into the palace and limited their food supply until a new pope was chosen. This was the first papal conclave: the cardinals were literally locked in until they elected a pope. *Conclave* is derived from two Latin words, *cum* (with) and *clavis* (key). The hungry cardinals finally elected Blessed Pope Gregory X on September 1, 1271.

Constantinople Returns to Byzantine Control

The Fourth Crusade of 1204 was supposed to rescue Palestine from the Muslims, but the soldiers never reached the Holy Land. French and Venetian troops sacked the wealthy city of Constantinople instead and placed a Western ruler on the throne. This action gave rise to an abiding hatred between the Byzantine East and the Latin West. It also impeded any real efforts toward unity. In 1261, the Latin Kingdom of Constantinople fell to the armies of the Greek Byzantine Emperor Michael VIII Palaeologus.

Charles of Anjou, the brother of St. Louis IX, King of France, made plans to regain the city by means of an attack from his strongholds in Sicily and Italy. To avert this calamity, Emperor Michael VIII asked the pope to intervene. The Holy Father assured him that Western rulers would not invade his territory on condition that the Greeks attend a general council. This presented an opportunity to heal the schism and bring about lasting unity between the East and West.

---

[202] "Sede autem vacante verba praedicta omittuntur." Ritus Servandis in Celebratione Missae—VIII. De Canone Missae usque ad Consecrationem.

[203] *Preces Ante et Post Missam,* Pustet, 1955, p. 120.

[204] *Vacante Apostolica Sede, loco invocationis* Ut Domnum Apostolicum et omnes ecclesiasticos ordines etc., *dicatur:* Ut omnes ecclesiasticos ordines etc., *Versus autem* Oremus pro *Pontifice nostro N. cum suo Responsorio, et Oratio pro eodem Pontifice omittuntur.* (Text printed in italic is printed in red, plain text is printed in black.)

The pope again chose Lyons as the most appropriate place, as he could expect the much needed help for the reconquest of Jerusalem only from lands on the western side of the Alps. Letters of invitation were sent to the Western hierarchy in April, 1273, to chapters, abbots and princes. Besides Emperor Michael and his patriarch, the leader (Catholicos) of the Armenians and the Mongolian Khan were invited.[205]

The Second Council of Lyons

The Second General Council of Lyons was possibly the most edifying held to that date. It was presided by a saintly pope, who almost worked himself to death in diligent and detailed preparation for it, and in constant sermons, addresses, arrangements, and personal interviews while it was in session. It had three purposes, all conceived on a high spiritual plane: the reunion of all Christians in firm faith and fraternal love, the organization of a great Crusade to redeem the Holy Lands, and the reform of flabby morals among clergy and laity.[206]

The six sessions of the council were held in the Cathedral of St. John between May 7 and July 17, 1274. There were 500 bishops from England, France, Germany, Italy and Spain present, plus five representatives of the schismatic Greek Church. Others attending the council included 60 abbots, over 1,000 minor prelates and delegates, King James I of Aragon, the ambassadors of England, France, Germany and Sicily and nearly 160,000 visitors. The number of attendees was so great that all minor prelates, plain abbots, priors and delegates were dismissed by the pope.

The great Theologian and Doctor of the Church, St. Thomas Aquinas (c. 1225-1274) had been invited to the council, but died on his journey to Lyons. The Superior General of the Franciscan Order, St. Bonaventure, was moderator of the council until his death on July 15, 1274.

A formal decree of union was signed between the Latin and Greek Church on July 6, 1274. Among other things the Greeks accepted Papal Primacy, the belief in Purgatory, Seven Sacraments and the teaching that God the Holy Ghost proceeds from the Father and the Son. Though the union was formalized on paper, schism remained in many hearts. Emperor Michael VIII desired union and had proposed compromises that encouraged the reunion with the Western Church,

---

[205] Francis Dvornik, *Ecumenical Councils*, p. 59.
[206] Msgr. J. Conway, *Times of Decision*, p. 177.

but lacked the support of the schismatic hierarchy and laity. His successor, Emperor Andronicus II, revived hatred for the West.

Pope Gregory's successor, Pope Martin IV, did nothing to help the situation. He even encouraged Charles of Anjou to invade Constantinople. Ironically, the Byzantine armies attacked first and much bloodshed ensued. The rift between East and West would remain permanent.

Canons of the Council

The council enacted 30 canons. Seven canons addressed the elections of bishops and abbots while others addressed proper church etiquette and decreed that legal proceedings were no longer to be held in churches.

One of the canons even condemned piracy, along with anyone who aided pirates in any way. "Furthermore, since corsairs and pirates greatly impede those travelling to and from that Land [the Holy Land], by capturing and plundering them, we bind with the bond of excommunication them and their principal helpers and supporters. We forbid anyone, under threat of anathema knowingly to communicate with them by contracting to buy or sell."[207]

"Gregory X's pontificate was also significant for the decree, formulated at the Second Council of Lyons (1274), that papal elections should be held within ten days after the death of a pope, in the city where the pope died, and with the cardinal-electors having no contact with the outside world."[208] "It [this decree] is often cited in the notes on the Constitution, *Vacante Sede Apostolica,* of Pope Pius X, 25 December, 1904, which is retained in the Code [of Canon Law]."[209]

Though this council had lofty aspirations, it achieved none of its goals. The clergy and general populace of the East had no desire for union with the West, the crusade to the Holy Land never materialized and no lasting reforms were effected. Years later the Council of Florence would make further attempts at reunion. Sadly, it too would be generally unsuccessful.

---

[207] Norman Tanner, S.J., *Decrees of the Ecumenical Councils, Vol. 1,* p. 311.
[208] Richard O'Brien, *Lives of the Popes,* p. 219.
[209] Archbishop Amleto Cicognani, *Canon Law,* p. 167.

CHAPTER FIFTEEN

Council of Vienne

1311–1312 AD

This council was held during the pontificate of Pope Clement V.

Pope St. Celestine V

Rome was in a state of turmoil at the close of the 13th century: plague decimated the population, civil war raged between the rival Colonna and Orsini families and the papal throne had been vacant for two years. A holy hermit warned the cardinals of future chastisements if they did not elect a pope soon.

Finally, on July 7, 1294 an 85-year-old hermit named Brother Peter Murone was elected pope and took the name Celestine V. Since he had no training in secular matters and had lived in a mountainous cave for years, Celestine soon realized that he was not "the man for the job." Pope St. Celestine V therefore decided to resign the papacy as had four of his predecessors: Popes Pontian, Silverius, John XVIII and Benedict IX.

On the morning of December 13, all the cardinals were summoned to the great hall of the palace. They entered in a group. There on the throne, fully dressed in all his pontifical robes, sat Celestine. He waited until the cardinals were gathered in front of him; then he began to read his resignation in a loud clear voice. A cardinal tried to interrupt, but Celestine silenced him with a glance. Finished, Celestine stood and began to disrobe, removing the beautiful garments one by one until he stood before the cardinals only in the long white alb. The cardinals watched him silently, some with quiet incredulity, some in soft amazement, some in tears. He left the room for a moment and when he returned he was dressed in the simple robe of a monk. He went to the throne, bowed to it, then sat on the lowest step.[210]

Pope Boniface VIII

Celestine's successor, Pope Boniface VIII, feared the possibility that the retired pope would become an antipope since the populace still revered him for his holiness and miracles. St. Celestine was therefore placed under guard, but somehow escaped to his mountain cave. He was later shipwrecked on another futile attempt at flight and was confined to a cell by Boniface VIII. He died ten months later from natural causes and was canonized by Pope Clement V in 1313.

The custom of cardinals wearing a red cassock to distinguish them from other prelates and the practice of the "Holy Year" which was first observed in 1300 were begun by Pope Boniface VIII.

King Philip the Fair

The waning years of the 13th century and the early years of the 14th century witnessed a protracted conflict between Pope Boniface VIII and King Philip IV, also known as Philip the Fair, of France. The pope wanted to keep the Church independent and free; the king wanted to control the Church.

"Unfortunately he [Pope Boniface VIII] lacked both the meekness and humility of a saint and the self-control of a statesman. His violent temper and his inconsiderate political measures created numerous enemies for him at Rome and abroad."[211]

---

[210] Glen Kittler, *Papal Princes,* p. 155.
[211] Fr. John Laux, *Church History,* p. 391.

Philip was inept in financial matters and deeply in debt. He was also a greedy, conceited ruler who used torture, bribery and blackmail to destroy his opponents. His minister, William of Nogaret, was as ruthless as his master. In order to obtain additional revenue to finance his war with England, Philip began to tax the clergy. Philip IV also took the liberty to judge clergymen before civil courts rather than the established ecclesiastical courts.

Pope Boniface VIII forcibly opposed this usurpation of Church authority. In April of 1302 the king retaliated by setting up a council at Notre Dame in Paris consisting of clergy, secular authorities and commoners. This "council" declared the misdeeds of the pope and called him a usurper. French representatives came to Rome to speak to the cardinals in order to depose the pope.

Philip was a power monger who would stop at nothing to achieve his ends. He found the papacy a stumbling block to his ambitions and sought to weaken or destroy it. Philip attempted to do this by altering the concept of the office and role of the papacy, while strengthening and enlarging the scope of the state.

The monarch incurred God's vengeance because he used religion to cloak his real intent. "The king was, at this moment, at war with the communes of Flanders. Only thirteen days after that audience the French were unexpectedly routed, with great slaughter, at the Battle of the Golden Spurs, and the three counsellors of the king whom the pope had denounced by name were among the slain."[212] As a result, King Philip and Pope Boniface were temporarily reconciled, but this peace was of very short duration.

A papal envoy who was later sent to admonish the sovereign for his abuse of power was cast into Philip's prison. Pope Boniface VIII then, in 1302, issued his famous papal bull[213] entitled *Unam Sanctam,* declaring the absolute authority of the pope over temporal rulers. The message was clear and unmistakable.

Attack on the Pope

The conflict reached its culmination when the pope attempted to excommunicate the king. On hearing this, Philip quickly dispatched armed

---

[212] Msgr. Philip Hughes, *Church in Crisis,* pp. 250-251.
[213] A formal document of the Holy See that the pope marks with a leaden seal.

knights, led by William of Nogaret, to the pope's summer palace in Anagni. Sciarra, who was the head of the powerful Roman Colonna family, rushed into the pope's residence, struck the pope in the face with his gauntlet, then forcibly divested him of the tiara and his pontifical robes. The pontiff defiantly refused to resign in spite of the ill treatment he so ignominiously received at their hands.

Three days later Pope Boniface VIII was rescued by Knights Templar and soldiers from Rome. The pontiff then made a triumphant entry into the Eternal City. He died about a month later on October 11, 1303 due to the injuries he had received from Philip's soldiers. Cardinal Boccasini was elected pope and took the name Benedict XI.

> 'This outrage at Anagni,' says the French publicist Carrère in his book *The Pope*, 'is without excuse because it is beyond all reason and devoid of any dignity. Otto, Henry III, Henry IV, Barbarossa, Frederick II treated the popes as enemies, but at least as kings. Philip behaved, not as one of the powerful of the earth at war with another power, but like a vindictive boor preparing an ambush and hiring with gold the cutthroats charged to carry out his vengeance.... Whatever may have been the errors of this pope, he was, none the less, the Vicar of Christ, recognized by all Christendom; he bore upon his forehead and upon his shoulders the insignia of his office, and he was an old man...'[214]

Blessed Benedict XI, who excommunicated William of Nogaret and the other soldiers who attacked his predecessor at Anagni, was found dead about a month later, allegedly after consuming a poisoned fig.

Pope Clement V

The cardinals were not anxious to elect a successor; thus the Chair of Peter remained vacant for nine months. Finally a compromise candidate, the Bishop of Bordeaux who had ties to both the French and the English thrones, was elected pope. The French cardinal was crowned Pope Clement V in Lyons in 1305 and remained in France. He then moved the papal court to Avignon in 1309, thus beginning the 68-year "Babylonian Captivity" of the popes (1309-1377).

---

[214] Fr. John Laux, *Church History*, p. 395.

But it was no novelty for the papacy to be located elsewhere than Rome. Between 1100 and the death of Clement's predecessor in 1304, the popes had spent only 82 years in the city of which they were nominally the bishops. The oddity of the 'captivity' was not that the Curia was established outside Rome, but that it was outside Italy.[215]

As a sign of things to come this pope created ten new cardinals: one Englishman and nine Frenchmen. Four of his nephews were among this number. The seven succeeding popes who resided in Avignon nominated 134 cardinals—113 of whom were French. The whole hierarchical structure of the Church was drastically changed and politics would play a major role in Church appointments for years to come. The papacy as an institution was weakened and the groundwork was laid for the Western Schism of 1378-1417.

Pope Clement V was a weak pope and a close friend of King Philip the Fair. Unfortunately, as the pope was dying of cancer he acquiesced to most of the king's demands including a trial of his predecessor Boniface VIII. This kangaroo court tarnished the memory of the deceased pope and stopped just short of total condemnation. Nogaret, on the other hand, was absolved from excommunication and told to make a pilgrimage to the Holy Land to make reparation for his crime.

The Knights Templar

Andrea Hopkins' book, *Knights,* explains the history of the Knights Templar:

For several years before the capture of Jerusalem in 1099, a group of knights had acted as guides and protectors of Christian pilgrims travelling through the lands of the hostile Seljuks. At the time of the First Crusade they lived in a hostel near the Temple of Solomon in Jerusalem,[216] and when Hugues de Payns and Geoffrey de St. Omer had the idea of formally incorporating the knights as a religious order in 1119, they took the name of the Poor Knights of the Temple of Solomon, or the Knights Templar. The order was formally recognized by the Church at the Council of Troyes in 1128, and St. Bernard of Clairvaux, the most influential

---

[215] Michael Walsh, *Illustrated History of the Popes,* pp. 129-130.
[216] ["...the Templars made their headquarters on the Temple Mount and converted the Dome of the Rock and Al-Aksa Mosque into churches."
Abraham Rabinovich, *Israel,* p. 51.]

Churchman of the day, was commissioned to write the Rule by which they should live.

...The idea of the military monk-knights was received with great enthusiasm. A group of Templars toured France and England to recruit members and also to solicit gifts of money and property so that the Order could support its military activities in the Holy Land. The gifts, especially grants of estates, poured in, and soon there was a Templar Commandery in every province and in most major towns and cities, where the knights were recruited and trained...

Their record of service defending the Christian kingdom of Jerusalem was distinguished, though somewhat marred by their relations with their rivals, the Hospitallers, which by the 1240s had deteriorated to the extent that knights for each Order were fighting openly in the streets of Acre. Because the great majority of knights on the eight crusades to the Holy Land returned home as soon as the military campaign was over, the task of keeping the kingdom against the Turks, and later the Egyptians, fell to the Templars and Hospitallers. They invested huge sums of money in the construction of a chain of massively fortified castles some of which were never captured by the enemy, but were abandoned when the knights withdrew from Palestine in 1291. They were famous for the ferocity of their fighting. After the disastrous Battle of Hattin in 1187, Saladin took prisoner about 200 Templars and Hospitallers, including both Grand Masters, and ordered them all to be executed, on the grounds that they were the 'firebrands of the Franks.'

Both the Templars and the Hospitallers entered into negotiations with various Muslim leaders over the years. Because they had to live permanently in the Holy Land, they often had a different perspective from that of the crusaders who appeared periodically in pursuit of short term military objectives. The Third Crusade came nearest to capturing Jerusalem which had fallen to Saladin after the Battle of Hattin.

...After the capture of Acre in 1291, the last outpost of the kingdom of Jerusalem had fallen. The Templars withdrew to their European estates. They had lost many of their best knights in the last desperate days of the siege and were demoralized by their failure and by the fact that with the loss of the kingdom they had lost their *raison d'être*. Over the years they had become heavily involved in banking and diplomacy; what had originally begun as a financial

> facility for pilgrims had grown to an international business which lent large sums of money to kings and governments. The Templars were perceived to be wealthy and corrupt and they became unpopular.
>
> Their wealth was untouchable because over the years they had won many privileges, including exemption from the payment of taxes and tithes. They were not subject to secular law, and were answerable only to the pope himself. This made them a law unto themselves in the countries of Western Europe where they had held lands and where they were very powerful.[217]

In 1139 the Knights Templar became an exempted Religious Order by decree of Pope Innocent II. Originally these knights protected Europe from the Muslims and the Mongols and more than 20,000 gave their lives during the Crusades. Once the Holy Land fell to the Muslim armies in 1291 there was little for them to do. Their 900 outposts had ranged from England to Egypt although their main power was concentrated in France.

> The power of the Templars grew swiftly, not so much because of their large land holdings as because they became notable as international bankers, and their Temple at Paris became the center of the world's money market. The role of international financiers fell quite naturally to them since the Templars' strongholds were scattered throughout both the East and the West, and made exchange with the East a possibility; their military power and discipline ensured safe transmission of the treasures entrusted to them; and their reputation as monks guaranteed their integrity in handling the funds.[218]

King Philip the Fair was deeply in debt and saw the suppression of the Knights Templar (who possessed great wealth) as a ready-made solution to his financial difficulties. "Around 15,000 knights, sergeants, chaplains, *confrères,* servants and laborers throughout the territories governed by France were rounded up in a single day."[219] This "unlucky" day was Friday October 13, 1307. Their castles and estates were likewise seized and became property of the Crown.

---

[217] pp. 86-88.
[218] Vergilius Ferm, *Encyclopedia of Religion*, pp. 420-421.
[219] Piers Read, *Templars*, p. 264.

The majority of the knights, who were subjected to the most atrocious tortures in Philip's dungeons (placed in irons, deprived of sleep and living on meager rations of bread and water), agreed to repeat whatever they were told to say. Those who claimed they were innocent were executed. William of Nogaret charged the Templars with worshiping the devil, denying Christ and engaging in immoral practices. Chaplains were even accused of omitting the words of consecration in the Mass.

Torture and Trial

One feature was common to all these trials: whenever, in France, the knights, free of the king's jurisdiction, appeared before the bishops they immediately revoked their confessions. Describing the tortures they had endured they declared they would have sworn to anything, and that if the horrors were renewed they would again admit whatever their tormentors demanded. This revocation, of course, could be dangerous—among the charges was heresy, the worship of an idol. The punishment for heresy could be death, and for the heretics who, once self-confessed, retracted their confessions, death was certain. And so, in May 1310, fifty-four Templars were burnt in a single execution at Paris, on the sentence of the Provincial Council. And, by a violent personal act of the king, the Grand Master himself was burnt, only a few hours after the ecclesiastical court had sentenced him to life imprisonment, because in his relief at the thought that his life was safe he solemnly retracted all his confessions, and vouched for the innocence of the order as such.[220]

Called to Judgment

King Philip the Fair and others who cruelly persecuted the Knights Templar experienced God's just punishment within the year: the king was gored by a wild boar, the minister perished soon afterwards and the pope died of cancer.

There is a story that as the Grand Master, Jacques de Molay, was fastened to the stake on that island in the Seine where he was done to death, he lifted up his voice and by name summoned his three oppressors to the judgment seat of God. ...Philip the Fair left three sons, young men, healthy, vigorous, well married. But not one of them had a son, and within fourteen years of his death the direct line of descent was extinct.[221]

---

[220] Msgr. Philip Hughes, *Church in Crisis*, p. 254.
[221] Hughes, 259.

The Holy Shroud of Turin

The Templar Knight, Geoffrey de Charnay is believed to have recovered the burial cloth of Christ (the Holy Shroud) during a military campaign in the East. In 1453, "Marguerite de Charny, a descendant of Geoffrey, gives the Shroud to Anna Lusignano, wife of the Duke of Savoy, who keeps it in Chambéry."[222]

The scorched marks visibly seen on the Holy Shroud today occurred when a fire broke out at Chambéry in 1532 partially melting the silver chest housing the sacred cloth. The Shroud eventually came to reside in the cathedral of St. John the Baptist in Turin, Italy in 1578 where it is honored today.

The March 2003 issue of *Reader's Digest* describes the extensive research that has been done on the Holy Shroud:

> The Council for Study of the Shroud of Turin's page, on the Duke University website says: Over 1,000 special tests were conducted and over 32,000 photographs were taken. These studies combine to make the Shroud of Turin the most intensely studied single object in history. The tests show clearly that the Shroud images are not any kind of artistic production, but are the result of physical / chemical changes in the linen fibers themselves.

A painting closely resembling the face of the Man of the Shroud was discovered in Templecombe, England in 1945. This life-size painting was probably modeled on the Shroud of Turin and revered by members of the Knights Templar who had an important outpost and training center there. Today this painting may be found in the Church of St. Mary the Virgin in Templecombe.

The Council of Vienne

The Council of Vienne that brought about the suppression of the Order of Knights Templar was convoked by order of Pope Clement V under pressure from King Philip IV. No other General Council of the Church is veiled in such obscurity as that of Vienne.

> The position that Clement gradually came to take in the affair is shown by his further decrees, one of which ordained that no one should aid a Templar by deed or word, and that the Knight who denied the charges should be put to the rack

---

[222] Lamberto Schiatti, *The Shroud: a Guide to the Reading of an Image Full of Mystery*, p. 32.

and [be] compelled to confess. The final decision was to be given in the General Synod of Vienne, which was appointed for the autumn of 1310, but which did not take place till the following year (1311), because of the long duration of the trial. By far the greater number of the Fathers, after the reading of the collected evidence, were of the opinion that the Order should be permitted to make a defense, and that it could not be condemned for heresy without offense to God and perversion of justice. A small minority, chiefly French, gave their votes for taking immediate action against the Order, and, as Philip soon appeared at Vienne, and again insisted on its abolition, his influence gave them the victory...[223]

First Session

Vienne is located on the Rhone River, just south of the city of Lyons. The Council of Vienne began on October 16, 1311 and all sessions were held at the Cathedral of St. Maurice, one of the largest cathedrals in southern France.

Politics played a major role in these proceedings since the pope and king worked out the final details of the council together. This was the first time in the history of Church councils that a monarch decided which prelates were to be present. Even many of the 165 bishops who were invited chose not to attend.

Four patriarchs, 20 cardinals, 29 archbishops, 79 bishops, and 38 abbots and their attendants were present at the council. For obvious reasons, Frenchmen and Italians had the greatest representation, but there were also prelates from England, Germany, Ireland and Spain.

Pope Clement V attended all three sessions of the council while King Philip attended only the second. The pope's opening discourse enumerated the desired ends of this council: a discussion of the Knights Templar, a new crusade to the Holy Land, the liberty of the Church and a reform of morals. Following the opening ceremonies, the council recessed until the following April.

---

[223] Francis Funk, *Manual of Church History*, Vol. II, p. 50.

Second Session

Despite the fact that the majority of the bishops opposed the dissolution of the Knights Templar on the grounds of insufficient evidence, Clement V suppressed the Order by the papal bull *Vox in excelso*[224] during the second session.

> There is no denying that their wealth [Knights Templar] had resulted in certain abuses, which necessitated a reform, but condemnations based on oral admissions obtained by torture are hard to justify. The rapaciousness of the administration of Philip the Fair accounts for this wicked trial and persecution. The King, however, did not derive all the profit he had expected from his enterprise... A papal Bull placed the goods of the Temple into the hands of the Hospitallers of St. John of Jerusalem, [Knights of Malta] who put them to good advantage in their warfare against the Turks.[225] But though this was done in Germany, in France and England most of it went to the crown. In Spain and Portugal the Order was simply refounded under new names.[226]

The Hospitallers founded the Hospital of St. John in Jerusalem for sick pilgrims. When they acquired the island of Malta from Emperor Charles V they became known as Knights of Malta. It seems ironic that the council proposed a crusade, and at the same time sought to dissolve the very Order of Knights that maintained the castles in the Holy Land. The proposed crusade never materialized since the time of crusades had long passed.

Third Session

The third session, which lasted three days, May 3-6, 1312, focused on doctrinal matters. The three dogmatic definitions were: "(1) The side of Christ was opened *after the death* of the Saviour; (2) the substance of the rational human soul is truly the *form* of the human body; (3) at baptism children and adults alike receive sanctifying grace and the virtues."[227]

Furthermore, Pope Clement V settled the controversy regarding evangelical poverty and approved the Rule of the Franciscan Order in the Constitution *Exivi de Paradiso*. Other legislation dealt with jurisdiction, duties of bishops and the

---

[224] April 3, 1312.
[225] Dom Charles Poulet / Rev. Sidney Raemers, *Church History, Vol. I*, p. 601.
[226] Andrea Hopkins, *Knights*, p. 88.
[227] Fr. Clement Raab, O.F.M., *Twenty Ecumenical Councils of the Catholic Church*, p. 117.

management of church property. The council also condemned the concept that usury was not sinful.

Peter Olivi, who was the leader of a group of Franciscan Spirituals and taught erroneous notions concerning poverty and the relationship of the human body and soul, was condemned during the council. A decree formulated at the third session of the Council of Vienne helped clarify this doctrinal matter.

Europe was also plagued with fanatical heretics called Beghards (male) and Beguines (female) who believed they could perform any carnal acts without committing sin. These self-professed "saints" claimed they had no need to observe ecclesiastical laws and did not have to avail themselves of the Mass or sacraments since they were already perfect. No external reverence was to be shown to the Blessed Sacrament since It was beneath their own elevated dignity. The Beghards and Beguines were condemned at the Council of Vienne.

The Feast of Corpus Christi had been established by Pope Urban IV on September 8, 1264 and was later ratified by Pope Clement V at the Council of Vienne. This feast in honor of the Blessed Sacrament is still celebrated with great solemnity in traditional Catholic churches throughout the world.

Unquestionably, the suppression of the Order of the Knights Templar was a great tragedy. However, the Council of Vienne is still numbered as one of the General Councils of the Catholic Church because of its decrees regarding Church doctrine and its denunciation of heretics.

Pope Clement V's successor, Pope John XXII, wanted the reforms of the council to be perpetuated. Therefore, after a slight revision, he gave the canons the force of law on October 25, 1317. These canons of the council were later published *(Clementines)* and were added to the existing Code of Canon Law.

CHAPTER SIXTEEN

Council of Constance

1414-1418 AD

This council elected Pope Martin V.

The Black Death

The era of Constance was one of schism, war, plague and social change: the Hundred Years War was raging, three men claimed the papacy and in England and Bohemia the seeds of Protestantism were being sown. This was also a time of unprecedented devastation throughout Europe, as the Black Death gripped the continent during the years 1347-1353. To our modern minds, the horrors of this plague seem almost unbelievable:

> As the plague advanced from town to town—for the rat filled, unclean cities suffered worst—normal life ceased. Physicians' remedies were powerless; priests feared to approach the dying and administer the last rites. The doors stood open, and no one dared or cared to enter and rob... At sea, ships, manned only by dead sailors, drifted derelict.

>...No one knows how many died in the Black Death, for medieval statistics were very emotionally compiled. But when we read that many villages were totally wiped out, that the papal authorities counted 1,500 dead in three days in Avignon, that five cardinals, 100 bishops, and 358 Dominicans succumbed in the same city, that at the end the Franciscan losses numbered 124,434 we may credit the specificity and accept the general conclusion that from a third to a half of Europe's population died. This was the greatest calamity ever visited on the Western world.
>
> The immediate results of the plague were worse than those of any war. A traveler would find whole villages tumbling into ruin, yielding to the assault of the elements. The countryside was noisome [putrid] with dead animals.
>
> ...To the clergy the Black Death dealt a cruel blow. Conscientious priests, administering the last rites, ensured their own. Many monasteries were completely wiped out. Petrarch's brother Gherardo, a Carthusian in the monastery of Montrieux, near Marseilles, tended his brother monks and buried them one by one; in the end only he and his faithful dog were left alive. (Dogs generally were more faithful than men.) The friars in particular, caring for the cities' sick, suffered appalling losses.[228]

Rats hosting infected fleas spread the Black Death and caused Feudalism as an institution to vanish. Although many turned to God and prepared for judgment, others knowing their end was near relentlessly pursued the pleasures of the passing world.

"Plague would reoccur every few years for the rest of the fourteenth and all of the fifteenth century, and initiate an era of depopulation that would last until the sixteenth century."[229]

Nuremberg, Germany suffered a 10% mortality rate due to good sanitation and hygienic practices. "The streets were paved and regularly cleaned. Trash and garbage could not be dumped in the streets, but had to be bagged and carted away. Pigs were not allowed to roam the city, and personal cleanliness was held in high regard, an unusual attitude in late medieval Christendom."[230]

---

[228] Morris Bishop, *Horizon Book of the Middle Ages,* p. 380.
[229] Robert Gottfried, *Black Death,* p. 130.
[230] Gottfried, 68.

John Wycliff and John Huss

Since England lost nearly half its priests to the plague, many unfit and poorly trained men were ordained to fill the decimated ranks. During this troubled time John Wycliff (1324-1384) and John Huss (Jan Hus) (1369-1415) emerged to kindle the flames of the Protestant Reformation nearly a century and a half before Martin Luther. John Wycliff, an English priest, was an anti-Catholic leader who denied the need for the Mass, the sacraments and a visible Church.

> He [John Wycliff] next attacked the Catholic doctrine of Transubstantiation, and the divine institution of the hierarchy, as well as Indulgences, Auricular Confession, Extreme Unction and Holy Orders. The Bible alone, without Tradition, was the sole rule of faith. The Church was composed only of the *predestined;* prayer and sacraments benefited only the predestined, and sins could not harm them. No temporal or ecclesiastical superior had authority when he was in a state of mortal sin. Here we have Calvinism a century and a half before Calvin. …His heretical teachings were condemned by the Council of London (1382), and he was deprived of his professorship at Oxford by royal order. He died two years later.[231]

Wycliff was a favorite at the English court and his circle of influence was extensive. His radical ideology found a new home at the University of Prague when King Richard II of England married Princess Anna, daughter of the Bohemian King, making the two nations allies.

John Huss, a Bohemian priest, professor at the University of Prague (1398) and preacher at the Bethlehem Chapel of Prague (1402) began to spread Wycliff's heresies throughout Bohemia. A national independence movement was sweeping the country among nobles and peasants and the Hussite concepts of rebellion and anarchy were used as a means to destroy German influence and authority. Huss is known for his utter contempt for the Catholic hierarchy and clergy. His teachings were similar to Wycliff's except that he believed in Transubstantiation. Huss would eventually be ordered to appear before the Council of Constance to answer charges of heresy.

---

[231] Fr. John Laux, *Church History,* p. 406.

The Avignon Popes

Seven successive popes ruled from Avignon, France, a city that from 1309-1377 was under the jurisdiction of the King of Naples. When King Louis IV of Bavaria invaded Italy and attacked Rome in 1327, he took possession of Naples, banished Pope John XXII and installed a Franciscan monk as "Pope" Nicholas V. This antipope (1328-1330 AD) was later reconciled with Pope John XXII.

Blessed Pope Urban V (1362-1370), one of the Avignon popes, returned briefly to Rome, but remained there for only three years. Unrelenting war, pestilence and anarchy left Rome in chaos with a population of a mere 10,000.

The move to Avignon was not totally detrimental to the Church. Not all the Avignon popes were controlled by the French monarchs as had been Pope Clement V. Avignon's location on the Rhone River in southern France made it easily accessible for travelers from most European countries. The unceasing power struggle between Roman families and factions was not found there, leaving it a much more stable and peaceful environment. The papacy survived in relative peace, though the cardinals grew worldly and powerful.

Prompted by the Dominican Tertiary, St. Catherine of Siena (1347-1380), Pope Gregory XI returned the Holy See to Rome in 1377. He died on March 27, 1378.

"Elect an Italian or Die!"

Gregory XI's death left the citizens of Rome demanding an end to French domination over the papacy. In order to insure that none of the cardinals would leave before the papal conclave, all roads leading out of Rome were barricaded and the oars and rudders of all boats in the Tiber were confiscated. "The cardinals themselves were threatened. The French Cardinal Jean d'Cros was warned 'give us an Italian or a Roman pope, or all the cardinals from beyond the Alps will be knifed.' "[232] As bonfires blazed in the streets, an angry mob burst into the room where the papal conclave was taking place.

> While the guards were fighting to hold them back, some of the cardinals hastily dressed the aged Roman cardinal, Tebaldeschi, in pontifical robes, put him on the throne, and left him to his fate. But he refused to continue with the masquerade telling the people 'I am not the pope. They have elected a better

---

[232] John Smith, *The Great Schism 1378*, p. 5.

one, the Archbishop of Bari.' The delay was, however, long enough for the French cardinals to get away. They climbed over the roofs and dropped out of windows to escape the swords. It was an ignominious end to an undignified night's work. Within a short time, several of them had barricaded themselves for safety in the Castel Sant'Angelo, Hadrian's mausoleum on the west bank of the Tiber. Others hid in odd corners of the city. But some merely went to their rooms in the Vatican and waited for the noise to die down. None of them was actually harmed in any way.[233]

Pope Urban VI

The cardinals unanimously chose a compromise candidate for pope, a man who had ties with both Italy and France. On April 8, 1378, they elected Bartholomew Prignano, who became Pope Urban VI (1378-1389). Prignano had previously been the Archbishop of Bari and Administrator of the Papal States.

Under the papacy of Gregory XI the Papal Palace had been moved from the Lateran Hill to Vatican Hill, an area that had been donated by the Roman Senate and given to Pope Gregory XI. Thus, Pope Urban VI was the first pontiff to be elected in the Vatican. He was crowned pope on Easter Sunday.

The cardinals, though fearful of the wrath of the crowds outside the conclave, admitted to having taken part in a free election and certified this fact on the following day when they met with the pope individually. They each agreed in the affirmative that the election was legitimate and coincided with canonical protocol, even signing a document to that effect.

Urban VI was sincere in his desire to reform the worldly lifestyle of the cardinals, but he often added insult to injury by his *modus operandi.* His lack of tact and his abrasive ways generated innumerable enemies.

> It may be said in favor of Urban's proposed reforms that there was too much pomp and wealth surrounding the lives of the cardinals of the 14th century; that bishops spent too much time away from their dioceses; that simony deserved to be punished; that the immorality, excessive luxury, and lascivity which had become proverbial while the papal court was at Avignon, should be banished from the Papal Curia at Rome. However, despite the recognition by churchmen of the urgency of reform in those areas, Urban's severe approach and insulting

---

[233] John Smith, *The Great Schism 1378,* p. 8.

methods lost him the sympathy and cooperation of many who would have made personal sacrifices to help him reform the Church—from top to bottom. Instead, the pope drove cardinals, bishops, and ambassadors from Rome with hurtful words, the Church remained unreformed, and, what was far worse and more destructive of bodies and souls, the ensuing conflict between Urban VI and the cardinals developed into a great rebellion.[234]

In a word, Urban undisputedly acted and ruled as pope. But it was during these crucial weeks following his election that he showed his true weaknesses: an uncontrolled temper, megalomania and extreme rudeness in consistory. The burden of the papacy was obviously too great for a man who was not born a ruler, but was an exemplary administrator. His aim as pope was to replace the oligarchy practiced at Avignon by the monarchy of the pope. ...What can hardly be doubted is the tactlessness and lack of wisdom he displayed in pursuing his policy.[235]

Conditions Ripe for the Western Schism

The predominance of French cardinals, the long exile from Rome and the mannerisms of Pope Urban VI all helped create the ideal conditions for the Western Schism (1378-1417). Since the Italian pope dwelt in Rome, the influence of France on the papacy began to wane. The French cardinals were mortified by his tirades and reforms and thought the new pope should return to France.

The fickleness of the cardinals during this period brings to mind an anecdote that was to take place centuries later. "It is said that Napoleon Bonaparte, so often at odds with the Vatican, once told a cardinal, 'The Church is my enemy. I will destroy Her.' The cardinal replied, 'I don't think you will. We cardinals have been trying to destroy Her for centuries and haven't been able to do it.' "[236]

Unfortunately, the general laxity, worldliness and personal ambition of the cardinals played a key role in the creation of the Western Schism. Cardinal Robert of Geneva, cousin of King Charles V of France, instigated the French cardinals against Urban VI and declared the election invalid on the grounds of duress and coercion. Years earlier, he had commanded the papal army in a war

---

[234] Daniel MacCarron, *The Great Schism*, p. 5.
[235] Walter Ullmann, *A Short History of the Papacy of the Middle Ages*, p. 294.
[236] Glenn Kittler, *Papal Princes*, p. 169.

against Florence and its allies acquiring the infamous name "Butcher of Cesena" for his massacre of 3,000 women and children during one of his campaigns.

Antipope Clement VII

The 13 French cardinals left Rome on September 20, 1378 and elected the antipope, Cardinal Robert, who took the name Clement VII (1378-1394). "The remarkable feature of this 'double election' was that one and the same College of Cardinals had elected two popes within a few months. In the numerous previous schisms this contingency had never occurred. The cardinals had acknowledged Urban VI as the rightful pope throughout the five months following the election; they had begged his favors even when they had repaired to Anangi and Fondi."[237]

> With Urban firmly installed in Rome, Clement was obliged to go to Avignon and settle there ten months after his 'election.' When Urban died in October 1389, Clement thought that his return to Rome was assured. But the opulence of his court and costs of his single-minded diplomacy meant that he had turned into a harsh tax collector, and this undermined his support. What is more, the schism caused by his election in 1378 and continued by that of Pope Boniface IX in 1389 was increasingly unpopular.[238]

Antipope Benedict XIII

The French cardinals pressured Clement to resign but he fell victim to a fatal apoplectic seizure before this occurred. Following Clement's death, the Avignon cardinals elected another antipope, Peter de Luna of Aragon, who took the name Benedict XIII (1394-1424). However, the clergy of France, on two separate occasions, withdrew their obedience to him because of his failure to put an end to the schism. The antipope was even abandoned by the King of France during the years 1398-1403.

A Divided Europe

As a result of the confusion, Europe itself was also divided. Northern and Central Italy, Corsica, Portugal, England, Ireland, Austria, Hungary, Scandinavia and Poland remained faithful to the Roman Pontiff. Scotland, Spain, France, Southern Italy, Sicily and Sardinia showed allegiance to the antipopes of Avignon.

---

[237] Walter Ullmann, *A Short History of the Papacy of the Middle Ages*, p. 295.
[238] P. Maxwell-Stuart, *Chronicle of the Popes*, p. 141.

Germany, Switzerland and the Central European nations shifted loyalties between the two opposing camps whenever it suited their purpose.

There were now two sets of cardinals and two claimants to the Chair of Peter: one in Rome and one in Avignon. Some parishes had two priests, each loyal to a different pope. Monasteries had multiple abbots. Families were divided. Nations were divided. The Church was divided. Even holy men and women, doctors of Canon Law and theologians were perplexed by the dilemma. A contemporary of the Western Schism, St. Antoninus, Archbishop of Florence, testified:

> There were many discussions about this matter; and many books written in defense of both sides. Through all the time that the division lasted, both parts (or obediences) could count among their supporters men exceedingly learned, both in theology and Canon Law, and also men of most holy life and (what is more striking still) outstanding by the miracles they wrought; yet it was never possible so to decide the question that no doubts remained in the minds of the majority of men.[239]
>
> It will be remembered that St. Catherine of Siena and St. Bridget declared themselves in favor of Pope Urban, while St. Vincent Ferrer and Blessed Peter of Luxemburg paid respect and obedience to the French [anti] Pope. Thus distracted, the Christian world was divided into two camps, and it was no uncommon sight to see two prelates or two abbots to settle their right to a benefice granted by the pope of their choice by force of arms.[240]
>
> At the grass roots level, however, the Church still functioned. Mass was celebrated, the gospel was preached, the sacraments were provided and works of charity went on. But for many, the papacy had lost credibility.[241]

Many people in good faith followed antipopes during this period since it was difficult to ascertain who was the legitimate successor of St. Peter. Their personal conviction was not a matter of faith; therefore they remained Catholic.

The Roman Line

In contrast to the antipopes, Urban VI was a legitimate pope who died in 1389 and was succeeded in turn by Popes Boniface IX (1389-1404), Innocent VII (1404-

---

[239] Chronicorum III, tit. 22; quoted by Edmund G. Gardiner, *St. Catherine of Siena,* 252.
[240] Dom Charles Poulet, *Church History, Vol. 1,* pp. 615-616.
[241] *Our Sunday Visitor,* September 16, 2001.

1406) and Gregory XII (1406-1415). The pontiffs of the Roman line are considered the legitimate popes.

The pontificate of Boniface IX did nothing to help end the Western Schism. He excessively taxed both clergy and laity as did many of the popes and antipopes of the period. "Though an able, even outstanding administrator, Boniface IX was infamous for his blatant nepotism and financial skullduggery. Because of the papacy's desperate need for money, he openly sold church offices to the highest bidders."[242]

The Illegitimate Council of Pisa

The Universities of Oxford, Paris and Prague believed that they could put an end to the schism by convoking a general council at Pisa. Sadly, they only made matters worse by the introduction of another antipope. Following the death of Pope Boniface IX, the Roman cardinals were willing to end the schism if the antipope of Avignon, Benedict XIII, would abdicate. Benedict refused and thus alienated his powerful allies—the French court and the University of Paris. In addition, his heavy taxation made further enemies.

Representatives from across Christendom met at the cathedral of Pisa on March 23, 1409 to put an end to the Western Schism. Most of the cardinals proceeded to abandon the two opposing popes, Gregory XII (Roman) and Benedict XIII (Avignon antipope) and elect another. Neither the Roman pope nor the Avignon antipope were in attendance. They were deposed and excommunicated by this Council of Pisa on June 5, 1409 and another new antipope, Alexander V was elected on June 26th.

> By the time the council opened in Pisa, almost the whole body of the followers of the rival popes had deserted to the neutral position of the cardinals and their council. It was numerically a splendid gathering and very representative: 500 active members, that is to say voters, at the great sessions where the popes were condemned—of whom 84 were bishops. There were besides, 100 representatives of cathedral chapters, representatives of 13 universities, and 300 doctors either of theology or of Canon Law—now, for the first time, here given a vote. The

---

[242] Richard O'Brien, *Lives of the Popes,* p. 250.

'general council' had indeed a new look. It greatly resembled a parliament, a single chamber parliament. Seventeen reigning princes sent ambassadors.

Another novel feature was the absolute unanimity of the council. ...The two rivals disposed of, i.e., excommunicated and deposed, it was the council that bade the cardinals set up a conclave and fill the presumed vacant throne. After ten days' seclusion they elected the archbishop of Milan, who took the style of Alexander V, and was duly crowned. He, too, was a very old man, and within the year he died. Whereupon the cardinals elected the strong man of the Council of Pisa, Baldassare Cossa, who called himself by a name that is lately familiar to all of us, John XXIII.[243]

The situation was an ecclesiastical nightmare. "There were now three popes, and three Colleges of Cardinals, in some dioceses three rival bishops and in some Religious Orders, three rival superiors."[244] "The schism called for immediate action; there were three popes now as there had been three hundred sixty five years before; and the emperor then had stifled the schism by deposing all three, might not a similar solution be possible in the present difficulty?"[245]

The Council of Pisa is considered to be an illegitimate council since it was never approved by the reigning pope (Gregory XII) and was conducted outside of the official auspices of the Church. In judging whether a council is legitimate or illegitimate, it should be noted that a general council is not considered legitimate until it is approved by the pope or his delegate. Based on this fact, a number of Church councils have been condemned in the past; some councils even taught blatant heresy.

The Western Schism

Roman Line (legitimate popes)	**Avignon Line** (antipopes)	**Pisan Line** (antipopes)
Urban VI (1378-1389)	Clement VII (1378-1394)	
Boniface IX (1389-1404)	Benedict XIII (1394-1417)	
Innocent VII (1404-1406)		Alexander V (1409-1410)
Gregory XII (1406-1415)		John XXIII (1410-1415)

---

[243] Msgr. Philip Hughes, *Church in Crisis,* p. 263.
[244] Fr. John Laux, *Church History,* p. 405.
[245] Eustace Kitts, *Pope John the Twenty Third and Master Hus of Bohemia,* pp. 2-3.

Dark Days for the Church

These were terribly dark days for the Catholic faithful, who once again found themselves unable to distinguish the true shepherds from the hirelings. Even a person's sanctity was no guarantee of his ability to recognize a true pope. Furthermore, those churchmen who held legitimate offices were themselves frequently scandalous individuals. As the months stretched into years and the years into decades, it must have seemed that the chaos would never end. "Forty years of wandering in the wilderness where no one knew with certainty who was head of the Church, forty years where unity of belief was marvellously preserved but in which administrative chaos reigned and there sprang up an abundance of anarchical theories about the nature of the papacy and its role."[246]

Yet this very depth of confusion—while distressing to those who endured it—served to illuminate with great brilliance the divine character of Holy Mother Church. It also indicated, very compellingly, how woefully inadequate are the perspectives of the human intellect. The Catholic Church remains the indestructible Bark of Peter, guided only in appearance by the calculations and maneuverings of men, but in reality by Christ Himself.

Ominous Signs

Rome was devastated by a tremendous storm on January 29, 1411. Some inhabitants were terrified, believing it to be a sign of impending calamity. On April 12, 1411, the antipope John XXIII finally gained control of the Vatican and triumphantly entered St. Peter's. During the illegitimate council held in Rome in 1412, a strange occurrence left an ominous feeling over the entire assembly.

> The Mass of the Holy Spirit had been said, the congregation were devoutly seated, and Pope [antipope] John had taken his place on his throne, when a ghastly bird of the night, a screech owl, flew with horrid outcry from a dark corner of the church, and perched opposite the pope with large threatening eyes. John reddened and perspired; finally he rose from his seat; and the congregation dispersed. But at the next assembly the bird again appeared, and again fixed its black eyes on the pontiff. Some of the cardinals laughed... John ordered them to chase the bird of ill omen away. They rose in a body, waved their staves,

---

[246] *A History of the Church*, III (New York), pp. 228-229.

shrieked at the owl, but it was some time before they made it budge. Finally they knocked it down and killed it.[247] But the memory of the evil omen remained.[248]

The antipope John XXIII signed a peace pact with King Ladislaus of Naples on June 15, 1412. As a result of the negotiations, Pope Gregory XII (the legitimate pope) was exiled from the city of Gaeta on October 31, 1412, finally reaching the port of Ancona on Christmas Eve, 1412. Pope Gregory then found refuge in the domain of Carlo Malatesta, the Lord of Rimini. This was the only area in Italy that remained faithful to the legitimate pope.

Emperor Sigismund

The Holy Roman Emperor Rupert of the Palatinate died on May 18, 1410 and three powerful kings vied for the throne. Sigismund, son of Emperor Charles IV, finally triumphed and was crowned on July 21, 1411. He believed the dilemma of having three "popes" and a kingdom with divided loyalties had to be remedied as soon as possible. Sigismund was the only individual who had the strength of character and resources to end the schism. His fluency in seven languages, his regal bearing and strength of character assured his ultimate success.

In 1414 King Ladislaus of Naples attacked Rome and threatened the rest of Italy. The antipope John XXIII feared that Ladislaus would attack Pisa next and therefore called upon Sigismund for aid. A deal was struck. Sigismund would come to his defense on the condition that John XXIII would convoke a general council in his domain. The antipope had no choice but to obey.

The Council of Constance

This council, which would be called the Council of Constance, would hopefully accomplish two things: it would put an end to the schism, for all three claimants to the papacy would be asked to resign and a new pontiff would then be elected; and it would put an end to the civil and religious strife caused by the heresies of John Huss in Bohemia and its environs.

The Church was also in dire need of reform. Although the Council of Constance would address the issue, it would remain for the Council of Trent

---

[247] Gratius, i. 402.
[248] Eustace Kitts, *Pope John the Twenty Third and Master Hus of Bohemia*, p. 131.

(1545-1563) to put an end to many of the abuses that plagued the Church, especially among the clergy. Most General Councils of the Church prior to the Council of Constance lasted for several months to a year. Constance would last for four long years; it began on November 16, 1414 and ended on April 22, 1418.

"All forty-five sessions of the council were held in the bishop's cathedral in Constance; ...the cathedral, built in the eleventh century on the foundation of a Roman fort, was the seat of one of the oldest bishoprics—and, as such, the logical location for a gathering of the church's highest officials."[249]

The city of Constance is today known as the twin cities of Konstanz, Germany and Kreuzlingen, Switzerland. In the 15th century it was known as a fishing village and a producer of fine linen. Its population of 10,000 grew tenfold from 1414-1418 as clergy, royalty and peasantry gathered for the historic council.

"Not all its members by any means were assembled by the opening date. But ultimately there were present, it is held, 600 ecclesiastics with a say in the council, 183 of them bishops, 300 doctors of theology and Canon Law; and an innumerable horde of less important clerics, and the suites of these magnificent ecclesiastical lords from Germany especially."[250]

Gallicanism

The writings of men who had lived years earlier began to have a profound effect on clergy and laity alike. William of Ockham (1280-1349) who opposed the abuses and worldliness of the Avignon popes advocated theories that destroyed the concept of the papacy as a divine institution. Ockham befriended the avowed enemies of the Avignon popes, Louis of Bavaria, Marsilius of Padua and Michael of Cesena.

The University of Paris was the catalyst for novel, erroneous concepts that were championed by clergy and laity alike during this period. The superiority of a general council over the pope and the fallibility of the pope were taught at the university and the Cardinal Bishop of Cambrai, Peter d'Ailly, echoed these erroneous concepts at the Council of Constance.

---

[249] Jay Jacobs, *Horizon Book of Great Cathedrals*, p. 219.
[250] Msgr. Philip Hughes, *Church in Crisis*, p. 264.

> Gallicanism may be defined in general as the tendency, while accepting the Papacy as of divine institution, to oppose or minimize the papal claims as they have been made in history. It has been of two kinds: political and theological. Political Gallicanism contested the claims to authority in the temporal order as asserted and exercised by Gregory VII, Innocent III and Boniface VIII; theological Gallicanism contested certain claims of the Papacy in the spiritual and religious order. These tendencies of course manifested themselves in other countries than France; they have received the name 'Gallican' because all through history it has been in France that they have found their chief expression.[251]

Gallicanism, also called Conciliarism, taught that a general council is superior to the pope and that a pope must pay obeisance to a general council. Marsilius of Padua, the rector of the University of Paris from December 1312-March 1313, claimed that authority ultimately resided in the people and that the pope received his jurisdiction from the State. This erroneous teaching destroys the concept that the pope receives his authority from Christ and the clergy thereby become mere representatives of the State.

> The main point of conciliarism was that power was not located in the papal monarch but in the Church itself as represented by the general council. In this system the pope was merely a representative of the general council and eventually of the Church. It was the latter from which he received power and to which he consequently remained responsible. Hitherto the master of the Church, he was now turned into its servant. The pope became an officer, an organ of the Church which could restrict, modify and take away the power conferred on him by the general council. Conciliarism was the exact opposite of the papal monarchy.[252]

Division into National Groups

Antipope John XXIII planned to legitimize his claim to the papal throne by means of the council since most of Europe already showed allegiance to him. In order to prevent John from using the council to his own advantage, it was decided that the nations of Europe would be divided into an electoral college.

---

[251] Dom Cuthbert Butler, *The Vatican Council 1869-1870, Vol. I*, p. 23.
[252] Walter Ullmann, *A Short History of the Papacy in the Middle Ages*, p. 299.

Each block of nations would receive equal representation and voting rights. The French, Italians, and Spaniards each had their own block. The German block included the Scandinavians, Hungarians, Dalmatians, Czechs, Croatians and Poles. The English block included the Scots and Irish. This procedure prevented any of the three claimants to the papal throne from seizing control of the council and allowed all nations an equal voice in the proceedings.

Antipope John XXIII

In January 1415 the Council of Constance started to seriously scrutinize the evil life of John XXIII. The bishops "...objected to his simoniacal intrigue at his election, his immorality, his faithless utterances and his irreligious conduct."[253]

Both Roman Catholic and Protestant church historians agree that John XXIII was a scoundrel of the first order. He seems to have been a pirate from a family of pirates prior to his ecclesiastical career. After entering the services of the Church, he so impressed Boniface IX with his ability to increase papal revenues that he was made a papal legate of Bologna. While serving in this capacity, he became the undisputed master of the city, and in the process incurred the wrath of Ladislaus, King of Naples and protector of Gregory XII. Cossa's elevation to the 'throne of Peter' did not change his moral standards, his greed, or his politics. He was feared and hated by his enemies; mistrusted and ridiculed by his friends.[254]

M. Creighton, in his authoritative work on the papacy says:

'It was a grotesque and blasphemous incongruity to look upon such a man as the Vicar of Christ.'[255] Though a churchman and a cardinal, he was still only a deacon, a layman in all but name; church routine occupied but little of his time, church matters had necessarily entered little into his thoughts. There were those who said he had never confessed nor taken the sacrament;[256] there were those who alleged that he believed not in the resurrection of the dead.[257]

"He was above all things a soldier, fitter for the sword than the cassock, taking more delight in buckler and helmet than in pall or vestments, an able man

---

[253] Roger Aubert, *Historical Problems of Church Renewal*, p. 43.
[254] M. Creighton, *History of the Papacy, Vol. 1*, p. 286.
[255] W.R. Estep, Jr., *John XXIII and the Papacy*, p. 3.
[256] Fink (*F.*), I, note.
[257] *Ibid, (B)*, 10.

in temporal matters but of no account in affairs spiritual;[258] he was a man who …would do better as king or emperor than as pope."[259]

A pamphlet was distributed listing many of the crimes of the former pirate, irreligious soldier and scandalous prelate. There were also allegations, which remain to this day, that he poisoned his predecessor, the antipope Alexander V.

Flight From Constance

John XXIII realized that he would have to resign his illegitimate claim to the papacy. To prevent this, he organized a sensational tournament for the emperor and for all those who attended the council on March 20, 1415. Under cover of darkness he escaped from Constance in the disguise of a stable hand and found asylum in the territory of Duke Friedrich of Austria in the city of Schaffhausen, Switzerland, 30 miles away. He remained there from March 21-29. John XXIII hoped this action would bring about the termination of the council proceedings.

Hundreds fled the city in fear and Sigismund found it necessary to ride on horseback through the streets of Constance threatening anyone who dared to leave the city before the council was completed. Thus, the bishops and theologians stayed in Constance and the council continued.

> Having thus calmed the public distress, the king then assembled all the prelates and secular dignitaries and assured them that he would, at the peril of his life, maintain the council. The king's resolution and courage appeased the tumult in all minds. The lords, spiritual and temporal, knew that the council was safe and would continue; the shopkeepers reopened their shops; the Florentine bankers and moneychangers were reassured; the town was quieted and the ordinary life of the place resumed its wonton aspect.[260]

Duke Friedrich of Austria and the antipope John XXIII would pay dearly for their cowardice and treachery. On March 25, 1415 Sigismund and the council declared that all subjects of the duke were released from their allegiance to him. All lands of the duke would become property of the emperor.

---

[258] Ciaconius, ii. 790; Mur. xix. 41.
[259] Eustace Kitts, *Pope John the Twenty Third and Master Hus of Bohemia*, p. 4.
[260] Kitts, 305.

John XXIII lost nearly all his supporters including his cardinals and close relatives. On Good Friday, March 29, 1415, the antipope and the duke left Schaffhausen with the emperor's army in hot pursuit. The cardinals scattered, some returning in disguise to Constance while others fled to Rome.

John XXIII next made his way through the Black Forest and finally reached Freiburg, Germany, just a few miles from the Burgundian border. Duke Friedrich joined the antipope, but the curtain was coming down fast as 40,000 soldiers of Sigismund's army were rapidly advancing. The duke's domains were being overrun and his allies deserted him. Their only hope lay in John of Burgundy who, however, feared a war with Sigismund and offered no assistance. He would leave them to their own fate.

Betrayed

Duke Friedrich was not of a character to be trusted. This man who had assassinated his own cousin in his rise to power would soon betray the antipope. An incognito John XXIII made a mad dash for liberty on April 25th. He found a contingent of the duke's cavalry and joined them as they made their way to the city of Neuenburg, Germany. The antipope then fled from the city during the night and arrived at Breisach, Germany, a broken man and a victim of Duke Friedrich's plan.

On April 27th, the duke handed John XXIII over to Sigismund in exchange for a merciful sentence for himself. John XXIII was apprehended within sight of the Burgundian border which he was never able to reach.

The antipope was finally arrested on May 17 and put on trial by Sigismund and the Council of Constance for his flight and for the serious crimes he committed before and after his supposed election. These included, among other things, the allegation of murdering his predecessor, piracy, simony, sacrilege, immorality, incest and adultery.

Although John XXIII was charged on 72 counts, many charges were dropped to avoid scandal. During the 11th session of the council, held on May 23, 1415, he was charged on 54 proven counts. The antipope was solemnly and formally deposed during the 12th session on May 29 and was sentenced to imprisonment at Heidelberg castle.

Putting an End to the Western Schism

Gregory XII [the legitimate pope], finding the moment opportune to abdicate from a sincere desire to give peace to the Church, in a bull to the Emperor Sigismund dated March 15, 1415, appointed Carlo Malastesta as his Procurator to His majesty, King of the Romans, and instructed Carlo to 'renounce all his rights, titles, and possession of the Papacy.' The bull was formally read to the council on May 13, and on July 4, 1415, Gregory officially resigned the Papacy forever. But before he abdicated Gregory ratified the Council of Constance as a true Ecumenical Council of the Church. The council, in gratitude for Gregory's benediction, confirmed everything he had done as a pope. But Benedict [the antipope] obstinately refused to abdicate under any consideration, and was deposed in July 1417, as follows:

'This holy ecumenical council declares Peter de Luna, called Benedict XIII, rebellious and contumacious. The holy council declares him to be an incorrigible and notorious schismatic and heretic.' The support the council received from St. Vincent Ferrer made it a success. It was generally believed that St. Vincent, as the Oracle of Spain and France, passed God's Judgment on Peter de Luna, when the latter, as Benedict XIII refused to abdicate. St. Vincent was a man of destiny, who placed his immense prestige as a miracle worker in the balance. Although every member of the council perhaps wanted him there, he did most of his great work for it from afar. What joy the Fathers at Constance must have felt on hearing that Vincent Ferrer had preached against the obstinacy of Peter de Luna before a huge crowd which included the Antipope himself! From that day Benedict's cause was lost; sympathy for him dried up...[261]

Benedict XIII never willingly resigned his claim to the papacy when requested by the Emperor Sigismund. Instead he isolated himself on a fortified island off the coast of Spain, obstinate to the end.

Final Work of the Council

The Council of Constance anathematized the heretics of that era. The 45 articles of Wycliff were judged to be heretical and his body, which was buried in consecrated ground, was ordered to be exhumed. The teachings of Jean Petit allowing political assassination were condemned.

---

[261] Daniel MacCarron, *The Great Schism*, p. 132.

Huss was condemned by the Council of Constance because he was what was afterwards known as a Protestant. He might venerate the Virgin Mary and believe the orthodox doctrine of transubstantiation, but he did not believe in the infallibility of the Church. He held the Protestant dogma that the written Word of God alone is the true standard and rule of faith; he rejected the Catholic dogma that there also exists a living authority, established by Christ in His Church, with His security against error, which can in cases of necessity issue decrees declaring what is true and what is false; he did not believe in Tradition, the unwritten Word of God, delivered by Christ to His apostles and by them to their successors. Therefore he was judged a heretic.[262]

At first, the council treated the heretic with mildness. After a long preliminary examination, the public trial of Huss took place on June 5th, 7th and 8th, 1415. The council rejected the heretical teachings of Huss, who refused to revoke them. Because of his refusal he was degraded from his sacerdotal dignity on July 6th, and handed over to the secular power for punishment. Huss remained obstinate to the end; ...He was burned at the stake on July 6, 1415.[263]

The flight of John XXIII from Constance caused a wave of antipapal feelings through the Council Fathers. The cardinals subsequently lost their prominence and influence over the council proceedings, though the various nations in attendance worked in concord to restore unity to the Church.

Other Legislation

"It is significant that during these days the bishops formulated the now famous 'Articles of Constance,' the heretical statements, declaring that a general council is superior to the pope."[264] This resentment toward the papacy, afterwards perpetuated by the Gallicanists, lasted for centuries.

Two decrees of the Council of Constance, *Frequens* and *Haec Sancta,* would cause havoc for years to come. Both decrees lacked an adequate system of checks and balances although they were written to prevent future problems. They only complicated matters by engendering a runaway council (Basel) and an antipope (Felix V). "*Frequens* declared that councils must assemble at regular intervals:

---

[262] Eustace Kitts, *Pope John the Twenty Third and Master Hus of Bohemia,* p. 395.
[263] Fr. Clement Raab, O.F.M., *Twenty Ecumenical Councils of the Catholic Church,* p. 133.
[264] Fr. John Murphy, *General Councils of the Church,* p. 134.

the first in five years after the close of Constance, the second in seven years after that, and each thereafter every ten years in perpetuity."[265]

The 51 canons enacted during the council treated a wide range of topics that included the deposition of antipopes, simony, clerical decorum and dress, dispensations, the age for taking religious vows and penalties for prelates who waged war.

Canon 45 of the Council of Constance is quite humorous when read today: "A further measure [Canon 45] complained of lords who took excessive advantage of the hospitality of religious houses, making the monks keep dogs and hunting birds for them, even pigs and cows to be fattened."[266]

The Election of Pope Martin V

On November 8, 1417, fifty-three electors entered the conclave prepared for them in the *Kaufhaus* (Merchant's Hall) at Constance, the College of Cardinals having been reinforced by six deputies from each of the conciliar nations. The Frenchmen's hope of securing the tiara for their countryman d' Ailly faded away. On November 11, Cardinal Otto [Oddo] Colonna, a member of the ancient and powerful Roman family, needed one vote for a two third's majority. At that moment a procession of intercession was passing by in the street and a large body of boys was singing the *Veni Creator Spiritus*. The chant sounded like an angelic choir. Thereupon two more cardinals with tears in their eyes, gave their votes to Colonna. 'Before the processional cross re-entered the minster,' Ulrich von Richental records, 'people outside the conclave began to shout: We have a Pope—Oddo Colonna, and everybody rushed to the Merchant's Hall, close to eighty thousand persons, both men and women.' Their joy was justified—the Church had once more an undoubtedly legitimate pope.[267]

---

[265] MANSI XXVII 1159; JEDIN, Conciliorum oecumenicorum decreta, 414-15. The best available work on Constance is a symposium: A. FRANZEN and W. MÜLLER (eds.), Festschrift: Das Konzil von Konstanz; Beiträge zu seiner Geschichte und Theologie, Freiburg i. Br. 1964. For biography, see also R. BÄUMER, Die Bedeutung des Konstanzer Konzils für die Geschichte der Kirche, in: Annuarium Historiae Concil. IV (1972) 26-45.
[266] Phillip Stump, *Studies in the History of Christian Thought, Volume LIII*, p. 154.
[267] Hubert Jedin, *Ecumenical Councils of the Catholic Church*, p. 95.

Reform of the College of Cardinals

The predominance of French cardinals in the earlier papal conclaves had helped bring about the Western Schism. Now the Council of Constance worked to reform the College of Cardinals to prevent this tragedy from recurring. The reform included limiting the number of cardinals to 24, establishing proper moral and intellectual standards for future cardinals and assuring that there was equal representation in the College of Cardinals.

Peace was finally restored to the Church. But what became of the last three claimants to the papacy of the Western Schism? God put His approbation on the legitimate claimant to the Chair of Peter, Pope Gregory XII (the nonagenarian), who had the courage to resign the papacy for the welfare of the Church.

"Gregory abdicated and retired with honourable appointments [was made bishop of Porto and perpetual legate of Ancona] and died in October 1417."[268] "He was buried in the cathedral of Recanati. In 1623, during a renovation of the cathedral, Gregory XII's tomb was opened. His perfectly preserved body was reclothed in pontifical vestments."[269]

> Benedict retreated to Spain, still obdurate in his refusal to surrender office, and died there in 1423 at the age of 90. After his death, three of his four remaining cardinals elected an antipope, Clement VIII;...[270]

> The party of this rival was so insignificant that none of his contemporaries took the trouble to record it, and Benedict XIV [another antipope elected by the one dissident cardinal] vanishes completely out of history.[271]

> One day, shortly after the middle of June 1419, as Pope Martin [V] was officiating in the cathedral at Florence, there appeared before him Baldassare Cossa, [the antipope John XXIII] an aged man before his time, broken down by nearly four years' captivity. He threw himself at Martin's feet and acknowledged him as the true and only, the canonically elected pope. All present were affected at the sight and wept for joy, more especially the former cardinals of the deposed pope.[272]

---

[268] P. Maxwell-Stuart, *Chronicle of the Popes,* p. 143.
[269] Richard O'Brien, *Lives of the Popes,* p. 252.
[270] Maxwell-Stuart, 143.
[271] Francis Funk, *Manual of Church History, Vol. 1,* p. 18.
[272] Eustace Kitts, *Pope John the Twenty Third and Master Hus of Bohemia,* p. 430.

Cossa died six months later as a cardinal of the Church at the home of Cosimo de' Medici on December 22, 1419.

Was the Council of Constance Legitimate?

Pope Martin V approved the acts of the council, with the exception of those that proposed Conciliarism. Some have questioned whether this was really a general council because of the difficulties involved, but in the light of many earlier councils, there should be no doubt. The sessions which took place after Martin V had been elected raise no problem at all, but his acceptance of the earlier decisions would be sufficient to make them of equal force.[273]

Conclusion

Although considered a legitimate council, not all 45 sessions of the Council of Constance were approved. Some of the propositions of the council, especially those dealing mainly with Papal Primacy and the relationship between popes and General Councils of the Church, were openly heretical and were condemned by subsequent pontiffs. We must keep in mind that many of those who attended the Council of Constance were exasperated by the Western Schism and did not want to see a repeat of the disaster. The actions of the fugitive antipope John XXIII only increased their frustration and anxiety.

After four long years of sessions, many were eager to return home. The inhabitants of Constance would finally have some peace and quiet. The council ended on April 22, 1418 and Pope Martin V departed from the city of Constance on the day after Pentecost, May 16, 1418.

> Amidst the rejoicing of the people he traveled through Berne to Geneva. From Geneva the pope went to Mantua; there he remained from October 1418 to February 1419. The critical conditions of the States of the Church [Papal States] compelled him to spend nearly two years in Florence, until he finally made his solemn entrance into the eternal City on September 30, 1420, where he was enthusiastically welcomed by the people of Rome as their deliverer.[274]

---

[273] Fr. John Murphy, *General Councils of the Church*, p. 137.
[274] Fr. Clement Raab, O.F.M., *Twenty Ecumenical Councils of the Church*, pp. 134-135.

CHAPTER SEVENTEEN

Council of Florence

1438-1443 AD

This council was held during the pontificate of Pope Eugene IV.

Background

The Council of Florence attempted to unite the Churches of the East and West. Its main sessions of were held in Ferrara (Jan. 8, 1438-Jan. 10, 1439), Florence (Feb. 26, 1439-April 26, 1442) and Rome (April 26, 1443-Aug. 7, 1445).

The Renaissance

The 14th and 15th centuries were times of dramatic change in Europe. The discovery of the New World and subsequent global exploration, the advent of the printing press and the renewed focus on art, humanities and higher learning had a tremendous impact on society.

A movement now known as the Renaissance attempted to resurrect the former glories of Rome and Greece. Cities and nations arose while the feudal system crumbled. The Renaissance was a period of unparalleled prosperity. As new trade routes opened, Genoa and Venice bustled with commerce and international trade. A middle class arose with money to spend on the finer things of life. Wealthy merchants such as the Borgias and the De Medicis sponsored great artists who flourished during that era. Because of this patronage, common people could enjoy the art of the Renaissance.

The Church employed such men as Michelangelo, Raphael, Bramante, Bernini, Fra Angelico, Piero, da Vinci and Perugino. Art, architecture and music began to embody the ideals of goodness and beauty in an unprecedented manner. St. Peter's Basilica in its perfection of form and unparalleled interior embellishments was constructed at this time. In contrast to the stiff, unnatural style of the Middle Ages, paintings and frescoes revealed great detail, vibrant color and spatial perception. Majestic ornamentation and Palestrina's awe-inspiring polyphonic chant helped raise the minds of Catholics heavenward.

The Dark Side of the Picture

The Popes of the Renaissance were great scholars and great politicians, but they were not always great spiritual leaders. As rulers of the Papal States, they allowed themselves to be put on the same level with other kings and princes and thus lost their influence for good in matters of eternity. Another evil which they allowed to prosper was *Nepotism*. This was the practice of putting their relatives into important positions in the Church. They made their nephews Cardinals, gave their brothers important posts in the government of the Papal States and in general enriched their own families. Of the thirteen popes who reigned from 1431 to 1534, all but three were related by blood to one of their predecessors or successors. It cost a great deal of money for the popes to support the artists and the literary men whom they gathered about them at Rome. ...In order to support them and also to pay for the many beautiful buildings and works of art which they created, it was necessary for the popes to make great demands for money upon all the Catholics of the world. This of course created a great deal of scandal and discontent.[275]

Pre Conciliar Years

In order to comply with the decree *Frequens* of the Council of Constance a council was held at Pavia, Italy attended by a handful of abbots and bishops.

---

[275] Fr. George Johnson, *Story of the Church*, pp. 298-299.

Circumstances were most unfavorable for such an assembly. England and France were engaged in a bloody conflict; Germany was laid to rest by the Hussites, and war with the Moors was raging in Spain. It was evident that the council which opened at Pavia on April 23, 1423, could not be adequately attended.[276]

The council then moved to Siena, Italy because of continued outbreaks of the plague, but Pope Martin V disbanded this council in March 1424 due to lack of interest shown by the bishops. Pope Martin V died on February 20, 1431 and was succeeded by Pope Eugene IV on March 11, 1431.

The Council at Basel

A new council, held at the cathedral Basel Minster in Basel (Basle) Switzerland, began on December 14, 1431. Due to its distant location, 700 miles north of Rome and situated in the Alps, very few bishops made the trip. Pope Eugene IV subsequently dissolved the council on December 18, 1431.

The French bishops were thoroughly tainted with Conciliarism, the theory which taught that General Councils were superior to the pope and could not be dissolved except by their own consent. Furthermore, these bishops believed that Church councils received their power directly from Christ and that no power on earth superseded that of General Councils. Diehard prelates along with powerful monarchs such as Charles VII of France, Henry VI of England and Sigismund, in whose domain Basel resided, opposed the dissolution of the council.

On February 23, 1432 the council continued its sessions despite the papal dissolution and divided its work into four categories:

- Matters of faith
- Reform of church discipline
- Attempt at union with the schismatic Greeks
- Common business

The Council of Basel functioned more like an efficient congress or parliament than a General Council of the Church. Unfortunately, there was no system of checks and balances and the situation was almost out of control.

---

[276] Fr. Clement Raab, O.F.M., *Twenty Ecumenical Councils of the Catholic Church,* p. 137.

The rebel Council Fathers muzzled the papal legates, claimed jurisdiction over matters reserved for the Holy See and dropped the prayer for the pope in the Mass. They even presumed to grant plenary indulgences to raise money for the council. A motion passed on September 26, 1432 which gave priests equal voice in the council proceedings. As a result, anarchy ensued.

To make matters worse, nobles getting their marching orders from the Council of Basel seized control of the Papal States. Under duress, Pope Eugene IV allowed the council to continue and ratified its acts.

Work with the Bohemian Hussites

In 1433, the council managed to achieve unity with the conservative Hussites who sincerely desired reform of the Church in Bohemia. Cardinal Cesarini, who presided over the early sessions of the Council of Basel, had previously served as papal legate to Bohemia and thus clearly understood the situation at hand. An amicable agreement approved by the council stated that:

> (1) The priests must always explain that the Body and Blood of Christ are equally and fully present under each species of the Eucharist; (2) every priest possesses the right to preach the Gospel but he must always remain subject to the approval of the bishop; (3) ecclesiastics have the right to hold temporal possessions...—but the Church has the power and the will to prevent or to reform abuses by wise regulations; (4) the right to punish public crimes belongs directly, in spiritual matters, to the ecclesiastical tribunals; in temporal concerns, to the civil magistrates.[277]

The Council of Ferrara

In the midst of this jurisdictional tug-of-war Pope Eugene IV issued a decree on September 18, 1437 dissolving the Council of Basel and transferring it to a city within the Papal States. Italian bishops who remained loyal to the pope flocked to the magnificent Romanesque cathedral of Ferrara where the council began its sessions on January 8, 1438. Meanwhile, the Eastern schismatic churches sent representatives to Pope Eugene IV in an attempt to achieve unity. Finally, the council would receive its *raison d'être.*

---

[277] Fr. Clement Raab, O.F.M., *Twenty Ecumenical Councils of the Catholic Church,* p. 141.

Antipope Felix V

Meanwhile, the schismatic clergy who had remained at Basel "suspended" Pope Eugene IV in 1438 and "deposed" him on July 25, 1439. On November 5, 1439 they elected Duke Amadeus VIII of Savoy who took the name Felix V. His electors consisted of one cardinal and 32 other clergymen. The antipope, who was recognized by Savoy and Switzerland, abdicated ten years later. On April 20, 1441 Pope Eugene IV excommunicated the clergy who remained at Basel. "The Middle Ages were full of antipopes, they continued off and on up to the Renaissance. After that no one thought it worth while to be one."[278]

A New Crusade?

As a result of the Greek Schism of 1054 AD the Church of Constantinople separated itself from the Church of Rome. Yet, Byzantine Emperor John VIII needed the support of the West against the Ottoman Turks. They had captured great expanses of his empire and actually threatened Constantinople whose population had dwindled from 1,000,000 to less than 50,000. Deno Geanakoplos has written: "...some of the Byzantines, especially of the court circles, came to view the West not only as the source of possible aid against the Turk but, still later, even as a place of refuge from Turkish domination."[279]

Sadly, no Western ruler came to John VIII's aid, or even attended the council. Why did Western monarchs fail to assist him in a campaign against the Turks? It is likely that occurrences during the Second and Fourth Crusades resulted in distrust and ill-will between East and West.

During the Second Crusade in 1148, it is alleged that Byzantine rulers had betrayed the Western crusaders by warning the Muslims of their approach. As a result, the Crusader army was ambushed and slaughtered. The Crusader armies retaliated during the Fourth Crusade by sacking Constantinople in 1204. Since both sides felt betrayed, a new Crusade to save Constantinople never materialized. Before long, the mighty city would fall to the power of the Turks.

> The fifteenth century Byzantine Emperors must have realized that the fall of the city was almost inevitable. There is a spirit of resignation in Byzantine writers of

---

[278] Alec Glasfurd, *The Antipope,* p. 11.
[279] *Greek Scholars,* p. 18.

the late Middle Ages: the Byzantines accepted their fate as God's punishment for their sins.

…Although Greek rulers and Constantinople's high officials and churchmen might be willing to agree to reunion with Rome in return for military help, this was never the wish of the Byzantine rank and file. Whether laymen or clergy, they preferred to be under Ottoman rule rather than recognize the hated Roman Church.[280]

The Attempt to Achieve Unity

There had been 30 attempts to unite the Byzantine East with the Latin West between the years 1054 and 1438. During the Council of Florence Pope Eugene IV would make another attempt. It was truly an ecumenical council since bishops from around the world took an active part in its proceedings.

The attendance at the first eight General Councils had been all but wholly Greek—the legates of the pope the only Latins in the assembly. At the rest of the series, the attendance had been just as exclusively Latin. Only at the Ferrara-Florence sessions of this council of Eugene IV, did Constantinople and Naples, Milan, and Ephesus ever sit down together. And the doctrinal business that brought them together was not the usual business of the condemnation of some new erroneous interpretation of the Christian faith, but Reunion, the demonstration—on the part of the Latins—that the Latin theology meant precisely the same as the Greek in matters where, for centuries now, the Greeks had been shunning the Latins as heretics.[281]

The Eastern Bishops were divided during the council. Bessarion of Nicaea and Isidore of Kiev represented those in favor of union with Rome while Mark of Ephesus, who was extremely hostile to union, represented those opposed to it. Cardinal Cesarini was the leading figure for the Latin Church and did much to bring about unity between East and West.

Disagreement Over Precedence at Ferrara

Geanakoplos describes the scene that unfolded as the Eastern delegates made their way to the pope: "On the 24th of November, 1437, in ships provided by the

---

[280] Jane Browne, *Mind Alive Encyclopedia—Early Civilization*, p. 174.
[281] Msgr. Philip Hughes, *Church in Crisis,* pp. 278-279.

pope, a huge Byzantine delegation of seven hundred ecclesiastics and laymen, headed by the Emperor John VIII Palaeologus, the Patriarch Joseph of Constantinople, and representatives of the three other patriarchs, finally set out for Italy."[282] Trouble began almost as soon as the three-month voyage had ended.

> Once they had landed in Venice, ...the division between the Greeks (as well as their extreme sensitiveness) became quite apparent. Even before they arrived, they seemed to have chosen their sides, for or against union. They also fell into minor disputes concerning the manner in which they ought to greet the pope, the proper order of precedence among the bishops, and the ever recurring problem at this council: the question of the financial reimbursement they were to receive. They arrived at Ferrara in full splendor; the details of precedence were all solved somehow, but not without a great deal of fuss concerning the position of the various thrones and their respective heights. At last, on April 9, a truly fantastic picture was unveiled in the Church of St. George. The Latins gathered on the Gospel side and the Greeks on the Epistle side. The emperor was present as well as his son, Demetrius (who happened to be against the idea of union). The pope was there also, as well as Joseph II, the patriarch of Constantinople—a sick, old man who favored the union and who had made this long journey for that reason, knowing full well that he would probably never return home.[283]

At times it seemed that the matter of canonical status and precedence would never be settled. Patriarch Joseph II absolutely refused to show Pope Eugene IV the customary reverence and threatened to sail back to Constantinople. Tactfully, the pontiff received the Eastern delegation privately and sought for suitable seating arrangements in the Cathedral of Ferrara for both East and West.

> After prolonged argument a solution was achieved whereby, as the Greeks insisted, the papal throne was placed on the side of the Latins. But it was, at the same time, elevated above all others including that of the emperor. Moreover, another throne, corresponding in every respect to that of the Greek Basileus, was set up on the Latin side for the Emperor of the West, despite the vacancy of the throne caused by the recent death of the western Emperor Sigismund.[284]

---

[282] *Byzantine East and Latin West*, p. 94.
[283] Fr. John Murphy, *General Councils of the Church*, p. 148.
[284] *Acta,* 11 (Mansi, 474E); Syrop., 103; and Andrea, XXXIB, col. 1436.

"The poor patriarch of Constantinople, his protests overruled, was in the meantime relegated to a place below both pope and emperors, a position, according to Andrea of Santa Croce, corresponding to that of the highest ranking cardinal."[285]

Ecclesiastics from the schismatic Eastern churches joined their Latin counterparts in council at Ferrara on April 9, 1438 and discussions on the main theological issues that divided the two churches commenced immediately. Some prelates became discouraged during the long hours of debate and at times it seemed that all the attempts for unity would be made in vain. The topics discussed included the Filioque question, papal primacy, Purgatory and the use of unleavened bread by the Western Church.

The Move to Florence

The situation became volatile as a Milanese army attacked the Papal States and major riots broke out in Rome. Pope Eugene IV fled incognito and sought asylum in Florence where the council continued its work on February 26, 1439.

Sessions of the councils were held at the great hall of the Dominican church of Santa Maria Novella in Florence and the liturgical ceremonies took place at the newly dedicated cathedral of Santa Maria del Fiore (St. Mary of the Flowers), also known as the *Duomo*. Construction began on the cathedral in 1296 and it was the first large dome constructed in Western Europe in nearly a 1,000 years.

The Filioque Question

The Latin word *Filioque*, meaning *and from the Son*, concisely summarizes the Catholic belief that the Holy Ghost proceeds from the Father and the Son. It was added to the Nicene Creed by Pope Benedict VIII in 1024 and is recited at every Sunday Mass in the Western Church.

"In Spain the clause Filioque had been inserted in the Creed, first in the Profession of Faith of the Synod of Toledo 447, and then in the Niceno-Constantinopolitan Symbol [Creed] of the council held at Toledo in 589."[286]

---

[285] Andrea, col. 1436: 'In oppositum primis cardinalis sedes patriarchae fuerat constituta.' The *Acta* does not specify the exact position.

[286] Francis Funk, *Manual of Church History, Vol. I*, p. 148.

The Athanasius Creed,[287] also known as the *Quaecumque,* uses similar terminology: "The Holy Ghost is not made, nor created nor begotten, but proceeds from the Father and the Son."[288]

The *Filioque* issue became a major cause of contention between Constantinople and Rome because the Greek Church claimed that the Western Church taught heresy by adding this word to the Creed. The matter was thoroughly debated and discussed.

> This proved the most lengthy of the council's tasks—a thorough investigation and criticism of all the old writers, the champions of orthodoxy at Nicaea, and Ephesus and Chalcedon, Athanasius, Gregory of Nazianzen, Cyril, and the rest. By June 8, 1439, the Greeks had been satisfied that the Latins, despite their use of the words 'and from the Son' (i.e. Filioque), did not hold a doctrine other than their own, and that the addition of the word Filioque to the original creed had been lawful since, at the time it was made, it was the sole means of warding off an heretical interpretation of the original text.[289]

Papal Primacy

The main stumbling block to unity at the council was papal primacy. The papal bull *Laetentur Coeli* of July 5, 1439 was an agreement on this pivotal issue signed by 33 Eastern and 133 Western prelates. The following tract summarizes Catholic belief on this important issue:

> In the name of the Holy Trinity... We, with the assent of the holy and General Council of Florence, define, in like manner that the holy Apostolic See and the Bishop of Rome, have a primacy [tenere primatum] throughout the whole world, and that the Bishop of Rome himself is the successor of St. Peter and the prince of the Apostles, and that he is the true Vicar of Christ, and the head of the whole Church, and the father and teacher of all Christians; and that to him in St. Peter there was committed by Our Lord Jesus Christ full power to pasture, to rule, and

---

[287] "It was commonly attributed to St. Athanasius (d. 373) but is certainly of late composition, written probably after the Council of Ephesus (431), condemning the errors of Nestorius and after the Council of Chalcedon (451), condemning those of Eutyches. Some say it was written in Southern Gaul towards the end of the fifth century, or in Spain in the sixth." J. O'Connell, *Simplifying the Rubrics of the Roman Breviary and Missal,* p. 55.

[288] Spiritus Sanctus a Patre et Filio: non factus nec creatus nec genitus, sed procedens.

[289] Msgr. Philip Hughes, *The Church in Crisis,* p. 282.

to guide the whole Church; as is also contained in the acts of the General Councils and in the sacred canons.[290]

Settling of Doctrinal Differences

The subject of Purgatory was hotly debated by Latins and Greeks for two weeks, though in the end, both sides concluded that they believed the same thing. In spite of differences in language, culture and customs, unity in doctrine was finally achieved. The Council Fathers concisely summarized this teaching:

> This dogmatic definition of the Union Council declares: that the Holy Ghost proceeds from the Father *and the Son;* that leavened bread or unleavened bread are equally valid matter of the Holy Eucharist, but commanded that each priest must follow the custom of his church; that the just, dying before their sins are entirely expiated, are purified in purgatory, and are there assisted by the sacrifices, prayers and alms of the faithful; that the completely purified soul is received into heaven there to enjoy the Beatific Vision of the triune God according to their merits; that those who die in actual mortal sin, descend into hell, there to undergo punishment; that the Roman Pontiff is the successor of Blessed Peter, Prince of the Apostles; that he is the true Vicar of Jesus Christ, the head of the Universal Church, and the father and teacher of all Christians; that Christ has given to him, in the person of Blessed Peter, the full power of teaching and governing the Universal Church.[291]

> The ailing Patriarch [of Constantinople], Joseph II died on June 10. Some of the other Greek bishops (as well as the learned layman, Scholarios) purposely left the council about the same time, before the solemn signing of the decree. One bishop stayed, steadfastly refusing to sign: Mark of Ephesus. This manner of avoiding the question of signing the decree is quite significant in view of what happened after the council had ended.[292]

The Greeks Depart For Constantinople

The work of the council seemed to be completed by July 6, 1439 and most of the Greeks began to depart for the port of Venice. Some had come to the council with a sincere desire for unity with the West; others had come with a

---

[290] Found in Denzinger's *Enchiridion Symbolorum,* no. 694.
[291] Fr. Clement Raab, O.F.M., *Twenty Ecumenical Councils,* pp. 153-154.
[292] Fr. John Murphy, *General Councils of the Church,* p. 151.

determination to remain independent from the Roman Church. The latter group may have decided to attend the council in order to experience the City of Florence at the peak of the Renaissance. Both groups set sail on October 19, 1439 and finally reached Constantinople in February.

Late Arrivals

In sharp contrast, leaders of other Eastern heretical and schismatic churches had traveled to Florence with a desire to be united to the Church of Rome.

> Most of them [the Greeks who attended the council] were still in Florence when there arrived another group of Orientals seeking reunion with the Roman See. These were Armenians from Constantinople and the Genoese colony of Caffa in the Crimea, but commissioned by their patriarch. They were Monophysites, their churches relics of the reaction that had followed the Council of Chalcedon, now a thousand years ago. 'We have come to you our head,' they said to the pope. 'You are the foundation of the Church. Every member that has left you is sick, and wild beasts have devoured the flock that has separated itself from you. …You have the power of the heavenly keys, open to us the gates of eternal life.'[293]

What a profound declaration on papal primacy!

The list below gives the names of the various Eastern schismatic and heretical churches that sought union with Rome and the year they came to the council.

Armenians (Armenia)	1439
Jacobites (Egypt, Ethiopia, Libya)	1442
Coptics (Egypt)	1442
Nestorians (Edessa)	1443
Nestorians (Mesopotamia)	1444
Jacobites (Syria)	1444
Nestorians (Chaldea)	1445
Monophysite Maronites (Cyprus)	1445

While the Council of Florence, like II Lyons, failed to bring about a lasting union, it is remarkably indicative of the action of the Holy Spirit in a council. Out of such a conglomeration of elements and cross motives, two particularly important results can be detected. One, the Church received its most clear and

---

[293] Msgr. Philip Hughes, *Church in Crisis*, p. 283.

explicit statement concerning the doctrine on the Holy Spirit, a formula worked out in the discussions between the Eastern and Western theologians. Moreover, the authority of the Roman Pontiff that had been so challenged after the Council of Constance, now emerged more firmly established in doctrinal matters than ever before.[294]

The papal bull of Pope Eugene IV, *Cantate Domino* of 1441 AD, strongly condemned the hardness of heart shown by many of the Orthodox who attended the Council of Florence in bad faith. In order to accurately understand its contents it is important to read it in the light of the times it was written.

The Council of Florence concluded in the fall of 1443. The remaining sessions were held at the Lateran in Rome and ended two years later. Little is known of these proceedings because once the majority of the attendees had departed from Florence, the official historian of the council packed his bags, too. As a result, no one knows when the council ended.

Tragically, the division between Catholic and Orthodox still continues today. It still endures in the Church of the Holy Sepulcher in Jerusalem which is divided between Roman Catholics, Egyptian Coptic, and Armenian, Ethiopian and Greek Orthodox. "Most of its history [is] marked by severe tensions between the Orthodox and Catholics; including an incident inside the church when a Catholic priest was beaten to death with a candlestick by an Orthodox clergyman."[295]

Greek Catholics

There are a variety of names used for the Greek Catholics who had always remained Catholic, as well as those who returned after the Greek Schism. Sometimes they are collectively referred to as Catholics of the Byzantine Rite.

> As Moscow grew in influence in the late Middle Ages, however, the church centered in Kiev [Ukraine] found itself squeezed between a Polish king who wanted to make them into Latin-rite Christians, and a Russian church that wanted the upper hand within Orthodoxy.
>
> In 1596, a majority of the bishops of the Kiev church voted to enter communion with Rome. The agreement is also called the union of Brest for the city in

---

[294] Fr. John Murphy, *General Councils of the Church*, p. 153.
[295] *Catholic Family News,* August 2001.

Belarusia in which it was signed. These Eastern believers maintained their ancient liturgical and theological traditions.

The word *uniate* is sometimes used to describe this church, but members regard it as pejorative, since it is often used in a dismissive fashion. The official term is 'Greek Catholic,' introduced by the Austrian empress Maria-Teresa in 1774.[296]

Rebellion at Home

Meanwhile, in Constantinople, the work accomplished at Florence was rapidly coming to naught. The emperor attempted to adhere to the agreement with the pope, as did his successor; but the people were opposed. In fact, thirteen years later the emperors had not yet dared to publish the decrees signed in Florence; this included Scholarios who had apparently undergone a change of heart; he had been in favor of union at first, but not at the close of the discussions. He had now become a monk and a most violent anti-unionist. The entire mentality of the period was summed up in the phrase: 'Better the turban of the Prophet than the tiara of the pope.'[297]

Emperor Constantine XI finally published the decree of union after Pope Nicholas V (1447-1455) sent him military aid. Yet, the hour was very late.

Constantinople

Constantinople had stood for more than 1000 years as the world's greatest city: the richest, strongest and most powerful capital of Christianity. Gold, silver, jewels, ivory, intricate glassware, silks, precious icons and manuscripts were found here in abundance. Though vast riches tempted many a conqueror, the city's defenses were formidable.

"Constantinople was built on a triangle of land with the sea on two sides and on the west a land wall. The long narrow sea inlet on the northern side formed the harbor known as the Golden Horn."[298] The city was protected by natural barriers, 14 miles of walls, three series of nearly impenetrable walls and 200 towers. A 60-foot moat 30 feet deep prevented ramming apparatus, portable towers and explosives from being used. A sea attack was often repulsed by sealing off the entrance of the harbor with a huge chain. The unfortunate ships

---

[296] *National Catholic Reporter*, July 13, 2001.
[297] Fr. John Murphy, *General Councils of the Church*, pp. 152-153.
[298] Jane Browne, *Mind Alive Encyclopedia—Early Civilization*, p. 174.

that made it through were quickly engulfed in flames once the flammable gel, Greek fire, was hurled at their vessels.

The Siege by the Ottoman Turks

The Black Death had so depleted the ranks of the Ottoman Turks that by the year 1397, the conquered Bulgarians and Serbians became mere vassals of their new overlords. Yet this conquest created a new platform from which their armies could attack the Byzantine Empire from the West.

In this ideal setting Mehmet II (Muhammad the Conqueror) emerged as the undisputed leader of the Ottoman Turks in the year 1451 at the young age of 19 years. His foremost ambition was to do what other sultans considered unthinkable: to capture the great city of Constantinople.

"The young new emperor was ruthless and determined and had announced that as soon as he controlled the reins of authority he would destroy 'the empire of the Romans and bring all the Christian Empires to naught.'"[299]

Mehmet II carefully prepared his campaign against Constantinople with unparalleled ingenuity and daring in February 1453. His plan was to surround Constantinople and attack it with a formidable army nearly 300,000 strong that included the elite Janissary troops. Cannons were positioned at strategic locations and a blockade of Constantinople began on April 2, 1453.

"His engineers now contrived to bring ships overland from the Bosporus into the Golden Horn. They were fixed on wheeled cradles and dragged over rollers by oxen—to the dismay of the Christians. On 22 April, about seventy Turkish ships made their appearance into the Golden Horn."[300]

> Over the centuries, the walls of Constantinople had withstood twenty-two sieges. Persians, Avars, Bulgarians, Slavs, Russians—all had been repelled; Attila the Hun himself had fallen back from them. For more than 100 years, they had been all that stood between an immature Europe and the risen power of the Arabs, who retreated from them in AD 718 with terrible losses. The walls' military worth had been reaffirmed during the sieges of 1402 and 1422. However, they had never been bombarded by cannon like those of Sultan Mehmet.[301]

---

[299] Jane Browne, *The Mind Alive Encyclopedia—Early Civilization*, p. 174.
[300] Browne, 176.
[301] Editors of Time-Life Books, *Voyages of Discovery—TimeFrame AD 1400-1500*, p. 81.

On April 12, Turkish artillery began pummeling the outer walls of the city, launching a bombardment that would last a month and a half. A massive 26-foot cannon which was capable of hurling a 1,500 pound projectile nearly half a mile joined in the assault. This deadly weapon was used to devastating effect although it could only be fired seven times a day because it took so long to cool.

Few battles have ever had as great an effect upon history as this Battle of Constantinople in 1453. Constantinople was defended by a mere 7,000 Byzantine troops together with 2,000 Genoese and Venetian soldiers, sailors and merchants.

"Eventually the defenders were exhausted by the toils of a continuous and hopeless conflict, while their ranks grew steadily thinner through death or wounds. The population gave no help and was content to taunt the Latins [the Genoese and Venetians who defended Constantinople], while waiting for a miracle of heaven that was to save them."[302]

> On the night of May 24, there was an eclipse of the moon; citizens recalled an ancient prophesy that their city would stand as long as the moon waxed in the sky.[303] During the days of 25-27 May there had been bad omens. The picture of the Mother of God had fallen to the ground as it was being carried in procession round the city; this was followed by a thunderstorm and a cloudburst and a dark fog; strange lights were seen playing over Santa Sophia, the cathedral of the Holy Wisdom. The emperor was advised to leave the city which God had abandoned, but he refused.[304]

The Fall of Constantinople

Mehmet finally ordered one last great assault that came in three waves. The first was a group of 'dispensable' warriors. Next came a wave of Turkish soldiers from his homeland. The third wave was that of the loyal, elite and fierce fighting Janissaries. Janissaries were Christian young men who had been taken captive by the Muslim leaders, converted to Islam and trained in the art of war. The fighting which began at one in the morning continued for over five hours with neither side gaining the advantage.

---

[302] Charles Herbermann, *The Catholic Encyclopedia, Vol. IV*, p. 305.
[303] Editors of Time-Life Books, *Voyages of Discovery—TimeFrame AD 1400-1500*, p. 87.
[304] Jane Browne, *The Mind Alive Encyclopedia, Early Civilization*, p. 174.

Two events turned the tide—leading to the utter collapse of Constantinople. Some attacking Ottoman soldiers noticed that one of the gates had been inadvertently left open and hordes of Turks began to rush in. Terrible hand-to-hand fighting ensued between the outer and inner walls.

> The presence of the Turks caused consternation, but even so, the Greeks might have managed to repel them if their entry had not coincided with an even greater disaster: While defending the stockade, Giustiniani was shot through the breastplate and wounded. For fifty-four days, the Genoese warrior had commanded the land-wall defenses with exemplary vigor and courage. Now his strength failed him. Although the emperor personally pleaded with him to stay, he insisted on being carried off to a Genoese ship waiting in the Golden Horn. The sight of his departure, coupled with the news that the Turks had entered the city to the north, spread panic among his Genoese compatriots, who abandoned their positions, leaving the Greeks and Venetians to fight on alone.[305]
>
> The Turkish entry was soon followed by panic amongst the Christians. Barbaro, a Venetian who was present, tells how everybody who could do so escaped by ship. But so many were killed that their heads in the Golden Horn and the sea of Marmora reminded him of melons floating in the canals of Venice. Certain quarters of the city seem to have been spared, probably because they voluntarily submitted to the Turks. Mehmet himself rode first to the church of the Holy Wisdom which was at once converted into a mosque; then he went to the imperial Great Palace, never fully repaired after the sack of 1204.[306]

The fall of Constantinople occurred on May 29, 1453, the Feast of Pentecost. Emperor Constantine XI on seeing the hopelessness of the situation, rushed headlong into the mass of attacking warriors and was cut down as he fought. The very last Roman Emperor died and with him 1,000 years of Roman-Byzantine history came to an end.

In 1472, less than 20 years after the fall of Constantinople, the union between East and West that was achieved at the Council of Florence was formally repudiated by the remaining Orthodox clergy of Istanbul. The attempt at union was again made in vain.

---

[305] Editors of Time-Life Books, *Voyages of Discovery—TimeFrame AD 1400-1500*, p. 89.
[306] Jane Browne, *The Mind Alive Encyclopedia—Early Civilization*, p. 176.

CHAPTER EIGHTEEN

Fifth Lateran Council

1512-1517 AD

This council was held during the pontificates of Popes Julius II and Leo X.

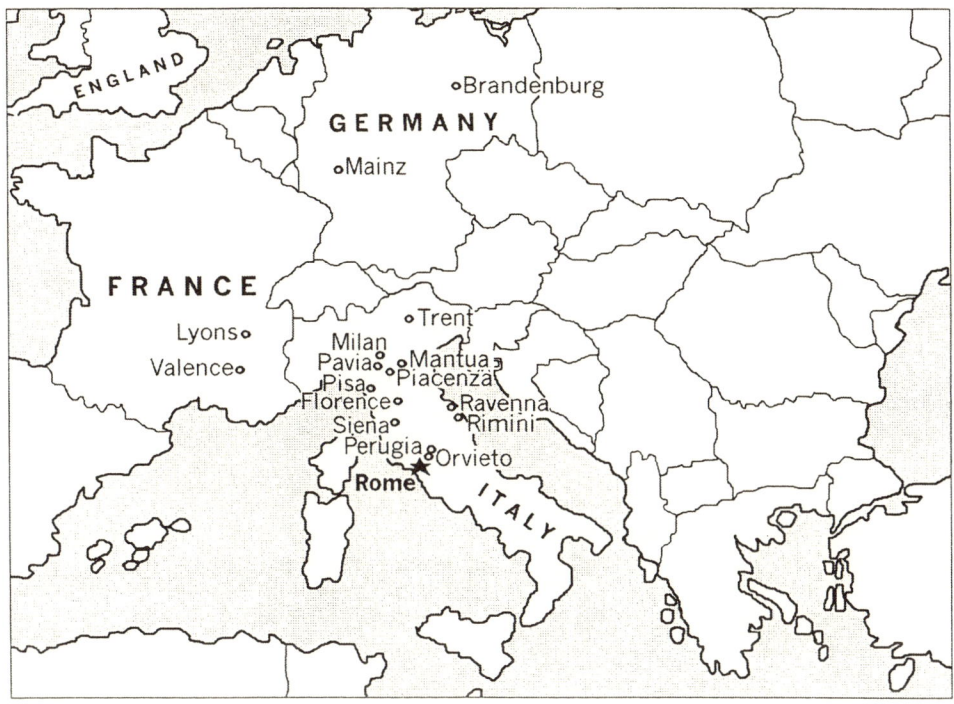

Background

The period surrounding the Fifth Lateran Council is one of the darkest chapters in Church history. The popes of this era were influenced by the humanism of the Renaissance and led scandalous lives. Reforms enacted by the council could have averted the devastation and tragic loss of souls caused by the Protestant Reformation. However, the council accomplished next to nothing and the Protestant Reformation erupted only seven and a half months after its conclusion.

Nepotism

Nepotism, the practice of placing family members into places of prominence in the Church while ignoring their lack of virtue and qualification, was a widespread abuse. Innumerable evils resulted from this practice because ecclesiastical posts were being filled by unworthy men and many popes of the period openly sold church offices in order to finance their elegant lifestyles.

Pope Innocent VIII

Flagrantly immoral was Innocent VIII (1484-1492), father of sixteen children whom he openly recognized and whose weddings he celebrated in the Vatican. To increase his income, he received an annual subsidy of forty-five thousand ducats, almost 1.7 million [dollars] from the Turkish Sultan Bayazid II for keeping as prisoner the latter's brother, a contender for the throne.[307]

"With the pontificate of Innocent VIII, the papacy sunk to the depths of worldliness—a fitting prelude to the most notorious pontificate in history, that of Alexander VI."[308]

Pope Alexander VI

Alexander VI, one of the worst popes in history, is known for his licentiousness, nepotism, simony and numerous other crimes. Yet in spite of his evil personal life, Pope Alexander VI was the legitimate descendant of St. Peter and never erred doctrinally while reigning as pope.

> Evil though he was, he never attempted to challenge or change the doctrines of the Church. 'Even his bitterest enemies are unable to formulate any accusation against him in this respect,' states Pastor. 'It seemed as though his reign was meant by Providence to demonstrate the truth that though men may hurt the Church they cannot harm Her. In the Church there have always been unworthy priests as well as bad Christians and... just as the intrinsic worth of a jewel is not lessened by an inferior setting, so the sins of a priest cannot essentially affect his power of offering sacrifice or administering sacraments or transmitting doctrine. ...The papal office belongs to a higher sphere than the personality of its occupant for the time being, and can neither gain nor lose its essential dignity by saintliness on one side, or unworthiness on the other.' Even the first Pope, St. Peter, had sinned deeply in denying his Lord and Master; and yet the office of Supreme pastor was given to him. In the words of the great St. Leo: 'The dignity of Peter is not tarnished by the unworthiness of his successor.'[309]

---

[307] Harold Grimm, *The Reformation Era 1500-1650*, p. 37.
[308] Richard McBrien, *Lives of the Popes*, p. 267.
[309] John Farrow, *Pageant of the Popes*, pp. 241-242.

Alexander VI fathered nine children, two of them during the time he was pope. His daughter, Lucretia, was left in charge of the Vatican whenever Alexander VI was absent. His son, Caesar Borgia, was made an archbishop at 17, a cardinal at 18 and later renounced both to follow a secular career. He married the sister of the King of Navarre and became the Duke of Romagna and Valence.

> Caesar methodically ousted the feudal dynasts of Romagna and the Marches, Umbria and Latium. One by one they were expelled or assassinated until by 1503, the year of Alexander's death, the whole papal state had passed into the personal possession of the Borgias.[310]

Caesar diligently applied the philosophy of his friend Machiavelli by eliminating all who stood in his way. Indiscriminately, fellow cardinals, relatives, civil leaders and close friends, even his own brother fell prey to his poisons and plots.

He decided that it was an ideal time to steal from the Church as his father, Pope Alexander VI, lay dying. "Caesar was too ill to visit him; but in the pope's last moments sent his confidential officer Michelotto, who with his dagger drawn extorted from the fears of the chamberlain the keys of the papal treasury, and carried off all the plate and 100,000 ducats in gold."[311] The jewels and plate that were unjustly confiscated at this time were valued at 300,000 ducats.

In spite of his ruthless tactics, tyrannical power and tremendous wealth, Caesar was not invincible. He was called before the Eternal Judge during the siege of the Castle of Viana on March 12, 1507. As he lay dying, his last words were: "I die unprepared."[312]

Pope Julius II

Pope Julius II (1503-1513) was a man of great courage and determination. "His abilities were those of a warrior statesman rather than those of an ecclesiastic."[313] "In 1506 he founded the Swiss Guards, who to this day defend with pikes and halberds and other archaic accoutrement all entrances to the

---

[310] Nicholas Cheetham, *Keepers of the Keys,* pp. 189-190.
[311] Burchard, iii., 239.
[312] John Chapin, *Book of Catholic Quotations,* p. 520.
[313] John Farrow, *Pageant of the Popes,* p. 243.

Vatican City."[314] Pope Julius II commissioned Bramante, Michelangelo and Raphael to commence their work on the new St. Peter's.

Pope Julius II began the Fifth Lateran Council in 1512 and issued the papal bull *Si summus rerum opifex*. "The bull provides briefly, among other things, that if anyone secures election as pope through simony, through bribes whether of money or of position or promise of favors, his election is null; and the elect, and those who have taken the bribes, are by the fact excommunicated, and they remain so until a pope lawfully elected absolves them."[315]

Pope Leo X

Pope Leo X (1513-1521) brought the Fifth Lateran Council to a conclusion. During his pontificate he placed family concerns above the welfare of the Church. "Born Giovanni de' Medici, son of Lorenzo the Magnificent, he was tonsured (i.e. admitted to the clerical state) at age seven, named a cardinal deacon of Santa Maria in Dominica at age thirteen, and was the effective ruler of Florence at the time of his election to the papacy on March 9, 1513, at age thirty-seven."[316]

He was elected pope on March 17, 1513 and though not as personally immoral as his predecessors, his was a court of pleasure. This is epitomized by his words to the Venetian ambassador at Rome, "Let us enjoy the papacy, since God has given it to us."[317]

Pope Leo X remained oblivious to the great evils prevalent in Rome and throughout the Church and to the many remnants of paganism found in the music, sculpture and architecture at the papal court. Under his orders the triumphal arch constructed for his papal coronation portrayed Moses flanked by Mercury and Diana while paintings of Venus, Jupiter, Bacchus, Apollo, Eros, centaurs, satyrs and nymphs filled the galleries of the Vatican.

> His gorgeous inaugural pageant alone cost 100,000 ducats and his court life was a continuous round of festivities, banquets, carnivals, theatrical shows, balls and hunting parties. ...Papal finances were more badly damaged by Leo's lavishness

---

[314] James Lee-Milne, *St. Peter's*, p. 135.
[315] Msgr. Philip Hughes, *Church in Crisis*, pp. 291-292.
[316] Richard O'Brien, *Lives of the Popes*, p. 272.
[317] Harold Grimm, *The Reformation Era 1500-1650*, p. 38.

than by the warlike operations of Julius, who in fact left a reserve of 700,000 ducats in the treasury. It was quickly dissipated and the Holy See lived from hand to mouth off credit from Roman and Florentine bankers... Although they charged him 40 per cent [interest], they themselves were seriously embarrassed by the pope's demands. In order to recoup his losses Leo multiplied the sale of offices and indulgences. ...His mass creation of 31 new members of the College [of Cardinals] in 1517 netted him half a million ducats. ...Not all the new creations were unworthy, but they included three professional financiers.[318]

Pope Leo X's worldliness was a cause of scandal as he literally sold out the Church in France in order to further his family interests.

Politically, he was concerned with preserving Italy, and especially his beloved Florence, from foreign domination. To do so, he entered into an unpopular treaty with France in 1515 (after a series of French military victories in Italy, including Milan). Leo X surrendered Parma and Piacenza in return for Florence's independence, under Medici control. He also arranged a concordat with France that would last until the French Revolution in 1789. The concordat conceded to the French crown the right of nomination to all higher church offices (bishops, abbots, and priors), reserving only lesser benefices to the pope.[319]

The Church in Financial Distress

Heavy taxes were imposed on the subjects of the pope; however, local rulers and officials took their cut first, leaving only the remaining third to reach the Vatican. "In 1484, Pope Sixtus IV had to pawn his tiara for 100,000 ducats. From 1471-1520 the Holy See was constantly in debt."[320]

Simony was at the heart of the curial system as it functioned before Luther. The popes had gained control of a large number of ecclesiastical appointments, and their sale was a lucrative... source of papal income. By the time of Leo X (d. 1521), it is estimated that there were some two thousand marketable Church jobs, which were literally sold over the counter at the Vatican; even a cardinal's hat might go to the highest bidder.[321]

---

[318] Nicholas Cheetham, *Keepers of the Keys,* p. 193.
[319] Richard O'Brien, *Lives of the Popes,* p. 273.
[320] Pierre Janelle, *The Catholic Reformation,* pp. 15-16.
[321] Thomas Bokenkotter, *Concise History of the Catholic Church,* p. 208.

The Pseudo Council of Pisa

Emperor Maximilian and King Louis XII of France, who had designs upon the papal lands, convened the anti-papal council of Pisa which lasted from the fall of 1511 until June of 1512. Nine cardinals who opposed Pope Julius II attended the proceedings. The clergy of Pisa barred the cathedral in order to prevent its use. Citizens of Pisa uttered death threats to the bishops and cardinals who attended the council. Armed French soldiers kept the violent crowds at bay. Seeking respite from the turmoil, the site of the council was transferred first to Milan and then to Lyons, where it soon dissipated with no tangible results.

Meanwhile, King Louis' armies occupied much of Northern Italy, yet failed to advance once General Gaston De Foix was killed in battle at Ravenna on April 11, 1512. Julius II returned to Rome and hastily convoked a general council which was scheduled to begin at the Lateran on April 19, 1512. The proposed council was to put an end to the schism and address the abuses in the Church.

On June 10, 1513, Swiss allies of the pope routed the French at Novara, near Milan, leading to an end of hostilities. Subsequently, King Louis XII sent a delegation to the Fifth Lateran Council on December 19, 1513, accepted its legitimacy and ended the schism.

The Fifth Lateran Council

The Fifth Lateran Council should have been engaged in the work of reforming morals of the Church hierarchy. Instead, it ranks as one of the greatest tragedies in the annals of Church history. Although the council condemned the illegitimate Council of Pisa and strengthened the claim of papal sovereignty, it did nothing to correct the abuses rampant in the Church.

> There was an average attendance at the council of about 90 to 100 bishops and almost all of them were from sees in one or other of the Italian states. ...There were no more than twelve public meetings of the council in all: four in 1512, four in 1513 and one in each of the years 1514, 1515, 1516, 1517. The legislation of the council appeared in the form of papal bulls, published in the several sessions. Of the organization of the council, and the discussions that preceded the drafting of these documents, we know very little, save that it was the Curia that decided what was to be enacted in the sessions of the council, in detail; and that the

bishops were allowed to elect a committee of twenty-four to discuss these drafts (or proposals) while in this formative state.[322]

Although there was talk of reform, nothing tangible occurred. The legislation limiting the number and use of benefices had too many loopholes, so the abuses continued.

The Camoldolese monks Giustiniani and Quirini sought for measures that would remedy the ignorance of the clergy in order to ensure that the laity would receive proper instruction on Sunday. Requisite qualifications for preachers were delineated in the papal bull *Supernae Majestatis Praesidio*[323] and it became the bishop's responsibility to oversee the matter.

The 20 decrees issued by Pope Leo X lessened the power of the Religious Orders, leaving local bishops the right to reform lax religious houses and to examine religious clergy on doctrinal and moral matters before their ordination.

The immortality of the individual human soul was the only theological matter discussed during the council. It was declared a dogma of faith during the eighth session, held on December 17, 1513.

The Tenth Session

The tenth session of the council dealt with problems that resulted from the advent of the printing press. Henceforth, bishops became the official censors of books and they were commissioned to warn the faithful of heretical works.

Another matter discussed at this session was the *Monti di Pietà* (Mountains of Benevolence). These charitable institutions loaned money without usury to the indigent. Other institutions of the time charged tremendous interest rates for loans; some moneylenders in Florence demanded a shocking 40% interest. Many of the bishops felt it was necessary to know more about these institutions before giving them their approbation.

> To prevent this oppressive exploitation of the needs of smaller townsfolk and of the poor, the Franciscans resolved to found institutions where anyone in want of ready money could obtain it in exchange for some pledge and without interest. The working capital of the scheme would be supplied by voluntary contributions,

---

[322] Msgr. Philip Hughes, *Church in Crisis*, pp. 290-291.
[323] December 19, 1516.

gifts and legacies; hence the name *'Monti di Pietà'*—*'Mountains* [Institutions] *of Benevolence.'* The first of these institutions opened in the Papal States; in Orvieto in 1463 and in Perugia in 1461. In both places the Franciscans were the originators of the plan. In fact, such great saints of the order, as St. Bernardine of Siena, St. John Capistrano and St. James della Marchia were indefatigable supporters and workers for these institutions. In the course of time similar benevolent banks were opened in Assisi, Mantua, Pavia, Ravenna, Verona, Ferrara, Parma, Rimini, and in so many other places. ...The extraordinary and rapid growth and spread of these institutions—to France, England, Bavaria—are the best proofs that they responded to a real want.[324]

Aftermath

The council finally ended on March 16, 1517, just months before Martin Luther began his revolt against the Church. In all probability this council could not have stopped the Protestant Reformation. Yet, true reform would not be achieved until nearly half of Europe had fallen to Protestantism.

Renaissance Rome was finally brought to its knees by violent means. The gleaming armor of 15,000 Italians, Spaniards and German Lutherans from the army of Emperor Charles V could be seen from the Eternal City on May 5, 1527. The vast majority were there for plunder and riches. Others considered it a holy war against the pope.

Rome fell to the invading armies who plundered the city for seven days. The mood around Rome, which for so many years had been one of frivolity and carnival, suddenly became sober. As a graphic representation of this new spirit, Pope Paul III commissioned Michelangelo to paint *The Last Judgment* in the Sistine Chapel. At this site, chosen for papal elections, the cardinals would be forcibly reminded to elect worthy candidates for so high an office. Years later, Pope Paul III would lead the Church in its true reformation at the Council of Trent.

---

[324] Fr. Clement Raab, O.F.M., *Twenty General Councils of the Catholic Church,* p. 166.

CHAPTER NINETEEN

Council of Trent

1545–1563 AD

This council was held during the pontificates of Popes Paul III, Julius III & Pius IV.

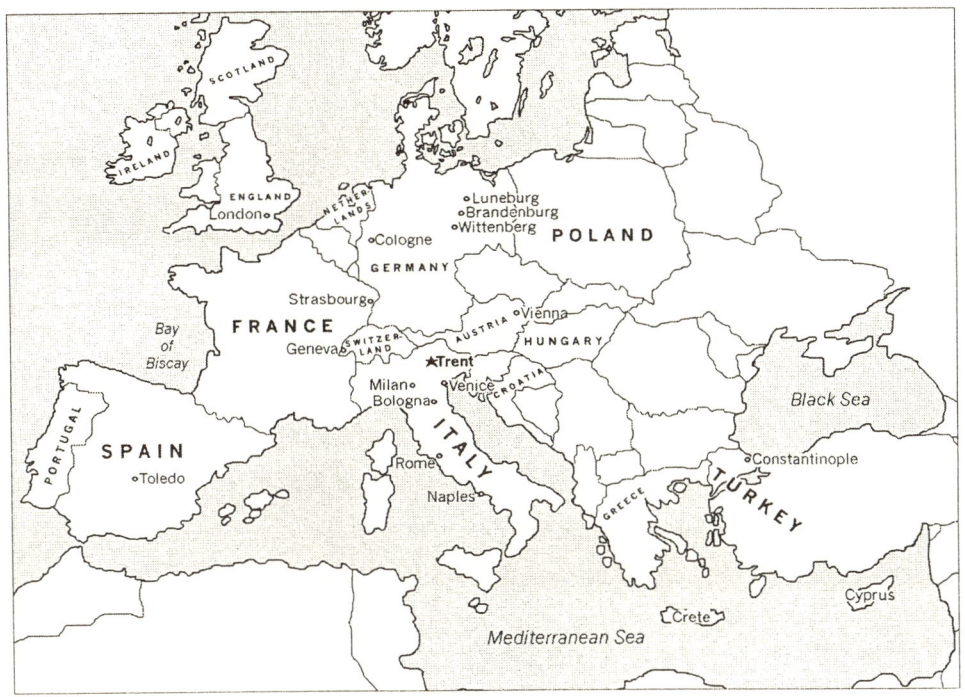

Causes of the Reformation

How was it possible that entire European nations such as England, Switzerland and the Scandinavian countries could abandon the Catholic Church and Her teachings during the Protestant Reformation? Many of the "reformers" were former Catholic clergymen. Archbishop Cranmer and the priests Luther, Zwingli and Knox worked from within the Church in their attempts to destroy it. This tactic is familiar, since we see history repeating itself in the post-Vatican II church.

The success of the Reformation in England and Germany was largely due to avarice. "By 1500 the Church owned, on a conservative Catholic estimate, about a fifth of all property in England."[325] The situation was similar in Germany because pious kings bequeathed property to the Church for the erection of convents, monasteries, oratories and pious institutions. Many greedy kings and princes rallied around the flag of Protestantism to justify their confiscation of Church lands through revolution or by force of arms.

Europe Before the Protestant Reformation

During the early 16th century, Europe was fertile ground for a great apostasy from the Church. Seminaries were nonexistent and immorality among the clergy was widespread, making the work of dedicated priests more difficult. Many pastors showed little concern for their flocks and resembled hirelings more than shepherds. Sunday sermons were the exception instead of the rule; well planned and instructive sermons were few and far between. These factors fostered general ignorance of the faith among many of the laity, which caused morals to decay.

Tremendous havoc was wrought as Church offices were bought and sold with little regard for the spiritual responsibilities involved. Worldly prelates chosen by monarchs were often ambitious and desirous only of worldly gain. Discipline was lax in a number of convents and monasteries and their vast tracts of land were coveted by many of the nobility.

In his book, *How the Reformation Happened,* Hilaire Belloc wrote: "It was a whole perverted aspect of the Catholic Church, affecting a great body of the hierarchy, established like a parasite *within* the organism, and threatening to starve and ultimately destroy its life." The laxity of the laity, the ignorance of many of the clergy and the avarice and worldliness of the popes, cardinals and bishops set the stage for the great conflagration to come.

Numerous heretics including the Cathars, Hussites, Lollards and Waldenses (who later became Huguenots) had prepared the soil for the seeds of discord and disbelief that would be sown by Calvin, Luther and Zwingli.

---

[325] Hilaire Belloc, *How the Reformation Happened,* p. 117.

Indulgences

The practice of bishops granting indulgences dates back at least to the First Council of Nicaea (325 AD).

> The word *indulgence* (Lat. *indulgentia*, from *indulgeo*, to be kind or tender) originally meant kindness or favor; in post-classic Latin it came to mean the remission of a tax or debt. In Roman law and in the Vulgate of the Old Testament (Is. 61: 1) it was used to express release from captivity or punishment. In theological language also the word is sometimes employed in its primary sense to signify the kindness and mercy of God. But in a special sense in which it is here considered, an indulgence is a remission of the temporal punishment due to sin, the guilt of which has been forgiven.[326]

By the 16th century the manner in which indulgences were granted became abusive, creating the need for reform. The granting of indulgences based upon a payment of money was initiated by Pope Julius II when he commissioned the rebuilding of St. Peter's Basilica in Rome. Since the project was very expensive he needed to find a means by which he could raise the necessary funds. "In 1513 the pope issued a bull announcing to the world that the new basilica would eclipse in size and magnificence every church in Christendom. Graciously he promised an extension of indulgences to those pious benefactors who agreed to pay contributions on an annual basis."[327]

This opened the door for unscrupulous individuals who took advantage of the situation. Upon his election to the archbishopric of Mainz, the 25-year-old Albrecht of Brandenburg owed 25,000 gold florins to the Roman Curia. In an attempt to cover this debt, Albrecht borrowed funds from the Fuggers banking house. Arrangements were then made with the Roman Curia allowing Albrecht of Brandenburg to get two-thirds of the proceeds collected when the indulgence for St. Peter's was preached in his domain.

"There is no doubt that the original bargain between the Curia and Albrecht, as well as the subsequent indulgence peddling, would have been

---

[326] Charles Herbermann, *Catholic Encyclopedia*, Vol. VII, p. 783.
[327] James Lee-Milne, *St. Peter's*, p. 146.

condemned by the early Church as a grave case of simony."[328] Although these abuses would finally be corrected by the Council of Trent, they gave the enemies of the Church an opening for attacks against Catholic belief and worship.

The Protestant Reformation

The 16th century movement against the Catholic Church directed by Martin Luther, John Calvin and others has been described by many historians as the Protestant Reformation. However, the term is a misnomer for they produced not reformation, but revolution. According to the *Merriam-Webster Collegiate Dictionary* the word "revolution" means "a sudden, radical or complete change."[329] The leaders of the uprising attacked the very foundation of the Catholic Church and were set on Her destruction. They did not bring about a true reformation. This is confirmed by history.

> The Reformation did not originate in a definite heresy, nor a new, nor a supposedly purified body of faith. Having arisen as an attack on priesthood and the Papal See, through anger against abuses in the priesthood and Holy See it kept this negative and formless character through all its first twenty years. Individuals speculated on doctrine and drew up this formula and that: but the spirit of the great affair was not for making a new organism. It was for destroying the old.[330]

Erasmus of Rotterdam lamented the temerity of the "reformers:"

> 'What do you want to do? You ask the world to despise and reject the traditions cherished by our fathers for centuries! Your new gospel lacks everything: prophesies, miracles, virtue, learning, the sanction of scholars, the testimony of martyrs; and yet you ask us to rush in and embrace this new gospel of yours? You want to make us believe that the Church was deprived of Christ for fourteen hundred years... There is no greater misfortune than to fall away from the Church. ...I see new hypocrites, new despots; but not the footprint of the Holy Spirit. Show me one man who has been made better by this new gospel. I, for my part, have not seen one who

---

[328] Joseph Lortz, *How the Reformation Came,* p. 94.
[329] p. 1575.
[330] Hilaire Belloc, *How the Reformation Happened,* p. 79.

has not become, on embracing the new opinions, a worse man than he was before, if possible. Wherever this new gospel prevails, learning falls to the ground and the writings of the ancient fathers are despised.'[331]

Martin Luther

Martin Luther (1483-1546) entered the Augustinian convent at Erfurt, Germany on July 17, 1505. Two years later he made his profession and was ordained a priest. This is considered a very short period of time, since today priestly ordination is not usually conferred until at least six years of studies are completed.

After his ordination, Luther continued his studies and filled various posts in the Order at Wittenberg and Erfurt. Even though, as a priest, he was bound under pain of mortal sin to recite the Divine Office daily, he neglected it for weeks at a time and then would inflict severe penances upon himself. His disregard of prayer ultimately led to his spiritual ruin.

> On 22 October [1512] he was formally admitted to the senate of the faculty of theology, and received the appointment as lecturer on the Bible in 1513. His further appointment as district vicar in 1515 made him the official representative of the vicar-general in Saxony and Thuringia. His duties were manifold and his life busy. Little time was left for intellectual pursuits, and the increasing irregularity in the performance of his religious duties could only bode ill for his future. He himself tells us that he needed two secretaries or chancellors, wrote letters all day, preached at table, also in the monastery, and parochial churches, was superintendent of studies, and as vicar of the order had as much to do as eleven priors; he lectured on the Psalms and St. Paul, besides the demand made on his economic resourcefulness in managing a monastery of twenty-two priests, twelve young men, in all forty-one inmates.[332]

When Martin Luther posted his *Ninety-five Theses* on the door of Wittenberg Castle Church on October 31, 1517 he sparked a religious revolution that changed the world.

---

[331] Fr. Richard Brennan, *History of the Catholic Church*, p. 239.
[332] DeWette, *Dr. Martin Luther's Briefe, I,* Berlin, 1825, p. 41.

Today "there are over 26,000 separate Christian denominations in the world."[333] Although many churches call themselves "Christian," Cardinal Henry Manning, himself a convert from Protestantism, wrote: "If Christianity is historical, Catholicism is Christianity."[334]

Soon Luther changed his focus from prevalent abuses in the Church to the Church's very doctrines. Bent on its destruction, he rejected the entire concept of indulgences and ultimately denied the papacy, the Holy Sacrifice of the Mass, and most of the sacraments. He constructed a new religion based on his own erroneous beliefs and the private interpretation of Scripture. Since Protestant theology contradicts many biblical teachings (e.g., Purgatory, the permanence of marriage, etc.) the "reformers" had to remove books from the Bible: Baruch, Ecclesiasticus, Judith, First and Second Machabees, Tobias, Wisdom and parts of Daniel and Esther. Equating faith with salvation, he further claimed that good works were not necessary for salvation and therefore there was no need for the Ten Commandments.

In his Commentary on Galatians, Luther stated:

'The law of the Ten Commandments did bind me. But against that law I have another law, even the law of grace; which notwithstanding is to me no law, neither doth it bind me, but setteth me at liberty. And this is a law against that accusing and condemning law; which law it so bindeth, that it hath no power to bind me any more.'[335]

Creation of the Lutheran Church

Pope Leo X, who thought the Lutheran movement was just a dispute between the Augustinians and Dominicans, condemned 41 theses from Luther's works on June 15, 1520 in the papal bull *Exsurge Domine*. Showing his contempt for the document, Luther burned the papal bull, together with works on canon law and theology books before a crowd of students, professors, monks and townsfolk near the east gate of Wittenberg on December 10, 1520 "where the town muck was deposited and criminals were put to death."[336] The revolution had begun.

---

[333] *Wanderer,* April 11, 2002, p. 3.
[334] Rod Bennett, *Four Witnesses,* p. 303.
[335] John Dillenberger, *Martin Luther, Selections from his Writings,* p. 125.
[336] Msgr. Philip Hughes, *A Popular History of the Reformation,* p. 125.

Martin Luther resided in the ancient Wartburg castle near Eisenach under the protection of Frederick the Elector from May 4, 1521-February 29, 1552. "If we may believe the story that he told in his anecdotage, he was disturbed, in the castle, by strange noises that he could explain only as the activity of demons. He professed to have seen Satan on several occasions..."[337] "Luther acknowledges himself that the devil once appeared to him in a visible shape and told him to abolish the sacrifice of the Mass and to deny the Real Presence of Our Lord in the Blessed Sacrament."[338]

In his work entitled *The Chief Points of Difference,* Fr. F. Laun relates:

It would be only fair to consider first the reason given by Luther for abolishing the Mass. He tells us that one night the devil appeared to him, and in fearful tones, curdling his very blood, declared that he, the learned Dr. Luther, had practiced idolatry every day for fifteen years by saying Mass. Although Luther was quite aware that the devil was not speaking the truth, he abolished the Mass and priestly ordination.[339]

The revolution proceeded. On September 22, 1521, Melancthon [an apostate priest and friend of Luther] administered communion in both kinds. ...On October 23 the Mass ceased to be said in Luther's monastery. On November 12 thirteen monks walked out of the cloister and headed for marriage; soon a similar exodus would empty half the monasteries of Germany. On December 3 some students and townsfolk, armed with knives, entered the parish church of Wittenberg, drove the priests from the altar, and stoned some of the worshippers who were praying before a statue of the Virgin. On December 4 forty students demolished the altars of the Franciscan monastery in Wittenberg.[340]

In conclusion, the soul for the Lutheran secession was not a question of indulgences, the Mass, the sacraments, the Papacy, priestly celibacy, or the predestination and justification of the sinner: it was an intolerance that the human race carries about fixed fast in its heart and which Luther had the

---

[337] Will Durant, *The Reformation,* p. 363.
[338] Fr. Michael Müller, C.SS.R., *The Holy Eucharist,* p. 25.
[339] p. 170. (Wittenb., Germ. Ed., VII, 443; Jena, VI, 87; Walch, XIX, 1489).
[340] Durant, 364.

daring to manifest openly: the intolerance of authority. Because the Church is the collective historical body of the God-Man [the Mystical Body of Christ], it draws its organic unity from a divine principle. ...The man who breaks that link loses the forming principle of the Christian religion.[341]

The Reformation Takes Hold in Germany

Martin Luther manipulated the German nationalistic spirit as a means of conveying his ideas to the populace. His general rejection of ecclesiastical authority and his radical doctrines inflamed the German peasants thereby inspiring the revolt of 1524-1525. Peasants, who had legitimate grievances, used force to achieve their ends. Needing the support of the nobility to further his teaching, Luther turned on the peasants. Historians relate that 100,000 serfs were slaughtered during the Peasants' Revolt of 1524-1525.[342] As a result, many rejected religious beliefs altogether and "relapsed into a state of mind which was not far removed from materialistic atheism."[343]

In his book, *The Reformation,* Will Durant relates: "The famished knights had waited impatiently for a chance to rise against princes, prelates, and financiers. In 1522 [Emperor] Charles V was far away in Spain; [Franz von] Sickingen's [Swabian] troops were fretfully idle; rich Church lands lay open to easy seizure."[344]

Fr. Hugh Smyth comments on the corruption spawned by Luther in his book, *The Reformation:*

> In opposition to the Catholic salvation by good works, the [Protestant] revolution had emphasized justification by faith alone. Some of the extreme Lutherans asserted that good works were prejudicial to salvation. In doing this they emptied faith of its essence and left little else than a mere acceptance of the dogmas of their church. Jacob Andreae, canon and chancellor of Tübingen, said that 'as the doctrine of justification by faith alone was preached, the ancient virtues vanished and a crowd of new vices appeared in the world.' Bucer, who helped establish Protestantism in

---

[341] Romano Amerio, *Iota Unum,* p. 25.
[342] See Lord Acton, *Cambridge Modern History: The Reformation,* pp. 185-195.
[343] Acton, 192.
[344] p. 380.

Strasburg, said that 'corruption makes further strides every day in the Evangelical Church.' Melancthon averred 'not all the waters of the Elbe would be sufficient for me to weep over the evils of the Reformation.' And finally Luther himself said 'that there is not one of our evangelicals that is not seven times worse than before he belonged to us.'

"The candid Melancthon 'avowed that in the triumph of the Reformation the princes looked not to the purity of doctrine, or the propagation of light, to the triumph of a creed, or the improvement of morals, but only regarded the profane and miserable interests of this world.' "[345]

Morals continued to decline as the Catholic Faith was abolished. Melancthon said: "The morals of the people, all that they do and all that they neglect to do, are becoming every day worse. Gluttony, debauchery, licentiousness, wantonness are gaining the upper hand more and more among the people, and in one word, everyone does as he pleases."[346]

Luther and his companions, Melancthon and Bucer, went so far as to allow Philip of Hesse to have two wives simultaneously! Luther's letter to Melancthon infers that faith alone will save an individual no matter what sins are committed:

> Sin and sin boldly; but let your faith be greater than your sin. It is enough for us, through the riches of the glory of God, to have known the Lamb of God who takes away the sin of the world. Sin will not destroy in us the reign of the Lamb, although we were to commit fornication or murder a thousand times in one day.[347]

In his book entitled *History of the German People at the Close of the Middle Ages,* Johannes Janssen adds:

> Monks and priests were flocking to the new altar of matrimony. At Nuremberg the Lorenzkirche and the Sebalduskirche resounded with 'God's

---

[345] Sie becümmerten sich gar nicht um die lehre, es sie ihnen blosz um die freiheit, und die herrschaft zu thun. Apud. Audin, p. 343.
[346] A. Guggenberger, S.J., *A General History of the Christian Era, Vol. II*, p. 220.
[347] "Sufficit quod agnovimus per divitias gloriae Dei Agnus qui tollit peccatum mundi: ab hoc non avellet nos peccatum etiamsi millies uno die fornicemur aut occidamus."— Epist. Melanc. 1 Aug. 1521. Apud Audin, p. 178.

Word'—the Reformers' phrase for a faith based solely on the Bible. 'Evangelical' preachers moved freely through northern Germany, capturing old pulpits and setting up new ones; and they denounced not only popes and bishops as 'servants of Lucifer,' but secular lords as 'iniquitous oppressors.'

"However, secular lords were themselves converts: Philip of Hesse, Casimir of Brandenburg, Ulrich of Württemberg, Ernest of Lüneberg, John of Saxony. Even the emperor's sister Isabella was a Lutheran."[348] The protection afforded Luther by Frederick the Wise (Elector of Saxony) and by German nationalists allowed him to continue his work devoid of fear from Emperor Charles V, his loyal vassals and ecclesiastical authorities.

Luther's ideas spread like wildfire across Europe by means of pamphlets, sermons and revised church hymns. "The printing press developed in Europe about 1450 also contributed to Luther's success. ...By 1523 about a million copies of Luther's pamphlets were in circulation."[349]

Ministers for the new religion came from the ranks of priests and monks, many of whom were poorly educated and unfit for their vocations. This is shown by the fact that so many set aside their vow of celibacy in order to marry.

> [Forty-year-old Professor Andreas] Carlstadt, who had a large following at the university [of Wittenberg] and was influential in the church of All Saints as archdeacon, made repeated acts upon clerical celibacy, the Mass and ceremonies. In his enthusiasm he tended to emphasize the significance of continuing revelation, thereby minimizing the importance of theological learning. On Christmas Day, 1521, he celebrated Communion in All Saints Church in both kinds without priestly vestments. In reading the service he omitted the passages referring to the sacrifice and did not elevate the host; he extended the bread and the cup to the communicants, though previously only priests had handled them. Moreover, having gone so far as to state that the clergy should be compelled to marry, he set an example by taking a wife [a 15-year-old girl] on January 19, 1522.[350]

---

[348] Will Durant, *The Reformation,* p. 380.
[349] Beverly Armento, *Across the Centuries,* p. 345.
[350] Harold Grimm, *The Reformation 1500-1650,* pp. 121-122.

Philip Melancthon used music as an effective means of spreading the new religion. Many Catholic hymns were retained by the "reformers" in order to leave the appearance that nothing had really changed. Others were altered in order to conform to the new gospel. Melodies encapsulating the new beliefs were an effective means of spreading the new theology among the populace.

Many idealistic humanists sincerely believed Luther would reform the Church and help remove the abuses that were prevalent at the time. However, when he began to attack the Mass, the sacraments and the authority of the Church, they parted company with him.

"Luther laid down the principle that the Bible was the only rule of faith, that anyone could read the sacred volume and the Holy Spirit enlightened each as to its meanings."[351] Christian humanists upheld the importance of Holy Scripture. They also realized that private interpretation of the Bible would ultimately lead to anarchy, and so it has. Since each individual can interpret Scripture differently there is not even complete unity of belief among Protestant congregations.

> Wherever it made its appearance its progress was marked by deeds of violence. Like a tornado, it swept every thing before it; and you might as easily trace its course by the ruins it left behind. Churches broken open and desecrated; altars stripped of their ornaments or pulled down; paintings and statues destroyed; the monasteries entered by mobs and pillaged of their effects; Catholic priests, monks, and nuns openly insulted and maltreated; the property of the churches and monasteries seized on by violence, after having been often pillaged and plundered: these were some of the ruins which the Reformation caused; these the sad trophies which it erected to celebrate its triumphs over the Catholic religion![352]

Luther, Melancthon, Bucer and Carlstadt themselves disagreed on doctrinal matters and modes of worship. Subsequently, Protestant churches reflect this diversity. Established religions such as Lutherans, Episcopalians and Baptists have fragmented into various groups holding conflicting beliefs.

---

[351] Rev. James Meagher, *History of the Protestant Churches,* p. 98.
[352] Archbishop M. Spalding, *History of the Protestant Reformation,* pp. 330-331.

The splintering and lack of unity persists even in the present as new independent churches arise and older ones continue to change.

A New "Mass"

The "reformers" deemed it necessary to fabricate a new "Mass" in order to embody their new beliefs. The Holy Sacrifice of the Mass was transformed into "the Lord's Supper"; altars were dismantled and tables were placed in a position facing the people. The "traditional liturgy could scarcely be recognized in Luther's 'German Mass.' The Offertory is no more, the Canon is reduced practically speaking to the Consecration, it has lost its Trinitarian structure."[353]

> The divine service, as arranged for Saxony,[354] had the name and exterior ceremonies of the Mass. Luther, however, omitted the Canon and everything in the collects that had reference to sacrifice. Yet, in order to mislead the people, he ordered this to be done in such a way that the common people should not observe it. With the same end in view, the Elevation was retained. Private Masses were entirely abolished. The remainder of the divine services consisted in singing, reading the Scriptures, and preaching.[355]

These changes are very similar to those that have taken place since Vatican II: the sacrificial character of the Mass and the Offertory have been eliminated. Various Eucharistic prayers have replaced the Canon of the Mass and nearly every reference to the Blessed Trinity has been eliminated.

Luther had an abiding hatred for the Holy Sacrifice of the Mass and the Papacy. These tendencies, which would remain with him until his dying breath, were conveyed by his own words, "When the Mass has been overthrown, I think we shall have overthrown the Papacy. I think it is in the Mass, as on a rock, that the papacy wholly rests... everything will of necessity collapse when their sacrilegious and abominable Mass collapses."[356]

---

[353] Georges Tavard, *Protestantism*, p. 3
[354] German princes assisted Martin Luther in the formation of the new liturgies.
[355] Dr. Heinrich Brueck, *History of the Catholic Church*, p. 164.
[356] Rama Coomaraswamy, M.D., *Problems with the New Mass*, p. 14.

The Establishment of Various Protestant Churches

"In the sixteenth century Protestantism did away with the authority of the Church, and constituted every man his own judge of the Bible; and what was the consequence? Religion upon religion, church upon church, sprang into existence, and new churches have never stopped springing up to this day."[357] Heretics such as the Waldenses, Albigensians, Wyclifites, Hussites, Calvinists and Zwinglians have found it necessary to attack the concept of a visible structured church in order to give credibility to their own.

> Luther's excommunication did not prevent the spread of his religion. His success emboldened Calvin, Cranmer, Knox, Zwingli, and others to imitate his example. Within a remarkably short time the Scandinavian countries, England, Holland, Scotland, and large sections of Switzerland and Germany became Protestant. For a time it seemed as if France, Poland and Hungary would also be lost to the Faith.[358]

Creation of the Church of England

England had been an integral part of the Church since 596 AD, when Saint Augustine and his forty monks arrived in the southeast coast, under instructions from Pope Gregory the Great. About the same time, some monks from Ireland began preaching in the northwest. Christianity gradually spread over the island. Its practice continued uninterruptedly until the days of Henry VIII.[359]

In *Pictorial History of the World,* published in 1855, John Frost describes conditions in Renaissance England as Henry VIII acceded to the monarchy:

> No prince ever ascended the throne of England with more advantages than Henry VIII. ...His power was respected by the great rivals of the continent, and his condition was no less happy as to the internal state of his kingdom. His title was not disputed; his treasury was full; his subjects in profound peace, and the vigor and comeliness of his person, his polished manners, and his manly dexterity, rendered his accession popular, while his proficiency in literature, and his reputation for talents made his character respectable. Everything seemed to prognosticate a happy and prosperous

---

[357] Fr. Edward McGolrick, *The Unchangeable Church, Vol. I,* p. 306.
[358] Stephen McKenna, C.SS.R., *A Brief History of the Church,* p. 22.
[359] Fr. C. Donovan, *Our Faith and the Facts,* p. 254.

reign, yet the death of no prince was ever less lamented than that of Henry. He ruled the people with a rod of iron, and drenched the scaffold with the best blood in the kingdom. Though a monster in private life, Henry affected a great zeal for religion, and by his tyrannical measures he succeeded in changing not only the national faith, but in a great measure the spirit of the laws of England.[360]

When Pope Clement VII (1523-1534) refused to annul the king's marriage to Catherine of Aragon, Henry declared himself the head of the Church of England. Thomas Cranmer (1489-1556) and Thomas Cromwell (c. 1485-1540)[361] thereafter helped form the Anglican Church.

As Protestantism spread, excuses for defection from the papacy and breaking from the Church became even more varied. Local lords divested the Church of its holdings in the name of the Crown, and for a small price, claimed former monasteries as ready-made estates and villas. "Even before the monasteries were closed, the great monastic shrines were destroyed and the jewels and treasure confiscated by the government."[362]

Since ornate candlesticks, chalices, ciboria and monstrances were not used in the new liturgies, they were melted down. "Henry's [VIII] armies were equipped with new cannons cast from melted-down church bells and the soldiers' muskets loaded with lead shot from the dismantled abbey roofs. By 1540 it was all over and England's great monastic tradition was finished."[363] "...The total spoils in goods and income accruing to Henry during his life may have been some 1,423,500 pounds."[364]

"All in all, 578 monasteries were closed, some 138 convents; 5,621 monks or friars were dispersed, [as well as] 1,560 nuns. Among these some fifty

---

[360] pp. 764-765.
[361] "Cromwell had obtained enormous wealth from his several offices, as well as from the plunder of the Church and the poor. He got about thirty of the estates belonging to the monasteries; his house, or rather palace, was gorged with the fruits of his sacking." William Cobbett, *History of the Protestant Reformation in England and Ireland*, p. 145.
[362] Tony McAleavy, *Life in a Medieval Abbey*, p. 59.
[363] Derry Brabbs, *Abbeys and Monasteries*, p. 16.
[364] Francis Cardinal Gasquet, *Henry VIII & English Monasteries*, Vol. II, pp. 386-387, 438.

monks and two nuns willingly abandoned the religious habit; but many more pleaded to be allowed to continue somewhat their conventual life."[365]

Changes in Worship and Belief

Cranmer, who was consecrated archbishop of Canterbury on March 30, 1533, was the driving force of the reformation in England by means of the new Bible, new catechism,[366] *Book of Common Prayer* (the new missal) and the *Administration of the Sacraments* (new rites for the sacraments).

Cromwell successively filled the offices of master of the rolls and secretary to the King.[367] Thomas Cromwell was responsible for the deaths "of thousands upon thousands whom he had quartered, hanged, burned or plundered."[368] He was arrested on a charge of treason on June 10, 1540 and executed 48 days later without the benefit of a trial. Cobbett believes that Henry may have been responsible for the charge since he became beneficiary of his ill-gotten goods.[369]

Interestingly, the work of transforming England into a Protestant nation was a joint effort. "Calvin was in close correspondence with Cranmer, Edward VI and the Duke of Somerset, and exerted a powerful influence throughout England."[370] John Knox also assisted in propagating the new gospel of the "reformers."

> Cranmer ...favored first Lutheranism then Zwinglianism, and lastly Calvinism, so that it may seem doubtful what form of Protestantism, if any, he really held. ...To him are chiefly due the legalization of the marriage of the clergy, the desecration and destruction of altars, for which tables were substituted, and of images and pictures, which gave place to the royal arms.[371]

---

[365] Gasquet, Vol. I, p. 363; II, p. 33, 323.
[366] "The catechism was mainly a translation of the Lutheran Catechism designed for Nuremberg, which Justus Jonas had translated into Latin. Cranmer's English version which contained numerous additions of his own, was printed in August, 1548." William Cobbett, *History of the Protestant Reformation in England and Ireland,* p. 155.
[367] "He had been made Earl of Essex; he had precedence over every one but the king; and he, in fact, represented the king in the Parliament, where he introduced and defended all his confiscating and murdering laws." Cobbett, 155.
[368] William Cobbett, *History of the Protestant Reformation in England and Ireland,* p. 147.
[369] "A very large sum of money and a great mass of monastic treasures were found in his possession. Probably the total value was hardly less than a quarter of a million of our money." (*v.* Gasquet *Henry VIII and the English Monasteries,* i., p. 431).
[370] Albert Newman, *Manual of Church History, Vol. II,* p. 263.
[371] Charles Herbermann, *Catholic Encyclopedia, Vol. V,* p. 447.

"Between 1535 and 1538 Cranmer as primate under Henry, declared indulgences useless and invalid, threw out of the calendar all the feasts of obligation except Sunday, and advised Henry to seize the property of all the monasteries."[372] He deposed bishops faithful to Rome (replacing them with others having Calvinist leanings) and invited fellow heretics from Europe, including Martin Bucer, to teach in the English universities and to assist in the formation of the Anglican Church. Like their Lutheran counterparts, many Anglican clergy married including Cranmer.

He denied the Real Presence of Jesus Christ in the Holy Eucharist and rewrote the Mass to conform to the new theology, denying its sacrificial character. "Already in Henry's reign, Cranmer had done his best to whittle away in the minds of his flock the traditional belief that Confirmation, Penance, Extreme Unction, Holy Orders and Matrimony were sacraments."[373] The "reformers" made gradual changes to the sacraments. Baptismal ceremonies omitted the exorcisms and the use of Holy Oils. Auricular confession was discouraged.[374] Common bread was often substituted for the hosts used in the Mass.

Many of the changes employed by the English "reformers" directly parallel the liturgical reforms of Vatican II, since the appearance of the Church remained while its essence was changed. "Reformers" in England, as well as those of Vatican II, introduced changes gradually, almost imperceptibly, in order to avoid resistance from faithful Catholics. In time, altars were destroyed and replaced with tables facing the people, crucifixes and statues were removed from the churches and the words *Mass* and *sacrifice* were no longer used. Prayers for the dead were no longer said and the Real Presence of Christ in the Holy Eucharist was denied.

The liturgical changes which began during the reign of Henry VIII continued to evolve. Sir William Cecil (1520-1598), a minister in the government of Queen Elizabeth I, was instrumental in destroying the Mass, perverting Catholic doctrine and training a new generation of believers for whom Catholic practices,

---

[372] William Gispin, *Life of Thomas Cranmer*, p. 65.
[373] Msgr. Philip Hughes, *The Reformation in England*, p. 84.
[374] Confession "told privately in the ear." John Barton, *Penance & Absolution*, p. 65.

belief and worship became a thing of the past. Cecil was clever in achieving his ends by means of slow, calculated change. The new changes in worship and belief slowly took root in the parish churches and were promoted by local clergy.

In order to enforce compliance with the new changes, Elizabeth fined all those who did not attend services on Sundays and Holy Days. "And thus by force or fraud it came to pass that the largest portion of the Catholics yielded by degrees to their enemies, and did not refuse from time to time publicly to enter the schismatical churches to hear sermons therein, and to receive communion in those conventicles."[375] As a result these former Catholics became members of the newly formed Anglican Church.

St. Thomas More / St. John Fisher

Those who opposed the "changes" were dealt with in a swift and stern manner. Priests and religious who resisted the changes, including Carthusian monks and Franciscan friars, were exiled or executed. Many faithful Catholics were fined, tortured and imprisoned, even quartered and beheaded. Cardinal (St.) John Fisher (1469-1535) and Sir (St.) Thomas More (1478-1535) were both sent to the Tower of London on April 17, 1534 for refusing to take the oath of Supremacy, which recognized the King as Head of the Church in England.

St. Thomas More witnessed firsthand the apostasy of England's clergy. "Through a window he watched the London clergy passing through the garden to take the oath; most were cheerful enough, slapping each other on the back and calling for beer at the Archbishop's buttery [dairy]."[376] His own daughter coaxed him to go along with the crowd. "More said to Margaret, if he were to swear the oath out of fellowship with his old companions, what should he say when he stands in judgment at the bar before the divine Judge?"[377]

The New English Mass

A new "Mass" was formulated to replace the old. The subtle rationale given by the reformers was that they merely wished to translate the Latin Mass into

---

[375] Rev. Dr. Nicholas Sander, *The Rise and Growth of the Anglican Schism,* pp. 266-267.
[376] Anthony Kenny, *Thomas More,* p. 72.
[377] Kenny, 78.

English so that the people could better understand it. Their insidious motives are shown by Msgr. Philip Hughes in his work *The Reformation in England:*

> In the *Order of Communion*, which appeared on March 8, 1548, the English tongue was, for the first time, used in the administration of this sacrament. The *Order* [the new Anglican Missal] is not, however, by any means a mere translation of the communion rite of the Latin Mass. It is a new thing and wholly different; and its author, Cranmer, modeled it closely on a rite lately devised by the Archbishop of Cologne, who had recently gone over to Lutheranism. It is, with certain modifications, the rite which has passed into the present Book of Common Prayer.

Sadly, the majority of the clergy joined the newly formed schismatic church. There were numerous reasons for the break with Rome: the clergymen who were educated at the universities had already imbibed the errors of Wycliff and the Lollards; many ecclesiastics were poorly educated or lacked a solid spiritual life, while others were preoccupied with secular employment. These men soon became an integral part of the Anglican Church and easily accepted the new beliefs, liturgy and sacraments.

> Two changes in religious belief sanctioned by the rite of this *Order of Communion* call for notice. In the exhortation, which the new rite contains, addressed to those about to receive the sacrament, it is implied that sorrow for sin and the prayer for absolution that is said before Holy Communion is administered suffice for forgiveness, without any necessity to confess the sins; those who communicate without ever going to confession are not to be regarded as less good Christians by those who prefer the old way—that is expressly said. Next, in the manner of speech about the presence of our Lord in the sacrament there are ambiguities designed to make the rite one which could be conscientiously used by those who did not believe that He was there present except to the communicant in the moment of receiving Holy Communion, and who believed that the presence, even at that moment, was not in what was received but only 'in the heart' of the receiver.[378]

---

[378] Msgr. Philip Hughes, *The Reformation in England,* pp. 101-102.

Msgr. Philip Hughes further relates additional changes in the Mass and the stringent fines that accompanied non-conformity:

> In 'The Supper of the Lord and the Holy Communion commonly called the Mass,' there are also changes full of meaning. ...the new rite was by no means, in the intention of those who devised it, meant to be just the Latin Mass in translation, the most cursory comparison of the two rites will reveal.[379] The *Order of Communion*, imposed in 1548, is now incorporated in a new service whose prayers are reminiscent of various sources, partly Catholic, but mainly Lutheran. From what has been kept of the Canon of the Latin Mass, all the numerous references indicating and implying that the action being done is a sacrifice, and that what the priest is offering as a sacrifice is the Body and Blood of Christ here really present—all this has been carefully cut out. The new Communion rite is already compatible with a denial of the Real Presence.
>
> The main effect, once more, was not to substitute English for Latin, but to produce a new rite, in which no words or ceremonies of the old were retained that gave any support to the Catholic doctrine that the role of the priest in the Holy Eucharist is to offer to God a real sacrifice—a sacrifice, that is to say, not merely of the good will and service of the priest and congregation, nor, again, of praise and thanksgiving, but a sacrifice of the Body and Blood of Jesus Christ actually present on the altar under the appearances of bread and wine. As the old Eucharistic rite had been replaced by a new rite, with changes meant to exclude the possibility of a Catholic interpretation of what was being done, so now, with the same motive of the same exclusion in their minds, Cranmer and those who thought like him in these matters drew up the new rite for ordination.
>
> Clergy who refused to use the Book of 1549, criticized it, or used any other (even in private chapels), were to lose a year's income and be imprisoned for six months; on a second conviction, to lose their benefices and go to prison for a year; on a third, to be imprisoned for life. For laymen who criticized or caused other rites to be celebrated, or hindered the new, there were also fines and imprisonment: [a fine of] 10 [pounds] or three months on a first conviction; [a fine of] 20 [pounds] or six months on a second; loss of all goods and life imprisonment on a third.

---

[379] For a detailed comparison, cf. E.C.M., I, 382-398.

In 1552, Parliament approved a revised Prayer Book with substantially new ceremonies for the ordination of priests and bishops. "No longer was a chalice and paten 'with the bread' to be handed to the man being ordained priest as tokens of the priestly powers and function, along with the Bible, but the Bible alone; and the new bishop was no longer given the pastoral staff."[380]

Words necessary for validity were purposely omitted or essentially changed. This alteration rendered the orders invalid due to defective *form* and *intention* as declared by Pope Leo XIII on September 13, 1896 in his encyclical *Apostolicae Curae*. Another parallel with the present—the "changes" that have been made in the rites for the ordination of priests and bishops since Vatican II mirror many of the "changes" that took place in England centuries earlier. These alterations leave grave doubt as to the validity of the new rites.

> The principal actors in this great work of English sacrilege—Cromwell, Somerset, Cranmer, and Northumberland—all perished by violent deaths; while Henry VIII and Elizabeth both died miserably, and Edward [VI] was cut off in the first bloom of boyhood. All of Henry's children were childless, and with them ceased forever the royal line of him who had sacrificed the faith of England to procure a male heir to his throne![381]

Yet, in spite of the upheaval, the Catholic Faith was not dead. In 1569 seminaries were established at Douai, Rheims and Rome and by 1585, 300 priests secretly entered England in order to preserve the Catholic Faith. As a result, many of these valiant Englishmen suffered martyrdom.

Zwingli's Iconoclasm in Switzerland

The heretical priest Ulrich Zwingli (1484-1531) of Zurich, Switzerland, with the blessing of the Archbishop of Constance, preached against indulgences. Zwingli then devised a new faith that revived iconoclasm.

> The Government of Canton seized the Church property and decreed the power of priests to marry. It was in 1522 that Zwingli had laid down the principle that the Bible under private interpretation, was the *sole* authority for doctrine. He denied all mystery in the Eucharist. By 1525 the Mass had been stamped out in Zurich,

---

[380] Msgr. Philip Hughes, *The Reformation in England,* p. 125.
[381] Bishop M. Spalding, *History of the Protestant Reformation,* p. 205.

and its departure had been preceded by violent iconoclasm committed by these mountaineers upon all the inheritance of beauty which their ancestors had left them for a guide. ...This was the first of the barbaric destructions. A host of others were to follow, through more than a century, ruining the art of Scotland, horribly maiming that of France and the Rhine and the Netherlands: murdering our ancestral wealth in living stone.[382]

Despite the opposition of the bishop of Constance and the Swiss diet [theological meeting], the canton of Zurich carried out religious reforms in a vigorous fashion.

During the year 1524, pictures, statues, crucifixes, candles, and other ornaments were removed from the churches and destroyed, decorated walls were whitewashed, the bones of the local saints were buried, altars were replaced by tables, organs were dismantled, and the singing by choirs was abolished. The congregational singing of hymns was not introduced until late in that century. Little remained but bare, cold edifices that would hardly distract the attention of the worshipers from the hearing of the simple, unadorned Word of God. Pilgrimages and processions naturally ceased, and the church year was reduced to four festivals: Christmas, Good Friday, Easter and Pentecost. Monasteries were dissolved and their properties were taken over by the state to be used for the care of the unfortunates and the education of the young.

During Holy Week in April, 1525, communion was celebrated according to the Zwinglian usage for the first time. ...Zwingli took his place at the head of a simple table that was covered with a white linen cloth and on which were placed Communion cups and plates of wood. After praying and reading in German the words of institution and pertinent Scripture passages, Zwingli and his assistants partook of the bread and wine and then distributed these sacred symbols among the people, going from pew to pew. Those parts of the liturgy that were retained in the Mass, that is, the Introit, the Gloria in Excelsis, the Creed, and a number of responses were read in the Swiss vernacular by the people, the men alternating with the women. The same year, Zwingli provided his followers with a simplified baptismal service in the vernacular, from which he had deleted the formula of exorcism and other parts...[383]

---

[382] Hilaire Belloc, *How the Reformation Happened,* pp. 76-77.
[383] Harold Grimm, *The Reformation 1500-1650,* p. 153.

The widescale destruction of altars, statues and crucifixes that took place after Vatican II parallels Zwingli's iconoclasm which had occurred centuries earlier.

John Calvin

John Calvin (1509-1564) was a stern French lawyer whose faith was strongly influenced by a Lutheran professor. He settled in Geneva, Switzerland where he founded a state-church and became a religious dictator.

> [Calvin denied free will and taught absolute predestination:] 'from all eternity God by an unchangeable decree of His omnipotent will saves or damns human souls and there is nothing that men can do about it. Men, therefore, do not 'receive' God's grace, but the elect may 'perceive' that they are predestined. The ultimate authority for all this is nothing else than the infallible interpretation of Scripture by Calvin, for 'God has designed,' as he said, 'to make known to me what is good and what is evil.'[384]

> He fled [from France] to Switzerland and eventually settled in Geneva where he established a theocratic state among its 20,000 inhabitants. Severe punishments were given for violations of the new legislation. The allowable color and the quantity of clothing, and the number of dishes permissible at a meal, were specified by law. Jewelry and lace were frowned upon. A woman was jailed for arranging her hair to an immoral height.[385]

> A first violation of these ordinances was punished with a reprimand, further violations with fines, persistent violations with imprisonment or banishment. Fornication was to be punished with exile or drowning; adultery, blasphemy, or idolatry, with death. In one extraordinary instance a child was beheaded for striking its parents.[386]

The Formation of the Presbyterian Church

Calvin's ideas were imbibed by John Knox (1510-1572) who formed the Presbyterian Church in Scotland in the mid-16th century. He was one of the first "reformers" to eliminate the practice of kneeling at the reception of Holy Communion and he called such action idolatry.

---

[384] The Knights of Columbus, *"The Reformation"—Was it Reform or Revolt?*, pp. 27-28.
[385] Villari, *Savonarola*, p. 491.
[386] Schaff, p. 491.

"Permeated with the spirit of the Old Testament and with the gloomy austerity of the ancient prophets, he displays neither in his voluminous writings nor in the record of his public acts the slightest recognition of the Gospel, or of the gentle, mild and forgiving character of the Christian dispensation."[387]

In August 1560, the Scottish Parliament rejected the authority of the pope and abolished the Mass. New laws were established that made attending or offering Mass three times a capital offense punishable by death.

Protestantism

Protestantism is essentially a movement of protest against the authority, worship and doctrines of the Catholic Church. Protestant churches often share several common characteristics: disdain for the Mass and sacraments, the papacy and hierarchy, and a stronger emphasis on faith than on good works. In Protestant churches the Holy Sacrifice of the Mass has been replaced with the Lord's Supper. In some cases, ceremonies bearing a resemblance to the Mass or sacraments were retained as mere "signs of faith" rather than means of grace. Statues, crucifixes, altars, communion rails, sacred vessels and other external manifestations of Catholicism were destroyed or sold. Wooden tables replaced altars, tabernacles were removed from the churches and external devotions to the Blessed Virgin were discouraged and ultimately discarded.

These changes took place slowly and were almost imperceptible by the laity. As a result many Protestants believed they were still Catholic because their churches retained some vestiges of Catholicism.

The founders of the new religions that stemmed from the Protestant Reformation claimed to teach the authentic gospel message, yet they disagreed on essential points of doctrine. Their churches were not established by Christ, but by mere men and women. With no central authority, ceremonies and beliefs differed from minister to minister, from church to church and from city to city. This splintering continues today.

---

[387] Charles Herbermann, *Catholic Encyclopedia, Vol. VIII*, p. 684.

The Threat from the East

Another factor that contributed toward the spread of Protestantism in the 16th century was the threat from the Muslims in Istanbul. "In the long reign of Suleiman the Magnificent (1520-1566) Ottoman armies reached as far as Algeria, Hungary,[388] the Persian Gulf (1535) and Aden [South Yemen] (1547)."[389] Vienna, Austria was attacked in 1529 and the Hapsburgs had to rally their forces to the defense of Europe. They had little time to put down rebellions by the German nobles who sided with Luther or the Swiss followers of Zwingli.

Alliances were formed between the Ottoman Turks and France against the Hapsburgs (Holy Roman Empire) and between the Persians and Austrians against the Turks. Europe, Asia and Africa were divided between Catholics, Protestants, Orthodox and Muslims.

> Mohacs made the Hapsburgs *realize* what they ought long to have known—that Suleiman had better material and a better military machine in recruitment, *morale* and methods than anything they could oppose to him. The Turk of that day was the superior of Europe—yes, even the Europe of the Renaissance—in men and guns and missiles, siegework and attack. He had larger, better and more numerous artillery. He invented the shell. He may almost be said to have invented the thought-out scheme of siege by trench-work, which dominated all our history for more than three hundred years.[390]

The Catholic Reformation

In the wake of the turmoil unleashed by Luther, the Catholic Church embarked on a true reformation of Her own. "The will to reform was unmistakably present. More than a few, bishops and priests alike, were keenly aware that all was far from well with their brother clerics. ...Where could be found tens of thousands of well-educated men of strong personal holiness eager for service in remote poorly paid parishes?"[391]

Pope Hadrian VI (1522-1523) pledged to: " 'Expend every effort to reform first this Curia, whence perhaps all this evil has come... We consider ourselves all the

---

[388] Following the Battle of Mohacs in 1526.
[389] Colin McEvedy, *Penguin Atlas of Modern History*, p. 32.
[390] Hilaire Belloc, *How the Reformation Happened*, p. 87.
[391] Martin Jones, *The Counter Reformation*, p. 33.

more bound to attend to this the more we perceive the entire world longing for such a reformation.' It was a point of view shared by many... The pope said: 'God permits this persecution to afflict His Church because of the sins of men, especially of the priests and prelates of the Church.' "[392]

In his book, *Church History*, Fr. John Laux describes the nature of the Catholic Reformation:

> Long before the Protestant revolt, all serious-minded Catholic men and women were convinced that the Church needed to be thoroughly reformed. Not the Catholic religion, as the Protestants maintained, but the people who professed that religion required reformation. 'Men must be changed by religion,' as one of the champions of true reform remarked,[393] 'not religion by men.' Reformation of the Church in Her Head and in Her members, this was the first part of the Catholic program of reform. The spread of error by the religious innovators [Protestants], who attacked the Divine Constitution of the Church and many of Her fundamental doctrines, imposed upon the Catholic leaders the duty of setting forth in unmistakable and authoritative terms the true doctrines of Christianity contained in Scripture and Tradition. There is no better proof for the divine origin and guidance of the Church than the fact that She not only survived the great apostasy of the 16th century, but emerged from the conflict rejuvenated and prepared to meet new ones.[394]

The movement known as the Catholic Reformation or Counter Reformation began about 1495 with the work of Cardinal Francisco Ximenes of Toledo, Spain and ended in 1563 with the conclusion of the Council of Trent. This reform movement enacted concrete measures to correct abuses and to restore good morals. It likewise clarified Catholic doctrines and promoted virtuous living for clergy and laity alike.

In the summer of 1536, Pope Paul III established a commission comprised of several ecclesiastics, among them Cardinals Contarini, Caraffa and Pole, to draft

---

[392] This statement of Adrian VI's in 1522 is part of his instruction to the papal nuncio Chieregati at the Diet of Nuremberg and is in CR, chap. 9.
[393] Egad of Viterbo, Fifth Lateran Council.
[394] p. 458.

a report concerning the need for reform in the Church. The lengthy document[395] lamented the widespread evils in the Church, especially in Italy:

> The first abuse in this respect is the ordination of clerics and especially of priests in which no care is taken, no diligence employed, so that indiscriminately the most unskilled, men of the vilest stock and of evil morals, [even] adolescents, are admitted to Holy Orders and to the priesthood, to the [indelible] mark, we stress, which above all denotes Christ. From this have come innumerable scandals and a contempt for the ecclesiastical order, and reverence for divine worship not only has been diminished but has almost by now been destroyed.[396]

> Another abuse of the greatest consequence is the bestowing of ecclesiastical benefices, especially parishes and bishoprics, in the manner of which the practice has become entrenched that provision is made for persons on whom the benefices are bestowed, but not for the flock and the Church of Christ. Therefore, in bestowing parish benefices and above all bishoprics, care must be taken that they be given to good and learned men so that they themselves can perform those duties to which they are bound, and, in addition, that they be conferred on those who will in all likelihood reside.[397]

> In this regard, most blessed Father, the abuse that first and before all others must be reformed is that bishops above all and then parish priests must not be absent from their churches and parishes except for some grave reason, but must reside, especially bishops, as we have said, because they are the bridegrooms of the Church entrusted to their care. For, by the Eternal God, what sight can be more lamentable to the Christian man traveling through the Christian world than this desertion of the churches? Nearly all the shepherds have departed from their flocks; nearly all have been entrusted to hirelings.[398]

Unfortunately, so entrenched were these errant practices that no real reforms were enacted until the Council of Trent, nearly a decade later. The history of the period testifies to the worldliness and immorality of many priests and bishops.

---

[395] *Consilium de emendanda ecclesia* of May, 1537.
[396] John Olin, *Catholic Reform*, p. 68.
[397] Regarding this important question see Hadrian VI's concluding remarks in his Instruction to Chieregati, in CR, chap. 9.
[398] "The calamity of our age," says Contarini, with reference to such widespread absenteeism and neglect, in his *De officio episcopi;* see CR, chap. 7.

However, the members of the mendicant orders (Augustinians, Dominicans and Franciscans) revived a sense of devotion and piety in their flocks that was sorely needed at the time.

> As a consequence, they, and not the parish clergy, had become the trusted leaders of the people. Their chapels were thronged by the common folk, and the better-disposed nobles and burghers took them for confessors and spiritual directors. ...The people, high and low felt that Bishops who rode to the Diet accompanied by their concubines disguised in men's clothing, and parish priests who were tavern-keepers or the most frequent customers at the village public-house, were not true spiritual guides.[399]

As a result of the Catholic Reformation the doctrines of the Church were more clearly set forth, discipline was restored and various abuses were corrected. Seminaries were established to properly train candidates for the priesthood in piety and Catholic theology. Meanwhile, new religious institutes arose to meet contemporary problems and replace the priests, monks and nuns who had apostasized. Older religious orders were also reformed.

New Religious Institutions

Because of the desperate need of revitalizing the Church in this troubled age, new religious institutes were established including the Theatines (1524), Capuchins (1525), the Society of Jesus (the Jesuits) (1534) and the Ursulines (1535).

Theatines produced numbers of saintly priests and bishops who would lead and govern the Church. Capuchins, numbering nearly 700 members by 1536, led virtuous lives and spread the faith among the infirm and indigent. Jesuits taught at schools and universities throughout Europe and sent missionaries like the zealous St. Francis Xavier to the ends of the earth to gain souls for Christ.[400] By 1556, there were more than 1,000 Jesuits. Ursulines instructed girls and young ladies in cities at a time when most nuns were cloistered.

---

[399] Lord Acton, *Cambridge Modern History, Vol. II, The Reformation*, p. 106.
[400] "From a rough calculation it would appear that, from 1540-1773, 21,000 Jesuits were employed in foreign missionary work. During this period 500 Jesuits are recorded to have won the martyr's crown." *Catholic Missions,* July 1886.

Though it was an age of sinners, it was also an age of saints. St. Bernardine of Siena, St. John of Capistrano and St. Antonius revived the faith in Europe; Thomas à Kempis composed his famous work, *The Imitation of Christ*—a book which has made such an impact that its popularity has lasted for over five centuries.

The long-awaited revival of scholastic philosophy, devotional practices and theological learning finally took place and came to be known as Christian Humanism. It preserved the philosophy, literature and art of the classical period yet did not fall into the paganism that created it. St. Thomas More represented this Christian humanism as did other saints of the period.

The Need for a New Council

The doctrines of the Catholic Church remained unchanged since the time of Christ, yet through the course of time, various abuses had crept in causing confusion, scandal and conflict. During the Renaissance, the Church had great financial difficulties that led corrupt popes to the practice of selling benefices and indulgences. Several of the worldly popes emptied the Church coffers in order to foster their own lives of comfort and self-satisfaction. Others lived scandalous lives and sought only to advance their family ambitions.

With the rampant abuses in the Curia by which ecclesiastical offices were purchased, many unworthy and worldly cardinals and bishops ruled the Church. The clergy were often poorly educated and many lacked the high morals and virtuous life necessary for so elevated a vocation. As a result, the laity received little instruction. It was this laxity of the laity and the avarice, immorality and worldliness of popes, bishops and priests which necessitated a new council to clearly define the Church's stance on morality and enforce it among its members.

> Even the doctrinal decrees of Trent, such as the very important one on justification, reflect this emphasis on the moral life of the Christian. Such a focus presupposes concern for the reform of the institutional Church as well, for if men are to be changed by religion, then religion itself must be correctly represented and faithfully imparted. ...And it explains why the Church's pastoral mission—the work of teaching, guiding, and sanctifying its members—must be given primacy and rendered effective. Thus it follows that

good men must be selected as bishops and must reside in their dioceses, the young instructed, that venality [greed] and other abuses must be rooted out in the service of Christ and the salvation of souls. The Bark of Peter was not to be scuttled or rebuilt but to be steered back to its original course with the crew at their posts and responsive to their tasks. The state of the clergy loomed large in Catholic reform. If their ignorance, corruption, or neglect had been responsible for the troubles that befell the Church, as nearly everyone affirmed, then their reform required urgent attention and was the foundation and root of all renewal. This involved personal reform, that of the priests and prelates who are the instruments of the Church's mission and the ones principally charged with the *cura animarum* [the care of souls]. The reform of the faithful would follow as the consequence, but the immediate objective was institutional or pastoral. The Church itself had to be revitalized and restored so that its true apostolate might be realized.[401]

Why Trent?

Why was a city located deep in the Alps (and known for its inhospitable seasons) chosen for this council? "Trent had been selected on account of its proximity to Germany, where the religious difficulties had sprung up, where reformation was most needed, where the Lutherans were to be found whom the council might reconcile to the Catholic Church. Also, the town lay within the dominations of the emperor whose support was sought above all others."[402]

Trent was close to the imperial palace in Innsbruck, Austria and was situated in a region relatively free from the threat of war. It was also an ancient Catholic city that had possessed a resident bishop since the fourth century.

Who Attended the Council?

Due to turbulent world conditions, its remote location and the length of its proceedings, few prelates attended the early sessions of the council. Religious wars raged throughout Europe and travel was both difficult and dangerous. Most of the prelates attending the council came from Italy, Spain and France. Attendance slowly increased as the years passed.

---

[401] John Olin, *Catholic Reform from Cardinal Ximenes to the Council of Trent 1495-1563*, pp. 35-36.
[402] Pierre Janelle, *The Catholic Reformation*, p. 80.

King Henry VIII's cousin, Cardinal Pole, alone represented England since a violent persecution raged there. During this persecution, the king had the cardinal's mother, the Countess of Salisbury, killed. She was "the last in a direct line of the noble race of Plantegenets, and the nearest living relative of Henry himself."[403]

On July 15, 1563, it [the number of attendees] rose to 235 including six cardinals, seven generals of orders, and six procurators of bishops. We have a full list of Fathers on that day, the diocese, abbey, or order of each being mentioned; yet it is no easy task to determine the national groups into which the assembly had naturally fallen, and to weigh the influence of the pope and the various European sovereigns. Many of the bishops resided in the Curia, and can hardly be considered as belonging to the countries to which their episcopal sees were situated. The difficulty of long journeys account for the fact that the assembly was mostly made up of those Fathers who were near at hand: Italian names are in a majority. This, however, is not, as one might think, equivalent to papal preponderance; for, as far as reckoning is possible, out of 135 Italians, 46 only depended upon the pope directly, as having their sees in the States of the Church. Among the rest, 40 belonged to the kingdom of Naples, 10 to the duchy of Milan, 15 to the territory of Venice; they were subjects of three sovereigns—the king of Spain, the emperor, the Venetian republic—who had not been noted lately for oversubmissiveness toward the Holy See. In fact, the emperor and Spain together could more or less command 95 votes (the Spanish alone numbering 75 Fathers, if Naples is counted in), while the king of France had sent 20 bishops, many of them strong Gallicans. The Germans—whether they were lukewarm toward the council, or kept at home by the religious troubles—were practically absent; but there were a good few representatives from the Venetian colonies Crete, Cyprus, Dalmatia, and the Greek Archipelago; together with a sprinkling from Portugal, Hungary, Croatia, Poland, Scotland, Ireland, Switzerland. Altogether, it would be a huge mistake to think that the pope had the assembly at his beck and call. It was frequently restive and submitted to the authority of the Holy See only because the latter had taken the lead in regard to reformation, and gained considerable moral prestige.[404]

---

[403] Bishop M. Spalding, *History of the Protestant Reformation, Vol. II,* p. 96.
[404] Pierre Janelle, *The Catholic Reformation,* p. 82.

The Council of Trent

The Council of Trent was the longest General Council of the Church for several reasons: it was interrupted four times, suspended for nearly 10 years and was not completed until it was freed from political interference.

> If the Fathers of the Council had been left alone to look after the interests of the Church, without political obtrusion, their work might have been soon accomplished. The sovereigns, however, and one in particular, claimed the right to interfere in the business of the Assembly, and long made real progress impossible. Charles V was mainly responsible for these complications; extremely distrustful of the Papacy, anxious to avoid breaking with the German Protestants and thus prevent trouble in his dominions. He thought that the council should be a friendly meeting-ground between Catholics and heretics, whereas the pope and the Church as a whole considered it rather as the occasion for a show-down which had become necessary even at the cost of circumstances.[405]

Though many attempts were made to draw Protestants back into the fold, these efforts remained fruitless. Luther and many of the Protestant leaders feared that a general council would condemn their new theology.

The Council of Trent discussed in great detail all the issues disputed by the Protestants—justification, original sin, the papacy, the Holy Sacrifice of the Mass, Baptism, Confession, Communion under both species, the priesthood, Purgatory, the honor shown to the saints and the veneration of images.

> 'No council in the history of the Church,' says Cardinal Hergenröther, 'has determined so many questions, established so many points of doctrine or made so many laws.' It was an immense achievement: after so much delay and opposition the Church managed to formulate with extraordinary vigor and absolute precision answers to the heretical thesis as well as to the criticism directed against Herself. Before long the Missal and Catechism, approved by the council and compiled by some of its members, would disseminate this teaching among the great mass of the faithful. Before long the seminaries advocated by the council would provide the Church with an altogether new type of clergy ready for the labor of reconquest. And before long the Papacy—which, in spite of all its faults, must be credited, in

---

[405] H. Daniel-Rops, *The Catholic Reformation*, p. 81.

the persons of Paul III and Pius IV respectively, with having initiated the council and brought it to a successful conclusion—would devote itself under Pius V to the task of injecting the reform into the blood and marrow of the Church.[406]

A Brief History of the Council of Trent

Due to religious wars, the Council of Trent was divided into three periods; however, the tremendous amount of dogmatic exposition, legislation and work of reform also made such interruptions necessary. All the while, the Council Fathers additionally had dioceses to oversee, souls to tend and administrative work to accomplish.

The Council of Trent spanned the reign of five popes: Paul III, Julius III, Marcellus II, Paul IV and Pius IV. Pope Paul III began the council with his legates presiding over the First Period. Pope Julius III's legates presided over the Second Period. Marcellus II had nothing to do with the council since his reign lasted only 21 days. Paul IV was staunchly opposed to the council because he believed the conversion of the Protestants could be effected in other ways. Nevertheless, Pope Pius IV reconvened the council after a ten-year hiatus and concluded it.

Sadly, this council never brought back to the Catholic Church the multitude of Protestants who had defected. It did, however, prevent the advance of Protestantism into Italy. "The Protestant 'share' of the European continent fell from 40 to 20 per cent between 1570 and 1650."[407] It also restored Church discipline, codified Catholic teaching and put an end to many of the abuses that plagued the Church, especially among the clergy.

First Period

Reigning Pope	**Sessions Held**
Pope Paul III	Dec. 13, 1545—Winter 1547

The first session of the council held in the Cathedral of St. Vigilius in Trent was attended by four cardinals, four archbishops, 21 bishops, five generals of religious orders, four priests and a number of theologians including four Servites, five Augustinians, five Carmelites, six Dominicans and 18 Franciscans.

---

[406] H. Daniel-Rops, *The Catholic Reformation*, p. 93-94.
[407] Geoffrey Barraclough, *The Times Atlas of World History*, p. 183.

Two of the papal legates present during this period of the council were later elected to the papacy: Cardinal Gian del Monte (later Pope Julius III) and Cardinal Marcello Cervini (later Pope Marcellus II). The third papal legate was Cardinal Reginald Pole of England.

During the first period the Council Fathers defended the Deposit of Faith by relying on the consistent teaching of the Catholic Church. They thoroughly explained and defined the sacraments and numbered them as seven. No previous General Council of the Church had ever needed to explain and define them to such a degree. The Council Fathers also refuted the Protestant attacks against the sacraments.

> During its first period (sessions I-VIII) the council established a precedent of doctrinal conservatism from which its collective action was never to deviate. It found the pope mainly interested in the definition of dogma, the emperor in disciplinary reforms, and hence it decided to treat both matters concurrently. It defied Lutheran teaching quite deliberately when it agreed that Scripture and tradition should have equal validity as sources of truth. It announced the sole right of the Church to interpret the Bible and upheld the primacy of the Vulgate text over all other Latin versions. It did not, however, exclude emendations of the Vulgate and it took no decisions concerning vernacular translations of the Scriptures. It asserted that while all Seven Sacraments were instituted by Christ and were necessary in general for salvation, not all were necessary to every man. The sacraments actually contained the grace they signified and they conferred it *ex opere operato,* irrespective of the qualities or the merits of the persons administering or receiving them. Sacramental doctrines, especially those touching Baptism and Confirmation, were defined in greater detail than hitherto. Yet by far the most important decree of the first period is the one promulgated in January 1547 concerning justification. By far the longest of all the Tridentine decrees, this consists of 16 chapters and 33 canons. Here the fathers condemn a number of beliefs, some of them either tendentiously summarized or in fact held exclusively by the extremists or the eccentrics of the Protestant Reformation.
>
> Among these condemned beliefs the following are characteristic: that man is passive under the influence of grace and lacks freedom of will; that good works executed before justification are sins; that nothing save faith is needed for justification; that man is justified solely by the imputation of the righteousness

of Christ; that the forgiveness of sins depends on a man's belief that he has been forgiven; that the justified man is bound to believe himself numbered among the elect; that the Gospel commands us only to believe; that the Ten Commandments have nothing to do with being a Christian; that Christ came only as a Redeemer and not as a Lawgiver; that a man once justified cannot sin or fall from grace; that lack of faith is the only mortal sin.[408]

On January 7, 1547, the Council Fathers approved the *Decree on Justification*. The Dominican Bishop Bertano of Fano had stated that the Lutheran formula of "faith alone" was deficient because it excluded hope and charity, making faith the sole basis of justification. St. Augustine's words verify the importance of good works: "He who made thee without thee will not save thee without thee."[409]

Fathers of the Council clarified the essential link between Apostolic Tradition and Sacred Scripture that had been previously rejected by the "reformers." The Council Fathers also discussed the papacy.

Catholic Reformers at the Council of Trent came to realize that the Church was not solely responsible for all the evils of the time. Secular rulers contributed in their own way toward laxity, worldliness and lack of piety in their subjects. The Council Fathers therefore found it necessary to give guidelines to secular rulers in order to help implement the Catholic Reformation movement throughout Christendom.

The untimely death of Martin Luther in 1546 was a major setback to the Protestant Revolt. Further German Protestant expansion was prevented by the peace of Augsburg of 1555 that gave equal rights to Catholics and Lutherans alike.

Move to Bologna

Because of an epidemic of typhus (spotted fever) which struck Trent on March 6, 1547, the council was transferred to the Church of San Petronio in Bologna. The council would remain there from April 21, 1547 until the pope suspended it in the early months of 1548. No decrees were issued and Emperor Charles V stubbornly commanded the bishops who resided in his territories to remain in Trent.

---

[408] A. Dickens, *The Counter Reformation*, p. 114.
[409] Hubert Jedin, *History of the Council of Trent Volume II*, p. 185.

While residing in Bologna the Council Fathers feared an invasion by Protestant princes. This threat, however, was removed when Charles V defeated the Schmalkaldian League (a Protestant alliance formed in 1531) at Mühlberg on April 24, 1547 and captured their leader, Johann Friedrich. The council continued its sessions until October 1549 although only 45 prelates were present. Finally, on May 1, 1551, the council resumed at Trent.

Second Period

Reigning Pope   **Sessions Held**

Pope Julius III   May 1, 1551—April 28, 1552

One cardinal, two prince-electors, five archbishops, 26 bishops and 25 theologians attended the sessions of the second period. These sessions dealt mainly with the Holy Sacrifice of the Mass and the Sacraments of Penance, Extreme Unction, Holy Orders and the Holy Eucharist. The Council Fathers refuted the erroneous concepts of the heretics of the Reformation and expounded on Catholic teaching by referring to Apostolic Tradition, Sacred Scripture, the writings of the Fathers and Doctors of the Church, the writings of the popes and the consensus of the Church. "By including all dogmas within an almost complete system the Council of Trent established the Catholic faith as an indivisible whole, against which heretical error would be powerless."[410]

> The Lutherans kept their promise and some of their delegates actually came to Trent during the autumn and winter of 1551. Remembering John Hus, they demanded that their safe-conduct be ironclad. They refused to deal with the papal legate, and would take no active part in the council unless it declared its superiority over the pope, after the manner of Constance. Diplomatic care was used, but no progress was made towards an understanding. It was at least 30 years too late for that.[411]

War raged as Lutheran armies under Maurice of Saxony advanced against Emperor Charles V. German bishops hastily returned to their sees and the

---

[410] H. Daniel-Rops, *The Catholic Reformation*, p. 100.
[411] Msgr. J. Conway, *Times of Decision: Story of the Councils*, p. 276.

council was suspended. The emperor entered the monastery of Geronimo de Juste in Spain, where he died. He was succeeded by his brother Ferdinand II.

Third Period

Reigning Pope	**Sessions Held**
Pope Pius IV	Jan. 18, 1562—Dec. 4, 1563

The leading figures during this period of the council were St. Charles Borromeo, Cardinal Morone, Cardinal Hosius, Cardinal Gonzaga and Cardinal Seripando. Pope Pius IV's nephew, St. Charles Borromeo, was made cardinal-archbishop of Milan and was appointed Secretary of State. He assisted the pope with planning the daily schema for the council. "During its first two periods the council had been concerned with the Lutherans, and the French had mostly stayed away—especially from the second period. Now it turned its attention to Calvinism in France and the Germans stayed away."[412]

The Holy Sacrifice of the Mass

The Council Fathers defined "that the Sacrifice of the Mass is the same sacrifice as that of the Cross, having the same High-Priest and the same Victim, and that the Mass may be offered up for the living and for the dead."[413] "Trent, of course, decreed that in the Mass the perfect sacrifice of the Cross which Christ offered once for all is *represented* and that the Mass is identical with the Cross, 'inasmuch as in this divine sacrifice which is celebrated in the Mass the same Christ who once offered Himself in a bloody manner is contained and immolated in an unbloody manner...' "[414] The various ceremonies of Holy Mass hold great meaning and significance, as the council decrees declare.

> And since the nature of man is such that he cannot without external means be raised easily to meditation on divine things, Holy Mother Church has instituted certain rites, namely, that some things in the Mass be pronounced in a low tone and others in a louder tone. She has likewise, in accordance with apostolic discipline and tradition, made use of ceremonies,[415] such as mystical blessings,

---

[412] Msgr. J. Conway, *Times of Decision: Story of the Councils*, p. 276.
[413] Fr. Clement Raab, O.F.M., *Twenty Ecumenical Councils of the Catholic Church*, p. 193.
[414] Sess. XXIII, ch. 1 and 2.
[415] Cf. *infra*, can. 7.

lights, incense, vestments, and a great many other things of this kind, whereby both the majesty of so great a sacrifice might be emphasized and the minds of the faithful excited by those visible signs of religion and piety to the contemplation of those most sublime things which are hidden in this sacrifice.[416]

The Establishment of Seminaries

A decree of the Council of Trent in 1563 commissioned bishops to establish seminaries in order to prepare young men for the holy priesthood. The Council Fathers realized that the establishment of seminaries would ensure the proper spiritual and intellectual training of future priests since ecclesiastics previously received their training from parish priests or at cathedral schools or colleges.

St. Charles Borromeo (1538-1584) established three seminaries in the city of Milan and three others within his diocese. St. Vincent de Paul (c. 1580-1660) created minor seminaries for young candidates and major seminaries where candidates completed their study of philosophy and theology.

In the seminary students were taught Philosophy, Dogmatic and Moral Theology, Canon Law, Scripture Study and Liturgy. Seminaries also helped assure the proper formation of future priests and provided them with a strong background in Catholic doctrine.

Tempers Rage

Due to the intense and drawn out nature of the council, one would expect tempers to flare. Personality conflicts, nationalistic tendencies and differences in theological views added to the tension. In March, 1563 wide-scale riots broke out between Spaniards and Italians in the streets of Trent. Realizing the gravity of the threat to the Faith caused by the rapid spread of Protestantism, both factions finally united under the papal banner and peace was restored.

> When a Greek bishop accused a Neapolitan of ignorance and perversity, the latter retorted by tearing out his antagonist's beard in handfuls. More typically, unpopular speeches were sometimes drowned by coughing and shouting. Yet alongside the vagaries of a quarrelsome, cocksure and uninhibited generation, there still runs through the Council of Trent an element which cannot be attributed to the mere exchanges of ambitious and opinionated men. A good

---

[416] Fr. H. Schroeder, O.P., *Canons and Decrees of the Council of Trent*, p. 147.

deal of this eloquence meant what it said; it betokened a genuine fervor, a capacity for self-criticism then rare in ecclesiastical assemblies, a passionate desire to reform and save the Holy Catholic Church.[417]

Gallican tendencies claiming that the council was superior to the pope and that his primacy was merely one of honor, not jurisdiction, remained very strong among the Spanish and French bishops. Pope Paul IV's animosity for the Spanish caused bitter feelings between these bishops and the Holy See. His successor, Pius IV, tactfully worked to achieve peace with Emperor Ferdinand I.

Rome itself was finally at peace and the reforms begun by the council were gradually implemented. Even visitors noted the welcome change.

> Fortune-seekers no longer flocked there; the cardinals led a more austere life; various societies were founded for the relief of the poor and for the education and protection of young girls; regulations were issued against excessive luxury, the pope himself, in August, 1564, dismissing over four hundred superfluous courtiers. The reform of religious orders was undertaken anew, and what was most important of all, seminaries were founded, largely under the guidance of the Jesuits.[418]

Popes of the period implemented the reforms of Trent:

- Simony was systematically abolished
- Episcopal visitations took place on a regular basis without remuneration
- The Roman Curia was refashioned and reformed

The decree on reformation successfully removed the worst abuses which had brought the Church and clergy into contempt. The authority of the bishops over the clergy, both secular [diocesan] and regular [belonging to religious orders], was considerably strengthened; and means were provided for the evil livers and the incompetent. The parochial clergy were compelled to preach; and the whole discipline of the Church was improved.[419]

---

[417] A. Dickens, *The Counter Reformation*, p. 112.
[418] Pierre Janelle, *The Catholic Reformation*, p. 102.
[419] Fr. Hugh Smyth, *The Reformation*, p. 152.

This is confirmed by James Robinson in *Medieval and Modern Times:*

> Although the Council of Trent would make no compromises with the Protestants it took measures to do away with certain abuses of which both Protestants and devout Catholics complained. All clergymen were to attend strictly to their duties, and no one was to be appointed who merely wanted the income from his office. The bishops were ordered to preach regularly and to see that only good men were ordained priests. A great improvement actually took place—better men were placed in office and many practices which had formerly irritated the people were permanently abolished.

Last Days of the Council

The Fathers of the Council of Trent on Saturday, December 4, 1563, had been in public session for two consecutive days, something that had happened never before in the annals of the great assembly. And now, in this, its twenty-fifth session, the ninth of its third convocation, after all the crises, all the deadlocks that more than once had threatened a collapse in failure; after having been twice suspended and reconvened, the council brought its gigantic labors to an end.[420]

Once the council ended, rivalry among the bishops ceased. A sense of relief and elation filled the Council Fathers as they eagerly returned to their homes.

> 'I cannot describe,' wrote an eyewitness, Paleotti, 'the spiritual joy of all, their gratitude to God, their act of thanksgiving when the council sat for the last time. I myself saw many of the most solemn prelates weep for joy, and those who had the very day before treated one another almost as strangers embrace with deep emotion. An astonishing outburst of cheers for the pope marked this final gathering.' The date was 4th December 1563. The decrees were solemnly signed by four legates, three patriarchs, twenty-five archbishops, one hundred and sixty-nine bishops, seven abbots, seven Generals of Orders, ten episcopal procurators and the ambassadors of all the Catholic powers. Confined to his palace, old and sick, suffering from asthma and rheumatism, but receiving daily reports on the progress of the council, Pius IV might well be proud to have been the instrument of this imposing and decisive work. Yet when his two intimate friends, Charles Borromeo

---

[420] Msgr. William McDonald, *The General Council,* p. 91.

and Philip Neri [both future saints] congratulated him upon his success, he replied simply: 'All was done by God's inspiration.'[421]

The Profession of Faith of the Council of Trent

"No account of the influence of Trent would be complete if it did not mention the influence of the Tridentine teaching on Catholic life itself. As Monsignor Michel has noted, the sessions on original sin, justification, and the sacraments constitute in themselves an admirable code of holiness."[422]

In stark contrast to the earlier unproductive councils, the reforms and clear teachings of Trent remain an integral part of the Catholic Faith. The inspiration of the Holy Ghost is clearly evident in the theological exactness, precision and intrinsic beauty of the canons and decrees of the council and the *Catechism of the Council of Trent.*

> The canons and decrees remain one of the greatest monuments of committee-thinking in the whole history of religion. Given their general purpose and outlook, their technical perfection and consistency are worthy of the highest admiration. In form and language they are models of clarity and care; they are serviceable documents well abreast of the modern idiom of their day; whatever their debts to scholastic theology, their language is uncluttered by the scholastic habits which had so little relevance to the needs of simple priests and literate laymen. To study them can be a fruitful, almost a moving experience, and this even for readers who normally inhabit very different worlds of thought.[423]

The Profession of Faith of the Council of Trent clearly defines many of the essential doctrines of the Church:

> ...The Apostolic ecclesiastical traditions and all other observances and constitutions of that same Church I most firmly admit and embrace. I likewise accept Holy Scripture according to that sense which our Holy Mother Church has held and does hold, whose [office] it is to judge of the true meaning and interpretation of the Sacred Scriptures; I shall never accept nor interpret it otherwise than in accordance with the unanimous consent of the Fathers.

---

[421] H. Daniel-Rops, *The Catholic Reformation,* pp. 93-94.
[422] Hefele-Leclercq, *Histoires des Conciles,* T.X. p. 1. p. xi.
[423] A. Dickens, *The Counter Reformation,* p. 133.

I also profess that there are truly and properly Seven Sacraments of the New Law instituted by Jesus Christ our Lord, and necessary for the salvation of mankind, although not all are necessary for each individual; these sacraments are Baptism, Confirmation, the Eucharist, Penance, Extreme Unction, Order [Holy Orders], and Matrimony; and [I profess] that they confer grace, and that of these Baptism, Confirmation, and Order cannot be repeated without sacrilege. I also receive and admit the accepted rites of the Catholic Church in the solemn administration of all the aforesaid sacraments. I embrace and accept each and everything that has been defined and declared by the Holy Synod of Trent concerning original sin and justification.

I also profess that in the Mass there is offered to God a true, proper sacrifice of propitiation for the living and the dead, and that in the Most Holy Sacrament of the Eucharist there is truly, really, and substantially present the Body and Blood together with the Soul and Divinity of Our Lord Jesus Christ, and that there takes place a conversion of the whole substance of bread into the Body, and of the whole substance of the wine into the Blood; and this conversion the Catholic Church calls transubstantiation. I also acknowledge that under one species alone the whole and entire Christ and the true sacrament are taken.

I steadfastly hold that a Purgatory exists, and that the souls there detained are aided by the prayers of the faithful; likewise that the saints reigning together with Christ should be venerated and invoked, and that they offer prayers to God for us, and that their relics should be venerated. I firmly assert that the images of Christ and of the Mother of God ever Virgin, and also of the other saints should be kept and retained, and that due honor and veneration should be paid to them; I also affirm that the power of indulgences has been left in the Church by Christ, and that the use of them is very salutary for Christian people. I recognize the holy Catholic and Apostolic Roman Church as the mother and teacher of all churches; and to the Roman Pontiff, successor of blessed Peter, chief of the Apostles, and vicar of Jesus Christ, I promise and swear true obedience.[424]

Pope St. Pius V

Pope St. Pius V, elected three years after the conclusion of the council, not only enforced the reforms of the council throughout the Church, but also applied

---

[424] Henry Denzinger, *Sources of Catholic Dogma,* pp. 302-303. Taken from the papal bull *Injunctum nobis* of Pope Pius IV of November 13, 1565.

them to his own life. The white cassock worn by popes developed from the white habit of the Dominican Order worn by Pope St. Pius V.

He prayed the Rosary, spent long hours meditating on the Passion, walked barefoot in processions of the Blessed Sacrament and also instituted the Forty Hours' Devotion in reparation for the sins of the time. What a contrast to the immorality and worldliness of the popes of the previous century!

As a means of further educating the clergy, this zealous pope ordered the publication of *The Catechism of the Council of Trent* (also called the *Roman Catechism*) along with the *Summa Theologicae* of St. Thomas Aquinas. *The Catechism of the Council of Trent* contained an outline for Sunday sermon topics that could be easily used by parish priests for instructing their flocks.

During this same period of time, St. Peter Canisius (1521-1597) wrote a catechism for the laity, often called the *Little Catechism*, which had a wide circulation and helped to reinforce the faith of the people.

Even though all Catholic priests at the time offered the same Mass, great diversity existed in minor details peculiar to various locations. Realizing that the Church would benefit greatly from a Breviary and Missal that could be shared by priests throughout the world, Pope St. Pius V completed the work of codifying the breviary on July 9, 1568 and Roman Missal *(Missale Romanum)* on July 14, 1570.

The *Missale Romanum* is the Latin altar missal that has been used by priests throughout the Latin Rite for over 400 years and is still used by priests offering the authentic Latin Mass. The Mass that is offered using this missal is called the "Tridentine Latin Mass," named after the Council of Trent. It is important to note that Pope St. Pius V did not create a new missal, but merely standardized the Curial Missal of the 13th century. Further, the early Latin Mass can be found in the writings of St. Justin (150 AD).

Even though Latin ceased to be a vernacular language between the 7th and 9th centuries, the Mass continued to be offered in Latin because much of the liturgy had already been established in that language. The Latin language has vividly come to portray the universality of the Church and has preserved the liturgy from doctrinal deviations through the centuries.

In 1570, the pontiff wrote the papal bull *Quo Primum,* which explicitly stated that no one, regardless of their rank or title, not even a pope, could substantially alter or rewrite the Mass. Since Christ personally instituted the Holy Mass it would follow that no one has the authority to essentially change it. The practice of popes adding feasts of new saints to the liturgical calendar does not fall under this prohibition since this does not in any way alter the Mass.

Quo Primum attempted to preserve for all time the sacred ceremonies and infallible doctrines contained in the liturgy. Pope St. Pius V further prohibited any tampering with the Mass, warning that anyone who would dare to substantially change the Mass would incur the wrath of Almighty God and the Apostles Peter and Paul.

The Council of Trent Towers Over All the Other Councils

This is true, first, because this council sums up broad areas of past teaching and brings to bear on its issues the teaching of past councils, as well as an extensive amount of Biblical patristic resource and joins to them an extraordinarily rich development of scholastic theology. Out of these doctrinal resources it produces a synthesis and explanation of Catholic teaching on a scale hitherto unknown.

Second, its main dogmatic concern is with what is the very heart of the Christian life, that is, grace and the sacraments, whereby the individual, through God's gifts is translated from the kingdom of darkness into the light and kingdom of the Son of God. Third, …is the fact that at the council, through its actual activity and direction is resolved an issue that has wracked and torn the teaching work of the Church for more than two centuries. This issue is the relation of the General Council to the pope.[425]

One of the most amazing features of the Council of Trent is the great span of time it took to complete its work. It began in 1545 and ended 18 years later in 1563. Few Council Fathers who attended the earlier sessions lived to see its conclusion. This council was able to successfully conclude its work in spite of the fact that it outlived four popes.

---

[425] Msgr. William McDonald, *The General Council,* pp. 6-7.

The Council of Trent transcends all previous General Councils of the Church by its clear, concise exposition of Catholic doctrine, its reforming disciplinary canons and decrees and by the doctrinally sound catechism that resulted from it. By the grace of God, the Council of Trent accomplished that which the six previous councils in 330 years had failed to achieve: a wholesale reform of the Church.

St. Charles Borromeo personified the Counter-Reformation and the work of the Council of Trent, as described by Thomas Cahill:

> He saw to it that his priests were morally upright, conscientious in their duties to their parishioners and well informed in theological matters. He built three seminaries for their education ...[and] created the Confraternity of Christian Doctrine, the driving force behind the reform of catechetical teaching—the weekly instruction of the faithful, especially children, in doctrine and morals—which had fallen so low. He insisted that vowed religious live in accordance with their vow of poverty—which meant in some cases the liquidation of prodigious possessions. One very rich and recalcitrant order, the Humiliati, became so opposed to the bishop that they decided to do away with him during Vespers, a plot that succeeded only in knocking Charles down, as the bullet that was meant to end his life bounced off his clothing and fell to the floor. The Humiliati were doubly humiliated.

> But if bullets did not harm him, the Milanese famine of the early 1570's and the plague of 1575 shortened Charles's life, as did his personal penances. The people of Milan, who were (and are) a worldly lot admired him especially for his faithfulness to them. As the nobles, the politicians (including the governor), and not a few clergymen escaped the city, Charles remained, inspiring many ordinary people to come down from the Alps to assist the sick and dying. As all commerce fled before the plague and severe malnutrition set in, the bishop managed to find food to feed some sixty to seventy thousand persons daily, exhausting all his resources and incurring great debts in the process. He nursed the sick, ministered personally to the dying, and wept openly—for others... When he died on a November night in 1584, at the end of a life full of incident, he was only forty-six years old.[426]

---

[426] *John XXIII*, pp. 99-100.

CHAPTER TWENTY

Vatican Council

1869–1870 AD

This council was held during the pontificate of Pope Pius IX.

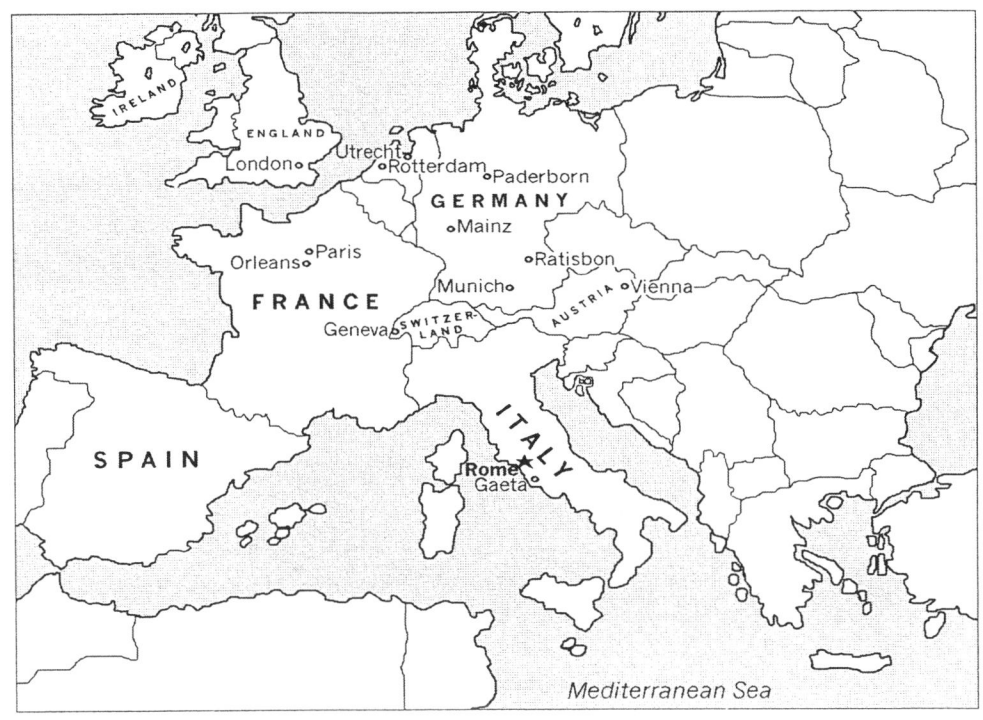

Background

Although the 19th century is primarily noted for the Industrial Revolution, it was also an era of social revolution, cultural upheaval and religious persecution. The revolutionary ideologies of Anti-Clericalism, Liberalism, Nationalism, Naturalism, Rationalism, and Social Atheism permeated European society. Nevertheless, the Oxford Movement, begun in 1833 by Dr. Keble, resulted in numerous conversions to the Catholic faith in England.

It was also an era of war and destruction. On May 26, 1865, the American Civil War came to an end; in 1866, Austria was at war with Italy and Prussia; in 1868, a revolution raged in Spain which caused Queen Isabella II to flee to France. In 1870, as if an omen of things to come, Nikolai Lenin was born.

Pope Pius IX

In the shortest papal conclave in 300 years, Giovanni Mastai-Ferretti was elected pope on June 17, 1846 and chose the name Pius IX. Liberals and Nationalists were elated at the election of the kind-hearted, 54-year-old pontiff because they envisioned that this politically liberal-minded pope would champion their causes. They also expected him to support or at least condone their plans for a united Italy. However, because of his firm resistance to political and religious ideologies that threatened the Church, Pope Pius IX had much to suffer during his 32-year reign, the longest in papal history.

> When Pius IX had been elected, in the year 1846, he had quickly become the most popular pope in modern history. This was because he had instituted a whole series of democratic reforms in his [Papal] States, and even granted a Constitution to his people. But these changes had gone to the heads of the populace—the radicals, extremists, Jacobins [revolutionaries] of Rome and Bologna—and they had tried to seize power for themselves, and the pope had been compelled to flee.[427]

> He set up a representative government for the Papal States, which was welcomed with enthusiastic acclamation by the people.[428] But the revolutionary element would not have it; the pope's Prime Minister, Count de Rossi was stabbed to death while entering the Chamber; the revolution broke out; the Roman republic was proclaimed; the pope was imprisoned in the Quirinal and had to escape from Rome in disguise, aided by the French Ambassador (1848). He found an asylum at Gaeta, in Neopolitan territory, where he stayed for a year, till restored to Rome by a French army, dispatched, be it said, through the efforts of the Catholic liberals, Falloux and Montalembert.[429]

> Returning from exile, the pope ceased his political changes.

> Moreover, after all that he had suffered at Rome, he denounced liberals, ...everywhere else, and especially in Italy, where he noticed that they were closing the monasteries and convents, seizing Church property and also, in their new enthusiasm for a politically united Italy, were occupying his own States, the

---

[427] E. Hales, *The First Vatican Council*, p. 12.
[428] Ozanam was in Rome and describes the great ovation given to the pope (*P. Ozanam,* Baunard, p. 245).
[429] Dom Cuthbert Butler, *Vatican Council: The Story Told from Inside, Vol. I,* p. 68.

States of the Church and demanding their allegiance to the King of Savoy, Victor Emmanuel or to Garibaldi. The sympathies of Protestant Europe as well as of America were emphatically and even violently on the side of Garibaldi, [and] the revolutionaries.[430] In 1849 a French army restored papal authority in Rome, and in 1850 back came Pius IX, thoroughly cured of liberalism.[431]

On December 6, 1854, Pope Pius IX conferred with the cardinals, expressing his desire to convoke a general council. The majority favored the idea, but six believed it was inopportune and only two cardinals strongly opposed the idea. Plans were therefore drawn up and arrangements made to prepare for this historic event, but once the proposed schema (agenda) for the council surfaced in the newspapers, many leading politicians and ecclesiastics voiced their strong opposition and sought to prevent the formation of the council.

Liberalism

Martin Luther and heretics of the 16th century had rejected the teaching authority of the Catholic Church and proclaimed the supremacy of the individual conscience in matters of religion. This ideology had a profound influence upon Western Europe. " 'The Mind of Europe,' writes Peter Wust, 'was *secularized,* the world stripped of its sacred meaning, the Church ruled out of public affairs, God dethroned in the soul of man.' "[432]

There are four basic principles inherent in Liberalism:

- The absolute sovereignty of the individual and his entire independence of God and God's authority.
- The absolute sovereignty of society in its entire independence of everything which does not proceed from itself.
- Absolute civil sovereignty in the implied right of the people to make their own laws in entire independence and utter disregard of any other criterion than the popular will expressed at the polls.
- Absolute freedom of thought in politics, morals, or in religion. The unrestrained liberty of the press.[433]

---

[430] E. Hales, *First Vatican Council,* pp. 12-13.
[431] Joseph Brusher, S.J., *Popes Through the Ages,* p. 510.
[432] Raymond Corrigan, S.J., *The Church and the Nineteenth Century,* p. 4.
[433] Fr. Felix Sarda y Salvany, *What is Liberalism?,* pp. 18-19.

Anne Carroll defines Liberalism as "a philosophy which rejects moral absolutes and authority, especially religious authority. It is usually opposed to hereditary monarchy. It emphasizes that men should be free to do whatever they want in moral matters. It usually approves the elimination of opposition, by violence if necessary."[434]

Liberalism is based on the absolute independence of the individual, society and the State from God and His Church. The Catholic Church is founded on the absolute subjection of the individual and society to the revealed law of God. These two ideologies are irreconcilable. Liberalism has been repeatedly condemned by a succession of popes from Gregory XVI to Pius XII because it is the very antithesis of Catholicism. Pope Leo XIII describes the inherent evils of this false philosophy:

> ...Man, by a necessity of his nature, is wholly subject to the most faithful and ever enduring power of God; and that, as a consequence, any liberty except that which consists in submission to God and in submission to His will is unintelligible. To deny the existence of this authority in God, or to refuse to submit to it, means to act, not as a free man, but as one who treasonably abuses his liberty; and in such a disposition of mind the chief and deadly vice of Liberalism essentially consists.[435]

Félicité de Lamennais, Henri Lacordaire and the Comte de Montalembert sought to Christianize liberalism in order to make the Church more acceptable to French society. This movement, known as Catholic Liberalism, was quickly repudiated by local ecclesiastical authorities and later by Rome for its compromise of principle and lowering of Catholic ideals. Liberty of conscience and worship are diametrically opposed to Divine Law and ultimately lead to religious indifferentism and social atheism. A spirit of Rationalism, derived from the French Revolution, permeated French society and infected many ecclesiastics.

---

[434] *Christ the King, Lord of History*, p. 312.
[435] *Libertas Humana (On the Nature of True Liberty)*, no. 36. Understood as it is in the encyclical, liberalism is in ethics and politics what naturalism or rationalism are in philosophy. ...It means the denial of any divine authority and the refusal to accept it as rule, or law, of the will. We are once more sent back to the fundamental tenet of naturalism which affirms the supremacy of the human reason (art. 15). Etienne Gilson, *The Church Speaks to the Modern World*, pp. 55-56.

When his book, *Paroles d'un Croyant*, was condemned for its radical and anarchistic content by Pope Gregory XVI in 1832, Lamennais lost faith in Rome and soon after, in Christianity itself. "Though he was never excommunicated, he ceased to perform his office as a priest and came to denounce the very priesthood itself and the basic articles of the Christian faith, finding 'the Truth' in the 'People' alone. Embittered and unreconciled, he died in 1852."[436]

In order to properly understand the Vatican Council it is important to realize that many statesmen and clergy of the 19th century were infected with the Liberalism of that era.

World Conditions

A united Italy was rapidly being formed which would eventually absorb the Papal States and Rome, ultimately making the pope "a prisoner of the Vatican." King Victor Emmanuel II of Sardinia defeated the papal army in 1860 and annexed most of the Papal States except a small territory around Rome. The same year, elections took place in Tuscany, Emilia, Romagna, Parma and Modena favoring union with Sardinia. Giuseppe Garibaldi's revolutionaries captured Palermo and Naples. Parliament proclaimed Victor Emmanuel II King of Italy in 1861 and nine years later Rome became the capital of a united Italy.

"Otto von Bismarck, the creator of modern Germany, declared war on the Church during Pope Pius' reign with his *Kulturkampf* [culture war] ...and for much of the time the pope felt himself alone against the whole world."[437] Also, Dr. Ignaz Döllinger, an influential history professor at the University of Munich, did all in his power to thwart the work of the council and helped form the schismatic Old Catholic Church.

The "Know-Nothing" Party persecuted Catholics and immigrants in the United States during the mid-19th century. Their motto was "Americans must rule America" and they gained political prominence in many states.

> When in 1853, a representative of the pope came to the United States, he was mobbed by members of this party in Cincinnati. There followed a bitter persecution of Catholics all over the country. Churches were destroyed. In

---

[436] E. Hales, *The Catholic Church in the Modern World*, pp. 92-93.
[437] *Our Sunday Visitor*, September 3, 2000.

Bangor, Maine, a Jesuit priest was tarred and feathered. There were riots at Louisville and St. Louis in which there was bloodshed, and everywhere, in spite of the fact that the Constitution of the United States guarantees religious liberty, everything possible was done to prevent Catholics from holding public office or even voting.[438]

By 1864, in spite of this tense setting, the council began to take a definite shape; however, it would not formally begin until five years later.

Attacking Modern Errors

Archbishop Pecci of Perugia, who would later become Pope Leo XIII, suggested compiling a list of contemporary errors in order to combat the many false ideologies prevalent at the time. This list, or syllabus of 80 modern errors called *The Syllabus of Errors* was promulgated by Pope Pius IX on December 8, 1864, along with the encyclical *Quanta Cura* (On Current Errors). The *Syllabus* was a compilation of errors already identified in past papal encyclicals, allocutions and apostolic letters. On September 8, 1907, Pope St. Pius X would also condemn many of these erroneous teachings in the encyclical *Pascendi* (Against Modernism).

There are 80 propositions in the *Syllabus of Errors:* 14 refer to Naturalism and Rationalism, 4 to Religious Indifferentism, 20 address errors concerning the Church and Her rights, Socialism, Communism and Bible Societies, 2 pertain to the temporal power of the pope, 17 refer to the relations between Church and State, 9 to Christian and natural morality, 10 to Christian marriage and 4 to Liberalism. "In the Syllabus is found the explicit and detailed condemnation of liberalism, whether philosophical, theological, religious or sociopolitical."[439]

> The enemies of the Church, interpreting the document in their own peculiar way, raised the cry that the pope had now declared the utter irreconcilability of the Catholic Church with modern progress, that the Church was opposed to liberty in all departments, and that the teaching of the Syllabus was out of harmony with the principles of modern government. History ...has proved how groundless

---

[438] Fr. George Johnson, *Story of the Church*, p. 429.
[439] Pietro Parente, *Dictionary of Dogmatic Theology*, p. 164.

were such assertions, but at the time, they were not without an effect upon many, both inside and outside the Church.[440]

With the secular press and the Church's enemies attacking the Syllabus and stirring up public opinion, Bishop Dupanloup of Orléans set his pen to work in defense of the pope. His pamphlet exposed the misinterpretations and calumnies of the Church's enemies and put forth the true meanings laid out by the Syllabus. The pope and at least 630 bishops from around the world wrote letters to congratulate Bishop Dupanloup and thank him for vindicating the Church's teaching with his pamphlet.

Dr. Döllinger and Lord Acton

Döllinger had not been sparing in his criticism of Rome, of the Papal States, of the Curia. He had been bitter in his contempt for Scholastic Theology. He had developed something very near hatred for the Jesuits. As early as 1850 he had propounded his grandiose dream of a German national church, not schismatic, it is true, but hardly Catholic with its domineering self-sufficiency. He was a protagonist, too, for 'public opinion.' And as he became more and more infatuated with 'liberal' ideas he became a source of anxiety to many of his former friends. The world still admired his immense learning and his undoubted intellectual powers. But not even Döllinger himself could have foretold whither they would lead him. Only by reading history backwards does one get the full significance of his appeal for deference to public opinion at the Munich assembly of 1863. ...His exclusion from the deliberations preparatory to the council was a final 'insult.' He threw his great weight into a most determined opposition.[441]

In 1860, Döllinger had expressed his bitter opposition to the dogma of the Immaculate Conception, primarily because of the manner in which the proclamation was accomplished. Pope Pius IX condemned many of Döllinger's erroneous beliefs in the *Syllabus of Errors*.[442]

Döllinger's fall, like that of Luther, stemmed from neglect of prayer. "In 1860, a certain countess asked him, 'When do you say Mass? I should like to be

---

[440] Fr. J. MacCaffrey, *History of the Catholic Church in the 19th Century*, pp. 440-441.
[441] Raymond Corrigan, S.J., *The Church and the Nineteenth Century*, pp. 190-191.
[442] See Proposition 13, D 2913.

present.' Döllinger answered, 'I do not say Mass. I have no time for it.' It was said of him that he had two brains and no heart. His apostasy was hardly a surprise."[443]

Sir John (later, Lord) Acton, a former student of Döllinger who was thoroughly imbued with the ideas of his age, envisioned a group of lay theologians who would work independent of ecclesiastical authority. Acton was muzzled and his theories condemned by the *Syllabus of Errors*. "Acton felt unable to continue his work; instead, as Regius Professor of Modern History at Cambridge University, he pursued the paths of secular history."[444] A few years later, the distinguished historian Acton displayed his bitter hostility to the work of the Vatican Council and the proclamation of papal infallibility. He also kept Döllinger abreast of the council proceedings.

Gallicanism

Papal infallibility had been assailed by an ideology called Gallicanism (Conciliarism) for more than 400 years prior to the Vatican Council. Gallicanism "tended to restrict the authority of the Church regarding the state (Political Gallicanism) or the authority of the pope regarding councils, bishops, and clergy (Ecclesiastico-Theological Gallicanism)."[445] These erroneous teachings were widely professed by the clergy of France (formerly called Gaul, hence the name) and later spread to Flanders, Ireland and England. Some prelates at the council followed the Gallican ideology and wished to make papal authority dependent on the bishops and the approbation of general councils.

> In the 14th century in consequence of the confusion in ecclesiastical and political affairs, the status of the papacy sank considerably. This was fatefully reflected in its effects on the teaching of the papal primacy. William of Ockham, in his battle against Pope John XXII, tried to undermine the divine institution of the primacy. Marsilius of Padua and John of Jandun directly denied it and declared the primacy to be a mere honorary primacy, and ascribed the supreme juridical power and doctrinal power to the general council. At the time of the great

---

[443] Bishop Johannes Pohlschneider, *Adsum, A Bishop Speaks to His Priests,* p. 63.
[444] E. Hales, *The Catholic Church in the Modern World,* p. 130.
[445] Pietro Parente, *Dictionary of Dogmatic Theology,* p. 108.

Western Schism (1378-1417) many reputable theologians, such as Henry of Langenstein, Conrad of Gelnhausen, Peter of Ailly and John Gerson, saw in the doctrine of the superiority of the general council over the pope (conciliary theory) the sole means of reuniting the Church. The viewpoint appeared that the general Church was indeed free from error, but that the Roman Church could err, and fall into heresy and schism. The Council of Constance (Fourth and Fifth Sessions) and of Basle (Second Session) declared for the superiority of the council over the pope. However, the resolutions referring to this did not receive the papal ratification and were consequently legally invalid (D 657 Anm. 2). In Gallicanism the theory of the superiority of a general council lived on for hundreds of years.[446]

Ultramontanism

Many Italians and Romans who opposed Gallicanism and defended the primacy and infallibility of the Roman Pontiff became known as Ultramontanists. "Ultramontanism [is] a term used to denote integral and active Catholicism, because it recognizes as its spiritual head the pope, who, for the greater part of Europe, is a dweller beyond the mountains (*ultra montes*), that is, beyond the Alps."[447] Ultramontanists stressed the monarchial role of the pope, his universal jurisdiction, his primacy over the Catholic Church and his infallibility in *ex cathedra* pronouncements.

The Chief Doctrinal Error of the Time

The conflict between these two groups is described by a contemporary writer:

Each council was convened to extinguish the chief heresy, or to correct the chief evil of the time. And I do not hesitate to affirm that the denial of the infallibility of the Roman Pontiff was the chief intellectual or doctrinal error as to faith, not to call it more than proximate to heresy, of our times.

It was so because it struck at the validity of the pontifical acts of the last 300 years, weakened the effect of papal decisions of this period over the intellect and conscience of the faithful. It kept alive a dangerous controversy on the subject of infallibility altogether, and exposed even the infallibility of the Church itself to

---

[446] Dr. Ludwig Ott, *Fundamentals of Catholic Dogma*, p. 289.
[447] Charles Herbermann, *Catholic Encyclopedia, Vol. 15*, p. 125.

difficulties not easy to solve. As an apparently open or disputable point, close to the very root of faith, it exposed even the faith itself to the reach of doubts.

Next, practically, it was mischievous beyond measure. The divisions and contentions of 'Gallicanism' and 'Ultramontanism' have been a scandal and a shame to us. Protestants and unbelievers have been kept from the truth by our intestine controversies, especially upon a point so high and so intimately connected with the whole doctrinal authority of the Church. Again, morally, the division and contention on this point, supposed to be open, has generated more alienation, bitterness and animosity between Pastors and people, and what is worse, between Pastor and Pastor, than any other in our day.[448]

The Bishops of France and Germany

It is necessary to understand the mind of the bishops who attended the Vatican Council in order to understand the council itself. Fr. James McCaffrey and Msgr. Hughes explain how the conflict over infallibility raged, especially in Germany: "The convocation of the council, while pleasing to the vast body of Catholic clergy and people, roused the bitter enmity of the radical-liberal party throughout Europe. Even in Catholic circles very sharp controversies broke out, especially in France and Germany."[449] "Also there were, in Germany, a very small number of great scholars who defiantly held that the pope was not infallible, and who grew more and more antipapal with each year that passed."[450]

> The bishops of Germany were in a peculiarly difficult position. Whether personally in favor of infallibility or opposed to it, they could not fail to be alarmed at the dangerous tendency of the movement. Under the circumstances, it was thought best to hold a meeting of their own body at Fulda in September 1869. The assembly was attended by sixteen bishops, one bishop-elect, professor Hefele, who had been appointed to the see of Rottenburg, and the procurators of three absent bishops. They determined to send a private letter to the pope, in which the arguments against the advisability of the definition, especially in so far as it would affect the Church in Germany, should be set forth. This document was signed by about two-thirds of those present. At the same time they issued a

---

[448] Cardinal Manning, *The Vatican Council and its Definitions*, pp. 41-42.
[449] *History of the Catholic Church in the Nineteenth Century*, p. 443.
[450] *The Church in Crisis*, p. 350.

pastoral letter to the Catholics of Germany, which was well calculated to allay the excitement and uneasiness that Döllinger and his friends had so industriously instigated. They pointed out that the council could not define any teaching that was not already contained in the Scriptures or in Tradition, that it could not define anything that would be opposed to the rights of the state or the interests of true science, and that, as Jesus Christ had promised that the Holy Ghost would be present to direct the Church till the end of time, the Holy Spirit would assist the deliberations of the council. The pastoral was read in all the Catholic churches of Germany, and made an excellent impression.[451]

Many of the provincial councils and the bishops in their assemblies at Rome had held language which showed that a proposal to define the pope's infallibility would meet with no opposition among the majority. With the German Catholics it was otherwise. There, many of the clergy were still educated at 'mixed' universities—many of the Catholic professors had already manifested their distrust of the 'Roman' theology, and some of them had come into collision with the Roman Congregations. They clung, in the supposed interests of science, to methods different from those that prevailed at Rome. And even in France there was a party, small in numbers, but strong in talent and character, which was attached to liberal principles in politics and distrustful of Roman interference in such matters. ...There were besides, Catholic statesmen in both countries who saw danger to the State in a definition of papal infallibility.[452]

Opposition to the Council

Powerful men throughout Europe feared the convocation of a General Council of the Church since it might condemn Communism, Liberalism, Rationalism, Religious Indifferentism, or other contemporary evils. Others feared that the council would consolidate or increase the power of the pope.

The eminent historian Lord Acton, who was a Catholic, but very much a liberal Catholic, and who was in Rome during the council, was so agitated when he discovered what was on the agenda, that he did all he could to persuade [English Prime Minister] William Gladstone to act in concert with the French government to cause the council to be dissolved. The Chancellor of the Austrian Empire,

---

[451] Fr. James MacCaffrey *History of the Catholic Church in the Nineteenth Century*, pp. 446-447.
[452] Fr. John McLaughlin, *Half-Hours with the Servants of God*, p. 182.

Beust, who was a Protestant, was strongly in favor of the same action. Gladstone, for a time, was persuaded by Acton, and if the Paris government had agreed with London and Vienna it is difficult to see how the council could have continued, since it depended on the protection of French troops at Rome. But Napoleon III was persuaded by his premier, Emile Ollivier, (who was also a Protestant) that it would be wiser to let the council run its course and to reserve political action until later, and then only to intervene in the eventuality that the council passed decrees inconsistent with a Frenchman's loyalty to the principles of his government. It was thus that Ollivier saved the life of the Vatican Council.[453]

The Vatican Council

The invention of the telegraph and the wide-scale circulation of newspapers kept the world informed of events during the 104 sessions of the Vatican Council that were presided over by Pope Pius IX and his legates. This was the first general council attended by Americans and the first legitimate council held at the Vatican. The five previous councils held in Rome had taken place at the Lateran.

Why did the non-Catholic world and the avowed enemies of the Church take such interest at the opening of the council and during its early sessions? It was both hoped and believed by these antagonists that during the council the liberal-minded bishops (called the "international opposition") would check and bring down the Roman Curia and the Ultramontane party, change the doctrines of the Church and strike down the definition of papal infallibility.

> Many publications had appeared in French, English, and German, from which it became evident that a common purpose and plan of co-operation had been formed. Certain notorious letters published in France, and the infamous book 'Janus,' [written by Dr. Döllinger] translated into English, French, and Italian, proclaimed open war upon the council. ...This alone was enough to set the whole anti-Catholic world on fire with curiosity, hope, and delight.

> A belief had also spread itself that the council would explain away the doctrines of Trent, or give them some new or laxer meaning, or throw open some questions supposed to be closed, or come to a compromise or transaction with other religious systems; or at least that it would accommodate the dogmatic stiffness of its traditions to modern thought and modern theology.

---

[453] E. Hales, *The First Vatican Council,* pp. 19-20.

It is strange that anyone should have forgotten that every general council, from Nicaea to Trent, which has touched on the faith, has made new definitions, and that every definition is a new dogma, and closes what was before open, and ties up more strictly the doctrines of faith.

But the interest excited by this ...was nothing compared to the exultation with which the anti-Catholic opinion and anti-Catholic press ...beheld, as they believed, the formation of an organized 'international opposition' of more than a hundred bishops within the council itself. The day had come at last. What the world could not do against Rome from without, its own bishops were going to do against Rome, and in the world's service, from within. [This is precisely what would occur later, at the Second Vatican Council.]

...In a moment, all the world rose up to meet them. Governments, politicians, newspapers, schismatics, heretics, infidels, ...revolutionaries, as with one unerring instinct, united in extolling and setting forth the virtue, learning, science, eloquence, nobleness, heroism, of this 'international opposition.' ...All who were against Rome received positive coverage in the press; all who were for Rome received negative coverage. The public eye and ear of all countries were filled, and taught to associate all that is noble and great with the 'international opposition,' all that is neither noble nor great, with those loyal to Rome.[454] [This too occurred at Vatican II.]

Triumphal Entry into St. Peter's

St. Peter's Basilica, the most magnificent church in the world, was chosen for the 20th General Council of the Church. It had been the work of great Renaissance artists and architects: Bramante, Michelangelo, Raphael, Della Porta, Maderno and Bernini. Although it took centuries to complete, it was finally dedicated in 1626.

Because of its enormous size (694 feet long, 376 feet wide—499 at transepts, 405 feet high) St. Peter's was able to accommodate the 50,000 people who packed into the basilica to view the spectacular opening ceremonies of the Vatican Council on December 8, 1869.

Archbishops and bishops put on white miters and copes in a room over the portico of St. Peter's, and at nine the procession started down the *Scala Regia* and moved across the porch of the basilica and into the central nave. Over 7,000

---

[454] Cardinal Manning, *The Vatican Council and its Definitions*, pp. 21-22.

prelates took part. Papal Zouaves [guards] kept a narrow passage clear as the fathers walked down the center of the church, uncovered their heads before the Blessed Sacrament exposed on the papal altar under the cupola, and turned to the right into the north transept. The council hall had been prepared there, complete with Brussels carpeting donated by the King of Prussia and with the fathers' places covered in red, purple, or green damask, according to their rank. Noble Guards and Knights of Malta stood at the main entrance and the Swiss Guard was posted at the other doors. ...The pope, who had been carried to the main door of St. Peter's in the *sedia gestatoria*, walked the length of the nave on foot, intoned some prayers before the Blessed Sacrament and entered the hall, where his throne was located at the far end, in front of the altar of Saints Processus and Martian. Cardinals and patriarchs took their places in the apse, and the rest of the fathers were ranged in long rows of choir stalls, eight rows deep, which ran the length of the chapel.

...Cardinal Constantino Patrizi celebrated Mass at 10:00 a.m., a full hour after the start of the procession. Before the Last Gospel a sermon was preached by Archbishop Luigi Puecher Passavalli, OFM Cap, a curial official. After the Mass, each of the fathers made his obedience to the pope; cardinals kissing his hand, bishops of all ranks his knee, and abbots and religious superiors his foot. A series of prayers and litanies followed and Pope Pius gave a brief exhortation. The session should then have been closed to the public, but the presence of a number of royal personages and ambassadors and the tribunes made this awkward, and so the hall was not cleared when Antonio Valenziani, Bishop of Fabriano and Matelica in the Papal States, read a formal decree declaring the council opened. The fathers gave unanimous approval to this by voice vote. A second decree announced the next public session would be held on January 6. The *Te Deum* was then sung, and the meeting adjourned. It was approximately 4:00 p.m. The services had taken seven hours.[455]

The Council Hall

The council assembled in the north transeptal arm of St. Peter's which was walled off from the rest of the church with what looked like a massive partition

---

[455] Granderath, II, 1, 20-33; Butler, I, 162-5; AAS, F.N. Blanchet Journal, December 8, 1869; "The First Oecumenical Council of the Vatican," *Catholic World*, X (1870), 693-705.

of solid marble in many colors, entering through a pair of bronze doors. In fact the whole thing was made to fold up like a screen. Reading-rooms, drawing-rooms and cloak-rooms were fitted in an ingenious way. Six hundred prelates sat on benches of eight tiers on either side of the transept. The opening session saw them resplendent in their silver copes and linen mitres.[456]

The cardinals sit in a large semi-circle on each side of the pope, and the patriarchs in a smaller and inner one; then there are eight or ten steps down to the floor, and the bishops are placed at each side of the hall in five rows of seats rising one above the other. The seats are very comfortable, and each one has a small table which hangs by hinges on the back of the bench in front, and can be used either sloping as a desk or flat like an ordinary table.[457]

Who Attended the Council?

Something like a thousand personages had the right to take part in the council, once the pope decided that titular bishops should be convoked as well as bishops actually ruling a territory. Of these thousand, some 75 percent actually attended the council, 744[458] of them, at one time or another, during the seven months it sat (December 8—July 18, 1870). Of these 744, 643 were bishops actually ruling a territory, and a bare 43 were bishops either retired from active work or consecrated as auxiliaries to some diocesan bishop, or because their high position in the Curia Romana carried with it episcopal dignity. The balance of the 744 was made up of cardinals resident in Rome and the general superiors of the religious orders. As many as 200, and even more, of these diocesan bishops were from Italy itself where, alone, the custom of the primitive church had continued, that each city should have its bishop.

Over 120 were English-speaking (from England 12, Ireland 19, the United States 46). From France came 70, Germany and the Austrian Empire 58, Spain 36, Latin America 30. There were 50 bishops from various churches of the Oriental rites, and 100 missionary bishops from Asia, Africa and Oceania.[459]

---

[456] James Lees-Milne, *St. Peter's*, pp. 315-316.
[457] Dom Cuthbert Butler, *The Vatican Council 1869-1870*, p. 165.
[458] R. Aubert, *Le Pontificat de Pie IX* (vol. 21 of F. and M., *Historie de l'Eglise*), 1952, 324.
[459] Msgr. Philip Hughes, *The Church in Crisis*, pp. 340-341.

Ground Rules for the Council

Pope Pius IX's apostolic letter, *Multiplices inter,* gave very specific guidelines for the council proceedings. This assured an efficient *modus operandi.*

> By this decree the right of proposing questions for deliberation was reserved to the pope. However, the pope would name a special congregation or committee of members of the council to which individual fathers might submit proposals. The apostolic letter provided for two types of meetings, the more common general congregations and the solemn public sessions. At general congregations, the fathers were to discuss *schemata* previously prepared by the preliminary commissions. Anyone could speak; it was only necessary that they register their names with the cardinal presidents. If the *schemata* needed revision, this would be done by one of four deputations to be elected by the fathers. When the final draft of a constitution had been completed, decrees would be voted upon in public session, in the presence of the pope. At general congregations three types of votes were possible, namely: approval *(placet),* disapproval *(non placet),* and conditional approval *(placet juxta modum).* In public sessions conditional votes were not to be allowed. All voting was to be by roll call, but in general congregations, written ballots were also acceptable. Finally, the apostolic letter reminded the fathers of their obligation to secrecy about the affairs of the council and informed them that they were not to quit Rome without explicit permission.[460]

The Proposed Schema

Prior to the formal beginning of the Vatican Council a number of commissions were assembled in order to draw up the schema. The commissions followed the pattern of the Council of Trent and the topics were systematically arranged so that the discussion could proceed in a scholastic manner. A cardinal oversaw each of the five preparatory committees that were established to prepare topics for discussion.

On December 10 the Council Fathers were given a copy of the schema and at a later date, a papal bull outlining the procedure to be followed during the council. The original schema contained 18 chapters detailing topics to be covered. The first 11 chapters were more general, dealing with current errors opposed to

---

[460] Mansi, L. 215-222.

Catholic teaching. Among those listed were divine revelation, mysteries, the nature of faith, the relation of faith to natural science, materialism, pantheism and rationalism. The final seven chapters dealt with specific doctrines including the Blessed Trinity, creation, the Incarnation and Redemption, Adam as progenitor of the human race, original sin, eternal punishment and grace.

Sadly, things did not move ahead as smoothly as many of the preparatory committee members had envisioned. It became obvious to all that the council would take many years to complete unless drastic changes were made and the schema simplified.

On January 6, 1870, the Council Fathers began the second session with a Profession of Faith and 22 general meetings followed. On February 22, 1870, the Council Fathers received a new set of regulations that were to be used for the remainder of the sessions. The council adjourned until March 18 in order to give the preparatory committees time to finish their work.

Political Developments

A new liberal government, the Third Republic, was formed in France on January 2, 1870. Its leader, Emperor Napoleon III, stationed imperial troops in Rome to protect the Vatican Council from political or outside interference. Ironically, the Catholic French foreign minister, Count Daru, did his utmost to exert pressure on the Vatican in order to prevent it from discussing any controversial topics: especially the relationship between Church and State and the formal definition of papal infallibility. On February 21, with the approval of Napoleon III, Daru sent a threatening dispatch to the French Ambassador in Rome. The French Prime Minister, Ollivier, was incensed and moderated the tone of the memo. On March 6, word finally leaked out that the council planned to discuss papal infallibility. By the middle of March, Pope Pius IX and many of the Council Fathers were terrified at the prospect of armed intervention by European powers that would effectively dissolve the council.

"Toward the end of March, the political situation became so tenuous and strained that some of the Council Fathers suggested omitting treatment of papal infallibility. Pio Nono's [Pius IX's] answer in effect was: Full steam ahead—'I have the holy Virgin with me: I will go on.' "[461]

> This special protection of the Blessed Virgin was more than ever necessary for the Church, because evil days were drawing nigh, days of direst distress, when the faithful and their august head were to be the objects of new and terrible persecutions. The Church had a presentiment of the impending struggle, and, led by the Holy Spirit, She prepared a providential concentration of Her forces by putting them all at the disposal of Her Supreme Head. In view of the shifting conditions of all human organizations, it was of utmost importance to the church that She possess one central authority, well-defined, universally acknowledged, and which could promptly and efficaciously intervene whenever need arose. Now the Vatican Council had time to render this most valuable aid to the Church. ...It proclaimed papal infallibility and thus sealed the promise made to Peter and on which is grounded the whole structure of the Church.[462]

On April 1, Pope Pius IX openly spoke on the matter of infallibility not only in his speeches, but also in his correspondence. Newspapers subsequently raised public alarm by forecasting disastrous results.

Meanwhile, French Foreign Minister Daru was not pleased with the reply he had received concerning his February 23 dispatch. On April 6 he issued a second memorandum in response.

> The French Ambassador was to present the [Daru] Memorandum to the Holy Father himself, but this was delayed, owing to Holy Week, until April 22, after it had already got in to the press. But Mgr. Forcade, Bishop of Nevers, one of the middle party of French bishops, who had been in Paris, had at the request of Daru undertaken to see the Holy Father privately and explain to him the attitude of the Government. He wrote to Ollivier on April 7 that he had had on that day a long, intimate and most affectionate audience.[463] Forcade 'ventured to insinuate' that the best way of avoiding the difficulties would be to postpone as long as possible the discussion of the schema 'de Ecclesia' in the whole matter of Church and State that was so irritating, till minds had had time to cool down; and so not

---

[461] Dom Cuthbert Butler, *The Vatican Council 1869-1870,* p. 282.
[462] Compilation of various authors, *Cabinet of Catholic Information,* pp. 198-199.
[463] *Lac* 1561; Ollivier, op. cit., II, 214.

allow the question to come on that year. This proposal was better received by the pope than Forcade had hoped for. The pope's desire was to avoid trouble, whether for the Church or for the Governments, over the matter of the relations of Church and State. Ollivier is very likely right in surmising that the decision to give precedence to the question of the papacy before the rest of the schema, was motivated partly by the desire to shelve subjects that might antagonize the Governments.

When the Ambassador on April 22 presented the Memorandum, the pope said he would consider it carefully, but he would not officially lay it before the council. At this juncture Daru resigned his place in the Cabinet, not on this issue, but on political grounds, but Ollivier for the time being took over the portfolio of foreign affairs. He at once reversed Daru's policy of intervention in the council, which he had never liked or believed in; and the telegram went from Paris to Rome: 'Daru se retire, Ollivier remplace, Concile libre.' [Daru retires. Ollivier replaces. The council is free.] And so it was; from that time forth there was no menace from the Governments interfering with the full liberty of the council.[464]

The Use of Latin

The unity of the Catholic Church was wonderfully portrayed in this assembly of bishops from around the world by the use of the Latin language. Cardinal Gibbons of the United States observed:

> Thanks to the Latin language, which all but a few Orientals understand, each bishop comprehended the discourses almost as clearly as if they had been spoken in his native tongue. Only the accent and pronunciation betrayed the nationality of the speaker. Sometimes a pleasant smile would play on the habitually grave countenance of an Italian cardinal while listening to the language of Cicero uttered with an inflection and a pronunciation unfamiliar to his ears. The accomplished Bishop of Geneva began a speech with a graceful apology for his French accent: 'My voice, Reverend Fathers, is French, but my heart is Roman.'[465]

Other Work of the Council

Although the Vatican Council is mainly remembered for its definition of papal infallibility, there were a number of other decrees and canons formulated

---

[464] Dom Cuthbert Butler, *Vatican Council: The Story Told from Inside, Vol. II*, pp. 24-25.
[465] Arline Boucher, *Prince of Democracy: James Cardinal Gibbons*, pp. 82-83.

at the council. "In the first [three] sessions the fundamental truths of Christianity: God's existence, nature and providence; the possibility and fact of revelation; the harmony between reason and revelation were defined, and the principal errors of the day: atheism, materialism, rationalism, and pantheism, were condemned."[466]

The Dogmatic Constitution Concerning the Catholic Faith (De Fide Catholica) was unanimously accepted by the 667 Council Fathers present and approved by Pope Pius IX during the third session of the council on April 24, 1870. In addition, 18 canons were written on the existence of a personal God and the means to know Him, the necessity of divine revelation, the nature of faith and the relationship between faith and knowledge.

What is Papal Infallibility?

The supreme head of the Church, he whose office is that of feeding the flock of Christ, must, in the essential matters of faith and morals, be actually unable to poison that flock with erroneous teaching. In a word, Peter (and his successors, each in turn) must be *infallible* when, as teacher and ruler of the whole Church, he speaks in definite pronouncement upon a matter of *faith* (what is to be believed as of Apostolic revelation) or *morals* (what is right or wrong, good or bad, in human conduct).

...But it is not only reasonable, but actually *requisite,* when we consider what the Supreme Pontiff has to do. Can he—teaching the whole Church in an essential matter of faith or morals in the name of Christ and by His authority—teach falsehood? Christ, then, is falsified! Can he—commissioned as he is to feed the flock of Christ—feed it the poison of error? As a man the pope may be weak, sinful, fallible; but when he speaks *officially* to the *whole Church* in a matter of *faith or morals,* then he is exercising the office Christ gave him to exercise; then he is speaking in the very power and authority of Christ Himself—and shall Christ's spokesman be able to teach falsehood to Christ's faithful? If so, then *Christ Himself is deceived and His word falsified,* for, if error could be definitely taught and universally accepted as truth in His Church, the gates of hell *could and would* prevail against the Church.[467]

---

[466] Fr. John Laux, *Church History,* p. 541.
[467] Msgr. Paul Glenn, *Apologetics,* pp. 246-247.

The pope is protected by papal infallibility from ever teaching anything contrary to the Deposit of Faith. When the pope defines a doctrine, he simply makes a public declaration of what has always been the teaching of the Church.

> It [the Catholic Church] exercises its infallible doctrinal authority in diverse ways: through its general councils, through the unanimous voice of the bishops dispersed through the universe but united with the pope; through its ordinary and uniform preaching; through the pope alone teaching 'ex-cathedra.'
>
> Granting the infallibility of the Church, it is natural to find the Church exercising that infallibility through the pope when as head and chief pastor of the whole Church, he pronounces decisions in matters of faith and morals binding the universal Church.
>
> From the earliest times, men turned to Rome as to the authoritative court of appeal and the teacher of Christian truth. When local synods disagreed and individual bishops judged each other to be heretics, from the chief pastor of the whole Church, men could learn what was the faith of the Church. Only by standing on the Rock of Peter could men be certain that they were in the Church of Christ and that their disputes were settled by competent authority.[468]

A Consistent Teaching of the Church

The vast majority of Catholics favored not only the idea of the council, but also the doctrine of papal infallibility, the dogmatic definition of which, as was well known, would crown the labors of that august assembly. Nor was Pius IX mistaken when he wrote: 'It is claimed that the Church seeks to introduce a new dogma. No, there is a question only of affirming a truth known and acknowledged by universal Catholic Tradition.' That was quite true. The theological proposition states that the pope, as trustee of the Holy Spirit, enjoys personal infallibility and has no need of the Church's express concurrence when as Shepherd and Teacher he proclaims an article of faith. The Jesuits had asked for its inclusion among the canons of Trent; Bellarmine had spent his life defending it; and, although questioned during the Jansenist and Gallican disputes, it had been admitted without dispute by the great mass of Catholics since the beginning of the eighteenth century. The Mendicants, the Jesuits and the Redemptorists, together with Joseph de Maistre's *Du Pape*, had done much to

---

[468] Charles Martin, *Catholic Religion,* p. 97.

secure its recognition. One may therefore say that most Fathers of the Council already accepted the doctrine long before they assembled at the Vatican.[469]

The Discussion of Papal Infallibility

When Pope Pius IX first proposed the convocation of a general council, two cardinals brought up the topic of papal infallibility. Although the primacy of the pope had been listed as a topic of discussion, papal infallibility was not included on the original schema. Providentially, the matter would be formally settled days before the forced ending of the council.

Archbishop Manning of Westminster, Bishop Martin of Paderborn, Bishop von Senestrey of Ratisbon and Bishop Spalding of Baltimore and 500 other bishops deemed it opportune for the council to formally define papal infallibility. Numerous world leaders and a minority of bishops strongly opposed such a definition. There were various opinions as to whether or not it would be expedient to define papal infallibility at the time, so the controversy continued.

Archbishop Manning approached the pope regarding this matter on April 19 at a time when the council was discussing various doctrinal issues. Ten days later the Council Fathers were informed that papal infallibility would take precedence over other topics. The Vatican Council found it necessary to address the definition of papal infallibility since this revealed truth had been obscured in the past and was at the time denied by an increasing number of people.

Papal infallibility had long been a stumbling block for heretics, liberals and Gallicans who were bold enough to deny or misrepresent it. Others opposed the formal definition in order to prevent further persecution of the Church.

> Seven months, however, was a long enough time for the council to tackle the most controversial and most widely discussed item of all, namely the nature of the infallibility of the pope. I have deliberately said the *nature* of the infallibility of the pope and not whether the pope was infallible, because it is quite erroneous to suppose that there was violent controversy within the church as to whether or not the pope, in certain special circumstances, spoke infallibly or not. Everybody within the Church was agreed that the Church was infallible, in Her dogmatic teaching on faith and morals. Everybody was agreed that the supreme authority

---

[469] H. Daniel-Rops, *The Church in an Age of Revolution 1789-1870*, p. 291.

within the Church was the pope. It therefore followed that when the pope defined dogma, in the sphere of faith or morals, he would be safeguarded from error by the promise of the truth given by Christ to the Church.[470]

Discussion Commences

The Fathers began formal discussions on papal infallibility on May 13 and continued until June 3. The primacy of the pope was discussed from June 6 until June 13. The final detailed discussion regarding the wording of the decree on papal infallibility took place between June 15 and July 4. The topic was debated by 57 speakers: 35 pro and 22 con. These speeches examined papal infallibility in the light of Scripture, Apostolic Tradition, the general councils and the history of the Catholic Church. The actions of Popes Liberius (352-366 AD) and Honorius I (625-638 AD) were debated at length as well as other events that posed apparent contradictions. (For additional information regarding Popes Liberius and Honorius I, refer to chapters 2 and 6.)

The Case of Pope Liberius

Pope Liberius reigned during the height of the Arian heresy and was exiled by order of the Emperor Constantius for his opposition to it. Some authors claim that the pope signed a document promoting Arianism. Frs. Rumble and Carty have refuted this false claim by asserting:

> Historical research has shown that it is doubtful whether he signed the document at all. ...St. Athanasius and St. Hilary, who thought he did sign, insist that no charge of heresy could be made against Liberius on the score that the document was not necessarily heretical. ...On his return from exile he defended the Nicene decisions against Arianism, and remained a most uncompromising defender of the orthodox doctrine until his death in 366 AD.[471]

Ballerini says that if Liberius compromised the faith, " 'which is by no means certain,' ...it was 'not the result of full free-will; for the fear of the Emperor Constantius was the motive; and still less in this fall was a definition of the faith involved.' "[472] "Many authors, like Socrates, Theodoret and Sulpicius Severus

---

[470] E. Hales, *First Vatican Council*, pp. 21-22.
[471] *Radio Replies, Vol. 3*, p. 99.
[472] Liberii lapsus non certus, nec si certus, voluntarius, nec in definitione fidei.
P. Ballerini de vi ac ratione primatûs, c. 15, 13, n. 30, p. 297, 299, 300.

testify in favor of Liberius. Of the testimonies brought against him, several are evidently spurious,[473] and even if they were genuine, they would show only a semi-Arian Catholicizing formula, but not an 'Arian creed.' "[474]

Hagemann in the *Journal of Theological Literature* notes: "Liberius can be accused, not of what he did, but what he omitted to do; he can, from a moral point of view, be blamed for his silence, for his weakness, while the dogmatic purity of his faith remains intact."[475]

The Case of Pope Honorius I

The council witnessed many heated debates concerning papal infallibility. Opponents to papal infallibility fabricated every objection possible in order to prevent or defer its definition, even claiming that Honorius I was a heretical pope.

Cardinal Manning refuted their false allegations:

> In the judgment of a cloud of the greatest theologians of all countries, schools, and languages, since the controversy was opened two hundred years ago, the case of Honorius has been completely solved. Nay more, it has been used with abundant evidence, drawn from the very same acts and documents, to prove the direct contrary hypothesis, namely, the infallibility of the Roman Pontiffs. ...They who have cleared Honorius of personal heresy, are an overwhelming majority compared with their opponents.
>
> It is vain for the antagonists of papal infallibility to quote this case as if it were certain. Centuries of controversy have established, beyond contradiction, that the accusation against Honorius cannot be raised by his most ardent antagonists to more than a probability. And this probability, at its maximum, is less than that of his defense. I therefore affirm the question to be doubtful; which is abundantly sufficient against the private judgment of his accusers. The cumulus of evidence for the infallibility of the Roman Pontiff outweighs all such doubts.

---

[473] The fifth fragment of Hilary is, according to Hefele, spurious; (Concil., vol. I, p. 605, *et seq.*), but, according to Reinkens, it is genuine (Hilarius, p. 216, *seq.*) Even Mr. Renouf sees himself forced to give up a portion at least of the Fragment; for the maintenance of it would have involved him in the most flagrant self-contradiction. (*Vide,* "The Condemnation of Pope Honorius," London, 1868, p. 41, *seq.* note.)

[474] Dr. Hergenröther, *Anti-Janus: An Historico-Theological Criticism of the Work, entitled "The Pope and the Council" by Janus,* (1870), pp. 76-77.

[475] (Bonn), February 1, 1869, No. 3, pp. 79-81.

...The following points in the case of Honorius can be abundantly proved from documents:

(A) That Honorius defined no doctrine whatsoever.

(B) That he forbade the making of any new definition.

(C) That his fault was precisely in this omission of Apostolic authority, for which he was justly censured.

(D) That his two epistles are entirely orthodox; though, in the use of language, he wrote as was usual before the condemnation of Monotheletism, and not as it became necessary afterwards. It is an anachronism and an injustice to censure his language, used before that condemnation, as it might be just to censure it after the condemnation had been made.

To this I add the following excellent passage from the Pastoral of the Archbishop of Baltimore: 'The case of Honorius forms no exception; for 1st, Honorius expressly says in his letters to Sergius, that he meant to define nothing, and he was condemned precisely because he temporized and would not define; 2nd, because in his letters he clearly taught the sound Catholic doctrine, only enjoining silence as to the use of certain terms, then new in the Church; and 3rd, because his letters were not addressed to a general council of the whole Church, and were rather private, than public and official; at least they were not published, even in the East, until several years later. The first letter was written to Sergius in 633, and eight years afterwards, in 641, the Emperor Heraclius, in exculpating himself to Pope John II, Honorius' successor, for having published his edict—the Ecthesis—which enjoined silence on the disputants, similar to that imposed by Honorius, lays the whole responsibility thereof on Sergius, who he declares, composed the edict. Evidently, Sergius had not communicated the letter to the Emperor, probably because its contents, if published, would not have suited his wily purpose of secretly introducing, under another form, the Eutychian heresy. Thus falls to the ground the only case upon which the opponents of infallibility have continued to insist. This entire subject had been exhausted by many recent learned writers.'[476]

---

[476] Cardinal Manning, *The Vatican Council and its Definitions,* pp. 245-246.

The Discussion Continues

The Council Fathers were able to prove beyond all doubt the fact that not a single pope had ever erred in his office as Universal Pastor of the Church. Numerous popes caused scandal by their personal conduct, including John XII, Benedict IX, Urban VI, Innocent VIII, Alexander VI and Leo X. Others, due to human frailty, had been weak and ineffective leaders. In spite of their shortcomings, God preserved them all from teaching doctrinal errors to His Universal Church.

After weeks of discussion, practically every facet of papal infallibility was covered from every conceivable angle. If it had been proven that any of the popes had ever formally promulgated heretical teachings on faith and morals, the secular newspapers of the time would have seized the opportunity to ridicule the Church and thus crush the matter once and for all. This did not occur.

For the past 300 years various writers have attacked the dogma of papal infallibility by alluding to the examples of Popes Liberius, Vigilius, Honorius and others. Manning stated that these objections have already been answered:

> I should hardly have thought... that any theologian or scholar would have brought up again the cases of Vigilius, Liberius, John XXII, etc. But as these often-refuted and senseless contentions have been renewed, I give in the footnote references to the works and places in which they are abundantly answered.[477]

Infallibility does not guarantee in any way the personal teachings or morals of a pope, but empowers him to protect the Deposit of Faith from all corruption.

Fr. Adolphe Tanquerey explains:

> The pope must be speaking not as a private teacher, nor as bishop of the city of Rome, nor as a temporal prince, but as a shepherd and teacher of the whole

---

[477] On the question of Vigilius, see Cardinal Orsi *De irreformabili Rom. Pont. In definiendis fidei controversiis judicio,* tom. i. p. i. capp. 19, 20; Jeremias a Benetti's *Privileg. S. Petri vindic.* p. ii. tom. v. art. 12, p. 397, ed. Roman. 1759; Ballerini *De vi et ratione primatus,* cap, 15; Lud. Thomassin, Disp. *xix, in Concil;* Petr. De Marca *Diss. De Vigilio;* Vincenzi in S. Gregorii Nyss. et Origenis scripta cum App. de actis Synodi V. tom. iv. and v. on the question of Honorius amongst older writers: Ios. Biner S.J. *in Apparatu eruditionis,* p. iii, iv, and xi.; Thomassin, op. cit. diss. xx.; Natalis Alex. Hist. Eccles. Saec. VII. diss. 2.; *Zaccaria Antifebrom.* p. ii. liv. iv. Amongst later authors, see Civilta Cattolica ann. 1864, ser. V. vol. xi. and xii; Schneeman, *Studia in qu. De Honorio;* Ios Pennachi *de Honorii I Romani Pontificis causa in Concilio VI.*

Church in virtue of his supreme authority; he must be teaching a truth of faith or morals; he must define, i.e. finally settle what is to be held with really interior faith; and the definition must impose an obligation on the universal Church.[478]

Divine Safeguard from Error in Matters of Faith and Morals

The popes have never erred in matters of faith and morals when addressing the universal Church and speaking officially as teacher, with the intention of obligating its members to assent to their definitions.

The fact that this council did indeed promulgate the doctrine of papal infallibility is proof that the Ultramontanists were able to masterfully refute every objection hurled against them by the Gallicans. They were able to establish beyond all doubt the fact that, since the foundation of the Catholic Church, not a single pope, even those who caused scandal because of conduct or weakness, had ever erred in his office as pope while using his supreme apostolic authority, when teaching the Universal Church in matters of faith or morals.

Our Lord entrusted St. Peter and the Apostles with the mission of imparting His teachings to all nations. Their mission was to continue until the end of the world, yet St. Peter and the Apostles were mortal men, destined to pass away. Jesus Christ assured us that His guidance would continue with their successors until the end of time: "Behold, I am with you all days, even unto the consummation of the world."[479]

Christ provided for the precise transmission of His immutable teachings from age to age by means of papal infallibility—a teaching authority that is divinely safeguarded from error in matters of faith and morals. The popes possess the same infallible teaching authority that was conferred on St. Peter, the first pope.

The pope can invent no new doctrines nor teach anything contrary to the Deposit of Faith, even if he claims divine inspiration. This is explained by Cardinal Gibbons:

> What, then, is the real doctrine of Infallibility? It simply means that the pope as successor of St. Peter, by virtue of the promises of Christ is preserved from error

---

[478] Dom B. Butler, *The Church and Infallibility*, p. 72.
[479] Matthew 28: 20.

of judgment when he promulgates to the Church a decision of faith or morals. The pope, therefore, be it known, is not the maker of the Divine Law; he is only its expounder. He is not the author of revelation, but only its interpreter. All revelation came from God alone through His inspired ministers, and was complete in the beginning of the Church. The Holy Father has no more authority than you or I to break one iota or tittle of the Scripture; and he is equally with us, a servant of the Divine Law.[480]

Archbishop Dechamps

Two great ecclesiastics championed the cause of papal infallibility, which was the majority opinion of the Council Fathers. One was the Primate of Belgium, Archbishop Dechamps of Mechelen (Malines), and the other, Archbishop Manning of Westminster, England. Both later became cardinals.

Archbishop Victor Dechamps, a Redemptorist, was a proficient writer. "His writings fill fourteen volumes. He was a highly trained theologian, and his speeches and pamphlets during the council were among the very best."[481] "It is probably true to say that no other bishop had so great a hand in the actual formulation of the two great dogmatic constitutions of the council. He was a man of great charm and attractive personality; and while uncompromising in urging his views, he was always friendly and conciliatory to opponents."[482]

Archbishop Manning

Archbishop Henry Manning of Westminster, a convert from Anglicanism, saw the definition of papal infallibility as a means of drawing converts to the Catholic Faith. He reasoned that the assurance of divine guidance and infallibility in matters of faith and morals when the pope addressed the universal Church would be a means of drawing lost sheep back to Christ. Manning worked tirelessly to bring about a definition of papal infallibility and gave his inspiring speech to the council on May 25, 1870.

---

[480] Canon Howe, *Stories from the Catechist*, p. 68.
[481] Dom Cuthbert Butler, *The Vatican Council: The Story Told from Inside, Vol. I*, p. 108.
[482] See Saintrain, *Vie de Cardinal Dechamps*; also Mourret, *Concile du Vatican*, p. 169.

Bishop Gasser

Prince-Bishop Vincent Gasser of Brixen, Austrian Tyrol gave a speech to the Council Fathers that lasted nearly four hours. He spoke of three main points of contention: the pope's *personal, separate* and *absolute* infallibility:

> In what sense is the pope's infallibility *personal?* It is personal in that it belongs to the Roman Pontiff, not the Roman Church, or the Roman See. The infallibility is personal in as far as it belongs to each legitimate occupant of the Roman See. But it is not personal as belonging to the pope as private person or private doctor. So we do not speak of personal infallibility although we attribute it to the person of the Roman Pontiff, not as an individual person, but as a public person, the Head of the Church in his relation to the Universal Church. Nor is the pope infallible simply as pope, but as subject to the divine assistance guiding him.[483]

> In what sense is the infallibility of the pope to be called *separate?* It may be called separate, or rather distinct, because it is founded on the special promise of Christ, and on the special assistance of the Holy Ghost, which is not the same as that enjoyed by the whole body of the teaching Church joined with its Head.[484]

> In what sense is the pope's infallibility *absolute?* In no sense is it absolute, because absolute infallibility belongs to God alone. The pope's is restricted by limitations and conditions, as set forth in the definition.[485]

Opponents to the Definition of Papal Infallibility

Because of the strong undercurrent caused by influential bishops, priests, laity and government officials a sense of suspicion and distrust pervaded the council until its final session. Many prelates who opposed the formal definition of papal infallibility were Gallicans who believed that the authority of the pope was subordinate to general councils and the consent of the Church.

Bishop Maret of Sura, the dean of the faculty of theology at the Sorbonne even wrote a book against papal infallibility that bordered on heresy. Lord Acton resided in Rome, gathering information about the council proceedings in order to mount an effective attack against papal infallibility.

---

[483] Dom Cuthbert Butler, *The Vatican Council: The Story Told from Inside, Vol. II*, p. 135.
[484] Butler, *Vol. II*, p. 136.
[485] Butler, *Vol. II*, p. 137.

Dr. Döllinger was also a determined opponent of the formal definition of papal infallibility. In letters purported to be from Rome, Döllinger, writing under the pseudonym Quirinus, attacked the work of the council. Numerous pamphlets attacking the doctrine of papal infallibility were disseminated and many of the news reports from the Vatican Council were intentionally falsified by the press.

Professor Hergenröther of Würzburg University wrote the book *Anti-Janus* to counter Döllinger's works. "Like Döllinger, he too, was professor of church history and held a leading position among Catholic scholars in Germany, but, unlike Döllinger, he knew how to combine thoroughly scientific investigation with due respect for the divinely constituted authority of the Church."[486]

Archbishop Friedrich Schwarzenberg of Prague and Archbishop Joseph Rauscher of Vienna were leaders of the Minority and voiced their opposition to the formal declaration of papal infallibility. They were not Catholic dissidents but rather stalwart defenders of the Catholic faith in Austria, especially after the revolutionary movements of 1848. The great revival of Catholicism throughout the Austrian empire was largely due to the zeal of these two prince-archbishops.

The two prelates—especially Rauscher—had also been primary negotiators of the Concordat of 1855 between the Holy See and the Austrian government. Their opposition to the formal definition proposed by the council was not indicative of any unorthodoxy on their part. They opposed the timeliness of the pronouncement because they feared it would result in a wide-scale persecution of the Church.

Some prelates claimed that the definition of papal infallibility would be an obstacle toward unity with the Protestant and Orthodox churches. A number of influential ecclesiastics (among them, Bishop Dupanloup of Orléans, Archbishop Darboy of Paris, Bishop Strossmayer of Sirmio, Archbishop Purcell of Cincinnati, Archbishop Kenrick of St. Louis, Bishop von Ketteler of Mainz and Bishop Hefele of Rotterdam) did all in their power to prevent the formal definition of papal infallibility. However, once the dogma was solemnly proclaimed, they obediently

---

[486] Fr. James MacCaffrey, *History of the Catholic Church in the Nineteenth Century*, p. 445.

assented and bade their clergy follow their example. According to the eyewitness account of Archbishop Manning:

> A certain number were found of the opinion that it was inopportune to define the infallibility of the Roman Pontiff. This was a question of prudence, policy, expedience; not of doctrine or of truth. It was thus that the Church was united twenty years ago [1854] in the belief of the Immaculate Conception, while some were still to be found who doubted the prudence of defining it. Setting aside this one question of opportuneness, there was not in the Council of the Vatican a difference of any gravity, and certainly no difference whatsoever on any doctrine of the faith. I have never been able to hear of five bishops who denied the doctrine of papal infallibility.[487]

Bishop Dupanloup of Orléans

We have already heard of the valor of Bishop Félix Dupanloup of Orléans in wielding his pen to defend the *Syllabus of Errors.* Nevertheless, he strongly opposed the formal definition of papal infallibility. Throughout February and March many bishops engaged in heated debates concerning this topic, voicing their opinions for or against the pronouncement. Bishop Dupanloup, however, surpassed the others in the intensity of his activities. He had six secretaries working to help propagate his message against the proclamation of infallibility and he circulated numerous letters and pamphlets promoting his opinion throughout Europe, especially in Paris and Munich.

Ironically, another of his writings—his doctoral dissertation—had been published many years earlier to defend the infallibility of the Roman Pontiff. His opposition to the proposed definition at the council did not indicate a renouncement of his belief in papal infallibility. Rather, he merely believed the time was inopportune for a universal proclamation.

Need for Papal Infallibility

There is an absolute need for God's protection over the Church in matters of faith and morals in order to assure the precise transmission of truth from age to age. "The Church guided by God, has always taught what it is teaching today. It

---

[487] *The Vatican Council and its Definitions*, pp. 32-33.

cannot change its teachings. It gives the same teaching in every nation, and every century of history."[488] In 1941, Fr. Martin Scott, S.J., expounded this topic in his work entitled, *Reasonableness of Infallibility*.

> No Church can be the Church of Christ which does not profess to be an infallible representative of the Infallible Founder of Christianity. Christ did not establish Christianity in order to have it either perish or mislead....
>
> Christ in establishing His Church endowed Her with an infallible voice which should define the truths of Revelation with Divine certainty when occasion should require it. This infallible voice does not proclaim a new Revelation, but only states definitely what has been Divinely revealed. In so defining Revelation, the pope is not inspired, as were the prophets of old, nor does he announce new doctrines, but simply declares the true sense of the Revelation which has been made once for all. In doing this, he has the guarantee of Jesus Christ that he will be assisted from on high, so that what he defines will be what God intended by the Revelation in question when it was given to mankind.

Fr. Joseph Fenton explains that the teachings of Christ have been preserved through the ages in various manners:

> (A) Not all of the doctrine entrusted to the Church as the content of divine public revelation was immediately, at the very outset of the Church's life, set down in writing by the Fathers [of the Church].
>
> (B) Not all of the ancient *monuments* of divine Apostolic Tradition (the writings and inscriptions of the early Christians) have survived until our time, even though the Tradition itself has survived and is just as perfectly possessed, guarded, and taught by the infallible Church today as it was in apostolic times.
>
> (C) Although the whole content of divine public revelation has always been guarded and presented infallibly by the Church, it has not always been, in its entirety, distinctly conceived and formally expressed.
>
> (D) A doctrine proposed as part of the divine Apostolic Tradition by the true Church of Jesus Christ at any one period in its history cannot possibly be in

---

[488] Parish Priests of Chicago, *Instructions for Non-Catholics*, p. 69.

opposition to what has been taught as divinely revealed by the Church at an earlier time.

(E) A doctrine proposed at any time within the true Church of God as part of divine public revelation must, by reason of the divine assistance promised and given to the Church, have been taught in the past at least in an implicit manner by the majority of the *ecclesia docens.* Moreover, such a teaching could never be denied by a majority of the authentic teachers within the Church.[489] [Yet, they were denied by Vatican II.]

Voting

The council hoped to produce a text of strict theological accuracy, neither supporting nor condemning any of the factions battling over papal infallibility. "The subject of the definition [was] not the controversial ideas of the moment but the traditional belief of the Church, the belief set out by such classic teachers as Bellarmine and St. Thomas."[490]

> The opposition, headed by Dupanloup, was for the most part unwilling openly to vote against the pope, and at the end of June [before the final vote] Dupanloup, and most of his supporters withdrew from Rome to their diocese, on the excuse that the approach of war between France and Germany required that they stand by their flocks.[491]

On July 13, at the 85th session of the council, a final vote could be taken to decide whether papal infallibility would now be formally defined. Of 601 bishops present, 451 voted in favor of the definition, 88 voted against it and 62—suggesting certain corrections to be made—gave their conditional assent. There was some consternation over the fact that one fourth of the bishops, including many noteworthy prelates, failed to give their full assent; however, it was apparent that the definition would be forthcoming.

Many who had voted their dissent opted to leave Rome quietly before the formal promulgation, so they would not be obliged to publicly oppose the decree. However, they declared beforehand their submission to the council's decision if

---

[489] *American Ecclesiastical Review, Vol. CXV,* July-December 1946.
[490] Msgr. Philip Hughes, *Church in Crisis,* pp. 360-361.
[491] E. Hales, *First Vatican Council,* pp. 25-26.

the pope were to promulgate this doctrine. The Franco-Prussian War began on July 19, 1870.

The Decree on Papal Infallibility—*Pastor Aeternus*

The decree that formally defined papal infallibility also addressed the various aspects of papal primacy: its institution, nature, power and infallibility.

> The Roman Pontiffs on their part, according as the condition of the times and circumstances dictated, sometimes calling together ecumenical councils or sounding out the mind of the Church throughout the whole world, sometimes through regional councils, or sometimes using other helps which Divine Providence supplied, have, with the help of God, defined as to be held such matters as they had found consonant with the Holy Scripture and with the Apostolic Tradition. The reason for this is that the Holy Spirit was promised to the successors of St. Peter not that they might make known new doctrine by his revelation, but rather, that with His assistance they might religiously guard and faithfully explain the revelation or Deposit of Faith that was handed down through the apostles. Indeed, it was this apostolic doctrine that all the Fathers held, and the holy orthodox Doctors reverenced and followed. For they fully realized that this See of St. Peter always remains untainted by any error, according to the divine promise of our Lord and Savior made to the prince of His disciples: 'I have prayed for thee, that thy faith may not fail; and do thou, when once thou hast turned again, strengthen thy brethren' [Luke 22:32].[492]

> Now this charism of truth and never failing faith was conferred upon St. Peter and his successors in this Chair, in order that they might perform their supreme office for the salvation of all; that by them the whole flock of Christ might be kept away from the poison of error and be nourished by the food of heavenly doctrine; that with the occasion of schism removed the whole Church might be preserved as one, and, secure on its foundation, stand firm against the gates of hell.[493]

> And so, faithfully keeping to the tradition received from the beginning of the Christian faith, for the glory of God our Savior, for the exultation of the Catholic religion, and for the salvation of Christian peoples, We, with the approval of the sacred council, teach and define that it is a divinely revealed dogma: that the

---

[492] D 1836.
[493] D 1837.

Roman Pontiff, when he speaks *ex cathedra,* that is, [1] when acting in the office of shepherd and teacher of all Christians, [2] he defines, [3] by virtue of his supreme apostolic authority, [4] doctrine concerning faith or morals [5] to be held by the universal Church, possesses through the divine assistance promised to him in the person of St. Peter, the infallibility with which the divine Redeemer willed His Church to be endowed in defining doctrine concerning faith or morals; and that such definitions of the Roman Pontiff are therefore irreformable because of their nature, but not because of the agreement of the Church.[494]

The Vatican Council's decree on papal infallibility included a section from Pope Eugene IV's papal bull *Laetentur Caeli* of the Council of Florence:

...that the Apostolic See and the Roman Pontiff hold primacy over the whole world, and that the Pontiff of Rome himself is the successor of the blessed Peter, the chief of the apostles, and is the true vicar of Christ and head of the whole Church and faith, and teacher of all Christians; and that to him was handed down in blessed Peter, by our Lord Jesus Christ, full power to feed, rule, and guide the universal Church, just as is also contained in the records of the ecumenical councils and the sacred canons.[495]

Cardinal John Henry Newman and the majority of the Church Fathers were very pleased with the final wording of the dogma of papal infallibility. On July 27, 1870 Newman wrote: "For myself, ever since I was a Catholic, I have held the pope's infallibility as a matter of theological opinion; at least, I see nothing in the definition which necessarily contradicts Scripture, Tradition, or History."[496]

Ex Cathedra

In his book, *The Vatican Council and its Definitions: Pastoral Letter to the Clergy,* Cardinal Manning explains the term *ex cathedra* and its historical significance:

The definition limits the infallibility of the Pontiff to the acts which emanate from him *ex cathedra.* This phrase, which has been long and commonly used by theologians, has now, for the first time, been adopted into the terminology of the Church; and in adopting it the Vatican Council fixes its meaning. The Pontiff speaks *ex cathedra* when, and only when, he speaks as the Pastor and Doctor

---

[494] D 1839.
[495] D 1836, July 6, 1439.
[496] Dom B. Butler, *The Church and Infallibility,* p. 15.

[Teacher] of all Christians. By this, all acts of the Pontiff as a private person, or a private doctor, or as a local bishop, or as a sovereign of a state, are excluded. In all these acts the Pontiff may be subject to error. In one, and one only, capacity he is exempt from error; that is, when, as teacher of the whole Church in things of faith and morals.

When a pope speaks *ex cathedra,* he simply makes a public declaration of what has always been the teaching of the Church.

And since the Church is where Peter is, and since Peter speaks through the Roman Pontiff and through his successors continues to live and exercise judgment and offer the truth of faith to those who seek it, therefore divine revelation must be accepted in that sense alone in which it is and has been held by the Roman chair of Blessed Peter, which is the mother and teacher of all churches and has ever kept the faith given by Christ the Lord whole and inviolate, and has taught it to the faithful, showing to all the path of salvation and the doctrine of incorrupt truth.[497]

Fr. Joseph Fenton concisely defines the term *ex cathedra* in his article in the *American Ecclesiastical Review* entitled *Infallibility in the Encyclicals:*

According to the teaching of the Vatican Council itself, the Holy Father speaks infallibly when he issues a definition *ex cathedra*, and he issues a definition ex cathedra when the following conditions are verified:

1) He speaks in his capacity as the ruler and teacher of all Christians.
2) He uses his supreme apostolic authority.
3) The doctrine on which he is speaking has to do with faith or morals.
4) He issues a certain and definitive judgment on that teaching.
5) He wills that this definitive judgment be accepted as such by the Universal Church.[498]

In recent years there have been some misunderstandings concerning the term *ex cathedra*. Literally taken, this term means "from the chair"; therefore some would say a pope must actually be seated in his chair in order to fulfill the requirements for speaking infallibly. This is erroneous. As the following

---

[497] Mansi, LI. 646-650.
[498] Vol. 128, p. 86, January 1953.

explanation illustrates, *ex cathedra* refers to the characteristics that must accompany an infallible proclamation:

> The quality and *condition* of the act of infallible definition is that the pope speaks *ex cathedra*. This term is received in the schools, and its meaning is defined as follows: 'When the pope speaks not as a private doctor, or as bishop of a diocese, but as exercising the office of supreme pastor, and teacher of all Christians.' Moreover, not every way suffices of propounding a doctrine, even as supreme pastor and teacher; but there must be the intention manifested of defining as doctrine, or of putting an end to controversy on some doctrine, by giving a definitive sentence, and propounding that doctrine as to be held by the universal Church. And this property and note of definition in the strict sense the pope should at least in some measure express when he defines a doctrine to be held by the universal Church.[499]

Even a cursory reading of the Vatican Council's definition of infallibility will reveal that it is possible for a pope to promulgate an infallible teaching on his own initiative, without seeking advice or concurrence from any other person. A pope may choose to consult advisors, and prudence might often prompt him to do so; however, the primacy of St. Peter's office endows the pope with power to make infallible proclamations without the collaboration of any others. Such proclamations are binding on the faithful whether the pope uses either his solemn teaching authority or his ordinary teaching authority. The only requirements that must be met are the five characteristics mentioned in *Pastor Aeternus*.

> The council does not so much recognize or define a limit to the pope's infallibility as defend it against those who would make it contingent on other factors—on the consensus of bishops, if not the decrees or canons of a general council. *Therefore such definitions of the Roman Pontiff are of themselves, and not by the consensus of the Church, irreformable.* In this last sentence of the council's definition is the key to its correct interpretation. Failure to take it into account is at the root of the decidedly un-Catholic belief that a pope is liable to err when he does not define a doctrine ex cathedra, even though he be speaking *ex officio*. ...The closing sentence of the council's definition expresses its very

---

[499] Dom Cuthbert Butler, *Vatican Council 1869-1870*, p. 393.

object and purpose, namely the infallibility of the Sovereign Pontiff even when speaking solely on his own authority.[500]

Lightning and Thunder

The last formal working day of the council was July 16, 1870, just two days before the solemn promulgation of *Pastor Aeternus*. An eyewitness described the dramatic scene at St. Peter's Basilica on the remarkable day of the final vote:

> The fateful day of the Public Session, Monday, July 18, dawned in rain, after a night of thunder and lightning. St. Peter's was opened at 7:30 and the Session began at 9. The crowd was not such as had filled St. Peter's to overflowing at the opening Session, December 8: the July heat had dispersed the visitors. The only royalty present was the Infanta of Portugal. A votive Mass of the Holy Ghost was celebrated 'sine cantu' by a cardinal. Then the pope entered and assumed pontifical vestments, the Litany of the Saints was chanted, followed by the hymn 'Veni Creator Spiritus', intoned by the pope. A bishop approached the throne and received from the pope the Constitution 'Pastor Aeternus', and mounting the ambo read it through in a loud and clear voice. Then he put the question: 'Right Reverend Fathers, do the decrees and canons contained in this Constitution please you?' And the voting by 'placet' or 'non placet' began. It was carried through under circumstances of unforeseen impressiveness.[501]

> The storm, which had been threatening all the morning, burst now with the utmost violence, and to many a superstitious mind might have conveyed the idea that it was an expression of divine wrath, as 'no doubt it will be interpreted by the numbers', said one officer of the Palatine Guard. And so the 'placets' of the Fathers struggled through the storm, while the thunder pealed above and the lightning flashed in at every window and down through the dome and every smaller cupola, dividing if not absorbing the attention of the crowd. 'Placet', shouted his Eminence or his Grace, and a loud clap of thunder followed in response, and then the lightning darted about the baldacchino and every part of the church and the conciliar hall, as if announcing the response. So it continued for nearly one hour and a half, during which time the roll was being called, and a more effective scene I have never witnessed. Had all the decorators and all the

---

[500] Bishop Robert McKenna, O.P., *Catholics Forever,* May 2000.
[501] Dom Cuthbert Butler, *The Vatican Council: The Story Told from Inside,* Vol. II, p. 163.

getters-up of ceremonies in Rome been employed, nothing approaching to the solemn splendor of that storm could have been prepared, and never will those who saw it and felt it forget the promulgation of the Constitution of the Church.

The storm was at its height when the result of the voting was taken up to the pope, and the darkness was so thick that a huge taper was necessarily brought and placed by his side as he read the words 'Nosque, sacro approbante Concilio, illa, ut lecta sunt, definimus et apostolica auctoritate confirmamus.' And again the lightning flickered around the hall, and the thunder pealed. The 'Te Deum' and their Benediction followed; the entire crowd fell on their knees, and the pope blessed them in those clear sweet tones distinguishable among a thousand.[502]

The great Session is over. The decree was voted by 533 'placets' to 2 'non placets' amidst the great storm. The lightning flashed into the aula, the thunder rolled over the roof, and glass was broken by the tempest in a window nearly over the pontifical throne and came rattling down. After the votes were given the pope confirmed it at once, and immediately there was a great cheering and clapping from the bishops, and cheers in the body of St. Peter's. Then the 'Te Deum' began, the thunder forming the diapason.[503]

The dogma of papal infallibility was formally declared on July 18, 1870. "Twenty-five Americans were present to vote *placet*. They were Archbishops Spalding, Alemany, Blanchet and John McCloskey, Bishops Amat, Bayley, Conroy, Dubuis, Elder, Gibbons, de Goesbriand, Heiss, Henni, Lootens, Loughlin, William McCloskey, Miége, O'Connell, O'Hara, Persico, Rappe, St. Palais, Shannahan, Williams, and Abbot Wimmer."[504] When they returned to their dioceses, the expected controversy over papal infallibility never materialized.

The two bishops who voted against the decree of papal infallibility were Edward Fitzgerald of Little Rock, Arkansas and Luigi Riccio of Cajazzo, Italy. However, both men subsequently offered their humble obedience to the pope and their submission to the formal decree of the council. The Franco-Prussian War broke out the following day.

---

[502] Dom Cuthbert Butler, *The Vatican Council 1869-1870*, p. 163.
[503] Butler, *The Vatican Council: The Story Told from Inside, Vol. II*, p. 416.
[504] Mansi, LII, 1337-1347.

The Last Days of the Council

Although the council was still officially in session many of the remaining bishops hastily left Rome and returned to their dioceses because political tension in Europe was mounting. During August and September, 120 prelates remained in the Vatican to complete the unfinished business of the council.

Once the French troops stationed in Rome were recalled by Napoleon III in early August 1870, the remaining Papal States were invaded by the Piedmontese army of Victor Emmanuel II. On September 19, 1871, 50,000 Italian troops under the command of General Cadorna were poised for a frontal attack on Rome. An artillery barrage on the following day created a 30-foot breach at Porta Pia at the Aurelian wall while invading forces stormed into the city.

The 12,000 men of the papal army were commanded by General Kanzler. They held their ground until Pope Pius IX requested them to surrender in order to prevent further loss of life. A white flag on the cross of St. Peter's Basilica signaled their final capitulation. Rome, the last papal stronghold, fell to the Italian armies.

> Persons suspected of sympathizing with the cause of the pope were murdered on the streets or thrown into the waters of the Tiber. Buildings were demolished. Confessionals, pulpits, kneeling benches, missals, rituals and other church furniture were brought out into the streets, heaped up and set on fire. Pictures, images and crucifixes were stolen and carried along the streets in derisive triumph.[505]

At the beginning of Pope Pius IX's reign the Papal States comprised 18,000 square miles. The terms of surrender stated that the sovereign pontiff's possessions would now consist solely of the 108 acres of the Vatican (the smallest independent state in the world), the Lateran and the papal summer residence at Castelgandolfo. The new Italian government also promised the Church freedom for councils and conclaves and an annual indemnity of 3,225,000 lires to the reigning pope. As a result of the political upheaval, Pope Pius IX suspended the council indefinitely on October 20 and it never resumed its work.

---

[505] Fr. Richard Brennan, *A Popular Life of Pope Pius the Ninth*, p. 253.

Aftermath

Bishop Dupanloup, who had worked so untiringly against the formal proclamation of papal infallibility, in February 1871 wrote to Pope Pius IX (once the hostilities had ended):

> 'It has been made known to me that Your Holiness wishes for something from me relative to the constitution of July 18. I have no difficulty in this matter; I have written and spoken only against the inopportuneness of the definition. As to the doctrine I have always professed it, not only in my heart, but in my public writings, ...I am preparing an ordinance in which I propose to promulgate the constitutions of April 24 and July 18.'[506] Soon after this, the pastoral was issued promulgating the decrees of the council, to which he gave his formal adhesion.[507]

The loyalty of Archbishop Darboy of Paris to the Catholic Church was later portrayed when he was taken hostage along with other Parisian clergy by a band of Communists during the Franco-Prussian War. They were brutally murdered by their captors on May 27, 1871.

Victor Emmanuel II died on January 9, 1878. "Twenty-nine days later the last Pope-King [Pius IX] passed away. One of the latest acts of Pius IX had been to send Monsignor Marinelli, his own father confessor, to the dying Victor Emmanuel with his blessing and with the Blessed Sacrament which was administered by the royal almoner, Canon Anzino."[508]

Foundation of the Schismatic Old Catholic Church

Dr. Ignaz Döllinger and J. Friedrich, his friend and biographer, were excommunicated on April 17, 1871 because of their refusal to accept the dogma of papal infallibility. Fellow dissidents from Germany, Switzerland and Austria formed the Old Catholic Church in that same year.

Professor Joseph Reinkens of the University of Breslau was consecrated bishop by the Dutch Jansenist bishop of Rotterdam to provide orders for the schismatic church. Today numerous Old Catholic sects are found in Germany, the Netherlands, Switzerland and the United States of America. Döllinger

---

[506] *Lac* 999.
[507] Dom Cuthbert Butler, *The Vatican Council: The Story Told from Inside, Vol. I*, p. 119.
[508] Lord Acton, *Cambridge Modern History, Vol. XII*, p. 216

disassociated himself from the schismatic church during the Second Old Catholic Congress of 1872. In 1887 he wrote, "I have no wish to be a member of a schismatic church. I am alone."[509]

> Though Döllinger was instrumental in organizing the Old Catholic movement, he never formally joined it. He attended Mass in Roman Catholic churches, but did not receive the sacraments. All attempts to reconcile him with the Roman Catholic Church were unsuccessful, and he received the last rites from Friedrich, now an Old Catholic priest.[510]

> This revolt did not break completely with Roman Catholicism. It rejected papal infallibility, the doctrine of the Immaculate Conception, compulsory celibacy of the priesthood, and in some instances the Filioque clause of the Nicene Creed, but kept much of the other doctrine, creed, customs, and liturgy of the Roman Catholic Church. It was also most anxious to preserve the orders and the Apostolic Succession of its priests and bishops, in as much as the Apostolic Succession was considered vital to valid Christian ministry. Much confusion has resulted in conflicting claims of succession and validity of orders, especially in American Old Catholic churches.[511]

Additional Information Regarding Papal Infallibility

Msgr. Van Noort writes in *Dogmatic Theology Vol. II*: "*The privilege of infallibility is not merely the absence of error,* but the *impossibility of erring.* It is of course a *supernatural gift,* and since it works not to the advantage of the recipients themselves but to that of the whole Church it is a *gratia gratis data* or charism. It is often called 'the charism of truth.' "

In its *Dogmatic Constitution concerning the Catholic Faith,* the Vatican Council of 1870 teaches that we must believe the Church's divinely revealed doctrines. These doctrines are proposed to us by both Her ordinary and extraordinary teaching authority: "Moreover, by divine and Catholic faith, everything must be believed that is contained in the written word of God or in

---

[509] William Whalen, *Separated Brethren,* p. 203.
[510] T. O'Brien, *Corpus Dictionary of Western Churches,* p. 271.
[511] Frank Mead, *Handbook of Denominations in the United States,* pp. 178-179.

Tradition, and that is proposed by the Church as a divinely revealed object of faith either in a solemn decree or in Her ordinary, universal teaching."[512]

Pope Pius XII reaffirmed this when he wrote:

> Nor must it be thought that what is expounded in Encyclical Letters does not of itself demand consent, since in writing such Letters the popes do not exercise the supreme power of their Teaching Authority. For these matters are taught with the ordinary teaching authority, of which it is true to say: 'He who heareth you, heareth me' (Luke 10: 16); and generally what is expounded in and inculcated in Encyclical Letters already for other reasons appertans to Catholic doctrine. But if the Supreme Pontiffs in their official documents purposely pass judgment on a matter up to that time under dispute, it is obvious that the matter, according to the mind and will of the same Pontiffs, cannot be any longer considered a question open to discussion among theologians.[513]

What is an encyclical? "Encyclicals are usually concerned with important matters that seriously affect the welfare of the Church and Her children. They explain the line of conduct to be taken in reference to urgent practical questions, prescribe remedies for evil foreseen or already existent, condemn some prevalent form of error, or exhort to a more perfect spiritual life."[514]

The Infallibility of Church Teaching

The Church may convey Her infallible teaching to us either on Her solemn or Her ordinary authority. With Her solemn authority She commands us to believe all doctrines contained in the four Creeds,[515] or, expressed in the Definitions of popes or general councils.[516] With Her ordinary authority She commands us to

---

[512] D 1792.
[513] *Humani Generis,* October 12, 1950.
[514] Charles Doyle, *Life of Pope Pius XII,* p. 223.
[515] The Apostles, the Nicene, the Athanasian, and the Creed or Profession of Pius IV. The last-named, issued in 1564, repeats the Nicene Creed and gives a summary of the doctrines defined by the Council of Trent; Pius IX inserted in it an acceptance of the decrees of the Vatican Council, "in particular of those affirming the Primacy and Infallibility of the Roman Pontiff"; and Pius X appended to it a solemn repudiation of the errors of Modernism.
[516] A General Council of the Church is a meeting of Bishops, representative of the entire Church, summoned by the pope, deliberating under his direction, and issuing decrees or condemnations, which however have no force unless he confirms them. That the concurrence and approval of the pope are necessary for the work of a general council follows from the doctrine of Apostolicity.

believe the doctrine which the pope and the bishops throughout the world, in the everyday exercise of their pastoral office, unanimously teach, as revealed truth. The Church is as infallible in Her ordinary teaching as She is in Her solemn teaching. The only points of distinction between the two which we need note are: (1) Her solemn teaching is made known at once to all the faithful by a most public and solemn declaration and always carries with a formal and express warning that its rejection means rejection of God's revealed word; it is thus a most effective organ of infallibility, a most effective means of combating widespread error. (2) Her ordinary teaching though less effective as an organ of infallibility, is of greater importance, because it is Her ordinary, every-day means of propagating and preserving the faith, and has gone on without interruption since Apostolic times. (3) Her solemn teaching is of rare occurrence and is never more than a clear and emphatic explanation of doctrines that have always formed part of Her ordinary teaching.[517]

Possessors of Infallibility

Dr. Ludwig Ott lists those who possess infallibility:

[These] Are the pope and the whole episcopate, that is, the totality of the bishops, including the pope, the head of the episcopate.

- The pope is infallible when he speaks ex cathedra. (De fide.)
- The totality of the bishops is infallible, when they, either assembled in general council or scattered over the earth, propose a teaching of faith or morals as one to be held by all the faithful. (De fide.)

The Vatican Council declares: "In the Apostolic See the Catholic religion has always been preserved untarnished" (D 1833). "The See of Peter always remains unimpaired by any error, according to the divine promise of our Lord" (D 1836).

"Peter is the foundation stone of the Church: of a Church which is invincible and for all time."[518] It is inconceivable that Jesus, who preached from Peter's vessel (which is a symbol of the Catholic Church), would allow Peter's successors to teach heretical doctrines.

---

[517] Bishop M. Sheehan, *Apologetics and Catholic Doctrine,* pp. 177-178.
[518] Msgr. Angel Herrera, *Preacher's Encyclopedia, Vol. III,* p. 308. "...and the gates of hell shall not prevail against it." (Matthew 16: 18)

The three tiers of the papal tiara symbolize the office of the pope: to teach, rule and sanctify. He is to teach the unblemished truth as Jesus did. He is to rule as Vicar of Christ on earth: correcting abuses and upholding God's law. He is to preserve intact the means of sanctification: the Holy Sacrifice of the Mass and the sacraments. "To define a doctrine is to be exact in teaching it, but to teach does not mean to invent. The Church in every age has defined doctrines, but has not invented any."[519]

Msgr. Van Noort summarizes the reasons for papal infallibility:

> It is evident from Christ's promises that the teaching office of the Church was endowed with infallibility so that it might be able to carry out its mission properly: to safeguard reverently, explain confidently and defend effectively the Deposit of Faith. If the Church were infallible only in the field of revealed truth and not in the matters annexed thereto, it would be like a general who was assigned to defend a city but was given no authority to build up defenses or to destroy the materiel which the enemy had assembled.[520]

Matters relating to infallibility include the Holy Sacrifice of the Mass, the Seven Sacraments and the teachings of the Catholic Church because they were established by Christ. Even the pope cannot substantially change these essential elements of the Catholic Faith.

Prussian Chancellor Bismarck erroneously claimed that papal infallibility limited the power of the bishops. This notion was refuted by 23 German bishops who attended the council and whose letter was approved by Pope Pius IX on March 2, 1875. Excerpts are given below:

> …We cannot call the pope's power over ecclesiastical matters an absolute monarchy. He is subject to Divine Law and to that which Jesus Christ had in mind for His Church. He cannot modify the Church's constitution which was given by its Founder…

> …The bishops are not the simple instruments of the pope, nor his mere functionaries without personal responsibility…

---

[519] Fr. Thomas Cox, *The Pillar and Ground of the Truth*, p. 236.
[520] *Christ's Church*, p. 111.

...As Vatican Council declared in clear and exact terms, infallibility belongs exclusively to the teaching power of the pope and this power extends exactly over the same area as the infallible teaching of the Church. This power is bound by the content of Sacred Scripture and Tradition, as well as to the doctrinal decisions that have been made by the Church in the past.[521]

A legitimate pope cannot contradict or deny what was first taught by Christ to His Church. An essential change in belief constitutes the establishment of a new religion.

A Heretical Pope—an Impossibility

The attribute of infallibility was given to the popes in order that the revealed doctrines and teachings of Christ would remain forever intact and unchanged. It is contrary to faith and reason to blindly follow an alleged pope who attempts to destroy the Catholic Faith—for there have been 41 documented antipopes. Papal infallibility means that the Holy Ghost guides and preserves the Catholic Church from error through the succession of legitimate popes who have ruled the Church through the centuries. All Catholics, including Christ's Vicar on earth, the pope, must accept all the unchangeable teachings of Christ and the Catholic Church, including the doctrinal pronouncements of the past popes. These infallible teachings form a vital link between Christ and St. Peter and his successors.

If a pope did not accept and believe this entire body of formulated teachings (the Deposit of Faith), he could not himself be a Catholic. He would cease to belong to Christ's Church. If he no longer belongs to the Catholic Church, he cannot be Her head.

One who, after baptism, retaining the name of Christian pertinaciously denies (rejects) or doubts a divinely revealed truth is a heretic[522] and by that fact ceases to be Catholic. A heretic incurs ipso facto excommunication,[523] i.e., (by that very fact) automatically, without sentence of law. A heretic is not a Catholic and the pope must be a Catholic.

---

[521] Paul Empie, *Papal Primacy and the Universal Church,* p. 150.
[522] *Codex Juris Canonici,* Canon 1325, no. 2.
[523] Canon 2314, no. 1.

In 1874, Cardinal Newman wrote an essay entitled *On Disobeying the Pope*:

> Cardinal Turrecremata says, '…To know in what cases he is to be obeyed and what not… it is said in the Acts of the Apostles, 'one ought to obey God rather than man'; therefore, were the pope to command anything against Sacred Scripture, or the articles of faith, or the truth of the sacraments, or the commands of the natural or Divine Law, he ought not to be obeyed.'

Theologians have debated whether a heretic could occupy the Chair of Peter. The eminent Doctor of the Church, St. Robert Bellarmine, stated:

> The pope simply and absolutely is above the Universal Church, in that he is the head of the whole Church on earth; so he is above a general council, and can recognize no judge upon earth above himself. He cannot be judged, punished, or deposed by a general council or by any human authority. But should a pope become a formal heretic he would by the very fact cease to be pope and could be judged and declared deposed by the Church.[524]

The Vatican Council stated: "For it is impossible that the words of Our Lord Jesus Christ who said, 'Thou art Peter and upon this rock I will build my Church' [Matt. 16: 18], should not be verified. And their truth has been proved by the course of history, for in the Apostolic See the Catholic religion has always been kept unsullied, and its teachings kept holy."[525]

A heretic, that is one who is not a member of the Church, is incapable of election to the papacy by Divine Law. Cardinal Billot says, "Given the hypothesis of a heretical pope, such a pope would automatically lose his power because he would be cast outside the body of the Church by his own will."[526]

Obviously, the pope cannot substantially change the faith, morals or worship of the Catholic Church. Fr. John O'Brien states:

> The pope has no authority to invent a new doctrine. He is not the author of revelation, but only its interpreter and expounder. He has no more authority to break a Divine Law or to distort an iota of Scripture than you or I. His function is to hand down unchanged the deposit of divine truth to all generations of men.[527]

---

[524] Dom Culbert Butler, *Vatican Council 1869-1870*, pp. 40-41.
[525] D 1833.
[526] *De Ecclesia Christi*, 5th ed., 1: 632.
[527] *Is Papal Infallibility Reasonable?*, p. 10.

Therefore, a heretical pope is deposed by his public sin against Divine Law. Were a pope ever to teach formal heresy, he would cease to be pope. There can be no such thing as a heretical pope. This is an oxymoron—heresy and the papacy are diametrically opposed and the terms are irreconcilable.

In his letter of May 25, 1999, Fr. Martin Stépanich, OFM says:

> If it is true, as some theologians reasonably maintain, that a true pope, one validly elected, *cannot become a heretic,* because of special divine protection, and cannot for that reason fall from the papacy, then the only logical conclusion to draw is that a heretic occupying the Chair of Peter was a heretic already *before* being elected, and could therefore not have been a legitimate valid candidate for election to the papacy to begin with.

If any baptized person (even an alleged pope) "pertinaciously denies or doubts any of the truths which must be believed by an obligation of divine and Catholic faith, he is a heretic; if he gives up the Christian faith entirely, he is an apostate..."[528] Obviously the pope cannot substantially change 2,000 years of Catholic faith, morals and worship. Canon Law states: "If one after the reception of baptism, while retaining the name of Christian, pertinaciously denies or doubts any of the truths which must be believed by an obligation of divine and Catholic faith, he is a heretic."[529]

A heretic ceases to belong to the Catholic Church and loses his office and authority. This is not a matter of "judging the pope," it is a recognition of fact. Popes and general councils don't create new doctrines; they merely clarify existing teaching.

"All apostates from the Christian faith, and all heretics and schismatics: 1. Are ipso facto excommunicated; 2. If after due warning they fail to amend, they are to be deprived of any benefice, dignity, pension, office, or other position which they may have in the Church, they are to be declared infamous, and clerics after a repetition of the warning are to be deposed."[530]

---

[528] John Abbo and Jerome Hannan, *The Sacred Canons,* p. 562. Canon 1325.
[529] *Codex Juris Canonici,* canon 1325, no. 2.
[530] Canon 2314, no. 1.

Canon Law lists eight cases in which clerics are deposed from ecclesiastical offices without any declaration by the public profession of heresy. Canon 188, no. 4, states: "Through tacit resignation, accepted by the law itself, all offices become vacant ipso facto and without any declaration if a cleric: …4. Has publicly forsaken the Catholic Faith."

> No one, unless he profess the Catholic Faith, can hold any office—that is, lay valid claim to authority in the Catholic Church. For the faithful to know this fact and refuse obedience, no formality is required; neither sentence passed by a court nor any other official pronouncement, nor a formally expressed resignation accepted by some official. Defection itself from the Catholic Faith constitutes resignation.[531]

Fr. John Sullivan discussed the possibility of a heretical pope. "Suppose that a pope becomes a heretic. Suppose that he openly rejected a truth of faith, which he is bound to believe as much as we are. What would happen? Theologians in general maintain that thereby he would cease to be pope, and that the Church would have the right and the power to judge him for heresy."[532]

St. Robert Bellarmine enumerated five opinions concerning the possibility of a heretical pope in his work entitled *De Romano Pontifice:*

1. The pope cannot be a heretic;
2. Falling into heresy, even merely internal, the pope loses the pontificate;
3. Even though he falls into heresy, the pope does not lose his charge;
4. The pope heretic is not deposed *ipso facto,* but must be declared deposed by the Church;
5. The pope heretic is ipso facto deposed at the moment in which his heresy becomes manifest.

He concluded his study by stating: "The fifth opinion [regarding a heretical pope] therefore is true; a pope who is a manifest heretic by that fact ceases to be pope and head [of the Church], just as he by the fact ceases to be a Christian."

---

[531] Benjamin Dryden, Canon 188.4 or *Where is the Church?*, p. 2.
[532] *Fundamentals of Catholic Belief,* pp. 124-125.

Concerning the deposition of a pope, the *Catholic Dictionary* states: "A pope can only be deposed for heresy, expressed or implied, and then only by a general council. It is not strictly deposition, but a declaration of fact, since by his heresy he has already ceased to be head of the Church. ...The deposition of antipopes was a different matter, for these had never in fact been pope."[533]

The question of a heretical pope was raised by one of the cardinals at the Vatican Council of 1870:

'What is to be done with the pope if he becomes a heretic?' It was answered that 'there has never been such a case; the council of bishops could depose him for heresy, for from the moment he becomes a heretic he is not the head or even a member of the Church. The Church would not be, for a moment, obliged to listen to him when he begins to teach a doctrine the Church knows to be a false doctrine, and he would cease to be pope, being deposed by God Himself. If the pope, for instance, were to say that the belief in God is false, you would not be obliged to believe him, or if he were to deny the rest of the creed; I believe in Christ, etc. The supposition is injurious to the Holy Father in the very idea, but serves to show you the fullness with which the subject has been considered and the ample thought given to every possibility. If he denies any Dogma of the Church held by every true believer, he is no more pope than either you or I.[534]

Conclusion

Christ established His Church upon the rock of Peter and promised that the gates of Hell would not prevail against it. St. Ambrose tells us that faith is the foundation of the Church; because of the faith, and not the person of Peter, the Church will always be preserved from error.

To guarantee the lifeline of truth, Our Lord gave the attribute of infallibility to His Vicar on earth. If it were possible at any time for the pope using his supreme apostolic authority to teach error on matters of faith and morals to the universal Church, it would affect the entire Church, thereby giving the gates of Hell power to prevail over Her.

---

[533] p. 389.
[534] Fr. James McGovern, *The Life and Work of Pope Leo XIII*, p. 241.

If the Vicar of Christ on earth could lead the Church astray, the devil would have prevailed over the immaculate Bride of Christ, the Church. This is an impossibility because we have Christ's guarantee that His Church, the Catholic Church, will last until the end of time, unvanquished by the lies and deceits of Satan. Jesus Christ, the Son of God, can neither deceive nor be deceived. He will protect His Church from false doctrine until the end of time.

The attribute of infallibility was given to the pope so that the revealed doctrines and teachings of Christ would remain forever intact and unchanged. Any pope who changes such teachings held for almost 2,000 years is a heretic and ceases to belong to the Catholic Church. A heretic is not a Catholic and therefore cannot be head of the Church.

Our study of the 20 General Councils of the Catholic Church (325 AD—1870) concludes with Vatican I. During that same period, there were also 20 false councils. Some were convoked by antipopes and many taught heresy. On which side would you place Vatican II?

St. Vincent of Lerins asserted: "Do not be misled by various and passing doctrines. In the Catholic Church Herself we must be careful to hold what has been believed everywhere, always and by all; for that alone is truly and properly Catholic."[535]

Part I now comes to a close. You have journeyed step-by-step through some of the most turbulent periods in Catholic history and have witnessed the endless waves of attack that have been crashing against the Rock of the Church since its inception.

Part II will reveal the amazing parallels between the doctrinal errors of the past and those emanating from Vatican II.

---

[535] (Commonitorium, 2, 5) 5th century.

Part II

Vatican II and Its Aftermath

(1962 to the present)

Introduction

Throughout Her tumultuous history, the Catholic Church has had to defend Herself against enemies both from within and without. Added to these assaults have been the cunning deceits employed by the devils to undermine the faith.

There are many important lessons we can learn from the past General Councils of the Church, since they parallel conditions today. As a result of the bishops rallying together under the authority of the pope during the 20 General Councils, the Church derived numerous benefits: Catholic truths were defended, heresies were condemned and the doctrines of the Faith defined more clearly and set forth more precisely. General councils further helped to restore ecclesiastical discipline, thereby reforming the morals of both the clergy and the faithful alike.

It has been, however, during the past 40 years that the Catholic Church has undergone some of the most radical and revolutionary changes in Her history: changes that have left members of the Church confused, frustrated and bewildered. Observing the devastating effects of these changes, many Catholics have asked themselves, "What has happened to the Catholic Church?"

The spiritual crisis of our day, the appalling decline of morals and universal loss of faith can be directly traced back to the Second Vatican Council (1962-1965). This council, better known as Vatican II, directly attacked the heart of the Catholic Faith—her immutable doctrines, the Holy Sacrifice of the Mass and the Seven Sacraments.

The 1960's, a "Decade of Tumult and Change,"[1] ushered in a new age which cast aside Christian morals and traditions. The world " 'underwent a social, political and spiritual transformation so wrenching that it ripped these societies apart, destroying traditional values and replacing them with a whole new set of notions about what's good and bad. ...An 'anything-goes' attitude pervaded society.' Russian author Aleksandr Solzhenitsyn stated: 'To destroy a people, you must first sever its roots.' "[2] Some of the Fathers of Vatican II seemed to have this very goal in mind when they set about severing the roots of Catholicism.

---

[1] *Life,* December 26, 1969.
[2] *Insight,* March 4, 2002, "Predicting the West's Decline," by Stephen Goode, pp. 24, 39.

A. The History and Origin of Vatican II
A New Council is Convened

On January 25, 1959, a mere 90 days after his election, John XXIII startled the world with the announcement that he intended to convoke a general council. "John's first Secretary of State, Cardinal Tardini, is said to have confessed that when the pope first mentioned to him his intention to summon a general council he thought that he must be out of his mind."[3]

> The thought of a council in the Roman Catholic Church was surprising. The fact that it was to be 'ecumenical' was puzzling. To Protestants and Orthodox believers the word 'ecumenical' suggested a gathering of all Christian churches. The radio announcement seemed to recognize other Christian churches as ecclesial communities, implying a willingness to deal with them directly. ...The official published wording of John's speech spoke rather of an invitation 'to the *faithful* of the separated communities' (emphasis added). ...One thing was sure: both texts spoke of 'unity,' and not of 'union' or unification,' both of which would have implied a 'return' to Rome and thus been unacceptable to Protestant and Orthodox Christians.[4]

Many bishops asked themselves, "Why is a council being called?" In the first half of the 20th century the Catholic Church experienced unprecedented growth. Catholic churches, schools, seminaries and convents were bulging. In the United States "seventy-five percent of married Catholics attended Mass every Sunday. Fifty percent received Holy Communion at least once a month. Eighty-five percent of single people went to Mass every Sunday, and fifty percent of them received Holy Communion monthly. College-educated Catholics were the most faithful of all."[5] Nevertheless, John XXIII insisted on calling a council.

Preparatory Work

Prior to the council a number of conservative[6] prelates, many from the Curia,[7] spent 45 months in preparation, drafting 75 traditional schemas (topics to

---

[3] Nicolas Cheetham, *Keepers of the Keys*, p. 293.
[4] Rev. Bob Bonnot, *John XXIII*, p. 156.
[5] Msgr. George Kelly, *The Battle for the American Church*, p. 455.
[6] Derived from the Latin *conserváre* which means "to preserve."
[7] Before Vatican II it consisted of various Congregations, offices and tribunals that assisted the pope in the government and administration of the Church.

be discussed during the council). However, shortly before the opening of the council, John XXIII scrapped the entire schema and drafted a new 20-point schema. Archbishop Marcel Lefebvre, the Superior General of the Holy Ghost Fathers and a member of the preparatory committee, reported that of the original schema "nothing remained, not a single sentence. All had been thrown out."[8]

John XXIII was indeed very crafty. By allowing the Curia and hierarchy to propose orthodox topics for discussion, he led them into believing that the teachings of Vatican II would parallel those of past general councils. Meanwhile, the Modernists and Ecumenists, under the direction of John XXIII, were taking control of the council to further their agenda of interfaith dialogue and worship. Through the 16 documents of Vatican II (2 dogmatic constitutions, 2 pastoral constitutions, 3 declarations and 9 decrees) they introduced a New Mass, doubtfully valid sacraments and major doctrinal changes.

Due to the last-minute scrapping of their schema (the fruit of four years of work) by John XXIII, many conservative prelates who came to the council were disorganized and unprepared for the Modernist onslaught that awaited them. "The council was born, so to speak, of itself, independently of the preparation which had been made for it. The paradoxical outcome of the council, the breaking of the council rules, and the setting aside of the council that had been prepared are passed over in silence [by many authors]."[9]

The international press often vilified those who voiced strong opposition to doctrinal changes as opponents of progress and ecumenism. The novel and sensational have always dominated the news—the usual and traditional have not. For this reason, since the Second Vatican Council was held in the presence of the media, those who were looking for change and novelty were the subjects of the news storylines, while the established and traditional were denounced.

There were a total of 2,860 Council Fathers from 79 countries who participated in the four sessions of Vatican II. Among the bishops there were 239 Americans and 430 Italians. Also attending the council were 200 *periti*

---

[8] *A Bishop Speaks* (Angelus Press, Kansas City, MO, 1985), p. 131.
[9] Romano Amerio, *Iota Unum*, p. 49. For an unbiased treatment of Vatican II, see *The Rhine Flows into the Tiber,* by Fr. Ralph Wiltgen, S.V.D.

(Modernist theologians) who accompanied their bishops and exerted tremendous influence on them. Vatican II opened on October 11, 1962, holding annual nine-week sessions during October, November and December. The council, which was held in the nave of St. Peter's Basilica, concluded on December 8, 1965.

Attacks from Without and Within

The pervasive spirit of worldliness and individualism strongly influenced and slowly undermined Catholic morality and personal responsibility. Archbishop Pell of Australia describes how situational ethics and secular humanism weakened family unity and destabilized society:

> [For] over two thousand years the Catholic Church has weathered persecutions, storms and trials, enemies from within and outside. Secularism will prove a more enduring challenge than Communism and the lethal influences on Catholic life, the acid rain, are coming from the society around us.
>
> In the nineteenth century the philosopher Nietzsche claimed that the newspaper had replaced daily prayer. Later television replaced the newspaper and now the Internet is replacing television. Last century G. K. Chesterton wrote that man has always lost his way, but modern man has lost his address.[10]

The Catholic Church was founded by Jesus Christ for the salvation of souls. Therefore, the devil and his agents have, throughout history, used all the means at their disposal in their attempts to destroy Her. Various world leaders from Nero[11] to Castro have persecuted and martyred millions of Catholics. The attacks continue.

> International Freemasonry and Communism: These are the two most terrible enemies the Church has so far had to face in Her long history. At times this persecution has been a bloody one and at times it has gone underground, to destroy and undermine all that the Church of God stands for in terms of faith or morals.[12]

---

[10] *Catholic World Report,* July 2003, "From Vatican II to Today."

[11] Nero began the persecution of the Christians in 64 A.D. "in which thousands of all ages in both sexes perished. Some were burned, some crucified, others bound and thrown to wild beasts, and others wrapped in pitch and set on fire to serve as lamps in the garden of the tyrant." John Frost, *Pictorial History of the World,* (1855), p. 354.

[12] Angel Cardinal Herrera, *The Preacher's Encyclopedia, Vol. IV,* p. 474.

Heretical bishops and priests have endeavored to destroy Her from within, using false pretenses—much like the Trojan Horse. Modernists have used the same ploy to "further" the Church during the last 40 years.

Communist Infiltration in the Church

Prior to the reign of John XXIII the Catholic Church represented the world's most effective opponent of Communism:

> Not so long ago one used to hear the remark, by both Catholic and non-Catholic, that the Catholic Church is in the forefront of the fight against Communism. This is as it should be, for the atheism and materialism of Communism are the antithesis of Christian doctrine; and the destruction of religion is a major Communist goal.[13]

Marxists were determined to destroy this bastion of religion and freedom.

> Bishop Fulton Sheen, auxiliary bishop of New York, while giving a discourse at Saint Suzanna of Rome revealed that in 1936 the American Communists recruited some agents for infiltrating the religious communities to destroy them from within. An appeal was made for volunteers to become priests and study in the seminaries.[14]

> Albert Vassart, a former member of the French Communist Party revealed in 1955 that Moscow had issued a 1936 order that carefully selected members of Communist youth to enter seminaries and, after training, receive ordination as priests. ...Manning Johnson, a former official of the Communist Party in America, gave the following testimony in 1953 to the House Un-American Activities Committee: 'Once the tactic of infiltration of religious institutions was set by the Kremlin... The Communists discovered that the destruction of religion could proceed much faster through the infiltration of the Church by Communists operating within the Church itself.'[15]

---

[13] Frank Brophy, *Catholics, Communists and the Commonweal.*
[14] André Mignot, *Les Fumees de Satan*, p. 45. "Mgr. Fulton Sheen, évêque auxíliarè de New York, dans un discoùrs prononcé à sainte Suzanne de Rome, révéla qu´en 1936 les communistes américains reçurent des consignes pour s`infiltrer au seìn des communautés religieuses pour les détruirè de l`íntérieur, un appel fut lancé à des volontaires pour entrer dans les ordres et faire des études dans les séminaires."
[15] *Communist Infiltration of the Roman Catholic Clergy*, Gregorian Press, p. 1.

Bella Dodd, a former member of the Communist Party of America, "herself had encouraged almost 1,000 young radicals to infiltrate the seminaries and religious orders."[16] " 'Young men who had neither faith nor morals,' was the way she put it. It seems legitimate at this point to wonder whether some of the horrendous sexual scandals that have rocked the Church in the United States are not traced to Bella Dodd's efficiency."[17] Alice von Hildebrand, who was a close friend of Dodd, has written:

> After dedicating 21 years of her life to the Enemy, she was so shattered when her eyes opened that she wanted to devote the years left to her to penance and to join the most severe penitential order. She turned for advice to Bishop Fulton Sheen. She opened her heart to him, went to confession and put herself under his guidance. He became her spiritual director and gave her the order to remain in the world and open the eyes of Americans to the deadly poison of Communism, its atheism, its hatred of God and the Church. She lectured extensively.
>
> ...I recall that one day my husband—who had become increasingly worried about what was dubbed 'the spirit of Vatican II'—said to her, 'Bella, at times I wonder whether the Church has not been infiltrated.' I can solemnly testify that she answered, 'Dear professor, you fear it; I *know* it. When I was a fanatic Communist, I was in close contact with four cardinals in the Vatican working for us. They are still active today.'
>
> ...One of the tasks of the KGB, the FBI and the CIA is to recruit double agents. There is not a single organization that does not aim at infiltration. If they don't, they will inevitably be defeated. Stalin (like every devil) was immensely clever. Being an ex-seminarian, he knew the power that faith exercises upon man's soul; he also knew best the means of weakening and destroying it. He would have been very stupid indeed had he not tried to infiltrate the Vatican.[18]

Communists have attempted by various means to destroy the Catholic Church. A document entitled *The Catholic Church in Cuba: A Program of Action* was published in numerous languages in the late 1960's and contained guidelines

---

[16] *Communist Infiltration of the Roman Catholic Clergy*, 1.
[17] *Crisis*, March 2003, p. 6.
[18] *Crisis*, "Letters to the editor," pp. 5-6.

on how to subvert the Church. It was successfully used in Poland, Czechoslovakia, Romania and China, and stated:

> The Catholic Church is a reactionary organization which promotes counter-revolutionary activities within the People's Democracies. If the People's Democracies are to continue to progress toward the Communist State, they must first and foremost put an end to the influence of the Catholic Church and its activities. We must not make the counter-revolutionist leaders of the masses [Catholic bishops and priests] appear like martyrs.

Their plan also included attempts to replace Christ's gospel with the social gospel. Bishop William Adrian has written: "On those few bishops and priests and lay people who dared to offer opposition to these Communist tactics, the smear [character assassination] was used, a favorite Communist tactic..."[19] As a result, many of the clergy refused to oppose Communism and remained culpably silent in spite of the fact that the laity needed their strong leadership.

Fr. Francis Fenton explains other Communist goals:

> To destroy religion and religious institutions, to eliminate belief in God and to break down traditional moral standards, to discredit the Church and the clergy—all of these have long been priority objectives of the Communist conspirators and their allies. The Communists well know that so long as belief in God and the practice of religion and obedience to the moral law are prevalent in a particular country, as long as the clergy remains effective in the performance of their spiritual duties, the subversive task of the Reds is nearly impossible. They quickly learned that a frontal attack upon the churches would get them nowhere, only exposing their hand. So, the strategy became one of infiltration, of gradually bringing this or that religious organization around to promoting some portion of the Communist line, of subtle and patient indoctrination of the innocent, of steady boring from within. ...The progress of Communism in the Catholic Church, then, has been a very slow process. Nonetheless, the termites have been at work. ...We know that the Communists are 'masters of deceit' and infiltration and subversion.[20]

---

[19] "The Threat to the Church in the U.S.," *The Wanderer,* February 20, 1969.
[20] *Review of the News,* October 16, 1968.

Pope Pius XI noted various means employed by the Communists to further their agenda in his encyclical *Divini Redemptoris* of March 19, 1937:

> Aware of the universal desire for peace, the leaders of Communism pretend to be the most zealous promoters and propagandists in the movement for world amity. Yet, at the same time, they stir up class warfare which causes rivers of blood to flow …They try perfidiously to worm their way even into professedly Catholic and religious organizations. They invite Catholics to collaborate with them in the realm of so-called humanitarianism and charity and at times make proposals that are in perfect harmony with the Christian spirit and the doctrine of the Church. …See to it, Venerable Brethren, that the faithful do not allow themselves to be deceived.

In his Christmas message to the world in 1942 Pope Pius XII condemned Communism because it "endangers the eternal salvation of mankind."[21] French Cardinals in 1949 collectively described the effects of Communism: "The atheism at the root of Communism and present like an active leaven in all its economical and social applications, leads logically to the degradation of man."[22]

The Communist infiltrators and their Modernist confreres worked together to create a new church. "Catholic" churches were "transformed into ideology-driven political clubs with the stress on 'social justice'… with worship reduced to trivialized entertainment, and with age-old doctrinal and moral teaching 'modernized' or diminished to the point of irrelevancy."[23]

"After the death of His Holiness Pope Pius XII (1958), the Modernists took leadership in the Vatican and without delay got in contact with Moscow. Thus officially started the pernicious era of false ecumenism. The goals of Modernists in Rome corresponded with the goals of Communists in Moscow, as both are the fierce enemies of the Roman Catholic Church."[24]

Alice von Hildebrand relates the history of Marie Carré's book on the infiltration of the Church by Communists in the March 2003 issue of *Crisis:*

---

[21] Henri Chambre, S.J., *Christianity and Communism*, p. 26.
[22] Chambre, 27. *Letter of September 8, 1949.*
[23] *The New American*, July 5, 1999, "Gramsci's Grand Plan," by Fr. James Thornton, p. 9.
[24] *Pabuskite ismiego*, Lithuanian apostolate publication, 1979.

She [Marie Carré] was a [French] nurse who received a call to take care of a man mortally wounded in a car accident. The dying man had no identification and no passport. All she found was a manuscript that she decided to publish in 1972 under the title *AA-1025—Memoirs of an Anti-Apostle.*

...A careful reading of the book shows that [the Communist agent] AA 1025 was much too clever to launch a direct attack on dogmas. His plans were much more subtle, much more 'professional,' to spread doubt, to weaken faith, to undermine tradition and to ridicule old-fashioned practices that alienate 'modern man' for failing to address themselves to his needs.[25]

Modernism

Of all enemies in the history of the Catholic Church, the Modernists are, perhaps, the most insidious and destructive. Modernism began in the late 19th century and rapidly spread like an epidemic among clerics and intellectuals. "In general we may say that Modernism aims at the radical transformation of human thought in relation to God, man, the world, and life here and hereafter, which was prepared by Humanism and eighteenth century philosophy, and solemnly promulgated at the French Revolution."[26]

The Dictionary of Dogmatic Theology describes Modernism as "a heresy, or rather a group of heresies, which have arisen in the very bosom of the Church under the influence of modern philosophy and criticism, with the pretense of elevating the ...Catholic Church by means of a radical renovation."[27] The popes have repeatedly warned the faithful against these modern errors in philosophy and theology which threaten to undermine the Catholic Faith: Pope Gregory XVI-*Singulari Nos* (1834), Pope Pius IX-*Qui Pluribus* (1846) and *Syllabus of Errors* (1864), Pope St. Pius X-*Pascendi, Lamentabile* (1907) and *Editae Saepe* (1910), Pope Benedict XV-*Ad Beatissimi* (1914) Pope Pius XII-*Mediator Dei* (1947) and *Humani Generis* (1950).

Modernism did not present itself to the philosophical and theological world as a definite and crystallized system. In such a form it would never have gained the

---

[25] Letter to the Editor, pp. 2, 4.
[26] Charles Herbermann, *The Catholic Encyclopedia, Vol. X,* p. 415.
[27] Pietro Parente, *A Dictionary of Dogmatic Theology,* p. 190.

sympathies of Catholics, but would have met with a speedy condemnation by the ecclesiastical authorities on account of its inherent and flagrant opposition to Catholic teaching.

By artifice and under guise of orthodoxy, its tenets were smuggled into Catholic schools. They were not propounded in their entirety, but only partially, as opportunity allowed; they were gradually, but with extreme caution and great reserve, applied to different subjects of history, sociology and finally invaded the territory of theology.[28]

Pope Gregory XVI described the traits of the Modernists:

Blind they are ...they pervert the eternal concepts of truth ...they are seen to be under the sway of a blind and unchecked passion for novelty ...despising holy and Apostolic Traditions they embrace other and vain, futile, uncertain doctrines, condemned by the Church.[29]

In 1907, Pope St. Pius X sounded the alarm that an effort was being made to dismantle the Church from within. He exposed and systematically refuted the doctrinal errors of the Modernist heresy in his encyclical, *Pascendi:*

Undoubtedly, were anyone to attempt the task of collecting together all the errors that have been broached against the faith and to concentrate into one the sap and substance of them all, he could not succeed in doing better than the Modernists have done. Nay, they have gone farther than this for ...their system means the destruction not of the Catholic religion alone, but of all religion.

...They lay the axe not to the branches and shoots, but to the very root, that is, to the faith and its deepest fires. And having struck at this root of immortality, they proceed to disseminate poison through the whole tree, so that there is no part of Catholic truth from which they hold their hand, none that they do not strive to corrupt.

---

[28] J. Godrycz, *Doctrine of Modernism and Its Refutation,* introduction.
[29] The encyclical *Singulari Nos,* June 25, 1834.

On April 24, 1870, the First Vatican Council lamented the widespread dissemination of such modern errors in philosophy and theology:

> Many, even children of the Catholic Church, have strayed from the path of true piety; and by the general diminution of the truths they have held, the Catholic sense has become weakened in them. For led away by various and strange doctrines, wrongly confusing between nature and grace, human science and divine faith, they are found to deprave the true sense of the doctrines which our Holy Mother Church holds and teaches, and to endanger the integrity and soundness of the Faith.[30]

Evolution of Dogma

History shows that changes in the Church are built upon a perduring [lasting and enduring] foundation, without change to that foundation itself. All genuine reforms within the Church have been based on old foundations; none have attempted to lay new ones. To attempt to lay them is the foundation of heresy, from the Gnosticism of the first centuries, to Catharism and the other medieval heresies regarding poverty, to the great German heresy of the sixteenth century.[31]

The Catholic Church has always taught that dogma is immutable since it is of divine origin. Contrary to this belief is the heresy of the evolution of dogma, on which Modernism is based. Modernists believe that the teachings of Christ, which have been faithfully retained from century to century by the Catholic Church, must change and adapt to the spirit of the world and to the standards of modern society. This heretical belief has no legitimate foundation and equally rejects Tradition, Scripture and past Church history.

The French Modernist priest Alfred Loisy, who was excommunicated in 1908, claimed that revealed dogmas "were merely fabrications of man that change from generation to generation as the need arises."[32]

Dr. Ludwig Ott taught the contrary and affirmed Catholic teaching when he wrote: "The ground for the immutability of dogmas lies in the divine origin of the Truths which they express. Divine Truth is as immutable as God Himself: 'The

---

[30] *Dogmatic Canons and Decrees,* pp. 216-217.
[31] Romano Amerio, *Iota Unum,* pp. 116-117.
[32] Ludwig Ott, *Fundamentals of Catholic Dogma,* p. 5.

truth of the Lord remaineth forever.' (Ps. 116, 2) 'Heaven and earth shall pass away: but My word shall not pass.' (Mark 13, 31)."[33]

The Catholic Church teaches that "a dogma is a truth revealed by God and proposed as such by the Magisterium of the Church to the faithful with the obligation of believing it."[34]

> As a matter of fact, the Church never establishes [defines] a dogma without a very long, careful, and profound examination of the question, taking into account not only the Bible, Tradition, history, and the Fathers, but also the reasons given by theologians and scientists.... Dogmas, therefore, cannot depend upon public opinion, because they are an essential prerogative of the Church; and for this reason they must be unchangeable likewise.

> [In direct opposition to this,] Modernists teach that the Church, by establishing unchangeable dogmas, put obstacles in its way for future development.[35] [We might ask here, "For the development of what?"]

The Vatican Council of 1870 declared:

> The doctrine of faith which God revealed has not been handed down as a philosophic invention to the human mind to be perfected, but has been entrusted as a divine deposit to the Spouse of Christ, to be faithfully guarded and infallibly interpreted. Hence, also, that understanding of its sacred dogmas must be perpetually retained, which Holy Mother Church has once declared; and there must never be recession from that meaning under the specious name of a deeper understanding.[36]

> How can the divine truths taught by Christ and carefully preserved in the Catholic Church by the divine assistance of the Holy Ghost, ever cease to be true with the passage of time or the change of circumstances? Christ's command to His Apostles 'to teach all nations all things' and His promise to be with His Church 'all days even to the consummation of the world' guarantee in every age the preservation of these divine truths.[37]

---

[33] p. 6.
[34] Pietro Parente, *Dictionary of Dogmatic Theology*, p. 81.
[35] J. Godrycz, *The Doctrine of Modernism and Its Refutation*, pp. 70-71.
[36] D 1800.
[37] Bishop Mark Pivarunas, CMRI, *Pro Grege*, September 3, 1995.

The Oath Against the Errors of Modernism

Pope St. Pius X, realizing that the poison of Modernism would lead to a loss of faith and, ultimately, to the loss of countless souls, relentlessly attacked it on all fronts. The Holy Father decreed that Modernists must be removed from positions of influence and authority in the Catholic Church and forbade anyone infected with Modernism to occupy teaching posts in seminaries and universities.

> Since efforts were made to continue to promote the Modernist cause, Pope St. Pius X, in his paternal solicitude, drew up and published on September 1, 1910, The Oath Against Modernism. This he imposed upon all seminarians before their ordination to the major orders, all professors of philosophy and theology in seminaries and universities, all confessors, pastors, preachers and religious superiors.[38]

The Oath Against Modernism reads:

> The doctrine of faith was handed down to us from the Apostles through the orthodox Fathers in exactly the same meaning and always in the same purport. Therefore, I entirely reject the heretical misrepresentation that dogmas evolve and change from one meaning to another different from the one which the Church held previously.

The warnings of Pope St. Pius X were prophetic. His requirement of taking the Oath Against Modernism was "just recently lifted [by the Postconciliar Church] because many attitudes of the Modernists are now accepted by contemporary Catholic scholars."[39]

In his encyclical letter *Editae Saepe Dei*, Pope St. Pius X further warned:

> These enemies of the Church are to be sought not only among the Church's open enemies; but... in Her very bosom, and are the more mischievous the less they keep in the open. These enemies are lay people and priests thoroughly imbued with the poisonous doctrines taught by the enemies of the Church and who put themselves forward as reformers of the Church.[40]

---

[38] Bishop Mark Pivarunas, CMRI, *Pro Grege*, September 3, 1995.
[39] Michael Glazier and Monika Hellwig, *Modern Catholic Encyclopedia*, p. 378.
[40] May 26, 1910.

Conditions in the Church Before Vatican II

Although Pope St. Pius X took severe measures to combat Modernism, especially through his encyclical *Pascendi* (1907), the poison had already been widely circulated. By the time Pope Pius XII assumed office in 1939, many of the Modernist clergy had attained prominent posts within the Church. During the final years of Pius XII's reign, he allowed the number of cardinals or papal electors to be reduced from its usual number of 70 members to 53, the lowest number in many years.[41] He refused to replace the cardinals who had died because he believed that many of the bishops were infected with Modernism.

Pope Pius XII's premonition that Modernists would control the next conclave was well founded. After the pope's death on October 8, 1958, the covert Modernists finally were able to obtain their long awaited freedom of activity because of the election of Angelo Roncalli on October 28, 1958.

John XXIII

In order to properly understand the Second Vatican Council we must first understand John XXIII (Angelo Roncalli). He was born in Sotto il Monte, Italy on November 25, 1881 and was ordained to the priesthood by Bishop Appotelli on August 10, 1904 at the church of Santa Maria in Monte Sacro.

The Modernist heresy, which emanated from France, quickly spread throughout Italy and the Catholic world, making inroads among priests, seminary professors and even prelates. The erroneous teachings were circulated by means of books, lectures, journals and meetings. Prior to his ordination, Angelo Roncalli embraced the teachings of Modernism and he completed his studies before the imposition of The Oath Against the Errors of Modernism.

Ernesto Buonaiuti, who assisted at Roncalli's First Mass, was a suspected Modernist who was excommunicated in 1921 and 1924. He was declared *vitandus* in 1926. *Vitandus* means that the pope personally expelled him from the Church.

Fr. Giacomo Radini-Tedeschi had been chaplain of Opera dei Congressi, an organization for Italian lay movements of social concern. Pope St. Pius X

---

[41] As of October 21, 2003, there were 194 cardinals. Of these, 135 are under 80 years of age and therefore eligible to vote in the next conclave.

suppressed the organization and attempted to neutralize Radini-Tedeschi by making him bishop of Bergamo, a small, nondescript town. It was here that Radini-Tedeschi chose Angelo Roncalli to be his secretary. Due to their Modernist and Socialist views, papal delegates were repeatedly sent to Bergamo to make diocese-wide investigations.

In 1909 Radini-Tedeschi gave vocal and monetary support to the Workers' League union which organized a strike against the Ranica textile factory near Bergamo. Commenting on these actions, the paper *Perseveranza* stated, "The bishop's alms is a consecration of the strike, a blessing given to a frankly Socialist cause."[42] Roncalli immediately countered with an article in the diocesan newspaper, *La Vita Diocesana,* defending the actions of Radini-Tedeschi. Roncalli's own radical political and religious beliefs were cleverly concealed under the façade of a concern for the poor:

> Here is Angelo in the first decade of the new century already anticipating the core insight of the Latin American liberation theologians of the 1970s... The article was clipped... and sent off to Cardinal Gaetano De Lai at the all-powerful Consistorial Congregation, the Vatican department that oversees seminaries and the appointment and (when necessary) deposition of bishops. It will remain in the growing file marked 'Roncalli,' next to the file marked 'Radini-Tedeschi.'[43]

After his ordination, Fr. Roncalli taught history and theology in the seminary. In 1913, he actively participated in Rezzara's socialist cause:

> Nicolo Rezzara, one of Roncalli's parishioners, advocated 'social progress' and 'civil strikes' as if the two existed hand in hand. Rezzara drew up a memorandum outlining his plans for 'justice, peace, and freedom.' These plans included all forms of civil violence directed mainly towards members of the Catholic Church. At the end of this document, among a great number of signatures, there stands out one for our concern: that of Angelo Roncalli.[44]

---

[42] Thomas Cahill, *Pope John XXIII*, p. 94.
[43] Cahill, 94-95.
[44] Zsolt Arade, *Pope John XXIII*, pp. 38-40.

On June 1, 1914 Angelo and the seminary rector traveled to Rome in order to discuss finances with Cardinal De Lai who became alarmed by Roncalli's persuasions. In a letter addressed to Roncalli, De Lai wrote:

> 'According to information that has come my way, I knew that you had been a reader of Duchesne [whose book, *History of the Early Church,* had been placed on the Index of Forbidden Books and used in Roncalli's seminary lectures] and other unbridled authors, and that on certain occasions you had shown yourself inclined to that school of thought which tends to empty out the value of Tradition and the authority of the past, a dangerous current which leads to fatal consequences.'[45]

This was indeed fatal "for, as Angelo knew, De Lai had the power to remove, defrock, excommunicate. Angelo's whole life was on the line."[46] The Holy Office then placed Roncalli under observation because of his unorthodox views and suspected Modernism. Roncalli did not heed Cardinal De Lai's letter.

In November 1924, Fr. Roncalli became professor of Patrology (the study of the Church Fathers) at the Pontifical Lateran Seminary in Rome and was appointed to the *Propaganda Fide.* Three months later he was relieved of both posts because of his Modernist beliefs. For the remainder of the year Roncalli fulfilled tasks of minor importance at the Vatican, while being closely watched. This scrutiny continued until his election in 1958.

On March 19, 1925, Fr. Roncalli was consecrated bishop by Cardinal Tacci at the Church of San Carlo al Corso in Rome and appointed apostolic visitor to Bulgaria and titular archbishop of Areopolis. This action was meant to neutralize his influence by positioning him in an obscure location where he could do little harm. In reality, this promotion was his first step to the papal throne.

In November 1934, Archbishop Roncalli was appointed Vicar Apostolic and Apostolic Delegate to Turkey and Greece where he frequently met with Orthodox leaders and worked closely with them. According to the June 9, 2002 issue of the *National Catholic Register,* he even "established scholarships so Orthodox priests could study in Rome."

---

[45] Thomas Cahill, *Pope John XXIII*, p. 105.
[46] Cahill, 105.

On December 22, 1944, Archbishop Roncalli was nominated Apostolic Nuncio to France. "The appointment as papal nuncio to Paris meant that Roncalli certainly would later become a cardinal and enter that select group eligible to be elected pope."[47] It was by default rather than by choice that Roncalli got this appointment. The two worthy men chosen by Pope Pius XII (Archbishops Valerio Valeri and Giuseppe Fietta of Buenos Aires) were rejected by French president Charles De Gaulle.

> It was not easy to fathom the mind of Pius XII, or to explain his choice of Roncalli for Paris. He certainly did not act on the recommendation of his own team in the Secretariat of State. There was little in Roncalli's record in Istanbul to commend him for such a position. One theory is that the angry Pius was showing De Gaulle his displeasure by sending him a second-echelon diplomat as nuncio.[48]

"It was a tradition for the head of the French state to be greeted at the New Year by the diplomatic corps and addressed by their dean, who was always the papal nuncio."[49] Before delivering his speech at the state dinner, "Angelo turned to the Russian ambassador, apologized for upstaging him, and promised to make his first diplomatic call to the Soviet embassy the very next day."[50]

The Socialist

As Apostolic Nuncio of France, Roncalli strongly supported the Communist worker-priest movement which placed priests as ordinary laborers in factories, so they could more easily approach the working class. Avro Manhattan described this association in *The Vatican Moscow Alliance:*

> The worker-priests and their supporters sympathized with the Communists on sociological and economic grounds. Their fellow-ideologues in the higher ranks did the same for ideological and diplomatic reasons. Certain key prelates, among whom were the Monsignori Roncalli and Montini [respectively, the future John XXIII and Paul VI] were active on both levels.[51]

---

[47] Wilton Wynn, *Keeper of the Keys,* p. 18.
[48] Wynn, 19.
[49] Thomas Cahill, *Pope John XXIII,* pp. 141-142.
[50] Cahill, 141-142.
[51] p. 26.

The worker-priest movement began during World War II. In 1942, the Nazis deported 800,000 Frenchmen to slave labor camps and refused to allow French priests to attend to their spiritual needs. Cardinal Suhard, archbishop of Paris, secretly smuggled 25 young priests who were not identifiable as such, among the prisoners. After the war, a number of these priests petitioned the archbishop to remain "worker-priests" and to live in close proximity with the laity. "To the Vatican...this was an innovation that could only result in scandal. Many of the priests were discovered and repatriated; two died in the camps."[52]

Thomas Cahill describes the many dangers of the worker-priest movement:

> The new worker-priests were dedicated to living with the pain of their people. This involved everything from sharing insalubrious [unwholesome] living quarters, working in factories and dockyards like ordinary laborers, befriending anarchists and Communists, and supporting radical labor demands to spending long nights in smoky cafés while discussing 'life' with the alienated young who took their cue not from preachers and theologians but from Sartre and Camus. Discovering that the rites of the Church meant nothing to workers, some priests began to say Mass while wearing factory uniforms, the eucharistic bread and wine laid out not on a gold-encrusted marble altar but on whatever surface was available, the *'Dominus vobiscum'* (The Lord be with you) transformed into *'Salut, copains!'* (Hello, mates!). Not a few worker-priests became gradually indistinguishable from the people they meant to help, more Communist or existentialist than Catholic; some lived openly with women, not only casting aside priestly celibacy but despising the bourgeois institution of matrimony.[53]

Realizing that the worker-priests were joining Communist controlled unions and persuading factory workers to accept Marxism, the Dominican and Jesuit superiors in 1954 finally forbade their priests to engage in this activity. Most priests went back to their parishes, while others left the priesthood and got married. Shortly after he was elected, John XXIII gave moral support to the French bishops supporting the worker-priest movement.

---

[52] Thomas Cahill, *Pope John XXIII*, p. 143.
[53] *Pope John XXIII*, p. 144.

On January 15, 1953, after appointment by Pope Pius XII, Roncalli received his cardinal's biretta from the President of the French Republic, Vincent Auriol, a Socialist and agnostic who had become one of Angelo's closest friends. Roncalli's words on this occasion were recorded by a journalist, "Now, with this red beret, I am more 'red' than you, my dear Vincent." That same day Roncalli was appointed patriarch of Venice and soon departed for Italy.

Shortly afterwards, he chose the Socialist sympathizer Monsignor Loris Capovilla as his personal secretary. Capovilla played an important role in shaping Vatican foreign policy after Roncalli's election in 1958, especially the *apertura a sinestra* (opening to the left) that helped the Italian Socialist party rise to power.

The 1958 Conclave

In order to be elected pope, a candidate must receive a two-thirds-plus-one majority of the valid votes. The outcome of the election is announced to those assembled in St. Peter's Square by means of smoke signals. If no candidate has received the necessary majority, the ballots are burned with damp straw. The resultant black smoke billowing from a special chimney informs the masses that a pope has not yet been selected. When a candidate has received the required number of votes the ballots are burned, creating a white smoke which announces to the world that a new pope has been elected.

With this in mind, certain occurrences surrounding the 1958 conclave are quite thought provoking. Wilton Wynn, the Vatican correspondent for *Time* magazine, described these events:

> On the first day of balloting, there were two false alarms. In the morning, the smoke that billowed out of the pipe from the Sistine Chapel at first looked white as cotton. An emotional Vatican Radio announcer screamed, 'Bianco, bianco, bianco, bello bianco!' ('White, white, white, beautiful white.') But his enthusiasm waned quickly; the smoke turned gray and then black. The same thing happened in the afternoon. [Since white smoke is the indication that a pope has been elected, the smoke usually appears black first then turns to white later, never vice versa.] Eventually it took four days to elect Roncalli, as the cardinals groped for a middle-of-the-road pope they thought they needed.

Roncalli sat serenely through the long days of balloting but never lost confidence. When finally he was elected [October 28, 1958] and asked by what name he would reign, he replied by pulling a well-prepared speech out of his pocket. He was ready.[54]

'I will be called John.' John? The electors who knew their history were confounded. The last John [XXIII] had been an antipope, a former pirate and a murderer... As with the name Henry in the British royal family, the last bearer of the name was thought to have rendered it unusable. What was Roncalli thinking of?[55]

Fr. Peter Stravinskas' *Catholic Dictionary* defines an antipope as "a pretender to the papal throne. One claiming to be pope in opposition to the one canonically elected." Popes had carefully avoided the designation John XXIII because they dared not dishonor their pontificate with the stigma of this notorious antipope. "One wonders why Angelo Roncalli chose to take the name of such a scandalous character."[56]

Neither scholar nor theologian, Roncalli was a cunning revolutionary whose ecclesiastical career was conspicuous for its support of Modernism, Ecumenism and Communism.

The foxy old Roncalli knew what the cardinals thought they were getting when they chose him. He later wrote: 'When the cardinals designated me to the supreme responsibility of the government of the Church, at 77 years of age, the belief was widespread that I would be a provisional pope of transition.'[57]

The Modernist

Roncalli had faced many hindrances and obstacles during his ecclesiastical career. After his election, John XXIII had access to the records of the Holy Office.[58] His curiosity led him to read the dossier which the Holy Office had been keeping on him for over 30 years. The documents carried the glaring caption "under suspicion of Modernism."

---

[54] Wilton Wynn, *Keeper of the Keys*, p. 23.
[55] Thomas Cahill, *Pope John XXIII*, p. 167.
[56] Norman Richards, *People of Destiny, Pope John XXIII*, p. 70.
[57] Wynn, 22-23.
[58] A Vatican Congregation established by Pope Paul III in 1542 in order to protect faith and morals and oppose heresy.

Modernism is not only a heresy, but in the words of Pope St. Pius X, it is the synthesis of all heresies! Consequently, 'under suspicion of Modernism,' can automatically be rendered as 'under suspicion of heresy.' Now, if the Holy Office, the president of which is the Sovereign Pontiff, would make such a damning remark as 'suspicion of heresy,' then it perforce follows that the theologians of that august body over the years had amassed ample evidence that Roncalli, if perhaps not guilty of actual heresy, had at the very least 'deviated from the Catholic Faith.'[59]

Cardinal Roncalli, an elderly man who was not expected to live long, was the short-term candidate chosen by the Modernists to bring about a revolution in the Catholic Church. This "provisional pope" would stack the deck with liberal cardinals, including Montini, and then implement doctrinal and liturgical changes by means of a General Council of the Church. The stage was set.

In 1959, to further his liberal agenda, John XXIII revoked canon 231 and the regulations of Pope Sixtus V which limited the number of cardinals to 70. In March of 1962, John XXIII increased this number to 85. This was the largest number of cardinals in 374 years, which allowed the Modernists to control the next conclave. By the end of his reign, John XXIII had appointed 55 cardinals.

Modernists achieved their greatest victory at Vatican II. Its teachings are permeated with Modernism since John XXIII and many cardinals, bishops and *periti* were Modernists. "In November of 1962 Italy's most respected daily paper, Milan's *Corriere della Sera,* published three articles which accused him [John XXIII] of Modernism. The author was a journalist to whom John had granted an interview in the spring of 1959."[60]

"The novelty of his pontificate consisted in his concern not so much to preserve the faith, or to present it afresh *(aggiornamento)* [Italian for "updating"], or even to spread it, as to provide for and to succor the whole of humanity; he seemed less preoccupied with the visible Church than with the world as a whole. Here, indeed, was a revolution."[61] "In spite of the fact that the

---

[59] Patrick Henry Omlor, *The "Unpersoning" of St. Philomena,* pp. 46-47.
[60] Rev. Bob Bonnot, *Pope John XXIII,* p. 225.
[61] E. Hales, *Pope John's Revolution,* p. 82.

term had directly a legalistic denotation, *aggiornamento* quickly came to denote much more. It became the term more typically connected with John and the Second Vatican Council. People understood that not only the Church's legislation needed updating, but the Church's meaning as well."[62] In June of 1961, John XXIII said: "Alongside our work on the conditions of the Church and for her *aggiornamento*, ...[let] there be added as well another objective... the recomposition of the whole mystical flock of Our Lord."[63]

The essential characteristic of John's reign was not a mere adaptation of the Church to modern times or a renewal of the Church, but the creation of a new liberal church that would be acceptable to the world. John XXIII viewed the primary mission of the Church as humanitarian rather than spiritual. "Good Pope John," who was so well liked by the world, was named *Time* Magazine's Man of the Year on January 4, 1963. Christ's followers generally have not been well received by the world for, as St. James declares "... whoever wishes to be a friend of this world becomes an enemy of God."[64]

His Encyclicals

John XXIII's *Mater et Magistra*[65] represents a striking departure from Catholic social principles. In this encyclical, he sought to further the general welfare of mankind through socialism rather than by the kingship of Christ.

John XXIII here shifts the primary mission of the Church from supernatural and spiritual to temporal and political. *Mater et Magistra* fails to condemn Communism but advocates socialism, and Chardin's term "socialization" is frequently used.

> The encyclical's title *Mater et Magistra* (Mother and Teacher), is intended as a description of the Church in its relation not only to Catholics or Christians but to all people. John presents a view of history that has much in common with the work of the silenced French priest-paleontologist Teilhard de Chardin, a vision of humanity coming gradually together from its primitive beginnings...[66]

---

[62] Rev. Bob Bonnot, *Pope John XXIII*, pp. 107-108.
[63] *Discorsi, Messagi, Coloqui del Santo Padre Giovanni XXIII*, 3: 574-575.
[64] James 4: 4.
[65] May 15, 1961.
[66] Thomas Cahill, *Pope John XXIII*, p. 191.

Socialization, says the encyclical, 'is an effect and a cause of the growing intervention of the state even in matters of such intimate concern to the individual as health and education, the choice of career, and the care and rehabilitation of the physically and mentally handicapped.'[67]

"[It] was the first encyclical ever to be addressed not only to Catholics but 'to all men of good will.' "[68] According to Wilton Wynn, "Just to make sure the point was understood, John had an advance copy sent to Nikita Khruschev in the Kremlin."[69] The encyclical called for dialogue with Communism and was responsible for one million Italian votes going to the Communist party. "The *Wall Street Journal* dismissed [John XXIII's encyclical] *Populorum Progressio* as 'souped-up Marxism,' which showed that it was to be taken seriously."[70]

The Ecumenist

John XXIII was thoroughly imbued with the concept that one religion is as good as another. "More than any other pope, John wanted dialogue with the world irrespective of creed."[71] On June 5, 1960 he established the controversial Secretariat for Christian Unity to promote ecumenism. This, in effect, would place all religions on an equal basis with the Catholic Church. It would also pave the way for interfaith worship.

Rev. Dr. Kissack, the British representative of the Methodist Conference at the council, noted that although John XXIII was very amicable to the Protestants, he never attempted to convert them. " 'In fact,' stated Kissack, 'the dear old pope is just like one of us.' "[72] He invited heretics and schismatics to roam about freely in the Vatican. "Never before had the presiding bishop of the Protestant Episcopal Church of the United States met with a reigning pope. Not since the fourteenth century had an archbishop of Canterbury set foot inside the Vatican, nor any Greek Orthodox sovereign since the time of the Byzantine Empire."[73]

---

[67] Thomas Cahill, *Pope John XXIII*, pp. 191-192.
[68] Alden Hatch, *A Man Named John*, p. 208.
[69] *Keeper of the Keys*, p. 239.
[70] Peter Hebblethwaite, *The Year of Three Popes*, p. 28.
[71] J. Kelley, *Oxford Dictionary of the Popes*, p. 322.
[72] Hatch, 235.
[73] Lawrence Elliott, *I Will be Called John*, pp. 264-265.

John's reign is remembered as an era of good feeling that not only stirred Catholics but also won the good will of Protestants, Orthodox, Atheists, Marxists, and Jews around the world. By 1962, John had already met more Anglican and Protestant leaders than any pope in history, and his excessive attention to all those non-Catholics irritated some old Vatican staffers. One conservative growled, 'It seems easier to see the pope if you are a Methodist.'[74]

When Pope John received Brook Hays, a U.S. Congressman from the Baptist South, Hays somewhat anxiously told John, 'I'm a Baptist!' The pope replied, 'Well, I'm John!' Indicating he was a Baptist too![75]

It was the final session of Vatican Council II, and some bishops began to say that the council, before closing, should make Pope John XXIII a saint by acclamation.[76] 'Don't do that,' several of the Protestant observers at the council said. 'The Good Pope John is a saint for all of us, Catholics and Protestants alike. If you box him into your canonical structures, he will no longer be our saint. And we don't want to lose him.'[77]

They didn't—John XXIII is listed on June 3rd in the *Lutheran Book of Worship*[78] under Lesser Festivals and Commemorations. The heretics Martin Luther, John Calvin and John Huss are also found in the same *Book of Worship*. This charade was carried even further when John XXIII was beatified by John Paul II on September 3, 2000.

His Death

John XXIII's radical beliefs caused great apprehension among conservative prelates. The Italian journalist Furno noted: "I remember a prelate telling me shortly before John's death, 'If the Lord doesn't open his eyes, let him at least close them.' "[79] John XXIII died of stomach cancer on June 3, 1963. "At his death,

---

[74] Wilton Wynn, *Keeper of the Keys*, p. 45.
[75] Rev. Bob Bonnot, *John XXIII*, p. 274.
[76] "Inside the council, progressive bishops mounted a campaign to canonize John by acclamation of the assembled prelates and thus bypass the rigorous church process. In part, their move was political: if the council proclaimed John a saint, progressives believed that they would also prevail against conservatives who were blocking various liberal reforms." *Newsweek*, September 22, 1997.
[77] *National Catholic Register*, September 16, 1994.
[78] Augsburg Publishing House, Minneapolis, MN, ©1978.
[79] L. Furno, "da un diario inedition," in *La Stampa*, June 3, 1973.

even the city of Belfast [Northern Ireland] lowered its flags to half-mast."[80] It was the first time in history that Protestants mourned the death of a pope.

Although he died less than five years after his election, he laid the foundation of a new church. In order to successfully deceive the masses, this new church founded by John XXIII is still controlled from the Chair of Peter and resembles the Catholic Church in certain customs and practices. John XXIII's revolution, which began with the Second Vatican Council, was continued by his successors: Paul VI, John Paul I and John Paul II.

Groundwork for Vatican II

In preparation for the Second Vatican Council, John XXIII sent the first seven schemas to the bishops of the world on July 13, 1962. Seventeen Dutch bishops met at s'Hertogenbosch to review the schema.

> There was general dissatisfaction with the first four dogmatic constitutions, entitled 'Sources of Revelation,' 'Preserving Pure the Deposit of Faith,' 'Christian Moral Order,' and 'Chastity, Matrimony, the Family and Virginity,' and general agreement that the fifth [the one composed by Modernist bishops and *periti*], on the liturgy, was the best. The proposal was then discussed and approved that a commentary should be prepared, and be widely distributed among the Council Fathers, pointing out the weaknesses of the dogmatic constitutions [the first four schemas], and suggesting that the schema on the liturgy be placed first on the council agenda.[81]

The Dutch Modernist, Fr. Edward Schillebeeckx, O.P.[82] anonymously composed a document promoting changes to the liturgy that had a tremendous influence on the Council Fathers. "Latin, English and French versions of the commentary were prepared. Close to 1,500 copies were printed in Rome... and were distributed to the bishops from all countries as they arrived for the council."[83]

---

[80] Article by Bishop Thomas Curry in *The Tidings*, November 1, 2002.
[81] Fr. Ralph Wiltgen, S.V.D., *The Rhine Flows into the Tiber*, p. 23.
[82] He believed that the words of consecration were not spoken by Christ, that Jesus did not intend to found a church and that the New Testament was not "a transcript of words that had been historically pronounced by Jesus." Carl Bernstein and Marco Politi, *His Holiness*, p. 417.
[83] Wiltgen, 23-24.

The European Alliance

A writer for *Time-Life* described Vatican II as a radically different council:

> In Rome the Church's four centuries of 'guard duty' [over the Deposit of Faith] since the Council of Trent were past, overturned by four years of revolution [Vatican II]. ...A 'liberal' movement began to appear, mainly among northern Europeans and the French, North and South Americans and the missionary bishops.[84]

This group, known as the European alliance (although not all of its members were European), was well organized, had a clear agenda and was responsible for the radical changes emanating from Vatican II. Many had the common thread of attending seminaries in Belgium, France or Rome which were permeated with the secular humanist and evolutionary existentialist theories of Jacques Maritain and Teilhard de Chardin.[85] The January 1963 issue of *Reader's Digest* reported, "Pitted against the traditionalists is a progressive bloc said to number 400. The progressives come mostly from the North, where the Protestant Reformation began: from Germany, Austria, Switzerland, the Netherlands, France, Belgium, Great Britain and Scandinavia." These men were appointed to key positions at the council by John XXIII and Paul VI and were given continued support and encouragement.

The European alliance and their allies carefully planned their objectives and strategies prior to, during and between sessions of the council. Their aim was to sway and control the hierarchy through their position of power and influence and thereby dominate the council. As a result, they could transform the Church into a vehicle to meet their own ends.

---

[84] Time-Life Special Report, *The Pope's Visit*, p. 92.
[85] Prior to Vatican II, Church authorities muzzled Chardin. "In 1927 Rome refused an imprimatur on his book, *Le Milieu Divin*. In 1933 he was ordered not to teach in Paris. In 1933 Rome refused him permission to publish *L'energie Humaine*. In 1944 his *Phenomene Humain* was banned. In 1948, summoned by his Superior General to Rome, he sought permission once more to publish his *Phenomene Humain*—and was refused. Again in 1949 and 1955 his printings and activities were restricted. In December of 1957 a decree from the Holy Office ordered the withdrawal of his works from Catholic libraries, seminaries, religious institutions and bookshops." Fr. Charles Coughlin, *Bishops Versus Pope*, pp. 215-216. "Although the faithful have twice been warned about dangers [to faith] in his work, Popes John XXIII and Paul VI have privately acknowledged his greatness." *Time*, October 16, 1964, p. 92.

The Most Influential Revolutionary Participants of Vatican II Were:

John XXIII and Paul VI

Cardinals:
Bernard Alfrink
Augustin Bea, S.J.[86]
Richard Cushing
Julius Döpfner
Joseph Frings
Franz König
Paul Léger
Giacomo Lercaro
Achille Liénart
Albert Meyer
Joseph Ritter
Leo Suenens

Patriarch:
Maximos IV Saigh

Archbishop:
Karol Wojtyla
(John Paul II)

Bishops:
Emile DeSmedt
Jan Willebrands
Joseph Wright

---

[86] "According to [Cardinal] König, 'Bea's role at the council cannot be rated high enough. He and his secretariat took over the responsibility for inviting and looking after the [non-Catholic] observers, who were by no means passive, as their designation might suggest, but played an increasingly influential role.'" *National Catholic Reporter*, March 7, 2003, "Cardinal chronicles impact of Vatican II," by Richard McBrien. John XXIII made Bea head of the newly created Secretariat for Christian Unity. By giving it the rank and status of a council commission "and entrusting it to Bea, he destined it to play a critical role in getting his purposes and ideas adopted by the Council. It was no accident. ...Bea was one of the persons permitted free access to John's apartment in the afternoons. ...In the nine years between his election to the cardinalate (at age 79 just recovered from serious illness) and his death in 1968 he generated some 250 publications, including ten books. In the nine months immediately preceding the opening of the Council alone, he held 25 news conferences. He traveled everywhere—Germany, Switzerland, France, England, the U.S.—lecturing about the Council and spreading significant ideas that would eventually be contained in conciliar documents. Together John and Bea dissipated an anti-ecumenical tone from other Roman sources, notably the Lateran and the Holy Office." Rev. Bob Bonnot, *John XXIII*, pp. 163, 169.

Priests who Served as *Periti* during the Second Vatican Council

Gregory Baum, O.S.B.	Hans Küng[87]
Marie Dominique Chenu, O.P.[88]	Frederick McManus
Yves Congar, O.P.	John Courtney Murray, S.J.
Jean Danielou, S.J.[89]	Karl Rahner, S.J.[90]
Henri De Lubac, S.J.	Joseph Ratzinger[91]
Godfrey Diekmann	Edward Schillebeeckx, O.P.
Bernard Häring, C.SS.R.	Gustave Weigel

---

[87] "On certain issues, including the Church's capacity to make binding and irreformable doctrinal definitions through the exercise of papal infallibility, he did not hold to be true, and he would not teach as true, what the Catholic Church held to be the truth. On December 15, 1979, the Congregation for the Doctrine of the Faith… [declared that Küng] 'could not be considered a Catholic theologian.' His ecclesiastical mandate to teach as a 'Professor of Catholic Theology' was withdrawn." George Weigel, *Witness to Hope,* p. 357. However, the Swiss priest continued to teach at the University of Tübingen from 1979 until his retirement in 1996 even though he continued to hold dissenting views on papal infallibility, the Eucharist and the scope of episcopal authority.

[88] A French Dominican who was an advisor for the worker-priest movement and whose work on St. Thomas Aquinas was placed on the Index of Forbidden Books.

[89] Paul VI made Danielou a cardinal deacon on April 28, 1969. According to James Hitchcock he was "the highest ranking Jesuit in the world." *The Pope and the Jesuits,* pp. 56-57. "Jean Cardinal Danielou, 69, died of a stroke in the Paris apartment of a young woman nightclub dancer, whom he had visited several times previously, the independent newspaper le Monde reported." *New York Post,* June 15, 1974.

[90] "He had more than 4,000 published works including 30 books and taught at Austrian and German Universities from 1937 until 1971." *Sacramento Bee,* April 1, 1984.

[91] "Closely connected with Ratzinger's claim that there is no pre- and post-conciliar church is his assertion that there is no pre- and post-conciliar Ratzinger. Though he is in disagreement with-and often investigating-the liberal theologians in whose company he began his career, he asserts that 'it is not I who have changed, but others.' " Peter Hebblethwaite, *Pope John Paul and the Church* (Sheed and Ward, 1995), p. 222. "But he has changed his position on many issues, and has been opposed to developments inspired by Vatican II in many areas. As the 1960s began, Ratzinger was serving on the board of the journal *Concilium,* and was friendly with the circle of those writing for it—Karl Rahner, Edward Schillebeeckx, Hans Küng, Johann Baptist Metz. At Vatican II he was a *peritus* for Cardinal Joseph Frings, a leader of the progressive majority. Ratzinger helped Karl Rahner create a new text to be substituted for the Curia's schema on the nature of the church—what became the document *Lumen Gentium.*" Garry Wills, *Why I am a Catholic,* pp. 256-257. "Yves Congar, another of the progressive *periti,* actually feared that the Ratzinger-Rahner document was 'too advanced' to be accepted by the council." Andrea Ricardi, "The Tumultuous Opening Days of the Council," in Giuseppe Alberigo, *History of Vatican II,* Vol. 2, (Orbis) p. 86.

"Two bold theologians, Murray and De Lubac[92] were not present at the opening of the council because their writings had earned reproof from their superiors. By the fourth session, however, they were not only among the most active *periti,* but were chosen to concelebrate a special Mass with the pope."[93]

To strengthen their position at the Second Vatican Council John XXIII and Paul VI turned many of these Modernists into trusted *periti.* Paul Bernier, SSS explains: "In the decade before that council [Vatican II], people like John Courtney Murray,[94] Henri De Lubac, Yves Congar,[95] Pierre Chenu, Teilhard de Chardin, even Karl Rahner were silenced by Rome [because of their unorthodox teachings]. All of them emerged as either *periti* (advisors) or as lights by which the council guided itself."[96] Thus, from the beginning of the council, liberal cardinals, bishops and *periti* held an iron grip on Vatican II by controlling the vital positions of the council.

---

[92] Pope Pius XII ordered that his writings be strictly censored and he was removed from his post as professor at Lyons, France after being accused of being a protagonist of the new theology. "De Lubac was silenced, forbidden to even live in a Jesuit house where there were students whom he might corrupt with his 'historical' theology..." Thomas Cahill, *Pope John XXIII,* p. 149. "Obligated by [the] Vatican to abandon all intellectual activities because of suspicions caused by [his] book *Surnaturel."* He was created a cardinal deacon on Feb. 2, 1983. <www.fiu.edu/~mirandas/bios-l.htm>

[93] *Life,* December 17, 1965, p. 73.

[94] Prior to Vatican II "Pressures from Rome began to mount and Murray found his outlets for publishing and lecturing cut off. A book with an article by him was cancelled by the University Press of Notre Dame. The head of the Holy Ghost Order in Rome was asked to have Murray 'disinvited' from an appearance at Notre Dame, which is run by that order. ...In 1957, Murray was told that he could not give permission to a German publisher to reprint one of his articles." Garry Wills, *Why I am a Catholic,* pp. 216-217. "Bishop William Scully of Albany wrote to complain to Murray's superior that a speech he gave on censorship would weaken the authority of the Legion of Decency (which banned certain movies for Catholics 'under pain of mortal sin')." Donald Pelottre, SSS, *John Courtney Murray: Theologian in Conflict* (Paulist), p. 55.

[95] "Congar was sent into exile in England, forbidden to converse with non-Catholics or even with his fellow Dominicans, because of his false irenicism." [ecumenism] Thomas Cahill, *Pope John XXIII,* p. 149. [During the pontificate of Pope Pius XII Congar was] "Forbidden by the Vatican to teach, lecture, or publish and banished to obscure posts in Jerusalem, Rome, Cambridge and Strasbourg due to his support of the priest-worker movement, 1954-1956." <www.fiu.edu/~mirandas/bios-c.htm> His writings were not put on the Index, but no new editions were permitted. He was a favorite theologian of Paul VI and was made a cardinal deacon on Nov. 26, 1994.

[96] *Eucharist Celebrating Its Rhythms in Our Lives,* p. 89.

The heretical tendencies of the prominent *peritus*, Hans Küng, were even noted by a Methodist minister who was present at Vatican II:

> I recall a lively discussion between Hans Küng and George Lindbeck, in which Küng claimed that *he* took Luther more seriously as a theologian than did Lindbeck—and Lindbeck was a Lutheran "observer"! But then Lindbeck takes St. Thomas [Aquinas] more seriously than Küng seems to.[97]

Vatican II

"The Second Vatican Council—Vatican II ...in the eyes of millions of contemporaries, Catholic and non-Catholic alike, ...was rightly seen as revolutionary."[98]

The intervention of John XXIII and his successor Paul VI assured the success of the Modernists. This relatively small group of revolutionaries and their allies were empowered to steer the course of the council and strongly influence the beliefs of 2,860 bishops from around the world. As a result, they achieved their goal during Vatican II—the creation of a new ecumenical church with new liturgy, sacraments and teachings. A new religion was born.

John XXIII appointed Modernist bishops and *periti* from Western Europe to compose the schema on the liturgy. They formed the International Theological Commission (ITC) and achieved a notable victory when the liturgy was chosen to be the first subject to be discussed during Vatican II. "Father Hans Küng asserted jubilantly that what had once been the dream of the *avant-garde* group in the Church had 'spread and permeated the entire atmosphere of the Church, due to the council.' "[99]

In June 1962 Cardinal Giovanni Montini addressed the Central Commission of the Council on the need for making sweeping changes in the Church. "It was after this speech that Cardinal Ottaviani was heard to murmur: 'I pray to God that I die before the end of the council—in that way I can die a Catholic.' "[100]

---

[97] Albert Outler, *Methodist Observer at Vatican II*, p. 67.
[98] Carl Bernstein and Marco Politi, *His Holiness*, p. 89.
[99] Fr. Ralph Wiltgen, S.V.D., *The Rhine Flows into the Tiber*, p. 59.
[100] Peter Hebblethwaite, *Pope John XXIII*, p. 414.

Non-Catholic Observers at the Council

Although the Catholic Church has consistently condemned ecumenical dialogue and interdenominational worship, it has nevertheless always and tirelessly sought the conversion of those who have separated themselves from Her through apostasy, heresy or schism.[101]

Several councils in the past invited non-Catholics to attend in order to attempt to convert them and thus bring them back to the true fold. The principal objective of the Second Council of Lyons and the Council of Florence was to achieve union with the schismatic Orthodox churches. Lutheran delegates were invited to the Council of Trent in 1551 in an attempt to convert them. Protestants and Orthodox were invited to the Vatican Council of 1870 in an attempt to bring about their return to the Catholic Church. Non-Catholic observers at Vatican II were invited for an entirely different purpose, however, which was evidenced by the active role they played in the council. They were definitely not there to be converted.

> Professor Oscar Cullmann of the Universities of Basel and Paris, who was a guest of the Secretariat for Promoting Christian Unity, ...pointed out that mistaken conclusions were being drawn from the presence of [non-Catholic] observers and guests at the council. He was receiving letters from both Catholics and Protestants who appeared to think that the purpose of the Council was to bring about a union between the Catholic and other Christian churches. That, however, was not the immediate purpose of the council, he said, and he feared that many such people would be disillusioned when, after the end of the council, they found that their churches remained distinct.[102]

The invitation of non-Catholics to Vatican II was John XXIII's way of promoting his agenda of ecumenism. This council was to be ecumenical not only in the sense that Catholic bishops from around the globe attended, but mainly in the sense of the modern connotation of the word *ecumenical*—the false belief that all religions may be brought to fraternal agreement and find a common spiritual base.

---

[101] Refer to *Mortalium Animos* of Pope Pius XI, January 6, 1928.
[102] Fr. Ralph Wiltgen, S.V.D., *The Rhine Flows into the Tiber*, p. 123.

The 93 official non-Catholic observers who attended the council represented various churches: Anglican, Church of Christ (Japan), Congregationalist, Disciples of Christ, International Association for Liberal Christianity, Lutheran, Methodist, Old Catholic, Orthodox (Armenian, Coptic, Georgian, Russian, Syrian), Presbyterian, Quaker and the World Council of Churches.

"And though the logistic problems would be awesome—accommodations would need to be found for 10,000 people; somehow 3,500 of them, including bishops and their assistants, would have to be seated in the nave of St. Peter's—he [John XXIII] himself intervened to assure that the [non-Catholic] observers would be given the best places."[103]

This fact is substantiated by Fr. Manton: "While bishops, so used to a throne front and center, were seated in what you might call the right and left field stands... 'Protestant Observers' (each the representative of some denomination) looked down from a special balcony that fairly overhung the papal altar."[104]

These non-Catholic observers were given free rein, exerted tremendous influence on the Council Fathers and became a driving force that would essentially alter Catholic belief and worship. Martin Niemoeller, the president of the World Council of Churches, was convinced that the Protestant observers at the council would be a means of reversing the Church's uncompromising opposition to interfaith worship. The *periti* and interpreters allowed each of the non-Catholic observers to follow everything the council did. Each received a copy of the agenda to be discussed at each session, had access to all conciliar documents and freely mingled with the Council Fathers.

Albert Outler, a Protestant observer at the council, called the new changes of Vatican II, "Reformation Roman-Style."[105] This fact was supported by another Protestant guest, Professor Oscar Cullman: "I am more and more amazed every morning at the way we really form part of the council."[106]

---

[103] Lawrence Elliott, *I Will Be Called John*, p. 281.
[104] *Straws From the Crib*, p. 289.
[105] *Methodist Observer at Vatican II*, p. 161.
[106] Fr. Ralph Wiltgen, S.V.D., *The Rhine Flows into the Tiber*, p. 124.

Bar Jonah / Bar-Mitzvah

Vatican II was actually a council within a council. The Modernists were well organized and had thoroughly discussed their predetermined agenda before any topic reached the council floor. Many of the other bishops simply settled into their national groups and had little impact upon the council proceedings. They were led to believe that the Second Vatican Council was merely rephrasing Catholic teaching in the light of modern conditions.

> The council met in formal session to hear interventions [speeches] (usually a dozen or so) in the mornings. A good deal of the real business, and certainly most of the human interaction, of Vatican II took place elsewhere—in, for example, the two coffee bars [where snacks, brandy, schnapps and espresso were served] that were set up inside St. Peter's [in the sacristy and inner vestibule behind the main altar] and immediately dubbed Bar-Jonah and Bar Mitzvah. Lunches, dinners and seminars, held in hotels, religious houses or the national seminaries in Rome where many bishops stayed, were other venues where things got talked out in a way that was often difficult, if not impossible, in the *aula* [council hall].[107]

Traditional Stand of the Church Against Communism

The Catholic Church has relentlessly opposed atheistic Communism since its inception. Pope Leo XIII defined Communism as "the fatal plague that insinuates itself into the very marrow of human society only to bring about its ruin."[108] Pope Pius XI declared Communism to be "intrinsically wrong" and forbade collaboration with Communism "in any undertaking whatsoever."[109]

> [This stand of the Church] …was reinforced during the reign of Pope Pius XII (1939-1958), especially through his strict prohibition against contact with Communist leaders. He rightly insisted that there be no dignity supplied to them, and that there be no negotiations or recognition of the kind reserved for legitimate national leaders. The numerous reports of typical Communist savagery meted out to prelates—from Stépinac in Yugoslavia [poisoned], Mindszenty in Hungary [tortured and later exiled], Walsh in Red China [tortured], and so many more—served only to stiffen the Church and its

---

[107] George Weigel, *Witness to Hope*, p. 161.
[108] *Quod Apostolici Muneris*, December 28, 1878.
[109] *Divini Redemptoris*, March 19, 1937.

admirers against the propaganda, subversion and terror that Communism was spreading everywhere.[110]

Communists inflicted horrific tortures on Catholic clergy:

Redemptorist Father Zenon Kovalyk was crucified on a wall of Lviv's Bryhidky prison in 1941, while 35-year-old Father Roman Lysko was sealed alive in a wall of another prison in 1949 after going insane under torture. ...Father Severan Baranyk, the prior of a Basilian order monastery at Drohobych, was arrested by the Soviet paramilitary NKVD police and found dead with cross-shaped knife slashes across his chest. Another Drohobych Basilian, Father Yakym Senkivsky, holder of a theology doctorate from Austria, was boiled alive in a prison cauldron. ...Meanwhile, in Russia, ...140 Catholic priests were shot in the 1937-1938 Great Purge alone...[111] Bishop Apor [of Hungary] was shot by the Soviets in his episcopal residence while protecting the chastity of the women and girls to whom he had given refuge while the Soviet army advanced westward in April, 1945. Shot on Good Friday, he died peacefully on Easter Sunday, offering his life as a pure oblation to the Lord.[112]

Atheism is the religion of the régime. Atheism is taught in the schools, preached in the conferences, propagated in the press, enforced on State employees and on the Army. Teachers in the elementary and middle (grammar and similar) schools are formally forbidden to frequent the churches. Teachers who do not obey this command are dismissed from their posts. In a State employee religiousness is considered to be the worst possible characteristic. Officers of the Yugoslav Army dare not even think of getting their children baptized.[113]

In 1949 the Holy See decreed that Communists, their supporters and those who voluntarily read their literature be denied the sacraments.[114] "A stronger penalty, excommunication, is applied automatically to all Catholics 'who profess, defend and spread the materialistic and anti-Christian doctrine of the Communists.' "[115]

---

[110] *New American,* December 2, 1985.
[111] *Our Sunday Visitor,* July 14, 2002, "Remembering Europe's Martyrs of Communism," by Jonathan Luxmoore.
[112] Fr. Maurice, *A Grain of Wheat,* Vol. 1, No. 8, November, 2002.
[113] Richard Patte, *The Case of Cardinal Aloysius Stepinac,* p. 493.
[114] AAS 42-142, December 20, 1949.
[115] Fr. Anthony Flynn, *Triumph of the Faith,* p. 416.

In his work *Murder by the State* (September 1997) Gerald Scully has written: "At least 170 million—and perhaps as many as 360 million—have been murdered by their own governments in this century. This is more than four times the 44 million deaths from civil and international wars." This includes World War I (10 million), World War II (17 million), the Korean War (approximately 3 million) and the Vietnam War (approximately 2 million). He continues:

- Communist regimes have killed the most people in this century, followed by Nazi Germany, which killed more than 16 million people between 1933 and 1945.
- The Soviet Union killed 54.7 million between 1917 and 1987 and China killed 35.6 million between 1949 and 1987.[116]

Statistics from the Judiciary Committee of the United States House of Representatives in 1964

The condition of the Catholic Church in the USSR and countries occupied by the Russians from 1917 to 1959 is appalling:

- The number killed: 2.5 million Catholic believers, 55 bishops, 12,800 priests and monks
- Imprisoned or deported: 10 million believers, 199 bishops, 32,000 priests
- 15,700 priests were forced to abandon their priesthood and forced to accept other jobs
- A large number of seminaries and religious communities were dissolved
- 1,600 monasteries were nationalized, 31,779 churches were closed
- Four hundred newspapers were prohibited, and all Catholic organizations were dissolved.[117]

At the time of Hitler's invasion of Russia after 24 years of the Soviet Regime, [1941] Russia had lost:

- 75% of its bishops
- 90% of its priests, the number falling from 50,960 to 5,665
- 96% of its monasteries, falling from 11,926 to 37
- 90% of its churches, falling from 40,474 to 4,225[118]

---

[116] National Center for Policy Analysis.
[117] Felician Foy, OFM, *1992 Catholic Almanac*, p. 363.
[118] Fulton Sheen, *Communism and the Conscience of the West*, pp. 178-179.

In Hungary alone:

- The Communist government of Hungary dissolved all Religious Orders in the nation (June 7-September 7, 1950), thereby imprisoning or exiling 10,000 members.[119]
- All Catholic Organizations were suppressed (1946).[120]
- All Catholic schools, colleges and institutions were suppressed (1948).
- The Catholic press was suppressed.

In Czechoslovakia the Catholic press was suppressed, schools were nationalized and Catholic organizations were suspended. During February 1953, 200 Catholic priests languished in Yugoslav prisons.

American Attitude Toward Communism in the 1960's

The 1960's were an era of high political tension between the United States and the Soviet Union. The construction of the Berlin Wall in 1961, the Cuban Missile Crisis of 1962 and the testing of nuclear weapons put both nations on high alert. *Life* carried a three part series dedicated to Communism and its threat to the U.S. from October 20-November 10, 1961. John Jessup wrote:

> There are only 36 million members of the [81] Communist parties of the world, but they control the governments, lives and destinies of a billion people; and they have dead serious designs on the other two-thirds of the human race. [The Communists are] ...gaining land and converts at a faster rate than any political or religious movement in history.[121]

The opposition to Communism became so pronounced in the United States that "the U.S. Gallup poll established that 81% of the American people preferred to fight a nuclear war rather than live under Communist rule."[122]

---

[119] "All were forbidden to engage in any pastoral activity, excepting for 400 priests who were permitted to carry out ecclesiastical tasks in the various dioceses, but without their religious vestments [habits]. Lino Gussoni and Aristede Brunello, *The Silent Church,* pp. 160-161. The Religious ran 9 hospitals, taught at 293 schools, were nurses at 90 state or provincial hospitals and ran 120 orphanages and homes for the needy.

[120] "More than 4,000 Catholic Associations were dissolved and their funds—more than ten million florins—taken over by the Ministry, or better, by the Communist Party since the money was passed on to Marxist organizations." Gussoni, 160-161.

[121] *Life,* October 27, 1961, "An Open Plot to Rule the World."

[122] *Life,* November 10, 1961, "What We Must Do To Defeat Communism," by John Jessup.

Vatican–Moscow Agreement of 1962

Even before his election, John XXIII had shown sympathy for the Communist cause which was in stark contrast to the Church's anti-Communist stand. He would not tolerate criticism of Communism in his presence nor did he condemn it during the Second Vatican Council.

> When John XXIII opened the windows of the Church, a truly friendly relationship sprang up between Rome and Moscow. The guests from Kremlin to Rome ceased to be a novelty. The big fishes Adzubej, Podgorny, Gromyko, Tito followed one another. Patriarch Aleksej sent his Metropolitan Nikodim to Rome several times and there were quite a few 'religious delegations' exchanging visits.[123]

In 1962, he arranged a secret meeting at Metz, France between Cardinal Eugene Tisserant and the Russian Orthodox Patriarch Boris Nikodim. Cardinal Tisserant's secretary, Msgr. George Roche, recently disclosed correspondence which confirms "the initiative for the talks was taken by John XXIII personally, at the suggestion of Cardinal Montini [later known as Paul VI], and that Cardinal Tisserant 'received explicit orders, both as to the signing of the accord and to ensuring that it was fully observed during the council.' "[124] "It was an unlikely friendship, perhaps, given the committed and unremitting atheism of the Soviet Union and the equally committed and unremitting condemnation of the Soviets [atheistic Communism] by every Roman Pope since Pius X."[125]

In the Vatican-Moscow Agreement (the accord mentioned earlier) John XXIII promised that his church would never condemn Communism. This fact was confirmed in the Marxist newspaper *France Nouvelle* which noted "that there would be no direct attack on the Communist regime at the council."[126] "Why, the word Communism doesn't appear even once in all of the documents and decrees that came out of the four years of meetings of Vatican II."[127] Millions of Catholics

---

[123] *Draugas,* May 6, 1970, "Communists used the Orthodox Church for their Goals."
[124] Mgr. Roche's letter in *Itinéraires,* No. 285, p. 153. *"A reçu des ordres formels, tant pour signer l'accord que pour en surveiller pendant le Concile l'exacte exécution."*
[125] Malachi Martin, *The Keys of This Blood,* p. 128.
[126] January 16, 1963.
[127] Fr. Francis Fenton, *The Treason of the Churches,* p. 7.

who had been tortured and martyred by the Marxists were betrayed—a betrayal that continues to this day.

Nikodim agreed to send two Russian Orthodox observers, the Archpriest Vitalyi Borovoi and Archimandrite (Abbot) Vladimir Kotliarov to the council. Nikodim, himself, came to Rome on the final day of the council. "It was no secret that Nikodim, known to be associated with the KGB, held his post as leader of the Russian church at the pleasure of Soviet officials."[128]

Opposition to Communism Ignored

Fr. Ralph Wiltgen, S.V.D., in his book *The Rhine Flows into the Tiber*, documents how the request of 450 Council Fathers to reaffirm the Church's condemnation of Communism was totally ignored by Paul VI:

> On December 3, 1963, the day before the second session ended, Archbishop Geraldo Sigaud of Diamantina, Brazil, personally presented to Cardinal Cicognani petitions addressed to Pope Paul and signed by more than 200 Council Fathers from forty-six countries. These called for a special schema in which the 'Catholic social doctrine would be set forth with great clarity, and the errors of Marxism, Socialism, and Communism would be refuted on philosophical, sociological and economic grounds.'
>
> There was no reply from the pope, but eight months later, on August 6, 1964, he published his first encyclical, *Ecclesiam Suam*. In it he called for dialogue with atheism. ...Josef Cardinal Beran, exiled archbishop of Prague, residing in Rome, received a Czechoslovakian newspaper clipping stating that the Communists had succeeded in infiltrating every commission at the Vatican Council.
>
> On April 7, 1965, while the schema was being revised, Pope Paul founded a Secretariat for Non-Believers, with the purpose of fostering dialogue with atheists. By September 14, 1965, the opening date of the fourth session, a revision of the atheism section in the schema on the Church in the Modern World was in the hands of the Council Fathers, but once again it contained no explicit reference to Communism.
>
> During the course of the council, 450 bishops—some one-sixth of the world's total—prepared a petition to the council, asking it to issue a condemnation of

---

[128] *New American,* December 2, 1985.

Communism. In it they pointed out that, if the council were to remain silent about the danger of Communism, this would be equivalent to a rejection of all that previous popes had said against it. But this did not seem to bother those who ran the council. The petition was blocked and ended in the wastepaper basket.[129]

"The petition called Communism and Marxism the 'greatest and most dangerous heresy of this century.' It said that the 'faithful will remain puzzled if the council does not treat a question of such great importance.' "[130] In spite of this, the commission that was formed to draft the pastoral *Constitution on the Church in the Modern World (Gaudium et Spes)* not only deliberately excluded any condemnation of Communism but also avoided mentioning it. "Economic, social and philosophical aspects of Communism were dealt with positively in other sections of the Constitution."[131] Archbishop Karol Wojtyla (John Paul II) was a leading member of the commission.

Bishops from Communist Countries

Communist governments took measures to prevent the formation of an organized anti-Communist bloc at Vatican II and kept many conservative cardinals and bishops from attending the council. As a result, only 49 bishops from Communist countries were allowed to attend Vatican II. "Several Communist governments [Albania and Romania] refused to allow bishops to attend, and some bishops living under repressive regimes were afraid that if they left their countries they would not be allowed back in. As a result, at least 274 bishops could not take part in the council."[132]

"Only one of three cardinals whose nations had been taken over by Communism was present, namely Cardinal Wyszynski, [who was both] the Primate of Poland, [and] the Archbishop of Warsaw."[133] Cardinal Slipyi, who remained in a Siberian prison camp where he had been a captive for 18 years, was released during the course of the council.

---

[129] Fr. Victor Mroz, O.F.M. Conv., *"Ecumenism" Leads to Apostasy*, p. 3.
[130] Floyd Anderson, *Council Daybook: Vatican II, Session 1*, p. 322.
[131] Walter Abbott, S.J., *Documents of Vatican II*, footnote 46.
[132] *National Catholic Reporter*, October 4, 2002, "A Council Primer" by Pat Morrison.
[133] Bishop Fulton Sheen, *Treasures in Clay*, p. 285.

"One of the most striking of all those from Red-dominated countries was a Yugoslav bishop [Anton Vovk of Ljubljana] who had gasoline poured over him and then had been set afire [on January 20, 1952]."[134] When he attended the Second Vatican Council, he seemed like a walking ghost due to his horrible disfigurement. Since Bishop Vovk's appearance inspired fear in all, the anti-Communist prelates could have used him as an example of the atrocities committed under Marxist domination, but they neglected to do so. Tragically, the council totally ignored the horrible persecution and torture endured by Catholics in Communist countries.

Communist leaders looked favorably upon Archbishop Wojtyla (the future John Paul II). There were "25 Polish bishops [who] applied for passports to travel to Rome for Vatican II... Fifteen were denied permission, but Wojtyla was one of the 10 who got a permit."[135] "Of the 61 Polish bishops and archbishops only 17, including Karol Wojtyla, were able to leave Poland to attend [the third session of the council]."[136]

In betrayal of all the faithful clergy who suffered torture under the Communists, Archbishop Wojtyla not only promoted dialogue with the atheists during Vatican II, but also placed Communism in a positive light, passing over its inherent evil. Even worse, he was instrumental in crushing the movement to formally condemn Communism during the council.

His position further revealed itself when the Polish primate, Cardinal Wyszynski, "asked the council to condemn Communism outright, and Karol Wojtyla did not back him up."[137] This in spite of the fact that, at the time 70,000 Polish citizens languished in Communist jails or concentration camps, and 2,000 Catholics were imprisoned for their beliefs, including 9 of Poland's 33 bishops and nearly 900 priests and one third of Poland's churches were closed.[138]

---

[134] Bishop Fulton Sheen, *Treasures in Clay*, p. 285.
[135] Robert Sullivan, *Pope John Paul II: Life a Tribute*, p. 52.
[136] Catherine and Jacques Legrand, *John Paul II*, p. 68.
[137] Legrand, 70.
[138] "In fact, 1,932 priests and clerics, 850 monks and 289 nuns would die during the war years [1939-1945]." Carl Bernstein and Marco Politi, *His Holiness*, p. 64.

"The Communist crime wave continues today. Ironically, there has been little done to call the Communists to account for their brutality which has claimed over 100 million victims since 1917."[139]

Mission of the Church—Supernatural or Natural?

Pope Pius XI described the mission of the Church as being primarily supernatural: "It is not, of course, the function of the Church to lead men to passing and perishable happiness only, but to that which is eternal."[140]

Francis Ripley puts it another way in his work, *The Last Gospel:*

> The Church has only one reason for its existence—the salvation of souls. Like its Head, it is the way, the truth and the life of men. He came to save souls; the Church continues His mission for all time. Everything in the Church's life has the same objective—sacraments, ceremonies, liturgical cycles, sermons, pastoral work, councils, synods, laws—there is no exception; every item is designed to assist the Church in the one, supreme task.

The Second Vatican Council sharply departed from this mission, placing its emphasis on worldly concerns: "Vatican II, especially in its *Pastoral Constitution on the Church in the Modern World,* has clearly directed Catholic thought and life to an emphasis on the present world."[141] This naturalism is manifest throughout the text: "...this involves not a lesser, but rather a greater commitment to working with all men towards the establishment of a world that is more human."[142]

Liberation Theology and the Social Gospel

The Catholic Church has always worked for social justice and the improvement of the lives of the people evangelized by its missionaries. It has never approved of liberation theology which is often nothing more than a cleverly disguised form of Marxism, a "movement of theologians and activists who believe that it is the church's duty to work for human rights for the poor and oppressed. Some of its more extreme proponents endorse the concept of Christ as liberator and see their mission in terms

---

[139] S. Astons, *Communism: the Unpunished Crime,* p. 6.
[140] *Worship, Vol. 31,* December 1956, p. 494.
[141] Bernard Cooke, *Christian Community: Response to Reality,* p. 32.
[142] Vatican II: *Pastoral Constitution on the Church in the Modern World,* Section 2, 57.

of a Marxist class struggle."[143] For example, in their literature "the Virgin Mary is shown as the spiritual mother of guerrillas. Jesus Christ is portrayed as a guerrilla murdered by Americans. ...Marxist guerrillas are the resurrected saints."[144]

"Bishop Sergio Mendez Arceo of Mexico has stated, 'Marxism is the only solution for Latin America.' "[145] Numerous clergymen have followed his advice as related in the October 17, 2003 issue of the *Wall Street Journal:* "Some priests exchanged rosaries for AK-47's and joined or founded guerilla groups."[146]

Why is Marxism so alluring to modern clergymen? Many once-religious people have lost their faith in God so they have used Socialism as a substitute. "...Claiming concern for 'the poor' is sought as a way of rationalizing and justifying a political career in place of lost spiritual convictions."[147] Jo Renee Formicola, in her book *Pope John Paul II: Prophetic Politician,* describes the essence of liberation theology: "Liberation theologians wanted to dilute the Church's spiritual mission by enlarging its temporal one..."[148]

The Formation of a New Church

The spirit of the French Revolution was embodied in the Second Vatican Council. Alberto Cavallari relates this in *The Changing Vatican:*

> Liberty, fraternity, and equality are in fact the keystones of the council doctrine concerning the Church and the modern world, toward the non-Christian religions, and towards the atheists. In contrast to Trent and Vatican I, Rome has now repudiated the 'medieval Catholic vision of the world' and integrated 'classical theocentrism with a new humanism.'

The devastation in the wake of Vatican II was so apparent that even secular magazines carried shocking headlines: "Catholic Revolution" (*Look,* Feb. 9, 1965) "New Currents Swirling Around Peter's Rock" (*Life,* December 18, 1965) and "Catholics and Communists, Strange New Bedfellows" (*Look,* May 2, 1967).

---

[143] *Time,* July 9, 1984.
[144] *The New American,* December 2, 1985, "Why Has Marxism Hooked Clergymen?," by John Utley.
[145] *Time,* February 5, 1979.
[146] Peter Mayer, "Pope John Paul II's Legacy: A Growning Flock, Widening Rifts."
[147] *The New American,* December 2, 1985.
[148] pp. 40-41.

The November 28, 1964 issue of *The Saturday Evening Post* carried a report that was the culmination of a ten-month study on the effects of Vatican II. It was entitled: "Momentous Changes Sweep the Catholic Church in America." Edward Sheehan arrived at the conclusion that a new church was being formed in the U.S.

Many books printed since Vatican II forcibly demonstrate this fact: *The Decomposition of Catholicism* (Bouyer), *The Torn Tunic* (Casini), *Has the Catholic Church Gone Mad?* (Eppstein), *Pope John's Revolution* (Hales), *The Runaway Church* (Hebblethwaite), *What Happened at Rome?* (MacEoin), *The Remaking of the Catholic Church* (McBrien), *What Has Happened to the Catholic Church?* (Radecki), *The Perplexed Catholic: A Guide Through Confusion* (Reedy & Andrews), *Catholic Revolution* (Roche), *Does Catholicism Still Exist?* (Schall), *Is It the Same Church?* (Sheed), *A People Adrift: The Crisis of the Roman Catholic Church in America* (Steinfels) and *Look What They've Done to My Church* (Urban).

Newsweek's article, "Has the Church Lost Its Soul?" of October 4, 1971 noted:

> Largely because of Vatican II and the turmoil that has followed, there is now as much diversity in theology and life-style among Catholics as there is among U.S. Protestants. A Catholic, in effect, is anyone who says he is, and his attitude toward the church is likely to be shaped essentially by his income, education and where he floats in America's still bubbling melting pot.

The First Session (October 11–December 8, 1962)

Before the opening of the council, the members of the European alliance feared interference from the conservative Roman Curia during Vatican II. "A leading curialist once passed a building which was being demolished. He commented… that was what Pope John was doing to the Church."[149] Unless the Curia was rendered ineffective, the plan of the European alliance would never materialize. Therefore, on the first working day of the council (October 13), two prominent members of the alliance, Cardinals Liénart and Frings, "were granted a postponement of several days for the bishops to consult with members of their national or regional conferences as to whom to elect to the council's commissions. This was in response to the basically predetermined curia-

---

[149] Rev. Bob Bonnot, *John XXIII*, pp. 223-224.

approved members of the various commissions, which likely would have led to the adoption of schemas already prepared."[150] This decisive move gave the Modernists the needed time to secure the appointments which would allow them to preside over the commissions, so they could thereby paralyze the Curia.

The heated debate between Traditionalists and Modernists on the Sources of Revelation reached such a level that "during the first session of the council, in November, 1962, fourteen cardinals sent a letter to Pope John expressing 'their disquietude over false doctrines' being aired on the floor of the council."[151] A number of Council Fathers, including Cardinals McIntyre (Los Angeles), Ottaviani (Holy Office), Ruffini (Palermo) and Siri (Genoa) defended traditional Catholic teaching and asserted that the two sources of Divine Revelation are Scripture and Tradition. This had been confirmed by the Council of Trent and the Vatican Council (1870).

> Cardinal Liénart from Lille, France, rose at once to lead the opposition. He insisted that the draft needed to be completely re-written because it did not deal accurately and well with the relationship of Scripture and Tradition. [He then uttered a heretical statement promoting the 'faith alone' theory of Martin Luther.] 'There are not and never have been two *sources* of revelation,' he claimed. There is only one source of revelation: the Word of God, announced by the prophets and revealed by Christ.[152]

Modernists such as Liénart and Wojtyla (John Paul II) disparaged Tradition by claiming that placing emphasis on Tradition would alienate Protestants who believe in Scripture alone. This was not a minor theological point. What it implied significantly altered Catholic teaching.[153]

---

[150] See Giuseppe Alberigo's *History of Vatican II*, 2:14-18.
[151] *Catholic World Report*, June 2003, "The Cost of Theological Dissent," by Ken Whitehead.
[152] Liénart, as quoted by Rynne, *Letters from Vatican City*, p. 143.
[153] St. Basil discusses this issue in the fourth century: "But it is against the Faith they make war. The common aim of all our adversaries, and of all *who are contrary to sound doctrine* (I Tim. 1: 10) is to overthrow the foundations of the Faith of Christ, by leveling the Apostolic Traditions to the earth and wholly destroying them." M. Toal, *Sunday Sermons of the Great Fathers, Vol. 3*, pp. 9-10.

The essence of the debate was explained by William Madges:

> Whereas the original draft had concentrated attention upon the 'sources' or 'founts' of revelation and the relationship between Scripture and Tradition, the revised draft focused upon the Sacred Scriptures themselves and their message. This new emphasis allowed for the validity of several modern theories concerning the biblical texts. It was precisely this modern acceptance of pluralism that Cardinal Ruffini of Palermo, Sicily opposed. During the debate on October 2, 1964, he repeated a point he had made previously: to encourage—as the present version of the text did—consideration of literary genres in determining the meaning of biblical texts was tantamount to admitting that the Church had not properly understood the Scriptures until quite recently. ...It does not claim that the Bible is materially insufficient in conveying Christian knowledge, but leaves open the possibility that the whole deposit of Christian faith is contained in the Bible.[154]

The verbal battle raged for almost two weeks. When no compromise could be achieved, John XXIII personally intervened and withdrew the document despite the fact that it lacked the two-thirds majority necessary to alter the draft. "He halted debate and sent the proposal to be rewritten by a new committee. ...Said Canadian Father Gregory Baum, 'This day will go down in history as the end of the Counter Reformation.'[155] Said the pope: 'Now begins my council.' "[156]

> By the time the session ended on December 8, however, the progressives, led by Suenens and Montini, and with some behind-the-scenes backing from John at crucial moments, had gained control. From now on it would be *their* council. No schema had been approved; all were sent back for rewriting; and a new organized committee, the Coordinating Commission, stuffed with a progressive majority, was set up to take control of agenda and procedures and to ensure that work would continue efficiently during the intercession [before the next session of the council].[157]

---

[154] *Vatican II: Forty Personal Stories,* pp. 112-114.
[155] [The Counter Reformation was the Catholic Church's response to the Protestant Reformation. The Council of Trent reaffirmed the tenets of Catholic belief and restored Church discipline.]
[156] *Reader's Digest,* April 1963, "Pope John's Great Gift," pp. 143-144.
[157] Thomas Cahill, *Pope John XXIII,* pp. 204-205.

Modernists Plan Their Strategy

Members of the European alliance met in Munich (February 5-6, 1963) and Fulda, Germany (August 26-29, 1963) to formulate a plan to further dominate and direct the council. Their methods are described in detail by Fr. Ralph Wiltgen:

> When the conference opened on August 26, there were present four cardinals and seventy archbishops and bishops, representing ten countries. Germany, Austria, Switzerland, and the Scandinavian countries were represented by nearly all of their archbishops and bishops. France, Belgium, and Holland had representatives; Cardinal Alfrink himself represented Holland. Cardinal Frings presided.

> The work carried out by the European alliance at Fulda was very impressive, and it is to be regretted that all national and regional episcopal conferences did not work with the same intensity and purpose. Had they done so, they would not have found it necessary to accept the positions of the European alliance with so little questioning. The council would then have been less one-sided, and its achievements would truly have been the result of a worldwide theological effort.

> Since the position of the German-language bishops was regularly adopted by the European alliance, and since the alliance position was generally adopted by the council, a single theologian might have his views accepted by the whole council if they had been accepted by the German-speaking bishops. There was such a theologian: Father Karl Rahner, S.J.

> Technically, Father Rahner was Cardinal König's consultant theologian. In practice, he was consulted by many members of the German and Austrian hierarchy, and he might well be called the most influential mind at the Fulda conference. ...The extent to which the bishops of Germany and Austria, and the entire Fulda conference, leaned on Father Rahner may be gauged by comparing his original observations with those submitted to the General Secretariat of the Council.

> ...A meeting of Council Fathers from so many nations was bound to interest the press, and a succession of newspaper stories appeared with references to a 'conspiracy' and an 'attack' upon the Roman Curia and its representatives. Some of the Council Fathers were styled 'progressives,' others 'traditionalists,' still others 'antiprogressives.'

Each of the German-speaking Council Fathers had been supplied with a total of 480 mimeographed pages of comment, criticism, and substitute schemas by the time he left for the second session. All this work was accomplished in connection with the Munich conference in February and the Fulda conference in August.[158]

The Second Session (September 29–December 4, 1963)

The new rules placed the responsibility for 'directing the activities of the council and determining the sequence in which topics would be discussed at the business meetings' in the hands of four Cardinal Moderators chosen from the membership of the Coordinating Commission, which had been expanded from six to nine [by Paul VI. He also chose four Moderators: Cardinals Döpfner, Suenens, Lercaro and Agagianian.]

...By these papal appointments the European alliance grew in power and influence, advancing from control of 30 per cent of the Council Presidency and control of 50 per cent of the Coordinating Commission to control of 75 per cent of the board of Cardinal Moderators. And since Cardinal Agagianian was not a forceful person, the three liberal Cardinal moderators often had 100 percent control.

...With a definite policy laid down at Munich and Fulda, which could be revised at the weekly meetings held in the Collegio dell'Anima; with 480 pages of comment and substitute schemas; with a German-speaking Council Father on every commission (the Bishop of Fulda was appointed by the pope to the Commission on Missions when an elected member died in the interim between sessions); with Cardinal Frings on the Council Presidency and Cardinal Döpfner on the Coordinating Commission and serving as one of the Moderators—no other episcopal conference was so well prepared to assume and maintain the leadership at the second session.

It was clear at this point how the discussions would develop. There would be a strong German influence which would make itself felt in nearly every council decision and statement of any importance. In every council commission, German and Austrian members and *periti* would be highly articulate in presenting the conclusions reached at Munich and Fulda. With the Munich and

---

[158] Fr. Ralph Wiltgen, S.V.D., *The Rhine Flows into the Tiber*, pp. 79-81.

Fulda conferences, the drastic changes that Pope Paul VI had made in the Rules of Procedure, and the promotion of Cardinals Döpfner, Suenens, and Lercaro to the position of Moderators, domination by the European alliance was assured.[159]

One can only be amazed when, scanning the roster of more than 2,000 bishops from practically every nation on the globe, he realizes that the only prelates who had any real influence on the council proceedings were a small minority of liberal cardinals, bishops and *periti* ("theologians"). Lamentably, many Council Fathers compromised their faith and finally succumbed to the pressure exerted by the Modernists and Ecumenists. These became known as *converso* from the Latin *convertere*—to change.

Collegiality

The pope, the Vicar of Christ, is the visible head of the Catholic Church. During the second session of the council the concept of collegiality was brought to the council floor, threatening to undermine papal primacy. The Modernist notion of collegiality is expounded in the Vatican II decree entitled *Dogmatic Constitution on the Church*: "Just as, by the Lord's will, St. Peter and the other Apostles constituted one apostolic college, so in a similar way the Roman Pontiff, as the successor of Peter, and the bishops as the successors of the Apostles are joined together" (No. 22). Paul VI went so far as to claim "that the national episcopal conference's function was nearly indispensible."[160] The conservatives among the assembly could foresee where this was headed, and they made a noble effort to oppose the issue.

The matter came to a head on October 30, 1963 when "the conservatives could not block the vote [on the resolution of collegiality], which went overwhelmingly against them—the articles on the bishops passed by majorities on the order of two thousand to three hundred. It was known beforehand that liberals were in a majority among the Council Fathers, but not that the scale was this great."[161]

Hindsight confirms the wisdom of the dissenters who opposed the October 30 resolution. Vatican II, with its emphasis on collegiality, has created an illusion

---

[159] Fr. Ralph Wiltgen, S.V.D., *The Rhine Flows into the Tiber*, pp. 82-84.
[160] Walter Abbott, S.J., *Documents of Vatican II*, p. 394.
[161] Xavier Rynne (F. X. Murphy), *Vatican Council II* (Orbis, 1968), pp. 213-215.

that the pope is a mere member of the College of Bishops—which is esteemed to be, of itself, a sort of supreme governing board of the Church. John Paul II wrote in his encyclical, *Ut Unum Sint,* "When the Catholic Church affirms that the office of the Bishop of Rome corresponds to the will of Christ, she does not separate this office from the mission entrusted to the whole body of Bishops, who are also 'vicars and ambassadors of Christ.' The Bishop of Rome is a member of the 'college,' and the Bishops are his brothers in the ministry."[162]

Albert Outler, a Methodist observer at the council, expressed his wonderment at the gradual loss of faith by the majority of the Council Fathers due to the influence of the liberals:

> There were those who found the protracted debates repetitious and boring. To me, they were the mirror in which one could trace the subtle cumulative shifts in 'the minds' of a council in the process of being formed. Their results were later registered in the successive revisions of the schemas. Moreover, I was mightily impressed by the sights and sounds of 2,000 bishops engaged in what still seems an extraordinary exercise in *reeducation.*[163]

The Third Session (September 14–November 21, 1964)

Conservatives left the second session badly shaken, but determined to take drastic measures to stop the revolution that was taking place before their eyes. Some already had the feelings Cardinal Giuseppe Siri of Genoa would later express: 'It will take a century for the church to recover from John's pontificate.'[164]

On the eve of the council's reconvening, a blistering letter signed by twenty prominent cardinals, several bishops, and the heads of twelve religious orders was sent to the pope [Paul VI]. Cardinal Ottaviani, though he did not sign the letter, supported it. The letter called into question the 'aims and methods' of the majority, saying their position on the college of bishops and other matters was reached in defiance of Scripture and previous councils, and reflected 'non-doctrinal' motives.[165]

---

[162] Libreria Editrice Vatican, 25 May 1995; n. 95.
[163] *Methodist Observer at Vatican II,* p. 16.
[164] Peter Hebblethwaite, *Paul VI,* p. 590.
[165] Hebblethwaite, 384-385.

The letter as much as said that the council's majority had become heretical, and that there was no compromise with heresy. Faced with that conviction on the part of much of his own cabinet, Paul became obsessed with proving that there *could* be a compromise, that he could soften the majority position enough to clear it of heresy in the eyes of the intransigents. ...When the minority made it clear to the pope that they would not accept the decree on collegiality, the pope took steps to water it down, sending 'from higher authority' an explanatory note to be appended to what the Fathers had decided....

- 'college' was not to be understood in any juridical sense
- episcopal ordination gives authority to a bishop, but its exercise must be regulated by the pope
- the college can act only with the pope; though the pope can act without the college

Though these propositions went against the logic of the document to which they were appended (which is the reason the minority demanded them), the majority, over an anguished weekend, decided to submit to the pope's interference in a debate that he said would be free. The case was made that getting any document to recognize the college (which had been anathema to the conservatives beforehand) was an important step. At least it was a development beyond Trent, where the idea of direct divine authorization of the episcopacy had been rejected.[166] The new council's document, *Lumen Gentium*, errantly said that the bishops' authority, 'which they personally exercise in Christ's name, is proper, ordinary and immediate.'[167]

The *Decree on Ecumenism (Unitatis Redintegratio)* and the Dogmatic Constitution on the Church *(Lumen Gentium)* were both promulgated on the final day of the third session on November 21, 1964.

The decree *[Lumen Gentium]* also moved beyond *Mystici Corporis*[168] and all previous Roman Catholic teaching by refusing to identify the Roman Catholic Church with the Church of Christ, stating instead that the Church of Christ 'subsisted in' the Roman Catholic Church, and not that it simply 'was' the Roman

---

[166] Garry Wills, *Why I am a Catholic,* pp. 232-233.
[167] *Lumen Gentium* 27, *The Sixteen Documents of Vatican II* (Pauline Books, 1999), p. 155.
[168] Encyclical Letter of Pope Pius XII on the Mystical Body of Christ, June 29, 1943.

Catholic Church. ...[this] opened the way to the recognition of the spiritual reality of other Churches and their sacraments and ministries.[169]

The Fourth Session (September 14–December 8, 1965)

"*Lumen Gentium* was not the only revolutionary document produced by the council."[170] The *Decree on Religious Freedom (Dignitatis Humanae)* and the *Constitution on the Church in the Modern World (Gaudium et Spes)* were ratified by the Council Fathers on the final working day of the council's fourth session on December 7, 1965. At both these critical times most bishops had their minds fixed on their return home and seemingly paid little attention to the heretical documents submitted for their approval.

> *Gaudium et Spes,* the 'Pastoral Constitution on the Church in the Modern World' (the Latin actually says 'in this world of time') represented a complete overturning of the Conciliar and papal denunciations of the 'modern world' which had been so regular a feature of the Ultramontane era.[171]

Also during the fourth session the term *separated brethren* was widely used. It implies a false type of unity and amicable relationship between the various religions—a relationship fully intended by the liberals.

In his historical survey of Lutheranism, Conrad Bergendoff describes the Protestant response to the "reforms" of Vatican II:

> The remarkable change which Pope John XXIII inaugurated when he called together the bishops of the Roman Church to chart a changed course in the modern world included an approach to Protestants as 'separated brethren,' which reversed a 400-year condemnation of the churches of the [Protestant] Reformation.
>
> ...The changes sanctioned by the [Second] Vatican Council, such as the celebration of the Mass in the vernacular, greater participation by the laity, and the admission of a collegiality of the bishops in the administration of the church are strangely reminiscent of demands made [by Martin Luther] 400 years ago.[172]

---

[169] Eamon Duffy, *Saints & Sinners: A History of the Popes,* p. 273.
[170] Duffy, 273.
[171] Duffy, 273.
[172] *The Church of the Lutheran Reformation,* p. 135.

Vatican II thus laid the foundation for a new church by introducing new doctrines and paving the way for the creation of a new liturgy and new sacraments. It would be a gradual, tedious process accomplished with great precision, determination and deception. Catholic teaching had to be chipped away slowly and subtly so nobody would suspect the true goal of the Modernists.

Paul VI

One of the most influential Modernists at Vatican II was Archbishop Montini of Milan who was later elected Paul VI. In his new office, he continued the doctrinal and liturgical revolution that was begun by John XXIII.

> If John was the pope of *aggiornamento* [updating], Paul has been called the pope of *avvicinamento,* which means neighborliness with other creeds and faiths. In Bombay he quoted with respect from the pre-Christian Indian sacred writings. In New York he even praised 'America's spiritual values,' a phrase which takes in Unitarians and humanists.[173]

Giovanni Battista Montini was born in Concesio, Italy on September 26, 1897. His father, Giorgio Montini, was a socialist who served in the Italian Parliament for three terms. "In 1916, he (Giovanni) received his college diploma from 'Arnold of Brescia Institute'—Arnold of Brescia was a medieval intemperate anti-papal and anti-clerical agitator!"[174] He was a political and religious revolutionary who was condemned and exiled by the Second Lateran Council.

Montini was ineligible for military service because of poor health so he began to study law. He eventually entered the Brescian seminary and was ordained a priest on May 29, 1920 by Bishop Gaggia. Fr. Montini continued his studies at the Gregorian Institute in Rome and the Ecclesiastical Academy. In June 1922, he was chosen for the Vatican diplomatic corps and in 1925 was made monsignor.

The Influence of Jacques Maritain

Jacques Maritain (1882-1973) is considered the father of the heresy of religious liberty. His Modernist teachings and existential Thomism had a profound influence upon clerical intellectual circles. Montini "nourished himself

---

[173] *Life,* October 15, 1965, "Pope Paul's Magnificent Risk," by John Jessup.
[174] Knights of Columbus, *Vicar of Christ, Paul VI,* p. 3.

with his political and social theses and acknowledged him as his mentor. These theses are, however, at the origin of 'liberation theology.' "[175] "Paul [VI] identified particularly with the Christian humanism of Jacques Maritain, even when Maritain was regarded by powerful conservative churchmen as a near-heretic."[176]

The motto of Pope St. Pius X was "To restore all things in Christ." "Jacques Maritain's motto, which would become that of Paul VI, was rather 'To restore all things in man.' "[177]

Maritain's *Integral Humanism* (1936) "later influenced the Second Vatican Council and its approach to the modern world."[178] His anti-Catholic teachings were widely circulated by books, conferences and retreats for priests and seminarians. Montini and other Modernists at Vatican II (including Chenu, Congar and Danielou) were disciples of Maritain.

"Over the years Montini had attracted a number of young priests who espoused his concept of Christian brotherhood for all human beings—regardless of choice of faith or the lack of it—and a downplaying of ritual and authority. Such men became known as 'Montinians' in Church circles and were widely regarded as ecclesiastical radicals."[179]

John Cogley describes Montini's early involvement with Modernism:

> ...as a very young priest he became associated with some of the most progressive thinkers of pre-Vatican II Catholicism, and though he served in increasingly important Vatican posts for three decades, his progressive ideas seemed an obstacle to his own advancement in the hierarchy. His vigorous defense of postwar French priests [worker-priests] who doffed their soutanes and took their place in factories, strikes and picket lines—the forerunner of today's clerical social activists—made him suspect in the eyes of the conservatives in the Holy Office, the official watchdogs of Catholic orthodoxy.

---

[175] Abbé Daniel Le Roux, *Peter, Lovest Thou Me?*, p. 61. [Liberation theology reduces Christianity to a mere social gospel; a social institution based on Karl Marx's class struggle.]

[176] *Life*, March 20, 1970, " 'Paul, poor fellow, has no friends.' " by John Cogley.

[177] Le Roux, 62.

[178] George Weigel, *Witness to Hope*, p. 139.

[179] *Four Popes*, March 1979, p. 59.

...The most recent changes in the Mass, which he highly commended, were the object of angry conservative demonstrations in Rome itself... Some of the most bitter opponents of the updated liturgy have gone so far as to call Paul a heretical antipope.

...A sympathetic priest in Rome who has known Paul for 40 years said recently: 'The pope knows better than anyone else that he is a failure. He has a strong sense of history. After the turmoil following the Vatican Council, it will take two or three generations to reconstruct Catholicism. ...The Vatican Council released demons.'[180]

Secretary of State

Montini held various offices in the Vatican from 1924-1954 including those of undersecretary of state (1937-1954) and joint pro-secretary of state (1944).

In 1954, when the Chinese Communists formed a schismatic church in an effort to destroy the underground Catholic Church, Msgr. Montini prevented correspondence of the heroic Chinese bishops who stood against the Communists from ever reaching Pope Pius XII. From his office in the Vatican Montini even dared to carry on negotiations with Moscow.

When the Lutheran Archbishop Brilioth of Uppsala became aware of this activity he notified Pope Pius XII. Being thus informed, the pope quickly removed Montini from his post as secretary of state and blocked his road to the papacy by refusing to make him a cardinal. Although it is theoretically possible for a non-cardinal to be elected pope, the last time it occurred was in 1378. Montini was thereupon exiled and made Archbishop of Milan on November 1, 1954.

Cardinal Montini

John XXIII removed obstacles to Montini's election to the papal throne by creating him a cardinal on December 5, 1958, saying "I am here to prepare the place for Montini."[181] Thus, following the death of John XXIII, Montini became one of the leading contenders for the papacy in spite of the fact that conservative cardinals from the Holy Office disliked Montini's liberal tendencies and had initiated a "stop Montini" campaign.

---

[180] *Life*, March 20, 1970, " 'Paul, poor fellow, has no friends.' "
[181] Wilton Wynn, *Keeper of the Keys*, p. 24.

In the early balloting, votes were diffused among a variety of candidates thereby preventing Montini from obtaining the necessary two-thirds plus one majority. The bloc of conservative cardinals, however, was not strong enough to hold back the liberal tide; at best they were only able to delay it. Cardinal Gustavo Testa protested against the conservative effort lest they "...destroy the patrimony left us by Pope John."[182] Testa swayed the votes in favor of Cardinal Montini, who was finally elected on June 21, 1963 and chose to be called Paul VI.

During his speech before the Protestant-dominated World Council of Churches in Geneva, Montini said: " 'The name which we have taken, that of Paul, fully indicates the orientation which we have wished to give our apostolic ministry.' Like the New Testament Paul, he meant to be a man of dialogue with other cultures and religions and to travel to many lands."[183]

Paul VI's words were mere deception, for St. Paul was one of the greatest missionaries of all time and converted countless souls to the Catholic faith. History records that Paul VI left no such legacy. During his reign the Catholic Church witnessed an unprecedented loss of faith, as millions left the Church and more than 30,000 priests were dispensed from their vows.

Collier's 1972 Encyclopedia Yearbook described the anarchy rampant during the reign of Paul VI: "Priests were leaving the active ministry in unprecedented numbers; vocations were at an all-time low; morale was slipping and aggressive independence was asserting itself among the laity."[184]

Paul VI's Legacy

Paul VI not only reconvened the Second Vatican Council, but also signed and formally promulgated its heretical constitutions, declarations and decrees. "During Paul's pontificate, every major liturgical rite of the Western church was revised... Extreme Unction was [essentially changed and] renamed the sacrament of the anointing of the sick... Penance came to be called the sacrament of

---

[182] Wilton Wynn, *Keeper of the Keys*, p. 30.
[183] Wynn, 8.
[184] p. 467.

reconciliation and penitents were given the option of sitting face to face with the priest in confession... bishops were permitted to authorize general absolution."[185]

Paul VI created 144 cardinals during his reign. His 1967 decree, *Regimini Ecclesiae,* excluded cardinals over 80 from voting in papal conclaves and limited the number of those voting in the conclave to 120. This legislation craftily eliminated many conservative cardinals and ensured that newly appointed liberal cardinals would control future papal elections.

The Ecumenist

> The key to understanding Paul VI's papacy lies in the late pontiff's innate belief that all men and women are naturally good and will totally reject evil once they are shown the difference between the two. The primary function of Christ's Church, he believed, was to make that difference clear to as many individuals as possible, not to convert the world... to Roman Catholicism.[186]

On January 4-6, 1964, Paul VI made a special trip to the Holy Land and conferred with Jewish, Orthodox and Muslim religious leaders. On May 19, 1964, he formed a Secretariat for the Development of Relations with Non-Christian Religions. In his first encyclical, *Ecclesiam Suam,*[187] Paul VI insisted on dialogue between Catholics and non-Catholic Christians, non-Christians, atheists and even Communists.

"He was a tireless host. He granted audiences to no fewer than ninety State visitors, a bizarre procession of sovereigns and presidents, dictators, democrats, and Communists, black and white, Christian and Jewish, Moslem and heathen."[188]

> Paul VI "initiated formal consultation levels and informal dialogue on international and national levels between Catholics and non-Catholics—Orthodox, Anglicans, Protestants, Jews, Muslims, Buddhists, Hindus and unbelievers. He and Greek Orthodox Athenagoras I of Constantinople nullified in 1965 the mutual excommunications imposed by their respective churches in 1054.[189]

---

[185] National Catholic News Service, *Nights of Sorrow, Days of Joy,* p. 6.
[186] Time-Life Report, *Four Popes,* p. 47.
[187] August 6, 1964.
[188] Nicolas Cheetham, *Keepers of the Keys,* p. 298.
[189] Matthew Bunson, *2002 Our Sunday Visitor's Catholic Almanac,* p. 252.

On March 23, 1966, Paul VI asked Archbishop Ramsey of Canterbury, the head of the Anglican Church, to bless the crowd assembled at St. Peter's Square. How could the "archbishop" bless the crowd when he lacked the powers of the priesthood? Pope Leo XIII had declared Anglican Orders to be invalid in 1896. Therefore, Ramsey had no priestly powers with which to bless anyone. The following day Paul VI gave the Anglican archbishop his ring. "The Bishop of Rome was, in effect, recognizing him as a fellow member of the episcopate, and in some sense the church he led as a 'sister' to the church of Rome."[190]

Paul VI prayed with the members of other religious denominations at the World Council of Churches in Geneva, Switzerland on June 10, 1969. On April 27, 1975, he invited 40 U.S. and Canadian Episcopal and Anglican clergy to perform a Protestant service in the Vatican.

Visit to the United Nations

During the fourth session of Vatican II, Paul VI traveled to New York in order to address the General Assembly of the United Nations. On October 4, 1965, he prayed in the United Nations' meditation room which has an altar to the "faceless god" and contains numerous Freemasonic symbols. The true goal of his visit was revealed nearly a year earlier on November 13, 1964 when he presented his papal cross, ring and tiara (items which have long symbolized the pope's authority as the Vicar of Christ) to U Thant, Secretary General of the United Nations. These papal insignia were replaced by an episcopal miter and a cross bearing a distorted, deformed Christ. The broken cross used by Paul VI and John Paul II depicts Christ in an indecent posture of defeat and despair. The gruesome features of this bent, grotesque cross are repulsive.

The profaneness of his visit was portrayed during his historic speech to the General Assembly when Paul VI called the atheistic United Nations the world's last hope: "The peoples of the earth turn to the United Nations as the last hope of concord and peace; We presume to present here, together with Our own, their tribute of honor and of hope."[191] Following this address, Paul VI spent more time

---

[190] *National Catholic Reporter,* October 17, 2003, "Pope Paul's gift marked moving moment of ecumenical drama," by John Allen Jr.
[191] Time-Life Report, *The Pope's Visit,* p. 26.

with Soviet delegates than any other; apparently he felt very comfortable in the company of atheists.

The Socialist

Why did Paul VI read Communist newspapers during breakfast? Why did he give moral support to Communist guerrillas in Spain and left wing parties? Why did Paul VI allow himself and his office to be exploited by the Communist government of North Vietnam in order to make their 1968 Tet offensive a reality? How could a shepherd of souls look favorably upon Castro's Cuba[192] and allow Marxist bishops and priests to say Mass? Why did Paul VI never utter a word of public protest against the suppression of the Church in Communist countries? How can we excuse his silence when Communist troops violently crushed the freedom fighters in Hungary, Romania and Czechoslovakia?[193]

Paul VI resumed diplomatic relations between Yugoslavia and the Vatican. This is "the first time the Holy See had reached such an agreement with an Eastern European Marxist state."[194] On March 25, 1971, he received Marshall Tito at the Vatican. Tito had been personally responsible for the torture and execution of hundreds of priests in Yugoslavia.

Nearly 34 million Chinese were executed during the regime of Communist dictator Mao Tse-tung. On July 5, 1973 *The New York Times* noted that "...a Vatican publication suggested recently that the teachings of Mao Tse-tung reflected Christian values. Shortly afterward a papal diplomat in Geneva publicly praised the Chinese Communist social system."

Americans are familiar with the fact that countless human rights violations are still occurring in Communist China. How could the Vatican under Paul VI praise such an individual as Mao and such a system of government—a government that forcibly advocates a one-child policy? Mao implemented the

---

[192] "On September 17 [1962] Castro expelled the auxiliary bishop of Havana and over 130 priests. He also padlocked all Catholic schools and in June confiscated 350 Catholic educational institutions." Louis Shore, *Collier's Encyclopedia 1962 Yearbook*, p. 541.
[193] See Gordon Thomas and Max Morgan-Witts, *Pontiff*, p. 32.
[194] Wilton Wynn, *Keeper of the Keys*, p. 200.

teachings of Antonio Gramsci: "Cleanse the people's memory of the past. Teach the people: 'Do not think. We will think for you.' "[195] This is the philosophy employed at Vatican II.

On September 26, 1974, the paper *Le Monde* reported a conversation between Paul VI and Archbishop Helder Camara of Brazil. Paul VI greeted Camara with the words, "Good morning, my Communist bishop. How are you?" The prelate replied, "And good morning to you, our Communist pope."[196]

> Paul VI received ...the Communist emissaries most cordially. The Vatican's official *L'Osservatore Romano* gives accounts of these visits with articles and profuse illustrations. It makes us sick to see how the Communist butchers are received, embraced, showered with gifts and blessings—all in the name of the Catholic Church.[197]

Other Communist leaders, including Hungary's Janos Kádár, Poland's Edward Gierek and Romania's Ceausescu were received with red carpet treatment at the Vatican even though at the same time 50 million Catholics were being persecuted behind the Iron Curtain. The terrible sufferings of all these Church members at the hands of the Communists were simply ignored.

Cardinal Mindszenty and other bishops behind the Iron Curtain stood as heroic symbols of resistance to Communism. Cardinal Beran said, "Christianity and Communism can never be reconciled. He who would attempt such an enterprise would prove that he did not understand history..."[198] Both cardinals had experienced Communist atrocities firsthand.

In order to establish better "diplomatic relations" with the Communist government of Hungary, Paul VI ordered Cardinal Mindszenty to leave the American Embassy in Budapest on September 29, 1971.[199] *Time Magazine*

---

[195] Malachi Martin, *The Keys of This Blood*, p. 128.
[196] Rama Coomaraswamy, M.D., *Destruction of the Christian Tradition*, p. 226.
[197] *Draugas*, May 6, 1970, "Communists used the Orthodox Church for their Goals."
[198] Lino Gussoni and Aristede Brunello, *The Silent Church*, p. 219.
[199] "On September 28 the *Osservatore Romano* actually portrayed my departure from Hungary as though this had removed an obstacle hampering good relationships between Church and state. ...I experienced my second disappointment when I learned that the Holy See had lifted the ban on the excommunicated peace-priests two weeks after my departure. I also encountered general indifference to my affairs." József Cardinal Mindszenty, *Memoirs*, p. 238.

reported that Paul VI appointed six new bishops in Hungary and allowed the clergy to take an oath of loyalty to the Communist government.[200]

One must keep in mind the words of Pope Pius XII to the Hungarian bishops 23 years earlier when he condemned Cardinal Mindszenty's arrest by the Communists:

> Now it is well-known what the totalitarian and anti-religious State demands and expects from her [the Church] as a price for its tolerance:

> ...A Church which is silent, when she should speak; a Church which weakens the law of God, adapting it to the tastes of human wills, when she should loudly proclaim and defend it; a Church which detaches herself from the unbroken foundation on which Christ has built her, to adapt herself on the moving sand of the opinions of the day or to abandon herself to the passing current...[201]

Sadly, this is the kind of church that was firmly established during the 15-year rule of Paul VI. He died of a heart attack on August 6, 1978. Monsignor Pasquale Macchi, who was his private secretary, promptly destroyed Paul VI's personal notes and correspondence. One must wonder why this was done. Was there anything among these papers that would have been incriminating?

Paul VI's legacy has been devastating. Many bishops and cardinals of the Roman Curia, "...had come to believe in the closing years of Paul's pontificate that, unless the slide was halted, by the end of the century there would no longer be a religious institution which they, in any event, recognized as the Roman Catholic Church."[202]

---

[200] September 25, 1964.
[201] The speech was given on February 20, 1949. Lino Gussoni and Aristede Brunello, *The Silent Church,* p. 202.
[202] Gordon Thomas and Max Morgan-Witts, *Pontiff,* p. 289.

How true this proved to be! Obviously, the havoc witnessed worldwide since Vatican II can be directly traced to Paul's destruction of the Holy Sacrifice of the Mass, his institution of the New Sacraments, his denial and total rejection of numerous Catholic teachings and the resultant universal loss of faith.

B. The Heresies of Vatican II

Ecumenism

The words *ecumenical* and *catholic* both derive from the Greek language and mean *universal*. Thus, the General Councils of the Church were called ecumenical since bishops from around the world attended them. However, Vatican II taught a new form of ecumenism—dialogue and joint worship with all the religions of the world.

Throughout the centuries a strong Catholic Church has stood as an obstacle to the amalgamation of churches into a one world church. Therefore, the liberals needed to essentially change the Catholic Church—"modernize" it and make it "acceptable" to the world. Their type of ecumenism is founded on the false belief and hope that all religions may, without great difficulty, be brought to fraternal agreement and find a common spiritual basis. In effect, this places the Catholic Church on the same level as all other religions, thereby implying that it is not the one true Church, and consequently, that there is not one true church at all. To them, "ecumenism... seemed to mean Catholics and Protestants sitting down together to decide what Catholics were not going to believe anymore."[203]

Foundation of the Ecumenical Movement

In his work, *What is Secular Humanism?* James Hitchcock describes the origin of the ecumenical movement and the motives that inspired it:

> As far back as the reformation a few people had, for religious reasons, advocated complete religious toleration. Later, many people espoused limited religious toleration as a way of avoiding destructive civil wars. In the eighteenth century, the intellectuals began to advocate religious toleration as a matter of principle. Their motives were somewhat mixed. In part they urged religious toleration out of respect for individual conscience. In part, however, it was out of the conviction that all religious beliefs were equally false and thus all should be equally tolerated. Voltaire rejoiced that, in a society where there were many religious groups, all of them would be weak.[204]

---

[203] August-September 1992, *Homiletic and Pastoral Review*, Quote by Colonel John Robertson.
[204] p. 39.

The ecumenical movement seeks the union of all churches into a single church, not necessarily holding the same religious beliefs. It began with a conference of Protestant missionaries in Edinburgh, Scotland (1910) and inspired the development of the International Missionary Council, the Universal Christian Conference on Life and Work (1925) and the World Conference on Faith and Order (1927). In fact, "the word 'ecumenism' was first coined about the year 1920, and refers to a movement among non-Catholics who seek a world union of Christians in some form of Christian faith."[205]

Early ecumenists engaged in religious dialogue and common social action. These efforts culminated in 1948 in the formation of the World Council of Churches, which consists of 147 independent Protestant and Orthodox churches. This council has served as a framework for uniting these churches. However, they remain independent. From its headquarters in Geneva, Switzerland, the WCC continues to vigorously further the work of ecumenism.

Catholics have always believed that the Church is united, has always been united in faith, government and worship and will remain united until the end of time. Protestants believe that the Church is currently divided and hope to achieve religious unity through good will and mutual understanding by means of the ecumenical movement.

> The official Catholic attitude toward this Protestant movement was very reserved, even negative. The Catholic Church sees itself as a visible institution founded by Christ, which has never lost its unity. The Catholic Church does not see the one Church of Christ as something synthetic, as a reunification of parts that today are scattered. Rather Catholicism is already this unity. ...[Vatican II] was based on the view that this unity has simply been lost and all that is now left is something residual, inasmuch as all baptized persons and all believers form one community which must 'manifest' itself as such.[206]

Attraction of False Ecumenism

The main deception of ecumenism lies in its appearance as something good. It distorts the truth. Christ said, "Do not judge, that you may not be judged."

---

[205] Paul Hallett, *Ecumenical Councils*, p. 9.
[206] Mario Von Galli, *The Council and the Future*, pp. 142-143.

(Matthew 7: 1) Catholics must not condemn others. This does not mean, however, that error and truth should have equal rights. This is contrary to reason. Believing that your neighbor thinks he is right is not the same as believing that he is right. A Catholic may think that his Protestant neighbor is acting in good faith, while still knowing that Protestantism is wrong.

One may ask the question, "Doesn't the ecumenical movement promote charity among Christians?" Pope Pius XI explains:

> These pan-Christians who strive for the union of the Churches would appear to pursue the noblest of ideals in promoting charity among all Christians. But how could charity tend to the detriment of faith? Everyone knows that John himself, apostle of love, ...who never ceased to impress upon the memory of his disciples the new commandment 'love one another,' nevertheless strictly forbade any intercourse [discussion] with those who professed a mutilated and corrupt form of Christ's teaching. 'If any man come to you and bring not this doctrine, receive him not into the house nor say to him God speed you.' (2 John 1: 10)[207]

There Can Only be One True Church

Erroneous beliefs pose a danger to our faith. Some concepts seem so basic and so simple that we do not think to question them, yet they are inherently wrong. When we accept these flawed ideas as the foundation of our religious thought, our Catholic faith is severely jeopardized. One such erroneous belief is that any religion is "right" for those who believe it, and that nobody has the right to denounce another's religion as false. This false premise is the foundation of the ecumenical movement.

Upon close examination we see that ecumenism is not only illogical, but also diametrically opposed to the first commandment which states explicitly: "Thou shalt not have strange gods before Me." The Book of Exodus affirms: "Thou shalt not adore their gods, nor serve them."[208] Moses condemned idolatry and false worship: "They provoked Him by strange gods, and stirred Him up to anger, with their abominations. They sacrificed to devils and not to God: to gods whom they knew not: that were newly come up, whom their fathers worshipped not. Thou

---

[207] *Mortalium Animos,* January 6, 1928.
[208] Exodus 23: 24.

hast forsaken the God that begot thee, and hast forgotten the Lord that created thee."[209] Jesus Himself denounced false worship, "The Lord thy God shalt thou worship and Him only shalt thou serve."[210]

These scriptural passages have nothing to do with charity or a lack of it. It would be false charity to pretend that all religions are true. It is true charity to bring others to the truth.

If there is a God who is absolute and perfect, His truths and His laws must also be absolute and perfect. There may be different viewpoints on who God is or what He taught or what He established, but it would be impossible for all those different viewpoints to be correct. Either the Blessed Trinity is God and Allah is not, or vice versa. Either Our Lady was conceived without Original Sin or she was not. Catholics believe she was, and Protestants and Orthodox believe she was not. The various religions of the world have conflicting beliefs; therefore they cannot all be true. Furthermore, there are now more than 26,000 Christian churches holding conflicting beliefs. Only one can be true.

There can be only two logical possibilities: either there is no God and all churches are false—as atheists believe—or there is only one true God and only one true religion. The Catholic Church is the one true religion because it alone can trace its origin to the Son of God.[211] All others were started by mortal men. Hence, the Catholic Church, Christ's Church, must teach and safeguard the truth for all time. It can never change its doctrinal and moral teachings nor contradict itself because it reflects God who is Truth Itself.

The Protestant and Orthodox churches cannot possibly be the true Church of Christ because they not only have conflicting beliefs, but all of them disappear when you go backwards in time. Most Orthodox Churches started in the 11th century and most Protestant Churches began in the 16th century. Furthermore, the founders of these various religions were mortal men. Not one of these false religions can truly claim Christ as its founder.

---

[209] Canticle of Moses, Deut. 32: 16-18.
[210] Matthew 4: 10.
[211] Jesus Christ claimed to be the Son of God. He proved His divinity by fulfilling the Messianic prophesies of the Old Testament (e.g. Isaias, Jeremias, Micheas, Osee, David, etc.) and performing miracles (especially His Resurrection from the dead).

It would be a contradiction of God's unity and truth to establish many different churches for He requires all to worship Him in one way and not in hundreds of different ways. Division implies weakness and opposition. Christ said, "Every kingdom divided against itself shall be brought to desolation."[212] Almighty God cannot be worshipped equally in truth and in error.

> Catholics, at least, should know that the Church is not author of Her own being, nor of Her essential qualities, or of Her sacraments. All these come from the Founder and are not subject to change. The Church's duty is to protect and to proclaim what has been entrusted to her. Any other course were treason; and from a practical point of view ineffectual. The *non possumus* of Rome, then, means precisely what it says: 'WE CANNOT.' We are without power in a matter upon which there is Divine Ruling.[213]

For this reason the teachings of the Catholic Church have remained the same since the time of Christ although, as time progressed, Her doctrines became clearer and more fully explained. This is similar to the operation of a camera lens bringing the same image into sharper focus.

Fr. Manton proves that two conflicting religious beliefs cannot both be true:

> We just cannot see how we can worship in a Protestant Church without doing a complete back-flip in basic logic. We reason that if Jesus Christ founded a Church (and in Scripture He never refers to My Churches but to My Church) then that Church and only that Church is the one true Church. This leads to the fearfully blunt conclusion that all other churches, however sincere and personally holy their members, however high their moral standards, however majestic their prayers and ceremonies, are themselves false; and as Catholics we cannot believe in only one true Church and at the same time casually worship in a false one.

> What we cannot accept is a blurry, fuzzy, foggy way of thought that purrs sweetly about accepting the broad spirit of Christianity and overlooking all these trifling denominational differences. In other words, some would have Christianity as a big wide living-room rug with a neutral color, all ready to harmonize with any

---

[212] Luke 11: 17.
[213] Fr. Hugh Smyth, *The Reformation*, pp. 227-228.

furniture anybody chooses to set around it. This might hold if the furniture were only a variation of hymns like "Rock of Ages" or "O Sacred Head." But when the furniture, the so-called denominational differences, extend to endorsement of divorce, approval of [artificial] birth control, denial of the Real Presence—how can a Catholic feel at home here? No Mass, no Purgatory, no Last Rites, no Confession, no Immaculate Conception—these are not tiny details, but tremendous differences. These are the very treasure-chest of the Catholic Church's ancient heritage.

Only if Christ had not founded one true Church could people logically say that all religions are equally good and that all distinctions are not important. The historical fact is, whether we like it or not, that He did not leave us a spiritual smorgasbord from which to select our own plate of pious preferences. He wrote the menu and it is not *a la carte.* Of the Church He founded He said, "He who hears you, hears Me."[214]

Pope Pius XII described the fallacy of modern ecumenism: "Hence they err in a matter of divine truth, who imagine the Church to be invisible, intangible... by which many Christian communities, though they differ from each other in the profession of faith, are united by an invisible bond."[215]

Fr. Francis Connell also clearly refuted the fundamental error of ecumenism:

> To characterize the relation between Catholics and Protestants as 'unity-in-diversity' is misleading, inasmuch as it implies that essentially Catholics are one with heretics, and that their diversities are only accidental. Actually, the very opposite is the true situation. For, however near an heretical sect may seem to be to the Catholic Church in its particular beliefs, a wide gulf separates them, inasfar as the divinely established means whereby the message of God is to be communicated to souls—the infallible Magisterium of the Church—is rejected by every heretical sect. By telling Protestants that they are one with us in certain beliefs, in such wise as to give the impression that we regard this unity as the predominant feature of our relation with them, we are actually misleading them regarding the true attitude of the Catholic Church toward those who do not acknowledge Her teaching authority.[216]

---

[214] *Straws from the Crib,* pp. 282-283.
[215] The encyclical on the *Mystical Body of Christ,* June 29, 1943.
[216] *Fr. Connell Answers Moral Questions,* p. 11.

The Church has consistently forbidden worship with non-Catholics. The Council of Laodicea[217] declared "No one shall pray in common with heretics."[218] St. Ambrose has written "…we are to understand that heretics and schismatics are also severed from the Kingdom of God, and from the Church. And so He [Christ] makes it clearly evident that every assembly of heretics and schismatics belongs, not to God, but to the unclean spirit."[219] However, the Church has always prayed for the conversion of those outside the fold: "That Thou [God] wouldst restore to the unity of the Church all who have strayed from the truth and lead unbelievers to the light of the Gospel, we beseech Thee, hear us."[220]

Practical Application

Msgr. Glenn, in his book *Ethics,* shows in a very practical way, the complete folly of modern ecumenism by applying it to the business world:

> Suppose an office manager said, 'We have many different systems of bookkeeping here; there is confusion, trouble and frequent arguments but that doesn't matter. All the clerks are working for the welfare of the business and so all are working for the same end'. 'As we examine further,' the manager explains, 'It is true that our systems are not all proper. Some of our clerks like to add, some like to subtract, some to multiply and unfortunately, some will only divide. But we do a great deal of figuring among us, one way or another, and so we'll all be sure to come out right in the end for we all have the good of the business at heart.'[221]

This type of reasoning would never be tolerated in the business world and yet these same principles are applied to religion, which deals with matters of utmost importance: our eternal salvation and where we will spend our eternity.

Ecumenism has poisoned the minds of many clergy, religious and laity who believe that all religions are more or less praiseworthy and are just different roads to the same end. Those who accept religious indifferentism ignore the inherent contradictions that are found in these false religions.

---

[217] 365 AD, Canon 33.
[218] John Chapin, *Book of Catholic Quotations,* p. 800.
[219] PL 15. Expos. in Lucam Lib. VII, 91-5.
[220] Litany of the Saints.
[221] pp. 156-157.

When we are about to die and gaze into the abyss of eternity, it will matter little what money and property we have acquired, what friends we have gained, or what is our eminence in society, if we find ourselves not in the state of friendship with God. It is God who lays down the terms of friendship and the conditions of salvation. The religion which He wills for men is not a collection of vague sentimental fantasies, subject to individual temperament and opinion. It is a sober reality to which we must conform ourselves, under pain of eternal loss. It consists of truths which we must believe on the authority of God; rules of conduct which we must obey; means of grace which we must use; worship which we must give. And if these are to have any efficacy in bringing us to eternal life, they must be authorized and established by Almighty God through His Son Jesus Christ. ...If God has willed one way of salvation, surely it cannot be a matter of indifference whether we use it or not.[222]

Compromise or Conversion

Having great insight, Pope Pius XII wrote the encyclical *Humani Generis* on August 12, 1950 in order to warn Catholics of the dangers of the ecumenical movement and to condemn the many false ideologies which threatened to undermine the foundations of the Catholic Faith. Many well intentioned Catholics, both clergy and laity, were being deceived because this false ecumenism concealed itself under a mask of virtue. In an effort to repel the attacks of atheism and modern unbelief, many of these Catholics, through an imprudent zeal for souls, endeavored to unite the various religions at any cost. In this encyclical, Pope Pius XII stated:

> Now if these only aimed at adapting ecclesiastical teaching and methods to modern conditions and requirements, through the introduction of some new explanations, there would be scarcely any reason for alarm. But some through enthusiasm ...seem to consider as an obstacle to the restoration of fraternal union, things founded on the laws and principles given by Christ and likewise on institutions founded by Him [The Mass and the sacraments], or which are the defense and support of the integrity of the faith... Some reduce to a meaningless formula the necessity of belonging to the true Church in order to gain eternal salvation.

---

[222] Franciscan Friars of Atonement Graymoor, *Indifference in Religion*, p. 2.

Ultimately there are only two ways of achieving unity among world religions. One way is through a genuine change of mind (conversion) leading individuals to believe and do all that God commands, as taught by the Catholic Church. The other way of achieving unity is an attempt to find common ground by discovering doctrinal beliefs that are shared.

Ecumenism would have been a noble and worthwhile endeavor had it been pursued as a means to convert non-Catholics. Pope Pius XI said that Christian unity can only be fostered by conversion: "There is but one way in which the unity of Christians may be fostered, and that is by furthering the return to the one true Church of Christ of those that have in the past fallen away."[223]

Prior to Vatican II the Catholic Church zealously engaged in extensive missionary activity to bring about such conversions to the true faith. Bishop Sheen declared: "In mission territories throughout the world near the end of 1961, there were 200,000 priests, Brothers and Sisters, 65,000 schools, 6,000 hospitals and dispensaries, 1,500 orphanages, 400 homes for the aged and 300 leper colonies."[224]

The number of converts has dropped dramatically since Vatican II. "Between 1965 and 2002, the number of converts decreased by 37 percent."[225] There were nearly twice as many converts in 1960 (146,212) as there were in 2002 (79,892).

When non-Catholics convert they become members of the one true Church of Christ; here they find a unity of doctrine, worship and government. "One faith, one Lord, one Baptism."[226] Vatican II's *Decree on Ecumenism* not only omits the term *conversion* and the concept of a *return* to the Catholic Faith but, in effect, holds it as unnecessary. The adoption of ecumenism by John XXIII and Paul VI succeeded in dismantling the extensive missionary work of the Church.

Cardinal Kasper, the Prefect of the Vatican's Pontifical Council for Promoting Unity, declared: "Today we no longer understand ecumenism in the sense of a return, by which the others would 'be converted' and return to being 'Catholics.'

---

[223] *Mortalium Animos.*
[224] Felician Foy, O.F.M., *1963 National Catholic Almanac*, p. 522.
[225] Kenneth Jones, *Index of Leading Catholic Indicators*, p. 66-67.
[226] Ephesians 4: 5.

This was expressly abandoned at Vatican II."[227] On January 20, 2003 John Paul II said, "The Second Vatican Council committed the Catholic Church 'irrevocably to following the path of the ecumenical venture...'"[228]

The modern ecumenical movement seeks unity through religious indifferentism. The *Baltimore Catechism* states that "Indifferentism is the error of those who hold that one religion is as good as another and that all religions are equally true and pleasing to God, or that one is free to accept or reject any or all religions."[229] It is the old, "I'm ok, you're ok, we're all ok."

However, if one religion were as good as another then they all become worthless and unnecessary. The question remains: Where will this all lead?

Did the ecumenists ever really hope to achieve an actual union—a unity of belief—with their doctrinal compromise? Hans Küng, one of the chief promoters of ecumenism, acknowledges that religious indifference does not lead to doctrinal unity:

> What we need is that both sides should create more and more common ground between us, until at last what separates us becomes insignificant and full unity is a reality. This 'perfect unity' will not be uniformity.[230]

Ecumenism, which promotes religious indifferentism, was expressly condemned by Pope Pius IX:

- Men can find the way to eternal salvation, and they can attain eternal salvation in the practice of any religion whatever.
- There is good reason at least to hope for the eternal salvation of all those who are in no way in the true Church of Christ.
- Protestantism is simply another form of the same true Christian religion, and it is possible to please God there just as much as in the Catholic Church.[231]

---

[227] *Adisti*, Feb. 26, 2001. English translation quoted from "Where Have They Hidden the Body?," by Christopher Ferrara, *The Remnant*, June 30, 2001.
[228] Speech of January 20, 2003 to the ecumenical delegation from Finland.
L'Osservatore Romano, Jan. 29, 2003, "Church: irrevocably committed to ecumenism."
[229] Q. 205, p. 124.
[230] Hans Küng, *The Council, Reform and Reunion*, p. 188.
[231] *Syllabus of Errors*, nos. 16-18, December 8, 1864.

To understand and to evaluate the Holy See's generally negative position on this matter, one must first examine its theoretical basis. This is to be found in the Catholic Church's understanding of itself, in the constant and deep conviction that it is the one and only true Church of Jesus Christ. …A great abundance of material from the documents of the Holy See can be adduced as evidence of this conviction; so great is the abundance that it is difficult to avoid the conclusion that what is involved here is indeed a matter of faith that cannot be altered. The one true Church of Christ, and it alone, has the right to honor God through the public worship willed by Him.[232]

Pope Pius XI clarified this point in his encyclical *Mortalium Animos:*

The one Church of Christ is visible to all, and will remain, according to the will of its Author, exactly the same as He instituted it. The Mystical Spouse of Christ has never in the course of centuries been contaminated, nor in the future can She ever be, as Cyprian bears witness: 'The Bride of Christ cannot become false to Her Spouse; She is inviolate and pure. …For since the Mystical Body of Christ, like His physical body, is one (I Cor. 12: 12), compactly and fitly joined together (Eph. 4: 15), it were foolish to say that the Mystical Body is composed of disjointed and scattered members. Whosoever therefore is not united with the body is no member thereof, neither is he in communion with Christ its Head.

The Decree on Ecumenism

"Dr. Oscar Cullman, a Protestant observer at the Council, has rightly said of the Decree: 'This is more than the opening of a door; new ground has been broken. No Catholic document has ever spoken of non-Catholic Christians in this way.' "[233] The heretical Vatican II *Decree on Ecumenism* specifically described the quest for religious unity as a "restoration" of a unity that had been lost, not as a conversion or return to the pre-existing unity of the Catholic Church.

---

[232] Wilhelm de Vries, S.J. "Communicatio in Sacris," *The Church and Ecumenism,* pp. 18-19.
[233] Walter Abbott, S.J., *The Documents of Vatican II,* p. 338.

Walter Abbott, S.J. noted that Vatican II's *Decree on Ecumenism* was in fact a revolutionary departure from previous Church doctrine:

> Many sentences and sections of Vatican II decrees are remarkable for the fact that they are there at all [because they are heretical]. It can truly be said that the whole *Decree on Ecumenism* is remarkable for that fact. In this Decree, the focus is more on a 'pilgrim' Church moving toward Christ than on a movement of "return" [conversion] to the Roman Catholic Church. In this Decree, the Council goes beyond the assertion that the Catholic Church is the true Church to assert that Jesus, in His Spirit, is at work in the Churches and Communities beyond the visible borders of the Catholic Church; the Council asserts that believers in Christ who are baptized are truly reborn and truly our brothers and that God uses their worship to sanctify and save them.[234]

The *Decree on Ecumenism* further states that, in spite of deficiencies "The spirit of Christ has not refrained from using them [other religions] as a means of salvation." Following the spirit of Vatican II the Postconciliar Church engages in dialogue with all religions, even to the degree of joining with them in formal worship. It does not seek the conversion of any.

Communicatio in Sacris—Interfaith Worship

When scrutinized, the heresy of such a stand becomes apparent. The Church forbids Catholics to actively participate in the religious services of non-Catholics *(communicatio in sacris)* because it implies approval of false beliefs and is a cause of scandal. The *Baltimore Catechism* states that "a Catholic sins against faith by taking part in non-Catholic worship because he thus professes belief in a religion he knows is false."[235] It is also obviously against the first commandment.

The 1918 *Code of Canon Law* declares: "A person who of his own accord and knowingly helps in any manner to propagate heresy, or who communicates in sacred rites with heretics in violation of the prohibition of Canon 1258, incurs suspicion of heresy."[236] Canon 1258 states: "The faithful are not allowed to assist actively in any way or to take part in the religious services of non-Catholics."

---

[234] Walter Abbott, S.J., *The Documents of Vatican II*, p. 338.
[235] Fr. Francis Connell, *Baltimore Catechism No. 3*, p. 124.
[236] Canon 2316.

Pope Pius XI forcefully stated: "It is clear that the Apostolic See can by no means take part in these assemblies, nor is it in any way lawful for Catholics to give to such enterprises their encouragement or support. If they did so, they would be giving countenance to a false Christianity quite alien to the one Church of Christ."[237] The Catholic Church cannot support the Ecumenical Movement.

The Vatican II *Decree on Ecumenism* explicitly contradicts these prohibitions and actually encourages *communicatio in sacris*:

> The sacred council exhorts all the Catholic faithful to recognize the signs of the times and to take an active and intelligent part in the work of ecumenism... Therefore, some worship in common *(communicatio in sacris)*, given suitable circumstances and the approval of Church authority, is not only possible but to be encouraged.

In his commentary on the *Decree of Ecumenism*, Walter Abbott, S.J. remarks:

> The Council here uses in a laudatory way an expression, *communicatio in sacris*, which, up to this time, had meant for students of canon law something simply prohibited (and, in fact, mentioned in tones akin to horror). The notion of worship connotes the official, public prayer of a Church or Community. Normally, it implies commitment to the faith or creed of that Church or Community.[238]

The *Decree on Ecumenism* discusses the relationship with churches separated from the Catholic Church. "...For men who believe in Christ and have been properly baptized are brought into a certain, though imperfect, communion with the Catholic Church."

Commenting on this text, Walter Abbott, S.J., notes that the novel doctrine of the *Decree* stands in direct contradiction to the previous teachings of the Church:

> The Decree stops short of saying outright that they are 'members' of the Church, probably because of the sentence in Pope Pius XII's encyclical 'Mystici Corporis' (The Mystical Body) issued in 1943: Only those are to be included as real members of the Church who have been baptized and profess the true faith, and

---

[237] *Mortalium Animos.*
[238] *Documents of Vatican II*, p. 352, footnote 37.

who have not been so unfortunate as to separate themselves from the unity of the Body, or been excluded by legitimate authority for serious faults.[239]

Samuel McCrea Cavert adds, "The assumption that the Holy Spirit is at work in 'ecclesial communities' outside the Roman Catholic Church is very different from the previous way of treating non-Roman Christians merely as individuals [heretics and schismatics] and ignoring their corporate life and structure."[240]

By encouraging common worship between Catholics and non-Catholics, Vatican II stands in direct opposition to the previous Church teachings of 260 popes and the 20 General Councils of the past 2,000 years. It also puts to folly the death and torture endured by millions of Catholic martyrs. The first 31 popes died for their faith rather than worship false gods. This example becomes "folly" in the shadow of Vatican II's teachings. The contradictions stand out boldly when the *Decree on Ecumenism* is read side by side with Pope Pius XI's *Encyclical on Promoting Christian Unity*[241] and the *Monita* (warnings) of the Holy Office.[242]

The documents of Vatican II teach that the Church of Christ is broader than the Catholic Church and that its many layers are composed of various ecclesial communities: Christian churches, non-Christian faiths and even atheists. How Vatican II's teachings can accept atheists (who do not in believe any God at all) as part of the Church of Christ is totally incomprehensible.

Paul VI expresses his Modernist views in the Apostolic Exhortation *On Evangelization in the Modern World:*

> The Church respects and esteems these non-Christian religions because they are the living expression of the soul of vast groups of people.... They possess an impressive patrimony of deeply religious texts.[243]

---

[239] *Documents of Vatican II*, p. 345, footnote 12.
[240] Walter Abbott, S.J., *The Documents of Vatican II*, p. 345.
[241] *Mortalium Animos.*
[242] June 5, 1948 (AAS 40-257) and December 20, 1949 (AAS 42-142).
[243] December 8, 1975.

Fr. Richard McBrien describes the results of three decades of ecumenical ventures in an article entitled "The State of Ecumenism" written in January 2002:

> Most mainline Protestants, Anglicans and [Postconciliar] Catholics simply take it for granted that they can work and pray together, receive the sacraments occasionally in one another's churches, and study in one another's seminaries and divinity schools. As far as many rank-and-file Christians are concerned, the ecumenical barriers have already fallen.[244]

This stands in stark contrast to the first draft of the *Dogmatic Constitution on the Church of Christ* at Vatican I (1870):

> Any societies whatsoever that are separated from the unity of the faith or from communion with the body [the Catholic Church] cannot in any way be said to be a part or a member of it. And it cannot be said to be diffused and distributed among the various Christian denominations; but it is an integrated unit, entirely coherent; and in its conspicuous unity, it shows itself an undivided and indivisible body, which is the true Mystical Body of Christ. The Apostle [St. Paul] says of it: 'One body, one spirit, even as you were called in one hope of your calling; one Lord, one faith, one baptism...' (Eph. 4: 4-6).[245]

Sadly, for the Catholic Church, the ecumenical experiment of the past 40 years has been a dismal failure and has led to a great loss of faith. Millions of Catholics have left the faith to join false religions after Vatican II, while the various non-Catholic religions still remain independent and show no signs of conversion.

Seeking conversions is an essential element of Christianity, as James Hitchcock confirms in his book, *Catholicism and Modernity:*

> The decline of the missionary impulse is of crucial importance, because Christianity is fundamentally a missionary religion. ...The missionary impulse is a crucial touchstone of the health of the Church, not only because it is an obedient response to the command of Christ but also because Christianity is a dynamic religion which must either grow or decline and cannot merely remain stable. ...The willingness or unwillingness of Christians to proselytize for their beliefs is an index of the firmness with which they hold those beliefs.

---

[244] *The Tidings,* January 25, 2002, p. 11.
[245] John Clarkson, S.J., *The Church Teaches,* p. 90.

> One of the open secrets of liberal Christianity is that, despite its talk of making the faith credible to nonbelievers, it has never been interested in conversions and is in fact made uneasy by them.[246]

Since Vatican II the work of Catholic missionaries throughout the world has become meaningless. Instead of working to convert natives to the Catholic faith, they often teach Hindus to become good Hindus, etc. Occasionally, postconciliar priests and missionaries even incorporate into the new liturgy the rituals of false religions, creating a new blend of paganism.

The Vatican II *Decree on the Sacred Liturgy* encouraged this liturgical inculturation. As a result, pagan ceremonies are sometimes incorporated into the New Mass. For example, in African "Catholic" churches ancestral worship and animal sacrifices are offered in conjunction with the new liturgies.

> In one recent incident at a township near Pretoria, a video recording was made of a priest blessing chickens and goats during Mass. The animals were then slaughtered and their sacrificial blood poured into a hole dug outside the church... Archbishop Tlhagale [of Bloemfonteinm, South Africa] has proposed that blood taken from an animal, whether it be a goat, chicken, sheep or cow, could be brought to the altar before the offertory during the Mass as 'a gift to the ancestors, not to God.'[247]

Although animal rights groups strongly oppose these practices, Church leaders are discussing the need to alter the interior of churches in order to accommodate these rituals.

Open Dialogue

The concepts embodied in the Vatican II *Declaration on the Relationship of the Church to Non-Christian Religions*[248] are unprecedented:

> The Church therefore has this exhortation for Her sons: prudently and lovingly, through dialogue and collaboration with the followers of other religions, and in witness of Christian faith and life, acknowledge, preserve and promote the spiritual and moral goods found among these men, as well as the values of their society and culture.

---

[246] p. 211.
[247] *Catholic,* May 2000.
[248] *Nostra Aetate,* October 28, 1965.

John Paul II has repeatedly demonstrated his belief in this ideology during his visits to predominantly non-Christian regions by his heretical speeches and active participation in non-Christian worship. For example, during his trip to Benin (a country situated between Togo and Nigeria on the West African coast) he addressed the adherents of Voodooism and praised the traditions of their ancestors:

> You have a strong attachment to the traditions handed on by your ancestors [witchcraft and false worship]. It is legitimate to be grateful to your forebears who passed on this sense of the sacred, belief in a single God who is good [not the Blessed Trinity], a sense of celebration, esteem for the moral life and for harmony in society.[249]

Many of the Documents of Vatican II (especially the *Decree on Ecumenism* and the *Declaration of the Relationship of the Church to Non-Christian Religions*) reject the mandate of Christ to "Go into the whole world and preach the gospel to every creature. He who believes and is baptized shall be saved, but he who does not believe shall be condemned."[250]

It would therefore follow that all the efforts of the Apostles who traveled throughout the world in order to convert those who had not yet been instructed in Christianity were all in vain and unnecessary. So were those of the innumerable Catholic missionaries who continued this work and journeyed to Asia, Africa and the New World in order to win souls for Christ and who sacrificed their lives in such an effort.

Vatican II's decrees on *Ecumenism* and *Religious Liberty* place all religions on an equal footing. In his pastoral letter, Bishop Pivarunas explains the absurdity of considering one religion to be as good as another:

> How does one 'in witness of Christian faith acknowledge, preserve, and promote the spiritual and moral goods' of false religions? Is Christianity, is Catholicism compatible and reconcilable with the worship of false gods!? What are the 'spiritual and moral goods' to be found in false worship?

---

[249] *L'Osservatore Romano,* February 10, 1993, p. 7.
[250] Mark 16: 16.

Should it be any wonder why so many Catholics since Vatican II have involved themselves in the practices of the Eastern religions of Hinduism, Buddhism, and Islamism? Should it be any wonder that since Vatican II, John Paul II and his Modernist clergy have publicly gathered together for worship in common with the leaders of these false religions and a multitude of other religions including Animism, Voodooism, Shintoism, etc.?[251]

The heretical Vatican II *Decree on Ecumenism* even goes so far as to declare that non-Catholic religions are channels of grace:

> The brethren divided from us also use many liturgical actions of the Christian religion. These most certainly can truly engender a life of grace in ways that vary according to the condition of each church or community. These liturgical actions must be regarded as capable of giving access to the community of salvation.
>
> It follows that the separated churches and communities as such, though we believe them to be deficient in some respects, have been by no means deprived of significance and importance in the mystery of salvation. For the spirit of Christ has not refrained from using them as means of salvation which derive their efficacy from the very fullness of grace and truth entrusted to the Catholic Church.

The *Decree on Ecumenism* further declares that "Sacred theology and other branches of knowledge, especially those of a historic nature, must be taught with due regard for the ecumenical point of view, so that they may correspond as exactly as possible to the facts."

What "facts?" This decree states that the Church must adapt its theology and alter its history in order to appease non-Catholics. As the saying goes, "If you don't like history—change it." Many religions already deny the Blessed Trinity, the Divinity of Christ, the sacraments and the teachings of the General Councils of the Church. Must Catholics likewise deny these teachings in order to placate non-Catholics? If non-Catholics do not themselves agree on these points—with which non-Catholic religions is the Church to align herself? Although the Postconciliar Church has made countless concessions and apologies, non-

---

[251] *Pro Grege*, June 29, 1994.

Catholics are still not satisfied and continue to verbally attack Catholic belief and worship. How many more treasured doctrines must be watered down and liturgical practices eliminated in order to placate non-Catholics?

Paul VI echoed the *Decree on Ecumenism* in speeches given on September 29, 1963 and March 29, 1964:

> Undoubtedly, the Catholic Church perceives, and with sorrow, the deficiencies, inadequacies and errors in many of these religious expressions, but she cannot refrain from addressing a word to them also, to remind them that the Catholic religion fully appreciates all that is true and good and human in them, [Even though they are man-made and false religions?] and that in order to preserve in modern society the religious sense and the worship of God...

> Every religion possesses rays of light which must neither be despised or extinguished, even if they are insufficient to enlighten men to the necessary extent [salvation?] and if they do not reach the miracle of Christian light in which truth and life meet...

This refrain is continued by Paul VI in his encyclical *Ecclesiam Suam:*

> Then to the adorers of God according to the conception of monotheism, the Muslim religion especially, is deserving of our admiration for all that is true and good in their worship of God. And also to the followers of the great Afro-Asiatic religions... [Buddhism, Hinduism, Islam, Jainism, Shintoism, Sikhism, Taoism, Voodoo, etc.].

It is a sin against the first commandment and, indeed, blasphemous to place the true Church of Christ, the Catholic Church, on a level with religions which worship animals and false gods, practice sorcery, spell casting or even perform blood sacrifices. Neither can the Catholic Church be placed on the same level with Monotheistic religions that deny the Blessed Trinity.

During his countless travels throughout the world, John Paul II routinely engages in dialogue and actively participates in worship with non-Catholic religions including Animist, Buddhist, Hindu, Islam, Jain, Jewish, Orthodox, Protestant, Shinto, Sikh, Snake Worshippers, Taoist, Voodoo and Zoroastrian. What kind of validation is he giving to these false religions?

One cannot help but wonder how the Postconciliar Popes would interpret Jesus' words when He said, "He who is not with Me is against Me, and he who does not gather with Me scatters." (Matthew 12:30) "I am the light of the world. He who follows Me does not walk in the darkness, but will have the light of life." (John 8: 12). "I am the way, and the truth and the life." (John 14: 6) "...Thou art Peter, and upon this rock I will build My Church." (Matthew 16: 18) "Go, therefore, and make disciples of all nations, baptizing them in the name of the Father and of the Son and of the Holy Spirit, teaching them to observe all that I have commanded you." (Matthew 28: 19-20)

Universal Salvation

Numerous Protestant terms were employed in Vatican II's *Dogmatic Constitution on the Church* and in other documents. This was confirmed by Dr. Albert Outler in his book, *Methodist Observer at the Council:* "In the course of the long debates in St. Peter's, I was repeatedly astonished... to hear Catholic bishops talking earnestly about 'the Word of God,' 'the People of God,' 'the priesthood of all believers,' 'the universal call to holiness'—phrases and notions that I could not classify otherwise than as 'evangelical.' "

> The 'Dogmatic Constitution on the Church' (*Lumen Gentium*) declared that all people are called to be 'church,' understood fundamentally as the assembly or people of God. And to the church, understood in this sense, 'belong, or are related in different ways: the catholic faithful, others who believe in Christ, and finally all of humankind, called by God's grace to salvation.'[252]

Yves Congar promoted the concept of "anonymous Christianity"—whereby everyone is a Christian, even without knowing it. According to Congar, the Church is the *People of God* and everyone is saved because all are called to salvation and belong to saved humanity. "Karl Rahner thinks that this is sufficient to justify extending the expression 'People of God' to all humanity."[253] It would follow from this system of belief that there is then, no hell. "In fact,

---

[252] *Lumen Gentium*, no. 13, in Flannery, *Vatican II*, p. 19.
[253] Cf. "L'Eglise sacrement universel du salut," *Eglise vivante* 17 (1965) pp. 641-642.

Rahner contended that the most important achievement of the Second Vatican Council was its *optimistic* attitude towards salvation, its implicit recognition of 'anonymous Christianity.' This means that even the agnostic or atheist 'who courageously accepts life... has already accepted God.' "[254]

"The basic idea, left half implied, is that all the baptized are members of God's People, but some of them, raised in a dissident church or ecclesiastical community, do not enjoy all the goods of the Covenant and do not have full communion with the body of the Church in which the Church of Christ and the Apostles exists."[255] Ecumenists teach that one religion is as good as another, although the Catholic Church is the preferred religion. If this is the case, one would logically have to ask, "Why would the Catholic Church be preferred?"

This novel concept of the "People of God" saves Catholics and Christians by their relation to Christ, non-Christians because they adhere to some type of religion and atheists because they are members of the human race. This erroneous belief leads not only to interdenominational worship but even to theological exploration into the different forms of atheism.

Fr. Richard McBrien says: "Vatican II insisted in its *Decree on Ecumenism* that the Body of Christ includes churches and ecclesial communities beyond the Catholic Church and that the quest for Christian unity is an ongoing responsibility for us all."[256]

The *Handbook for Today's Catholics* confirms this ideology: "In speaking of the Church, the Second Vatican Council emphasizes the image of the people of God more than any other one. Strictly speaking, all people are the people of God. ...'The Catholic community is not the whole of God's people.' "[257]

Pope Pius XI declared the fallacy of the new theology of Vatican II:

They presuppose the erroneous view that all religions are more or less good and praiseworthy, inasmuch as all give expression, under various forms, to that

---

[254] Karl Rahner, *I Remember,* Translator's Forward, p. 3.
[255] John Miller, C.S.C., *Vatican II: an Interfaith Appraisal,* p. 204.
[256] *The Tidings,* March 30, 2001, "The Pope and Vatican II."
[257] The Catholic People of God, [781-786], pp. 27-28.

innate sense that leads men to God and to the obedient acknowledgement of His rule. Those who hold such a view are not only in error; they distort the true idea of religion, and thus reject it, falling gradually into naturalism and atheism. To favor this opinion, therefore, and, to encourage such undertakings is tantamount to abandoning the religion revealed by God.[258]

Archbishop Fulton Sheen describes the evil results of indifference:

In religious matters, the modern world believes in indifference. Very simply, this means it has no great loves and no great hates; no causes worth living for and no causes worth dying for. It counts its virtues by the vices from which it abstains, asks that religion be easy and pleasant, sneers the term 'mystic' at those who are spiritually inclined, dislikes enthusiasm and loves benevolence, makes elegance the test of virtue and hygiene the test of morality, believes that one may be too religious but never too refined. It holds that no one ever loses his soul, except for some great and foul crime such as murder. Briefly, the indifference of the world includes no true fear of God, no fervent zeal for His honor, no deep hatred of sin, and no great concern for eternal salvation.[259]

In such a secular, humanistic religion, "Where does God, where does sanctity, where does the supernatural or the sacramental life, come into this? Nowhere. The result is a kind of common denominator of social cooperation as a substitute for faith, which, if it goes on long enough, completely distorts the sense of values upon which Catholic Christianity rests."[260]

Intercommunion

In an attempt to promote ecumenism, the Postconciliar Church allows non-Catholics to receive the eucharist in Vatican II churches and Postconciliar Catholics to receive communion in non-Catholic churches.

The Vatican II *Decree on the Catholic Eastern Churches:*

Permits Eastern Christians not in full communion with the Apostolic See of Rome [schismatics] to be admitted to the Sacraments of Penance, of the Eucharist and of the Anointing of the Sick when they find themselves in the specified circumstances. It equally authorizes Catholics to request these same

---

[258] *Mortalium Animos,* January 6, 1928.
[259] *The Hymn of the Conquered,* Huntington, Indiana: Our Sunday Visitor, pp. 26-27.
[260] John Eppstein, *Has the Catholic Church Gone Mad?,* pp. 134-135.

sacraments from Eastern priests whenever necessity or a genuine spiritual benefit call for it and access to a Catholic priest is physically or morally impossible.[261]

This position was later expanded to give even more latitude for non-Catholic reception of other Catholic sacraments which have always presupposed membership in the Catholic Church. The Secretariat for Promoting Christian Unity issued a decree, approved by Paul VI on May 25, 1972, permitting non-Catholics to receive communion at Catholic churches when "in danger of death or urgent need (during persecution, in prisons, etc.) if the separated brother has no access to a minister of his own communion... " The decree further states: "Such cases are not confined to situations of suffering and danger. Christians may find themselves in grave spiritual necessity and with no chance of recourse to their own community."[262]

Another decree issued on October 17, 1973 further declared:

…Admission to Catholic Eucharistic communion is confined in particular cases to those Christians …who experience a spiritual need for the eucharistic sustenance, who for a prolonged period are unable to have recourse to a minister of their own community, and who ask for the sacrament of their own accord; all this provided that they have proper dispositions and lead lives worthy of a Christian.[263]

The *New Code of Canon Law* of 1983 further allows intercommunion between Catholics and non-Catholics.

Whenever necessity requires or genuine spiritual advantage suggests... it is lawful for the faithful for whom it is physically or morally impossible to approach a catholic minister, to receive the sacraments of penance, the Eucharist, and anointing of the sick from non-catholic ministers in whose Churches these sacraments are valid.

---

[261] *On the Position of the Catholic Church on the Celebration of the Eucharist in Common by Christians of Other Confessions,* AAS 62 (January 7, 1970).
[262] *The Instruction Concerning Cases When Other Christians Can Be Admitted to Eucharistic Communion in the Catholic Church.*
[263] *Note Interpreting "Instruction Concerning Cases When Other Christians Can Be Admitted to Eucharistic Communion in the Catholic Church Under Certain Circumstances."*

Catholic ministers may lawfully administer the sacraments of penance, the Eucharist, and anointing of the sick to members of the eastern Churches not in full communion with the catholic Church, if they ask spontaneously for them and are properly disposed.[264]

This permission for non-Catholics to take Communion has been expanded by John Paul II, where "at mixed marriages, between a Catholic and a baptized Christian who is not in full communion with the Catholic Church" a "eucharistic sharing" is possible.[265] His encyclical *The Eucharist, Source of the Church's Life* of April 17, 2003 renews permission for intercommunion:

> It is a source of joy to note that Catholic ministers are able, in certain particular cases, to administer the Sacraments of the Eucharist, Penance and Anointing of the Sick to Christians who are not in full communion with the Catholic Church [non-Catholics] but who greatly desire to receive these sacraments, freely request them and manifest the faith which the Catholic Church professes with regard to these sacraments. Conversely, in specific cases and in particular circumstances, Catholics, too, can request these same sacraments from ministers of Churches in which these sacraments are valid.[266]

Condemnations of Intercommunion

The practice of non-Catholics receiving Holy Communion in Catholic churches is completely contrary to the Church's teachings of the past 2,000 years.

> [Pope] John XXII, in a letter of October 11, 1322, to the Latin Patriarch of Constantinople, condemned a practice prevalent in Akhaia. Latin Catholics were going to the schismatics' Mass and were there receiving the sacraments; and in turn they were admitting non-Catholics to the services in the Catholic churches. This involved danger to souls, the divine majesty was offended and considerable harm was done to the Christian religion. Therefore, under threat of ecclesiastical penalties, this practice was to be strictly forbidden.[267]

---

[264] Canon 844 (2) and (3).
[265] *Directory for the Application of the Principles and Norms of Ecumenism,* June 8, 1993.
[266] No. 46: AAS 87 (1985), 948.
[267] *Codific. Canonica Orientale, Fonti, Serie III* (Vatican, 1943), Vol. VII, 2, pp. 120-l, n. 204.

The Council of Florence declared "For union with the body of the Church is of such importance that the sacraments of the Church are helpful to salvation only for those remaining in it."[268]

The Council of Trent condemned the proposition that faith alone was a sufficient preparation for receiving the Sacrament of the Holy Eucharist.[269] The *Code of Canon Law* of 1918 states: "It is forbidden to administer the sacraments of the Church to heretics or schismatics, even if they err in good faith and request the sacraments, unless they shall have previously rejected their errors and have been reconciled to the Church."[270] This concurs with the reply of the Holy Office:

> 'May material schismatics at the point of death, who ask in good faith for absolution and Extreme Unction, be given these sacraments without an abjuration of their errors?' The reply was: 'No, but it is required that to the best of their ability they reject their errors and make a profession of faith.'[271]

Msgr. Mannion explains why intercommunion is forbidden:

> Put as simply as possible: When a non-Catholic comes to Communion, he or she is expressing complete unity with the Catholic Church. ...Receiving Communion is more than a matter of receiving Christ's Body and Blood—as central as that is. To receive Communion in the Catholic Church is to state acceptance of the dogmas of Catholicism, to express adherence to the Catholic moral system and to recognize the authority of the Catholic bishops and the pope.[272]

Religious Liberty

On December 7, 1965 Paul VI promulgated the heretical *Declaration on Religious Freedom (Dignitatis Humanae)*. This document contained teachings that had been explicitly condemned by previous popes and because of this, many of the Council Fathers opposed it until the very end.

> Cardinal Ottaviani said that the declaration stated a principle which had always been recognized, namely, that no one could be forced in religious matters. But the text was guilty of exaggeration in stating that 'he is worthy of honor' who

---

[268] *Decree for the Jacobites*, February 4, 1441.
[269] Session XIII, Canon II *On the Most Holy Sacrament of the Eucharist*.
[270] Canon 731.
[271] May 17, 1916.
[272] *Our Sunday Visitor*, December 16, 2001, "Pastoral Answers."

obeys his own conscience. It would be better to say that such a person was deserving of tolerance or of respect and charity. 'The principle that each individual has the right to follow his own conscience must suppose that the conscience is not contrary to the Divine Law.'[273]

Cardinal Quiroga y Palacios, of Santiago de Compostela, Spain, called for the complete revision of the text. From its style and language, its dominant preoccupation appeared to be to favor union with the separated brethren, without sufficient consideration of the very serious dangers to which it thereby exposed the Catholic faithful. The text was filled with ambiguities, he charged, new doctrine being favored at the expense of traditional doctrine, and the Council was being invited to give its solemn approval to the liberalism which the Church had so often condemned.[274]

The *Declaration on Religious Freedom* is diametrically opposed to the consistent teaching of the Catholic Church. This irreconcilable contradiction was even noted by the principal author of the document, Fr. John Courtney Murray, when he admitted, "The course of the development between the *Syllabus of Errors* (1864) and *Dignitatis Humanae Personae* (1965) still remains to be explained by theologians."[275]

In order to understand the implications of the *Declaration on Religious Freedom* one must first recognize the vast difference between the meaning of the terms, *freedom* and *right*. Almighty God created us with the gift of free will—the ability to choose between good and evil. A *free act* "is an act ...that is under *control* of the will, an act that the will can do or leave undone."[276] Morality does not consist in freedom itself, but in the conformity of our actions to the Eternal Law of God. Man, therefore, may have the *freedom* to commit sin and to promote error, but he does not have the *right* to do so.

> A right is "...a moral power residing in a person—a power which all others are bound to respect—of doing, possessing, or requiring something. Right is founded upon *law*. For the existence of a right in one person involves an

---

[273] Fr. Ralph Wiltgen, S.V.D., *The Rhine Flows into the Tiber*, p. 164.
[274] Wiltgen, 165.
[275] William Abbot, S.J., *The Documents of Vatican II*, p. 673.
[276] Msgr. Paul Glenn, *Ethics*, p. 11.

obligation in all others of not impeding or violating that right. Now, it is only law that can impose such an obligation. And whether this law, upon which right is based, be the natural law or positive law, it is (as all true law) founded ultimately upon the Eternal Law.[277]

As a consequence, man does not have the right to do wrong or to freely promote false teachings on religious matters in society. He does not have the *right*—the *moral power*—to teach and proselytize Atheism, Agnosticism, Satanism, Witchcraft and other false religions. He has the freedom to do such, but not the right to do so. In contrast, the *Declaration on Religious Freedom* says, "Therefore, the right to religious freedom has its foundation, not in the subjective disposition of the person, but in his very nature."[278]

The *Declaration on Religious Freedom* falsely proclaims that those in error have the right to promote their error publicly, even if they are in bad faith:

> In consequence, the right to this immunity continues to exist even in those who do not live up to their obligation of seeking the truth and adhering to it. ...Religious Communities also have the right not to be hindered in their public teaching and witness to their faith, whether by the spoken or written word.[279]

Concerning the term *right,* Pope Leo XIII taught in *Libertas Humana* that "Right is a moral faculty, and as we have said, and it cannot be too often repeated, it would be absurd to believe that it belongs naturally and without distinction to truth and to lies, to good and to evil."

Pope Pius XII explicitly taught that error and false religions cannot be the object of a natural right:

> It must be clearly affirmed that no human authority, no State, no Community of States, of whatever religious character can give a positive mandate or a positive authorization to teach or do anything contrary to religious truth or moral good... Whatever does not respond to truth and the moral law has objectively no right to existence, nor to propaganda, nor to action.[280]

---

[277] Msgr. Paul Glenn, *Ethics,* p. 136.
[278] This decree teaches that "religious liberty" is a natural God-given right.
[279] Vatican II *Declaration on Religious Freedom.*
[280] Pope Pius XII, *Ci Riesce,* December 6, 1953.

Thus, although individuals have the *freedom* to disobey and disregard the laws of God, they do not have the right to do so. They have neither the right to be indifferent to their duties to God, nor the right to worship God in any manner they wish. They do not have the right to sin. Pope Leo XIII declared in his encyclical *Libertas:*

> Wherefore, when a liberty such as We have described is offered to man, the power is given him to pervert or abandon with impunity the most sacred of duties, and to exchange the unchangeable good for evil; which, as We have said, is no liberty, but its degradation, and the abject submission of the soul to sin.[281]

Pope Gregory XVI described the evil fruits resulting from religious liberty:

> This is the most contagious of errors, which prepares the way for that absolute and totally unrestrained liberty of opinions which, for the ruin of the Church and State, is spreading everywhere and which certain men, through an excess of impudence, do not fear to put forward as advantageous to religion. Ah, 'What more disastrous death for souls than the liberty of error,' said St. Augustine.[282]

Tragic events followed the promulgation of the *Decree on Religious Freedom,* as once Catholic nations revised their constitutions to adapt to this decree. As a result, the Catholic Faith no longer remained the state religion and various Protestant religions and other sects began a vigorous campaign to proselytize these nations, thereby winning millions of converts. In the meantime, Catholic missionary activity was greatly curtailed. Emphasis has been placed on ecumenism and dialogue rather than conversion.

> When we compare the Declaration on Religious Freedom of Vatican Council II with the texts produced by the general assemblies of the World Council of Churches in Amsterdam (1948) and New Delhi (1961), we see at once that there is a large measure of agreement. Furthermore, if we disregard the theological reasoning on which they are based, we see that, insofar as the principle itself and its practical application are concerned, the texts are often almost identical.[283]

---

[281] On June 20, 1888.
[282] *Mirari Vos,* August 15, 1832.
[283] Lukas Vischer, *Religious Freedom and the World Council of Churches,* p. 58.

Spain's concordat of May 1958 was modified on January 10, 1967 to conform to the *Decree on Religious Freedom,* allowing any sect to freely proselytize.

And what followed? With the circulation of all manner of opinions and beliefs, Spain eventually legalized pornography, contraceptives, divorce, sodomy and abortion. This example is by no means just limited to Spain. Other Catholic countries with constitutions and concordats which once prohibited proselytism by religious sects had to change their laws and to grant religious freedom to all religions. In Brazil, the National Conference of Brazilian Bishops acknowledges that each year approximately 600,000 Catholics leave the Church to join false religions.[284]

Practical Application

It has been more than 40 years since the beginning of Vatican II, and the tangible fruits of the *Decrees on Ecumenism* and *Religious Liberty* can be easily seen. Following Vatican II, modern Catholic churches have experienced a dramatic decline in Sunday Mass attendance, baptisms and conversions, while during the same period there has been, even in former Catholic countries, a tremendous expansion and growth of Protestant religions, various cults, Eastern Religions and Islam.

Vatican II has rejected the belief that the Catholic Church is the one, true Church and has relegated it to the level of being merely another selection in the cafeteria of religions. The Vatican II church is simply another choice—a choice that in the eyes of many people doesn't really matter.

---

[284] Bishop Mark Pivarunas, CMRI, *Pro Grege,* February 29, 1995.

Since the Postconciliar Church's goal is not the salvation of souls, its members have been leaving in droves or have simply given up the practice of their faith altogether. This cannot be the fruit borne from a good tree.

C. The Tridentine Latin Mass and the New Mass

In order to understand what has occurred in the Church since Vatican II it is necessary to have a basic knowledge of the Mass and Sacraments as they have been preserved through the centuries in the Catholic Church. The *Baltimore Catechism* defines the Mass as "the Sacrifice of the New Law in which Christ, through the ministry of the priest, offers Himself to God in an unbloody manner under the appearances of bread and wine." St. Irenaeus (120-c. 202 AD) affirms that "Christ taught us the Sacrifice of the New Law [the Mass]."[285] "The end of the Sacrifice of the Mass is identical with that of the Sacrifice of the Cross—the salvation of men."[286]

The term "Mass" (*Missa* in Latin) first appears in the writings of St. Ambrose (+397) to describe the Eucharistic Liturgy. "Some derive it from the Hebrew word *Missach*, which signifies a *free gift* or *offering*. Others are of the opinion that it comes from the Latin word *dimissio*, meaning *dismissal*, from the circumstances that in the first five or six centuries of the Church the faithful were solemnly dismissed at the end of the Mass by the deacon."[287]

Traditional Catholic priests carefully follow precise rubrics during Mass as they focus their attention on divine worship.[288] They offer the Holy Sacrifice of the Mass upon the altar while facing both the tabernacle and the crucifix because our worship is directed to Almighty God. The priest does not face the people for much the same reason that a bus driver does not face his passengers. To turn the driver around to face the passengers would lead to disastrous consequences.

Placement of the Tabernacle

It has been noted "that it was principally through the influence of St. Charles Borromeo in the latter half of the sixteenth century that tabernacles began to be permanently attached to the main altar. The *Roman Ritual* (1614) then explicitly called for the tabernacles to be either on the main altar or on a minor altar. An 1863 decree of the Congregation of Rites was decisive in making this practice

---

[285] Lib. 4, cap. 32.
[286] Dr. Pius Parsch, *The Liturgy of the Mass,* pp. 172-173.
[287] Fr. Shadler, *Beauties of the Catholic Church,* p. 325.
[288] Rubrics are actions, movements, etc. printed in red ink in the *Missale Romanum*.

universally observed."[289] "To separate the tabernacle and the altar is to separate two things which should remain united by their origin and nature."[290]

The Postconciliar Church has replaced the Holy Sacrifice of the Mass with a commemoration of the Lord's Supper. Since this new service focuses on a celebration of the Christian Community, the priest or presider now faces the people. In the new liturgy, the people, not God, have become the center of attention. This view is portrayed by the placement of the tabernacle in an inconspicuous location, while the presider's chair has been placed in a position of central prominence. In most cases the tabernacle has been relegated to the side of the church or even to a separate room.

The new liturgy gives "the celebrant an opportunity for genuine self-expression, [and, at times, even showmanship] ...appropriate for eliciting community response and prayer."[291] Individual prayer is replaced by that of the Christian Community. Sacred ceremonies that have been observed for centuries have been replaced with novel liturgical practices that differ from parish to parish.

Languages Used for Holy Mass

"Aramaic, previously known as Chaldean, was the language spoken by Christ."[292] Therefore, Our Lord spoke Aramaic at the Last Supper.

As the Catholic Church spread throughout the world, liturgies were named after the Apostles who composed them or in whose missionary territories they were offered. Eastern Churches (Greek, Russian, Turk, Coptic, Slav, Armenian and Bulgarian) adopted the Liturgy of St. James. Africans (including the Ethiopians and Abyssinians) used the Liturgy of St. Mark. Western Europe adopted the Liturgy of St. Peter, which is today known as the Latin rite. These liturgies were substantially the same insofar as they contained the three essential elements of the Mass: Offertory, Consecration and Communion.

Various rites of the Catholic Church have used vernacular languages in their liturgies for centuries. Through the course of time, some of these languages

---

[289] *Worship, Vol. XL,* Jan. 1966, "Altar and Tabernacle," Godfrey Diekmann, O.S.B., p. 505.
[290] *Worship, Vol. XL,* Jan. 1966, pp. 494-495.
[291] *Worship, Vol. XL,* Jan. 1966, p. 117.
[292] Eric North, *Book of a Thousand Tongues,* p. 19.

became "dead" languages. Since they were no longer commonly spoken, they could not be changed and therefore were kept by the Church in order to assure the integrity of the liturgy.

Msgr. Gamber lists the various rites of the Church which have diversity of language and customs, yet retain unity in belief and worship:

> In the Western Church, in addition to the Roman rite, there are the Gallican rite [France] (now defunct), the Ambrosian rite [Milan, Italy], and the Mozarabic rite [Toledo, Spain]; and in the East, among others, the Byzantine rite, the Armenian rite, the Syriac rite and the Coptic rite [Egypt].[293]

The Latin Language

During the first centuries of Christianity, when the rites as we know them today were in the process of formation, the ceremonies that were used were largely of eastern origin. During these centuries, too, the Greek language enjoyed the first position among the languages used in Church documents and ceremonies; the use of Latin in the Church ceremonies waited until the third century.[294]

Latin eventually replaced Greek as the official language of the Roman Empire. The writings of Saints Justin (150 AD) and Hippolytus (215 AD) refer to the Latin Mass. By the year 250 AD, the Latin Mass was offered throughout most of the Roman world including the cities in Northern Africa and Northern Italy. The Church of the West adopted Latin for liturgical use by 380 AD and the Latin Canon as we know it was completed by 399 AD.

> Latin enters history in the 6th century BC, as one of the three primary languages of the Italian peninsula (with Umbrian and Oscan). ...Throughout the Middle Ages, Latin remained the preferred language of books, correspondence, and learned discourse. Its continued popularity over any of the developing European vernaculars is due primarily to its identification with the Church, which was then the center of European cultural and intellectual life. At the end of the 16th century Latin began to wander, but it was so well entrenched that it remained in considerable use until the 18th century. It was still the tutorial language of the Italian universities in the 1800's, but aside from the liturgical and administrative

---

[293] *Reform of the Roman Liturgy*, p. 30.
[294] Edward Finn, S.J., *A Brief History of the Eastern Rites*, p. 12.

affairs of the Roman Catholic Church and a narrowing circle of classical and theological scholars, Latin may now be said to have passed out of use.[295]

Our Lord established His doctrines to stand for all time and they are as unchangeable as He is Himself. His Church and His teachings were never intended to be improved, modernized or arbitrarily altered in order to fit the lifestyle of the time. Nor did He ever intend that His teachings be ambiguous. The Latin language providentially protected the Deposit of Faith from material change. The Church in Her wisdom adopted Latin as Her universal language in order to guarantee the immutability of doctrine and liturgy as established by Christ. In this way the Mass, the Sacraments and the very teachings of the Church throughout the centuries have remained intact.

Present day Catholics throughout the world speak nearly 800 different languages—a fact that would cause division were it not for the uniting force of Latin. In sharp contrast to this uniformity which Latin has so long guaranteed is the fact that since Vatican II "On any given Sunday in the Los Angeles archdiocese Mass is said in as many as 80 languages."[296] This division is further exemplified in Miami, Florida where 134 different languages are spoken. Without a common liturgical language it is nearly impossible for clergy to minister to those of diverse ethnic backgrounds in their own vernacular languages. It also leaves room for ambiguity since languages are always evolving.

Cardinal Avery Dulles, S.J. said, "I don't think we can really abandon Latin without abandoning a lot of our own tradition; more than 1,500 years of theology and liturgy and literature will be lost."[297] Pope Pius XII declared, "The use of the Latin Language, customary in a considerable portion of the Church, is a manifest and beautiful sign of unity as well as an effective antidote for any corruption of doctrinal truth."[298]

The Church in our days must strenuously guard the purity of Her faith, and, beyond doubt, ecclesiastical Latin serves Her as an excellent means to that end.

---

[295] Eric North, *Book of a Thousand Tongues*, pp. 251-252.
[296] *National Catholic Reporter*, March 27, 1998.
[297] *Catholic World Report*, September / October 1992, p. 30.
[298] *Mediator Dei*, November 20, 1947.

The unchanging truth of the one objective faith must be proclaimed throughout ever modifying areas in which countless errors in the guise of truth are being disseminated by means of ambiguous ideas and expressions. The Latin language secures to the Church solid ground amid the morass of modern civilization; it serves as a megaphone to all the nations; it is a sure protection for the preservation of the true faith.[299]

The *Los Angeles Times* carried an article by Lesley Chamberlain entitled "The Mysteries of Latin—how a dead language continues to live," which underscored the importance of the Latin language:

> Not so long ago, Latin was part of everyday life. It was the …attractive language of the Western Church and its music, the language of memorials and tombstones, and of doctors' notes.
>
> …Latin was a sign of universality when people believed the West was the universe. But it was also convenient that educated men from different countries had a common language. For several centuries international diplomacy was conducted in Latin (conferences in Latin were still proposed in the early 20th century). The universality of Latin suggested potential peace and unity.[300]

The Holy Sacrifice of the Mass

Protestant heretics of the 16th century denied both the Real Presence of Christ in the Holy Eucharist and the sacrificial character of the Mass. Subsequently, the Catholic Church explicitly codified Her teachings on the Holy Sacrifice of the Mass and the Seven Sacraments (which had been in use continually since the time of Christ) at the Council of Trent. The idea that the Canon of the Mass contained errors and was in need of alteration was also condemned.[301] The Council of Trent stated that "the Canon of the Mass was composed from the very words of Our Lord, the traditions of the Apostles, and the pious institutions also of holy pontiffs."[302]

In 1570, Pope St. Pius V formulated the *Missale Romanum* or Roman Missal, thus standardizing the *Curiae Missale* which had been used in Rome for many

---

[299] *Worship, Vol. XXVI*, pp. 279-280, "The Problem of Language in Liturgy."
[300] July 21, 2002.
[301] Session 22, Canons 3 and 6.
[302] Session 22, Chapter 4, September 17, 1562.

years. The *Missale Romanum* is the Latin altar missal that has been used by priests throughout the Latin rite since 1570 and is still used today by Catholic priests offering the authentic Latin Mass. The term *Tridentine Latin Mass* is derived from the word *Trent,* and is often used to denote the Latin Mass that is offered from the *Missale Romanum* of Pope St. Pius V.

> The Mass goes back to Calvary. Its liturgy goes back farther even than the Catacombs. [St.] Peter's chasuble is still preserved in the Church of Paris. Pope Clement, at the end of the First Century, saw a definite uniformity in the celebration of this clean oblation. St. Leo and St. Gregory associated their great names with the majestic rite of Rome; St. Basil and St. Cyril with the more beautiful rites of the Orient; St. Chrysostom, St. Ambrose and St. Isidore of Spain left their mark on the setting of the Sacrifice [the various rites of the Church].

> ...whether it was Greek or Syrian, Armenian or Coptic, Roman or Ambrosian, Mozarabic or Gallican or Celtic ...the Mass is the center of all our worship. It is more, for it is the compendium of all our history and theology.[303]

> That the Apostles were in the habit of saying Mass we learn from Holy Scripture and the lives of the Apostles. St. Matthew was stabbed at the altar while offering the Holy Sacrifice. Tradition relates of St. Andrew that he said to the judge: 'I offer daily to the Almighty God upon the altar, not the flesh of oxen or the blood of goats, but the spotless Lamb of God.' ...From all that has been said, it follows that Mass was celebrated in the Church from the very beginning and that it has at all times been regarded as the True Sacrifice of the New Testament.[304]

St. Thomas Aquinas says that the Mass "contains in itself all the elements of sacrifice and is essentially a representation of the sacrifice of the Cross, where 'Christ offered Himself a Victim to God.' (Ephesians 5: 2)"[305]

"Pope Leo XIII declared that the 'Mass is not an empty or bare commemoration of His [Christ's] death, but a true and wonderful, though unbloody, renewal of it.' "[306] Trent condemned the notion that the Mass was merely a sacrifice of praise and thanksgiving and not one of propitiation.

---

[303] Msgr. Francis Kelley, *Dominus Vobiscum,* p. 147.
[304] Fr. Martin von Cochem, *The Incredible Catholic Mass,* pp. 9-10.
[305] P. 3, q. 79, a. 7; q. 83, a. 1.
[306] Martin Harrison, O.P., *Credo,* p. 59.

Pope Pius XII wrote: "Therefore, the august sacrifice of the altar is not a simple commemoration of the sufferings and death of Jesus Christ, but a true, genuine act of sacrificing, whereby the High Priest by an unbloody oblation accomplishes what He has already done upon the cross."[307]

> As to the effects of the two sacrifices, Calvary was the actual atonement for the sins of the world, past, present and yet to be committed until the end of time, by the terrible suffering and death of Christ willingly accepted under obedience by Him as the innocent victim of sin. The Mass is the practical application of this infinite atonement to the individual soul...[308]

Cardinal Newman, a convert to the Catholic Church, writes, "To me nothing is so consoling,... so thrilling, so overcoming, as the Mass... It is not a mere form of words—it is a great action, the greatest action that can be on earth.[309]

"The traditional Mass of the Roman rite is, as Fr. Faber expressed it, 'the most beautiful thing this side of heaven.' "[310] St. Francis de Sales (1566-1622) writes in *An Introduction to the Devout Life* that the Mass is "the most holy, sacred and royal sacrifice... the center of the Christian religion, the heart of devotion, the soul of piety; an ineffable mystery which embraces the untold depths of divine charity, and in which God, giving Himself to us, bestows upon us freely all His favors and graces." James King beautifully describes the Mass:

> The Mass is the very core of the Catholic way of life. The graces of the Eucharistic Sacrifice should permeate every fiber of a Catholic's being, every action of his day, influencing his thoughts, vivifying his life, uniting him in ever-closer bonds of love with Christ and with His members. His active presence at Sunday Mass should climax his week, for in the Mass Christ Himself is here in person. 'Here is His entire redemptive activity, working on us, transfiguring us, divinizing us, reshaping us into His own image and likeness.'[311] ...A college student put it this way: 'Surrounded by the materialistic ideals of the world, we must make headway in our trek toward salvation, we must grow in the

---

[307] *Mediator Dei,* November 20, 1947, Section II, Par. 68.
[308] Martin Harrison, O.P., *The Everyday Catholic,* pp. 62-63.
[309] Cardinal Newman, *Loss and Gain,* p. 20.
[310] *Christian Order,* Vol. 30, Number 11, p. 541.
[311] John H. Miller, C.S.C., S.T.D., *Fundamentals of the Liturgy* (Notre Dame: Fides Publishers Association, 1959), pp. 213-214.

knowledge and love of Jesus Christ; but where else shall we find more incitement to humility, where purer, more health-giving and strengthening food of souls for a virtuous life than in the Mass? All that is mysterious and divine, majestic and sublime, instructive and edifying, is combined and enclosed in the liturgy of the Mass. In the Mass, our Lord mystically accomplishes, in the presence of the faithful, the entire work of redemption, offering His life of sacrifice and His sacrificial death, and He thus appears in the closest proximity to us as the most illuminating model of virtue and holiness. The Eucharistic Sacrifice is the most glorious crown of the great work of salvation and at the same time, the living memorial of all the mysteries of Christ. Anyone who considers this devoutly in the spirit of a lively faith cannot fail to grow strong and increase in virtue and merit.'[312] We are missing the richest, most purifying, most enlightening, most sanctifying experience of our lives when we miss a Mass.[313]

Visits to the Blessed Sacrament

Prior to Vatican II, many Catholics expressed their devotion to the Holy Eucharist by visiting Our Lord in the Blessed Sacrament. This fact is supported by John Reedy S.C.S.:

> In a great many parishes, a person who observed the church closely during the week would probably be surprised at the number and variety of people who dropped in to spend time in prayer before the Blessed Sacrament. The grade-school kids bouncing in and out, but showing just enough reverence in a fleeting expression to convey some of the wonderful simplicity of a child's faith; the mothers, with preschoolers who would stop in on their way to their shopping; the old people whose eyes and prayers were clouded with memories. In the downtown churches there was a constant traffic of young girls from offices and a fair number of businessmen who stopped by during their lunch hour or after work.[314]

---

[312] George Van Hollebeke, *The Mass,* pp. 7-8.
[313] *The Liturgy and the Laity,* pp. 60-61.
[314] *The Perplexed Catholic: a Guide Through Confusion,* p. 102.

The Devotional Aspect of Catholicism

The beautiful ceremonies and devotional practices that have been disregarded after Vatican II are still retained in traditional Catholic parishes throughout the world. These are described by William Bausch:

> ...Ember days, fish on Fridays, the cult [veneration] of the saints, parish missions, the habits of the nuns, the cassocks of the priests, incense, miraculous medals, novenas, sodalities, weekly or monthly confession, the Latin Mass, the Angelus, first Fridays—all blended into the rhythm of the liturgical year. ...[The church had] a feel: the smudge of ashes on your forehead on Ash Wednesday, the cool candle against your throat on St. Blaise's day, the waferlike sensation on your tongue in Communion. It had a look: the ...silky vestments on the back of the priest as he went about his mysterious rites [offering the Mass] facing the sanctuary wall in the parish church; the monstrance with its solar radial brilliance surrounding the stark white host ...the indelible impression of the blue-and-white Virgin and the shocking red image of the Sacred Heart. It even had a smell, an odor: the pungent incense, the extinguished candles with their beeswax aroma floating ceilingward and filling your nostrils, the smell of olive oil and sacramental balm. It had the taste of fish on Fridays and unleavened bread and hot cross buns. It had the sound of unearthly Gregorian Chant and *flectamus genua* and the mournful *Dies Irae.* The church had a way of capturing all your senses, keeping your senses and being enthralled.[315]

Satan's Hatred of the Mass

The devils have an indescribable hatred for the Holy Sacrifice of the Mass because it renews in an unbloody manner the Sacrifice of the Cross which inflicted the greatest harm on Satan and his efforts to ruin souls. The evil spirits are fully aware of the great spiritual blessings that are imparted to the Church, the faithful and the world during each Mass.

On May 28, 1902 Pope Leo XIII spoke of the great treasures of grace we receive from the Holy Eucharist in his encyclical *Mirae Caritatis:*

> In a word, this Sacrament is, as it were, the very soul of the Church; and to it the grace of the priesthood is ordered and directed in all its fullness and in each of

---

[315] *Brave New Church,* pp. 54-55.

its successive grades. From the same source the Church draws and has all Her strength, all Her glory, Her every supernatural endowment and adornment, every good thing that is Hers; wherefore She makes it the chiefest of all Her cares to prepare the hearts of the faithful for an intimate union with Christ through the Sacrament of His Body and Blood, and to draw them thereto. And to this end She strives to promote the veneration of this august mystery by surrounding it with holy ceremonies.

Therefore, it is no wonder that Satan inspired the Modernists and Ecumenists to target the Mass at Vatican II. Spurned on by the devils, they aimed to destroy the very heart of the Church, the Holy Sacrifice of the Mass, and to do away with it once and for all.

The Foreshadowing of the New Mass

Modernists attempted to introduce liturgical changes as early as 1937 under the pretense of elevating the Church by means of radical renovation:

> The bishop of Linz, Austria (Province of Vienna), found it necessary to rebuke extreme liturgists in his diocese who wish to turn the altar around and celebrate Mass facing the congregation, to remove the tabernacle from the altar and to reserve the Blessed Sacrament in a safe in the wall, to have the faithful receive Holy Communion standing and to forbid the recitation of the Rosary during Mass.[316]

These actions were quickly denounced by the Church.

> The Archbishop of Fribourg [Switzerland] censured those who wished to dispense altogether with the use of black vestments and who exaggerated the part which the laity should take in the offering of the Sacrifice. A circular letter to the hierarchy of Greater Germany, issued in 1943 by the Archbishop of Breslau at the direction of the Holy See, also condemns the tendency to upset the rubrics on the plea of returning to the practices of the earliest ages of the Church. It is reasonable to conclude that this extreme enthusiasm for antiquity condemned by the Holy Father [Pope Pius XII] led in some places to attempts to set up altars modeled on the most primitive table altars.[317]

---

[316] Vide *Periodica,* 1937, p. 163.
[317] Gerard Montague, *Problems in the Liturgy,* pp. 318-319.

Many of these changes were specifically condemned by Pope Pius XII:

> Thus to cite some instances, one would be straying from the straight path were he to wish the altar restored to its primitive table-form; were he to forbid the use of sacred images and statues in churches; were he to order the crucifix so designed that the Divine Redeemer's Body shows no trace of His cruel sufferings; and lastly were he to disdain and reject polyphonic music or singing in parts, even where it conforms to regulations issued by the Holy See.[318]

In the early 1950's various authors throughout the world attempted to condition Catholics to accept liturgical change. In his book, *Holy Mass: Approaches to the Mystery*, Fr. A. Roguet, O.P. subtly used terms that would become prevalent during the council: *Liturgy of the Word, the Liturgy of the Eucharist, sacrifice of praise, community, meal, cup and table.* He and other Modernists often made ambiguous remarks in their writings. For example Roguet stated, "Yet it is of faith for Catholics that the Mass is a true sacrifice." Roguet's very next sentence contradicts the previous one: "This word [sacrifice] no longer has a precise meaning for civilized people of the 20th century." No wonder so many clergy and laity were confused by the nuances of Vatican II!

Constitution on the Sacred Liturgy

Undoubtedly, the Mass has been essentially changed since Vatican II. How did this happen? The *Constitution on the Sacred Liturgy* of the Second Vatican Council was the medium by which radical changes were introduced into the liturgy. The Modernists who drew up this document intentionally used equivocation to achieve their ends. "These inexact formulations were deliberately introduced so that the hermeneutics could gloss or reinforce whichever ideas they liked."[319] Fr. Schillebeeckx described their cunning plan: "We will express it in a *diplomatic* way, but after the council we will draw out the implicit conclusions."[320]

> The first matter for discussion at the council was the sacred liturgy: There were few outside the clergy, and not all in it, who really understood the core

---

[318] *Mediator Dei,* November 20, 1947.
[319] Romano Amerio, *Iota Unum,* p. 107.
[320] *De Bazuin,* no. 16, 1965.

significance of this issue. On the surface, it sounded like little more than an idea for dropping the traditional Latin in certain parts of the Mass and permitting those parts to be said in the language of the people. But most of the Council Fathers, and certainly all of the traditionalists among them, understood clearly that to deprive the Curia of its historically held right to decide all liturgical matters was to open the door to decentralization.[321]

Following the council, the liberals justified their sacrilegious liturgical experimentation by citing Vatican II's *Constitution on the Liturgy* since it was purposely vague and ambiguous. Under the direction of John XXIII, Paul VI and John Paul II, the Vatican enacted numerous liturgical changes that were implemented through nearly 120 postconciliar documents on the liturgy. "The number of postconciliar documents on the liturgy is very great, greater than in any other postconciliar area."[322]

Warnings Against Changing to the Vernacular Languages

Fr. Wiltgen describes the adverse consequences resulting from the use of the vernacular: "As long as Latin texts and Latin rites were universally used in the Church, the Roman Curia would be competent to check and control them. But if hundreds and even thousands of local languages and customs were introduced into the liturgy, the Curia would automatically lose this prerogative."[323]

On October 23, 1962 Cardinal McIntyre of Los Angeles addressed the council and voiced his strong opposition to the draft of the *Constitution on the Liturgy:*

> The schema on the Liturgy proposes confusion and complication. If it is adopted, it would be an immediate scandal for our people. The continuity of the Mass must be kept. The tradition of the sacred ceremonies must be preserved. …changes are not needed.[324]

Cardinal McIntyre was convinced that the Latin language was instrumental in preserving the integrity of the Church's doctrines and Her liturgy.

> In recent times, even in materialist North America, the growth of the Church was magnificent with the liturgy being kept in Latin. The attempts of the Protestants

---

[321] Lawrence Elliott, *I Will Be Called John*, pp. 291-292.
[322] Augustine Flannery, O.P., *Vatican II Conciliar & Postconciliar Documents*, p. 37.
[323] *The Rhine Flows into the Tiber*, p. 42.
[324] Fr. Francis Weber, *His Eminence of Los Angeles: James Cardinal McIntyre, Vol. II*, p. 7

have failed, and Protestantism uses the vernacular. We ask again: Why the change, especially since changes in this matter involve many difficulties and great dangers? All of us here at the Council can recall the fundamental changes in the meaning of words in common use. Thus it follows that if the sacred liturgy were in the vernacular, the immutability of doctrine would be endangered.

...The introduction of the vernacular should be separated from the action of the Mass. The Mass must remain as it is. Grave changes in the liturgy introduce grave changes in dogmas.[325]

Centuries before Vatican II, attempts had been made to introduce vernacular languages into the Mass. Pope Pius VI forbade this practice in his bull *Auctorem Fidei* of 1794.[326] However, the Church does allow the use of the vernacular in certain blessings and some of the nonessential elements of the Sacraments.

Bishop António de Castro Mayer of Campos, Brazil said:

The use of a language not readily understood 'lends a certain dignity to the divine service, giving it a mysterious tone, which, in a certain degree is natural for things pertaining to God.' ...And since a variety of missals are available with the Mass text translated into living languages, it was not necessary for the priest to say the Mass in the vernacular. Bishop Mayer doubted that a spiritual revival among the people and nations would necessarily follow upon the introduction of the vernacular in the Mass as some have claimed.[327]

Kilian McDonnell, O.S.B. noted that "From a study of the history of curial, papal and conciliar[328] documents it must be said that the *Constitution on the Liturgy* [of Vatican II] marks a departure of some significance from the earlier documents."[329]

---

[325] Fr. Francis Weber, *His Eminence of Los Angeles: James Cardinal McIntyre, Vol. II*, p. 393. Speech of November 5, 1962.
[326] D 1566.
[327] Fr. Ralph Wiltgen, S.V.D., *The Rhine Flows into the Tiber*, p. 40.
[328] From the 20 General Councils of the Church.
[329] *Worship, Vol. XLI*, January 1967, "Themes in Ecclesiology and Liturgy."

Forging Ahead

Nevertheless, the push for liturgical changes continued, including the introduction of the vernacular Mass that was spearheaded by the European alliance. Their members held an iron grip on Vatican II by serving as council moderators and by controlling its committees; a grip which was established and sanctioned by both John XXIII and Paul VI.[330] In turn, any doctrinal battles on the council floor between traditionalists and liberals often ended with the muzzling or the ridiculing of those Council Fathers who were brave enough to speak against radical doctrinal or liturgical changes. This is evidenced in the case of Cardinal Ottaviani, the most powerful cardinal in the Roman Curia and prefect of the Holy Office. On October 30, 1962, Cardinal Alfredo Ottaviani addressed the council:

> Are we seeking to stir up wonder, or perhaps scandal, among the Christian people, by introducing changes in so venerable a rite that has been approved for so many centuries and is so familiar? The rite of Holy Mass should not be treated as if it were a piece of cloth to be refashioned according to the whim of each generation.[331]

Cardinal Ottaviani "demanded to know whether the Fathers were planning a revolution. The liturgy was sacred ground," he said. "Changes in the Mass would scandalize and alienate the faithful."[332] Ottaviani, who was hard of hearing, kept speaking after his allotted ten minute time limit had expired. The moderator, Cardinal Bernard Alfrink, ordered the technician to turn off his microphone. "After confirming the fact by tapping the instrument, Cardinal Ottaviani stumbled back to his seat in humiliation. The most powerful cardinal in the Roman Curia had been silenced, and the Council Fathers clapped with glee."[333]

Shrewdly, the Modernists knew that their changes had to be made, at first, subtly and slowly. Later, once their plan was in full operation, they could forge

---

[330] These facts are documented by Fr. Ralph Wiltgen, S.V.D., in his book *The Rhine Flows into the Tiber.* Wiltgen, the founder of the Council News Service, was an unbiased eyewitness to the day-to-day workings of the council.

[331] Fr. Ralph Wiltgen, S.V.D., *The Rhine Flows into the Tiber*, p. 28.

[332] Lawrence Elliott, *I Will Be Called John,* p. 291.

[333] Wiltgen, 29.

ahead. "After nearly a month of intense debate, the council approved certain limited liturgical reforms, among them the right of the bishops to decide whether parts of the Mass could be said in the language of their own countries."[334] This *modus operandi* of the Second Vatican Council allowed the bishops essentially to do whatever they pleased. These seemingly "limited" reforms opened the floodgates to the terrible abuses we see in the new liturgies today.

The American liberal, Fr. Godfrey Diekmann, who later helped found the International Commission of English in the Liturgy (ICEL), had a tremendous role in changing the Mass and in the implementation of the New Mass:

> A persistent advocate for using the vernacular in the liturgy and revising the Church's sacramental rites, he was made a member of Vatican II's Preparatory Committee on the Liturgy and took a lead role in drafting the council's 'Constitution on the Sacred Liturgy.' He then served on the Consilium, the Vatican agency that oversaw the implementation of the council's liturgical reforms.[335]

The Canon—the Heart of the Mass

The Canon of the Mass, as preserved in the Tridentine Latin Mass, was essentially composed by Christ Himself. It is most pleasing to God and is truly His work. Francis Amiot asserts that the Canon was written before the Gospels:

> The text of the Roman Canon does not entirely resemble any of the four accounts of the institution [of the Eucharist] in the New Testament; it represents very possibly an even older tradition; the Eucharist had already been celebrated for something like a quarter of a century when in 55 or 56 [AD], St. Paul wrote his account of the Lord's Supper in his First Letter to the Corinthians.[336]

Joseph Husslein S.J., says that the early Church Fathers taught that "Christ Himself had personally instructed His Apostles in regard to that entire portion of the Mass, which in the early Church was known as the Eucharistic Prayer, but in the Eastern Church [it] corresponds to the *Anaphora*, and in the West to the *Preface* and the Canon combined."[337]

---

[334] Lawrence Elliott, *I Will Be Called John*, pp. 291-292.
[335] *National Catholic Reporter*, March 8, 2002.
[336] *History of the Mass*, p. 90.
[337] *Mass of the Apostles*, p. 319.

Fr. Gassner, O.S.B. continues:

The Canon had its history, development, changes, reforms, until it became the 'unchangeable rule' of offering the Eucharistic sacrifice. Not so the words of consecration. Our Lord's words remained unchanged in the Eucharistic rite from the time when the first Canon was written, even from the time before any Canon and any Gospel were written, from the Eucharistic celebration of the Apostles to our own days. This stability of the words of Christ, around which the prayers of the Canon grew up, were unfolded like rose leaves round a shining diamond, is in itself a most solemn testimony for the perennial faith of the Church, that with the words of Christ, and exclusively through them, transubstantiation is accomplished.[338]

Introduction of St. Joseph in the Canon

Beginning in 1815, hundreds of thousands of signatures of clergy and laity were sent to the Vatican requesting permission to insert the name of St. Joseph into the Canon of the Mass. One of the reasons assigned for making the request was because many persons had a particular devotion to the saint. The Sacred Congregation of Rites steadfastly refused to grant the petition. Even though the addition of St. Joseph's name would not be an essential change, the Church remained firm in Her refusal which was binding throughout the world. "So careful is the Church to prevent innovations from entering into this part of the Mass that She forbids anyone to meddle with it under pain of incurring Her most severe censures."[339]

The campaign to promote this change became quite intense, even just prior to Vatican II. Monsignor Joseph Phelan of St. Joseph's Church in Capitola, California launched a drive which netted 150,000 signatures. It didn't take the Modernists long to use this seemingly innocent request to the benefit of their devious purpose. Long before the council, booklets containing a petition were circulated to the Council Fathers. The Modernists, under the guise of promoting devotion to St. Joseph, soon became actively involved in this movement to include St. Joseph in the *Communicantes* of the Mass. The insertion of St. Joseph

---

[338] *The Canon of the Mass*, p. 247.

[339] Fr. John O'Brien, *A History of the Mass and Its Ceremonies in the Eastern and Western Church*, p. 296.

would serve as a wedge to break open the Canon and authorize change to the very words of the Consecration, the Modernists' ultimate target.

The Cardinal Secretary of State, on November 13, 1962, announced to the council that John XXIII had decided to insert the name of St. Joseph in the Canon of the Mass immediately after the name of the Most Holy Virgin. John XXIII had taken this independent action while the Second Vatican Council was in session. This was indeed a bold move, because no changes had been made to the Canon of the Mass since the time of Pope St. Gregory I (590-604 AD); however, even he made no essential changes, but only minor ones.

> The whole Canon in its present structure was already in existence before [Pope] Gregory I. His additions are: *diesque nostras in tua pace disponas* [and provide that our days be spent in Thy peace] inserted in the *Hanc Igitur* [prayer] which he ordained as a regular prayer; [the] addition of [the names of the saints] Matthias, Barnabas, Agatha and Lucia; and the rearrangement in hierarchical order.[340]

Pope St. Pius V (1566-1572 AD) threatened with the wrath of Almighty God and the Apostles Peter and Paul anyone who would dare to change the Mass in any substantial way.[341] The liturgical Modernists ignored this perilous warning, disregarded tradition, history and the work of Christ and attempted to change the unchangeable, the *fixed rule,* the Canon of the Mass. A revolution was unleashed that would culminate with the creation of the New Mass *(Novus Ordo Missae).*

Suppression of the Last Gospel

Ominous clouds appeared at the advent of Vatican II when John XXIII ordered changes to be made to the Church calendar, the Divine Office and the Mass. These changes which went into effect on January 1, 1961 decreed:

> The preparatory prayers at the foot of the altar are to be omitted on a few occasions during the year; the Creed is not to be said or sung as frequently as before; the words, 'Benedicamus Domino,' are to be used for the dismissal at Mass only when the Mass is followed by a procession; the Last Gospel is omitted in sung Funeral Masses and whenever a procession follows the Mass; additional

---

[340] Fr. Jerome Gassner, O.S.B., *The Canon of the Mass,* p. 216.
[341] *Quo Primum,* July 19, 1570.

prayers or commemorations (collects) are strictly limited in number; ...at sung Masses the celebrant does not recite the Epistle and the Gospel, which are chanted by the subdeacon and the deacon respectively.[342]

Three years later, in the Vatican's first instruction on the implementation of the *Constitution of the Sacred Liturgy (Inter Oecumenici)*, the Modernists advised that the destruction of the Mass and Sacraments should be carried out cautiously: "The general reform of the liturgy will be better received by the faithful if it is accomplished gradually, and if it is proposed and explained to them properly by their pastors."[343]

The shrewd Modernists introduced many seemingly minor liturgical changes in order to condition Catholics to accept the eventual fundamental changes in doctrine that would follow. In *Inter Oecumenici* the Vatican declared, "the Last Gospel is omitted; the Leonine Prayers are suppressed."[344] The term *Last Gospel* refers to a section of St. John's Gospel that is recited at the conclusion of Mass (the first 14 verses of chapter one). These scriptural verses are also used in the rite of exorcism.[345]

Ironically, the suppression of the Last Gospel is in direct contradiction to the *Liturgical Constitution* of Vatican II: "Sacred Scripture is of the greatest importance in the celebration of the liturgy. ...Hence in order to achieve the restoration, progress and adaptation of the sacred liturgy it is essential to promote that warm and lively appreciation of Sacred Scripture to which the venerable tradition of Eastern and Western rites gives testimony."[346]

Liberals suppressed the Last Gospel not only because it contains an explicit profession of faith in the divinity of Christ, but also because it contains the unecumenical phrase: "He came unto His own, and His own received Him not."[347]

---

[342] Felician Foy, O.F.M., *1963 National Catholic Almanac*, p. 282.
[343] *Inter Oecumenici,* chapter 1, no. 4, September 26, 1964.
[344] *Inter Oecumenici,* chapter 2, no. 48j.
[345] *Rituale Romanum*, p. 682.
[346] *Constitution on the Sacred Liturgy*, no. 24.
[347] John 1: 11.

Other Changes in the Mass

- The first use of the vernacular in the Mass occurred when the Vatican decreed on April 24, 1964 that the priest say the words "Corpus Christi" (Body of Christ) in the vernacular as he distributed Holy Communion. The communicant was to respond "Amen."
- Additional changes to the Mass were introduced gradually and craftily.
- "By November 29, 1964, all the parishes in the United States had begun to pray the portions of the Mass in the official interim Missal in English."
- By March 7, 1965, the commission on... the *Constitution [on the Sacred Liturgy—the 40 member Consilium]* told us that "the 'liturgy of the word,' that is, the early instructional part of the Mass, was to be celebrated away from the altar."[348]

Tables Replace Altars

Early changes eventually escalated into major ones. The sanctuary was rearranged, replacing the altar with a table at which the priest now faced the congregation. Craftily, liturgists claimed that they were reviving the practice of the early Church. In reality, it was a revival of exactly what had taken place during the Protestant Reformation and was the very thing that Pope Pius XII had warned against. Msgr. Hughes describes how, in an earlier century, altars were removed from the churches and tables placed in their stead:

> On November 24, 1550, the king's council [in England] ordered all the altars to be destroyed. Every parish was now to provide a table of wood, and on communion days this was to be used by the minister. The council issued, with these orders, an official explanation which makes crystal clear the nature of the official changes since 1547. The form of the table shall move the simple from the superstitious opinions of the Popish Mass unto the right use of the Lord's Supper. 'For the use of an altar is to make sacrifice upon it; the use of a table is to serve men to eat upon it.'[349]

---

[348] Gerald Sloyan, *Worship in a New Key*, p. 32.
[349] *A Popular History of the Reformation*, p. 225.

Over 415 years later, these same changes were implemented by Vatican II under the semblance of a valid council:

> This innovation 30 years ago entailed an architectural revolution and radically changed attitudes to the celebration of the Eucharist throughout the Catholic world. The altar was detached from the apse. The priest no longer turned his back on the people but faced them.
>
> According to German Liturgist [Klaus Gamber] this was totally wrong and should be corrected. 'It was thought that by doing this they revived a custom of primitive Christianity,' writes Gamber in the posthumous translation of his book. 'But it can be proven beyond all doubt that there never was a celebration *versus populum* [facing the people] in the Eastern or the Western Church and that at all times everyone (priests and faithful) were turned toward the East to pray *ad Dominum* [to the Lord].' Towards the East, the place where salvation was manifest.[350]

> ...Priest and people should face in the same direction, toward the altar, toward God, especially for acts of prayer and sacrifice directed toward God. When Mass is so celebrated, the priest is at the head of the people, leading them as it were, expressing by his position the part he takes in divine worship.[351]

Church Architecture

Pope St. Pius X explains the two ends of the liturgy as being "the glory of God and the sanctification and edification of the faithful."[352] Catholic cathedrals and churches throughout the world prior to Vatican II contributed to both these ends.

"One of the oldest terms used to describe the Christian church is *porta coeli*, the gate of heaven."[353] The Gothic cathedrals of Cologne, Germany and Amiens, France embody this concept in a wonderful manner as colored light streams through their stained glass windows, illuminating the breathtaking vaulted ceilings, delicately carved high altar and the beautiful depictions of the saints.

Medieval cathedrals were often called "the poor man's Bible" since the message of Christ and biblical themes were depicted in glass and stone to instruct

---

[350] *30 Days*, No. 5—1993, "Altar Out of Place," by Lucio Brumnelli.
[351] *Worship*, XXXIX, Jan. 1965, p. 125, "Mass Facing the People," by Frederick McManus.
[352] Motu proprio on Church Music: *Tra le Sollectudini*, November 22, 1903.
[353] Fr. Robert Barron, *Heaven in Stone and Glass*, p. 119.

the common people about the faith. G. Coulton, in his book *Art and the Reformation,* tells us, "In many ways, therefore, churchman and artist were natural allies, and art was kept in natural touch both with the religious idealist up above and with popular ideas down below."

These magnificent works of art were often constructed in a cruciform shape in order to remind the faithful of the sacrifice of Christ on Calvary. In his book *Heaven in Stone and Glass,* Robert Barron sheds light upon the architectural features of the great cathedrals:

> What we spontaneously call the front of a cathedral—the façade and towers—is in fact the back. Almost all the Gothic Cathedrals are oriented, that is to say, they face the rising sun, and the eastern point of these churches is not the façade but the apse. When the medieval priest celebrated Mass he was situated in the apsidal end of the cathedral and he looked to the east—away from the people and the main portals. This orientation was of great spiritual moment, for all of Christian life is a looking to the one who called Himself the Light of the World...[354]

The cathedral also personifies the battle between God and Satan:

> ...But when we turn toward something, we inevitably turn away from something also; to set our face is also to set our back. Therefore the backside of the cathedral symbolizes the Christian resistance to all that is opposed to the light of Christ. If the apse faces the rising sun, the façade confronts the setting sun and all the powers of darkness. It is the Church's great 'no' to violence, self-absorption, and hatred—all the works of the Devil. And this of course is why there is a fierce, bristling, looming quality to so many of the Gothic fronts: they are the fighting face of Christianity.[355]

Since Vatican II, all this has radically changed. "A prominent Catholic architect, for example, says that 'Churches are a thing of the past' and, 'It's not the church that's needed, it's the community center.' "[356] Why are so many modern churches so barren or even ominous? Consider the recently constructed

---

[354] p. 55.
[355] Fr. Robert Barron, *Heaven in Stone and Glass,* cover jacket.
[356] Patrick Quinn, quoted in *National Catholic Reporter,* May 17, 1974, p. 15.

$195 million Los Angeles Cathedral. "Some critics have compared the cathedral's austere, modernist look to a prison."[357]

David Littlejohn described the new cathedral in the September 11, 2002 issue of the *Wall Street Journal:*

> The 5.5-acre cathedral precinct stands on a small rise, just on the edge of the Hollywood Freeway. So, thousands of people will see it from the outside every day, and they will probably be disappointed by what they see. The blue construction fence has been replaced by an unwelcoming tan concrete wall. The shapes that rise over it, with the possible exception of a freestanding 150-foot-tall bell tower on the edge of the freeway, and a gigantic cross in a box illuminated at night like a Las Vegas hotel sign, cannot be called inspiring. The cathedral itself- 128 feet tall… colored in beigy-tan, chopped into odd angles and decorated with horizontal stripes is hard to comprehend from a distance.

Changing the Unchangeable Mass

The Holy Sacrifice of the Mass was established by Christ Himself and is therefore an indispensable part of the Catholic Faith. It is not just a ceremony that can be changed arbitrarily every few years.

> To change any of its essential elements is synonymous with the destruction of the rite in its entirety. This is what happened during the Reformation when Martin Luther did away with the Canon of the Mass and made the words of consecration and institution part of the distribution of communion. [Ironically, these same changes have been made after Vatican II.] Clearly, this change destroyed the Roman Mass, even though it appeared that traditional liturgical forms continued unchanged—initially even the vestments and choral chant remained.[358]

Monsignor Klaus Gamber also noted that "unlike the appalling changes we are currently witnessing, the changes made in the Roman Missal over a period of almost 1,400 years did not involve the rite itself. Rather, they were changes concerned only with the addition and enrichment of new feast days, Mass formulas and certain prayers."[359]

---

[357] *Oakland News,* September 3, 2002.
[358] Msgr. Klaus Gamber, *The Reform of the Roman Liturgy,* p. 31.
[359] p. 11.

The Use of Deception

Although the argument is used over and over again by the people responsible for creating the new Mass, they cannot claim that what they have done is what the [majority of the] Council [Fathers] actually wanted. The instructions given by the Liturgy Commission were general in nature, and they opened up many possible ways for implementing what the Commission stipulated, but the one statement we can make with certainty is that new *Ordo* of the Mass that has now emerged would not have been endorsed by the Council Fathers.[360]

Certain stipulations were included in *The Constitution on the Liturgy* to imply that the Holy Sacrifice of the Mass would not be drastically altered:

- (4) ...in faithful obedience to tradition, the Sacred Council declares that Holy Mother Church holds all lawfully recognized rites to be of equal right and dignity; that she wishes to preserve them in the future and to foster them in every way. The Council also desires that, where necessary, the rites be revised carefully in the light of sound tradition, and that they be given new vigor to meet present-day circumstances and needs.
- (23) In order that sound tradition be retained ...there must be no innovations unless the good of the Church genuinely and certainly requires them, and care must be taken that any new forms adopted should in some way grow organically from forms already existing.
- (36, 1) The use of the Latin language, with due respect to particular law, is to be preserved in the Latin rites.
- (114) The treasury of sacred music is to be preserved and cultivated with great care.
- (116) The Church recognizes Gregorian Chant as being specially suited to the Roman liturgy. Therefore, ...it should be given pride of place in liturgical services.

The Modernists knew full well that this was merely for the sake of deception. All these laudatory guidelines were summarily rejected as the new liturgical changes were introduced.

---

[360] Msgr. Klaus Gamber, *The Reform of the Roman Liturgy*, p. 61.

The Formation of a New Mass

Once the clergy had been desensitized to change, Paul VI proceeded to ignore these passages and replace the Holy Sacrifice of the Mass with a New Mass or *Novus Ordo Missae*. On January 3, 1964 Paul VI commissioned Fr. Annibale Bugnini to work with a group of advisors *(Consilium)* to create the New Mass. Bugnini said, "We must strip from our Catholic liturgy everything that can be the shadow of a stumbling block for our separated brethren, that is the Protestants."[361]

Later, allegations of Fr. Bugnini's affiliation with Freemasonry became known. "This accusation was made public in April 1976 by Tito Casini, one of Italy's leading Catholic writers. The accusation was repeated in other journals, and gained credence as the months passed and the Vatican did not intervene to deny the allegations."[362] Subsequently, Bugnini served as Apostolic Pro Nuncio to Iran from 1976-1982.

Paul VI chose six Protestant ministers (Raymond George, Ronald Jasper, Massey Shepherd, Friedrich Künneth, Eugene Brand and Max Thurian) to assist Bugnini in composing a New Mass which would be acceptable to Protestants and non-Catholics. This special commission became known as the Consilium for the Implementation of the Constitution on the Sacred Liturgy. The head of the Consilium was the liberal Cardinal Lercaro, whom Cardinal Antonio Bacci described as "Luther resurrected."[363]

The fact that Protestants collaborated in formulating the New Mass was confirmed by an article in *The Detroit News* entitled, "Protestants helped Revamp Catholic Mass, Priest Says."

> Protestant scholars, including an American Episcopalian, have had a voice in recent changes in the Catholic Mass and other liturgy, it was revealed today by the leading American spokesman on church unity. Msgr. William W. Baum of Washington, told delegates to the general synod of the United Church of Christ (UCC) that the Papal Consilium on Liturgical Reform has 'turned to Protestant theologians and liturgists, who sit in regularly on meetings...'

---

[361] <www.d.umn.edu/~mich0212/Mass/whatis.html> "What is the Tridentine Mass?"
[362] *Christian Order*, November 1989, p. 538.
[363] Tito Casini, *The Torn Tunic*, preface.

In a private interview, Msgr. Baum said the Protestant liturgical scholars at the Vatican represent the world Anglican Communion, the Lutheran World Federation and the World Council of Churches. The Anglican representative, he said, is Dr. Massey Shepherd, California liturgist and professor at the Church Divinity School of the Pacific at Berkeley. 'I think this development is highly significant, but it has been overlooked,' said Msgr. Baum.

'They [were] not simply there as observers, but as consultants as well, and they participate fully in the discussions on Catholic liturgical renewal. It wouldn't mean much if they just listened, but they contribute.'[364]

The fact that six non-Catholic ministers were allowed to create a new "Mass" for the Catholic Church is so absurd, it is difficult to believe that this was actually done. It would be just as ridiculous to entertain the idea, for even a moment, that the Protestant churches or any other church for that matter, would allow a group of six traditional Catholic liturgists to write a new worship service for their religion. Nevertheless, Protestant collaboration in the formulation of the New Mass is a documented fact. This alone reveals the heretical nature of Vatican II.

The French philosopher, secretary and confidant of Paul VI, Jean Guitton, revealed in a radio interview in the mid-1990's:

The intention of Paul VI with regard to what is commonly called the Mass, was to reform the Catholic liturgy in such a way that it should almost coincide with the Protestant liturgy—but what is curious is that Paul VI did that to get as close as possible to the Protestant Lord's Supper... There was with Paul VI an ecumenical intention to remove, correct or at least relax, what was too Catholic, in the traditional sense, in the Mass and, I repeat, to get the Catholic Mass closer to the Calvinist Mass.[365]

What has become of those responsible for the creation and promulgation of the New Mass? The "reformers" of Vatican II have sealed their own fate, for in the papal bull *Quo Primum*[366] Pope St. Pius V condemned such persons with the "wrath of Almighty God and the Apostles Peter and Paul."

---

[364] June 27, 1967.
[365] Reported in *Apropos,* No. 18, 1966, (Scotland) p. 122.
[366] July 19, 1570.

Comparison Between the Latin Mass and the New Mass

Paul Bernier explains the sacrificial nature of the Mass and the meal aspect of the *Novus Ordo* in his book *Eucharist—Celebrating Its Rhythm in Our Lives*:

> Before the Second Vatican Council, the eucharist [the Holy Sacrifice of the Mass] was conceived as essentially a ritual performed by the priest... as a sacrificial personage, much after the model of Old Testament priests. This sacrificial role was exercised especially during the eucharistic prayer [the Canon of the Mass], which, as proper to the priest, was said silently. Such a eucharist stressed the vertical relationship between God and creation, and the adoration owed to God on the part of his creatures.
>
> In contrast to this emphasis on eucharist as eternal sacrifice, the days following the council began to see a greater emphasis placed on the horizontal dimension of the eucharist. In rediscovering the meal aspects of the liturgy,[367] with the appropriate awareness of the interrelatedness of people gathered around a common table, the mass became a celebration and expression of fellowship.[368]

New Ecumenical Lectionary

The *Lectionary* is a new ecumenical liturgical book published shortly after Vatican II. It contains the scriptural readings for Sundays and weekdays that are used for the New Mass. The *Lectionary* was the result of "several years' work by a full-time staff and 800 consultants—Protestants, Catholics, and Jews—[who] brought it to its present form. ...Episcopalians (BCP, 888-931), Lutherans (LBW, 13-41) and Presbyterians (WB, 167-175)[369] have made their own version of it."[370] Because Catholics, Jews and Protestants differ on important issues: God, the Bible, worship, sin, salvation, saints, sacraments, justification, the Holy Eucharist etc., numerous scriptural passages were altered in order to accommodate the beliefs of these religions.

The *Lectionary* is built on a three-year cycle and liturgical calendar that is used jointly by Protestants and postconciliar Catholics. The Postconciliar Church

---

[367] The Catholic Mass has never been a meal; it has always been a sacrifice.
[368] p. 79.
[369] *Book of Common Prayer, Lutheran Book of Worship and Worship Book.*
[370] James White, *Introduction to Christian Worship Revised Edition*, p. 81.

has eliminated the seasons of Pentecost and Epiphany and replaced them with the generic Sundays in Ordinary Time.

Invalid Matter in the New Mass

Wheaten bread and grape wine are the essential matter for the Sacrament of the Holy Eucharist. For validity: "The bread must be made from wheat, mixed with natural water, baked by the application of fire heat (including electric cooking) and substantially uncorrupted."[371] "Bread made with milk, wine, oil, etc., either entirely or in a notable part, is invalid matter."[372]

For liceity (lawfulness): "The bread must be of wheat *flour* and only in case of necessity a white material thrashed or crushed from wheat."[373] It must be unmixed with any other substance besides wheat flour and water. It is gravely unlawful to consecrate with doubtful matter.[374] "In the Oriental [Eastern Rites of the] Church the minister is gravely bound to use leavened bread (except the Armenians and Maronites who use unleavened bread); Latin priests must use only unleavened bread."[375]

The Congregation of Sacred Rites declared: "Therefore, the valid matter of this sacrament must be in the common estimation of men bread made from wheat and not mixed notably with something else so that it is no longer wheat."[376]

Nevertheless, "...Pope [John Paul II] has permitted bread to be replaced by cakes made of millet or cassava root, grape wine by corn wine."[377] Concerning this obvious repudiation of Divine Law, Fr. Francis Fenton has written:

> The Church's teaching is crystal clear on the subject of what constitutes valid matter for the Holy Sacrifice of the Mass and *no one* may make any substantive change of that matter without invalidating the Mass... To suppose that an authentic pope would render invalid the very Consecration of the Mass—is not this totally contrary to the most elementary common sense? Is not such a

---

[371] Canon 815, 1.
[372] Fr. Nicholas Halligan, O.P., *The Administration of the Sacraments*, p. 100.
[373] Ruling of the Holy Office, 23 Jun. 1852.
[374] Halligan, 101.
[375] Council of Florence, D 692, Canon 816.
[376] March 26, 1929.
[377] Solange Hertz, *The Remnant*, April 30, 1990, *La Croix*, August 9, 1989.

supposition utterly absurd? Assuredly it is and no theological expertise whatsoever is required to arrive at that conclusion.[378]

Various ingredients are used for altar breads in modern Catholic churches today with seemingly little regard for validity and lawfulness. Recipes for altar breads found on the Internet[379] include brown sugar, buttermilk, honey, molasses, oil, shortening, wheat germ and Bisquick.

Eucharistic Meal Replaces the Holy Sacrifice of the Mass

At first the true intentions of the Modernists were couched under the pretense that they were merely translating the Latin liturgy into the vernacular. However, if liturgical reform meant that the Tridentine Latin Mass was merely to be translated into the vernacular, Catholic linguists, not Protestant ministers, should have overseen the project. In reality, even this wasn't needed, for the Latin Mass had already been translated into most of the vernacular languages and printed in missals (prayer books). Cardinal James McIntyre noted that prior to Vatican II "very many of the faithful read the whole Mass assiduously and privately with the help of missals. These missals are written either in the vernacular or with the Latin on the same page."[380] However, the Modernists never intended to accurately translate the Mass into the vernacular, nor even to paraphrase it. Their real intent was to create a totally new, ecumenical service.

Paul VI was determined to destroy the Holy Sacrifice of the Mass. This is evident in his official definition of the New Mass:

> The Lord's Supper is the assembly or gathering together of the people of God, with a priest presiding to celebrate the Memorial of the Lord.[381] For this reason the promise of Christ is particularly true of a local congregation of the Church: 'Where two or three are gathered in my name, there am I in their midst' (Matt. 18:20).[382]

---

[378] *The Athanasian,* July 5, 1990. *"To Prove That John Paul II Is Not A True Pope—How Many Examples Are Required?"* p. 1.
[379] <http://www.osb.org/liturgy/altarbread.html>
[380] Fr. Francis Weber, *His Eminence of Los Angeles: James Cardinal McIntyre, Vol. II,* p. 387.
[381] *Presbyterorum Ordinis,* no. 5; CSL, no. 33.
[382] *Roman Missal* (1970), p. 9.

Since this definition explicitly denies the sacrificial character of the Mass it was amended by Paul VI because of numerous protests made by Catholics throughout the world. "The Lord's Supper or Mass gathers together the people of God, with a priest presiding in the person of Christ, to celebrate the memorial of the Lord or Eucharistic sacrifice."[383]

The liturgical "reformers" thus rejected the sacrificial nature of the Mass in favor of a memorial meal or celebration. The new Eucharistic Prayers, which have replaced the Canon of the Mass, are a mere narrative of the Last Supper. The New Mass is "all told, a simplification so sweeping as to signal a veritable revolution in the spirit of our public worship as well as in its practice."[384] In spite of the objection of the majority of the first general assembly of the 1967 synod of bishops, Paul VI continued its development.

In his work *The Reform of the Roman Liturgy,* Msgr. Klaus Gamber writes:

> In spite of the careful advance work that had already been done and the skilled manipulation and management of the sessions themselves, the first general assembly of the 1967 Synod of Bishops *did not approve* [emphasis added] with the required two-thirds majority vote the so-called *Missa normativa,* the forerunner of the new [Novus] *Ordo Missae.* Even so, the development of the new Ordo Missae continued anyway.[385]

In his study of the *Novus Ordo Missae,* Cardinal Alfredo Ottaviani, former prefect of the Holy Office, states:

> To abandon a liturgical tradition which for four centuries stood as a sign and pledge of unity in worship, and to replace it with another liturgy which, due to the countless liberties it implicitly authorizes, cannot but be a sign of division—a liturgy which teems with insinuations or manifest errors against the integrity of the Catholic Faith—is, we feel bound in conscience to proclaim, an incalculable error.[386]

---

[383] *Sacramentary* (1974), p. 33.
[384] *Worship, Vol. XL,* p. 116.
[385] p. 61.
[386] *Ottaviani Intervention,* p. 55.

He further declares that the New Mass "represents, both as a whole and in its details, a striking departure from the Catholic theology of the Mass as it was formulated in Session 22 of the Council of Trent."[387] The Modernists, nevertheless, continued with their agenda. It did not take them long to attack the very heart and essence of the Mass itself—Christ's words of Consecration.

Transubstantiation

Transubstantiation is the miracle that took place at the Last Supper and is repeated during the Consecration of the Mass, whereby the bread and wine are changed into the Body, Blood, Soul and Divinity of Jesus Christ. The Council of Florence declared that transubstantiation takes place during Mass when the priest uses the proper *matter* (material), *form* (words) and *intention*. Each is essential for the validity of the sacrament.

> The words of the Savior, by which He instituted this sacrament, are the form of this sacrament; for the priest, speaking in the person of Christ effects this sacrament. For by the power of the very words the substance of the bread is changed into the body of Christ, and the substance of the wine into the blood; yet in such a way that Christ is contained entire under the species of bread, and entire under the species of wine.[388]

Transubstantiation does not take place in the Mass if the *matter, form* or *intention* are essentially changed; the bread and wine remain merely bread and wine. This is explained by St. Thomas Aquinas (1226-1274): "Now it is clear, if any substantial part of the sacramental form be suppressed, that the essential sense of the words is destroyed; and consequently the sacrament is invalid."[389] The great Doctor of the Church St. Alphonsus Liguori (1696-1787) asserted: "If anyone abbreviates or changes something of the form of consecration, and the words do not signify the same thing, he does not confect the sacrament."[390]

---

[387] p. 27.
[388] *Decree for the Armenians* from the bull *Exultate Deo,* November 22, 1439.
[389] *Summa Theologica III,* Q. 60, Art. 8.
[390] Patrick Henry Omlor, *Questioning the Validity of Masses Using the New, All-English Canon,* pp. 78-79.

The *De Defectibus Decree,* which is found in every Roman Missal published prior to Vatican II, is almost identical to the wording of this passage.[391] This decree explains in minute detail that defective *matter* (bread and wine), *form* (words of consecration), *minister* or *intention* invalidates the Mass. The decree further says, "If he [the priest] should add anything which would not change the meaning, he would indeed confect, but would sin gravely." The *form* required for the validity of the Sacrament is found not only in the *De Defectibus Decree* of the *Missale Romanum,* but also in the *Catechism of the Council of Trent.*

Our worship reflects our beliefs. This truth is expressed by the idiom, *lex orandi, lex credendi* (the law of praying is the law of believing). Therefore, the Postconciliar Church had to destroy the Holy Sacrifice of the Mass because it contradicted the heresies of Ecumenism and Modernism and was a significant obstacle to the formation of a one-world church.

The Consecration of the Host

When Our Lord instituted the Sacrament of the Holy Eucharist at the Last Supper He used the words *For this is My Body*[392] to consecrate the host. The new "reformers," following the example of Martin Luther, added the words, "which will be given for you" to this formula. It may seem to be an insignificant change, but there was a specific reason for the alteration. The traditional words of consecration denote an event that is taking place here and now. The new terminology denotes a future event and leaves room for various interpretations.

This would also explain why the blessing of the offerings prior to the Consecration was dropped by the Episcopalians, Lutherans and the "reformers" of Vatican II. In the true Mass the priest asks Almighty God that the bread and wine "may become for our good, the Body and Blood of Thy dearly beloved Son, Jesus Christ Our Lord."[393] These words were far too explicit for the Modernists and Ecumenists, so they conveniently discarded them.

---

[391] *Missale Romanum, De Defectibus,* Ch. V. Par. 1.
[392] *Hoc est enim Corpus Meum.*
[393] Prayer *Quam Oblationem,* Fr. Walter Van de Putte, C.S. Sp., *St. Pius X Missal,* p. 503.

The Consecration of the Wine

The essential words necessary for a valid consecration of the wine are: *Hic est enim calix Sanguinis mei, novi et aeterni testamenti, mysterium fidei, qui pro vobis, et pro multis effundetur in remissionem peccatorum.* (For this is the chalice of My Blood of the new and eternal covenant; the mystery of faith; which shall be shed for you and for many unto the forgiveness of sins.)

The *De Defectibus Decree* states clearly: "If one should take away from, or change anything of the form of the consecration of the Body, and of the Blood, and in the very change of the words, the words should not mean the same thing, he would not confect the Sacrament."[394]

St. Thomas Aquinas explains why Our Lord used the words "for many" at the Last Supper:

> The blood of Christ's Passion has its efficacy not merely among the elect among the Jews, to whom the blood of the Old Testament was exhibited, but also for the Gentiles; not only for the priests who confect the sacrament, or others who receive (partake) but likewise for those whom it is offered. And therefore He says expressly: for you—the Jews, and for many, namely the Gentiles; or for those who partake, and for many for whom it is offered.[395]

The *Catechism of the Council of Trent* specifically defines the form of the Holy Eucharist in order "to guard against shameful mistakes on the part of priests, at the time of consecration, due to ignorance of the form."

> We are then firmly to believe that it [the form for the consecration of the wine] consists in the following words: *This is the chalice of My blood of the new and eternal testament, the mystery of faith, which shall be shed for you, and for many, to the remission of sins.* Of these words the greater part are taken from Scripture; but some have been preserved in the Church from Apostolic Tradition. …it is plain that no other words constitute the form.[396]

---

[394] V. De Defectibus Formae.
[395] *Summa Theologica III*, q. 78, a. 3, 8.
[396] On the Sacrament of the Holy Eucharist, p. 225.

With reason, therefore, were the words 'for all' not used, as in this place the fruits of the Passion are alone spoken of, and to the elect only did His passion bring the fruit of salvation.[397]

On April 3, 1969 Paul VI promulgated the New Mass in his Apostolic Constitution *Missale Romanum*. Note that the words for the consecration of the wine have been essentially changed in the vernacular translations of the New Mass.

> In every Eucharistic Prayer, therefore, we wish these words to be as follows: Over the bread: 'Take this, all of you, and eat it; this is my Body which will be given up for you.' Over the wine: 'Take this, all of you, and drink from it; this is the cup of my Blood, the Blood of the new and everlasting covenant. It will be shed for you and FOR ALL MEN [emphasis added] so that sins may be forgiven. Do this in memory of me.' The words, 'The mystery of faith,' spoken by the priest are to be taken out of the context of the words spoken by our Lord, and used instead to introduce an acclamation by the faithful.[398]

When Paul VI replaced Christ's words "for many" with the words, "for all" he changed the essential words of the Consecration of the Mass. Our Lord died for the salvation of all, but His Passion and Death were efficacious only for the many who are saved. In other words, Christ redeemed all, but not all are saved. This is what is signified in the true words of consecration.

St. Alphonsus Liguori says:

> The words 'Pro vobis et pro multis' ('For you and for many') are used to distinguish the virtue of the blood of Christ from its fruits; for the blood of Christ is of sufficient value to save all men, but its fruits are applicable only to a certain number and not to all, and this is their own fault.[399]

If Christ wanted to use the words "for all" at the Last Supper He would have done so since the Aramaic language has words that mean "all", "all the inhabitants of the earth" or "all mankind."[400] Obviously, He chose to use the

---

[397] p. 227.
[398] Austin Flannery, O.P., *Vatican Council II: The Conciliar and Post Conciliar Documents*, p. 139.
[399] *The Holy Eucharist*, p. 44.
[400] See: *The Robber Church* by Patrick Henry Omlor, pp. 114-115.

word "many," the word that the Catholic Church has retained in Her liturgy for nearly 2,000 years.

Our Lord's words that His Precious Blood would be shed for you (the Apostles) and for many have always been understood to refer to the efficacy, and not the sufficiency of His sacrifice. "Since the new 'form' [the faulty translation] contains a lie and a sacrilegious mutation of the words of Christ as recorded in Holy Writ [Scripture], *how can it conceivably* be a valid form for this Most Holy of Sacraments?"[401]

Invalid Form

The Protestant liturgies created by the "reformers" of the 16th century were invalid due to defect of form, since they changed the wording. Isn't it paradoxical that the *New Mass* which was drafted after Vatican II employs the same changes made by the Protestants? Is it possibly because six Protestant ministers were active in its creation? Would it not follow that the "Masses" and "consecrations" used in Postconciliar Churches are also invalid due to defect of form?

Shortly after the conclusion of the Second Vatican Council, a New Mass *(The Novus Ordo Missae)* was formulated in which substantial changes were made to the words of Consecration. These essential changes have rendered the New Mass invalid, as stated by the *Catechism of the Council of Trent, the De Defectibus Decree* of Pope St. Pius V and by St. Thomas Aquinas and St. Alphonsus Liguori. Therefore, because the *matter, form* and/or *intention* of the Mass were essentially changed, *transubstantiation* does not take place; the elements remain merely bread and wine.

Knowing full well that the changes made to the words of Consecration were in complete contradiction to the words of Christ and the teachings of the Church, Paul VI nevertheless promulgated the New Mass. In one of the greatest deceptions ever perpetrated, Paul VI misled millions of Catholics into believing that the New Mass was simply a vernacular translation of the Tridentine Mass.

---

[401] Patrick Henry Omlor, *Questioning the Validity of Masses Using the New, All-English Canon*, pp. 60-61.

In order to couch his deception, Paul VI even went so far as to retain the correct form of the Sacrament of the Holy Eucharist to the point of including the words "pro multis" (for many) in the Latin translation of his Apostolic Constitution *Missale Romanum*.[402] Paul VI ordered his liturgical commissions to translate the New Mass into the vernacular with the foreknowledge that "he would reserve to himself the power to approve directly all the translations into the vernacular of the sacramental forms."[403]

Even though the official Latin words "pro multis" can only be correctly interpreted as "for many" it is not surprising (knowing Paul VI's obvious intentions) to find that in every vernacular translation of the New Mass, the official Vatican approved words for the consecration of the wine were substantially altered to the translation—"FOR YOU AND FOR ALL MEN" and later to "FOR YOU AND FOR ALL." Thus, Our Lord's own words "…FOR MANY" were insidiously replaced with "…FOR ALL."

Paul VI officially decreed that on March 22, 1970 the *Novus Ordo Missae* become mandatory throughout the world. It is unthinkable that a true pope could promulgate an invalid Mass containing such obvious doctrinal errors.

He tried to soften the blow by saying that Catholics should prepare themselves to be disturbed by these changes, adding, "that pious people will be those most greatly disturbed."[404] If everything including the council were good, true and valid, then why would the pious be disturbed?

Are Not the Words "This is My Body, This is My Blood" Alone Sufficient?

Regarding the words of consecration, "Father Suarez says that, according to the common opinion of theologians, not merely the words of the form, 'this is the Chalice of My Blood,' but all the words from take to remission of sins, were pronounced by Jesus Christ."[405]

---

[402] A.A.S., #4, April 30, 1969.
[403] Congregation for Divine Worship, circular letter of the Secretary of State: A.A.S. 66 (1974): 98-99.
[404] *New York Daily News*, November 27, 1969.
[405] M. Gavin, S.J., *The Sacrifice of the Mass*, p. 105.

Concerning the necessity of the complete form for the validity of the Sacrament, St. Thomas Aquinas has written: "Some have maintained that the words *This is the chalice of My Blood* alone belong to the substance of the form, but not the words which follow. Now this seems incorrect, because the words which follow them are determinations of the predicate, that is, of Christ's Blood; consequently, they belong to the integrity of the expression."[406]

Some theologians hold the opinion that "This is My Body, This is My Blood" constitute the essential form of the Holy Eucharist. However, despite the speculative opinions of theologians, in practice, the minister of a Sacrament may never use a probable form. He must always use a certainly valid form, not a doubtful one.

> In practice, the very raising of questions or doubts about the validity of a given manner of confecting a Sacrament—if this question is based on an apparent defect of matter or form—would necessitate the strict abstention from use of that doubtful manner of performing the sacramental act, *until the doubts are resolved*. In confecting the Sacraments, all priests are obliged to follow the *medium certum* [that is, 'the safer course.'][407]

Fr. Jone reaffirms this in his *Moral Theology* when he says: "Matter and form must be certainly valid. Hence one may not follow a probable opinion and use either doubtful matter or form."[408]

This fact is supported by Father Henry Davis, S.J.:

> In conferring the sacraments, as also in the consecration in Mass, it is never allowed to adopt a probable course of action as to validity and to abandon the safer course. The contrary was explicitly condemned by Pope Innocent XI (1670-1676). To do so would be a grievous sin against religion, namely, an act of irreverence towards what Christ Our Lord has instituted. It would be a grievous sin against charity, as the recipient would probably be deprived of the graces and effects of the Sacrament. It would be a grievous sin against justice, as the recipient has a right to valid Sacraments.[409]

---

[406] *Summa Theologica III*, q. 78, a. 3.
[407] Quote from Fr. Lawrence Brey in *Questioning the Validity of Masses Using the New, All-English Canon*, Patrick Henry Omlor, p. 15.
[408] Fr. Heribert Jone, OFM Cap., *Moral Theology*, p. 308.
[409] *Moral & Pastoral Theology*, Vol. 2, p. 27.

Is Not One Valid Consecration Sufficient?

Fr. Brey asks several weighty questions:

Even if the Consecration of the Wine is invalid by reason of defect of form, and therefore the entire Mass is invalid, does the priest nevertheless truly consecrate the *Bread* in such a Mass? Even if the wine does not become truly consecrated, would we not at least have validly consecrated Hosts, the true Eucharistic Body of Christ, provided that the Consecration of the Bread be performed using the proper matter and form? And therefore could not our people at least be certain they are receiving the true Body and Blood of Jesus at Communion time in such a Mass?

The answer to these questions is a qualified *no*, for one could not be *certain* that the hosts are truly consecrated; at least there is a real and practical *doubt*. In fact, some theologians hold with *certainty* that under such circumstances the bread is *not* validly consecrated.[410]

Fr. M. Gavin, S.J. explains:

The Consecration, according to our Lord's command, must ever be under both kinds, since it is only from the double Consecration that the Blessed Eucharist has the character of a Sacrifice. The separate Consecration of bread and wine represents in a mystical way the death of Christ, the parting of the Body and Blood on the Cross. That Blood was shed really on the Cross: mystically in the institution of the Eucharist and daily at Mass on our altars.[411]

Since the Holy Eucharist is a Sacrament and a Sacrifice, the consecration of both species is required. This is confirmed by the moralists Noldin and Schmitt:

As often as the sacrifice is offered, the consecration of both species is required, according to the Will and institution of Christ. For Christ at the Last Supper, consecrating each species, commanded: 'do *this* in commemoration of Me' (Cf. I Cor. 11, 24-25).... the very notion of sacrifice ...demands the consecration of both species.[412]

---

[410] Patrick Henry Omlor, *Questioning the Validity of the Masses Using the New, All-English Canon*, pp. 120-121.
[411] *The Sacrifice of the Mass*, p. 106.
[412] *De Eucharistia, Summa Theologiae Moralis III.*

Fr. Adolph Tanquerey writes: "The consecration of both species is required by Divine Law for the essence of the Sacrifice: this we know from Christ's very (words of) Institution, and from the precept and practice of the Church, so that it is necessary in order that a true representation of the Sacrifice of the Cross be had."[413]

Fr. Brey continues:

...The *Sacrament* of the Body and Blood of the Lord was given to us *only and exclusively* in the context of the *Sacrifice* of the Body and Blood of Christ... IF NO SACRIFICE, THEN NO SACRAMENT. Nor is there any indication anywhere that Christ willed the *Sacrament* of the Eucharist to be confected apart from the propitiatory *Sacrifice* of the Mass. Indeed, 'the notion of the *Sacrament* in the Eucharist, according to the Will of Christ, *cannot be separated from the notion of Sacrifice.*'[414]

Indeed, in practice, Church law absolutely forbids, without any exception, the consecration of only one species without the other. Canon 817 of the Code of Canon Law states: 'It is forbidden, even in extreme cases of necessity, to consecrate one species without the other...' The *Roman Missal*, in its section, 'De Defectibus,' prescribes that a Mass interrupted after the Consecration of the Host (because of illness or death of the celebrant) *must* be continued by another priest, i.e., that the wine must be consecrated to complete and effect the Sacrifice (Cf. *De Defectibus*, X, 3).[415]

The Offertory has been Radically Changed

The New Church has supplanted the Mass with a new ecumenical service. The traditional offertory prayers denote an offering being made to God and acknowledge that the bread and wine will soon become the Body and Blood of Christ. It was therefore of paramount importance to the liturgical Modernists that the offertory prayers be removed. They have been replaced with a Jewish blessing before meals in order to eradicate the concept of sacrifice from the Mass. Luther also practically eliminated the offertory from his liturgy.

---

[413] *Brevior Synopsis Theologiae Dogmaticae.*
[414] Noldin-Schmitt, Innsbruck, 1940.
[415] Patrick Henry Omlor, *Questioning the Validity of the Masses Using the New, All-English Canon*, p. 122.

Forms Used in the Eastern Rites

In their efforts to defend the validity of the New Mass some liturgists mistakenly claim that the Eastern rites used the words "For you and for all." The error of this claim is apparent when one reviews the forms used by the Eastern rites for the consecration of the wine.

THE BYZANTINE LITURGY:

"This is my Blood of the New Testament, which is shed for you and for many for the forgiveness of sins."

THE ARMENIAN LITURGY:

"This is my Blood of the New Testament, which is shed for you and for many for the expiation and forgiveness of sins."

THE COPTIC LITURGY:

"For this is my Blood of the new Covenant, which shall be shed for you and for many unto the forgiveness of sins."

THE ETHIOPIC LITURGY:

"This is my Blood of the New Covenant which is shed for you and for many for the forgiveness of sin."

THE SYRIAN LITURGY:

"This is my Blood, of the New Covenant, which shall be poured out and offered for the forgiveness of the sins and eternal life of you and of many."

THE MARONITE LITURGY:

(The form is identical to that which was always used in the Latin Rite.)

THE CHALDEAN LITURGY:

"This is my Blood of the New Eternal Covenant, the mystery of faith, which is shed for you and for many for the forgiveness of sins."

THE LITURGY OF MALABAR:

"For this is the chalice of my Blood of the New and Eternal Testament, the mystery of faith, which is shed for you and for many for the remission of sins."[416]

---

[416] Quotations and excerpts are from Donald Attwater's *"Eastern Catholic Worship."* Devin-Adair Co., New York, 1945. Patrick Omlor, *The Robber Church,* pp. 158-159.

Ecumenical Nature of the New Mass

The phrase: "Christ has died. Christ has risen. Christ will come again." was borrowed from the *Lutheran Book of Worship.* In a spirit of ecumenism the Postconciliar Church has even adopted the same three-year liturgical calendar that is used by the Episcopalian and Lutheran churches.

In an effort to accommodate other religions, the very architecture, floor plans and interiors of Catholic Churches began to change and take on a Protestant look. The ceremonies and church interiors of these religions are often indistinguishable from one another save for the sign posted out front.

Innovations were introduced in order to fashion churches that would be more acceptable to non-Catholics. Benediction, rosary processions and novenas are few and far between. Altars, communion rails and statues have all but vanished. Tabernacles have been moved to the side or placed in a separate room in an effort "not to offend" those of other religions. Is the New Church unconcerned about offending God?

Postconciliar Churches

Knowing that these subtle changes influenced the way people believe, novelties such as communion in the hand,[417] "liturgical dancers," Polka Masses and general absolution were introduced. Churches were transformed from quiet places of worship into community centers for socialization and entertainment.

Most postconciliar churches reflect the emptiness of their religion. Altars have been abandoned or removed in favor of tables. The presider's chair now holds the place of prominence once only reserved for the tabernacle. Crucifixes depicting the sufferings of Our Lord have been replaced with a Risen Christ. Great cathedrals have been gutted and refashioned into cold, bare edifices to accommodate the new beliefs—beliefs that are as empty and cold as the structures that mirror them.

---

[417] "Several participants at the recent Toronto World Youth Day [July 18-28, 2002] were scandalized by the way singing, dancing and boisterous laughing were going on at a Mass while bishops and cardinals were concelebrating. It wasn't clear when the festivities ended and the Mass began. More serious still was the distribution of Communion in cardboard boxes by girls while hundreds of priests remained at their seats." *Latin Mass Magazine,* Fall 2002, "Roman Landscape," Alessandro Zangrando.

Reverence is gone as people enter, sit and talk, waiting for the celebration to begin. The meeting hall often resounds with laughter or clapping and music from guitars, drums, accordions and mariachi bands. In contrast to the Traditional Mass, the New Mass is not bound by rigid liturgical guidelines, but has numerous variations. Consequently, the liturgy often differs from parish to parish and may even include liturgical dancers, tribal rites, clowns and balloons.

Frederick McManus characterizes the New Mass:

> The new Instruction marks a definite break with the traditional pattern of rigid, precise rubrical directions. Choices, alternatives, variations are opened up, especially in the 'Liturgy of the Word,' to use the expression employed by the Fathers of the Second Vatican Council. This means that much more is left to the judgment and responsibility of the individual pastor and celebrant. Circumstances, varying from church to church and indeed from Mass to Mass, will dictate some of the details.[418]

Summary

In 1851, Fr. Faber foretold that in the last age of the Church "there will be hardly any Mass and the majority of Christians will apostasize."[419] This prophecy has been fulfilled. The Postconciliar Church dismembered the Mass and replaced it with a shell of what it had once been. The new ceremony, which closely resembles a Protestant service, is not a Catholic Mass.

The New Church has destroyed the essence of the Mass by changing the words of Consecration—the very words of Christ. Most of the exterior signs of adoration (genuflection, kneeling, bells, signs of the cross, prayerful silence, etc.) denoting the mystical and sacred nature of the Mass have also been eliminated.

Charles Davis dispels any doubts regarding the aims of the liturgical reforms:

> Let no one, then, underestimate the significance and power of the [new] liturgical movement. What is taking place is not the increasing popularity of a private hobby or interesting sideline, not a touching-up of ritual anomalies, but a change, a renewal in the pastoral work of the Church. And the concern is not with incidentals, but with the fundamentals of doctrine.[420]

---

[418] *Worship, Vol. XXXIX,* January 1965, p. 67.
[419] *Notes on Doctrinal and Spiritual Subjects Vol. II,* pp. 16-17.
[420] *Liturgy and Doctrine,* p. 123.

It is obvious that the *Novus Ordo* is not a vernacular translation of the Tridentine Latin Mass, but is rather a complete rewrite containing many essential changes. The Mass has always been the center of the Catholic religion for it is in the Holy Sacrifice of the Mass that the relationship between God and man is most perfectly expressed. All Catholic spiritual, social and moral behavior stems from this relationship.

The Catholic Church is God-centered because it was established by Jesus Christ, the Son of God. The New Mass is man-centered in that it emphasizes the memorial meal aspects of the Mass and social interaction between parishioners instead of spiritual interaction between God and worshipper. The Tridentine Mass is a sacrifice; the Novus Ordo Mass is a social celebration. The New Mass is invalid, sacrilegious and an affront to God.

If man is at the center of the New Mass, then man is at the center of this new religion. If man is at the center of this new religion it follows that spiritually, morally and socially this religion must be whatever people say it is. From this secular humanistic philosophy (which guided the Second Vatican Council) have followed the inconsistent and confusing spiritual, moral and social teachings of our time. Vatican II has imposed a religion founded on the cult of man.

In retrospect, we can see when new religious leaders have appeared throughout history they claimed their beliefs were signs of enlightenment and progress, necessary for the good of the people. The New Church used the same rationale, claiming that this was going to modernize the Church so it would conform to the times. Most Catholics, believing Vatican II to be a valid council, at first accepted these proscribed alterations of belief and worship, especially since the Modernists proceeded in such a gradual way. In time, many Catholics became desensitized to additional and less subtle changes that were being imposed upon them. A minority finally realized what was happening and left the Postconciliar Church in search of the traditional Catholic Church they once knew.

Tragically, the majority accepted the radical changes and heretical teachings of the New Church. Wanting to be part of the new faith community they (often unwittingly) became members of this new religion. Since the Postconciliar Church is not that different from other religions, millions of former Catholics simply left and joined other religions.

The evolution of the new church of Vatican II reads much like the story of cooking a live frog. One places the frog in cold water and then gradually increases the temperature. At what point, if any, does the frog realize he is being slowly cooked and jump out before it's too late?

An Even Newer Mass

The missal has been revised three times since Vatican II: 1969, 1975 and 2002. On March 18, 2002, John Paul II gave his formal approbation to the latest edition of the Roman Missal and the new General Instruction of the Roman Missal (GIRM). The headline from the *National Catholic Register* reads: "New Roman Missal Means Mass Changes—Added Eucharistic Prayers, Recent Saints, New Creed Options and More."[421] John Paul II authorized the following changes:

- There are now 10 Eucharistic Prayers from which to choose: 4 common, 2 with a Reconciliation theme and 4 new ones.
- The Apostles' Creed may be substituted for the Nicene Creed on Sundays during Lent and Easter time.
- "The tabernacle is not, the new instruction makes clear, to be on the same altar where Mass is offered."[422]
- A genuflection to the tabernacle is to be made at the beginning and end of the service but not during it.
- The calendar has been changed again.

U. S. Catholics Barred from Kneeling for Communion?[423]

Prior to Vatican II, Catholics throughout the world (barring physical ailments) knelt to receive Holy Communion. This was an outward expression of

---

[421] April 7, 2002, Article by Raymond De Souza.
[422] *National Catholic Register,* April 7, 2002.
[423] Headline of the Catholic World News Website, August 23, 2002.

their adoration and reverence toward the Blessed Sacrament, as masterfully explained by Judy Tarjanyi in the *Toledo Blade:*

> If Catholics were known for anything before the 1960s, it was their habit of kneeling. Kneeling [genuflecting] on entering the church, kneeling on leaving. Kneeling during the Mass and especially, kneeling when receiving communion.
>
> Since the liturgical reforms of the Second Vatican Council swept the Catholic Church clean of many such pious practices, however, standing has replaced much of the knee bending in Catholic worship life.[424]

Leon Suprenant Jr. explains the profound significance of kneeling during religious worship: "From biblical times to the present, kneeling has been considered not merely a penitential posture in the Church but also a posture of adoration and profound reverence."[425]

When Catholics go to Holy Communion they receive the Body, Blood, Soul and Divinity of Jesus Christ, who unites Himself to them in the most intimate manner. The Blessed Sacrament, therefore, should be treated with great honor and respect. When the Blessed Sacrament is exposed for adoration, the faithful kneel in profound reverence. We express our love and devotion in many ways, including kneeling and folding our hands in prayer. As we enter the church we genuflect, thereby outwardly manifesting our belief in the Real Presence of Christ in the Holy Eucharist.

"The Second Vatican Council radically altered the theology of the Eucharist, and standing is the only posture compatible with this new theology."[426] The Bishops' Committee on the Liturgy declared in its July [2002] newsletter:

> 'The bishops of the United States have decided that the normative posture for receiving Holy Communion should be standing. Kneeling is not a licit posture for receiving Holy Communion in the dioceses of the United States of America unless the bishop of a particular diocese has derogated from this norm in an individual and extraordinary circumstance.'[427]

---

[424] January 11, 2003.
[425] *National Catholic Register,* January 26, 2003, "Standing Up (& Not Kneeling) For The Church."
[426] *Adoremus Bulletin,* March 2003, p. 2.
[427] Catholic World News—News Brief—August 23, 2002.

"The General Instruction of this new Roman Missal 'notes that Communion should not be denied a person who kneels to receive, but that if the case arises, the priest should provide additional catechesis to help the person understand the reason for common posture.' "[428]

Although this directive seems to imply that the parishioners are at liberty to stand or kneel, many are humiliated for continuing to kneel. Julia Baltrinic, who attends services at Christendom College, asks the simple question: "Why is kneeling to receive our Lord such an awful thing?"[429] Bobby Ryan "finds it hard to give up the devotional kneeling he has learned since he became a Catholic in 1995. 'For people who have knelt all their lives, and a bishop saying you shouldn't kneel, there's something wrong. ...I'd think it would make a bishop happy to have people in his diocese who want to kneel.' "[430]

Lex orandi, lex credendi.—The law of praying is the law of believing. Discouraging the faithful from kneeling to receive Communion displays a lack of faith in the Real Presence. However, if the host is only a symbol of Christ, it would be appropriate to stand to receive it. Perhaps this is why it is a common Protestant practice.

Kenneth Jones gives the percentages of Catholics who believe the Eucharist merely a 'symbolic reminder' of Jesus:

- Catholics aged 65 and older: 45%
- Catholics aged 45-65: 58%
- Catholics aged 18-44: 70%
- Catholics who attend Mass every Sunday: 51%[431]

The Indult Mass

Since the introduction of the *Novus Ordo Missae* in 1967, tens of thousands of concerned Catholics have sent petitions to the Vatican requesting the restoration of the Latin Mass. Although Paul VI granted permission for the Latin Mass,

---

[428] *Our Sunday Visitor*, December 29, 2002, "New norms aim for fewer Mass surprises."
[429] *National Catholic Register*, January 26, 2003, "A College Readjusts to No-Kneeling Rule," by John Burger.
[430] *National Catholic Register*, September 29, 2002, "No-Kneeling-For-Communion Rule Sparks Widespread Outcry," by John Burger.
[431] *Index of Leading Catholic Indicators: The Church Since Vatican II*, p. 80. Taken from *New York Times / CBS Poll*, 1994.

restrictions were such that, in many cases, it was the New Mass, not the Tridentine Mass, that was celebrated in Latin. This was done in order to placate traditional Catholics and lead them into thinking that the Tridentine Mass was being said when, in reality, it was not. It makes little difference whether the New Mass is celebrated in Latin or the vernacular—it is still essentially a non-Catholic service.

> According to the notices issued by the Congregation for Divine Worship June 1, 1971 and Oct. 28, 1974: (1) Bishops may permit the celebration of Mass in Latin for mixed-language groups; (2) bishops may permit the celebration of one or two Masses in Latin on weekdays or Sundays in any church, irrespective of mixed-language groups involved (1971); (3) priests may celebrate Mass in Latin when people are not present; (4) the approved revised order of the Mass [the New Mass] is to be used in Latin as well as vernacular languages; (5) By way of exemption, bishops may permit older and handicapped priests to use the Council of Trent's Order of the Mass [the Tridentine Mass] in private celebration of the Holy Sacrifice.[432]

On October 3, 1984 John Paul II granted an indult allowing the Latin Mass to be celebrated using the 1962 edition of the Roman Missal which conveniently contained the liturgical changes approved by John XXIII. Once again, this was not the Tridentine Mass and the permission granted is only temporary as indicated by the term "indult." "The word *indult* means granted by way of indulgence. ...The favor may be a faculty, permission, dispensation, etc. but an indult usually denotes a favor granted only for a time."[433]

The conditions for the indult granted by John Paul II stipulated that the New Mass should be placed on a par with the Latin Mass and that both need be accepted on an equal basis. The Indult Mass was a clever attempt to abolish the Tridentine Latin Mass.

---

[432] *2003 Our Sunday Visitor Catholic Almanac,* p. 193.
[433] T. Lincoln Bouscaren, S.J., *Canon Law: A Text and Commentary,* p. 19.

The principal condition for the celebration was: 'There must be unequivocal, even public, evidence that the priest and people petitioning have no ties with those who impugn the lawfulness and doctrinal soundness of the Roman Missal [the New Mass—*Novus Ordo*] promulgated in 1970 by Pope Paul VI.'

- The letter, from the Pontifical Commission *Ecclesia Dei,* said in part: The Tridentine Mass can be celebrated in a parish church, so long as it provides a pastoral service and is harmoniously integrated into the parish liturgical schedule.
- When requested, the Mass should be offered on a regular Sunday and holy day basis, 'at a central location, at a convenient time' for a trial period of several months with 'adjustment' later if needed.[434]
- Celebrants of the Mass should make it clear that they acknowledge the validity of the postconciliar liturgy [New Mass]. Although the commission has the authority to grant the use of the Tridentine rite to all groups that request it, the commission 'would much prefer that such faculties be granted by the Ordinary himself [local bishop] so that the ecclesiastical communion may be strengthened.'
- While the new lectionary in the vernacular can be used in the Tridentine Mass, as suggested by the Second Vatican Council, it should not be 'imposed on congregations that decidedly wish to maintain the former liturgical tradition in its integrity.'
- Older and retired priests who have asked permission to celebrate Mass according to the Tridentine rite should be given the chance to do so for groups that request it.[435]

Serious Problems with the Indult Mass

There are good reasons to believe that the Vatican allows the Indult Mass in order to appease those who oppose the New Mass. The Indult Mass can be said to be a "Compromise" Mass insofar as it only *appears* to be the Tridentine Mass which Catholics have been requesting for so many years. It is also very insidious

---

[434] "The Congregation for Bishops approved July 4, 1992 a resolution of the U.S. bishops to waive the Mass attendance obligation for the holy days of Mary, the Mother of God [used to be called the Circumcision of Our Lord] (January 1) the Assumption of Mary (August 15) and All Saints (November 1) when the solemnities fall on a Saturday or Monday." Matthew Bunson, *2003 Our Sunday Visitor Catholic Almanac*, p. 193.
[435] Bunson, 195.

as it is only temporary and requires the participants to accept the New Mass and the perverted doctrines of Vatican II along with it.

Should Catholics Attend the Indult Mass?

The priests who celebrate the Indult Mass also offer the New Mass, thereby revealing their position as one of compromise. They should be suspect since they promote both liturgies on an equal basis. Truth and error, sacrifice and sacrilege cannot be accepted on equal terms. Furthermore, it is difficult for many to detect whether the priest is using the traditional *form* of Consecration, since some priests think nothing of substituting it with the *form* used in the New Mass.

Because Indult Masses are offered in the same churches in which the New Mass is celebrated, priests often takes hosts from the tabernacle that were previously "consecrated" at a New Mass. As the priest distributes Communion, one must wonder whether the communicant receives the Body, Blood, Soul and Divinity of Jesus Christ or simply a wafer of bread.

Many older priests in the Postconciliar Church have not celebrated the Latin Mass for decades. It is likely that they have forgotten many of the basic rubrics, even some essential ones. Other priests may omit parts of the Mass or they may combine the old with the new.

Since the rite of ordination has been essentially changed, any priest or bishop ordained in the new rite (after June 18, 1968) may not be a priest at all. Therefore, since their ordination is at best doubtfully valid, their Masses are likely to be invalid.

Finally, it is difficult to know which Latin Mass the priest is offering. Some offer the Latin Mass but apply the rubrics of John XXIII. Others deceitfully offer the New Mass in Latin. One must be proficient in Latin in order to ascertain which Mass is being offered.

Due to these considerations, Catholics should only attend the Tridentine Latin Mass and avoid the Indult Mass because it poses numerous dangers to the faith. The Tridentine Latin Mass is offered in most major cities and, with prayer and research, you should be able to find one in your locale. Be aware that if your diocese offers the Latin Mass it is the Indult Mass, not the Tridentine Latin Mass.

Conclusion

The following words of warning, (even though written in the late 1800's), seem prophetic for our time:

> The Church appears to be reaching the time when She will be mystically crucified with Her Lord. The powers of darkness are evidently allowed a strange power of temptation: 'It is their hour.' Even many of Our Lord's own have fallen away... We see that the Church is visibly afflicted, that the powers of Hell are leagued more strongly than ever against Her... The Church has already commenced that season of persecution, trial and temptation, in which She will in herself represent again the Passion of Our Lord.[436]

Indeed these words ring true, for the Second Vatican Council has become the avenue whereby Christ is being re-crucified. He, along with His Church, has been taken, once again, in chains and is now being led to Calvary. Just as when Our Redeemer was crucified and all seemed lost, so too it might appear today. As the Pharisees of old rejoiced in the death of Jesus Christ, so also do the liberals and Modernists of today rejoice in the destruction of the Mass and Christ's Church. However, just as Our Lord's crucifixion was not His defeat, but was rather His victory over Satan, so too, the true Mass and the Catholic Church have not been nor can ever be destroyed—they live on in the faithful who hold to traditional Catholic teaching and the Tridentine Latin Mass.

The creation of the sacrilegious New Mass did not obliterate the old. The true Mass, as established by Christ and codified by Pope St. Pius V from its already existing liturgical tradition, has not been destroyed. The Catholic Church remains preserved under the promised care and protection of Our Lord Himself. The Holy Sacrifice of the Mass continues to be offered to Almighty God daily by the Church's loyal clergy.

Just as, a faithful remnant stood by the Cross of Christ in His darkest hour, so do traditional Catholics remain loyal to the faith as pockets of light in a world shrouded in darkness.

---

[436] Mother Mary Potter, *The Path of Mary,* pp. 15-16, 18.

D. The Seven Sacraments and the New Sacraments

Once the Mass had been dismembered, the sacraments became the next target of the Modernists. The Church has always held that the Seven Sacraments would never have need of alteration or reform since Jesus Christ Himself instituted them.[437]

The Council of Florence described the elements necessary for the validity of the sacraments: "All these sacraments are brought to completion by three components; by things as matter, by words as form, and by the person of the minister effecting the sacrament with the intention of doing what the Church does. And if any of these three is lacking, the sacrament is not effected."[438]

Once again, contrary to the teachings of the Catholic Church for nearly 2,000 years, Vatican II introduced changes to the essence of the sacramental rites. Several sacraments even have new names: Initiation (Baptism), Reconciliation (Penance) and Anointing of the Sick (Extreme Unction). Because several of the sacraments have been modified extensively, their validity is in no way guaranteed.

The Church is Not Above Christ

The Catholic Church can change the nonessential ceremonial aspects of the sacraments; however, it cannot change the substance of the sacraments since the Church did not institute them—Our Divine Redeemer did. Bernard Leeming, S.J. in *Principles of Sacramental Theology* says: "In fact, if the matter of any sacrament has been fixed by Christ, not even the pope or general council can change it." Pope St. Pius X wrote: "It is well known that to the Church there belongs no right whatsoever to innovate anything touching on the substance of the sacraments."[439]

This is confirmed by Msgr. Joseph Pohle: "Solid arguments can be adduced in support of the proposition that Christ Himself so determined both the *matter* and the *form* of all the sacraments not only *in genere* [generally], but likewise *in*

---

[437] Council of Trent, Session 7, Canons 1 and 13.
[438] *Exultate Deo,* November 22, 1439.
[439] The encyclical *Ex Quo Nono,* December 26, 1910.

specie [specifically], that the Church has never made any essential changes in regard thereto, and could not make such a change if she would."[440] The Catholic Church has received from Christ the duty of safeguarding the holiness of divine worship by preserving the Mass and the sacraments for all time. The Church is not above Christ.

In his Apostolic Constitution *Sacramentum Ordinis,* Pope Pius XII declared:

> For these sacraments instituted by Christ our Lord, the Church in the course of centuries never substituted other sacraments, nor could she do so, since, as the Council of Trent[441] teaches the Seven Sacraments of the New Law were all instituted by Jesus Christ our Lord, and the Church has no power over the 'substance of the sacraments,' that is, over those things which, as is proved from the sources of Divine revelation, Christ the Lord Himself established to be kept as sacramental signs.[442]

The Seven Sacraments of the Church are instruments of God's power and goodness, instituted by Christ for the spiritual welfare of mankind. They are divine actions: divine in their origin and divine in their efficacy. They sanctify, they cleanse, they strengthen, they heal. They bring supernatural life to the soul, endow it with beauty, enrich it with virtue, preserve it from sin and entitle it to eternal life. Yet these marvelous sacraments are enshrined in delicate elements: in the words of human speech, in symbolic actions and in sacred signs that depend for their very being on the ministry of men.

Prior to Vatican II priests received thorough training in the seminary regarding the administration of the sacraments, leaving one confident that the sacraments offered in Catholic churches were valid. The same cannot be said of the priests of the Postconciliar Church; ceremonies often differ from parish to parish and are, to a great degree, contingent upon their whims.

The Vatican II *Constitution on the Liturgy* "introduced certain modifications in the very *essence* of the sacramental rites."[443] The changes, expressing the new

---

[440] *The Sacraments, Vol. I,* p. 108.
[441] Session 7, Canon 1, March 3, 1547.
[442] November 30, 1947.
[443] *L'Osservatore Romano,* November 7, 1974.

theology of Vatican II, consisted of alterations, deletions and insertions. Did the formulators of Vatican II dare think they could improve on the work of Christ, or were they casting His work aside in order to promote their own agenda?

The New Rite of Baptism—Initiation

The Sacrament of Baptism cleanses our souls from original sin, making us adopted children of God and heirs of heaven. As a result of Vatican II, the sacrament has been significantly changed. The new ceremony, called the Rite for the Christian Initiation of Infants, was introduced on June 1, 1970.

Luther's Revisions

Martin Luther held erroneous beliefs about Baptism. The Catholic Church teaches that Baptism removes original sin. Luther, however, taught that "original sin remains in the baptized until their death."[444] "In his earlier baptismal order of 1523, Luther, in order not to offend weak consciences, had retained as many of the traditional ceremonies as possible."[445]

"In 1526, he [Luther] yielded to the urging of his friend Nicholas Hausmann in Zwickau and published a revised form of *The Order of Baptism* which introduced some important changes. Omitted were the exsufflation, the first of the two opening prayers, the giving of the salt, the first of the two exorcisms, the salutation before the Gospel, the Ephphata ["Be though opened."—Our Lord used these words to cure a man who was deaf and dumb.], the two anointings before and after Baptism, and the placing of a lighted candle in the child's hands."[446] The postconciliar Rite of Christian Initiation adopted many of Luther's changes.

Teilhard de Chardin

Teilhard de Chardin was a French Jesuit priest who attempted to reconcile Christianity with Darwin's evolutionism and Hegel's philosophy.[447] "...Teilhard could not accept the definite and detailed Catholic doctrines on creation, the

---

[444] *Table Talk: Luther's Works, Vol. 54*, p. 20.
[445] *Liturgy and Hymns: Luther's Works, Vol. 53*, p. 106.
[446] *Liturgy and Hymns*, 106.
[447] "God does not exist; but will exist when good and evil will have completely assimilated one another in fusion. ...As I love to say the synthesis of the Christian God (of the above) and the Marxist God (of the forward)... is the only God whom henceforth we can worship in spirit and in truth." Fr. Coughlin, *Bishop Versus Pope*, pp. 211, 215-216.

explanation of miracles, the existence of Original Sin, the personal responsibility for actual sin, the Resurrection and personal Life Everlasting."[448] In his "Cosmic Christ" concept "the person of Christ is dissolved into the universe and Christ no longer has a personal identity."[449] Some priests and deacons have adopted the erroneous teachings of Chardin regarding Original Sin. This has caused them to have false views of Baptism.

Notable Changes

- The prayer of exorcism and the anointing with oil of catechumens are omitted.[450]
- A saint's name is no longer required.
- Baptized non-Roman Christians are rarely baptized conditionally.
- In place of a second Catholic baptismal sponsor, a Christian of a Protestant denomination who may be a relative or friend of the family may serve as a Christian witness of the baptism with a Catholic sponsor. A Catholic, incidentally, can do the same for a member of a Protestant denomination.[451]
- An even closer participation is permitted when the person to be baptized is a member of one of the separated Eastern Churches. A member of one of these churches may be a godparent, together with a Catholic godparent, at the baptism of a Catholic infant or adult.[452]
- In the new rite of reception of baptized Christians into full communion with the Catholic Church the requirement of absolution from excommunication is now suppressed and no abjuration of error is made.

Before Vatican II, parish priests instructed converts to Catholicism. Their seminary training in dogmatic and moral theology allowed them to give converts a sound foundation in the truths of the Catholic Faith. This has all changed since the Second Vatican Council and the introduction of the RCIA.

---

[448] Fr. Coughlin, *Bishop Versus Pope,* p. 214.
[449] *Our Sunday Visitor,* April 20, 2003, "What is the 'Cosmic Christ'?," Msgr. F. Mannion.
[450] ICEL, *The Rites of the Catholic Church as Revised by the Second Vatican Ecumenical Council, Vol. I,* p. 423.
[451] John Dietzen, *The New Question Box,* p. 206.
[452] *Directory Concerning Ecumenical Matters of the Secretariat For Promoting Christian Unity,* May 14, 1967, no. 48.

RCIA

Many modern Catholics are familiar with the RCIA (Rite of Christian Initiation for Adults). The RCIA religious educational program was established on January 6, 1972 in order to impress upon the minds of adult converts the teachings and ideals of Vatican II. Prospective converts are required to complete a lengthy series of classes directed primarily toward community participation. Sadly, RCIA members rarely receive orthodox and comprehensive instruction in Catholic doctrine. The results:

- Seemingly high dropout rate within a few years of RCIA.
- A perceived lack of knowledge about Church teaching, not only among participants, but often among the Catholics giving instruction.
- An emphasis on the 'experience' of community, rather than on the substance of our common Catholic faith, which sets participants up for a fall when the program is over. ...And, on occasion, those responsible for RCIA are themselves uncomfortable with Church teaching or unwilling to support it boldly.[453]

Experimentation

Although numerous changes were introduced into the new Rites of Christian Initiation, the essential words, "I baptize you in the name of the Father, and of the Son, and of the Holy Spirit (Ghost)," have been retained.

However, this does not always assure the validity of the new rite because following the Second Vatican Council, radical priests sometimes experiment with the essential rites of the sacraments, including Baptism. Instead of using the correct words, some priests make up their own formula or alter the essential words or change key elements in the Rite of Christian Initiation. Others perform the ceremonies carelessly. These alterations, deletions and insertions have rendered many baptisms doubtfully valid and others certainly invalid.

The Intention of the Minister

The Church teaches that even a heretic or an unbaptized person can validly and licitly baptize. This fact is supported by Fr. John Murphy, "The validity of Baptism does not depend on the minister or the kind of person he may be, but on

---

[453] Editorial in the March 2, 2003 issue of *Our Sunday Visitor*.

the fact that, wishing to administer the Baptism of Christ, he uses the correct rite."[454] "He must, however, perform the ceremony correctly and have the intention of 'doing what the Church does,' namely, of performing the ceremony that is usual among Catholics."[455] Fr. Bouscaren, S.J. has written in his commentary on Canon Law: "It must of course be clearly understood that a right intention, that is, an intention of doing what the Church of Christ does, is always necessary for the validity of the sacrament."[456]

> The minister of a sacrament can invalidate the rite by not intending to accomplish a sacramental rite at all, even though he goes through this ritual quite scrupulously... However, just what sort of intention must the minister have? He must have 'the intention of doing what the Church does.'

> ...It is at least certain that the minister not need personally believe that the Church's doctrine is true: provided he intends to do what the Church does... Of course, if the minister intends, positively, to do something different from what the Church does, he has not the requisite intention.[457]

Are the baptisms performed in the Postconciliar Church valid? Due to occasional carelessness in the Rite of Christian Initiation, the safest course is to investigate each case. If the minister of Baptism used the proper *matter* and *form* and *intended* to confer the Baptism of Christ ("to do what the Church does") the Baptism is valid.

In all other cases we should follow the wise guidelines found in *The American Ecclesiastical Review*: "If the inquiry brings to light that Baptism was conferred either invalidly or not at all, the sacrament is to be administered absolutely; if the point of validity or invalidity remains doubtful, the sacrament is to be conferred conditionally."[458] In view of the fact that Baptism is necessary for salvation, "the repetition of the sacrament ought to be done where its validity is doubted—or rather, so long as its validity is not morally certain."[459]

---

[454] Fr. John Murphy, *The Sacrament of Baptism*, pp. 55-56.
[455] Fr. Francis Connell, C.SS.R., *Baltimore Catechism*, p. 187.
[456] T. Bouscaren, *Canon Law: A Text and Commentary*, p. 559.
[457] C. Martindale, S.J., *The Sacramental System*, p. 55.
[458] Ulrich Beste, *American Ecclesiastical Review, April 1950*, pp. 260-261.
[459] Beste, 268-269.

Sacrament of Penance / Rite of Reconciliation
Divine Forgiveness

Among the most consoling words ever spoken or written are those by which Our Lord gave to His Apostles and their successors the power to forgive sins: "Whose sins you shall forgive they are forgiven them and whose sins you shall retain they are retained." (John 20: 23) St. John Chrysostom wrote: "God has confided a power which neither angels nor archangels ever attained, ...for what the priest does here below God ratifies in heaven... Can there be a greater power than this?"[460]

Our Savior's words imply that we must confess our sins to a priest in order to obtain absolution, for how could a priest forgive or retain sins if people did not confess them? The fact that Catholics have availed themselves of this sacrament and confessed their sins to priests for nearly 2,000 years is a testimonial that Christ instructed the Apostles that sins should be forgiven in this manner.

The Sacrament of Penance was instituted by Christ to serve as a medicine for our souls in order to restore them to spiritual health and to strengthen us to avoid sin in the future. The graces of this sacrament are sorely needed, since we have a strong inclination to sin and easily consent to temptation.

> The Council of Trent declares: *For those who fall into sin after Baptism the Sacrament of Penance is as necessary to salvation as is Baptism for those who have not already been baptized.*[461] The saying of St. Jerome that Penance is *a second plank,*[462] is universally known and highly commended by all subsequent writers on sacred things. As he who suffers shipwreck has no hope of safety, unless, perchance, he seize on some plank from the wreck, so he that suffers the shipwreck of baptismal innocence, unless he cling to the saving plank of Penance, has doubtless lost all hope of salvation.[463]

"The Church universal has always understood that Christ, when He instituted the Sacrament of Penance ...instituted as well an integral confession of sins, and that such confession is necessary, of divine right, for all who have fallen after

---

[460] Msgr. Angel Herrera, *The Preacher's Encyclopedia, Vol. II,* p. 459.
[461] Sess. vi. de Just. cap. 14; Sess. xiv. De Poenit. cap. 3.
[462] In Isa. iii.
[463] On the necessity of the Sacrament of Penance. See Summa Theol. 3a. 84. 5. 6.

Baptism."[464] This sacrament is so essential to preserve morals and virtue that Pope St. Pius V writes: "Give us fit confessors, and surely the whole of Christianity will be reformed."[465]

The Concept of Sin

Sadly, we are not sinless, and since temptations are often difficult to overcome and virtue requires effort, we are in need of heavenly assistance. There are two different personal responses we can have towards sin—contrition or rationalization. Contrition has been defined by the Council of Trent as "sorrow of soul and a detestation for sin committed with the purpose of not sinning in the future."[466] After we have sinned, we can experience peace of soul only when our conscience is clear and our friendship with God restored. Just think for a moment of the billions of people across the globe.

> They are not all wicked by any means, yet all sin and the overwhelming majority promptly justify themselves. It is at this point that the sublimity of our holy religion becomes manifest: Instead of denying the existence of sin, we define it most carefully; instead of burying the memory of sin, we recall it to mind by examining our conscience; instead of justifying ourselves, we accuse ourselves; instead of carrying the burden of sin around with us, we have the certainty of forgiveness. This is all so wonderful, so splendid and so unnatural that it is clearly divine.[467]

The *Baltimore Catechism* and the postconciliar *Catechism of the Catholic Church* define *sin* in a completely different manner. The pre-Vatican II catechism is clear and concise: "Actual sin is any willful thought, desire, word, action or omission forbidden by the law of God."[468] The post-Vatican II catechism is vague and nebulous: "Sin is an offense against reason, truth, and right conscience; it is a failure in genuine love of God and neighbor caused by a perverse attachment to certain goods. It wounds the nature of man and injures human solidarity."[469]

---

[464] Council of Trent, D 899.
[465] Dentur idonei confesarii; ecce omnium Christianorum plena reformatio.
[466] Sess. 14. c. 4. (D 897).
[467] Bryan Houghton, *Mitre and Crook,* pp. 153-154.
[468] Q. 64, p. 39.
[469] Part III, art. 8 II. The Definition of Sin, p. 453.

Priests have a duty to provide moral guidance and instruction, exhorting their parishioners to avoid sin and the near occasions of sin. Bishop Angel Herrera says, "The preacher's mission is not to create an easy Christianity, but to explain it as it really is."[470] On the contrary, the priests of the Modern Church "rarely preach about contraception—or about sexual morality or abortion or divorce and remarriage or the reality of mortal sin and the need for absolution for those who commit it."[471]

Frequent Confession Prior to Vatican II

Frequent confession (weekly or monthly) was a common practice among devout Catholics prior to Vatican II. "During the pontificate of Pope Pius XII [1939-1958], the sacrament was used more widely than at any other time in the history of the Church."[472] Catholics were taught to frequent the sacrament and churches provided ample, scheduled times for confession.

> Historian James O'Toole writes anecdotally of what most older Catholics can recall: an endless stream of Saturday confessions, of 60 percent of parishioners in a given parish going to confession at least once a month. He tells of a small Idaho parish in 1952 where two priests tabulated that they heard 9,431 confessions that year, an average of about 182 per week. And then it all disappeared, virtually overnight. In response to a national survey in the mid-1980s, 65 percent of American priests reported that they were hearing fewer than 20 confessions per week—a far cry from Fr. [Patrick] Healy's 175 in a single day [in 1896].[473]
>
> In the United States from the end of the 18th century until the Second Vatican Council, confession was "a distinctive marker of Catholic identity; it was something Catholics did that their Protestant and Jewish neighbors did not do. Within the Catholic community, it served as a yardstick; priests sometimes measured a parish's spiritual well being by the frequency with which

---

[470] Bishop Angel Herrera, *The Preacher's Encyclopedia, Vol. II*, p. 5.
[471] *Crisis*, March 2, 2003, "Ignoring the Obvious: the Unreality of American Catholicism," by Russell Shaw, p. 27.
[472] *The Tidings*, March 6, 1992, Article by Hermine Lees.
[473] *Boston College Magazine*, Fall, 2000, p. 34.

parishioners went to confession. For more than a century Catholics confessed more often than they partook of communion."[474]

Conditions after Vatican II

Perhaps the most striking feature of the history of confession in the United States is the speed with which it collapsed. Catholic commentators began to note the falling numbers of penitents shortly after the close of the Second Vatican Council in 1965. ...In 1968 a priest wrote in the Passionist Fathers' *Sign* magazine that "people are staying away from confession in droves."[475]

Houses of religious women and seminaries, where only a few years ago the canonical rule of weekly confession was practiced quite rigorously, have now given up either in theory or at least in practice such a regimen. One is surprised at the number of Catholics both clerical and lay who will admit that they have not been to confession in the last year or two or three.[476]

This concurs with the observation of Charles Curran in 1969, when he remarked that many children do not go to confession before making their First Communion. In the early 1970's many parishes in the United States began delaying first confession until fourth grade or later, on the grounds that confession at an early age could be psychologically disturbing to young children. Does this mean that an individual beyond the age of reason, although young, does not sin? If so, does anyone sin? Does sin even exist anymore?

Since Vatican II, most U.S. Catholics have given up the practice of confessing their sins. In 1960, 75% of U.S. Catholics who attended Sunday Mass "would have gone to confession at least monthly. By 1977 the number of Catholics saying they went to confession every month was down to 18 percent, and by 1995 that rate was down to just 8 percent."[477] These results concur with the Scripps-Howard news service survey of the 1980's where "26% of active, church-going Catholics never went to confession, while another 35% went only once a year."[478]

---

[474] *Boston College Magazine,* Fall, 2000, p. 25.
[475] *Boston College Magazine,* Fall 2000, p. 27.
[476] *Worship, Vol. 43,* January 1969, "The Sacrament of Penance Today," p. 510.
[477] See David Gibson, *The Coming Catholic Church,* p. 64.
[478] *National Catholic Register,* April 6, 2003.

The New Rite of Reconciliation

"Penance, as a sacrament of the 'forgiveness of sin,' obviously presupposes the existence and importance of sin. ...If there is no real importance attached to sin and sinfulness, then the Sacrament of Penance becomes meaningless."[479]

Vatican II is directly responsible for this undoing. In its *Constitution on the Sacred Liturgy* (n. 72) it called for changes in the rite and formulae of the Sacrament of Penance "so that they may more clearly express both the nature and effect of the sacrament." On February 7, 1974 the Congregation of Divine Worship issued a new ritual for reconciliation. Its usage became mandatory in the United States on February 27, 1977.

Prior to the introduction of the new rite, the sacrament was called *Confession* or *Penance,* which indicated sorrow for offending Almighty God through personal sin. After the revised ritual was formulated the sacrament became commonly known as the *Rite of Reconciliation,* a term which emphasizes the social aspect of sin. The emphasis is no longer upon the overcoming of one's sins; the primary focus is now upon our shared responsibility within the Christian Community. This impersonal approach is conducive to rationalization rather than to individual responsibility. Thus, a certain levity has ensued which has lowered this sacrament to the level of a mere apology.

While the new *form* of the sacrament (the words of absolution) includes a petition that pardon and peace may be granted by God through the ministry of the Church, the essential *form* of the sacrament (I absolve you from your sins in the name of the Father and of the Son and of the Holy Spirit) has been retained.

This new Rite of Reconciliation can be celebrated in any of three ways: traditional, communal and communal with general absolution. With the introduction of the new Rite of Reconciliation, Catholics noticed that confessionals were quickly replaced with reconciliation rooms for face-to-face conversation with the priest.

Since the traditional manner of confessing one's sins is still available, many older Catholics continue to go to confession as before. However, the new rite

---

[479] *Worship, Vol. 43,* p. 515.

contains some additional optional elements: "reception of the penitent... an exhortation by the confessor to trust in God; a reading from Scripture; ...praise of God's mercy and dismissal in peace."[480]

The results of a national survey taken in the mid 1980's indicated that most Catholics are uncomfortable with the reconciliation rooms and prefer the traditional confessional: "...a majority (58 percent) of those few lay people still going to confession said that they preferred the anonymity of the confessional box to a more open-ended, personal conversation with their confessor in a newly redesigned 'Reconciliation room.' "[481]

The atmosphere is now one more of levity rather than of compunction. The face-to-face counseling sessions that have replaced confession often promote the rationalization of sin. The new rite allows individuals to more easily make excuses for their sins by blaming them on others or on the everyday stress of life. This may be socially satisfying, but it is spiritually debilitating. Our realization of the evil of sin followed by contrition, absolution and penance gives great peace of soul and weakens our inclination to sin. While confession of sin is painful because we are forced to humbly own up to our offenses against God, receive absolution and perform a penance, it results in the forgiveness of our sins, a spiritual strengthening and it reduces our propensity to sin.

> There is today a general loss of a sense of sin and confusion about what is sinful. In his popular book, *Whatever Became of Sin?*, Karl Menninger points out how our society is losing its sensitivity to moral wrong. A growing secularism seems to be succeeding in numbing our consciences to the evil we call sin. Today, when it comes to discerning what is morally right or wrong, it seems too many Christians are more anxious to listen to the voices of their culture and its media than to the voice of Jesus in the Gospels. Then, too, conflicting responses from priests regarding moral issues often cause confusion about sin.[482]

The grating of the confessional allows the penitent to remain anonymous. Therefore, it is less difficult for one to reveal his sins, even if they are mortal.

---

[480] Matthew Bunson, *2002 Catholic Almanac,* pp. 204-205.
[481] *Boston College Magazine,* Fall 2000, p. 34.
[482] Rev. Eamon Tobin, *The Sacrament of Penance,* pp. 5-6.

However, the face-to-face reconciliation rooms do not provide this security. Thus it is reasonable to believe that, on occasion, numerous confessions in the Postconciliar Church are incomplete because it is likely that some penitents deliberately conceal shameful mortal sins through fear of human respect.

Communal Reconciliation

The second form of reconciliation is a general communal reconciliation service. The new rite emphasizes the role of the whole Christian community and includes the reading of Scriptural verses, joint confession of sins and prayer for forgiveness. The communal reconciliation rites are to be followed by individual confession and absolution, but this is sometimes omitted. In some cases, this type of confession is now accepted as sufficient in itself.

The new theology implies that the most offensive aspect of sin is its damage to the community; it de-emphasizes the spiritual damage done to the sinner who offends God. The emphasis has shifted away from the confession of personal sins and disobedience to God's commandments, such as unchecked anger, immorality and dishonesty. As a result, when confessing their sins, some penitents are unaware of what is important and what isn't. Therefore, communal reconciliation services often focus upon "sins" for which the entire Christian community shares a responsibility (poverty, war, racism, injustice, poor housing conditions, etc.) rather than personal offenses against the laws of God.

Communal Reconciliation and General Absolution

When a number of penitents are present, the third rite is often celebrated with general confession and general absolution—"a communal approach common in Protestantism."[483] Prior to Vatican II, general absolution was employed only in extraordinary circumstances.[484] For example, during the First and Second World Wars military chaplains occasionally made use of general absolution when large numbers of Catholic soldiers went into dangerous battles

---

[483] *Atlanta Constitution*, February 28, 1976.

[484] C'est ainsi que le Sainte-Office, le 2 mars 1679, a condamné la proposition que prétendait autoriser l'absolution générale un jour de grande fête ou de grand pèlerimage, alors que des confesseurs sont à disposition. André Mignot, *Les Fumees de Satan*, p. 63.

and there was little time for individual confessions. If a soldier survived the conflict, he was still obliged to confess any serious sins to a priest.

Once again the Modernists were very careful not to cause too much wonderment. The Congregation of Divine Worship decree *Ordo Paenitentiae* of February 7, 1974 established the use of general confession and general absolution. It was stated that it may be used in:

1) Danger of death, when there is neither time nor priests available for hearing confession;
2) Grave necessity of number of penitents who, because of a shortage of confessors, would be deprived of sacramental grace or Communion for a lengthy period of time through no fault of their own.

It further stated that persons receiving general absolution are obliged to be properly disposed and resolved to make an individual confession of the grave sins from which they have been absolved; this confession should be made as soon as the opportunity to confess presents itself and before any second reception of general absolution.

They included the specifications that norms regarding the general absolution, issued by the Congregation for the Doctrine of the Faith in 1972, are not intended to provide a basis for convoking large gatherings of the faithful for the purpose of imparting general absolution, in the absence of extraordinary circumstances. Judgment about the circumstances that warrant general absolution belongs principally to the bishop for the place, with due regard for related decisions of appropriate episcopal conferences.[485]

Despite these restrictions, modern bishops have authorized priests to absolve penitents without individual confession. General absolution has become a common practice, especially in the United States and Australia, although "Canon 960 [of the 1983 Code of Canon Law] states that 'physical or moral impossibility alone excuses' a penitent from 'individual and integral confession,' allowing 'other means' for attaining reconciliation such as general absolution."[486]

---

[485] Matthew Bunson, *2002 Catholic Almanac,* p. 205.
[486] *Catholic World Report,* May 2002, "General absolutions continue," by Michael Gilchrist.

When the sinner is "reconciled" to the community in the new rite, the damage to the community may be repaired (though it is unclear how this is done), but is the specific sin absolved and forgiven by God?

John Paul II recently issued an apostolic letter concerning Reconciliation and general absolution. "Despite press reports that the pope is tightening up Church law, *Misericordia Dei* ('The Mercy of God'), issued on May 2, [2002] actually breaks no new ground according to Dominican Father Giles Dimock, dean of the Dominican House of Studies in Washington, D.C."[487] The regulations set down in the new Code of Canon Law are reiterated and general absolution, although it is only to be used on special occasions, will still remain a common practice.

The laity often have a hard time distinguishing between communal penance with individual confession (the second rite) and general absolution (the third rite). To make matters worse "some hybrids of the second and third rites have cropped up in which penitents are instructed to confess only one type of sin, or perhaps are exhorted to simply confess being a sinner."[488]

Individual confession of sin demonstrates admission of guilt and personal sorrow for sin. Msgr. Mannion describes the harmful effects of general absolution without individual confession: "Consider the medical equivalent: a medical doctor dispenses cures to patients without ever hearing about or analyzing their ailments. ...Just as medicine has no reality unless personalized, so the Sacrament of Penance, to be properly effective, must be personalized."[489] How can the priest help penitents avoid sin and overcome temptation if he is unaware of their spiritual problems?

"General absolution has not worked to enhance the sanctity of people. All too often, it has worked the other way by clouding the reality of sin and thereby diminishing what we all must understand is required truly to be followers of Christ."[490]

---

[487] *Our Sunday Visitor,* May 19, 2002, "Pope seeks to correct misuse of general absolution," by Ann Carey.
[488] *Our Sunday Visitor,* May 19, 2002.
[489] *Our Sunday Visitor,* March 16, 2003.
[490] *Our Sunday Visitor,* June 2, 2002, "Confronting sin face-to-face," by Msgr. Owen Campion.

A Changed Attitude Toward Sin and Confession

The majority of worshipers in the modern Church receive the eucharist, yet numerous polls indicate a steep decline in Mass attendance and in the number of confessions since Vatican II. Now, rather than any type of reconciliation at all, some individuals prepare for Sunday communion simply by offering a silent prayer of contrition. This reflects the view that only the most grievous sins, if any, should preclude one from the reception of the eucharist.

Since Vatican II, the attitudes of Catholics toward confession changed considerably as a result of the widespread circulation of erroneous teachings concerning the nature of sin, contrition, penance, Purgatory and Hell. Consequently, the vast majority of clergy and laity seldom, if ever, go to confession. Many modern Catholics have adopted the Protestant practice, where confession is a private matter between the believer and God. Instead of confessing one's sins to a priest in a reconciliation room or confessional, it has become more and more a do-it-yourself project for the believer—a "One-on-one with God."

The Postconciliar Church teaches a new morality that condones situational ethics. As a result, individuals decide for themselves what is right and wrong, rather than basing the morality of their actions upon the Ten Commandments and the teachings of Jesus Christ. This has led to a diminished sense of a person's own sinfulness and is reflected by the dwindling use of confession and a lack of comprehension of the salutary graces of the sacrament.

A survey by the National Association of Scholars found "that three-fourths of college seniors report being taught that right and wrong depend 'on differences in individual values and cultural diversity.' Only a quarter of the students reported that their professors adhered to the more traditional understanding of morality, namely, that there are uniform standards of right and wrong."[491]

If modern Catholics still believe in mortal sin, they display no anxiety about the effects of mortal sin on their own prospects for salvation. Unfortunately, many believe that confession and penance for sin are unnecessary because no one really goes to hell. This outlook is spiritually harmful because when we do

---

[491] William Donohue, *Catalyst*, September 2002, Vol. 29, No. 7.

wrong we <u>should</u> feel a sense of guilt and shame. We feel guilt because we have offended Almighty God by sin; shame, because our sins not only lessen us in the esteem of others, but mostly because we have been so ungrateful to such a good and loving God. Sadly, this entire experience has been lost to a great extent among modern Catholics.

Hell

Although Hell is a very unpopular topic today, "A May 2001 Gallup Poll of adults nationwide found that 71 percent [still] believe in hell. They just don't want to hear about it."[492] According to the same poll only 70% of Catholics believe in the devil.[493]

"Hell's fall from fashion indicates how key portions of Christian theology have been influenced by a secular society that stresses individualism over authority and the human psyche over moral absolutes."[494] Denis de Rougement has written: "…if there is no heaven, there is no hell; if there is no hell, then there is no sin; if there is no sin, then there is no judge; and if there is no judgment then evil is good and good is evil."[495]

"A week after telling the Roman Catholic faithful that heaven was not up in the clouds, Pope John Paul II said Wednesday [July 26, 1999] that hell was not a physical place either."[496] He further stated: "Whether or not any human beings are in hell 'is not something we can know.' "[497]

> …Pope John Paul II made headlines by saying that hell should not be seen as a fiery underworld, but as the 'state of those who freely and definitively separate themselves from God, the source of all life and joy.'
>
> As much as that seemed like a departure from Church beliefs, the pope's words weren't all that new. The Roman Catholic Church in the 1960's [the Postconciliar Church] moved away from the view of hell as a gothic torture chamber as part of the Second Vatican Council's modernization of Church teachings.

---

[492] *The News Tribune,* July 6, 2002, "Today, hell hath no fury—at all," by Mike Anton.
[493] See: *National Catholic Register,* March 9, 2003, "Two-Thirds of Americans Believe in the Devil, Gallup Poll Finds," (Religion News Service).
[494] *Los Angeles Times,* June 19, 2002, "Hold the Fire and Brimstone," by Mike Anton.
[495] *The Devil's Share,* (New York: Pantheon Books, 1944), p. 46.
[496] *Detroit News,* July 28, 1999, "Pope: Hell not a real place," by Jude Webber.
[497] *Our Sunday Visitor,* August 22, 1999.

'…When you take [hell] away as a threat, everything changes,' said Martin Marty, professor emeritus of religion and culture at the University of Chicago Divinity School. 'Who goes to confession anymore? Time was, a church had 16 booths and people snaked around the block. Today, a church might have one left.'[498]

In no uncertain terms Jesus Christ declared: "Enter by the narrow gate. For wide is the gate and broad the way that leads to destruction, and many there are who enter that way. How narrow the gate and close the way that leads to life! And few there are who find it."[499] "The angels will go out and separate the wicked from among the just, and will cast them into the furnace of fire, where there will be the weeping and the gnashing of teeth."[500] "Few things are more frequently referred to by Jesus Christ in the Gospels than this doctrine. And if we reject this doctrine, then we must also reject every other doctrine taught by Christ, if we wish to be consistent."[501]

One of the seers of Fatima, Sr. Lucia dos Santos, described a vision of Hell she witnessed on July 13, 1917:

> We saw as if into a sea of fire, and immersed in that fire were devils and souls in human form, as if they were transparent black or bronze embers floating in the fire and swayed by the flames that issued from them along with clouds of smoke, falling upon every side just like the falling of sparks in great fires, without weight or equilibrium, amidst wailing and cries of pain and despair that horrified and shook us with terror. We could tell the devils by their horrible and nauseous figures of baneful and unknown animals, but transparent as the black coals in a fire.[502]

In 1954, Father Lombardi, S.J., went to Portugal to preach at Fatima and other places, in order to make known the movement of which he was the chief promoter, under mandate from the Holy Father [Pope Pius XII], the *Movement for a Better World.* The bishop of Coimbra authorized him, by special privilege, to pay a visit to Sr. Lucy.

---

[498] *Los Angeles Times,* June 19, 2002.
[499] Matthew 7: 13.
[500] Matthew 13: 50.
[501] Fr. Clement Crock, *Discourses on the Apostles' Creed,* p. 264.
[502] *Mother of Christ Crusade,* pp. 63-64.

This is the account which Fr. Lombardi gives of his interview: Behind the parlor grill I saw the young girl to whom the Blessed Virgin confided her revelation. A simple face, a clear voice, nothing put on, as one might expect. I asked her: 'Tell me. Is this *Movement for a Better World* the Church's answer to the words Our Lady spoke to you?' 'Father,' she answered, 'this great renovation [amendment of life] is certainly needed. If this does not come about, and humanity is allowed to go on as it is doing today, only a small portion of the human race will be saved.'

'Do you really believe that many souls go to Hell? I trust that God will save the greater part. I have even written a book which I entitled: *The Salvation of the Unbeliever.*' 'Father, many are damned.' 'Certainly this is a sinful world; but there is always hope for salvation.' 'No, Father. Many, many are lost.'

'We have to remember,' Father Lombardi comments, 'that [Sister] Lucy had once had a vision of Hell, and even to read about it makes one shutter with fear. I was greatly impressed by her words. I went back to Italy nursing this warning in my heart.'[503]

It is indeed tragic that people today often do not take personal responsibility for their sins. Mortal sin is no longer looked upon as a deadly sin since "everyone does it" and the prospect of eternal punishment in Hell for unrepentant mortal sin is looked upon as being a medieval concept. Sadly, horror for mortal sin and fear of hell no longer grip the minds of modern "Catholics." Basically they think that they're "ok."

The Devil

We cannot afford to be indifferent about the devil or to have warped ideas about him and his power. The demons are living realities, powerful enemies, dangerous, ingenious, treacherous and furious foes. If we believe in Christ, we must also believe in the devil for Christ told us about him, warned us against his snares and taught us how to conquer his temptations.

We then know Satan, as a malicious liar and deceiver. What else does revelation tell us about him? First, he is no mere personified abstraction: the Scriptures always present him as a real being, a mighty spirit, a great intelligence, inflexibly

---

[503] Georges Panneton, *Heaven or Hell,* pp. 196-197.

given over to evil. …he is God's creature, originally the highest of angels, called like all the angels to eternal joy in God. But the joy was not forced on him: it was to be won by the exercise, under grace, of his own freedom, it was his to choose; and in fact he chose otherwise. Instead of standing in the truth in which he had been created[504] he deliberately abandoned it, impelled, it would seem, by pride;[505] and with him there fell away a great number of the angels.[506] Thus by their own choice they were …excluded from heaven and bound forever to the evil they had chosen.[507] Their rebellion stripped them of all their supernatural life and power; but their natural power and activities remained to them, and these are henceforth devoted to expressing their pride and their enmity.[508]

Devils attack us systematically; they work together to deceive and seduce us. Their power over us depends on our degree of resistance. The less opposition we give them, the greater control they gain over us. Henri-Irénée Marrou wrote in the 1948 edition of *Études carmélitaines*:

> I am certain that among the Christians of our day there are very few who *believe* really in the Devil: …for many people Satan is merely a personification of Evil, a figure of speech …detached from any real personality. …And this attitude has the serious disadvantage of misrepresenting the nature of the moral struggle which is the basis of human life here on earth. We are fighting, or so we imagine, against abstractions which, though very real to us, yet appear only to be static adversaries, and not intelligent, cunning, spiteful enemies eager to destroy us, to overcome whom we must call on God, the good angels and the saints for help.[509]

Nicolas Corte asserts: "Satan can remain hidden in the wings and preserve what has been described as his incognito. He is quite prepared for man to deny him, provided that they also deny God. He who, as the expression goes, 'believes in neither God nor the Devil', is just the man for him."[510]

---

[504] John 8: 44.
[505] I Tim. 3: 6.
[506] Apoc. 12: 4.
[507] II Peter 2: 4.
[508] Gerald Vann, O.P. and P. Meagher, O.P., *The Temptations of Christ*, pp. 34-35.
[509] Nicolas Corte, *Who is the Devil?*, pp. 112-113.
[510] p. 115.

This denial of hell and the devil is now more evident than ever before when viewed in conjunction with the latest change in the rite of exorcism decreed by the Vatican. The rite of exorcism employed by the Catholic Church for centuries was composed by Pope Paul V in 1614. Fr. Amorth, the chief exorcist of Rome, laments that in the new rite, "some effective prayers were cancelled, prayers with 12 centuries of history. New ineffective prayers were written in."[511]

He also stated that in its new wording the Postconciliar Church infers the devil is not even an actual being, but an evil force that influences people. One can find this same type of belief in many false religions.

> Fr. Amorth was asked, 'What do you see as Satan's greatest success?' He replied: 'The fact that he has managed to convince people that he does not exist. He has almost managed it, even within the [Postconciliar] Church. We have a clergy and an episcopate who no longer believe in the Devil, in exorcism, in the exceptional evil the Devil can instill, or even in the power that Jesus bestowed to cast out demons.'[512]

Furthermore, if one does not believe in the devil, it would probably follow that he does not believe in hell either, for one is basically dependent on the other. Following from this, "…Eternal damnation—once clearly insisted upon—has almost entirely disappeared from the active teaching of many teachers, pastors and theologians."[513]

Not only are mortal sin and the danger of eternal punishment hardly ever mentioned in sermons or religious instruction, but few people think of hell as a possibility. "Only one per cent of *Catholic Digest* readers in 1983 thought there was a chance they might go to hell, compared with twelve per cent of the readers in 1952."[514] Today, this percentage has declined even further.

These same people do not read, or do not want to believe, what is mentioned repeatedly in the Bible, for it explicitly teaches that mortal sins have

---

[511] Fr. Gabrielle Amorth, *30Days*, No. 6, 2001, p. 31,
"The Smoke of Satan in the House of the Lord," by Stefano Paci.
[512] *30Days*, No. 6, 2001.
[513] *National Catholic Register*, August 1, 1999.
[514] *Sacramento Union*, March 9, 1985, "How the clergy views eternal damnation," by Richard Dujardin.

deadly consequences and exclude sinners from Heaven. St. Paul states, "that they who do such things will not attain the kingdom of God." (Gal. 5: 21) In his First Epistle to the Corinthians (6: 9) he also enumerates a number of mortal sins that debar the soul from eternal life.

In Scripture, Our Lord describes hell as a place of endless suffering where "the fire is not quenched,"[515] where there is an "everlasting fire which was prepared for the devil and his angels." (Matt. 25: 41) Jesus Christ said: "And do not be afraid of those who kill the body but cannot kill the soul. But rather be afraid of him who is able to destroy both soul and body in hell."[516] In the Apocalypse St. John declares hell to be, "a pool of fire," a place where "the smoke of their torments goes up forever and ever."[517]

"Men are afraid of prison, yet they are not afraid of hell fire. They fear temporal punishments, but dread not the torments of eternal fire."[518] "He who continually fears hell, will never fall into it; but he who is negligent, will undoubtedly fall."[519]

Confession is a strong deterrent against sin. The universal disorder and depravity in society today, even among Catholics, can be attributed to a denial of sin and its consequences and infrequent confession. Invalid Masses and sacraments have resulted in a loss of grace. The *Catechism of the Council of Trent* describes the social evils resulting from the rejection of confession:

> Abolish sacramental confession, and, at that moment, you deluge society with all sorts of secret crimes—crimes, too, and others of still greater enormity, which men, once that they have been depraved by vicious habits, will not dread to commit in open day. The salutary shame that attends confession, restrains licentiousness, bridles desire, and coerces evil propensities of corrupt nature.[520]

---

[515] Mark 9: 46-47.
[516] Matthew 10: 28.
[517] Apocalypse 19: 20, 20: 9, 15; Apocalypse 14: 11.
[518] S. Austin in Baradius.
[519] S. Chrys. in Baradius.
[520] *Confession, Its Importance IV*, p. 272

A Very Serious Problem

Can priests of the Postconciliar Church even absolve from sin? Priests ordained in the traditional rite (prior to 1968) are valid priests and have received the power to forgive sins. However, the essence of the priesthood has changed radically since Vatican II. The postconciliar priest is ordained not to offer sacrifice, but to merely preside over the Memorial of the Lord. Thus, a basic element of the Sacrament of Holy Orders has been altered. As a result, those who have been ordained in the new rite are, at best, doubtfully valid priests and may not be priests at all. Bishops ordained in the new rite are almost certainly invalid due to the complete change to the essential form of the sacrament. If they are not valid priests and bishops, they do not possess the power to forgive sins.

Confirmation

The word *confirmation* is derived from Latin, and signifies to make strong, firm or steadfast. "Confirmation may be defined as a sacrament in which those already baptized, through the imposition of the hands, anointment and the prayer of the bishop, receive the power of the Holy Ghost, by which they are enabled to believe firmly and to profess the faith boldly."[521]

Through the reception of the Sacrament of Confirmation, a baptized person receives the grace and strength of the Holy Ghost to persevere steadfast in the faith and resolutely and fearlessly to confess it before others. The Sacrament of Confirmation fortifies us against dangers to our Faith and gives us strength to conquer the temptations of the world, the flesh and the devil. The strengthening graces of Confirmation enable one to be a strong and perfect Christian and a soldier of Jesus Christ.

Vatican II's *Constitution on the Sacred Liturgy* [522] mandated a revision of Confirmation that was implemented by Paul VI in his Apostolic Constitution *Divinae Consortium Naturae* of August 15, 1971. A completely new rite of Confirmation was introduced. Paul VI brazenly declared that "the very essence of the sacramental rite" had been changed.[523] He promulgated the revised rite,

---

[521] Msgr. Joseph Pohle, *The Sacraments, Vol. I*, pp. 276-277.
[522] December 4, 1963.
[523] *Divinae Consortium Naturae*, August 15, 1971.

which became mandatory on January 1, 1973. This definitely raises doubts about Paul VI, for any attempt to change the substance of a sacrament is contrary to Divine Law and obviously could not come from legitimate Catholic authority.

The Essential Matter of Confirmation

Dr. Ludwig Ott notes, "There is no dogmatic decision regarding the essential *matter* of the Sacrament of Confirmation. Theologians are divided in their opinions."[524] Some theologians believe that the imposition of hands is the sole *matter* of Confirmation while others contend that it lies in the imposition of chrism. Many theologians state that both are required and others maintain that either is sufficient. Despite these theoretical differences of opinion, most traditional theologians maintain that the essential *matter* of Confirmation consists in the anointment with chrism and the imposition of hands. This concurs in the rite of the Catholic Church when administering this sacrament.

When the bishop confers Confirmation he imposes his hands upon the confirmandi (the person being confirmed), following the example of the Apostles who administered this sacrament in this manner.[525] The imposition of hands "signifies the descent of the Holy Spirit, and particularly the protection of God under which the Christian is henceforth to remain."[526]

Fr. Pourrat has stated: "In Apostolic times the *matter* of Confirmation was the imposition of hands; after the second century, it was, besides, the anointing with holy chrism."[527] This opinion is supported by Dölger who thinks that possibly "the Apostles conferred Confirmation by that imposition of hands, and that the anointment with chrism, as the external sign, was introduced at their behest only toward the close of the Apostolic age."[528]

The New Rite of Confirmation

In his book *The Reform of the Liturgy,* Annibale Bugnini gives a detailed account of the "revision" of Confirmation. Paul VI entrusted this project to the Consilium (a Modernist team of "liturgical experts"). The Consilium drafted the

---

[524] *Fundamentals of Catholic Dogma,* p. 361.
[525] Acts of the Apostles 8: 14.
[526] Leonard Goffine, *Goffine's Devout Instructions,* p. 470.
[527] *Theology of the Sacraments,* p. 85, footnote.
[528] *Das Sakrament der Firmung,* p. 190.

complete text of the new rite in 1968, yet it took three years until the "revised" sacrament was introduced since the proposed changes were quite radical.

Because this new rite was such an utter departure from the sacrament instituted by Christ, it had to be submitted in couched and ambiguous terms in order to be approved as "similar" but not "essentially" different. When Paul VI eliminated the imposition of hands, this was a clear departure from Scripture and Tradition and also a significant alteration because some canonists and theologians[529] regard the imposition of hands as the sole *matter* of Confirmation. Their chief argument is that Holy Scripture[530] always describes Confirmation as a laying-on of hands, never as an unction.[531]

Bugnini and his fellow Modernists were faced with an obvious perplexity, for this raised serious doubt regarding the validity of the new sacrament.

> The position of the Consilium and the Congregation for Divine Worship had been clear from the beginning: assign equal value to the two actions—the general laying on of hands and the chrismation—and remove from the latter the laying on of the hand that was prescribed in the rubric of the former Pontifical: 'the right hand being laid on the head of the confirmandi.'[532]
>
> The final determination of the sacramental matter by the constitution reflects the hesitation felt by the Congregation for the Doctrine of the Faith, which did not want to lose the reference to a laying on of the hand in the act of chrismation [primarily to keep the traditionalists from being alarmed].[533]
>
> In his letter of May 10, 1969, to the SCDW [Sacred Congregation for Divine Worship], Cardinal Seper made known the decision of the SCDF [Sacred Congregation for the Doctrine of the Faith]: "What is laid down in canon 780 of the [1918] Code of Canon Law is to be maintained; accordingly, by the laying on of hands which is required for the validity of the sacrament is meant only the laying on which takes place in the act of anointing, as in the tradition.[534]

---

[529] Notably Aureolus *(Comment. in Sent.,* IV, dist. 79, q. 1), Isaac Habert, Petavius, Sirmond, (Migne, *Theol. Curs. Compl.,* XXI, p. 769).
[530] Acts of the Apostles 8: 14ff, 19: 1ff.
[531] Msgr. Joseph Pohle, *The Sacraments,* Vol. I, p. 288.
[532] Annibale Bugnini, *Reform of the Liturgy 1948-1975,* pp. 623-624.
[533] Bugnini, 624.
[534] Bugnini, 624, footnote 27.

Subsequently, members of the Congregation for the Doctrine of the Faith, who were also aware of the obvious change to the essential *matter* of Confirmation, suggested some other formulations such as " 'the anointing, which is necessarily accompanied by a laying on of the hand is essential for the sacrament,' 'an anointing which by its nature implies a laying on of the hand;' 'the laying on of the minister's hand in the act of anointing.' "[535]

Employing the ambiguity so common in the decrees of Vatican II, Paul VI declared in his Apostolic Constitution on the Sacrament of Confirmation:

> But the laying on of hands on the elect, carried out with the prescribed prayer before the anointing, is still to be regarded as very important, even though it is not of the essence of the sacramental rite: it contributes to the complete perfection of the rite and to a more thorough understanding of the sacrament.[536]

With this suppression of the individual imposition of hands, Paul VI clearly departed from both Scripture and Tradition. He thereby directly contradicted the Acts of the Apostles, consistent liturgical practice and Canon Law. This can only leave serious doubts regarding the validity of the new rite.

Holy Chrism

Holy Chrism is a mixture of olive oil and balsam that is consecrated by the bishop on Holy Thursday and used for the administration of several of the sacraments, including Confirmation. Pope Fabian (236-250 AD) testified that the Apostles received the composition of Chrism from Our Lord and transmitted it to us.[537] Holy Chrism is used in Confirmation to indicate the effects of the sacrament. "The oil signifies inward strength for the struggle against the enemies of our salvation. Oil was formerly used by soldiers and athletes to make their limbs supple and strong. As oil strengthens the limbs of the body, so does the Holy Spirit strengthen our souls for combat with sin."[538] The balsam signifies "that he who is confirmed receives grace to keep himself pure from the

---

[535] Annibale Bugnini, *Reform of the Liturgy 1948-1975*, p. 624.
[536] ICEL, *The Rites of the Catholic Church as Revised by the Second Vatican Ecumenical Council, Vol. I*, pp. 477-478.
[537] *Cat. Rom.*, P. II, c. 3, n. 7.
[538] Leonard Goffine, *Goffine's Devout Instructions*, p. 470.

corruption of the world, and by a pious life give forth the sweet odor of virtue."[539] "It is necessary for validity that the *matter* used for Confirmation be pure olive oil mixed with balsam."[540] "It is never allowed to administer Confirmation without chrism or to receive the chrism from heretical or schismatical bishops."[541]

In 1971 a directive from the *Congregation of Divine Worship* permitted the use of other oils from plants, seeds or coconuts in place of the traditional olive oil and balsam. The use of various vegetable oils in place of olive oil leaves grave doubts as to the validity of this sacrament.

The Form of Confirmation

"The *form* of the sacrament [in the Latin rite] consists of the words 'I sign thee with the Sign of the Cross, and I confirm thee with the chrism of salvation. In the name of the Father, and of the Son, and of the Holy Ghost.' "[542] The *form* used by the Eastern rites is much shorter but essentially the same, "The sign [or seal] of the gift of the Holy Spirit."[543] The *forms* used by both the Western and Eastern Churches express the two concepts necessary to effect the sacrament: the act of signing or sealing and the grace of the Holy Ghost.

When Paul VI introduced the new rite of Confirmation he deceptively claimed he was merely reverting to "the very ancient formulary belonging to the Byzantine [Eastern] rite."[544] However, he craftily added the words "receive" or "be sealed" *(áccipe)* to this Byzantine *form*. This addition was enough to change the sense of the words. This subtle change has made the sacrament simply a passive request to accept what is offered and does not necessitate any power on the part of the minister. Hence, even priests in the New Church regularly administer Confirmation.

---

[539] Leonard Goffine, *Goffine's Devout Instructions,* p. 470.
[540] D 697. The Council of Florence, *Decree for the Armenians.*
[541] S. C. Sac. 20 Maii 1934; "Spiritus Sancti munera," n. 25.
[542] N. Signo te signo Cru+cis et confirmo te chrísmate salútis: In nómine Pa+tris et Fí+lii, et Spíritus+Sancti. Amen. *Pontificale Romanum Pars Prima,* p. 4.
[543] Arthurus Vermeersch, *Theologiae Moralis,* Tomus III, p. 219.
[544] *Divinae Consortium Naturae,* August 15, 1971.

Further, in the new rite the confirmandi is merely asked to passively receive the gifts of the Holy Spirit, a change which is consistent with Protestant belief. This is the complete opposite of what occurs in the traditional rite, in which the bishop actively confers the sacrament upon the recipient.

Minister of the Sacrament

In the Eastern Churches, according to a long-standing custom, the parish priest is the ordinary minister of Confirmation. Even today, Greek Catholic priests administer Confirmation to infants shortly after Baptism. However, this practice was never universally authorized or adopted in the Western Church.[545] The 1918 Code of Canon Law declares that "the bishop alone is the ordinary minister for Confirmation"[546] in the Western Church.

"The extraordinary minister is the priest to whom this faculty has been granted either by common rite or by a particular indult by the Holy See."[547] For example, Fr. Junipero Serra, an early missionary to California, received a temporary indult to confirm those under his care. In 1946 Pope Pius XII authorized pastors or their equivalent to confer Confirmation on their subjects who are in danger of death in order to provide this important sacrament to Catholics who would otherwise be deprived of its graces.[548] It is to be understood that the priest must have validly received Holy Orders in order to possess this power to confirm.

In the Postconciliar Church, the bishop's role has been diminished. He is no longer defined as the "ordinary minister" of the sacrament, but is now called the primary minister. Priests now commonly administer the sacrament, especially during the Easter Vigil and for the reception of adult converts into the Church. Since in the Western Church the priest is not the ordinary minister of Confirmation, the validity of many postconciliar Confirmations is very doubtful.

---

[545] "In fact it was the custom in Spain for children around two or three years of age to be confirmed." Fr. Alexio Lepicier, ORD. SERV. B.M.V., *Tractatus de Baptismo et de Confirmatione,* (1923), p. 366.

[546] Canon 782-1.

[547] Canon 782-2.

[548] *Spiritum Sancti Munera,* September 14, 1946.

No Longer Soldiers of Christ

In the traditional Sacrament of Confirmation, the bishop delivers a slight blow to the cheek of the confirmed. This ritual is an adaptation of the symbolic sword stroke of the medieval knighting ceremony. The gentle blow to the cheek and the red gowns often worn at Confirmation signify that the recipient, as a soldier of Christ, must be willing to suffer and die for Him if necessary. It is intended to impress upon the mind of the person being confirmed that he must be prepared to suffer patiently every insult or injury for his religion's sake.

This meaningful ceremony has been replaced with "a sign of peace after the anointing," usually a handshake or a hug. The new rite of Confirmation has thus been reduced to a meaningless ceremony. According to *Time* magazine, "The soldier days are over."[549] There is never a formal commitment to the Catholic Church as the one true Church *per se,* but rather a general enrollment into the Christian community.

Customary Age

What is the customary age for receiving Confirmation? Prior to the changes of the Second Vatican Council, Confirmation was usually administered to children between the age of seven and their early teens. The mind of the Church is that the sacrament be received prior to the age of puberty, before the beginnings of adulthood, when spiritual and moral armor is needed.[550] Through the abundant grace of Confirmation, Catholic youth become strong in the Faith and are empowered to meet the trials of adolescence.

> [Since Vatican II, in the Los Angeles Archdiocese] the focus is placed on committed faith response to the parish along with community service. Recent practice requires those who desire to be confirmed to complete a two-year program of instruction and formation at their parish during their high school years, even if they attend religion class every day at school.[551]

---

[549] *Time*, September 27, 1971.
[550] Canon 788, A.A.S., 1932, p. 271.
[551] *The Tidings*, December 9, 1994 and April 26, 1996.

The new rite of Confirmation is often administered during the teen years.[552] However, most active high school students readily admit that the prospect of taking additional classes, which are usually held at night, is not appealing. Homework, babysitting, sports, band and other extracurricular activities leave little time or energy for two years of evening classes, especially during the most active period of their lives.

The practice of postponing Confirmation for young people until their teen years is absurd.[553] Preparation and fortification are needed before a battle, not after the battle is nearly over. Children need to be fortified and strengthened before the onslaught of their teen years and before their course in life is set, not after they are well underway.

One may ask, "Why has the age for receiving Confirmation been moved up?" The Postconciliar Church is employing the same rationale used by Protestants in delaying Baptism. However, this approach is both illogical and spiritually debilitating.

Doubtful Validity

Fr. John Coleman summarizes the practice of the Church in the past regarding Confirmations conferred by heretics and schismatics:

> She found heretical confirmations to be invalid in some instances for want of some essential element, and in such cases she confirmed [absolutely]. In other instances she found that heretical confirmation had the required elements, and therefore she abstained from a repetition of the ceremony.[554]

In cases of doubtful validity, the sacrament was administered conditionally.

The new rite marks a radical change from the traditional Sacrament of Confirmation as found in the *Roman Pontifical and Ritual*. The Postconciliar rite of Confirmation is likely invalid, and, at best doubtfully valid due to substantial

---

[552] "Because the Council gave to bishops the freedom to make adaptations in rites for their own countries, the United States bishops made the early teen years the normal age for celebrating the sacrament of confirmation in the United States. In other countries, the practice may be different, and there are even some variations in our own country." Joseph Martos, *The Church's Sacraments: Confirmation*, p. 14.

[553] "In the Los Angeles Archdiocese, candidates are accepted once they enter the ninth grade." *The Tidings*, June 6, 1997.

[554] *The Minister of Confirmation*, p. 55.

changes in *matter*, *form* and *minister*. The change from olive oil to the use of other oils from plants, seeds or coconuts and the suppression of the individual laying on of hands at the time of the actual anointing raise serious doubts as to the validity of the new rite.

The essential words *(form)* have also been substantially changed. In addition, Postconciliar bishops ordained in the new rite (which was introduced on June 23, 1968) are almost certainly invalidly consecrated. Therefore, these are not Catholic bishops at all and cannot even consecrate Holy Chrism, which is an integral element to the sacrament. Priests cannot confer Confirmation except in danger of death and under specific guidelines. As a result, the numerous confirmations regularly administered by postconciliar priests are most likely invalid because they do not fulfill these necessary conditions. As a practical guideline, those who have been confirmed in the new rite of Confirmation (which was first introduced on August 15, 1971) should be at least conditionally confirmed by a traditional Catholic bishop because the new rite is very doubtful.

Matrimony

Even the Sacrament of Matrimony has not escaped the ravages of Vatican II. The two essential qualities of marriage, unity and permanence, have been seriously weakened by the tens of thousands of annulments granted annually by the Postconciliar Church during the past two decades. The Vatican is presently developing new legislation that will make the obtaining of annulments even faster and easier.

> Though the final text is not yet available, experts familiar with the document say a draft version contained a provision that will be of strong ecumenical interest. It would recognize the marriage law of other Christian churches—especially the Orthodox and Anglican—as part of Catholic Canon Law. Thus, if a marriage were nullified under Orthodox law, it would be considered invalid for Catholics as well, and a formal judgment of validity would not be needed.
>
> The new document is formally known as an 'instruction on the nullity of marriage,' and it will replace the previous set of rules for processing annulment requests, called *Provida Mater,* that dates from 1936, during the pontificate of

Pius XI. ...The United States produces by far the largest number of annulments in the world, some 60,000 a year.[555]

What percentage of annulment requests are granted by marriage tribunals? "In a letter, Dr. Vasoli [author and retired associate professor of sociology at Notre Dame] said that in the year 2000, the latest year for which Vatican statistics were available, U.S. tribunals granted annulments in 97% of the cases heard, a total of 44,861 decrees of nullity. That number is higher than for all tribunals in the rest of the world put together."[556]

The Primary Purpose of Marriage

The *Baltimore Catechism* explains important truths about matrimony:

The end to which marriage is primarily directed is that children be brought into the world and properly reared for happiness in this life and in the next. Hence, when a married couple make use of their right to sexual union but perform the act in such a way that the conception of children is positively frustrated, they are guilty of a grave sin. This sin, known as contraception or [artificial] birth control, is very common nowadays. It was severely condemned by Pope Pius XI in his Encyclical on Christian Marriage.[557] Other purposes of marriage are the love and assistance that the husband and wife mutually give and the opportunity of satisfying reasonably and lawfully the inclination to sexual gratification, which is so strong an impulse in human nature.[558]

Modern times have seen the primary purpose of marriage, the procreation of children, being relegated to a secondary role or even an unnecessary one. This is evident by the widespread use of contraceptives and the high abortion rate even among Catholics. Tragically, the abortion rate among postconciliar Catholics has surpassed that of Protestants. According to the Alan Guttmacher Institute of New York, "Catholics are as likely as women in the general population to have an

---

[555] *National Catholic Reporter,* April 26, 2002, "Vatican May Simplify Annulment Rules," by John Allen, Jr. In 1991, 63,933 annulments were granted.
[556] *National Catholic Reporter,* April 26, 2002.
[557] *Casti Connubii,* December 31, 1930.
[558] Fr. Francis Connell, C.SS.R., *Baltimore Catechism,* p. 271.

abortion, while Protestants are only 69% as likely and evangelical or born-again Christians are only 39% as likely."[559]

Promises in a Mixed Marriage

Of all the requisite factors to be considered in the choice of a partner for life, religion should be, by far, the most important. Even more important than the mutual affection and cooperation between spouses is that same commitment on the spiritual level. Each partner is intended by God to help the other toward personal sanctification. Through marriage as their vocation and way of life they must work out their eternal salvation—not alone, but together.

The primary purpose of marriage is the procreation, education and Catholic upbringing of children. This serious moral obligation, particularly the Catholic upbringing of children, becomes incredibly difficult when a Catholic shares parenting responsibilities with a non-Catholic. Unequally yoked partners, instead of pulling together and helping each other bear the load, are inclined to pull against each other in opposite directions, thereby splitting the team.

The sixth law of the Church is: "To observe the laws of the Church concerning marriage." This law has been abandoned by the modern church as indicated in paragraphs 2041-2043 of the (1994) *Catechism of the Catholic Church.* This is not a minor omission, but one that often leads to a loss of faith. "Experience shows that mixed marriages [marriages between Catholics and non-Catholics] are the greatest source of loss of the Catholic faith or loss of the practice of Christian morality."[560]

In the Old Testament, God forbade the Chosen People to marry unbelievers. In the New Testament, the Catholic Church—while not absolutely forbidding them—opposes mixed (religion) marriages and marriages with non-Christians. A dispensation is needed to validate such a union. Before such a dispensation is granted, the non-Catholic party must promise to allow the Catholic partner to practice the faith and raise the children in the Catholic Faith.

---

[559] The results of a 1994-1995 national survey of 9,985 abortion patients by Stanley Henshaw and Kathryn Kost.
[560] Parish Priests of Chicago, *Lessons in the Catholic Faith,* p. 81.

- The non-Catholic party must guarantee to the Catholic spouse the free exercise of their religion.
- Both parents must agree to baptize their children and instruct them in the Catholic Faith.
- The Catholic party must promise to endeavor to convert the non-Catholic spouse to the Catholic religion—especially through frequentation of the sacraments, prayer and good example.

The Postconciliar Church has eliminated all these requirements.

Formerly, both Catholic and non-Catholic partners signed promises to raise the children Catholic. This was changed by Pope Paul VI in a document on interfaith marriages ('Matrimonia Mixta') in 1970. ...The procedure today is this: The non-Catholic partner signs or promises nothing. The Catholic partner signs two statements. The statements are basically as follows:

- I reaffirm my faith in Jesus Christ, and intend to continue living that faith in the Catholic Church
- I promise to do all in my power to share my faith with our children by having them baptized and raised as Catholics[561]

Since the non-Catholic is no longer required to agree to allow the Catholic the free practice of the faith nor to the Catholic upbringing of their children, this can lead to serious problems, often resulting in a broken marriage or loss of faith. It is difficult enough to practice our religion under ideal conditions, let alone under persecution from a non-Catholic spouse.

Children, being astute, will observe that their parents are divided over religion and will invariably ask:

'Which is the true religion?' Who is to answer? Mother or father? If both reply, the child faces a confusion too great for his immature mind. Suppose, seeing that his father is a good man who never goes to church on Sunday, your son begins to imitate him. Suppose one by one all your children do likewise. What are you going to do? Tell them their father is wrong? Both parents are intended

---

[561] John Dietzen, *The New Question Box,* p. 241.

by God to be the child's most effective teachers. What can a child learn from teachers who disagree?[562]

Furthermore, children need a sense of security. Parents who disagree upon religion (whether the dissent be silent or vocal) add to the insecurity of their children, especially in this very crucial area of their life—their religious upbringing. They observe their parents united and in agreement on other things such as college, a nice home, nice cars, etc. This further proves to the children that religion is not as important as other things so they, in turn, place it at the bottom of their priority list, if it even makes the list at all. The children will quite likely come to the conclusion that religion isn't really important anyway since it is obviously not held as an object of value by their parents.

Holy Orders

"Christ gave the power to teach, to rule and to sanctify the members of His Church to the Apostles, the first bishops of the Church."[563] Our Lord intended that this power should be passed on to the various ministers of the Catholic Church through Holy Orders because the Church must endure until the end of time.

Since it is received in preparatory steps or degrees, this sacrament is called Holy Orders. There are various orders in the Church: four minor orders (porter, lector, exorcist and acolyte) and three major orders (subdeacon, deacon and priest). These orders possess varying degrees of dignity and power. The bishop alone possesses the fullness of the priesthood. It is his duty to govern with care and vigilance both the clergy and laity of the Church in order to promote their salvation. He alone ordains priests, consecrates bishops and is the ordinary minister for Confirmation. The priest's powers are more limited. He has the office of second rank and assists the bishop in caring for souls.

The Council of Trent describes the office and role of the priest and bishop:

> ...By divine precept it is enjoined on all to whom is entrusted the *cura animarum* [the care of souls] to know their sheep,[564] to offer sacrifice for them, and feed

---

[562] Dorothy Grant, *So, You Want to Get Married!*, pp. 106-107.
[563] Fr. Francis Connell, C.SS.R., *Baltimore Catechism*, p. 81.
[564] John 10: 1-16; 21: 15-17; Acts 20: 28.

them by the preaching of the divine word, the administration of the sacraments, and the example of all good works...[565]

Jesus Christ established the priesthood and episcopacy in order to perpetuate His mission on earth. This work is accomplished by offering the Holy Sacrifice of the Mass, dispensing the Seven Sacraments and preserving and promulgating His teachings for the salvation of souls. Priests and bishops act as representatives of Christ and are invested with the power and grace to fulfill their vocation.

The Sacrament of Holy Orders is vital to the Catholic Church:

> If one attentively considers the nature and essence of the other sacraments, it will readily be seen that they all depend upon the Sacrament of [Holy] Orders to such an extent that without it some of them could not be constituted or administered at all; while others would be deprived of all their solemn ceremonies, as well as of a certain part of the religious respect and exterior honor accorded them.[566]

Traditional Ordination to the Priesthood

Pope Pius IV (1559-1565) defined Holy Orders as "a sacrament which gives grace and power to perform the public functions connected with the worship of God and the salvation of souls. ...The sensible sign is the prayer of the bishop [*form*] and the imposition of hands [*the matter*]."[567] The imposition of hands by the bishop on the ordinand (the one being ordained) is the *matter* in both the Eastern and Western Church. This is confirmed by the Fathers of the Church, the General Councils of the East, the Council of Trent and by Pope Pius XII.

In 1947 Pope Pius XII settled the controversy concerning the ceremonies and words (*matter* and *form*) necessary for the validity of Holy Orders in his Apostolic Constitution *Sacramentum Ordinis*. He also declared that any substantial alteration in the rite would render the sacrament invalid.

> In the Ordination to the Priesthood, the matter is the first imposition of hands of the Bishop which is done in silence... And the form consists of the words of the 'Preface,' of which the following are essential and therefore required for validity:

---

[565] Chapter I, Session 23, July 15, 1563.
[566] John McHugh, O.P. *Catechism of the Council of Trent*, p. 317.
[567] Session 23, July 15, 1563.

Da, quaesumus, omnipotens Pater, in hunc famulum tuum Presbyterii dignitatem; innova in visceribus ejus spiritum sanctitatis, ut acceptum a Te, Deus, secundi meriti munus obtineat censuramque morum exemplo suae conversationis insinuet.[568]

We beseech Thee, Almighty Father, invest this Thy servant with the dignity of the priesthood. Do Thou renew in his heart the spirit of holiness, so that he may persevere in this office, which is next to ours in dignity, since he has received it from Thee, O God. May the example of his life lead others to moral uprightness.

The priest is ordained to offer the Holy Sacrifice of the Mass as is shown from the various prayers of the rite of ordination:

'May they change by the holy words of consecration bread and wine into the Body and Blood of Thy Son. ...I admonish you, my dear sons, before celebrating Mass, to learn carefully from well-instructed priests the order of the whole Mass. ...May the blessing of Almighty God, Father, Son and Holy Spirit descend upon you—that you may offer for the sins and offenses of the people, the sacrifice of propitiation to Almighty God.'

'Receive the power—to celebrate Mass.' Here is the first and the greatest of the priestly powers; here is the highest function of the ministry and the most perfect fulfillment of the office of mediator between God and men; here is the principal reason for ordination and consecration. A priest, before and above all else, perpetuates on earth, by means of the Holy Mass, Our Savior's immolation on Calvary.[569]

The New Rite

Completely disregarding Pope Pius XII's Apostolic Constitution, Paul VI approved new ordination rites for deacons, priests, and bishops in his Apostolic Constitution *Pontificalis Romani*.[570] The revised rites went into effect in 1970. The Motu Proprio of Paul VI of August 15, 1972 eliminated the rite of Tonsure and the orders of Porter, Lector, Exorcist, Acolyte and Subdeacon. On June 29, 1989, the ordination rite was again altered.

---

[568] Apostolic Constitution *Sacramentum Ordinis,* November 30, 1947, AAS 40-45.
[569] Fr. John Dougherty, *Unto the Altar of God,* pp. 208-209. The second paragraph was written for priests and had to be slightly changed in order to convey the same ideas to the laity.
[570] June 18, 1968.

Paul VI changed the *form* of the ordination rite of priests:

> Almighty Father, grant to these servants of yours the dignity of the priesthood. Renew within them the spirit of holiness. As co-workers with the order of bishops may they be faithful to the ministry that they receive from you, Lord God, and be to others a model of right conduct.[571]

The essential words of the new rite are similar to the traditional *form* although the Latin word *ut,* which means "in order that" is omitted, thus breaking the link between the graces of the office and the order of the priesthood. To many, this may seem an insignificant change, but it has serious ramifications.

> The deletion of the word *ut* (meaning 'so that') removes the causal relationship between the two sentences. No longer is it made clear that the ordinand receives the 'office of the second rank' as a result of the 'renewal of the Spirit of Holiness.' Whether or not this invalidates the rite is open to question and much depends on the reason why *ut* was deleted.[572]

Parallels With Anglican Orders

The changes in the new ordination rite closely parallel those made in England by the Anglican Church nearly 500 years ago. Historically, all Anglican bishops derive their orders from Dr. Matthew Parker, the first Anglican Archbishop of Canterbury, who was consecrated by William Barlow on December 7, 1559. "The question regarding the validity of Anglican Orders [Holy Orders received in the Anglican Church] gave rise to a long controversy, which was definitively decided by [Pope] Leo XIII in his Apostolic Constitution *Apostolicae Curae* of Sept. 13, 1896."[573]

The pope declared Anglican Orders to be invalid because the *Edwardine Ordinal* of 1549 (new ritual) changed the essential words *(form)* and the *intention* necessary for the bestowal of priestly powers. Pope Leo XIII noted that "the words used in their ordination rite, 'Receive the Holy Ghost,' certainly do not in

---

[571] ICEL, *The Rites of the Catholic Church as Revised by the Second Vatican Ecumenical Council, Vol. II*, p. 198.
[572] Rama Coomaraswamy, M.D., *The Problems with the new post-Conciliar Sacraments,* p.36.
[573] Msgr. Joseph Pohle, *The Sacraments, Vol. IV*, p. 70.

the least definitely express the Sacred Order of Priesthood, or its grace and power, which is chiefly the power *'of consecrating and of offering the true body and blood of the Lord.'* "[574]

> Now, if the form is 'indeterminate,' [as in the post-Vatican II rite] and if the remainder of the rite fails to specify that it intends to ordain sacrificing priests, then the new rite suffers from exactly the same defects as its Anglican prototype...
>
> In vain has help been recently sought for the plea of the validity of Anglican Orders from the other prayers of the same Ordinal. For, to put aside other reasons which show this to be insufficient for the purpose of the Anglican rite, let this argument suffice for all. From them has been deliberately removed whatever sets forth the dignity and office of the priesthood in the Catholic rite. The 'form' consequently cannot be considered apt or sufficient for the sacrament which omits what it ought essentially to signify.[575]
>
> 'It is clear,' says St. Thomas, 'that if any substantial part of the sacramental form be suppressed, the essential sense of the words is destroyed, and consequently the sacrament becomes invalid.' This principle explains the custom existing long before the Leonine decision (practically since 1554) of conditionally reordaining converted Anglican clergymen. The orders conferred under the Edwardine Ordinal were declared null and void by [Pope] Paul IV as early as 1555.[576]

Those who composed the Anglican rite of Ordination intended to "invent a new rite for a new type of ministry that is totally different from that of the Catholic Church."[577] Pope Leo XIII wrote:

> If the rite be changed, with the manifest intention of introducing another rite not approved by the Church and rejecting what the Church does, and what by the institution of Christ belongs to the nature of the sacrament, then it is clear that not only is the necessary intention wanting to the sacrament, but that the intention is adverse to and destructive of the sacrament.

---

[574] Council of Trent, Sess. XXIII, de Sacr. Ord., Can. 1.
[575] Rama Coomaraswamy, M.D., *The Problems with the new post-Conciliar Sacraments*, pp. 35, 56-57.
[576] Cfr. Pohle-Preuss, *The Sacraments, Vol. IV*, p. 71.
[577] *Letter of Patrick Henry Omlor,* September 21, 2003.

Cardinal Vaughn asserted that the Anglican rite for Holy Orders was "set up in opposition to the Catholic rite, with the express object of rejecting that kind of priesthood for the conveyance of which the Catholic rite was instituted."[578]

The New Ordination Rite is Acceptable to Anglicans

After expressing surprise that there was no mention of the power of absolution in the new 1968 ordination rite of the Postconciliar Church, the *Anglican Church Times* of May 30, 1969 published the following appraisal of the new rite:

> Though this omission happens to be of particular interest to Anglicans because our own ordinal lays such stress upon the words from St. John 20: 23 [Receive the Holy Spirit; whose sins you shall forgive, they are forgiven them; and whose sins you shall retain, they are retained], perhaps of greater significance are the other changes and omissions which show a distinct movement away from medieval and counter-Reformation [Catholic] theology.
>
> For instance, that prayer has been eliminated which spoke of the power 'to transform bread and wine into the Body and Blood of Christ… Equally significant is the new emphasis upon the proclamation of the Word… To sum up: it is an 'oecumenical' ordinal in the best sense, in that it avoids much questionable [Catholic?] terminology and is clearly expressive of the theological aggiornamento of Vatican II…

The editorial contained in the 1977 issue of *Approaches* questions the validity of the Postconciliar ordination rite:

> Since the new rite is acknowledged by Anglicans to be virtually indistinguishable from their own ordination rite, and since there is nothing in the new Catholic ordination rite as such that indicates that those about to be ordained are being ordained to say Mass or forgive sins, the question arises: Is the new rite certainly valid?

Priest or Presider over the People of God

In the pre-Vatican II ordination ceremony the bishop tells the candidate that he is ordained "to offer sacrifice, to bless, to guide, to preach and to baptize."[579]

---

[578] *A Vindication of the Bull 'Apostolicae Curae,'* p. 35.
[579] A. Biskupek, S.V.D., *Ordination to the Holy Priesthood,* p. 92.

In the new rite the ordinand is told: "You will celebrate the liturgy and offer thanks and praise to God throughout the day, praying not only for the people of God but for the whole world."[580] This new rite enumerates duties that correspond identically with Anglican Orders.

According to Pope Leo XIII, Anglican Orders are invalid because:

> ...In the whole [Anglican] ordinal not only is there no clear mention of the sacrifice, of consecration, of the priesthood [or *sacerdotium*], and of the power of consecrating and offering sacrifice, but, as We have just stated, every trace of these things which had been in such prayers of the Catholic rite as they had not only entirely rejected, were deliberately removed and struck out.[581]

The office of the priest is to offer the Holy Sacrifice of the Mass to God and to administer the sacraments of the Church. This is powerfully portrayed in the pre-Vatican II rite of Holy Orders. The bishop presents to the kneeling ordinand a chalice containing wine and water and a paten with the host lying upon it, saying, "Receive the power to offer sacrifice to God, and to celebrate Masses, both for the living and for the dead. In the name of the Lord." This important ceremony is not contained in the postconciliar rite of ordination and has been replaced by several queries by the bishop to the candidate.

> Bishop: Are you resolved, with the help of the Holy Spirit, to discharge without fail the office of priesthood in the presbyteral order as a conscientious fellow worker with the bishops in caring for the Lord's flock? Candidate: I am.
>
> Bishop: Are you resolved to celebrate the mysteries of Christ faithfully and religiously as the Church has handed them down to us for the glory of God and the sanctification of Christ's people? Candidate: I am.
>
> Bishop: Are you resolved to exercise the ministry of the word worthily and wisely, preaching the Gospel and explaining the Catholic faith?
> Candidate: I am.[582]

---

[580] ICEL, *The Rites of the Catholic Church as Revised by the Second Vatican Ecumenical Council, Vol. II*, p. 41.
[581] *Apostolicae Curae.*
[582] ICEL, *The Rites of the Catholic Church as Revised by the Second Vatican Ecumenical Council, Vol. II*, p. 42.

With the exception of the phrase "explaining the Catholic faith," this section of the ordination rite could conceivably be used for the induction of a Protestant minister. *Novus Ordo* priests do not offer the Holy Sacrifice of the Mass, but merely preside over the "memorial of the Lord" or "Lord's Supper."[583] They preside over "the mysteries of Christ" and "the ministry of the word" which is not a propitiatory sacrifice, but rather a sacrifice of thanksgiving and praise[584] similar to Protestant liturgies.

Joseph Martos sheds light on the subject: "When Protestants attend something like a Mass in their own churches, they don't call it a Mass; they call it communion service or Lord's Supper."[585]

Pope Leo XIII declared Anglican Orders to be invalid due to a defect in form and intention. The new rite for the ordination of priests, like the Anglican Ordinal, represents a radical departure from the traditional rite of ordination. Not only has the form been changed, but also the primary function of the priest, to offer sacrifice to God, has been eliminated. Therefore, the new rite is most probably invalid, or at best quite doubtful.

"But if all this is not enough to cast doubt on the validity of Postconciliar ordinations, there is yet more. Obviously, one of the requirements for valid ordination of a priest is a validly ordained bishop. No matter how correct the rites used for the priesthood are, the absence of a validly ordained bishop would make the rite a farce."[586]

---

[583] *Sacramentary*, p. 33.
[584] Condemned by the Council of Trent at Session 22, Chapter 9, Canon 3, Sept. 17, 1562.
[585] *The Church's Sacraments: Eucharist*, p. 3.
[586] Rama Coomaraswamy, M.D., *The Problems with the new post-Conciliar Sacraments*,
   p. 38. It is pertinent that the "bishops" selected for ordaining the priests of the Society of St. Peter ("The Pope's own Traditional Order") are Ratzinger and Meyer. Both of these received their episcopal "consecration" by the new rites to be discussed in the body of this text. If they are in fact not bishops, all the priests they ordain—even if they use the traditional rites as they state they intend to do—are no priests at all and have no more priestly power than laymen do.

Traditional Rite for the Consecration of Bishops

The ceremonies necessary for valid consecration of bishops are explicitly defined in *Sacramentum Ordinis:*

> ...the matter is the imposition of hands which is done by the bishop consecrator. The form consists of the words of the 'Preface,' of which the following are essential and therefore required for validity: Perfect in Thy priest the fullness of thy ministry and, clothing him in all the ornaments of spiritual glorification, sanctify him with the heavenly anointing.[587]

New Rite for the Ordination of Bishops

Paul VI totally disregarded Pope Pius XII's definition in *Sacramentum Ordinis* and composed an entirely new rite for the consecration of bishops in his Apostolic Constitution *Pontificale Romani.*[588]

The traditional ceremony used for the consecration of bishops contains five acts of faith professing belief in the Blessed Trinity. These professions of faith, which most likely date back to the First Council of Nicaea (325 AD), have been removed by the Postconciliar Church because they are unecumenical.

The new rite eliminated the traditional instruction given to the bishop-elect: "It behooves the bishop to judge, to interpret, to consecrate, to ordain, to offer sacrifice, to baptize and to confirm."[589] "Nowhere in the new rite is it stated that the function of the Bishop is to ordain, or to confirm, much less to judge."[590]

According to the teachings of the Church, a sacrament must signify what it effects and effect what it signifies. Therefore the *form* of Holy Orders must externally portray what occurs in the soul of the recipient: the conferral of the episcopacy. The new *form* of Paul VI is extremely vague, mentioning neither the role nor the graces of the episcopal office. Although the laying on of hands *(matter)* has been retained, the *form* employed in the new rite is completely different from the essential sacramental *form*. The only similarities between the

---

[587] *Comple in sacerdote tuo ministerii tui summum, et ornamentis totius glorificationis instructum coelestis unguenti rore sanctifica.*
[588] June 23, 1968.
[589] *Pontificale Romanum,* p. 336.
[590] Rama Coomaraswamy, M.D., *The Problems with the new post-Conciliar Sacraments,* p. 56.

two *forms* are the words: "and," "by," "him," "of," and "the." This can be demonstrated by a side-by-side comparison.

THE PRE-VATICAN II FORM FOR THE CONSECRATION OF BISHOPS:	THE POST-VATICAN II FORM FOR THE ORDINATION OF BISHOPS:
Perfect in Thy priest the fullness of Thy ministry and, clothing him in all the ornaments of spiritual glorification, sanctify him with the heavenly anointing.[591]	So now pour out upon this chosen one that power which is from you, the governing Spirit whom you gave to your beloved Son, Jesus Christ, the Spirit given by him to the holy apostles, who founded the Church in every place to be your temple for the unceasing glory and praise of your name.[592]

The sacramental form for the new rite of episcopal consecration (1968) presents the essence of the episcopate not as the fullness of the priesthood, but rather as something called the *spiritus principalis*. *Spiritus principalis* was first translated into English as "that excellent spirit" and then several years later as "that governing spirit." What is meant by the term, *governing spirit?* The authors of the new rite (including Annibale Bugnini) even disputed with each other over what *governing spirit* is really supposed to mean. Bugnini stated, "There are difficulties in understanding and readily translating into the vernaculars, the term 'Spiritus principalis' in the ordination prayer."[593]

The phrase occurs in only one place in Sacred Scripture (Psalm 50) and, as the *Consilium* who composed the new text admitted, its meaning there is unclear because the manuscripts at that point are slightly corrupted.

Even if the term "governing spirit" refers to the Holy Ghost, the new *form* is still doubtfully valid according to the teaching of Pope Leo XIII. He declared that the mere mentioning of the Holy Ghost in Anglican Orders was insufficient for validity. The Postconciliar rite for consecrating bishops, together with the

---

[591] Msgr. Phelan, *The Ceremony of Consecration of a Bishop*, p. 15.
[592] ICEL, *The Rites of the Catholic Church as Revised by the Second Vatican Ecumenical Council, Volume II*, p. 73.
[593] *Reform of the Liturgy*, p. 714, footnote 16.

Anglican rite, are defective and inadequate because they "certainly do not in the least definitely express the Sacred Order of Priesthood, or its grace and power."[594]

For the validity of a sacrament the *form* must adequately convey the spiritual reality taking place. Since *governing spirit* is so vague that it could mean almost anything, its use raises a positive doubt about all episcopal consecrations performed according to the new rite. Catholics should not assist at Masses offered by priests whose ordination is doubtful. This is over and above the consideration that one should stay away from the New Mass, the Indult Mass and the clergy of the Priestly Fraternity of St. Peter because they teach and profess the false religion of the Postconciliar Church.

Pope Leo XIII stated in the encyclical *Apostolicae Curae* that ordinations of the Anglican Church are invalid due to defect of *form* and *intention:* "Therefore, the Episcopate can in no wise be truly and validly conferred by it; and this is the more so because among the first duties of the Episcopate is that of ordaining ministers for the Holy Eucharist to offer sacrifice." The Postconciliar Church embodies these same invalidating changes.

The 16th century Anglican reformers did not restore Holy Orders to its ancient form, but they substantially changed the rite, thus invalidating it. The "reformers" of Vatican II used the same stratagem.

> Under the pretext of restoring the order of the liturgy to its primitive form, they corrupted it in many respects to bring it into accord with the errors of the innovators. As a result, not only is there in the whole [1968] Ordinal no clear mention of sacrifice, of consecration, of priesthood (*sacerdotium*), of the power to consecrate and offer sacrifice, but, as We have already indicated, every trace of these and similar things remaining in such prayers of the Catholic rite as were not completely rejected, was purposely removed and obliterated. [The same changes were introduced into the 1549 Anglican Ordinal.]
>
> As the *Vindication of the Bull Apostolicae Curae* points out: The fact that the Anglicans added the term 'Bishop' to their form did not make it valid because doctrinally they hold the Bishop to have no higher state than that of the

---

[594] *Apostolicae Curae.*

priest—indeed, he is seen as an 'overseer' rather than as one having the 'fullness of the priesthood.'[595]

Pope Leo XIII concluded his epoch decision by saying: "Therefore adhering to the decrees of the Pontiffs, Our Predecessors, on this subject, and fully ratifying and renewing them by Our authority, on Our own initiative and with certain knowledge, We pronounce and declare that ordinations performed according to the Anglican rite have been and are completely null and void."

He further condemns the notion that various other nonessential ceremonies *(significatio ex adjunctis)* validate the rites used for the ordination of priests and the consecration of bishops in spite of defective *matter, form* and/or intention.

What are the consequences of changing the Catholic ordination rite in such a way that it parallels Anglican Orders? If the rite of ordination of priests is thereby invalid, it would follow that a man ordained in the new rite is not a priest at all. Bishops ordained in the new rite do not receive a valid sacrament and therefore cannot validly ordain priests or bishops or confer Confirmation. Further, even if a bishop were to use the old rite of ordination, the fact that the bishop was consecrated with the new rite makes him, *de facto*, an invalid bishop and therefore all his ordinations would be invalid.

Clerical Immorality

In every line of work, there are many who honorably discharge their duties as well as others who, unfortunately, disgrace their profession. Everyone knows there are heroic law enforcement officers, dedicated doctors and saintly priests and also corrupt police officers, unethical physicians and immoral clergymen. It certainly seems possible that invalid ordinations and consecrations could play a large part in the scandals involving *Novus Ordo* priests.

The teachings of the Second Vatican Council have transformed priests into social workers and masters of ceremonies. "The theological emphasis in this rite [Holy Orders] is no longer on spiritual power, as it was in earlier centuries, but on ministry and service."[596] This loss of faith and grace certainly has contributed

---

[595] Rama Coomaraswamy, M.D., *The Problems with the new post-Conciliar Sacraments*, p. 43.
[596] Joseph Martos, *The Church's Sacraments: Holy Orders*, p. 22.

to the widespread pedophilia and ephebophilia (immoral conduct with post-pubescent minors) by the postconciliar clergy. This breakdown of morals is a direct result of the de-emphasis on sin and the focus on self-expression—resulting from Vatican II.[597]

Although the mass media has dwelt almost exclusively on pedophilia, the greater problem is actually one of homosexuality. "Well over 90% of the victims in abuse cases involving priests were adolescent boys, indicating not a problem of pedophilia—abuse against pre-pubescent boys and girls—but of ephebophilia, or predatory homosexuality."[598] "The number of gay priests is not known but experts say it could be as high as 50%."[599]

In his *Encyclical on the Holy Priesthood*, Pope Pius XI stated clearly and firmly that bishops and seminary rectors should not only develop and strengthen vocations, but also "discourage unsuitable candidates and in good time send them away from a path not meant for them."[600] These warnings have been ignored.

St. John Eudes explains how evil, lax priests are a scourge to the world:

> The most evident mark of God's anger and the most terrible castigation He can inflict upon the world are manifested when He permits His people to fall into the hands of clergy who are priests more in name than in deed, priests who practice the cruelty of ravening wolves rather than the charity and affection of devoted shepherds. Instead of nourishing those committed to their care, they rend and devour them brutally. Instead of leading their people to God, they drag Christian souls into hell in their train. Instead of being the salt of the earth and the light of the world, they are its innocuous poison and its murky darkness.[601]

Priests and bishops " 'must be outstanding by the sanctity of their lives' (Pope Pius XII); 'Sanctity is the chief and the most important endowment of the

---

[597] See *The Chicago Tribune,* June 3, 2003, "Scandals draw attention to obscure condition: Ephebophilia," by Lou Carlozo.
[598] *Wanderer,* June 27, 2002, "Bishops' Actions Expose More Corruption," by Michael Rose.
[599] *National Catholic Reporter,* February 28, 2003, "About half of priests leave for love or sex, study says," p. 7. This figure is similar to one given in an NBC report on celibacy. See William Bausch's *Brave New Church,* p. 106.
[600] *Ad Catholici Sacerdotii,* December 20, 1935.
[601] St. John Eudes, *The Priest: His Dignity and Obligations,* p. 9.

Catholic priest' (Pope Pius XI); 'Sanctity alone makes us what our vocation demands, and if this be lacking in a priest, all things are lacking' (St. Pius X)."[602]

"St. Gregory the Great says that priests and pastors of souls will stand condemned before God as murderers of any souls lost through neglect or silence."[603] He also states "that nothing more angers God than to see those whom he set aside for the correction of others, give bad example by a wicked and depraved life."[604] Bad priests are more culpable than others for their sins because of their unique vocation.

Corrupt Bishops

Many postconciliar bishops have been neglecting the spiritual welfare of their flocks due to their excessive involvement in political and financial matters. When they received numerous warnings regarding the immorality rampant among their priests, these corrupt bishops ignored the situation and continued to allow such abusers to be involved in parish work or, at worst, merely transferred these priests to other parishes. Sadly, few parishioners were aware of the predators in their midst and as a result suffered terribly.

Author George Weigel believes " 'incompetent or malfeasant' bishops not only coddled sinful clergy, but also allowed dissent to flourish, failing to defend the morals and disciplines of 'classic Catholicism.' "[605]

American bishops have known about clerical immorality for decades. At their annual meeting in 1971 they were given a report on this topic by the famous Catholic psychologist, Dr. Conrad Baars, who warned them of a " 'crisis in the priesthood' due to homosexual clerics."[606] In May 1985, the U.S. bishops were given a second warning when they received a 92-page document outlining the problem.[607]

---

[602] Fr. John Dougherty, *Unto the Altar of God,* p. 219.
[603] Homil. 12 super Ezech.
[604] Homil. 27 in Evang.
[605] *The Detroit News,* July 27, 2003, "Calls mount for Catholic reforms," by Richard Ostling.
[606] *Wanderer,* May 23, 2002, "Insiders' Knowledge of Homosexuality in Priesthood Becomes Public," by Paul Likoudis.
[607] Fr. Michael Peterson, director of St. Luke's Institute in Silver Springs, Maryland, Fr. Thomas Doyle, Dominican canonist in Washington, D.C. and attorney Ray Mouton spent five months composing the document.

It was 'backed with more than 100 pages of supporting evidence. The report covered the civil, canonical, and psychological aspects of priests' sexual involvement with children. ...At the June 1985 meeting of the U.S. bishops at St. John's Abbey in Collegeville, Minn., the bishops were quietly briefed on the report's contents. But, according to [Fr. Thomas] Doyle, the committee headed by [Cardinal] Law never followed through on the promise to create the ad hoc committee.'[608] ...The document, reportedly referred to in more than 100 lawsuits, is well known to the bishops.[609]

Lamentably, the immorality continued and the prophetic warning has come back to haunt those who did nothing to stop it. "It is interesting (and quite revealing, too) that at the special convention of Novus Ordo bishops at Dallas in June [2002], a motion was made, but denied, to discuss the homosexuality that pervades the ranks of the clergy."[610]

Many bishops who were aware of problems merely transferred the immoral priests or tried to cover up the situation by quietly settling legal cases out of court. "In its April 15 [2002] issue, *Business Week* magazine cited estimates by plaintiffs' lawyers that U.S. dioceses have spent as much as $1 billion in sex-abuse settlements since 1985."[611] "The church has long attempted to keep priest-abuse cases quiet through the paying of hush money—estimated at a billion dollars so far—to families instructed to sign confidential agreements."[612] There are numerous cases reported in nearly every American state and in 116 U.S. dioceses.[613] Immorality among the clergy has become a worldwide problem.[614]

The future of the postconciliar priesthood appears very bleak as hundreds of priests have been incarcerated, removed or simply resigned because of immoral behavior. Many young men who previously felt called to the priesthood have

---

[608] *National Catholic Reporter,* May 17, 2002, "What they knew in 1985," by Thomas Fox.
[609] *National Catholic Reporter,* May 17, 2002.
[610] *Reign of Mary, Vol. 33,* No. 110, "Letters to the Editor," by Fr. Casimir Puskorius, CMRI.
[611] *National Catholic Reporter,* April 19, 2002.
[612] *The Wall Street Journal,* April 19, 2002, "The Pope Steps In," by Peggy Noonan.
[613] *Toledo Blade,* December 1, 2002, "Shame, sins and secrets," by Michael Sallah and David Yonke.
[614] Cases have been documented in Argentina, Australia, Austria, Britain, Canada, Chile, France, Ireland, Mexico, Poland, South Africa and Wales.

been sickened by these scandals and are now pursuing other fields, leaving seminaries with few candidates to replace the priests who retire annually.

Rod Dreher addressed the culpability of the bishops of the Postconciliar Church in his article in the *National Review:* "Aside from not addressing the root causes of the scandal, the bishops refused to accept personal accountability for their paramount role in the scandal. Not one resigned. Not one was asked to resign, at least publicly. Words of apology ring hollow when not followed by action."[615]

Diogenes, in his article "Holding Bishops Accountable," shows that modern bishops are personally responsible for the moral decay and loss of faith today:

> The hierarchy which is unable to react when a young boy is abused is the same hierarchy which has been unable to reply effectively when the universities and colleges were secularized, when religious education was gutted, when parents were pointing out that sex-ed programs were violating their children's innocence, when it was revealed that two whole generations were wholly ignorant of Catholic doctrine, when Mass attendance dropped by 60% in 30 years, when people were hurt and felt betrayed by liturgical abuses. This is not an isolated problem.
>
> The bishops have acted in a way that suggests their first loyalty is not to Christ, or his Church, or the care of their people. Their loyalty is to the clerical establishment.[616]

The Solution?

Some have suggested that married priests would resolve the problem. Since the problem is predominantly a homosexual one, marriage would not help. Others push for women priests; some say that this would resolve the sex scandals! This isn't the solution either. The solution is simple—a return to the conditions under which the Catholic Church and Catholics flourished—the traditional Mass, sacraments and teachings.

---

[615] David Gibson, *The Coming Catholic Church,* p. 32.
[616] *Catholic World Report,* February 2002.

Lay Ministers

David Gibson describes the foundation of the lay ministry and its prevalence in the American Church of today:

> Vatican II declared "that lay people were part of the 'priesthood of all believers,' a phrase that had been a governing principle of the sixteenth-century Reformation as Luther and his followers sought to throw off the shackles of clericalism.
>
> A 1999 study by the National Pastoral Life Center estimated that nearly 30,000 lay ecclesiastical ministers worked in full- or part-time pastoral roles in more than two-thirds of the nation's 19,000 parishes, a 35 percent increase from 1992. Combined with the estimated 30,000 lay ministers currently undergoing training, lay people—mainly women—will soon outnumber the nation's 47,000 priests.[617]

Lay deacons, who are so common today, are a by-product of Vatican II. Saints Stephen (the first Christian martyr), Lawrence (martyred by being roasted on a gridiron) Vincent (a Spaniard who was tortured and died for his faith) and Francis of Assisi are deacons who observed lifelong celibacy. This practice goes back to the earliest ages of the Church.

Lay deacon is a contradiction of terms since prior to Vatican II deacons in the Western Church were bound to celibacy, obliged to pray the Divine Office daily, were to complete their studies and be ordained as priests.

Vatican II changed all that. David Gibson explains:

> Since 1971, when the first class of seven [lay] deacons was ordained in the United States, the number of [lay] deacons has exploded. In 2002 there were more than 13,500 [lay] deacons in 67 percent of all parishes, with another 2,500 in various stages of training. That accounts for well over half of all [lay] deacons worldwide. Europe has about 7,500 [lay] deacons. In all of Asia there are just 142 [lay] deacons, and in Africa just 331.
>
> But [lay] deacons exist in a new clerical gray area. While they are dismayed at being considered lay people, which happens frequently, they certainly *look* like laymen, not priests. Some 90 percent of [lay] deacons are married, with most of

---

[617] *The Coming Catholic Church*, p. 53.

the rest widowed or divorced. Just 3 percent have never married. They have jobs and families, and don't dress in black.[618]

The precipitous decline in the number of seminarians and priests since Vatican II attests to the fact that the establishment of lay deacons and lay ministers has minimized the need for Catholic clergy.

Extreme Unction / Anointing of the Sick

Catholics who are in danger of death from sickness, accident, or old age should receive the Sacrament of Extreme Unction for the strengthening of their souls and the remission of their sins.

"The term is called Extreme Unction because it is the last of the holy anointings to be administered in life."[619] The Council of Trent enumerates its salutary effects upon the soul:

> For the thing signified is the grace of the Holy Spirit Whose anointing blots out sins if any remain to be expiated, and also the remains of sin, and raises up and strengthens the soul of the sick person by exciting in him a great confidence in the Divine Mercy, sustained by which he bears more lightly the troubles and pains of his illness, and resists more easily the temptation of the devil who lies in wait for his heel; and sometimes when expedient for the welfare of his soul restores bodily health.[620]

Therefore, Extreme Unction produces three principal effects:

- It confers grace and remits sins.
- It comforts the sick.
- It restores health to the body if it is for the good of the soul.

In his epistle, St. James describes the administration of Extreme Unction in the early Church: "Is any man sick among you? Let him bring in the priests of the Church, and let them pray over him, anointing him with oil in the name of the Lord. And the prayer of faith shall save the sick man: and the Lord shall raise

---

[618] *The Coming Catholic Church,* p. 55.
[619] Nicholas Halligan, O.P., *The Administration of the Sacraments,* p. 617.
[620] Conc. Trid. 1, 14, ch. 2.

him up: and if he be in sins, they shall be forgiven him."[621] The Council of Trent explains the great consolation afforded by the reception of this sacrament:

> He [Christ] prepared the greatest aids, whereby during life Christians may preserve themselves whole from every more grievous spiritual evil, so did He guard the close of life, by the Sacrament of Extreme Unction, as with a firm defense. For though our adversary [the devil] seeks and seizes opportunities all our life long to be able in any way to devour our souls; yet is there no time wherein he strains more vehemently all the powers of his craft to ruin us utterly and, if he can possibly, to make us fall even from trust in the mercy of God, than when he perceives the end of our life to be at hand.[622]

The Matter of Extreme Unction

The Catholic Church teaches that "the valid matter of Extreme Unction is olive oil duly blessed for this purpose by a bishop or a priest who has obtained the faculty to do so from the Apostolic See."[623] The *Catechism of the Council of Trent* says: "Its element, then, or matter, as defined by Councils, particularly by the Council of Trent, consists of oil consecrated by the Bishop. Not any kind of oil extracted from fatty or greasy substances, but olive oil alone."[624]

"St. James in saying, 'Anointing with oil,' employs the Greek word ελαιον, which literally means oil of olives. Consequently oil of olives is the remote matter of the Sacrament of Extreme Unction. This deduction is expressly confirmed by the *Decretum pro Armenis* [D 700]. All other oils, such as that derived from nuts, sesame, etc., are not valid matter for Extreme Unction."[625]

Anointing of the Sick

Perhaps the most tragic and treacherous alteration in the sacraments occurred in Extreme Unction, for it simply does not exist in the New Church. The Vatican II *Constitution on the Sacred Liturgy* decreed that the "prayers accompanying the rite of anointing are to be revised."[626] Extreme Unction has

---

[621] James 5: 14-15.
[622] Session XIV, Chapter IX, November 25, 1551.
[623] *Code of Canon Law* (1918), Canon 945, Council of Trent, D 908.
    This is confirmed by the Council of Florence—D 700.
[624] Part II, p. 309.
[625] Msgr. Joseph Pohle, *The Sacraments, Vol. IV*, pp. 16-17.
[626] Chapter 3, no. 75.

been replaced with an Anointing of the Sick, thus depriving hundreds of millions of the numerous graces of this sacrament. Paul VI changed the *matter* and *form* in 1972. The new rite became mandatory on January 1, 1974.

The Matter of the Anointing of the Sick

In order to validly confer Extreme Unction, a priest must use olive oil that is validly consecrated. Paul VI authorized the use of various types of vegetable oil for the anointing of the sick, although this is in direct opposition to the teachings of the Catholic Church which specifically require olive oil for the validity of this sacrament. Doubtful matter could invalidate the rite.[627] Msgr. Joseph Pohle affirms that the oil of the sick must be blessed by a bishop:

> Tradition since Pope Innocent I [401-417 AD] insists on the oil being blessed by a bishop, which indicates that this blessing is the condition for validity. ...In 1842, the Congregation of the Holy Office, reaffirming a previous decree, replied negatively to the query whether a parish priest, in case of necessity, could validly use oil blessed by himself.[628]

The Postconciliar Church in defiance of previous declarations, "empowers" priests to bless the oil of the sick. "In case of necessity, a priest himself may bless the oil. (A draft of the rite, which appeared in 1970, would have allowed the priest to do the blessing whenever it seemed pastorally appropriate.)"[629] This action assures the invalidity of the rite.

The Form is Changed

Extreme Unction has specific prayers for the anointing of each sense: "Through this holy unction and His own most tender mercy, may the Lord pardon you whatever sins you have committed by (sight, hearing, smell, taste, speech, touch and walking)."[630]

---

[627] See footnote 606.
[628] Msgr. Joseph Pohle, *The Sacraments, Vol. IV*, p. 18.
[629] Michael Glazier and Monika Hellwig, *Modern Catholic Encyclopedia*, pp. 761-762.
[630] Fr. Paul Griffith, *Priest's New Ritual*, pp. 77-79.

The *form* used in the (Vatican II) Anointing of the Sick is: "Through this holy anointing may the Lord in his love and mercy help you with the grace of the Holy Spirit. Amen. May the Lord who frees you from sins save you and raise you up. Amen."[631]

At first sight, the wording for the Anointing of the Sick may seem to be very similar to Extreme Unction. Nevertheless, upon further examination it is found to be very ambiguous. The new form also omits the important words "May the Lord pardon thee whatever sins you have committed." These words express the primary effects of the sacrament: the healing and strengthening of the soul, the remission of venial sins and the cleansing of the soul from the remains of sin. According to St. Thomas Aquinas, Extreme Unction was instituted for "...the health of the soul which is effected by strengthening of the soul through grace and by the remission of sins."[632]

In his encyclical *Apostolicae Curae,* Pope Leo XIII taught that the sacraments "...ought both to signify the grace which they effect and effect the grace which they signify." He also declared, "That form consequently cannot be considered apt or sufficient for the sacrament which omits what it ought essentially to signify." Accordingly, the change in wording has resulted in an essential change in meaning, more than likely rendering this sacrament invalid.

The Recipient of Extreme Unction

Concerning the recipients of Extreme Unction, the *Baltimore Catechism* teaches: "All Catholics who have reached the use of reason and are in danger of death from sickness, accident, or old age should receive Extreme Unction." According to the new rite, "People no longer need to be dying or even look sick, to receive the [new] Sacrament of the Anointing of the Sick."[633] The American bishops even issued guidelines expressing that the illness need not be physical, but could be an emotional or spiritual crisis. "It can be performed for an

---

[631] ICEL, *The Rites of the Catholic Church as Revised by the Second Vatican Ecumenical Council, Vol. I,* p. 825.
[632] St. Thomas Aquinas, *Summa Theol.* Suppl. 29, 1.
[633] John Dietzen, *New Question Box,* p. 429.

individual, a group or at a special Mass of anointing in a parish, hospital or home for the aged."[634]

During their last moments on earth, whether caused by sickness or sudden accident, Catholics customarily call upon a priest to administer the Last Sacraments of Penance, Extreme Unction and Holy Eucharist.[635] As their eternity hangs in the balance and they prepare to meet their Judge, devout souls seek the sacrament of pardon and reassurance. At this critical moment, Postconciliar Catholics are denied Extreme Unction and receive merely the spiritual equivalent of a get well card due to essential changes in the sacrament.

Doubtful Validity of the New Sacraments

The new sacraments of the Postconciliar Church are substantially different from those instituted by Christ. At this point one must pose the question, if a particular item (*matter, form* or *intention*) was not important, why has the Church used specific ceremonies for the sacraments for nearly 2,000 years? Why has it been so careful to preserve them in their exact form? Who gave the Modernists of Vatican II the authority to declare that the sacraments are now subject to arbitrary change? Did Christ make a mistake when He first instituted the sacraments? Has He suddenly changed His mind? Were the previous popes and 20 General Councils of the Church wrong? If a priest can simply change the sacraments by his own authority, willy-nilly, how can we be sure of their efficacy?

The new rites of Confirmation, Holy Eucharist, Holy Orders (especially the Ordination of Bishops) and the Anointing of the Sick have been altered to such an extent that at best, their validity is extremely doubtful.

Conditional Sacraments

The Catholic Church specifically teaches us what to do in case of doubt regarding the reception of the sacraments: "When the invalidity of a sacrament is certain, the sacrament must be repeated absolutely; when the invalidity is doubtful, it must be repeated conditionally."[636]

---

[634] Joseph Martos, *The Church's Sacraments: Anointing of the Sick,* p. 14.
[635] Holy Viaticum—food for the journey.
[636] Fr. Henry Davis, S.J., *Moral and Pastoral Theology, Vol. III,* p. 25.

Fr. Henry Davis, S.J. further clarifies this point:

The repetition of the sacrament ought to be done where its validity is doubted—or rather, so long as its validity is not morally certain—in cases when the sacrament is necessary, whether absolutely and of its nature, as Baptism, or relatively and in respect of the good of others, as Ordination, absolution, Extreme Unction. Consequently, in doubt as to validity, Baptism, Ordination, absolution of the dying, Extreme Unction of the unconscious, and consecration of doubtfully consecrated hosts, must be repeated.[637]

---

[637] *Moral and Pastoral Theology, Vol. III,* p. 25.

E. Statistics

Our Lord gave us an infallible rule to discern truth from error: "By their fruits you will know them. …Every good tree bears good fruit, but the bad tree bears bad fruit. A good tree cannot bear bad fruit, nor can a bad tree bear good fruit."[638]

The Catholic Church thrived in America before Vatican II. Historians have recorded the frequent reception of the sacraments, regular attendance at Sunday Mass and the unparalleled growth of the Church.

> It has been said that in 1669, the [Catholic] faithful [in the United States] numbered 2,000; in 1708, 3,000; in 1755, 7,000…[639] An expert in ecclesiastical history, Reverend I. J. Laux, has said that 'the advance of the Catholic Church in the United States by leaps and bounds, from 25,000 faithful at the time of the Revolution [1776] to 20,000,000 in 1931, is an outstanding phenomenon in Church history.'[640]

> Between 1940 and 1960 American Catholics grew in number from 20 to 40 million; priests from 25,000 to 50,000; religious from 50,000 to 100,000. About 75% of these Catholics were at Mass on a given Sunday and 80% were validly married. They had a high birth rate and a low crime rate. Upwardly mobile graduates of Catholic schools were rising to executive positions, forming a voting bloc in industrial centers, and molding public opinion through organizations like the Legion of Decency.[641]

In contrast, the Postconciliar Church has borne the bad fruits of heresy, loss of faith and defection from the Catholic Church.

- Numerous seminaries and convents have been closed.
- Religious habits have been discarded.
- Multitudes of priests and Religious have abandoned Christ to follow the spirit of the world.

---

[638] Matthew 7: 16-18.
[639] Alfonso Zaratti, O.C.D., *The Work of the Catholic Church in the United States of America*, p. 359.
[640] *The National Encyclopedia*, (Collier), New York, 1934, VIII, p. 518.
[641] *The Catholic World Report,* March 2002, p. 52.

- Mass attendance has plummeted while Catholic churches now often resemble non-denominational or Protestant churches.
- Statues, altars and tabernacles have all but vanished.

Msgr. Kelly cited depressing statistics based on figures for 1976, "indicating that there had been a collapse in every aspect of Catholic life subject to statistical verification, and that most of those still claiming to be practicing Catholics were not very Catholic in what they practiced: Perhaps as many as 10,000,000 Catholics stopped regular attendance at Sunday Mass—a 30% decline."[642]

Weekly Mass Attendance in the United States

Catholic churchgoing [in the United States] has dropped to its lowest level ever.[643] In the wake of the sex-abuse scandal of the past year [2002], Sunday Mass attendance rates among American Catholics plummeted from a discouraging one in three to a disastrous one in four, according to the Gallup Organization.[644]

The decline in church attendance among Catholics is part of a long-term phenomenon that precedes the current scandals afflicting the Church. Gallup data from the 1950s and 1960s show that about three-quarters of Catholics reported attending church within the last seven days, compared with just half or fewer of Protestants at that time. Catholic attendance continued to fall through the late 1960s, 1970s and early 1980s, but remained higher than Protestants' attendance.[645]

Loss of Faith in the United States

There are no numbers to show how many have left the Church [in the U.S.], how many are thinking about coming back, or how many have indeed returned. But people in the 'business' of apologetics [defense of the Catholic Faith], like Patrick Madrid, editor of *Envoy* magazine, report that wherever they go, they see the same thing.

---

[642] G. Kelly, *The Battle for the American Church,* p. vii.
[643] *Jackson Citizen Patriot,* December 26, 2002, "Fewer Catholics than ever attend church, poll finds," by David Gibson.
[644] *Crisis,* March 2003, "Ignoring the Obvious: the Unreality of American Catholicism," by Russell Shaw, p. 28.
[645] *The Wanderer,* January 2, 2003, "Religious Scandals Top News Stories," by Paul Likoudis. This concurs with a recent study made by the University of Notre Dame.

In his book *Search and Rescue: How to Bring Your Family and Friends Into—or Back Into—the Catholic Church,* Madrid writes: I've given countless seminars throughout the country about Christ and the Catholic Church. In each seminar, I ask the same question: 'How many of you have a family member or a friend who has abandoned the Catholic Church and gone into another religion?' Whether it's 50 people or 5,000, the answer is always the same, always unanimous: everyone in the audience raises a hand.[646]

Even Hispanic Catholics are leaving the church. "Many Hispanics who arrive in the United States have already left the Catholic Church behind."[647] "According to Father Greeley's statistics, since 1972 the equivalent of one in seven Hispanics has left Catholicism. In 1972, 78% of Hispanics were Catholic. By the mid-1990's, that number has dropped to 67%. An estimated 23% of U.S. Hispanics are now Protestant, and the leakage continues at the rate of approximately 600,000 people a year. He adds that if the trend continues for the next twenty-five years, half of all American Hispanics will not be Catholic."[648] "Findings from the American Religious Identification Survey 2001 showed that the number of Hispanics who declared no religious affiliation more than doubled from 1990 to 2000, from 6% to 13%, from 926,000 to 2.9 million."[649]

Religion in the United States

The fact that the majority of Americans aren't in church can be seen in the Sunday traffic jams at malls, movie theatres and grocery stores. ...Nearly 100 million Americans live without a connection to a church, synagogue or temple, says pollster George Barna, president of the Barna Research Group in Ventura, California. Most of them are unconcerned about this state of affairs. ...According to the 2001 American Religious Identification Survey released in January, more than 29.4 million Americans have no religion—double the number 11 years ago. That's 14% of the nation, up from 7.5% in a similar 1990 survey.[650]

---

[646] *Crisis,* December 2002, "Why Young Catholics Leave the Church," by Kathryn Lopez.
[647] David Gibson, *The Coming Catholic Church,* p. 74.
[648] *Our Sunday Visitor,* November 16, 1997.
[649] Gibson, 75.
[650] *Insight,* May 27, 2002, "Americans Keep Faith, Lose Religion," by Julia Dunn.

Worldwide Loss of Faith

The loss of faith by former Catholics subsequent to the Second Vatican Council is keenly felt in the Province of Quebec. "Though nearly all of the province's six million French-speakers have Catholic roots, less than 10% attend Mass regularly, compared to 90% a few decades ago. Government statistics say 24% of Quebec families are headed by unmarried couples, nearly twice the national average."[651] "Birth rates in the province [of Quebec] have plummeted from one of the highest in the world to one of the lowest (1.5 children per family)."[652]

"In Latin America—which many Americans consider solidly Catholic—12,000 people leave the faith every day."[653] "In Latin America evangelical conversions within Christianity are transforming bad Catholics into good Protestants. ...Christian missionary traffic has gone into reverse gear."[654]

Mass attendance in Australia has dropped from 50% to 17% since Vatican II. Argentina claims that 84% of its population is Catholic, but a 2002 Gallup poll found "only 24% attended Mass at least once a week; another 40% went to Church between once a month and once a year; and 34% attended Mass "rarely" or "never."[655]

"It has been almost 100 years since Hilaire Belloc pronounced of Catholicism: 'Europe is the faith and the faith is Europe.' "[656] This is surely not the case today. " 'Where religion is concerned,' a European writer says, the attitudes of many have passed 'from incredulity and distaste to something colder: the absence of any sort of interest or engagement.' "[657]

The tremendous decline in Mass attendance, the loss of vocations and the disregard of Catholic moral teaching in Ireland is staggering. St. Patrick's work is being eroded in spite of the fact that 88.4% of the Irish call themselves Catholic.

---

[651] *Catholic,* January / February 1998.
[652] *Our Sunday Visitor,* August 9, 1998.
[653] *National Catholic Register,* June 23, 2002, p. 15.
[654] *Insight,* August 26, 2002, "Is Europe Losing Its Faith?," by John O'Sullivan.
[655] *Catholic World Report,* April, 2003, "Hunger, Physical and Moral," by Marco Navas.
[656] *Insight,* August 26, 2002.
[657] *Our Sunday Visitor,* August 25, 2002, "Why Europe is no longer 'the faith,' " by Russell Shaw.

According to census figures, the number of people who said they had no faith increased from 66,000 to 140,000 between 2002 and 2003.

> Since Vatican II, Ireland has experienced a major decline in weekly Mass attendance. "In the 1960's, more than 90% of the population attended weekly Mass."[658] "The figure dropped from 87% in 1981 to 60% in 1998."[659] A poll taken by Ireland's state broadcaster-RTE in September 2003 found that "only half of the Catholics in Ireland attend Mass weekly."[660]

So much for the fallacy that the changes were enacted and the liturgy put into the vernacular in order to draw more people to church. Jonathan Luxmoore relates that "in 2000, only 14% of the 18-24 age group saw Mass attendance as 'important,' while only one in five Catholics claimed to follow Church teachings when making 'serious moral decisions.'[661] Many Irish Catholics are losing their faith: "38% do not believe that the pope is infallible, 13% do not believe in Mary's perpetual virginity, 10% do not believe in transubstantiation, and 5% do not believe that Jesus is the Son of God."[662]

The article "Is Europe Losing Its Faith?" written by John O'Sullivan, Editor in Chief of United Press International (UPI), gives shocking statistics on current Mass attendance: "Missionaries are certainly needed in Western Europe. Regular church attendance there has sunk to single digits—7% for most Christian denominations in Britain, even lower in France and Germany. In Holland and Belgium, Mass attendance rates are around 3%."[663] "Only about 23% of Italians regularly attend Mass; 60% never go to confession."[664]

"Close to 85% of Spaniards claim to be Catholics, but more than 40.3% go to church only for weddings, funerals or some other special occasion, according to a new study."[665] According to a survey conducted by the Sociological Research Center, only 21% of Spaniards attend church services on Sundays and Holy Days.

---

[658] *The Catholic World Report,* February 2000.
[659] *Our Sunday Visitor,* September 29, 2002, "Who'll minister to Ireland's Catholics?"
[660] *Catholic World Report,* November 2003, p. 13.
[661] *Our Sunday Visitor,* September 29, 2002.
[662] *Catholic World Report,* November 2003, p. 13.
[663] *Insight,* August 26, 2002.
[664] 1995 poll for the Italian Bishops' Conference. Carl Bernstein, *His Holiness,* p. 512.
[665] *National Catholic Register,* May 20, 2000.

Cardinal Cormac Murphy-O'Connor confirmed the sad state of affairs in England when he told London's *Daily Telegraph* on January 20, 2003 that "after 1,500 years of Christianity, Britain has become largely a pagan country in the course of only 50. The cardinal, who leads the [modern] Catholic Church in England and Wales, said Britons faced a religious vacuum in which people are willing to believe virtually anything—except in Christ."[666] "In England the number of Catholics attending Mass is declining by 50,000 a year. If that continues, Catholicism will be extinct in 30 years."[667]

In Catholic schools throughout England and Wales, the majority of pupils and their parents no longer go to Mass. This has been the case for some time, and the problem shows no sign of going away. Whereas in the 1970s, most pupils in any given class would attend Sunday Mass on a regular basis, the opposite is true of children attending Catholic schools today. These days only a minority of pupils will go to church on a regular basis and an even smaller group will know the basic tenets of their faith.[668] Of pupils in Catholic schools here [the author is writing from Scotland], 90% lapse from religious practice before leaving.[669]

Catholic Priests in America[670]

1967	2003
59,193	44,487

Shortage of Priests in the United States

According to the November 20, 1998 issue of the *Detroit Free Press*, the Motor City has experienced tremendous change during the past 30 years:

- More than 30 parishes have closed.
- There are approximately half as many priests in Detroit as there had been 30 years ago.
- There are 24 priests who are 70 years old or older running parishes.
- The average age of diocesan priests assigned to parishes is 53.

---

[666] *National Catholic Register*, February 2, 2003, p. 6.
[667] *The Spectator*, December 14, 2002, "Is the Pope Catholic?," by Gerald Warner.
[668] *Catholic World Report*, April 2003, "Grim Future Prospects," by Tara Holmes.
[669] *The Spectator*, December 14, 2002, "Is the Pope Catholic?,' by Gerald Warner.
[670] Statistics given in this chapter are taken from *1961, 1963, 1965, 1967, 1968, 1969, 1970, 1972, 1990, 1999 National Catholic Almanac.* Felician Foy, O.F.M., and the *2002, 2003 and 2004 Our Sunday Visitor's Catholic Almanac,* Matthew Bunson.

Conditions have dramatically worsened in the U.S. since Vatican II according to Peter Steinfel's book, *A People Adrift:*

> In 1965, the average age of diocesan priests was 46. In 2002, it was almost 60. …In 1965, there was one priest for approximately every 800 Catholics. In 2002, there was one priest for every 1,400 Catholics. Because priests are aging, there is now one non-retired priest for approximately 1,900 Catholics."[671]

Bishop Banks of Green Bay, Wisconsin lamented today's priest shortage:

> [He] projected that by 2005 only 20 to 25 of his 198 parishes would be 'independent,' that is, having a pastor who was not shared with other parishes. These independent parishes are expected to have no fewer than 4,000 households each. In 2000, 102 parishes were sharing pastors and in some places a priest was pastor of as many as six parishes.[672]

Greg Erlandson's article entitled "The Forgotten Crisis" sheds new light on an emerging crisis in the Postconciliar Church:

> Do you expect a priest to celebrate your funeral Mass? Or preside at the marriages of your children or the baptisms of your grandchildren? Do you expect Sunday Mass always to be available at your parish church? Don't.
>
> While the Church in the United States has been fixed on scandals and media exposés, a crisis far more wide-ranging and far less amenable to solution is looming. Within the next several years, priests in the last great wave of vocations will be reaching retirement age. The steady decline will become precipitous, and the number of new ordinations will be not enough to staunch the decline. …Add to this fact that 59% of priests are over 55, as opposed to 26% of the laity, and there is an ominous picture of the tsunami [tidal wave] about to hit in most U.S. dioceses.[673]
>
> More than 3,300 U.S. parishes [out of 19,000] are led by administrators who are not priests[674] and about 2,400 are forced to share a pastor. Some 13% of dioceses report closing parishes because there is no pastor to staff them.[675]

---

[671] p. 29.
[672] Michael Rose, *Good Bye Good Men,* p. 212.
[673] *Our Sunday Visitor,* September 1, 2002.
[674] *National Catholic Reporter,* October 17, 2003, "Just how bad is it?, by Joe Feuerherd.
[675] David Gibson, *The Coming Catholic Church,* p. 56.

What happened to the vocations? Gone! Why? Because the concept of the priesthood itself has changed. With the introduction of the Novus Ordo and extraordinary eucharistic ministers, lay persons were permitted to serve as lectors and distribute communion. Permanent deacons could marry and baptize people. Why make a commitment to the priesthood when you can do all these things as a lay person and have the best of both worlds?[676]

According to David Gibson "Priestly ordinations have been dropping at a rate of 7% per decade."[677] The December 20, 2001 issue of *USA Today* reported there are 20% fewer priests than in 1965. Priests are aging and there are few replacements. One fourth are over age 70.[678] "More priests are over 90 than under 30 and 20% of parishes have no resident priest."[679]

The disheartening situation only worsens with time. "…By 2010 the number of active diocesan clergy (just over 15,000) will be less than the country's 19,000 parishes …even as seminaries graduate only one new priest for every three clerics… who retire, die or resign."[680]

"Among the 110,000 married priests worldwide, there are over 20,000 married priests in this country—or, to put it into perspective, one out of every three priests in the United States is married."[681] These "fallen away" priests forsook the priesthood in order to get married.

The statistics speak for themselves

Seminaries in America

1962	2003
454	213

Seminarians in America

1962	2003
46,189	4,522

Academic weaknesses in seminaries result in priests who are ill-equipped to teach and preach the Faith effectively and may even lead those priests to

---

[676] *Reign of Mary,* Vol. 33, No. 108, "I Will Put Enmities Between Thee and the Woman," by Bishop Mark Pivarunas, CMRI.
[677] *The Coming Catholic Church,* p. 154.
[678] See ABC News.com, April 4, 2002, "The Preaching Life," by Geraldine Sealey.
[679] *Time,* April 1, 2002, "Can the Church be Saved?," by Hanna McGeary.
[680] *Inside the Vatican,* January 2003, p. 31, Pat Buchanan's list of "grim statistics of Catholicism's decline in the United States."
[681] William Bausch, *Brave New Church,* pp. 208-209.

embrace heterodoxy or dissent. But the consequences of weaknesses in a seminary's formational program are even more serious. Problems in this area can keep the seminarian from developing the virtues and dispositions that will be absolutely necessary for him to function (and even survive) as a priest.[682]

Shortage of Priests Worldwide

"In Latin America, ...as many as one in every four priests leaves the priesthood, mostly to get married. ...To compound the problem, there are fewer and fewer seminarians; this is true in all of the Western world. In Canada, for example, there were 445 seminarians 20 years ago. Today, there are 48."[683]

Things are no better in Europe. "In 1944 there were 178 ordinations to the priesthood in England and Wales. The number rose to 230 by 1964, but in 1999 ordinations had plunged to 43, while 121 priests died the same year; that is three deaths for every ordination. This is not a crisis but a catastrophe. There will soon be only two seminaries in England in place of the five before Vatican II."[684]

"With seven times as many priests dying as being ordained each year, France's Catholic clergy has dropped from 45,000 in 1945 to 15,000 today and could plummet to 5,000 over the next decade."[685]

The August 9, 1996 issue of the *National Catholic Reporter* carried some shocking news concerning the Church in Italy: "Vocatio, the organization of Italian married priests, says one third of Italy's practicing priests are involved with women, *The European Magazine* reported in July. Vocatio also says up to 10,000 of Italy's 57,000 priests have left the ministry and are married."

"In Spain, where 41% of priests are past retirement age, almost half the Church's 68 Catholic dioceses had no seminary admissions this year, Church sources reported."[686] "In the past 50 years, the number of seminarians in Spain has dropped from 7,052 to 1,797."[687]

---

[682] *Crisis,* May 2003, "What's Wrong With Our Seminaries?," by Rev. Robert Johansen.
[683] William Bausch, *Brave New Church,* pp. 93-94.
[684] Michael Davies, *Una Voce—Buffalo,* February 2003, "The Church in Collapse."
[685] *Our Sunday Visitor,* July 6, 2003, "Eldest daughter' still desperately seeks faith," by Jonathan Luxmoore.
[686] *Our Sunday Visitor,* May 11, 2003, "East trumps West in Europe's seminaries."
[687] *Catholic,* April 2003.

In Switzerland, zero admissions were reported for the first time at seminaries in Geneva, Fribourg, Lausanne and Sion... In France, where 111 priests were ordained for 75 Catholic dioceses in June [2002], seminary admissions fell from 1,210 in 1991 to 927 in 2001.

Meanwhile, in predominantly Catholic Belgium, where seminary enrollments have fallen by half in five years, just 26, mostly foreign, seminarians began studies last October, said the Le Soir daily. ...In Lithuania ...a third of Catholic parishes still lack resident pastors.[688] Today only a few more than 200 men from dioceses in England and Wales are training to be parish priests.[689]

In Ireland "in 1965, 282 men were ordained as diocesan priests, and 377 more into religious orders. Today, those numbers stand at around 50 and 30, respectively."[690] "Clergy are roughly half those of the mid-1960's."[691]

St. Patrick's College was the seventh seminary to recently close in Ireland. "In the 1960s, its seminary had 130 students but was reduced to two or three a year by the 1990s...—leaving the Pontifical University of Maynooth as Ireland's only college still training priests. Maynooth, which boasted up to 600 students in the 1960s, now has approximately 110."[692]

Religious Orders in America

For religious orders in America, the end is in sight. In 1965, 3,559 young men were studying to become Jesuit priests. In 2000, the figure was 389. With the Christian Brothers, the situation is even more dire. Their number has shrunk by two-thirds, with the number of seminarians falling 99%. In 1965, there were 912 seminarians in the Christian Brothers. In 2000, there were only seven.

The number of young men studying to become Franciscan and Redemptorist priests fell from 3,379 in 1965 to 84 in 2000.[693]

---

[688] *Our Sunday Visitor,* May 11, 2003.
[689] *Catholic World Report,* August / September 2003, "Who Wants Priestless Parishes?," by Tara Holmes.
[690] *Our Sunday Visitor,* September 29, 2002, "Who'll minister to Ireland's Catholics?," by Jonathan Luxmoore.
[691] *Our Sunday Visitor,* September 29, 2002.
[692] *Our Sunday Visitor,* September 29, 2002.
[693] *Conservative Focus: Church & State,* December 18, 2002, p. 17, "An index of Catholicism's decline," by Pat Buchanan.

Religious Sisters (Nuns) in America

Ann Carey, in her book *Sisters in Crisis,* tells the important role Religious Women have played in the Catholic Church in America:

> Catholic sisters have been the backbone of the Catholic Church in the United States for more than one hundred fifty years. Sisters literally built the parochial school system as well as the Catholic health care and social service systems.
>
> Sisters helped Catholic dioceses and parishes spread the Catholic faith to the unchurched while at the same time ministering to the spiritual needs of the Catholic people. Perhaps most importantly, sisters have dedicated their lives to giving visible witness to the transcendence of God and to the spiritual aspect of our humanity.[694]
>
> Sisters have nearly disappeared from many Catholic institutions, and some of the sisters who are still visible seem to be very angry with the Catholic Church in general and with the male hierarchy in particular. In many orders, the sisters themselves seem to be divided about how religious life should be lived, as some wear religious garb and continue to work in Catholic institutions, while other sisters in the same order live alone in apartments and work in secular occupations.[695]

There has been a tremendous decline in Religious Sisters since Vatican II:

1964	2003
180,015	74,698[696]

In 1965, there were 104,000 teaching nuns.[697] In 2003, there are only 7,389.

Women Religious, who once were revered as models of deep spirituality and Christian virtue, now have a reputation as the most rebellious group within the Church. The names of sisters are prominent in organizations which challenge the Church on issues such as abortion rights, women's ordination, and internal authority structures of the Church. In many orders of women Religious, sisters no longer live together, pray together, or work together. Sisters, who once were

---

[694] p. 7.
[695] Ann Carey, *Sisters in Crisis,* p. 7.
[696] "…their average age is 69. There are 6,000 Sisters of Mercy, but only 240 are under the age of 45." *Our Sunday Visitor,* February 9, 2003, "Who is the weaker sex?" by Amy Welborn.
[697] *Conservative Focus: Church & State,* December 18, 2002.

the backbone of Catholic institutions, have left those institutions in growing numbers to pursue 'ministries' in the secular sphere that have little to do with the Church or the vows they profess as consecrated women.

As a result, numerous Catholic institutions have closed because of lack of personnel even as the Catholic population has grown. ...During that time frame, [1965-1996] nearly half of all Catholic grade and high schools closed, and many Catholic health care institutions were secularized or forced to close. Also in the years between 1965 and 1996, the number of sisters declined by half, and many of the communities of women Religious have unraveled to the point that their survival is questionable, for the median age in many orders has soared into the seventies because young women are not attracted to the sisters' new self-styled way of life.[698]

Catholic Schools in the United States

Between 1900 and 1920, the number of Catholic elementary schools in the country had doubled to more than 6,500. Catholic school enrollment reached an all-time high of 5.3 million students in 1960... In 1965, the parish schools mirrored the demographics of Catholic schools across the country, in which 95% of teachers and staff belonged to Catholic [religious] orders. 'There was the sister with a piece of chalk in front of a class of 60 kids. She didn't earn a salary,' says Professor Joseph O'Keefe of Boston College.[699]

The Catholic Church in the United States built "the largest system of Catholic schools in the world."[700] In 1964, one half of Catholic children attended Catholic schools.[701] "...There have been dramatic changes in Catholic schools, students and teachers. There are fewer Catholic schools, fewer students in these schools (especially in seminaries and in diocesan and parochial schools), and fewer teachers who are priests, brothers, sisters or scholastics."[702]

"A recent report by the National Catholic Educational Association found that 140 Catholic schools consolidated or closed last year, the majority in cities. Over

---

[698] Ann Carey, *Sisters in Crisis,* pp. 311-312.
[699] *U.S. News & World Report,* May 5, 2003, "Echoes of a Scandal," by Anna Mulrine.
[700] Herbert Muller, *Religious Freedom in the Modern World,* p. 79.
[701] See Herbert Schneider, *Religion in 20th Century America,* p. 44.
[702] *The Tidings,* August 16, 2002, "Dramatic changes in Catholic school totals."

the past decade, 394 Catholic schools, most built to serve Irish, Italian and Polish immigrant communities, have closed."[703]

U.S. Catholic Schools

	1962	2003
Elementary Schools	10,630	7,142
Students	4,451,893	1,873,217
High Schools	1,435	1,376
Students	945,785	686,651
Colleges and Universities	278	237

Peter Steinfels in his book *A People Adrift* states: "Between 1965 and 2002, the number of sisters, brothers and priests teaching in these schools declined from 114,000 to 9,000. Today, almost 95% of the teaching staff are laypeople, Catholic and non-Catholic."[704]

The decline of vocations is a worldwide crisis. The number of Sisters in Germany has dropped from 82,166 in 1970 to 41,257 in 1998. Canada has seen a similar decline from 45,761 in 1970 to 25,716 in 1998.[705]

Catholic Marriages in America

1971	2003
416,924	241,727

"Nationwide, according to Purdue University sociologist James Davidson, the number of marriages in general declined 9% from 1975 to 1995. Church-sanctioned marriages dropped by 23% during that same period."[706]

Marriage Annulments in America

"From 1952-1956 only 392 annulments were granted worldwide."[707] Today, nearly 50,000 marriage annulments are granted in the United States and "less than 10% of annulment applications are denied."[708] According to John Allen, Jr., Rome correspondent for the *National Catholic Reporter*, "Americans compose

---

[703] *U.S. News & World Report,* May 5, 2003.
[704] Peter Steinfels, *A People Adrift,* p. 212.
[705] See Kenneth Jones, *Index of Leading Catholic Indicators,* p. 108.
[706] *National Catholic Register,* March 2, 2003, "Cohabitation Seen as Reason for Sharp Decline in Church Marriages," p. 3.
[707] F. Sheed, *The Nullity of Marriage,* p. 127.
[708] *The Detroit News,* November 9, 2003, "Church split over ending of marriages," by David Crary of the Associated Press.

only 6% of the world's Catholics but are granted 80% of the annulments."[709] The April 20th issue of *The Washington Post* gave the following shocking statistics: "Half of all Catholic marriages now end in divorce, the same as the general population." William Donohue, president of the Catholic League said: "There's hardly a Catholic family that doesn't have someone in it who's divorced."[710]

Marriage Annulments in America

1968	2000
450	49,069

"Birthrates in Europe are so low—especially in Spain, Portugal, and Italy, countries that traditionally have been Catholic—that they are now below replacement level. ...Divorce rates continue to climb (one out of every three marriages in Europe fails)."[711] "The French scourge, however, is that it has the highest out-of-wedlock birthrate of any European nation. 'The problem with France is marriage,' Father Suaudeau said. 'People live together and have children. But they are not getting married.' "[712]

Family Life in the United States

John Paul II marked the 40th anniversary of the Second Vatican Council by commenting that its documents are a 'secure compass' for modern Catholics. On the contrary, if we take a look at the state of the Catholic family in the United States it becomes apparent that things have only worsened after Vatican II.

> In fact, surveys show that the last 40 years have shown a decline in happiness among all married people, according to the National Marriage Project, a think tank at Rutgers University in Piscataway, N.J.
>
> Dave Popenoe, Rutgers professor of sociology and co-director of the project, says marriage has dissolved from a respected social institution upheld by economic, legal and religious components to a private agreement based on feelings and emotions.[713]

---

[709] *National Catholic Reporter,* November 22, 2002.
[710] *The Oakland Press,* November 8, 2003, "Annulment common but unpopular with conservatives and liberals," by David Crary.
[711] *National Catholic Reporter,* January 5, 2001, "Real disregards ideal," by John Allen, Jr.
[712] *National Catholic Register,* December 15, 2002.
[713] *National Catholic Register,* May 11, 2003, "Married-and Happy?" by Barb Ernster.

The report by the Chicago's National Opinion Research Center is blunt in its documentation of the rapid disintegration of family life in the last 25 years.

- The most common living arrangement today is two unmarried adults with no children; nearly one-third—32%—of all United States households are composed that way, as compared with 16% in 1972.
- Just 51% of all children live with their two natural parents compared with 73% two decades ago.
- More than 18% of U.S. children live in single-parent homes compared with 5% in 1972.
- Only 26% of United States households are made of married couples with children; in 1972, the figure was 45%, and 'married with children' was the most common living arrangement for adults.
- Today, 56% of adults are married; in 1972, the number was 75%.

That these figures have lost their shock value is only another sign that the family, as it has been known in Western civilization for two millennia, is fast becoming a thing of the past.

…The effects of the devastated family on individuals, especially children, are immense. We can't begin to calculate the future social toll that will result from a generation of children growing up in a household that doesn't include their two original parents.[714]

Double Standard

Many American Catholics follow a double standard; their faith does not seem to influence their daily lives, their decision-making process or moral practices. David Kelley says: "The most striking thing to me about American Christians is that so few of them seem to feel any conflict between their religious beliefs and the secular values that are so clearly part of American culture."[715] Consider the many divorced Catholics who speedily receive annulments, remarry and are in good standing with the Postconciliar Church.

Though the number of U.S. Catholics has risen by 20 million since 1965, [Kenneth] Jones' statistics show that the power of Catholic belief and devotion to the faith are not nearly what they were.

---

[714] *Our Sunday Visitor,* December 12, 1999, "The Kids Aren't All Right."
[715] *Crisis,* May 2002, "Christianity from the Outside," by Eve Tushnet.

...Only 10% of lay religious teachers now accept church teaching on contraception. Fifty-three percent believe a Catholic can have an abortion and remain a good Catholic. Sixty-five percent believe that Catholics may divorce and remarry. Seventy-seven percent believe one can be a good Catholic without going to Mass on Sundays. By one *New York Times* poll, 70% of all Catholics in the age group 18 to 44 believe the Eucharist is merely a 'symbolic reminder' of Jesus.[716]

The Abortion Issue

One of the greatest tragedies of modern times is the staggering number of abortions and their acceptance by so many people. In the United States alone, 1.4 million helpless, innocent babies are murdered each year by means of abortion. If this number is extended over a 10-year period it is "the equivalent of butchering every man, woman and child in Los Angeles."[717] According to Connecticut attorney Albert Hilburger, "one in four women of childbearing age in the United States has had an abortion."[718] "America currently has the most permissive abortion laws in the world. More than a million abortions take place every year—and have since 1973—right up to through the ninth month of pregnancy."[719]

The irrationality of abortion is exposed in the October 2003 issue of *Reader's Digest* by a Boston Ob-Gyn, Dr. Eric Keroack: "A fetus is considered so precious that we spare no expense to save its life; yet it's also so worthless that it can be legally disposed of."

Since the legalization of abortion on January 22, 1973 through 2002, there have been 43,358,592 abortions in the United States.[720] "Forty million. There isn't a country in the world with an army that big. Many don't have a population that big."[721]

---

[716] *Conservative Focus: Church & State,* December 18, 2002, p. 17, "An index of Catholicism's decline," by Pat Buchanan.
[717] *Insight,* October 15, 2002.
[718] *National Catholic Reporter,* March 23, 2003, "Lies of Abortion Meet Their Match," by Connie Pilsner.
[719] *National Catholic Reporter,* March 23, 2003, "Popes, Presidents and Power," by J. Zmirak.
[720] *National Right to Life News,* January 2003.
[721] Peggy Noonan, *Catholic World Report,* March 2003, "The Next Roe," p. 58.

Sadly, abortion is not just an American tragedy. The annual figure of abortions performed throughout the world is appalling. According to Dr. Marie Peeters Ney, "60 million abortions occur worldwide yearly."[722]

> It is evident that Catholicism cannot have a future without Catholics. The birthrate necessary for a nation to reproduce itself is 2.2 children per couple. In Europe as a whole it is 1.4; in France 1.7 (the highest birthrate in Europe), in England 1.64, ...Germany with a birthrate of 1.3 kills 350,000 babies each year by abortion, filling more coffins than cots.[723]

Italy and Ireland had the European Union's lowest divorce rate, but birth rates also ranked among the lowest. "The fact that Italy has the lowest birth rate in the world—1.2 children per couple—comes as a shock to many. ...There are 530,000 births in Italy per year and 130,000 abortions."[724]

In Russia, conditions are much worse: "For every baby born, two are aborted. Official statistics also reveal that 60% of first pregnancies end in abortion. After decades of being an officially atheistic state, few Russians believe abortion is morally wrong."[725] As a result, there were 1.7 million abortions in 2002 and Russia's population is dropping by 700,000 annually.

Since the Second Vatican Council, a permissive attitude has dominated both church and society regarding the abortion issue. The New Code of Canon Law still retains the excommunication attached to abortion.[726] Nevertheless, a proportionately high percentage of Catholics have abortions and many "Catholic" politicians maintain a strong pro-choice or pro-abortion platform.

Numerous "Catholic" politicians consistently promote abortion in spite of a recent Vatican document that says: "Those who are directly involved in lawmaking bodies have a grave and clear obligation to oppose any law that attacks human life."[727]

---

[722] *National Catholic Reporter,* January 16, 1998.
[723] *Catholic World Report,* March 2003.
[724] *National Catholic Register,* December 15, 2002, "Once Family-Oriented, Italians Choosing to Have Fewer Babies," by Sabrina Arena Ferrisi.
[725] *Our Sunday Visitor,* September 21, 2003, "Russia: Where have all the babies gone?"
[726] See Canon 1398, 1983 Code.
[727] Congregation of the Faith's: *Doctrinal Note on Some Questions Regarding the Participation of Catholics in Political Life,* November 24, 2002.

"The note mentions specifically that Catholics cannot support legislation endorsing abortion, divorce, same-sex marriage, scientific research involving the destruction of embryos or 'modern forms of slavery'—defined as prostitution, drug addiction and the trafficking of humans."[728] Despite the strong rhetoric, there is no penalty of excommunication for politicians who endorse these evils, so the *status quo* will likely be maintained.

M. Rita Patterson asks some serious questions regarding the large number of pro choice (pro abortion) "Catholic" politicians who would lobby to save whales but allow the murder of unborn children: "Why is it that these *Catholics* are rarely contradicted and never seem to be held accountable to the truth? How long will we tolerate those priests and bishops who implicitly or explicitly support this or that heresy? What is so difficult to understand?"[729]

Loss of Faith Among Young Adults in America

"According to an April 2002 ABC News/BeliefNetpoll, 11% of American Catholics said they may leave the Church in the next few years."[730] The majority of young Catholic adults in the Postconciliar Church do not practice their faith. This is verified in a recent survey of young adult Catholics between the ages of 18-39. The study shows:

> About 30% of today's young adult Catholics remain Catholic and religiously active during their teenage years and their 20s. These young adults are actively involved in many youth programs and campus ministries. They also are likely to be the backbone of their parishes and dioceses in the years ahead.
>
> But what happens to the other 70%?
>
> Three to four percent drop out of religion altogether. Another six to eight percent leave the Catholic Church for some other faith. ...By far, the largest number of young adults (about 60%) continue to think of themselves as Catholic but become religiously inactive. On average, they drift into religious inactivity when they are 20 years old. ...About half of this 60% never returns to any

---

[728] *Our Sunday Visitor,* Feb. 2, 2003, "Rome: Catholic pols must be 'morally coherent,'" by Andrea Kirk.
[729] Letter to the Editor, *Our Sunday Visitor,* October 6, 2002.
[730] David Gibson, *The Coming Catholic Church,* p. 83.

church. However, the other half does bounce back and in over 80% of the cases, it is to the Catholic Church.[731]

Are Catholic Colleges Leading Students Astray?[732]

An article written by Patrick Reilly in the March 2003 issue of the *Catholic World Report* describes the declining morals and theological dissent of Catholic colleges in America, as shown in a report conducted by HERI.

A survey of students at 38 Catholic colleges—including major universities like Creighton, Loyola Marymount, Notre Dame, and St. John's of New York—reveal that graduating seniors are predominantly pro-abortion, approve of 'homosexual marriage,' and only occasionally pray or attend religious services. Nine percent of Catholic students abandon their faith before graduation.

The annual survey conducted by the Higher Education Research Institute (HERI) at the University of California—Los Angeles [UCLA], is important because it provides the only useful data on Catholic colleges that cuts across institutions. There simply isn't any other publicly available assessment of the student experience for the 223 Catholic colleges in the United States. ...

- In 1997, 45% of incoming freshmen at Catholic colleges said they support keeping abortion legal, with 55% opposed. Four years later, the same students were 57% pro-abortion, 43% pro-life. Similarly, students' support for legalizing homosexual 'marriages' increased from 55 to 71%. Approval of casual sex increased from 30 to 49%.
- In 1997, more than two-thirds of Catholic freshmen at Catholic colleges attended religious services frequently, while the remaining third attended occasionally. By senior year, 13% stopped attending services altogether, and nearly half attended only occasionally.
- Similarly, only 37% of seniors at Catholic colleges said they prayed or meditated more than one hour a week. Almost one-third of the students reported that they do not pray at all.[733]

---

[731] Survey results from *Young Catholic Adults* as recorded in *The Tidings*, July 12, 2002, "How many young adults leave the church and why?" by James Davidson.

[732] "A nationwide survey raises concerns about the impact that American colleges have on the faith and morals of Catholic students," *Catholic World Report*, March 2003.

[733] pp. 38-39.

A recent University of California-Los Angeles Higher Education Research Institute survey suggested Catholic colleges, far from instilling the faith in students, are just as likely to cause students to lose their faith. That scares parents who don't want to pay for a Catholic education only to see their child taught that the faith isn't true.[734]

Suicides

Suicide has been traditionally held as a form of cowardice and despair. "It was thus condemned by early Church Councils and Church Fathers—[St.] Basil, [St.] Clement of Alexandria, Tertullian, [St.] Augustine."[735]

Teen suicide has been a national crisis for many years, but many people are unaware of the fact that "the suicide rate among seniors is actually 50% higher than among the nation as a whole."[736] The vast number of suicides by senior citizens suggests a tremendous lack of faith and a disbelief in an afterlife.

"Older couples account for about 20% of murder-suicides, or as many as 500 a year. But in senior-heavy Florida, the percentage of murder-suicides is double the national average."[737] "Suicide rates among Quebec youths have soared to one of the highest of any region in North America."[738]

Conclusion

Is the world better or worse since Vatican II? Are Catholic marriages stronger or weaker? Are the Ten Commandments being observed and moral standards upheld or are they both disregarded? Does fervor reign or general apathy? Do Catholic schools lead to a deeper faith or to a loss of faith? Are these schools turning out exemplary Catholics and fostering numerous religious vocations? You be the judge: Do these statistics reflect good fruits from a good tree or bad fruits from a bad tree?

---

[734] *National Catholic Register,* July 6, 2003, "Notre Dame to Parents: We Won't Tell," by Tim Drake.
[735] *Our Sunday Visitor,* May 14, 1996.
[736] "There were 5,306 suicides among people 65 and older in 2000 (latest figure available). 18% of the nation's 29,350 total." *USA Today,* February 20, 2003, "Senior suicides too increase as U.S. ages," by Deborah Sharp.
[737] *USA Today,* February 20, 2003.
[738] *Our Sunday Visitor,* August 9, 1998.

F. The Third Secret of Fatima

Our Lady appeared to three shepherd children (Lucia dos Santos and Francisco and Jacinta Marto) in Fatima, Portugal in 1917. During her six apparitions, the Blessed Virgin Mary told Catholics to amend their lives and avert God's chastisement through prayer and penance. She also revealed three secrets to the children. The first secret applies to the vision of Hell which the children saw on July 13, 1917. In her second secret, she disclosed to them the threat of war and Communism and the importance of devotion to the Immaculate Heart of Mary. Only the first two parts of the Secret of Fatima were revealed in 1941. Francisco and Jacinta died shortly after the apparitions and Lucia entered a convent.

Sr. Lucia dos Santos received permission from Heaven to disclose the first two parts of the Secret of Fatima. This permission, however, did not apply to the third part of the secret. On July 26, 1941 the bishop of Leiria asked Sr. Lucia to put in writing all that she thought suitable to reveal. Sr. Lucia obediently replied by sending a document to the bishop on August 31, 1941.

"Is there any explanation why these could not have been revealed earlier? Lucia, in her memoirs, says that of the second part at least, had she revealed them she would have been regarded as a prophetess and it was Our Lord's will that they be revealed only at that time."[739]

During an interview with several historians in 1946, Sr. Lucia stated:

I think that in 1917 He could have commanded me to speak, whereas He commanded me to keep silent, and His order has been confirmed by His representatives. I think then …that God did not want to make use of me except to remind the world of the necessity of avoiding sin and of making reparation for offense against God by prayer and penance.

Q. At what actual stage are we of the period mentioned in the secret?

A. I think that you are at the period when false doctrine shall propagate its errors throughout the world.[740]

---

[739] Vincent-Marie Goldstein, *A Fatima Catechism,* p. 25.
[740] Fr. V. Montes De Oca, C.S. Sp., *More About Fatima,* p. 56.

The Third Secret of Fatima, nevertheless, still remains hidden. It was written down by Sr. Lucia and sent to Pope Pius XII in 1957. When questioned in 1917 about the content of the Third Secret the three Fatima children replied, "Good for some, for others bad." During Jacinta's serious illness her mother asked if the secret was good or bad. "It is good for those who believe, Mother," Jacinta told her. "Believe in what?" "In God, Mother."[741]

In December, 1941, Sr. Lucia added the following words to the second secret of Fatima: "In Portugal, the dogma of the Faith will always be preserved." These words are believed to be the first words of the Third Secret. "If 'in Portugal, the dogma of the Faith will always be preserved,'... it can be clearly deduced from this that in other parts of the Church these dogmas are going to become obscure or even lost altogether."[742]

On February 4, 1946, Fr. Jongen questioned Sr. Lucia about the Third Secret of Fatima. "You have already made known two parts of the secret. When will the time arrive for the third part?" She replied, "I communicated the third part in a letter to the Bishop of Leiria, but it cannot be made known before 1960."[743]

Cardinal Ottaviani visited Sr. Lucia in Coimbra on May 17, 1955 and asked her, "Why wait until 1960?" She replied, "Because then it will seem clearer."[744]

Historians record that in the 1960's revolutionary changes occurred in religion, music, art, fashions and morality. Beginning in 1960, John XXIII gradually introduced significant changes to the Holy Sacrifice of the Mass that eventually led to the formation of the New Mass *(Novus Ordo Missae)*. Perhaps, Our Heavenly Mother chose to have her secret revealed in 1960 in order to forewarn Catholics of the dangers threatening the Church.

Even though the Third Secret of Fatima was to be revealed in 1960, this was not done. John XXIII read the secret, put it in a sealed envelope and had it taken to the secret archives of the Vatican. John XXIII further dismissed Our Lady's words by saying, "It does not concern my pontificate."[745]

---

[741] Costa Brochado, *Fatima in the Light of History,* p. 134.
[742] *La Verdad sobre el Secreto de Fatima,* p. 80.
[743] *Revue Mediatrice et Reine,* October 1946, pp. 110-112.
[744] *Doc. cath.* March 19, 1967, col. 542.
[745] Frere Michel de la Sainte Trinite, *Whole Truth About Fatima: The Third Secret,* p. 557.

The Portuguese news agency ANI (Agencia Nacional de Informacao) announced on February 8, 1960, "According to Vatican sources, the [Third] Secret of Fatima will never be disclosed."[746] John XXIII began implementing changes in the liturgy and the rest is history. Paul VI read the secret and ordered Cardinal Ottaviani to tell the world that it would not be revealed.

Many informed sources speculate that the Third Secret of Fatima describes a universal apostasy and loss of faith which would begin in approximately 1960. In his book *The Secret of Fatima,* Fr. Alonzo writes, "It is completely probable that the text [of the Third Secret] makes concrete references to the crisis of faith within the Church and the negligence of the pastors themselves."[747]

On September 16, 1970, Sr. Lucia wrote to Mother Martins:

> It is painful to see such a great disorientation and in so many persons who occupy places of responsibility... It is because the devil has succeeded in infiltrating evil under the cover of good and the blind are beginning to guide others, as the Lord tells us in His gospel, and souls are letting themselves be deceived. Gladly I sacrifice myself and offer my life to God for peace in His Church, for priests and for all consecrated souls, especially for those who are so deceived and misled.[748]

To someone who questioned her on the content of the Third Secret, Sr. Lucia replied, "It's in the Gospel and the Apocalypse. Read them."[749] "We even know that [Sr.] Lucy one day indicated chapters 8-13 of the Apocalypse."[750]

The Vatican refused to reveal the authentic secret of Fatima in 1960 because of its content. However, on June 26, 2000 it finally revealed "the secret." Officials produced a document which is obviously a counterfeit. For instance, Our Lady's words at Fatima are clear and concise while the new "secret" is vague and nebulous. Also, the Vatican version does not correspond harmoniously with the

---

[746] Fr. Martins dos Reis, *O Milagre do Sol e o Segredo de Fatima.*
[747] *Uma Vida,* pp. 380-382.
[748] *Uma Vida,* 377-379.
[749] Frere Michel de la Sainte Trinite, *The Whole Truth About Fatima: The Third Secret,* p. 788.
[750] de la Sainte Trinite, 33.

message of Fatima. It is worth noting that the Third Secret of Fatima which was fabricated by the Vatican contains nothing objectionable to the modern Church. After ignoring the Third Secret of Fatima as of no concern for 40 years, why bring up the document now, especially if its message is apparently of no great importance?

The Secret of La Salette

During her apparition to Maximin Giraud and Melanie Mathieu at La Salette, France on September 19, 1846, the Mother of God foretold that mankind would be severely punished for their sins. Our Lady wept over the prevalent desecration of Sundays and the widespread profanation of God's name.[751] After thorough examination by Church authorities, the apparition at La Salette was approved and declared worthy of belief:

> The Bishop [of Grenoble] ordered a thorough investigation of the apparition and the cures. After examining all the testimony and evidence, he satisfied himself that the appearance had been authentic. He founded the Missionaries of Our Lady of La Salette to carry out her command: 'You will make this known to all the people.' Pope Pius IX approved the devotion of La Salette. His successor, Leo XIII, built a great basilica on the mountain.
>
> Five years after the apparition, Pope Pius IX said he would like to know the secrets. The children agreed to write them provided they would be placed in sealed envelopes and delivered directly to the Pontiff.[752]

In his book, *The Holy Mountain of La Salette,* Bishop Ullathorne gives additional facts about the secret of La Salette:

> Seeing that the children were so determined not to deliver their secret open, as the Cardinal [Archbishop of Lyons] had intimated a wish they should, and that they were

---

[751] St. John Bosco "undertook to speak of it on every possible occasion. In 1850 he had published a pamphlet of which 30,000 copies were distributed. In it he told the story and dwelt on its meaning. To him it was clear that Our Lady asked reform of men's thinking, choosing, living." John Kennedy, *Light on the Mountain,* p. 167. St. John Vianney at first had his doubts, but eventually concluded that the apparition was authentic: "I have been represented as not believing in it. That boy [Maximin] and I did not understand each other. But I have asked heaven for signs to shore up my faith, and I have had them. I tell you, one can and one *must* believe in La Salette." Kennedy, 129. Also see Abbé Francis Trochu, *The Curé D'Ars,* pp. 385-387.

[752] Don Sharkey, *Madonna in Tears,* pp. 7-8.

as firmly resolved to give it to no one but the Pope, the Bishop of Grenoble appointed certain witnesses, respectable laymen as well as clergymen, to be present, while Maximin and Melanie wrote each their secrets. They were introduced into the same room, and were seated at separate tables.

Maximin put his head into his hands in an attitude of reflection, and then wrote his letter rapidly... So far only is positively known of it, that it is written in seven paragraphs, each of which is numbered, and that it begins with these words: *'Most Holy Father, on the 19th of September, 1846, a Lady appeared to me; they say it is the Blessed Virgin; you will judge whether it was by what follows.'* Whilst writing, Maximin asked how the word *Pontiff* was spelled.

It is said that Melanie betrayed much emotion whilst she wrote her letter, but was in no way embarrassed, and wrote rapidly. She suddenly stopped, and asked the meaning of the word *infallibly*. ...She also asked the orthography and meaning of the word *Antichrist*. The secret of Melanie is of considerably greater length than that of Maximin. They each sealed their letters themselves in the presence of the witnesses, and they were then sealed with the seal of the Bishop of Grenoble.[753]

...The Bishop of Grenoble deputed M. Rousselot, one of his Vicars-general, and M. Gerin, the Curé of his Cathedral, to convey the secrets to Rome. ...When they were presented to His Holiness, he took the sealed letters from their hands, opened them, and began to read that of Maximin. *'Here,'* he observed, *'is all the candor and simplicity of a child.'*

Then, that he might read the letters more easily, His Holiness went up to a window and opened the shutter. ...As he read the letter of Melanie, his lips became strongly compressed, and his face seemed moved with considerable emotion. *'These are scourges,'* he said, *'with which France is threatened, but she is not alone culpable. Germany, Italy, all Europe is culpable and merits chastisement. I have less to fear from open impiety than from indifference and human respect... It is not without reason that the Church is called militant...'*

On the following day they had an audience with Cardinal Fornari, at which [time] his Eminence said to the two envoys: 'I am terrified with these prodigies; we have

---

[753] pp. 120-121

everything that is needed in our religion for the conversion of sinners; and when Heaven employs such means, the evil must be very great.'

...After his return from Rome, M. Gerin said to Melanie, 'I know not what you have written to the Pope, but he appeared much affected by it.' ...It is Melanie's impression that, when the Apparition disappeared, the last looks of the Blessed Virgin were mournfully cast towards Rome.[754]

Cardinal Lambruschini, Prefect of the Sacred Congregation of Rites, said: 'I have known the fact of La Salette for a long time and as a bishop I believe it; as a bishop also I have preached it in my diocese of Porto and remarked that my sermons produced a deep impression. Besides, I know the shepherds' secrets. The Holy Father has communicated them to me.'[755]

The Holy See then addressed Bishop de Bruillard and told him "that he might do whatever he judged expedient with regard to La Salette."[756] Bishop de Bruillard gave his formal approval of the apparitions in a pastoral letter written on December 13, 1847: "We judge that the apparition of the Blessed Virgin to two cowherds on the 19th of September, 1846, on a mountain of the chain of the Alps, situated in the parish of La Salette, in the archpresbytery of Corps, *bears within itself all the characteristics of truth, and that the faithful have grounds for believing it indubitable and certain.*"[757]

Years later the Pope [Pius IX] said: "Do you wish to know the secret? This is it: 'Unless you do penance, you shall all perish.' "[758]

---

[754] pp. 124-126.
[755] James O'Reilly, *The Story of La Salette*, pp. 105-106.
[756] O'Reilly, 106.
[757] O'Reilly, 111.
[758] Don Sharkey, *Madonna in Tears*, p. 8.

G. The Rosary

The Blessed Virgin Mary gave the Rosary to St. Dominic in 1214 as a spiritual weapon to combat the Albigensian heresy and to rekindle the Catholic Faith. She told Blessed Alan de la Roche: "When you say the Rosary the angels rejoice, the Blessed Trinity delights in it, my Son finds joy in it too and I myself am happier than you can possibly guess. After the Holy Sacrifice of the Mass, there is nothing in the Church that I love as much as the Rosary."[759]

"The Rosary is the world's most popular prayer"[760] and has been prayed throughout the world for nearly eight centuries. It is a combination of vocal and mental prayer (meditation). As we meditate upon the lives of Jesus and Mary we recite vocal prayers which are counted on the Rosary beads. The Rosary is, according to Pope Pius XII, "A synthesis of the whole Gospel: meditation on the mysteries of the Lord, an evening sacrifice, a garland of roses, a hymn of praise, a family prayer, a compendium of Christian life, a sure pledge of heavenly favors, a defense while we await our expected salvation."[761]

In 1858, Our Lady of Lourdes appeared to St. Bernadette, bearing a Rosary. "…At Fatima, the Rosary was offered to men with much greater insistence than at Lourdes."[762] In 1917, Our Lady of Fatima, known as "the Lady of the Rosary," told Catholics to amend their lives and pray the Rosary in order to avert spiritual and temporal calamities. One of the visionaries, Sr. Lucia dos Santos, remarked:

> The Most Holy Virgin in these last times in which we live has given a new efficacy to the recitation of the Rosary to such an extent that there is no problem, no matter how difficult it is, whether temporal or above all, spiritual, in the personal life of each one of us, of our families, of the families of the world, or of the religious communities, or even of the life of peoples and nations that cannot be solved by the Rosary.
>
> There is no problem I tell you, no matter how difficult it is, that we cannot resolve by the prayer of the Holy Rosary. With the Holy Rosary, we will save

---

[759] St. Louis Marie de Montfort, *The Secret of the Rosary,* p. 120.
[760] According to author Kevin Johnson in *The Wanderer,* October 24, 2002.
[761] *Letter to Philippinas Insulas,* July 31, 1946.
[762] John Johnson, *The Rosary in Action,* p. 42.

ourselves. We will sanctify ourselves. We will console Our Lord and obtain the salvation of many souls.[763]

Meditation on the Mysteries of the Rosary

Meditation is the heart and soul of the Rosary. As we "say" the prayers of the Rosary—we "think" of the chief events in the lives of Jesus and Mary. In the Rosary, the prayers are counted on the beads, but through the beads there runs a chain—a chain of thought. As we say the words, we are supposed to think of the joys, sorrows and glories of Jesus and Mary. The ten Hail Marys in each decade of the Rosary simply measure the time we dwell on the mysteries or events in the life of Christ. Meditation on the mysteries of the Rosary can be compared to a talented musician singing at a piano. His hands are on the keys, his voice is on the notes, but his mind is on the spirit of the piece. As our fingers glide over the Rosary beads, our lips recite the prayers, but our mind and heart focus on the principal events in the life of Christ.

We learn and understand the chief mysteries of the Faith through the recitation of the Rosary. It strengthens our souls, confirms our faith and protects us from error. Through the Rosary the poor find help, those who grieve find comfort, those who are tempted find peace and those who are enslaved to sin have their bonds broken. The Rosary is an excellent means to grow in virtue and conquer sin. It is a remedy for evil and the source of many blessings.

The Rosary has a special efficacy to aid in living a Christian life, acquiring the spirit of prayer and avoiding the corrupting influence of the world. It is said that one cannot persevere in a habit of mortal sin and in the daily recitation of the Rosary: One must give up one or the other.

This prayer offers an easy way to impress the chief doctrines of Catholicism upon the mind. Many Catholics are so busy with the various activities of life that they wander into matters of little importance. Unless we frequently meditate on heavenly truths, the doctrines of Faith are gradually forgotten. Then, faith begins to grow weak and may even die.

Some people say, "I don't pray the Rosary because I don't get anything out of it." The reason they don't get anything out of it is that they don't put anything

---

[763] Frere Michel de la Trinite, *The Whole Truth About Fatima, Vol. I*, p. 508.

into it. For example, you cannot enjoy football if you have no knowledge of the game. In like manner, if you have a poor understanding of the Rosary you will find it tedious. The Rosary will become more appealing as you broaden your knowledge by reading *The Secret of the Rosary*[764] and studying the New Testament. Rosary meditation books and depictions of the mysteries will help you visualize the events of the Life, Death and Resurrection of Jesus Christ.

You will not get anything out of the Rosary if you do not pray it properly. It is really sad to see how astonishingly fast some people say the Rosary. Sometimes it is recited as quickly as possible just to get it finished. Everyone needs to break away from their duties for a few moments each day in order to spend time in intimate communication with God. Pope Pius XI wrote:

> We must not, then, despair at the sight of present evils, or even of greater that may come. We must pray to God with confidence, and take as our intermediary and patroness the Blessed Virgin, through whom it is His will we should have all. We must say her Rosary, and by meditation on its mysteries obtain the true, serene, perspective view of life, death, and eternity which they present. Especially the 'family Rosary' is to be maintained.[765]

The New Ecumenical Rosary

Catholics are familiar with the 15 mysteries of the Rosary given to us by the Blessed Virgin Mary: five joyful, five sorrowful and five glorious. Yet, even the Rosary was not immune to Vatican II's reckless spirit of innovation. John Paul II introduced the five "luminous" mysteries of the rosary on October 16, 2002: Jesus' baptism in the Jordan, the Marriage of Cana, Jesus' proclamation of the Kingdom of God, the Transfiguration and the institution of the Eucharist.[766]

John Paul II's document is conspicuous for what it fails to say:

> There is no mention of St. Dominic ...nor is there any mention of the heavenly origin of the Rosary. There is plenty of talk of ecclesial communities and the like, but we do not encounter the word *Catholics* even once.[767]

---

[764] Written by St. Louis Marie de Montfort.
[765] *Ingravescentibus malis,* September 29, 1937.
[766] Apostolic letter *Rosarium Virginis Mariae.*
[767] James DePiante, *The Catholic Voice,* "Shedding More Light on the Mysterious Mysteries—Part II, p. 11.

In his encyclical *On the Rosary,* John Paul II wrote: "Perhaps, too, there are some who fear that the Rosary is somehow unecumenical because of its distinctly Marian character. ...If properly revitalized, the Rosary is an aid and certainly not a hindrance to ecumenism!" He further claimed that without his luminous mysteries "...there is a risk that the Rosary will not only fail to produce the intended spiritual effects, but even that the beads, with which it is usually said, could come to be regarded as some kind of amulet or magic object, thereby radically distorting their meaning and function."[768]

Numerous saints, popes, prelates, clergy, laity including famous statesmen, scientists, inventors and common folk have prayed the Rosary for centuries. Why would the absence of the luminous mysteries for the past eight centuries cause the Rosary to be less effective? Catholics do not use rosaries as some sort of talisman or good luck charm, but as blessed sacramentals. Why does John Paul II put so much emphasis on these new mysteries?

John Paul II insolently thought that he could improve the Rosary when he said: "In its favor one could cite the experience of countless saints. This is not to say, however, that the method cannot be improved. Such is the intent of the new series of *mysteria lucis* [mysteries of light] to the overall cycle of mysteries..."[769] What audacity! Did the Blessed Virgin make a mistake?

Were the changes made to the Rosary in order for people to discontinue this devotional practice? When familiar prayers are changed, people often get discouraged or confused and abandon them altogether. It is important for Catholics to understand their traditions and heritage. When prayers are essentially changed, such as the Holy Sacrifice of the Mass and the Rosary, Catholic generations are gradually dissociated from one another. They can no longer pray together; their faith becomes weakened and may even be lost. The changes made to the Rosary are just another example of an "improvement" implemented by Modernists—much like their "improvements" made to Mass and sacraments.

---

[768] *Rosarium Virginis Mariae,* chapter 3, section 28.
[769] *Rosarium Virginis Mariae,* chapter 3, section 28.

H. How Could This Have Happened?

If the changes of Vatican II took place all at once there would have been a universal rebellion against them. Since these changes took place gradually under the auspices of a "council of the Church," many people didn't notice the destruction of their faith.

The study of history confirms the fact that cultural changes rarely occur overnight, but are the culmination of slow, incremental change where time is an ally and speed an enemy. The most effective way to change attitudes and beliefs is through gradual steps—not great leaps. People get alarmed at sudden changes, but easily adapt to gradual ones. When new ideas are slowly presented, many people are hardly aware of what is happening. Hence, many political, social and religious changes take place very slowly.

The Formulation of Ecclesiastical Laws

Many of the ecclesiastical laws contained in the *Code of Canon Law* have been taken from the canons of the 20 General Councils of the Church and are used as a norm for clergy throughout the world in disciplinary and doctrinal matters. Church law is also a compendium of what has been taught and upheld through the centuries. Msgr. Van Noort states in his writings that the Church cannot introduce universal laws that would harm souls:

> *The Church's infallibility extends to the general discipline of the Church.* This proposition is *theologically certain.* By the term 'general discipline of the Church' are meant those *ecclesiastical laws passed for the universal Church for the direction of Christian worship and Christian living.* Note the italicized words: 'ecclesiastical laws,' 'passed for the universal Church.'
>
> The imposing of commands belongs not directly to the teaching office but to the ruling office; disciplinary laws are only indirectly an object of infallibility, i.e., only by reason of the doctrinal decision implicit in them.
>
> ...But the Church is infallible in issuing a doctrinal decree as intimated above —and to such an extent that *it can never sanction a universal law which would be at odds with faith or morality or would by its very nature be conducive to the injury of souls.*

The Church's infallibility in disciplinary matters, when understood in this way, harmonizes beautifully with the *mutability* of even universal laws. For a law, even though it be thoroughly consonant with revealed truth, can, given a change in circumstances, become less timely or [even] useless, so that prudence may dictate its abrogation or modification.[770]

The Catholic Church, often through the actions of popes or General Councils, has changed, added or removed disciplinary laws (canons) when necessary. However, it is important to note that canons dealing with Catholic doctrine are immutable by their very nature since they are based on Divine Law. They can never be altered, abrogated or repealed.

Until the promulgation the 1918 Code of Canon Law, the primary source of Church legislation dates back to the Council of Trent and Pope Pius IV's Constitution *Benedictus Deus* of January 26, 1564. Pope St. Pius X ordered a revision of this Code that was completed on May 27, 1917 by his successor, Pope Benedict XV, and became effective on May 19, 1918. This revision, however, did not change Catholic doctrine, nor did it abrogate any essential beliefs which had been preserved for nearly 2,000 years.

New Code of Canon Law

Legitimate councils of the Catholic Church always condemned heresies and clarified Catholic doctrines. The Second Vatican Council, on the contrary, officially promulgated the heresies of ecumenism and false religious liberty.

An entirely new religion was formed during Vatican II with new teachings, a new liturgy and new sacraments. Therefore, it was absolutely necessary to formulate a new code of Canon Law that would reflect these changes in belief and worship. Some Catholics were shocked when they discovered that not only disciplinary laws were changed, but also some laws that were derived from the Divine Law itself. For example, the new Code of Canon Law allows intercommunion and formal worship with non-Catholics.

> The revision process was formally inaugurated on November 20, 1965. On that occasion, Pope Paul VI, in an address to the Pontifical Commission for the Revision of the Code, proposed two goals which set the course for the task ahead.

---

[770] Msgr. G. Van Noort, S.T.D., *Christ's Church, Vol. II*, pp. 114-115.

First, the Holy Father noted that the revision was to be a 'reformation' of Canon Law, not merely a reworking of the 1917 codification. Second, the decrees and acts of the 'Second Vatican Council' were to supply the parameters of the legislative renewal...[771]

The formulation of a new Code of Canon Law would epitomize and legitimize, in the eyes of the world, the beliefs and practices promoted by Vatican II. On January 25, 1983, John Paul II officially promulgated this new Code of Canon Law through his Apostolic Constitution *Sacrae Disciplinae Leges*. These new laws reflect revolutionary changes in belief and the formation of a new church.

New Catechism

The *Catechism of the Council of Trent* is a veritable compendium of Catholic teaching that has been used by countless bishops, priests, seminarians and college students for nearly 400 years. Its clear, concise and thorough exposition of Catholic doctrine is unparalleled.

The doctrines contained in the *Catechism of the Council of Trent* stand in opposition to the teachings of Vatican II. Therefore, the Modernists found it necessary to compose a new catechism that would encapsulate their new beliefs and morals. The resultant 865 page *Catechism of the Catholic Church* is vague, indeterminate and filled with ambiguities paralleling the teachings of Vatican II.

There has also been a drastic change in Catholic terminology since Vatican II. The formal references to God (Thou, Thy, Thine) once found in Catholic catechisms and prayerbooks have been replaced with "you" and "yours." The meaning of the words sacrament,[772] eucharist,[773] grace and liturgy have changed significantly. The new terms: reconciliation, People of God and Christian Community have a broad, ecumenical connotation.

---

[771] Editors' Preface, *The Code of Canon Law: A Text and Commentary*, (1983 Edition), p. xv.
[772] The Modernist Fr. Schillebeeckx, O.P. refers to Christ as a "sacrament."
[773] Consider these book titles:
Eucharist—Celebrating Its Rhythm in Our Lives (Paul Bernier)
The Future of Eucharist—How a New Self Awareness Among Catholics is Changing the Way They Believe and Worship (Bernard Cooke)
The Eucharist—Yesterday and Today (M. Pennington).

What Has Happened to the Catholic Church?

New religious leaders who have appeared throughout history have claimed their beliefs were signs of enlightenment and progress, necessary for the good of the people. The New Church used the same rationale by gradually incorporating changes in belief and worship. In time, the subtle alterations desensitized the masses who inadvertently became part of a new religion without realizing it.

In 1678, Pere Claude Texier wrote in his work entitled *Panegyrique des Saints:*

> Read ecclesiastical history and you will not find an age in which hell has not vomited forth some new heresy, and where the devil has not succeeded in seducing some member of the Church to arm and fight against the body. You will see that there is not a single article of the Creed which has not been assailed, not one article of the faith for the destruction of which the devil has not even distorted the words of Holy Scripture and the power of the Word of God.
>
> ...I confess that nothing demonstrates the goodness and the miraculous protection of Almighty God so much as the preservation and augmentation of the Church in the midst of heresies.
>
> A vast number of heresies have attacked the Church, a thousand storms have raged over it, but in the midst of tempests this ship, though battered by many rolling billows, has not been shattered or engulfed. Truth remains, error passes away.[774]

Nearly three centuries later Fr. Francis Fenton laments:

> What has happened to our beloved Church since Vatican Council II is nothing short of a disaster, a tragedy of gigantic proportions surely without parallel in the history of the Christian centuries. Humanly speaking, the Roman Catholic Church is today in a shambles, a stark fact which... [no one] can honestly deny unless he be totally out of touch with reality...
>
> To contend, however, that all of this just 'happened' or that it is the consequence of needed change or that it is, God forbid, the work of the Holy Spirit—how anyone... can seriously accept any of these contentions is beyond my comprehension. Surely, a far more logical explanation, and the one I fully accept, is that the destruction of the

---

[774] Fr. John McLaughlin, *Half-Hours With the Servants of God*, pp. 128-129, (1889).

Church which we are witnessing today is by no means an accident but that it has been *planned that way*. 'An enemy hath done this.'[775]

The Devil's Hand in Vatican II

Satan's influence was strongly felt during Vatican II. A German theologian who attended Vatican II remarked, "The devil, too, was there at the council. Sometimes you could almost pinch him."[776] During the council Satan attacked the heart of the Catholic Faith—her immutable doctrines, the Holy Sacrifice of the Mass and the Seven Sacraments.

Throughout the New Testament the devil appears as the enemy of Christ's Church, the little flock that He has patiently gathered together. In the parable of the sower and the seed, the devil snatches the seed of grace from men's hearts.[777] In the parable of the cockle and the wheat, the evil spirit prowls about at night sowing noxious weeds.[778] Above all, it is Satan's aim to secure the downfall of the clergy and those who work for the salvation of souls.

St. Peter compares the devil's strength and raging hatred to that of a roaring lion ready to attack.[779] Like lions, the demons are cunning and stealthy predators. They even go so far as to appear as 'angels of light'[780] in order to deceive. The devils are our enemies and have only one goal: to drag us into hell with them. They work incessantly to bring about the loss of souls and the destruction of the Church, the Holy Sacrifice of the Mass and the means of grace.

Satan's triumphs in the Modern Church are manifold:

- Universal disbelief in the existence of the devil and an eternal Hell
- Rationalization of sin
- The use of sacramentals (holy water, rosary etc.) is ridiculed
- De-emphasis on prayer and self-denial
- Universal apathy in all that pertains to God
- Concept of universal salvation encourages spiritual complacency

---

[775] *An Open Letter to Priests,* November 15, 1977.
[776] Mario Von Galli, *The Council and the Future,* p. 94.
[777] Luke 8: 12.
[778] Matthew 13: 25-28.
[779] I Peter: 5: 8-9.
[780] II Cor. 11, 14.

- The Last Gospel and Leonine Prayers dropped (September 26, 1964)
- Exorcisms during baptism eliminated (January 6, 1972)
- The Minor Order of Exorcist abolished (August 15, 1972)
- Laity are forbidden to use Pope Leo XIII's Prayer to St. Michael (September 29, 1984)[781]
- The Rite of Exorcism rewritten and virtually eliminated (June 4, 1990)

Sr. Lucia, to whom Our Lady of Fatima appeared, described this raging battle:

> The devil does all in his power to distract us and to take away from us the love of prayer. ...the devil knows what it is that most offends God and which in a short space of time will gain for him the greatest number of souls.
>
> The Most Holy Virgin made me understand that we are living in the last times of the world. She told me that the devil is in the process of engaging in a decisive battle against the Blessed Virgin, and a decisive battle is the final battle where one side will be victorious and the other side will suffer defeat. Hence from now on we must choose sides. Either we are for God or we are for the devil. There is no other possibility.[782]

Even the *Wall Street Journal* commented on the apprehension felt by many Americans concerning the great battle between God and Lucifer. "Up to 40% of Americans believe that we are living in the last days, says historian Paul S. Boyer, and that history is racing toward an apocalyptic clash between the forces of good and evil."[783]

The Leonine Prayers

In 1884 and 1886, Pope Leo XIII ordered special prayers—the *Ave Maria* thrice, [three Hail Marys], the *Salve, Regina* [the Hail, Holy Queen] and two other prayers—to be recited after a private Mass in all churches for the needs of the Church. This prescription was renewed by St. Pius X (1903) and by Benedict XV (1915). Pius XI, in a Consistorial Allocution on June 30, 1930, ordered these prayers to be said for [the conversion of] Russia.[784]

---

[781] *Inde Ab Aliquot*, Congregation of the Doctrine of the Faith.
[782] Fr. Freire, *O Segredo de Fatima*, pp. 504-508.
[783] April 21, 2003, Robert Bartley, "Religious Crossfire Hits the President."
[784] Fr. J. O'Connell, *The Celebration of Mass*, p. 172.

On October 13, 1884, Pope Leo XIII had a vision concerning the future of the Catholic Church. After the pontiff had finished his Mass at the Vatican, he suddenly stopped at the foot of the altar. He stood there for about 10 minutes, as if in a trance, his face ashen white. When asked what had happened, he explained that as he was about to leave the foot of the altar, he suddenly heard two voices.

> In front of the tabernacle, he had heard a confrontation between Jesus and Satan. Satan boasted that if he had enough time and enough power, he could destroy the Church. Jesus asked him: 'How much time and how much power?' Satan replied that he would need a century and greater influence over men who would give themselves to him. Jesus said, 'So be it.' The twentieth century is the century given to Satan to do his best to destroy the Church.
>
> Apparently, Leo was then permitted a horrible vision of the attacks that would be waged by evil spirits against souls in the Church, as well as a consoling vision of the Archangel Michael thrusting Satan and his legions back down into the abyss of hell.[785]

Going immediately from the chapel to his office, the pope composed a prayer to St. Michael, with an instruction that it be recited by priests throughout the world.

Freemasonry

Secret Societies have played a major role in bringing about the present crisis in the Catholic Church. Freemasonry is, and always has been, diametrically opposed to Catholicism. The History Channel's documentary "Secret Brotherhood of Freemasons" describes these Secret Societies:

> Freemasonry: to some the word suggests a harmless social club with a taste for colorful pageantry; others envision a sinister Kabal with bloody oaths and a hidden network of powerful and highly placed men. ...Freemasonry is an organization with mysterious roots. It is generally acknowledged as a fraternity of men bound by secret oaths and rituals... Throughout history the brotherhood has also brought together men of learning and influence around common causes.

---

[785] Peter Kwasniewski, *Catholic Faith,* September/October 2001, "Leonine Prayers After Mass."

Albert Lantoine, an atheist and 33rd degree Freemason, declared: "Freemasonry seeks to exalt Man; the Church to exalt God. ...we are the servants of Satan. You, the guardians of truth, are the servants of God."[786]

> In the October, 1902 edition of the French Freemasonic magazine *L'Acacia,* we read: 'Freemasonry is an association, an institution ...it is more than that. Let us take away all the veils, lest we provoke protests. Freemasonry is a church, the counter-church, counter-Catholicism, the other church, the church of heresy, the church of free-thinking.'[787]

The October 8, 1956 issue of *Life* magazine featured a comprehensive article explaining the ceremonies and the various degrees of American Freemasonry:

> Throughout its 239 year history[788] Freemasonry found that its secrecy and rituals have both attracted members and aroused enemies. When cathedral-building in England decreased in the mid-17th Century many guilds of stoneworkers, known as Freemasons apparently because they were free to move from town to town, became purely social groups. They often initiated nonmasons as members, calling them speculative Masons. In 1717 four London Lodges composed largely of speculative Masons formed the Grand Lodge of England.[789] ...Wherever Englishmen went they founded Masonic Lodges. ...The antagonism to the Roman Catholic Church that grew with the Enlightenment [French Revolution of 1789] was reflected in the anticlerical attitudes of leading Masons. This aroused the hostility of Pope Clement XII who in 1783 denounced the order, 'for if they were not acting ill, they would not... have such a hatred of the light.'[790]

"The papacy was the only power which clearly recognized the peril which Freemasonry presented, and that almost from its beginning."[791] Freemasonry

---

[786] *Lettre au Souverain Pontife,* pp. 44, 168-169.
[787] Quoted in Msgr. Henri Delassus, *Le problème de l'heure présente,* p. 393.
[788] As of October 8, 1956 when the article was written.
[789] "Two Protestant clergymen, Dr. John Theosophilus and Dr. James Anderson, were instrumental in setting up the self-styled governing body [at the Apple Tree Tavern in London]. Not all lodges were willing to submit to the rule of the new Grand Lodge but by 1725 the original four lodges had grown to 64 of which 50 were in London." William Whalen, *Christianity and American Freemasonry,* p. 15.
[790] "U.S. Masons: The Order's History Here and Abroad," p. 120.
[791] G. Bord, *La Franc-Maçonnerie en France des origines à 1815,* pp. 194-196.

was explicitly condemned by Popes Clement XII, Benedict XIV, Pius VI, Pius VII, Leo XII, Pius VIII, Gregory XVI and Pius IX. Fr. McLaughlin noted:

> Freemasonry is the system of the Freemasons, a secret order and pantheistic sect, which professes, by means of a symbolic language and certain ceremonies of initiation and promotion to lay down a code of morality founded on the brotherhood of humanity only. Some writers apply the term Freemasonry not only to the Freemasons proper, but also to all secret organizations which seek to undermine Christianity and the political and social institutions that have Christianity for their basis.[792]

Pope Leo XIII described the goals of Freemasonry:

> Their ultimate aim is to uproot completely the whole religious and political order of the world, which has been brought into existence by Christianity, and to replace it by another, in harmony with their way of thinking. This will mean that the foundation and the laws of the new structure of society [New World Order] will be drawn from pure Naturalism. ...Let us remember that Christianity and Freemasonry are fundamentally irreconcilable, so much so that to adhere to the one is to cut oneself off from the other.[793]

According to Pope Pius XII, Freemasonry is a catalyst of the anti-Christian movement: "The roots of modern apostasy lay in scientific atheism, dialectical materialism [Communism], rationalism, illuminism, laicism, and Freemasonry—which is the Mother of them all."[794] Freemasons and Communists often work for the same ends. "Freemasons achieve their ends by secretly subversive means, Communists by openly subversive movements."[795]

Alta Vendita Instruction

The Alta Vendita was the highest lodge of the Carbonari, a group of Italian Freemasons. In the early 19th century they composed a secret document, *The Permanent Instruction of the Alta Vendita*, which describes their long-range plans to infiltrate and subvert the Catholic Church.

---

[792] *Half-Hours with the Servants of God*, p. 33, (1889).
[793] *Humanum Genus*, April 20, 1884.
[794] *Address to the 7th Week of Pastoral Adaptation*, May 23, 1958.
[795] *Declaration on Freemasonry by the Plenary Assembly of Cardinals, Archbishops and Bishops of Argentina*, February 20, 1959.

The following excerpts were taken from the correspondence of the Italian *Alta Vendita* which is commonly supposed to have been, at the time, the governing center of European Freemasonry. The documents were seized by the Pontifical Government in 1846. They were communicated by Pope Gregory XVI to Cretineau-Joly (March 1846), who, with the approval of Pope Pius IX, published them in his work *L'Eglise en face de la Revolution*:

> Our ultimate end is that of Voltaire and of the French Revolution—the final destruction of Catholicism, and even of the Christian idea. The work which we have undertaken is not the work of a day, nor of a month, nor of a year. It may last many years, a century, perhaps; in our ranks the soldier dies; but the fight goes on...[796]
>
> It is not in the blood of an isolated man, or even of a traitor, that it is necessary to exercise our power: it is upon the masses. Let us not individualize crime: It is necessary to generalize it... Let us not then make more martyrs; but let us spread vice broadcast among the multitude; ... let them breathe it through their five senses; let them drink it in, and become saturated with it...
>
> Make men's hearts corrupt and vicious, and you will no longer have Catholics. Draw away the priests from the altars, and from the practice of virtue. Strive to fill their minds and occupy their time with other matters. ...it is the corruption of the masses we have undertaken—the corruption of people through the clergy, and of the clergy by us—the corruption which ought one day to enable us to lay the Church in the tomb... The best poinard with which to strike the Church is corruption.[797]

The *Alta Vendita Instruction* called for "the dissemination of liberal ideas and axioms throughout society and within the institutions of the Catholic Church so that laity, seminarians, clerics and prelates would, over the years, gradually be imbued with progressive principles."[798]

The Freemasons further intended to produce a liberal pope who would fulfill their aims. This gradual process would be achieved by indoctrinating the young clergy.

---

[796] Fr. E. Cahill, S.J., *Freemasonry and the Anti-Christian Movement*, p. 101.
[797] Cahill, 103.
[798] John Vennari, *The Permanent Instruction of the Alta Vendita*, p. 2

Now then, in order to secure to us a Pope in the manner required, it is necessary to fashion for that Pope a generation worthy of his reign. ...Let the clergy march under your banner in the belief that they march under the banner of the Apostolic Keys. ...Lay your nets like Simon Barjona. Lay them in the depths of sacristies, seminaries and convents, rather than in the depths of the sea, and if you will precipitate nothing you will give yourself a draught of fishes more miraculous than his. The fisher of fishes will become a fisher of men. You will bring yourselves as friends around the Apostolic Chair. You will have fished up a Revolution in Tiara and Cope, marching with Cross and banner—a revolution which needs only to be spurred on a little to put the four quarters of the world on fire.[799] [This goal was nearly accomplished as early as 1903.]

Cardinal Rampolla

During the papal conclave of August 2, 1903, Mariano Cardinal Rampolla Del Tindaro was nearly elected pope. Providentially, the Austro-Hungarian Emperor Franz Josef vetoed the nomination of Rampolla.[800]

The conclave assembled, the doors were locked, and the first three ballots were in his [Rampolla's] favor but suddenly to prevent his election the solemn proceedings were dramatically halted by Cardinal Puzyna[801] who rose and, white-faced and tremulous of voice for his was a disagreeable task, informed his startled colleagues that on behalf of Emperor Franz Josef of Austria he was forced to exercise the right of veto. There was consternation among the scarlet-clad voters but after a formal protest the candidature of the former Secretary of State was withdrawn with dignity and with manifestations of relief on his part.[802]

"It was only in subsequent years that the true motive for Franz Josef's veto was revealed. The Emperor was privy to a very closely held secret: Cardinal

---

[799] "Permanent Instruction of the Alta Vendita," *Grand Orient Freemasonry Unmasked*, pp. 93-95.

[800] This Cardinal, who was Secretary of State to Pope Leo XIII (1878-1903), is mentioned in a Masonic publication called *The Equinox*, published in Detroit, Michigan (vol. 3, March 1, 1919). The journal lists him, together with other notable personalities such as Richard Wagner and Goethe, as belonging to the O.T.O., the *Ordo Templi Orientis* (Order of the Eastern Temple), which was a particularly sinister form of Freemasonry. *Catholic Restoration* July-August 2003, "The Role of Freemasonry in the Destruction of the Catholic Order," by Bishop Donald Sanborn.

[801] Of Kraków.

[802] John Farrow, *Pageant of the Popes*, p. 372.

Rampolla had joined the Lodge of the Freemasons."[803] Giuseppe Cardinal Sarto was elected pope on the seventh ballot and chose the name Pius X. During the first conclave of the twentieth century the Freemasons[804] nearly achieved their goal of electing their own pope.

Bishop Rudolph Graber, in his book *Athanasius and the Church of our Time*, quoted the Freemason Yves Marsaudon (member of the Supreme Council of France, Scottish Rite) who declared that "the goal [of Freemasonry] is no longer the destruction of the Church, but to make use of it by infiltrating it." Marsaudon further said, "The sense of universalism that is rampant in Rome these days is very close to our purpose for existence ...with all our hearts we support the revolution of John XXIII."[805] What had failed with Rampolla became a reality with John XXIII in 1958.

Was John XXIII a Freemason?

Freemasonry is a secret society that has been repeatedly condemned by the Church. "Any Catholic who affiliates with the Masonic lodge is automatically excommunicated, forfeits any share in the public prayers of the Church, and is denied a Christian burial; any Mason who wishes to enter the Church must sever all ties with the lodge."[806] Yet, in spite of these harsh censures, there is evidence to suggest that John XXIII was a Freemason.

> In a recent edition of *30Days*, an influential international monthly published in several languages, we find the startling news that, Archbishop Angelo Roncalli, when he was in Paris as Papal Nuncio, was initiated into the Masonic Order and that he participated in the works of the Masonic Lodges when he was in Istanbul, Turkey. This statement was made by Virgilio Gaito, Grand Master of the Oriente, regarded as the official Masonry of Italy.
>
> Gaito used the words, 'It seems that Pope John XXIII has been initiated in Paris and has participated in the works of the Lodges in Istanbul.' The Grand Master

---

[803] Malachi Martin, *The Keys of This Blood*, p. 678.
[804] Today there are O.T.O. lodges in nearly 40 countries. The grandfather of modern Satanism, Aleister Crowley, belonged to the O.T.O.
See *"Did a Freemason Almost Become Pope?—The Story of Cardinal Rampolla,"* by Craig Heimbichner, *Catholic Family News*, August 2003.
[805] Rama Coomaraswamy, M.D., *The Destruction of Christian Tradition*, p. 84.
[806] William Whalen, *Christianity and Freemasonry*, p. 1.

of Italy's Freemasons would be in a position to know with certainty if Angelo Roncalli had been initiated into the Order in Paris.

It would be incredibly reckless of him to make such a sensitive statement, if he did not. The implications of this are tremendous. In the late forties, the initiation into the Masonic Order incurred automatic excommunication.[807] [Could John XXIII lead an institution from which, *de facto,* he had been expelled?]

Since Freemasons were not able to obliterate Christ's Church, they planned, instead, to use it against itself. By infiltration, the Masons hoped not only to eradicate the influence of Catholicism in society, but they would thereby be able to advance their own principles and goals by making the Church their personal instrument for "renewal," "progress" and "enlightenment."[808]

Cardinal Jose Caro y Rodriguez, archbishop of Santiago, Chile in 1957, warned of the Freemasonic infiltration into Catholic societies and clergy:

> ...the revolutionary spirit entered among many members of seminaries, among them many priests of poor theological preparation, to the point where the Supreme Head of the Church was alarmed, as we can see in the ecclesiastical reports of the time, and especially in Cretineau Joly (L'Eglial, en face de la Revolution. The Church facing a Revolution). It is well known that in Brazil there were religious confraternities dominated by Masonry...[809]

Ultimately, the pope fashioned by the Freemasons, accompanied by his liberal hierarchy, would lead countless souls away from the true Church by means of a false sense of obedience. According to the diabolical plan of the Masons, the misguided masses would apostasize from the Catholic Church yet "all the while believing themselves to be faithful Catholics."[810]

In his Prayer to St. Michael the Archangel, Pope Leo XIII referred to the Freemasonic goal of placing their agent upon the Chair of Peter:

> That malignant dragon [Satan] is pouring abroad, like a foul stream, into the souls of men of ruined intellect and corrupt heart the poison of his wickedness,

---

[807] *Catholic,* June 1994, "Was John XXIII really a Pope?," by Robert Bergin.
[808] John Vennari, *The Permanent Instruction of the Alta Vendita,* p. 2.
[809] *The Mystery of Freemasonry Unveiled,* pp. 229-230.
[810] Vennari, 3.

the spirit of lying, of impiety and blasphemy, the pestilent breath of impurity and of all vice and iniquity. Most cunning enemies have filled with bitterness and drenched with gall the Church, the Spouse of the Lamb without spot, and have lifted impious hands against all that is most sacred in it. *Even in the holy place where the See of Blessed Peter and the chair of truth was set up to enlighten the world, they have raised the abominable throne of their impiety with the iniquitous hope that the Shepherd may be stricken and the flock scattered abroad* [emphasis added].[811]

This dark state of affairs would be evidenced by a major upheaval within the Catholic Church. Traditional beliefs and liturgy were discarded in order to create a new church. The new theology, based on Modernism and Liberalism, directly contradicts previous Catholic theology. This insidious deception is clearly evidenced in the *Alta Vendita Instruction* which planned "a revolution in tiara and in cope, marching with the cross and the banner…"[812] This revolution attempted to fulfill the ultimate goal of Freemasonry—"the final destruction of Catholicism and even of the Christian idea."[813]

Notable Predictions of Canon Roca

The writings of the 19th century revolutionary, Canon Roca, are almost prophetic concerning the current crisis in the Church. In 1858, Roca was ordained to the priesthood and became an honorary canon in 1869. "He was very well-versed in the occult sciences and disseminated extensive propaganda, in particular among the youth. Because of this he came into conflict with Rome" [and was excommunicated.][814] Canon Roca "preached revolution and church 'reform' and predicted a subversion of the Church that would be brought about by a council."[815]

Roca described the formulation of a "new religion," "new dogma," "new ritual" and "new priesthood," a "new church, which might not be able to retain anything of scholastic doctrine and the original form of the former church

---

[811] *Raccolta*, 1898.
[812] John Vennari, *The Permanent Instruction of the Alta Vendita*, p. 10.
[813] Fr. E. Cahill, S.J., *Freemasonry and the Anti-Christian Movement*, p. 101.
[814] Dr. Rudolf Graber, *Athanasius and the Church of our Time*, p. 34.
[815] Vennari, 6.

[traditional Catholicism, but] will nevertheless, receive consecration and canonical jurisdiction from Rome."[816] He foresaw a movement for revolutionary liturgical "reform," stating, "...the Roman Church will shortly undergo a transformation *at an ecumenical council.*"[817] [Emphasis added.] According to Canon Roca, "The papacy will fall; it will die under the hallowed knife which the fathers of the last council will forge."[818] Most of Roca's predictions have become a reality.

The battle cry of the French Revolution "to overturn throne and altar"[819] has successfully been carried out by means of the Second Vatican Council. The Postconciliar Church has become a deviant church, a church which no longer echoes with the prayers of the Holy Sacrifice of the Mass, but rather generally resounds with the social gospel of secular humanism.

Vatican II—An Illegitimate Council

A legitimate council of the Catholic Church cannot possibly alter the teachings of Christ nor substantially change the Mass or the sacraments. These have been preserved intact for nearly 2,000 years and are unchangeable by their very nature. A council that would undertake such actions would be null, void and heretical. How could a pope dare to pursue such changes and not be a heretic? There are historical precedents for our present situation when we consider the 19 false councils and the 41 antipopes. Vatican II is an illegitimate council because it is the very antithesis of previous legitimate councils of the Church.

> According to the Catholic doctrine, the true Church of Christ possesses four essential marks by which she may be ever recognized, namely, *she is One, Holy, Catholic and Apostolic.* The Church has for her the promise of Christ that He would remain with her *'all days,'* even to the consummation of the world (Matt. 28: 20); that against her, founded on the rock (Peter), the gates of hell [hostile evil powers] would never prevail (Matt. 16: 18); that the Paraclete, the Spirit of truth, would abide with her *forever,* and teach her all truth (John 14: 16-18). There

---

[816] John Vennari, *The Permanent Instruction of the Alta Vendita,* pp. 16-18.
[817] Dr. Rudolph Graber, *Athanasius and the Church of our Time,* p. 35.
[818] Graber, 35.
[819] Vennari, 38.

cannot be a single moment in history at which the Church is bereft of this assistance; she can never fall away from the truth; she is not merely in the days of the Apostles, not merely in the first six or seven centuries, but at all times the 'pillar and ground of the truth' (I Tim. 3: 15). She is at all times in possession of the truth;[820] 'she has at all times the tradition of the Apostles;'[821] never can it be said she has experienced a falsification of the true doctrine until this or that reformer came to her aid.[822] She is inundated with the light of the Lord, and she pours forth her rays over the whole surface of the earth. She is the Bride of the Lord, can never be an adulteress; she is inviolate and pure.[823] She is unconquerable; and it were easier for the sun to become extinct, than for her to be annihilated.[824] All in the Church is guided by God.[825]

The new, man-made church created since Vatican II has implemented many of the same changes introduced by Luther 445 years earlier. It bears little resemblance to the Catholic Church: It is Diverse—not One; Secular—not Holy; Regional—not Catholic; Contemporary—not Apostolic. It is not the true Church, but rather poses as the Catholic Church while attempting to destroy it.

We know that the Catholic Church is indefectible and indestructible since Our Lord promised that she will endure until the end of time. Christ, however, did not promise that His Church would not undergo trials. Thus, from 1870 to our present age, the Church has traversed through very tumultuous times which continue to threaten her very existence. Communists, Freemasons and Secular Humanists have fiercely and relentlessly attacked her not only from without, but

---

[820] Iren. adv. haer., iii. 4: depositorium dives veritatis.
[821] Tert. adv. Marc., i. 21: Non alia agnoscenda erit traditio Apostolorum, quam quae *hodie* apud ipsorum ecclesiae editur.
[822] Loc. cit., i. 20: O Christe, patientissime Domine, qui tot annis interversionem praedicationis tuae sustinuisti, donec tibi scilicet Marcion subveniret! Cf. de praescript., c. 28.
[823] Cypr. de unit. Eccles., c. 5, 6, p. 214. Ed. Vendob. 1868. (Corp. script. eccl. lat. ed. impens. acad. Caes., t. iii., p. 1) Even the words following, which we omit for the sake of brevity, are worthy of all consideration.
[824] Chrys. Hom. 4 in illud: Vidi Dominum, n. 2 (Migne lvi., pp. 121, 122): "Learn the force of truth, that it is easier for the sun to be extinguished, than for the Church to disappear."
[825] Cypr. ep. 59 (al. 55) ad Cornel., n. 5, p. 177: Cum ille (Dominus Matth., 10, 29) nec minima fieri sine voluntate Dei dicat, existimat aliquis *summa et magna* aut non sciente aut non permittente Deo in *Ecclesia Dei* fieri et sacerdos, id est dispensatores ejus, non de ejus sententia ordinari? *Hoc est fidem non habere,* qua vivimus, hoc est Deo honorem non dare, cujus nutu et arbitrio regi et gubernari omnia scimus et credimus.

they, along with Modernists and Ecumenists, have infiltrated her very ranks and continue their deadly assault from within.

Apostate Bishops

"The Church in America had gone into Vatican II as arguably the strongest in the world, vibrant, growing, devout. Look at it now. The dismantling has been from within and could not have been done without the collusion of our bishops."[826] These bishops are not shepherds, but ravening wolves, seeking the ruin of souls. They are culpable for sacrilegious liturgies and sterile homilies, the loss of faith experienced at Catholic schools and colleges, for the decline in religious vocations and for the tremendous drop in Mass attendance.

Besides their apathy at the loss of faith, the bishops have been silent concerning the immoral entertainment industry that has caused tremendous moral decay in their flocks. Fr. Jerome Treacy, S.J. of Clarkston, Michigan writes:

> Movies, television, and magazines and novels are producing an immoral, sex-drenched culture which is an occasion of sin for young and old, while our bishops sit idly by, too timid or too unperceptive to do anything about it.
>
> In view of the disastrous results of the perverse climate, such as illegitimacy (unmarried teenage pregnancy has doubled since 1960), abortion (40% of those teen pregnancies are aborted), divorce (increased almost 200%), acceptance of the homosexual lifestyle as moral, and so on, the bishops' failure to face up to this problem and lead Catholic people—almost a quarter of the nation—to combat and correct it must be recognized as the great pastoral scandal of our times.[827]

The Great Apostasy

Our Lord foretold in Sacred Scripture that cunning men, inspired by the devil, would lead multitudes astray. Jesus Christ repeatedly warned His flock against their wily attacks:

> Beware of false prophets, who come to you in sheep's clothing but inwardly are ravening wolves. By their fruits you will know them. Do men gather grapes from

---

[826] *Crisis,* April 2002, "The Shame of the Shepherds," by Ralph McInerny, p. 64.
[827] *Catholic World Report,* April 2002, "Letters," p. 4.

thorns or figs from thistles? Even so, every good tree bears good fruit, but the bad tree bears bad fruit. Every tree that does not bear good fruit is cut down and thrown into the fire. Therefore, by their fruits you will know them.[828] And take care that no one leads you astray.[829] And many false prophets will arise, and will lead many astray.[830]

St. Paul declared that these false prophets (heretics, schismatics and antipopes) would be wolves in sheep's clothing: "I know that after my departure, fierce wolves will get in among you, and will not spare the flock. And from among your own selves men will rise speaking perverse things, to draw away the disciples after them."[831] "For they are false apostles, deceitful workers, disguising themselves as apostles of Christ."[832] This age has now fallen upon us.

The abandonment of the faith by the majority of Catholics (known as the great apostasy) was also predicted by St. Paul: "Let no one deceive you in any way, for the day of the Lord [the Second Coming of Christ] will not come unless the apostasy comes first and the man of sin is revealed, the son of perdition [Antichrist]."[833]

> No man has a right to establish a religion; no man has a right to dictate to his fellow man what he shall believe and what he shall do to save his soul. Religion must come from God, and any religion that is not established by God is a false religion, a human institution, and not an institution of God; and therefore did St. Paul say in his Epistle to the Galatians: 'Though we Apostles, or even an angel from heaven, were to come and preach to you a new Gospel, a new religion, let him be anathema.'[834]

---

[828] Matthew 7: 15-20.
[829] Matthew 24: 4.
[830] Matthew 24: 14.
[831] Acts of the Apostles 20: 29.
[832] II Corinthians 11: 13.
[833] II Thessalonians 2: 3-4.
[834] Fr. Edward McGolrick, *The Unchangeable Church*, p. 307.

I. Who is Ultimately Responsible for the Universal Loss of Faith?

Through the course of this book one can't help but notice that the various decrees, bulls and encyclical letters of the popes, the canons of the general councils and various excerpts from Canon Law have a wonderful uniformity in content and composition. In spite of diversities of the times and circumstances in which they were written, these documents all seem to have emanated from one pen. The clarity, precision and simplicity of these works are unmistakable: truly the work of the Holy Ghost.

However, with Vatican II and its aftermath, a stark, new picture emerges. The decrees of John XXIII, Paul VI, John Paul I and John Paul II are so ambiguous that they can mean whatever one wants them to mean and thus can be acceptable to the various religions of the world. Included are "hard-line" documents such as *Humanae Vitae, Dominus Jesus* and *Liturgiam Authenticam.* Others, such as *The Church's Respect for Authentic Islam* (September 24, 2001) and John Paul II's Catechesis of September 9, 1998, *'Seeds of Truth' in the World Religions,* openly condone heresy and false beliefs.

How can the changes of the Second Vatican Council be from God when this new church offers an invalid Mass, has doubtfully valid sacraments and many of its teachings (ecumenism, religious liberty, etc.) are opposed to the Gospel?

Can John XXIII, Paul VI, John Paul I and John Paul II be legitimate popes when they have condoned and promulgated heresy and actively participated in nearly every type of non-Catholic worship? These men, spurred on by their insidious agenda, have created a new church, a church based on the spirit of the world and designed to accommodate all beliefs. A legitimate pope could not attempt to abolish the Holy Sacrifice of the Mass and replace it with a Protestant Eucharistic celebration. It is inconceivable that a true Vicar of Christ would invalidate the sacraments or officially teach heresy.

John Paul I

John Paul I was elected on August 26, 1978 "by the 111 cardinals participating in the largest and one of the shortest conclaves in history. The quickness of his election was matched by the brevity of his pontificate of 33 days."[835] John Paul I was merely installed in a simple inaugural service in which he insisted upon not being crowned with the papal tiara. Why?

Dr. Philip Potter, the director of the World Council of Churches said, "By choosing to be known as John Paul, the new pope identifies himself with the Vatican II tradition of his... predecessors."[836] *Newsweek* also noted that "He was the first pope since Simon Peter to have borne two names."[837]

A brief summary of his life is given below:

- Born: Oct. 17, 1912, in Forno di Canale (Canale d'Agordo), Italy
- Educated: Minor seminary, Feltre; major seminary, Belluno
- Ordained: July 7, 1935
- Served: Vice rector of Belluno seminary, 1937-1947
- Appointed: Vicar general in Diocese of Belluno, 1947
- Earned: Doctorate in theology, Gregorian University, 1950
- Consecrated: Bishop of Vittorio Veneto, Dec. 27, 1958
- Attended: All sessions of the Second Vatican Council 1962-1965
- Elevated: To archbishop and patriarch of Venice, Dec. 15, 1969
- Given: Red hat of a cardinal, March 5, 1973
- Published: His book 'Illustrissimi,' 1976
- Elected: Pope John Paul I, Aug. 26, 1978
- Died: In the Vatican, Sept. 28, 1978[838]

John Paul I is often portrayed as a humble, saintly prelate of the Church. His doctrinal stand was very questionable as evidenced by his pastoral letter of 1967 in which he advised his clergy to "see if, instead of uprooting and throwing down [error], it might be possible to trim and prune it patiently, bringing to light the core of goodness and truth which is often not lacking even in erroneous opinions."[839] This is like a doctor telling his patient "I won't take out all the cancer; it may be good for you."

---

[835] Matthew Bunson, *2002 Our Sunday Visitor Catholic Almanac*, p. 253.
[836] *Newsweek,* September 4, 1978, p. 88.
[837] September 4, 1978, p. 81.
[838] *Our Sunday Visitor,* September 28, 2003, "I am just poor dust," by Russell Shaw.
[839] *Our Sunday Visitor,* September 28, 2003, "Celebrating the Smiling Pope," by Lori Pieper.

Although he was not so liberal as to attract the hostility of conservatives, Luciani had shown a progressive inclination when he expressed kind words for the parents of a 'test-tube baby' at a time when such experiments were condemned by the Vatican. Another evidence of his liberal tendencies was the fact—revealed later by his secretary—that when he went into the conclave, Luciani had resolved to vote for Brazilian Cardinal Aloisi Lorscheider, who had gained widespread attention for his support of movements associated with liberation theology in Latin America.[840]

His sudden death on September 29, 1978 was shrouded in mystery. Before his untimely death, John Paul I had attempted to remove Freemasons from prominent ecclesiastical positions. He also planned to take drastic measures to resolve serious problems at the Vatican Bank.

Author David Yallop, who thoroughly researched the matter for three years, asserts that John Paul I was murdered. He believes members of the secret P-2 Lodge in Rome and prominent prelates including Bishop Paul Marcinkus (in charge of the Vatican Bank), Cardinal Jean Villot (Vatican Secretary of State) and Cardinal John Cody (archbishop of Chicago) may have been responsible for his untimely death.

> [The P-2 Lodge] was founded in 1877 as a temple of convenience for provincial Freemasons visiting Rome. ...Among the P-2's 962 members were 43 members of parliament, 43 generals, eight admirals (including all the heads of the Italian armed services), all the heads of the state security services, sundry government officials, police chiefs, businessmen, media stars, and journalists (including the editor and publishers of a major Italian newspaper).[841]

Michele Sindona, Licio Gelli and Roberto Calvi, all members of the P-2 lodge, may have had a leading role. Yallop states that these men definitely had motives to have John Paul I terminated. Michele Sindona's "financial empire crashed in 1974, and he was poisoned in 1986 while serving a prison sentence for murder."[842] Licio Gelli "eluded the law for decades but was finally arrested in Cannes in 2002 and brought

---

[840] *Time,* October 9, 1978.
[841] *Crisis,* July / August 2003, "A Quiet Death in Rome: Was John Paul I Murdered?," by Sandra Miesel, p. 15.
[842] *Crisis,* 17.

back to Italy to answer for his crimes."[843] Roberto Calvi was also threatened by John Paul's intended measures and died a violent death.[844]

> But some Grand Orient brethren [Freemasons] still managed to do dramatic harm in 1981 by scamming the Vatican's bank out of millions and by conspiring against the Italian government in the P-2 Lodge scandal. Although none of the thousand men enrolled in P-2 was a Catholic cleric, the notion that the Church, particularly the Italian Church, is packed with secret Masons lives on.[845]

"The evidence the pope had acquired indicated that within the Vatican City State there were over one hundred Masons, ranging from cardinals to priests."[846] John Cornwell, who compiled his findings five years later, believes John Paul I died at his desk and was later placed in bed after suffering "pulmonary embolus due to a condition of abnormal coagulability of the blood."[847] "Cornwell's book is also interwoven with conversations which reveal the Vatican as it has seldom been revealed before: a world of personal rivalries, small daily intrigues, great disorganization, of pious lies and congenial incompetence."[848]

The official Vatican version that John Paul I died peacefully in bed while reading the *Imitation of Christ* has numerous discrepancies and is obviously untrue. He died either on the night of September 28 or the following morning. "Yallop fixed on digitalis as the poison, administered in liquid medicine that

---

[843] "*Crisis,* July / August 2003, "A Quiet Death in Rome: Was John Paul I Murdered?," by Sandra Miesel, p. 17.
[844] "BBC. Oct. 25-Just 20 years ago, Roberto Calvi, a leading figure in the secretive world of Italian banking, was found hanging from a bridge in London, an apparent suicide. A panel of forensic judges in Rome have examined his body—exhumed four years ago at his family's insistence—and judged that he must have been murdered. According to the BBC, Calvi's neck showed no signs of the damage usually inflicted by hanging, and his hands had not handled the stones found in his pocket. ...His death came just days after the sudden collapse of the Vatican-sponsored Banco Ambrosiano, which lost more than a billion dollars under his management. His death brought on one of the greatest scandals in post-war Italy, according to the BBC, 'with widespread speculation about Mafia involvement and links to a shadowy Masonic group, known as P2 ...a secret right-wing Masonic lodge.'" *National Catholic Register,* November 10, 2002. "At least two of the suspects being questioned in connection with his death reportedly have ties to the Italian Mafia." *Catholic World Report,* October 2003, p. 8.
[845] *Crisis,* December 2002, p. 43.
[846] David Yallop, *In God's Name,* p. 4.
[847] *A Thief in the Night,* p. 331.
[848] *30Days,* June 1989, "Like a Thief in the Night," by Robert Moynihan, p. 15.

John Paul was taking for low blood pressure. Half a teaspoon of digitalis would indeed cause a fatally frantic heartbeat."[849] The one detail Vatican officials, David Yallop and John Cornwell agree upon is that he died alone and without receiving the Last Sacraments. Despite the mysterious circumstances surrounding his sudden and untimely death, no autopsy was ever performed.

John Paul II

John Paul II is one of the most charismatic religious leaders in history. His international popularity is vividly portrayed on the cover of *Time Magazine* (October 15, 1979) as the smiling photogenic prelate, pictured with the caption "John Paul II, Superstar."

During the past 25 years John Paul II has traveled more than 774,200 miles and visited nearly 1,000 cities in 133 countries.[850] "Cumulatively, more people have turned out to see John Paul II than any other figure in history."[851] According to *The Los Angeles Times*, his trip to Toronto for World Youth Day (July 18-28, 2002) was "...a week long event that feels like a combination of Woodstock, the Olympics and an old-fashioned revival meeting headlined by Pope John Paul II."[852]

Like a chameleon which can rapidly change skin color in order to blend in, John Paul II adapts his beliefs to fit his surroundings. In India, he received cow dung ashes from a Hindu priestess in honor of the god Shiva;[853] in Japan he praised Buddhism; in Morocco, he lauded Islam; in Africa, he prayed with animists and dialogued with voodoo chiefs and while in Canterbury, he prayed with the Anglican archbishop. On his international travels he habitually

---

[849] *Crisis*, July / August 2003, "A Quiet Death in Rome: Was John Paul I Murdered?," by Sandra Miesel, p. 16.

[850] As of September 15, 2003.

[851] *National Catholic Reporter*, August 16, 2002, "23-year odyssey," by John Allen, Jr., p. 5.

[852] July 27, 2002.

[853] Hinduism is an ancient religion that is difficult to describe. Its roots are based in pantheism and polytheism. "A world of supernatural beings, genii and demons, form the retinue of this array of major and minor gods and lesser divinities of the Hindu religion who are all so many aspects of the single divinity. They can change their shape at will and are usually grouped under a leader. Their influence can be good or harmful—sometimes both at once." Solange Lemaître, *Hinduism*, p. 67.

dialogues and worships with non-Catholics and makes no attempt to convert them.

His Early Life

Karol Wojtyla was born in Wadowice, Poland on May 18, 1920. At the age of 15 he began a successful acting career which lasted six years. According to his classmate, Antoni Bohdanowicz, Wojtyla "devoted every free moment to the theatre."[854] In the play *Balladyna*, on May 14, 1937, he masterfully filled two separate roles (the leading role and that of a missing actor whom he had to replace). John Paul II's phenomenal charisma, witnessed in his later life, quite likely can be attributed to his early training in the theatre.

The Wojtylas moved to Kraków in August 1938 in order for Karol to pursue studies in philosophy, theatre and poetry. A month later, Karol began his literary studies at the Jagiellonian University. "He became heavily involved in Kraków's theatrical scene and was well known for his powerful and beautiful voice, often reading epic Polish poetry [or others of his own composition] at public meetings."[855]

Nazi & Soviet Invasions of Poland

"On September 1, 1939, Hitler's panzer [armored] divisions rolled across the Polish frontier, and despite the gallant attempts of the Polish Army, Poland was overrun with alarming speed. On the 17th, the Soviets also invaded Poland, quickly swallowing up the eastern third of the country, and effective opposition soon ceased."[856]

Karol's studies suddenly ended on November 6, 1939 when the 183 university professors were arrested by the Nazis and transported to slave labor camps. The Catholic University of Lublin was "shut down by the German Occupation, with numerous professors imprisoned, tortured, or killed outright."[857] The Soviets were just as ruthless and eliminated all who stood in their way.

On March 5, 1940, the Politburo ordered the shooting of at least 22 thousand [Polish] officers who were labeled 'inveterate and incorrigible enemies of Soviet

---

[854] See Carl Bernstein and Marco Politi, *His Holiness*, p. 35.
[855] Patrick Edwards, *Pope John Paul II*, p. 10.
[856] Edwards, 10.
[857] George Weigel, *Witness to Hope*, p. 131.

power.' The slaughter was carried out in the Katyn forest, and many of the bodies were then thrown into common graves. Immediately afterwards, 61 thousand of the victims' family members were transferred, so to speak, to Kazakhstan.[858]

In September 1940, in order to avoid being sent to a labor camp, Wojtyla began to work at a quarry as an explosives helper. The following year he was transferred to the Solvay chemical factory outside Kraków. Tragedy followed tragedy as Karol experienced the death of his mother Emilia (April 13, 1929), brother Edmund (December 4, 1932) and father Karol (February 18, 1941).

It is remarkable that in spite of the horrible atrocities committed by the Nazis and Communists against the Polish people, Karol Wojtyla always escaped unharmed. Many biographers note that those around him (including bishops, priests and university professors) were often imprisoned or executed. For example: "May, 1942: Gestapo arrests Wojtyla and others. His worker's card gets him off. The others are shot at Auschwitz."[859] Did Karol fraternize with the Nazis and Communists? On December 24, 1965, allegations surfaced in a letter published in the *Gazetta Krakowska* written "by the workers of the former Solvay factories, where he himself [Karol Wojtyla] worked during the war, of [Wojtyla] having been a 'collaborator' throughout this period and of working for the National Socialists."[860]

In December 1942, Karol attended classes for the priesthood at Cardinal Sapieha's residence in Kraków. Three years later he became an assistant professor at Jagiellonian University where he taught the history of dogmas and detailed systematic theology.

Wojtyla's Priesthood

After completing four years of studies, Karol was ordained to the priesthood on November 1, 1946 by the cardinal archbishop of Kraków. Fr. Wojtyla obtained his degree in theology at the Angelicum in Rome on July 2, 1947 and a doctoral degree from the Jagiellonian University Faculty of Theology on December 16, 1948.

---

[858] Gian Svidercoschi, *Stories of Karol,* pp. 26-27.
[859] *The Globe and Mail,* (Toronto, Ontario), October 12, 1998, " 'Countercultural' Pope wins hearts, loses minds."
[860] Catherine and Jacques Legrand, *John Paul II,* p. 71.

Karol served as assistant priest at a parish in Niegowíc for seven months and held the position of parish priest at St. Florian's Church in Kraków from 1948-1951. As a young priest, Wojtyla organized frequent outings with young people. "Rising early, his day always began with a solitary swim. Then he said Mass for his young followers, on an improvised altar: upturned kayaks. As for the crucifix, it was made from a couple of crossed paddles."[861] He continued the outings and "informal" style of Mass even after he became a bishop. All the while, the Communist government tightened its control in Poland.

> But it was hard for the Communist government at Warsaw to make headway so long as Cardinal Hlond, the Archbishop of Warsaw, remained alive, for he had been a prisoner of the Germans and nobody could doubt his Polish as well as his Roman loyalty [to the pope]. After his death in 1948 the government made more progress... an agreement was reached, without consultation with Rome, between the Polish hierarchy and the government in April 1950... Less than six months had passed before the Polish hierarchy found itself compelled to protest against numerous violations of the agreement. But the Communist masters at Moscow were well satisfied, and in August 1950 they procured a similar agreement in Hungary. Under the aegis of the 'Orginform,' established in the same year to undertake the training of those entrusted with the special task of dispelling the Faith (for which purpose they would pose as priests), an all-out effort was made by the Communists to sow religious confusion in eastern Europe generally, in particular by undermining allegiance to the pope.[862]

Lino Gussoni describes the conditions in Poland during the early 1950's in his 1954 book, *The Silent Church: Facts and Documents Concerning Religious Persecution Behind the Iron Curtain:*

> One of the most painful aspects of the condition of the Church in Poland is that many priests are under surveillance, that many have been arrested and sent to jail without a previous trial. The clergy and the Episcopate feel painfully the vexing system of continuous control, the repeated summonings to the offices of the police or the local authorities. Many have been arrested in churches, in confessionals, ...The surveillance extends even to bishops who, during their

---

[861] Catherine and Jacques Legrand, *John Paul II*, p. 58.
[862] E. Hales, *The Catholic Church in the Modern World*, pp. 283-284.

journeys to assemblies or their visits to the Dioceses, are accompanied by many police.

It is difficult to say just how many priests are presently in prison [1954], but it would be more than 700, averaging about 35 from each diocese.

Higher, instead, is the number of members of religious orders who were deported or who 'disappeared.' It is believed that these may total twelve hundred.[863]

Approximately 80 percent of the Church's property had been seized, including 2,143 places of worship, 1,110 monastic houses, 229 publishing houses and 85 schools.[864]

Father Karol Wojtyla's academic teaching career began in October 1953, when he took over a course in Catholic social ethics in the Jagiellonian University's faculty of Theology. When the faculty was suppressed by the [Communist] regime in early 1954, Wojtyla continued to teach the social ethics course in the school of theology that was quickly organized for seminarians, who now had no university-based theology courses to attend. Like his Jagiellonian course, these seminary courses ran for two hours a week, and Wojtyla taught them throughout the 1950s.[865]

In spite of the Communist movement to dispel the Catholic faith, Fr. Wojtyla was allowed a great deal of freedom. There are some questions that need to be answered regarding his teaching career. Why was he allowed to travel to Rome? Why was he allowed to teach? Why was Fr. Wojtyla appointed to the philosophy department of the Catholic University of Lublin on October 12, 1954 at a time when the Communists arrested the rector and nine of its professors? Why wasn't he arrested? Why was he allowed such a free lifestyle: acting, camping, kayaking, hiking, and skiing, while Poland was suffering under Nazi and Communist occupation? Cardinal Mindszenty specifically noted that anyone under Communist occupation who was allowed to travel freely must be a collaborator.

---

[863] pp. 99, 107.
[864] *Our Sunday Visitor,* October 12, 2003, "How the future pope beat the Communists," by Jonathan Luxmoore.
[865] George Weigel, *Witness to Hope,* p. 130.

Ascending the Ladder

Cardinal Stefan Wyszynski, Primate of Poland, who had been placed under house arrest for three years by the Communists, strongly opposed Wojtyla's ideas regarding ecumenism and changes to the Mass. Archbishop Baziak bypassed Wyszynski and insisted on the appointment of Wojtyla as auxiliary bishop of Kraków on July 4, 1958. On July 8, Fr. Wojtyla met with the cardinal and merely asked, "Where do I sign?

> That July 8 remained fixed in the primate's memory: It was the first time he had been bypassed in the appointment of a Polish bishop. Since the authorities had made it so hard to conduct Church business, Pius XII had granted Wyszynski the extraordinary privilege of selecting and keeping on hand a list of future bishops already approved by the pope. When Wyszynski wanted to appoint someone, he would send a secret message to Rome, and as soon as he got a coded signal from the pontiff, would go ahead with the appointment. Karol Wojtyla's name was not on Wyszynski's list.[866]

Wojtyla received episcopal consecration on September 28, 1958.

> Karol was not among those favored for the post, partly because of his age [he was the youngest person to ever become a bishop in Poland—he was only 38], and partly because he was too involved in his research and the theological aspects of the priesthood to be able to find time for this essentially pastoral role.[867]

"Karol Wojtyla lived in Kraków for exactly forty years, including four years as auxiliary bishop, two years as *de facto* leader of the archdiocese, and fourteen as its archbishop."[868] His appointment as archbishop, in itself, is quite interesting.

Archbishop Eugeniusz Baziak of Kraków died on June 15, 1962 and the vacancy needed to be filled. As a result of the Communist occupation of Poland, the state usurped the right to approve the episcopal nominees of the Polish Primate Cardinal Wyszynski. The decision ultimately fell to Zenon Kliszko, "the Communist Party's second ranking figure ...he was the Party's chief ideologist and the guardian of Polish Communist orthodoxy."[869]

---

[866] Carl Bernstein and Marco Politi, *His Holiness*, p. 88.
[867] Catherine and Jacques Legrand, *John Paul II*, p. 63.
[868] George Weigel, *Witness to Hope*, p. 186.
[869] Weigel, 184.

"Kliszko, who did not lack ego, was very pleased with himself for having vetoed all seven names the Primate [Wyszynski] had proposed over the past year and a half. 'I'm waiting for Wojtyla,' Kliszko said, 'and I'll continue to veto names until I get him.' "[870] "They had rejected them [the other candidates] because they [the Communists] were convinced they could find—in that careful student of Marxism, Karol Wojtyla—an interlocutor who was more conciliatory and malleable than the cardinal primate."[871] "It was the first time in 13 years that Poland's Communist rulers had permitted the appointment of a residential archbishop."[872]

Wojtyla was obviously favored by the Communists. "...It was the Communist regime that pushed for his appointment to the critical see of Kraków, because the Communists thought he was a bishop they could work with."[873]

Jonathan Luxmoore relates new information taken from the archives of the Polish Secret Police (Sluzba Bezpieczenstwa) from the book *Teczki Wojtyly (Wojtyla Files)*:

> From the party's viewpoint, Bishop Wojtyla was a preferable candidate for archbishop of Krakow to two others being considered by the Church: Bishop Jerzy Stroba, who was 'a decided opponent of all state cooperation,' and Father Tadeusz Federowicz, who was 'totally subservient to the Church Hierarchy.'
>
> It was said the regime had deliberately waited for Bishop Wojtyla's name to come up. In a letter to Cardinal Wyszynski a month later, Poland's Communist premier, Jozef Cyrankiewicz, noted tersely that he had 'no reservations' about the 42-year-old's appointment.[874]

Bishop Vida Elmer dispels a common misconception about Karol Wojtyla:

> While living in Poland, Karol Wojtyla did not suffer persecution. The assumption that he did is gratuitous. The fact that JP 2 [John Paul II] came from a Communist land earned him a great deal of sympathy in the West. Many good-

---

[870] George Weigel, *Witness to Hope,* p. 184.
[871] Gian Svidercoschi, *Stories of Karol,* p. 146.
[872] *Our Sunday Visitor,* October 12, 2003, *Why he's the pope of the 'new evangelization,'* " by Russell Shaw.
[873] *The Los Angeles Times*, August 17, 1997.
[874] *Our Sunday Visitor,* October 12, 2003, p. 4.

hearted people have taken it for granted that Karol Wojtyla had to endure the same (or similar) hardships as the other members of the Catholic clergy did. I can say, this assumption gives a free and unearned credit to Wojtyla out of the sufferings of the other priests and bishops who really endured persecution. At one time or other, the Communist regime of Poland threw into jail hundreds of priests. Even Cardinal Wyszynski was under house-arrest for a long period of time. Meanwhile, Karol Wojtyla enjoyed his freedom traveling inside and outside of the country. He was given the opportunity to visit schools and universities abroad, to learn several languages, to hold lectures inside and outside of Poland. Evidently, he was a favored son of the government. No subject of a Communist government can enjoy such rare privileges without performing proportionate services to the regime.[875]

Wojtyla's Role at Vatican II

Bishop Wojtyla attended every session of Vatican II and in the fall of 1963 joined the council's discussion of the Church as the "People of God." He was appointed archbishop of Kraków on December 30, 1963.

His stand on atheism deeply puzzled many of the bishops, especially those from Communist countries. Archbishop Wojtyla believed that the human person should find the truth on their own and that conversion was unnecessary.

> Wojtyla was deeply convinced that personalist ethics—which stresses the uniqueness and inviolability of the human personality—would never allow the imposing of ideas on anyone. He took the same line when the council discussed the problems of atheism—a question that vexed the Council Fathers almost from the beginning to the end of Vatican II. 'It is not the Church's role to lecture unbelievers,' Wojtyla declared on taking the floor on October 21, 1964. 'We are involved in a quest along with our fellow men. ...Let us avoid moralizing or suggesting that we have a monopoly on the truth.' ...Talk at the council of actual 'relations with atheism' meant dialogue with Marxists.[876]

These were revolutionary ideas, especially at a time when the West braced for nuclear war and when much of the world was held captive under Communist

---

[875] *Monograph,* No. 66, May 1983.
[876] Carl Bernstein and Marco Politi, *His Holiness,* pp. 102-103.

tyranny. He further expressed his ecumenical and Modernist persuasions a week later.

> He began with several previously expressed comments on the Church and the world and the president of the session was on the point of stopping him, when he quickly and skillfully captivated his audience and silenced all the noise in the auditorium. In a loud and distinct voice, he clearly explained that the Church should no longer pose as the sole dispenser of Truth and Goodness... She should, he went on, be in the world but not above it. ...The Church must alter her teaching: she should encourage Revelation and no longer dictate it.[877]

> Although he was only forty-two when the council opened, Wojtyla made eight oral interventions in the council hall, a rather high number, and often spoke in the name of large groups of bishops from Eastern Europe. (Altogether he made 22 interventions, oral and written.) He was an unusually active member of various official drafting groups for *Gaudium et Spes,* and even a chief author of what was called the 'Polish draft.' His voice was crucial to the passage of the document on religious liberty.[878]

The Modernists Yves Congar, Henri de Lubac and Jean Danielou worked closely with Archbishop Wojtyla to draft the *Pastoral Constitution on the Church in the Modern World.* In his speeches of September 22 and 28, 1965, Wojtyla championed the heresy of religious liberty and encouraged dialogue with atheists.

> "Archbishop Wojtyla then took up the question of atheism as a pastoral issue, as a part of the Church's 'dialogue with everyone.' ...The Church's dialogue with atheism should begin not with argument or proofs about the existence of God, but with a conversation about the human person's 'interior liberty.' "[879] George Weigel describes Wojtyla's rise to prominence:

> By the end of the Council in 1965, the young bishop who arrived in Rome in 1962 as the unknown vicar capitular of Kraków was one of the better-known churchmen in the world, to his peers, if not to the world press. And he was

---

[877] Catherine and Jacques Legrand, *John Paul II,* p. 68.
[878] William Madges and Michael Daly, *Vatican II: Forty Personal Stories,* p. 33.
[879] George Weigel, *Witness to Hope,* pp. 168-169.

known, not primarily by contrast to the overwhelming personality of his Primate, Cardinal Wyszynski, but as a man with ideas and a striking personal presence in his own right.[880]

On June 26, 1967, as a reward for his loyalty to Vatican II, Paul VI made Archbishop Wojtyla a cardinal at the age of 47. The young cardinal ascended the ladder quickly. He was named to the Vatican Congregations of Catholic Education, the Clergy, the Liturgy and the Oriental Church and was made a special consultor to the Council on the Laity. In 1974, he was elected to the council of the world bishops' synod. Wojtyla also conducted the Lenten retreat for the household of Paul VI in 1976. Communist Poland's Department of Religions even noted Cardinal Wojtyla's rapid rise to power as he was "becoming an increasingly important figure in the arena of world Catholicism."[881] His facility in English, French, German, Italian, Latin, Polish, Russian and Spanish enabled him to greatly expand his circle of influence.

Building a New Church

Nowa Huta [New Foundry], Poland was known for its Lenin Steelworks.

> Throughout the Communist period the shortage of church buildings has been the most meddlesome problem. After the war's destruction, and increase in population and the move of peasants to industrial 'new towns' Polish Catholics needed large numbers of new buildings. But the Communist government which has control of building permits and supplies, played a maddening cat-and-mouse game of rejection and delay. John Paul's most telling achievement in Kraków was the erection of a modernistic concrete-and-steel church at Nowa Huta.[882]

This was an interesting accomplishment, since no Catholic church was allowed in Nowa Huta under the Communist regime. Through Cardinal Wojtyla's persistent efforts and ten years of labor by the Polish people, the Ark Church was finally dedicated on May 15, 1977. Although it seemed as though Catholics had achieved a great victory through its construction, the structure is unrecognizable as a Catholic church both from within and without.

---

[880] p. 158.
[881] *National Catholic Register,* July 6, 2003, "Polish Book Details Secret Police Surveillance of Future Pope," CNS.
[882] *Time,* June 11, 1979.

The incongruous church embodies the concept that "Architecture was a very important weapon in the hands of the creators of a new social order. ...In this great work [of social transformation] a crucial role fell to an architect who—'is not merely an engineer creating edifices and streets but an engineer of human souls.' "[883]

Taking the Second Vatican Council very seriously, "...Karol Wojtyla initiated one of the most extensive implementations of the council of any diocese in the world."[884] This was clearly evidenced by the entire design of the Ark Church, even down to the tabernacle itself. "The tabernacle was a gift from the diocese of Sankt Pölten in Austria, and was shaped like a model of the solar system; its decoration included a piece of moon rock, given to Paul VI by an American astronaut."[885]

Two Conclaves

Following the death of Paul VI on August 6, 1978, Wojtyla took part in the papal conclave which elected John Paul I. Only 33 days later, John Paul I died suddenly. Wojtyla again returned to Rome to participate in another conclave. Cardinal Franz König was instrumental in drawing support for Wojtyla even though a non-Italian had not been elected in 455 years. Wilton Wynn noted Wojtyla's unusual behavior during this papal election:

> Wojtyla always takes along some reading matter wherever he goes, and during those long periods of voting in the conclave he was calmly perusing a book of political theory by Karl Marx. When a fellow cardinal asked if he didn't feel it sacrilegious to read such an author in that sacred place, he answered with a good natured smile, 'My conscience is clear.'[886]

On October 16, 1978 the 58-year-old Cardinal Wojtyla received a majority of votes and took the name John Paul II. He, like John Paul I before him, was installed in a simple inaugural service in which he, too, insisted upon not being crowned with the papal tiara. Why? Wojtyla said that he chose the name John

---

[883] Welcome to Nowa Huta, "The Principles of Social-Realism," www.nowahuta//nh.pl/english/socrealism.htm.
[884] George Weigel, *Witness to Hope*, p. 155.
[885] Weigel, 190.
[886] Wilton Wynn, *Keeper of the Keys*, p. 39.

Paul II, out of "reverence, love and devotion to John XXIII and also to Paul VI, who has been my inspiration, my strength."[887] Two days later *The Los Angeles Times* carried the headline: "Polish Communist Party praises choice of pope."

The Socialist

Newsweek featured an article describing the Marxist beliefs of John Paul II: "With faith in Christ and borrowings from Karl Marx, John Paul II builds his own challenging gospel of work. He is not only the first pope from a socialist country, he may also be described as the first socialist pope. What he did learn from books was how to think like a Marxist as well as a Christian."[888] Where does John Paul II really stand? Pope Pius XI in his *Encyclical on Atheistic Communism* wrote: "No one can be at the same time a sincere Catholic and a true socialist."

His theological leanings are hard to decipher. "Never has any man who sat upon the papal throne been the subject of so many articles and books with conflicting ideas about his beliefs. His seemingly self-contradictory stands have been a puzzlement to the press—to religious as well as secular writers."[889] According to Thomas Langan, professor of philosophy at the University of Toronto: "Arguably in the entire history of the papacy—and that goes back two millennia—there has been no more radical pope than John Paul II."[890]

"John Paul II paid homage to the Soviet dictator Yuri Andropov (who imprisoned, tortured and executed untold Christians while serving as KGB chief and USSR premier) by sending his condolence to the Communist leaders at their ruler's death with the assurance of 'special thoughts for the illustrious deceased one.' "[891] Why?

Cardinal Casaroli was the architect of the *Ostpolitik* of Paul VI, opening the doors for dialogue with Communists. John Paul II appointed Casaroli as Secretary of State, the second highest position in the Church. In February 1984, he signed the new concordat with the Italian government which replaced the

---

[887] Thomas Cahill, *Pope John XXIII*, p. 224.
[888] June 20, 1983.
[889] *The Athanasian*, March 1, 1984, "Who is John Paul II?, Part I," by John Weiskittel.
[890] *The Globe and Mail*, October 12, 1998, (Toronto, Ontario), " 'Countercultural' Pope wins hearts, loses minds."
[891] *The Athanasian*, March 1, 1984.

Lateran Treaty of 1929. "Under the new provisions, Roman Catholicism no longer will be the state religion of Italy, and Rome's status of 'sacred city' will disappear. In addition, the agreement will ease the choice of Italian parents who oppose religious education for their children in public schools."[892]

The Ecumenist

In the March 26, 1979 issue of *Newsweek,* Kenneth Woodward wrote:

John Paul II's [1st] encyclical *[Redemptor Hominis]* is important for what it says to the church as well as to the world. Both, he writes, are anchored in the mystery of the Incarnation, by which all people are reunited with God through the humanity of Jesus Christ. Indeed, the Pope sounds almost Protestant in proclaiming that the church must measure its performance by its faithfulness to the 'person' of Jesus Christ.

On November 17, 1980, John Paul II visited a Lutheran Church in Germany on the anniversary of Martin Luther's birth and praised the 'profound religiosity and spiritual heritage' of Martin Luther. "Imagine a vicar of Christ praising an ex-priest who hated the Church and who well may have done more harm to the Church than any other one person. JP II did so and the person he praised was Martin Luther. Strange isn't it?"[893]

"In August 1983, John Paul II began a biennial series of summer humanities seminars at Castel Gandolfo [the pope's summer palace]. Unique in the annals of the modern papacy, these seminars brought Christian, Jewish, agnostic and atheistic philosophers, historians, and other scholars into conversation with the Pope, for whom serious intellectual exchange remained a passion."[894]

The Oriental Orthodox Churches have been called *Monophysite Churches* because of their adherence to the Monophysite heresy which taught that Jesus Christ did not have a human will. This heresy was condemned at the Third Council of Constantinople in 681 AD. Nevertheless, on June 23, 1984, John Paul II signed a joint statement with Syrian Orthodox Patriarch Ignatius Zakka declaring that "the respective Churches confess one and the same faith in the mystery of

---

[892] *Miami Herald,* February 19, 1984.
[893] Fr. Francis Fenton, *The Athanasian,* June 1, 1985.
[894] George Weigel, *Witness to Hope,* p. 466.

the word incarnate"⁸⁹⁵ even though these churches have not rejected their heretical teachings.

On August 8, 1985, John Paul II assisted in pagan rites at the sacred forest of the snake worshippers at Tara and Togoville in Togo, Africa (a country located between Ghana and Benin in West Africa). The Associated Press described the event: "The high priests and sorcerers seldom emerge from the forest, which is considered sacred, and their appointment with the pope was interpreted as a special sign of respect for him." "The French periodical *La Croix* (August 13) quoted John Paul as follows: 'The prayer meeting in the sanctuary at Lake Togo was particularly striking. There I prayed for the first time with the animists.' "⁸⁹⁶

John Paul II received the tika (which is a mark on the forehead) and vibhut (cow dung ashes) in Madras, India from a Hindu priestess on February 2, 1986. This pagan ritual is in honor of the false god Shiva (the Destroyer).

On February 5, 1993 the Associated Press reported that during John Paul II's visit to Cotonou, Benin he "sought common ground with believers in voodoo."

> On the second day of his 10th African pilgrimage the pope held an emotional meeting with priests of the vodun, as the ancestral gods are known in the Fon language. The Catholic Church seeks to maintain a dialogue with voodoo followers but frowns on superstitious practices. Voodoo worshippers believe in one god but also in lesser deities. Snakes and fetishes are important in the ritual.

The Vatican newspaper *L'Osservatore Romano* also describes voodoo rituals:

> Voodoo ceremonies consist of rituals invoking the spirits and the great god and are marked by drums and songs accompanying an animal sacrifice. The rite culminates in a trance in which a ritual dancer is thought to be possessed by a divinity [devil?]. Ceremonies are conducted by a man *(hungan)* or a woman *(mambo)*, who are often knowledgeable about witchcraft as well.⁸⁹⁷

John Paul II's ultimate goal seems "to empty the Christian religion of its supernatural and spiritual content and give it a unique political twist."⁸⁹⁸

---

⁸⁹⁵ Matthew Bunson, *2003 Our Sunday Visitor's Catholic Almanac*, p. 585.
⁸⁹⁶ Patrick Henry Omlor, *Sedevacantists and the "Una Cum Problem,"* p. 4.
⁸⁹⁷ February 10, 1993.
⁸⁹⁸ John Eppstein, *The Cult of Revolution in the Church*, p. 15.

He has engaged in dialogue with Bahais, Buddhists, Hindus, Jains, Jews, Muslims, Orthodox, Protestants, Shintos and Sikhs and worshiped or joined in formal prayer with their religious leaders in churches, mosques, synagogues and temples. Some naively believe he is trying to lead non-Catholics to the Catholic Faith. This is definitely not the case. His intention has never been to convert them, but rather to accommodate the religions of the world. In 1954, Cardinal Stritch forcibly condemned interfaith dialogue:

> The Catholic Church does not take part in these organizations or in their assemblies or conferences. She does not enter into any organization in which the delegates of many sects sit down in council or conference as equals to discuss the nature of the Church of Christ or the nature of her unity, or to propose to discuss how to bring about the unity of Christendom, or to formulate a program of united Christian action.
>
> She does not allow her children to engage in any activity or conference or discussion based upon the false assumption that Roman Catholics too are still searching for the truth of Christ.
>
> For to do so would be to admit that she is but one of the many forms in which the true Church of Christ may or may not exist... such an admission she can never make, for she is now as she has always been, the one and only Spouse of Christ, the one and only Mystical Body of Christ, the one and only Church of Christ.
>
> Now this unity, clear and obvious as it is, exists in the Church of Christ today. It is found in the Roman Catholic Church and in her alone. She and she alone is the true Church of Jesus Christ. There is only one way to the unity so anxiously sought by some men. That is through entrance into the fold of the Church of Christ, participation in her life, submission without reserve to her teaching and ruling authority.[899]

Fr. Gianni Bozzo remarked "that John Paul's travels promote 'universality at the price of ambiguity.' "[900] This point was elucidated in John Paul II's Catechesis of September 9, 1998 where he manifested his conviction that all religions possess

---

[899] *The Tidings,* July 9, 1954.
[900] *National Catholic Reporter,* August 16, 2002, p. 5.

the truth and that the Holy Spirit was instrumental in the foundation of all religions.

> In *Nostra Aetate,* the Declaration on the Relation of the Church to Non-Christian Religions, the Second Vatican Council teaches that 'the Catholic Church rejects nothing of what is true and holy in these religions. She has a high regard for the manner of life and conduct, the precepts and doctrines which, although differing in many ways from her own teaching, nevertheless often reflect a ray of that truth that enlightens all men.'[901]

> ...The 'seeds of truth' present and active in the various religious traditions are a reflection of the unique Word of God...

> ...It must first be kept in mind that every quest of the human spirit for truth and goodness, and in the last analysis for God, is inspired by the Holy Spirit. The various religions arose precisely from this primordial human openness to God. At their origins we often find founders who, with the help of God's Spirit, achieved a deeper religious experience. Handed on to others, this experience took form in the doctrines, rites and precepts of the various religions.

> ...The Holy Spirit is not only present in other religions through authentic expressions of prayer. 'The Spirit's presence and activity,' as I wrote in the encyclical letter *Redemptoris Missio,* 'affect not only individuals but also society and history, peoples, cultures and religions.'[902]

> ...May the Spirit of truth and love, in view of the third millennium now close at hand, guide us on the paths of the proclamation of Jesus Christ and of the dialogue of peace and brotherhood with the followers of all religions![903]

John Paul II wanted to clear up any misunderstanding after the declaration *Dominus Jesus* of September 5, 2000 when he said 13 days later that "the commitment of the Catholic Church to ecumenical dialogue is irrevocable."[904]

On December 9, 2000 an article in *The Los Angeles Times* further stated: "Tempering a controversial Vatican declaration on salvation [*Dominus Jesus*],

---

[901] *Nostra Aetate,* n. 2.
[902] N. 28.
[903] *The Pope Speaks,* May / June, 1999, " 'Seeds of Truth' in the World Religions," pp. 147-149.
[904] *National Catholic Reporter,* October 1, 2000.

Pope John Paul II said this week [December 9, 2000] that all who live a just life will be saved, even if they do not believe in Jesus Christ and the Roman Catholic Church." Following John Paul II's example, modern Catholics throughout the world have embraced ecumenism to the extent that many have lost their Catholic Faith because to them it doesn't really matter anymore.

Conversion to the Catholic Church is not the object of John Paul II's ecumenical dialogue with world religions. This was expressed on June 28, 2003, in his Apostolic Exhortation, *Ecclesia in Europa (Preaching the Gospel of Hope to Agnostic, Rootless Europe)*: "…The new evangelization is in no way to be confused with proselytism (conversion), without prejudice to the duty of respect for truth, for freedom and for the dignity of every person."[905]

Fr. Richard McBrien, summarizes the state of the Postconciliar Church during the pontificate of John Paul II: "The number of Catholics who attend church and the number of religious vocations have plummeted, and the 'greatest crisis since the Reformation, [besides the havoc caused by Vatican II] the sexual crisis, occurred on his watch.' "[906]

The concept of God as envisioned by John Paul II is not the Blessed Trinity (Three Persons in one God), but a form of the Arian and Macedonian heresies that denied the divinity of both Jesus Christ and the Holy Ghost. John Paul II's speech of September 23, 2001 manifests these beliefs:

> 'There is one God.' The apostle proclaims before all else the absolute oneness of God. This is a truth that Christians inherited from the children of Israel and which they share with Muslims: it is faith in the one God, "Lord of heaven and earth" (Lk 10:21), almighty and merciful.
>
> In the name of this one God, I turn to the people of deep and ancient religious traditions…[907]

---

[905] *The Pope Speaks,* November / December 2003, p. 341.
[906] *USA Today,* May 12, 2003, "John Paul at 83: 'Ministry of presence,' " by Cathy Grossman.
[907] *The Pope Speaks,* July/August, 2002, "Religion Must Not Be a Reason for Conflict," pp. 193-194.

John Paul II has met with Muslim leaders on more than 60 occasions. According to the *Wall Street Journal,* this is "more than all other Popes combined." He has "repeatedly called Muslims 'brothers in Abraham,' the common progenitor of Judaism, Christianity and Islam. 'As I have often said in meeting with other Muslims,' the Pope said in 1985, 'your God and ours are one and the same. And we are brothers and sisters in the faith of Abraham.' "[908]

Meetings of World Religions at Assisi

John Paul II held a Day of World Prayer for Peace at Assisi, Italy which was attended by 160 representatives from 12 different religions on October 27, 1986. Each faith held separate prayer meetings in the various Catholic churches. Buddhists even placed a statue of the Buddha on the tabernacle of the church of San Pietro.

"Among the participants: Dalai Lama, self-exiled Buddhist leader of Tibet, and John Pretty-on-Top, Crow medicine man from Montana. Buddhist monks waved incense; African snake worshippers paraded through cobblestone streets. Jews, Muslims, Hindus, Zoroastrians, Sikhs, Jains, Bahais, Protestants and other Christians also took part. Even Libya sent a Moslem representative."[909]

All the delegates then returned to the basilica of St. Francis for a final outdoor peace service where John Paul II was seated next to Dalai Lama (the Buddhist god-king) whom the Buddhists consider an "incarnate god."[910]

On January 24, 2002, John Paul II organized a meeting at Assisi, Italy with 250 representatives of: African Animists[911] (adherents of Voodoo), Anglicans, Baptists, Buddhists, Confucians, Hindus, Jains, Jews, Lutherans, Mennonites, Methodists, Moravians, Muslims, Orthodox Churches, Pentecostals, Quakers,

---

[908] September 25, 2000.
[909] *USA Today,* October 28, 1986.
[910] "The Dalai Lama is believed to be a reincarnation of the Buddha. When he dies, his soul is thought to enter the body of a newborn boy, who, after being identified by traditional tests, becomes the new Dalai Lama." MSN Learning & Research Plus— Dalai Lama from Encarta.
[911] "Animism has two fundamental components: a belief in the spirit of nature and a cult of the dead." F. Bergounioux, O.F.M. and Joseph Goetz, S.J., *Primitive and Prehistoric Religions,* pp. 108-109.

Reformed Churches, Shintos, Sikhs, the Salvation Army, followers of Tenrikyo (a faith healing sect), Zoroastrians and the World Council of Churches.

> The different religions went into different rooms in the convent of the Franciscan Friars to pray at the same time, but not together. The Franciscans removed the crucifixes from the vaulted rooms where the different leaders went to pray and provided prayer carpets for the Muslims. The Buddhists, however, had to contend with a large nativity scene in their room, as it was affixed to the room and could not be moved.[912]

During his closing speech, John Paul II prayed: "In the name of God, may every religion bring upon the earth Justice and Peace, Forgiveness and Life, Love!" Praying for peace is very beneficial but such ecumenical prayer is forbidden by Divine Law. Many of the religious leaders that were present do not believe in a personal God; many deny the Blessed Trinity; some of them worship idols and others openly worship the devil. Therefore, which god were they invoking? Is the First Commandment now obsolete? This is illogical and even blasphemous. John Paul II obviously believes that there are no false gods and that there is no one true God. What kind of church does he represent?

John Paul II continues to have amicable relations with the "Sister Church"—the Anglican Church—as evidenced by his welcoming speech to Rowan Williams, the new archbishop of Canterbury:

> I am confident that, with God's help, we can make progress along the path toward unity, in order to experience anew 'how good and pleasant it is when brothers dwell in unity!' (Psalm 133:1) I send my best wishes for your new and demanding ministry.
>
> 'I have had the opportunity to know and work closely with your predecessors, Archbishop Runcie and Archbishop Carey, in the shared task of promoting understanding between the Anglican Communion and the Catholic Church.'[913]

On February 28, 2003 John Paul II sent Williams congratulatory greetings and a pectoral cross through the Vatican's chief ecumenical official, Cardinal Walter

---

[912] *National Catholic Register,* February 3, 2002.
[913] *National Catholic Register,* August 4, 2002.

Casper. The June 7, 1982 issue of *Time* shows how such actions are contrary to the past teachings of the Church:

> Catholics believe a priest must be ordained by a bishop historically tied to bishops who are linked all the way back to Peter and the Apostles: the apostolic succession. ...In 1886 Pope Leo XIII declared that Anglican Orders are, and always have been, 'absolutely null and utterly void,' mainly because the 16th century ordination rite omitted the power of priests to offer a sacrifice to Christ in the Mass. Therefore Anglican Primate Runcie and other bishops [including his successor Rowan Williams] are technically, in papal eyes, not ordained priests at all.

According to Pope Leo XIII's encyclical *Apostolicae Curae,* the current leader of the Anglican Church, Rowan Williams, is a mere layman. Why did John Paul II acknowledge him as otherwise? The Anglican Church has indeed maintained a semblance of Catholicism, although its liturgy is invalid and it has embraced heretical beliefs. Archbishop Williams has ordained a homosexual priest who was living with another man and "supports not only the ordination of women as priests, but also their consecration as bishops. He also has no theological problem with the remarriage of divorced men and women."[914]

"Now, some Episcopal churches in Canada are blessing same-sex unions, and the Episcopal Church of the United States has confirmed the election of Rev. Gene Robinson, who left his wife and children to live in an openly homosexual relationship, as bishop of New Hampshire."[915] The installation ceremony took place on November 2, 2003.

---

[914] *Our Sunday Visitor,* August 11, 2002.
[915] *Our Sunday Visitor,* November 2, 2003, "How one gay bishop makes ecumenical road rocky," by Thomas Szyszkiewicz.

The *London Times* on July 19, 2002 reported that Williams is also a Druid:

> As the sun rises over a circle of Pembrokeshire bluestones, the Archbishop of Wales, the Most Reverend Dr. Rowan Williams will don a long white cloak while druids chant a prayer to the ancient god and goddess of the land. He was accepted into the 'white druid order,' the highest of the three orders of the 'gorsedd of bards, the Welsh body of poets, musicians, writers and artists,' according to the *Times*.[916]

The Assyrian Orthodox Church and the Postconciliar Church

The Congregation for the Doctrine of the Faith issued a directive allowing Catholics of the Chaldean rite to receive communion at schismatic Assyrian Orthodox churches and for Assyrian Orthodox parishioners to receive communion at Chaldean Catholic churches:

> The guidelines are revolutionary in character. For the first time in modern history, the [Postconciliar] Catholic Church has recognized the validity of a eucharistic prayer (the Anaphora of Addai and Mari) [of the Assyrian Orthodox Church] without the words of institution ('This is my body, This is my blood'), more commonly referred to as the words of consecration. ...If someone had suggested then—or now, for that matter—that even without the words of consecration, Christ could become really and truly present in holy Communion, they would have been scoffed at and dismissed as either frivolous or heretical.
>
> But the Vatican has now ruled that this is, in fact, the case. In recognizing the validity of the Anaphora of Addai and Mari, proclaimed since the earliest centuries in portions of the East and still used today by the separated Assyrian Church of the East, the [Postconciliar] Catholic Church now officially acknowledges and teaches that Christ can become sacramentally present at Mass without the traditional words of consecration.[917]

Serious doctrinal problems must be addressed. The words of consecration that Our Lord used at the Last Supper to change the bread and wine into His Body and Blood are nowhere to be found in the Anaphora of Addai and Mari.

---

[916] *Adoremus Bulletin*, September 2002, p. 2.
[917] See: *Guidelines for Admission to the Eucharist between the Chaldean Church and the Assyrian Church of the East*, October 25, 2001.

Therefore, the bread and wine remain bread and wine just as they do in Protestant liturgies. Yet, John Paul II personally approved this heretical decree.

The Assyrian Orthodox are sometimes called Nestorians for they, like the heretic Nestorius who was condemned at the Council of Ephesus in 431 AD, deny the Divine Maternity of the Blessed Virgin Mary. The Chaldean rite, however, returned to the Catholic Faith during the reign of Pope Innocent XII in 1692.

Saints March In / Others March Out

The September 7, 2000 issue of *The Wanderer* carries an interesting article written by James Drummey regarding the Canonization of Saints:

> The first thing to remember is that every holy person who dies and goes to Heaven is a saint, whether he or she is ever officially canonized or not. Second, saints were proclaimed in the early centuries of the Church by the acclamation of the faithful; there was no investigation or pronouncement by the church. Third, the first officially recorded papal canonization was that of St. Ulric [bishop of Augsburg, Germany] by Pope John XV in 993. Fourth, in 1234, the *Decretals* of Pope Gregory IX laid out for the first time the guidelines for beatification and canonization. Fifth, the first solemn beatification at St. Peter's Basilica in Rome was that of St. Francis de Sales in 1622 by Pope Alexander VII.

Pope Alexander III (1159-1181) decreed that no one could be publicly honored by the faithful without papal approbation. Pope Urban VIII (1623-1644) drafted the ecclesiastical legislation that has been used for the canonization of saints for centuries.

Time periods for canonizations of different saints have varied. St. Anthony of Padua was canonized in the same year of his death, St. Francis of Assisi the year following his death, St. Thérèse of Lisieux, 28 years after her death, St. Joan of Arc and St. Thomas More almost 500 years after their deaths.

There are three steps in the canonization process: Venerable, Blessed and Saint. The first step may begin shortly after death, as the virtue and writings of the servant of God are scrutinized. The sanctity of the individual must be confirmed by authentic miracles. The entire canonization process may take 50 years or even centuries. There are nearly 2,000 saints, and they may be found in the *Roman Martyrology* and *Butler's Lives of the Saints*.

What Happened to St. Christopher?

Vatican II's *Decree on the Liturgy* prescribed changes to the liturgical calendar "to suit the conditions of modern times." On January 1, 1970, Paul VI removed many saints from the Catholic calendar and demoted others, claiming that they were mere legends and therefore never really existed. Such popular saints as St. Christopher, St. Patrick and St. Philomena were deleted from the common list. *Life* and *Newsweek* featured articles entitled, "Out Go the Beloved Saints" and "Drooping Halos."

> Newspapers told their uninformed readers that saints had been 'purged', 'dethroned', and 'pensioned off after years of honorable service.' ...A few priests took the cue from them and told their faithful to stop lighting candles to St. Barbara, because she did not exist. While this was going on, the blood of St. Januarius, who had been removed from the universal calendar, liquefied as usual and on time in Naples.[918]

Since 1970 more than 100 saints have been demoted, "lost their jobs" or "were forced into early retirement." This included: St. Valentine, St. Christopher, patron of travelers; St. Lucy, patroness of the blind; St. Philomena, patroness of the children of Mary; St. Patrick, patron of Ireland; St. George, patron of England; St. Vitus, patron of epileptics; St. Barbara, patroness of firemen; St. Catherine of Alexandria, patroness of philosophers; St. Nicholas of Myra (Santa Claus) and the patron of hunters, St. Eustace.

Although Modernists claim these saints were not de-canonized, they questioned their authenticity despite historical evidence. Many of the saints who have been purged from the Postconciliar Church were remarkable for the miracles obtained through their intercession. God Himself has been pleased to assist those who have prayed to them. However, the doctrine of the Communion of Saints is unecumenical and offensive to Protestants. Therefore, many of the saints had to be "de-canonized" and their statues were removed from the churches to placate them.

---

[918] *L'Osservatore Romano*, September 25, 1969.

Tragically, the Postconciliar Church no longer venerates notable saints found in Scripture, including: St. Simeon who held the Infant Jesus at the Presentation, St. Dismas the good thief, St. Longinus the soldier who pierced the side of Christ, St. Cornelius the centurion, St. Mary Salome, St. Mary of Cleophas and even the Magi (the Three Kings) who visited Bethlehem.

Saint Factory?

On February 7, 1983, John Paul II altered the age-old rules for canonization and beatification and has "beatified or canonized more people than all of his predecessors combined."[919] From 1588-1958, the popes canonized a total of 296 saints and beatified 808 individuals (the step before canonization). "The process normally takes decades, sometimes centuries."[920] By streamlining the canonization process he beatified 1,318 and canonized 477 individuals in less than 25 years.[921] The office of "devil's advocate," which carefully scrutinized the lives of candidates for sainthood, has been eliminated and "the reduction of the necessary miracles from four to two [for sainthood] also made it easier for the congregation [for Sainthood Causes] to advance particular causes."[922]

Carl Bernstein describes the flood of canonizations:

> Under John Paul II, the Catholic Church [Postconciliar Church] was becoming a saint factory. The pope was canonizing and beatifying Christian heroes at a rate of almost one a week. ...Until Wojtyla's papacy, the Congregation for the Causes of Saints had had to certify two miracles for each person beatified; John Paul II lowered the bar to one miracle.[923]

Why did the Vatican, during the past 40 years, eliminate over a hundred popular saints and then create hundreds of new ones? On nearly every trip abroad, John Paul II performs numerous beatifications or canonizations,

---

[919] *Toronto Sun*, October 21, 2002.
[920] *National Catholic Reporter*, October 17, 2003, "Pope considered declaring Mother Teresa blessed, saint in one ceremony," Religious News Service and CNS.
[921] Figures as of November 26, 2003.
[922] *National Catholic Register*, Oct. 12, 2003, "John Paul the Saint-Maker," by Tim Drake.
[923] *His Holiness*, p. 393.

representing the countries and cultures he visits. These actions immensely increase his popularity and influence worldwide.

Politicians meticulously analyze their audiences in order to tell them what they want to hear. What better way to endear himself to the masses and keep them loyal to his church than by creating saints in many of the countries he visits?

Consider the spectacle of John Paul II's visit to Korea on May 16, 1984:

> The Mass that John Paul II celebrated in Seoul for the Korean martyrs was one of those gigantic ceremonies that seemed designed by the pope and his aides to stun the world. A cross 130 feet high had been raised over the papal platform. A million faithful were present—in a country with barely 1.7 million Catholics. A fifteen-hundred-voice choir sang, while 800 priests and 1,200 deacons and subdeacons went into the crowd to distribute communion. Amid this imperial pomp, the pope wore gold-colored satin vestments, embroidered with a white cloud and a dragon, the emblem of Korea's royal dynasty.[924]

> ...Beneath the eye of the camera, his global evangelization came to life. ...People watched him against the background of exotic panoramas: sailing down tropical rivers, standing on the slopes of sacred volcanoes or walking in the shadow of soaring skyscrapers—like some omnipresent Master of the Universe.

> Masses celebrated by Pope Wojtyla became epic performances. He preached and prayed in stadiums and at racetracks, on the tarmacs of airports and in meadows of clover. [He also worshipped in churches, mosques, synagogues and temples of every major religion.] Wherever he appeared in cities, a Super Bowl atmosphere prevailed. Local organizers felt compelled to create more and more fantastic stage designs for his open-air events, turning the papal platforms on which John Paul II celebrated masses into gargantuan Hollywood sets. ...Sometimes the canopy above the tabernacle was shaped like a vast sail or an enormous dove or the walls to the side would form a pyramid, decorated with cultural symbols from whatever nation the pope was visiting. In his honor bands played, choirs sang, dancers swayed. Liturgical acts were transformed

---

[924] Carl Bernstein and Marco Politi, *His Holiness*, p. 394.

into spectacle. ...Before his throne, bread, fruits, fabrics, arts and crafts, even babies in cradle passed in review.

...On the TV screen, as the pope and Navarro-Valls [Vatican spokesman] well understood, glory would invariably overshadow problems, emotion would overwhelm insight. Any uncomfortable questions from print reporters would be drowned out.[925]

All Roads Lead to Rome

In an editorial in the *Wall Street Journal* entitled "The Pope Has Let Us Down," Rod Dreher asks numerous questions regarding John Paul II's lack of concern regarding the crisis in the Church today:

Why has he allowed so many American bishops, nearly all of whom he has appointed, to eviscerate the liturgical, catechetical and pastoral life of the church...

[There are many] serious questions, but they fade into abstraction when one is confronted by the horror of the sex-abuse scandal, and decay of faith and morality among the American priesthood and episcopate, which has left so many trusting Catholic laymen and their children vulnerable.

...When considering how this intolerable state came to pass, all roads lead to Rome. In Catholic teaching, the chief responsibilities of a bishop, including the Bishop of Rome, are to teach, sanctify and govern.

...Who retains in office a host of American bishops defiled by their indifference to the victims of depraved priests under their authority? Who could remove them with a stroke of his pen? It is hard to judge John Paul, because we don't know what he's had to fight behind the scenes. Still, I find it impossible any longer to give him the benefit of every doubt, as is the custom of many papal loyalists. John Paul must bear partial responsibility for the catastrophe that has befallen us.[926]

Even Hans Küng admitted that John Paul II's reign has been a dismal failure. He "told the Swiss weekly *Sonntagszeitung*, 'For the Catholic Church, this papacy was a disaster despite some positive aspects. Don't be fooled by the Masses at big

---

[925] Carl Bernstein and Marco Politi, *His Holiness*, pp. 399-400.
[926] August 20, 2002. Mr. Dreher is senior writer for *The National Review*.

papal events. During this papacy, millions have fled the church or quietly turned inward.'"[927]

Is Not the Pope Infallible?

The subject of papal infallibility is one, which, for various reasons throughout history, has often been denied or misrepresented. Basically, the term means that when a pope in his official capacity as successor of St. Peter and Vicar of Christ promulgates a decision on faith and morals to the Universal Church he is preserved from error. Papal infallibility is a form of God's protection over His Church whereby the pope is protected from ever teaching anything contrary to the Deposit of Faith.

The dogma of papal infallibility has been attacked for more than 600 years. Even during the Vatican Council of 1869-1870 several bishops objected to this doctrine by referring to the examples of Pope Liberius and Pope Honorius I. However, the Council Fathers were able to prove beyond all doubt that not a single pope erred in his office as Supreme Pastor of the Church, and they formally declared papal infallibility a Dogma of the Faith.

Infallibility has nothing to do with the personal conduct of the pope and it does not mean he cannot sin. It is an essential part of his office as defender of the Deposit of Faith. In spite of the fact that several popes caused scandal by their immoral lives and others were weak and ineffective leaders, nevertheless God preserved each pope from teaching doctrinal errors, thereby safeguarding the truths of the Faith. From the foundation of the Catholic Church until the time of Vatican II, not a single pope had ever taught formal heresy or erred when teaching the Universal Church in matters of faith and morals.

A pope cannot invent any new doctrines nor teach anything contrary to the Deposit of Faith. The pope is not the maker of Divine Law; rather, he is only its expounder. He is not the author of Catholic doctrine, but only its guardian for Divine Revelation was complete at the time of the death of the Apostles. A pope has no more authority than you or I to change one iota of the Deposit of Faith or Divine Law.

---

[927] *National Catholic Reporter,* November 7, 2003, "World Briefs," by Dennis Coday.

The office of the papacy is clearly expressed by Wladimir D'Ormesson, who lived at the time of the Vatican Council (1869-1870):

> Papal infallibility embraces the whole of Divine Revelation, but it is confined to that revelation. The pope can impose nothing beyond what forms part of the deposit of revelation. His mission is to profess it, to teach it, to maintain it and to preserve it. He has an immense task of conservation and exposition. It is not for him to establish new doctrine. The revelation is complete.[928]

Schism, Heresy and Apostasy

Schism, heresy and apostasy immediately separate one from the Catholic Church, whether that individual is a lay person or the highest official in the Church.[929] Pope Pius XII reaffirms this fact in his encyclical *On the Mystical Body of Christ*, "For not every sin, however grave it may be, is such as of its own nature to sever a man from the body of the Church, as does schism, heresy or apostasy."[930]

A Heretic Cannot be Pope

Cajetan says in order to be the head of an organization, you must first be a member. Since a heretical pope is no longer a member of the Catholic Church, it follows that he cannot be its visible head. "And so a man lacking faith is in the classification of a heretic and is not a member of the Church, therefore he is not the head of the same, and because of this when a pope is nothing other than the (visible) head of the Church, he himself cannot be the pope because he is without faith."[931] St. Robert Bellarmine, in his work entitled *De Romano Pontifice*, declares: "A pope who is a manifest heretic by that fact *[per se]* ceases to be pope and head [of the Church], just as he by the fact ceases to be a Christian."[932] "This

---

[928] *The Papacy*, p. 115.

[929] "All apostates from the Christian faith and all heretics and schismatics are ipso facto excommunicated… " Canon 2314 further states that clerics who have publicly fallen away from the Catholic faith lose their office as noted in Canon 188, 4. This legislation is similar to the Constitution *Apostolicae Sedis*, C.S.O. February 19, 1916.

[930] June 29, 1943.

[931] "Et sic, homo carens fide, qualis est haereticus, non est membrum Ecclesiae, igitur non est caput ejusdem, ac per hoc, cum Papa nihil aliud sit quam caput (visibile) Ecclesiae, eo, ipso quod fit sine fide, fit non Papa." (Tract. 1 de auctorit. Papae et Concilii.)

[932] "…papam haereticum manifestum per se desinere esse papam et caput, sicut per se desinit esse christianus et membrum corporis Ecclesiae;" Xisto Cardinal Sforza, *S.R.E. Cardinalis Roberti Bellarmini Politiani, S.J., Opera Omnia*, p. 420.

is the judgment of all the early Fathers [of the Church] who teach, that manifest heretics immediately lose all jurisdiction."[933]

The eminent Doctor of the Church confirms this teaching by stating that according to the early Fathers of the Church (St. Athanasius, St. Augustine, St. Cyprian and St. Jerome) a manifest heretic cannot be pope.[934]

The papal bull *Cum ex Apostolatus* of Pope Paul IV states:

> ...If ever at any time it shall appear that... the Roman Pontiff, prior to his promotion or his elevation as cardinal or Roman Pontiff has deviated from the Catholic Faith or fallen into some heresy: (i) the promotion or elevation, even if it shall have been uncontested and by the unanimous assent of all the cardinals, shall be null, void and invalid; (ii) it shall not be possible for it to acquire validity ...through the acceptance of the office, of consecration, ...nor through the putative enthronement of a Roman Pontiff... (v) each and all of their words, deeds, actions and enactments... shall be without force (vi) those thus promoted or elevated shall be deprived automatically and without need for any further declaration, of all dignity, position, honor, title, authority, office and power, without any exception in respect of those to which they may have been promoted or elevated before they deviated from the Faith, became heretics, incurred schism, or provoked or committed any or all of these.[935]

John XXIII and his successors have embraced the heresies of Modernism, false Ecumenism, Religious Indifferentism and false Religious Liberty. Their adherence to heresy prior to their elections made them ineligible candidates for the papacy because they had already severed themselves from the Catholic Church.

Such obvious invalidation can be more easily understood when applying this reasoning to the United States presidential election. One of the requirements for

---

[933] "Haec est sententia omnium veterum Patrum, qui docent, haereticos manifestos mox amittere omnem jurisdiction." Sforza, 420.

[934] "Non Christianus non potest ulla modo esse papa, ut Cajetanus fatetur in eod. lib. cap. 26. et ratio est, quia non potest esse caput id quod non est membrum; et non est membrum Ecclesiae is qui non est Christianus: at haeriticus manifestus non est Christianus, ut aperte docet Cyprianus lib. 4. epist. 2. Athanasius ser. 2. cont. Arian. Augustinus lib. de grat. Christ. cap. 20. Hieronymus cont. Lucifer et alii; haeriticus igitur manifestus papa esse non potest." Xisto Cardinal Sforza, *S.R.E. Cardinalis Roberti Bellarmini Politiani, S.J., Opera Omnia*, pp. 419-420.

[935] February 15, 1559.

a person to become President of the United States is that he must be an American citizen. If perchance one were elected President, and it was later discovered that he was not an American citizen, then, *de facto,* that individual who was ineligible for the office could not be considered head of the country to which he does not belong. Americans, in turn, would have no obligation to follow his invalid directives since he would have no legitimate authority to mandate them.

The teachings of Pope Paul IV, which deal with a cleric losing his office because of abandonment of the Catholic Faith, were incorporated into Canon Law: "All [ecclesiastical] offices shall be vacant *ipso facto* by tacit resignation through the operation of law, automatically and without any declaration... when a cleric publicly abandons the Catholic faith."[936]

Every word of this canon is significant including: *cleric*—which includes all ecclesiastics without exception, from porter to pope, from tonsure to tiara; *defects from* or *forsakes the Catholic faith*—this takes place not only when a Catholic apostasizes completely, but even if he falls into just one heresy. Hence, whether a man is invalidly elected pope, or whether he *de facto* removes himself from office by heresy (which has never occurred in the history of the Church), the Chair of Peter becomes vacant. Theologians have said, "A heretic pope is no pope."

Wolves Amid the Fold

Our Lord foretold that cunning men, inspired by the devil, would lead multitudes astray. Jesus repeatedly warned His flock against the wily attacks of false prophets:

> Beware of false prophets, who come to you in sheep's clothing, but inwardly are ravening wolves. By their fruits you will know them. Do men gather grapes from thorns, or figs from thistles? Even so, every good tree bears good fruit, but the bad tree bears bad fruit. Every tree that does not bear good fruit is cut down and thrown into the fire. Therefore, by their fruits you will know them. (Matt. 7: 15-20)

---

[936] "Ob tacitam renunciationem ab ipso jure admissam quaelibet officia vacant ipso facto et sine ulla declaratione... si clericus: A fide catholica publice defecerit." Canon 188, 4.

The wolves of the Second Vatican Council have even retained the name "Catholic" in order to more easily deceive the unwary. These heretics appropriately fit the words of St. Paul:

> ...Fierce wolves will get in among you, and will not spare the flock. And from among your own selves men will rise speaking perverse things, to draw away the disciples after them. (Acts 20: 29) For they are false apostles, deceitful workers, disguising themselves as apostles of Christ. And no wonder, for Satan himself disguises himself as an angel of light. It is no great thing, then, if his ministers disguise themselves as ministers of justice. But their end will be according to their works. (II Cor. 11: 13)

Perpetual Successors in the Primacy

Confusion has arisen over the Vatican Council's teaching of July 18, 1870 concerning "perpetual successors in the primacy over the Universal Church."[937] Fr. Martin Stepanich, O.F.M. explained this topic very well when he wrote:

> The important thing here is to understand just what kind of 'perpetual succession' in the papacy Our Lord established. Did Our Lord intend that there should be a pope on the Chair of Peter every single moment of the Church's existence and every single moment of the papacy's existence?
>
> You will immediately realize that, no, Our Lord very obviously did not establish that kind of 'perpetual succession' of popes. You know that, all through the centuries of the Church's existence, popes have been dying and that there then followed an interval, after the death of each pope, when there was no 'perpetual successor,' no pope, occupying the Chair of Peter. That chair became vacant for a while whenever a pope died. This has happened more than 260 times since the death of the first pope. But you also know that the death of a pope did not mean the end of the 'perpetual succession' of popes after Peter.
>
> You understand now that 'no pope' does not mean 'no papacy.' A vacant chair of Peter after the death of a pope does not mean a permanent vacancy of that chair, a temporary vacancy of the Chair of Peter does not mean the end of the 'perpetual successors in the primacy over the Universal Church.'

---

[937] See D 1824 *Dogmatic Constitution on the Church of Christ,* Chapter 2.

Even though Our Lord, had He so willed it, could have seen to it that, the moment one pope died, another man would automatically succeed him as pope, He nevertheless did not do it that way. Our Lord did it the way we have always known it to be, that is, He allowed for an interval, or interruption, of undesignated duration, to follow upon the death of each pope.

That interruption of succession of popes has, most of the time, lasted several weeks, or a month or so, but there have been times when the interruption lasted longer than that, considerably longer. Our Lord did not specify just how long that interruption was allowed to last before a new pope was to be elected, and He did not declare that, if the delay in electing a new pope lasted too long, the 'perpetual succession' was then terminated, so that it would then have to be said that 'the papacy is no more.' Nor did the Church ever specify the length or duration of the vacancy of the Chair of Peter to be allowed after the death of a pope.

Most important of all, never forget that men cannot put an end to the 'perpetual succession' of popes, no matter how long public heretics may occupy Peter's chair. The Catholic papacy comes from God, not from man. To put an end to the 'perpetual succession' of popes, you would first have to put an end to God Himself.[938]

Whether there is a legitimate pope, no pope or an antipope—the Catholic Faith remains the same. Even if the chair is vacant, the papacy still exists. Jesus Christ is the Head of the Catholic Church and the pope is His vicar on earth. (For additional information regarding papal infallibility refer to Chapter 20.)

The Authors' Position

The fourth commandment obliges us to obey the legitimate orders of our lawful superiors, and we know we must obey the true pope. The promulgators of Vatican II, as experts in deceit, banked on Catholics' obedience to the Church—especially to the papacy. However, at the onset of the heretical changes of Vatican II, many Catholics failed to remember that they are not to obey any sinful or heretical directive, regardless from whence it derives. As St. Paul wrote, "But even if we or an angel from heaven should preach a gospel to you other than

---

[938] Letters of November 30, 2002 and March 25, 2003.

that which we preached to you, let him be anathema!" (Gal. 1: 8) Therefore, we cannot obey anyone who commands us to sin, even if the man be called "pope."

Tragically, most Catholics after Vatican II blindly followed the directives of the Postconciliar Popes and bishops, even when they attacked Christ's teachings and the Ten Commandments. So accustomed were they to obey and not question orders that many failed to realize that their first obligation is to obey God. In the final analysis, we should remember the words of St. Peter: "We ought to obey God rather than men."[939]

Since Catholics were accustomed to accepting the directives of the pope, the bishops and their parish priests without question, the architects of Vatican II exploited this characteristic to create the Postconciliar Church. New doctrines, a new Mass and new sacraments were created to replace the old. Laity were told that the Church needed to "get with the times." The few who questioned the "authority" of the new "reformers" who dismantled what Christ had created were subjected to ridicule or ostracized for their non-compliance. As a result, centuries of tradition, faith and belief were universally discarded by the majority.

- The documents of Vatican II contain numerous heresies, including the false doctrines of ecumenism and religious indifferentism. These heresies, although previously condemned by the Catholic Church, have been officially promulgated by the Postconciliar Popes. They have even given official recognition to non-Christian religions (many of which are polytheistic) and actively promote interfaith worship.
- The New Mass or *Novus Ordo Missae* formulated after Vatican II is not a propitiatory sacrifice offered in atonement for sin, but is merely a Protestant memorial of the Last Supper.
- The words of Christ used in the sacramental form of the Holy Eucharist, since the time of the Apostles, have been substantially altered in the New Mass. These essential changes invalidate the Mass according to the teachings of Pope St. Pius V *(De Defectibus)*.

---

[939] Acts of the Apostles 5: 29.

- The substantial changes to the sacraments place serious doubts as to their validity.

One cannot reconcile these obvious doctrinal errors with the infallible teaching Magisterium (the authority of the popes and bishops of the Catholic Church) throughout history. The hierarchy of the Postconciliar Church does not represent the Magisterium of the Catholic Church. A true pope cannot promulgate invalid, sacrilegious ceremonies, rites or disciplines for the Church. It is impossible for a true pope to promulgate error by means of the ordinary universal Magisterium. One who has placed himself outside the Catholic Church by the profession of public heresy cannot be a valid pope.

Traditional Catholics throughout the world reject the Postconciliar Popes because of their formal heresy. This is based on:

- the indefectibility of the Church
- the dogma of papal infallibility
- the writings of the Fathers and Doctors of the Church regarding a "heretical pope."

Many wonder what has brought about the devastation that followed in the wake of Vatican II. Some claim that the hands of the Postconciliar Popes were tied by the liberal cardinals and bishops surrounding them. This is wishful thinking. The facts reveal otherwise.

On numerous occasions, the Postconciliar Popes have given positions of power and prestige to Modernists and Socialists by elevation to the episcopacy and even promotion to the College of Cardinals itself. In addition, John Paul II carefully planned and organized the details of the interfaith services in Assisi. He was not forced to do things contrary to his will. If, in fact, he was unduly pressured by the hierarchy, he would only have needed to hold a press conference and millions would have risen to his defense.

It cannot be stated that any of the Postconciliar Popes acted against their wills. In its section on offenses and penalties, Canon Law declares that when the law is violated (e.g. heretical teaching), a bad intention is presumed. Canon 2200 states, "...when an external violation of the law occurs, in the external forum the existence of malice is presumed until the contrary is proved because in the ordinary case man acts knowingly and freely."

Ultimately the reader cannot help but question and weigh the opposing sides. Who is right—the past 260 popes or the four "popes" since 1958? Which teachings are correct—those of the Catholic Church for nearly 2,000 years or the teachings of Vatican II and the "popes" of the past 40 years?

One can only conclude that John XXIII, Paul VI, John Paul I and John Paul II have led millions astray with their new Mass and sacraments, heretical beliefs and false ecumenism. Yet they deceptively still call this new religion the "Catholic Church" and continue to mislead countless souls.

The authors, along with many Catholics throughout the world, share the view expressed in a 1983 declaration by Bishop Carmona and Bishop Zamora:

> We hold that the Apostolic See has been vacant since the death of Pope Pius XII by virtue of the fact that those who were elected to succeed him did not possess the canonical qualifications necessary to be legitimate candidates for the papacy.
>
> ...Based upon the Bull *Cum Apostolatus Officio* of Pope Paul IV, we hold that Angelo Roncalli [John XXIII] was never a legitimate pope and that his acts are completely null and void.
>
> We declare that the New 'Mass' is invalid. ...We declare that the introduction of this New 'Mass' also signals the promulgation of a new humanistic religion in which Almighty God is no longer worshipped as He desires to be worshipped...

J. Conclusion

The radical changes of Vatican II have hurled many unsuspecting Catholics into a new church that has the semblance of Catholicism but lacks many of its essential elements. Many find themselves bewildered by this modern religion of convenience, confusion and inconsistency. Sweeping changes have resulted in a faith based on the fads and beliefs of the time. The modern liturgy is so unpredictable and changeable that publisher Eliot Kapitan claims, "There's nothing [no book] available today that conforms perfectly with the new laws and regulations."[940] Yet, in the Postconciliar Church the liturgy continues to change.

While the formal dogmas of the Catholic Church and the Canon of the Mass are unchangeable by their very essence, the New Mass, new sacraments and new teachings that have emanated from Vatican II are changed at the least whim, just as if they were written on an Etch A Sketch.[941] If any think that these modern changes in faith and worship are from God, then they have to conclude that the Catholic Church has been wrong for 2,000 years—a fact that contradicts both Scripture and history.

Since Vatican II we have witnessed widespread irreverence, a disintegration of the sacrificial character of the Mass, an absence of the concept of personal sin and an unprecedented loss of faith. Universal consensus of belief, once the hallmark of Catholicism, has all but vanished.

Following St. Paul's lead, we must "stand firm and hold the traditions"[942] which we have learned from Christ and His Apostles. We all need to hold on to Tradition because it is deeply rooted in the past, supports us in the present and guides us along the safest path to the future.[943] By discarding Apostolic Tradition the New Church has lost its foundation of faith and its very soul. Something is

---

[940] *National Catholic Reporter,* December 13, 2002, "Under pressure from bishops, publisher pulls liturgical books," by Robert McClory.
[941] An Ohio Art toy that has a white screen and two dials: one for vertical drawing, another for horizontal drawing. The screen becomes blank when shaken—erasing the previous image so new ones can be drawn. The process can go on indefinitely.
[942] 2 Thess. 2: 14.
[943] The word *tradition* means "handed down," "customary."

terribly wrong when centuries of beliefs and worship are contemptuously discarded.

Interestingly enough, even the secular world has noted this defection with shocking headlines: "Has the Church Lost Its Soul?" (*Newsweek,* October 4, 1971), "Can the Church Save Its Soul?" (*U.S. News & World Report,* April 1, 2002) and "Can the Catholic Church Save Itself?" (*Time,* April 1, 2002).

In retrospect, with the view of the 20 General Councils of the Church behind us, we can see that the results of Vatican II have, sadly, paralleled the Protestant Reformation. During that revolution "All the theological notions, all the institutions, the whole discipline of the Church, were thrown into disorder. Luther concentrated in one nearly universal denial, all the errors which former heresies had successively opposed to each separate dogma of our faith. Strictly speaking, he was not inventing a system of errors, but merely collecting all past heresies into the great pandemonium called Protestantism."[944]

The Protestant Reformation attacked the very foundation of the Catholic Church: Apostolic Tradition, the Holy Sacrifice of the Mass, Dogmas of the Faith and the Seven Sacraments. Vatican II followed the same pattern.

Peter Ackroyd, in *The Life of Thomas More,* compares the manmade religion of Luther to the Catholic Faith, which alone traces its foundation to Christ:

> Where Luther would characteristically write 'I think thus', or 'I believe thus', More would reply with 'God has revealed thus' or 'the Holy Spirit has taught thus'. His [More's] was a church of order and ritual in which the precepts of historical authenticity were enshrined. All this Luther despised and rejected.[945]

Nearly 500 years after Luther, another church has been formed which likewise rejects and despises the doctrines, moral standards and traditional liturgy of the Catholic Church. Since Jesus Christ instituted very specific doctrines, liturgy, sacraments and moral standards, no one can arbitrarily change them. Vatican II was indeed the "work of human hands," not the work of God. Although its stated goal was "to adapt the Church to the times," the enemies of the Church used the

---

[944] Abbe J. Darras, *A General History of the Catholic Church, Vol. IV,* p. 65.
[945] Peter Ackroyd, *The Life of Thomas More,* p. 229.

Second Vatican Council as an attempt to destroy the Catholic Church from within.

Satan successfully caused unwary clergymen to deviate from the teachings of Christ, even in the early ages of the Church; why should we think he would be less active today? The powers of darkness have always sought to eradicate the light of Christ and His Church.

Those who are teaching modern heresies are not shepherds, but wolves disguised in sheep's clothing, even though they claim to belong to Christ's true Church. Tragically, the majority of Catholics have been misled by these heretical clergy into following erroneous beliefs, perverted liturgy and lax moral standards. Many of these Catholics never realized they were gradually adopting beliefs and practices of a church that was not founded by Christ.

For encouragement and edification, let us consider briefly how one great hero of the past dealt with just such a situation. He bravely defended the Faith against the overwhelming majority of his countrymen, clergy and government.

In 1534 St. Thomas More and a relatively small number of faithful Catholics refused to sign King Henry VIII's *Oath of Supremacy* because it amounted to a denial of the Catholic Faith. "If More had sworn the oath as it was presented to him... he would have concurred the forcible removal of the Pope's jurisdiction and the effective schism of the Church in England. This he could not do, even at the cost of his life."[946]

When St. Thomas More stood before Parliament he was taunted by Audley, Duke of Norfolk:

'Indeed, Master More, you wish to be held wiser than all the bishops, all the nobility, all the realm entire!' It was the old sneer he had heard so often, and now he flung back challenge for challenge in a voice ringing with the glory of belonging to Christ's Mystical Body. 'My lord, for one bishop of your opinion I have a hundred saints of mine; for one Parliament of yours, and God knows of what sort, I have all the General Councils of a thousand years; for one kingdom I have all the Kingdoms of Christendom!'[947]

---

[946] Peter Ackroyd, *The Life of Thomas More*, p. 364.
[947] Richard Smith, *John Fisher and Thomas More: Two English Saints*, p. 271

Unafraid of the violent death awaiting him, the saint joked with the executioner as he mounted the rickety scaffold: "I pray you, sir, see me safe up, and for my coming down let me shift for myself."[948] More's last words portrayed his deep faith and courage: "I am dying in the faith and for the faith of the Catholic Church, the king's good servant and God's first."[949]

It would be a mistake to claim that traditional Catholicism is false simply because it is not what most people now believe. As we have seen in our thorough examination of Church history, the Catholic Church is distinguished by the purity of its doctrine, not defined by the number of followers. In the fourth century, such multitudes of the faithful were seduced by the Arian heresy, that it appeared to be Catholicism's great defender "(St.) Athanasius against the world."

Catholicism is not defined by the possession of church buildings. During the sixteenth century hundreds of Catholic churches were occupied by "Catholic" priests who were, in fact, subtly replacing the true Faith with Protestantism. Catholicism is not guaranteed by those who bear titles of authority; during the Western Schism of the fourteenth and fifteenth centuries, several of the men who bore the title of "pope" were not popes at all.

The New Church created by Vatican II is not the Catholic Church. Because its "popes" are illegitimate, there is no moral obligation to follow such men or their new religion. On the contrary, we are obliged to follow the doctrines handed down by Christ and His Apostles and to avoid this New Church as we would any other false religion.

In order not to be deceived by heretical teachings or exposed to an invalid Mass and questionable sacraments, we encourage the readers to locate a church in your area that still offers the Tridentine Latin Mass and the authentic sacraments and teachings of Jesus Christ. Satan has not triumphed over the Catholic Church and Christ will remain with His Church until the end of time. Let us remember that "the gates of hell" will never prevail against the Church Christ founded.

---

[948] Msgr. Leon Cristiani, *The Revolt Against the Church*, p. 87.
[949] Linda Proud, *2000 Years of Christianity in England*, p. 16.

Traditional Catholics of today are often criticized because they do not accept Vatican II's new heretical teachings. Nevertheless, these Catholics and their families retain the rich heritage that has been handed down from time immemorial. Their credibility lies with Christ Himself and His Church of 2,000 years. It stands in preservation of the faith of 260 popes, 20 General Councils, countless saints, Catholic clergy and Religious, faithful lay men, women and children and the multitudes of martyrs who gave their lives in defense of these same beliefs.

The Catholic Church still exists, but not in the barren framework of the new religion established since Vatican II. It is found worldwide in Christ's flock of Traditional Catholics and faithful clergy who still follow the teachings of Jesus Christ as they have been handed down through the centuries. These sacred beliefs still remain as clear and precise as when the Apostles first heard them from the lips of Christ. The Catholic Faith lives on as it did in the time of the catacombs and will, as Our Lord promised, continue until the end of time.

In the traditional Catholic liturgy the priest faces the crucifix and the tabernacle, not the congregation; the Mass is an unbloody renewal of the sacrifice of the Cross, not a social event, and the preeminent place is given to Christ in the tabernacle, not to the chair of the presider. Here one finds no empty table in a bare hall, but the Real Presence of Our Lord in the Holy Eucharist adored in a surrounding that bespeaks of the mystical and the supernatural. Women kneel with modest dress, heads covered, and hands folded in prayer. Men and children also worship in humble silence before the tabernacle. Here one is able to experience the unchanged Tridentine Latin Mass and liturgy derived from the time of Christ and the Apostles. It is here that you will be able to recapture the stability and worship you thought had disappeared and that you have been searching for.

We conclude with the *Letter of St. Athanasius to His Flock:*

May God console you!... What saddens you... is the fact that others have occupied the churches by violence, while during this time you are on the outside. It is a fact that they have the premises—but you have the apostolic faith. They can occupy our churches, but they are outside the true faith. You remain outside the places of worship, but the faith dwells within you. Let us consider: what is more important, the place or the faith? The true faith, obviously. Who has lost and who has won in this struggle—the one who keeps the premises or the one who keeps the faith?

True, the premises are good when the apostolic faith is preached there; they are holy if everything takes place there in a holy way...

You are the ones who are happy; you who remain within the Church by your faith, who hold firmly to the foundations of the faith which has come down to you from apostolic tradition. ...They are the ones who have broken away from it in the present crisis.

No one, ever, will prevail against your faith, beloved brothers. And we believe that God will give us our churches back some day.

Thus, the more violently they try to occupy the places of worship, the more they separate themselves from the Church. They claim that they represent the Church; but in reality, they are the ones who are expelling themselves from it and going astray. Even if Catholics faithful to tradition are reduced to a handful, they are the ones who are the true Church of Jesus Christ.[950]

---

[950] *Coll. Selecta SS. Eccl. Patrum,* Caillau and Guillou, Vol. 32, pp. 411-412.

K. Plan of Action

Prayer

St. Paul assures us that we haven't a chance in our conflict against the devil if we try to fight him bare-handed. The devil's keen intelligence and stupendous power is far superior to all our willpower, all our human prudence and cleverness, and all our strength of character. "Our wrestling is not against flesh and blood but against the Principalities and Powers, against the world-rulers of this darkness, against the spiritual forces of wickedness on high."[951]

However, Almighty God has provided us with many spiritual weapons with which to defend ourselves against the allurements and attacks of the devil. The most effective means of overcoming temptation are prayer, penance, frequent Confession and Holy Communion and avoidance of the near occasions of sin.

According to St. Bernard, "The powers of hell are mighty but prayer is stronger than all the devils."[952] "For as St. [John] Chrysostom says 'Prayer is a strong weapon, a defense, a port and a treasure.' "[953] " 'There is nothing more powerful than a man who prays,'[954] because such a one is made a partaker of the power of God."[955] St. Alphonsus asserts that prayer "…is a weapon sufficient to overcome every assault of the devil; it is a defense to preserve us in every danger; it is a port where we may be safe in every tempest; and it is at the same time a treasure which provides us with every good."[956]

"St. Augustine says that prayer is a key which opens heaven to us; the same moment in which our prayer ascends to God, the grace which we ask for descends to us: 'The prayer of the just is the key of heaven; the petition ascends, and the mercy of God descends.' "[957]

---

[951] Ephesians 6: 12.
[952] "Oratio daemoniis omnibus malis praevalet."—*De modo bene viv.* s. 49.
[953] "Magna armatura precatio tutela portis et thesaurus."—*Hom. In Ps.* 145.
[954] "Nihil potentius homine probo orante."—*In Matt. Hom.* 58.
[955] St. Alphonsus Liguori, *The Great Means of Salvation and of Perfection*, p. 62.
[956] Liguori, 52.
[957] "*Serm. 47, E.B. app.* Liguori, 86.

Concerning prayer, St. John Chrysostom has written:

'The angels have a great esteem for fervent prayer, and consequently do much to promote it. The devils, on the contrary, have an intense dislike for it and as a result strongly combat and disturb it.' The same Saint tells us that the angels greatly respect those who are united to God by means of prayer. While the latter are praying, they stay near them in profound silence, and when they have finished, they praise them.[958]

Prayer is the strongest weapon to conquer temptations. Like the Apostles beaten about by the stormy winds of the Sea of Galilee we cry out in prayer, "Lord save us! we are perishing!"[959] and the peace and strength of Christ comes to our aid in the struggle against the world, the flesh and the devil.

To banish temptations, immediate resistance, humility, confidence in God and watchfulness are necessary, but according to the testimony of the saints prayer is by far the most efficacious means to win the combat. Our entire life, then, should be fortified with daily prayer for it is crucial to our survival in this battle with the demons.

Use of Sacramentals

Sacramentals also serve as powerful weapons against the devil and his temptations. Wear a blessed medal (e.g. Miraculous Medal or a St. Benedict Medal) and a brown scapular, not as a charm against the devil, but as a sacramental. Trust that through the prayer of the Church in blessing the medal and scapular and through your confidence and reliance on the blessing of both, you will be protected against the devil. Carry a blessed Rosary or a blessed crucifix with you; call upon the Holy Names of Jesus, Mary and Joseph and make the sign of the cross using holy water.

Keep a supply of holy water in your home and have holy water fonts throughout your home. Use holy water frequently on yourself and on your children, and teach them how to use it reverently as a sacramental. Begin when they are very young. This sacramental is very powerful and repels the devil.

---

[958] *Spiritual Diary*, pp. 184-185.
[959] Matthew 8: 26.

Spiritual Guidelines

1) Attend the Tridentine Latin Mass exclusively. For information on where to locate Tridentine Latin Masses, please check the *Official Catholic Directory of Traditional Latin Masses and Resource Book For the United States and Canada* compiled by Veritas Press, P.O. Box 1704, Santa Monica, CA 90406-1704. (We recommend only the Masses of those priests who hold to the position that the Chair of Peter is at least materially vacant.)

2) Receive Holy Communion frequently and go to Confession often.

3) Pray the Rosary daily and foster a deep devotion to the Blessed Virgin Mary, for she is more powerful than all the devils.

4) Say the Morning Offering and ask God to help and protect you.

5) Offer up aspirations of love and gratitude to God throughout the day.

6) Pray the Act of Contrition before retiring and implore God's protection throughout the night.

7) Remember that when you are alone you are least alone: God and your Guardian Angel are with you.

8) Recall that your body is the temple of the Holy Ghost and is destined for a glorious resurrection. Keep it pure.

9) Keep yourself occupied with work or play. Resist the very first suggestion of sin by saying a quick prayer and then turn your mind to some other subject.

10) Keep away from persons, places or things that are for you an occasion of sin.

11) Read traditional Catholic periodicals (*The Reign of Mary*, 8500 N. St. Michael's Rd. Spokane, WA 99217) and spiritual books, including the lives of the saints.

12) View the video: *The Vacancy*. It is a documentary of the current situation in the Church. The price of the video is $12.50 each plus $3.85 shipping and can be obtained by writing to: The Vacancy, P.O. Box 220208, Newhall, CA 91322.

13) Do your own research by reading the suggested reference books suitable for research which are designated by asterisks (*) in front of the titles found in the bibliography.

14) Refrain from indecent styles of clothing and from immoral music, TV and movies. If you would be ashamed to have Jesus with you, don't wear the clothes, listen to the music or watch the program. While we cannot control what is shown on TV, you can control what is being watched in your home.

15) Pray and make sacrifices for the conversion of sinners.

Amid the storms of adversity and winds of change the Catholic Church stands as an indestructible lighthouse guiding souls through the darkness of heresy to the safe haven of God's truth and grace.

Appendix

Summary of the 20 General Councils of the Church

Chart of the 20 General Councils

Chart of the Founders of the Various Religions

Heresies Combated by the General Councils

List of the Illegitimate Councils

List of the Legitimate Popes

List of the 41 Antipopes

Brief Description of the Crusades

15 Promises of the Rosary

Pope Leo XIII's Prayer to St. Michael the Archangel

Summary of the General Councils of the Church

Council	Date	Pope

1. Nicaea I 325 St. Sylvester I
   Acts: Condemned heresy of Arius; defined clearly that the Son of God was consubstantial (homoousios) with the Father; formulated the Nicene Creed.

2. Constantinople I 381 St. Damasus I
   Acts: Condemned heresy of Macedonius; defined the divinity of the Holy Ghost; confirmed and extended the Nicene Creed.

3. Ephesus 431 St. Celestine I
   Acts: Condemned heresy of Nestorius; defined that there was one Person in Christ and defended the Divine Maternity of the Blessed Virgin Mary.

4. Chalcedon 451 St. Leo I
   Acts: Condemned heresy of Eutyches (Monophysitism); declared Christ had two natures, human and divine.

5. Constantinople II 553 Vigilius
   Acts: Condemned, as savoring of Nestorianism, the so-called Three Chapters, the erroneous books of Theodore of Mopsuestia and the teaching of Theodoret of Cyrrhus and Ibas of Edessa.

6. Constantinople III 680-681 St. Agatho (confirmed by St. Leo II)
   Acts: Declared against the Monothelites, who taught one will in Christ, by defining that Christ had two wills, human and divine.

7. Nicaea II 787 Hadrian I
   Acts: Condemned the heresy of the image-breakers (Iconoclasm).

8. Constantinople IV 869-870 Hadrian II
   Acts: Deposed the usurper, Photius and suppressed the Greek Schism.

9. Lateran I (Rome)   1123   Calixtus II

    Acts: Called to confirm the peace between Church and State after the settlement of the Investiture Question.

10. Lateran II   1139   Innocent II

    Acts: Suppressed last remnants of the schism of Anacletus II; reaffirmed principles of the Gregorian Reform; silenced and banished from Italy Arnold of Brescia; condemned the heresy of Peter of Bruys.

11. Lateran III   1179   Alexander III

    Acts: Reformed ecclesiastical discipline; decreed papal elections by two-thirds majority of cardinals at conclave; confirmed Peace of Venice (between Alexander III and Barbarossa).

12. Lateran IV   1215   Innocent III

    Acts: Condemned errors of Albigenses, Joachim of Floria and Almaric of Bena; prescribed annual Confession and Communion for all; promoted ecclesiastical discipline; ordered crusade for the recovery of the Holy Land.

13. Lyons I   1245   Innocent IV

    Acts: Called in behalf of the Holy Land, and on account of the hostility of the Emperor Frederick II toward the Holy See.

14. Lyons II   1274   Bl. Gregory X

    Acts: Called to promote ecclesiastical discipline; to effect union of the Greeks with the Latin Church; to aid the Holy Land.

15. Vienne   1311-1312   Clement V

    Acts: Condemned the extreme views of Olivi and the heresies of Fraticelli, Dulcinists, Beghards, and Beguines; suppressed the Knights Templar; sought aid for the Holy Land.

16. Constance   1414-1418   Gregory XII, Martin V

    Acts: Suppressed Western Schism; ecclesiastical reform in "head and members"; Wycliff and Hus condemned.

17. Florence   1438-1443   Eugene IV

    Acts: Called to effect union of Greeks and other Oriental sects with the Latin Church; to re-establish peace among Christian princes.

18. Lateran V   1512-1517   Julius II, Leo X

    Acts: Defined relations of pope to General Councils; condemned certain errors regarding nature of the human soul; called for crusade against Turks.

19. Trent   1545-1563   Paul III, Julius III, Pius IV

    Acts: Called to combat heresies of so-called Reformers of the 16th century; proclaimed Bible and Tradition as the Rule of Faith; issued canons on the Sacraments and decrees of purgatory, indulgences, justification, invocation and veneration of saints, veneration of images and relics; published decree on the "Index" of forbidden books.

20. Vatican I   1869-1870   Pius IX

    Acts: Promulgated canons relating to faith and the Constitution of the Church; defined solemnly the infallibility of the pope (adjourned but not closed).[1]

---

[1] *The Catholic Almanac,* St. Anthony's Guild: Paterson, NJ, 1955. Vatican I was never officially closed.

The Twenty General Councils of the Catholic Church

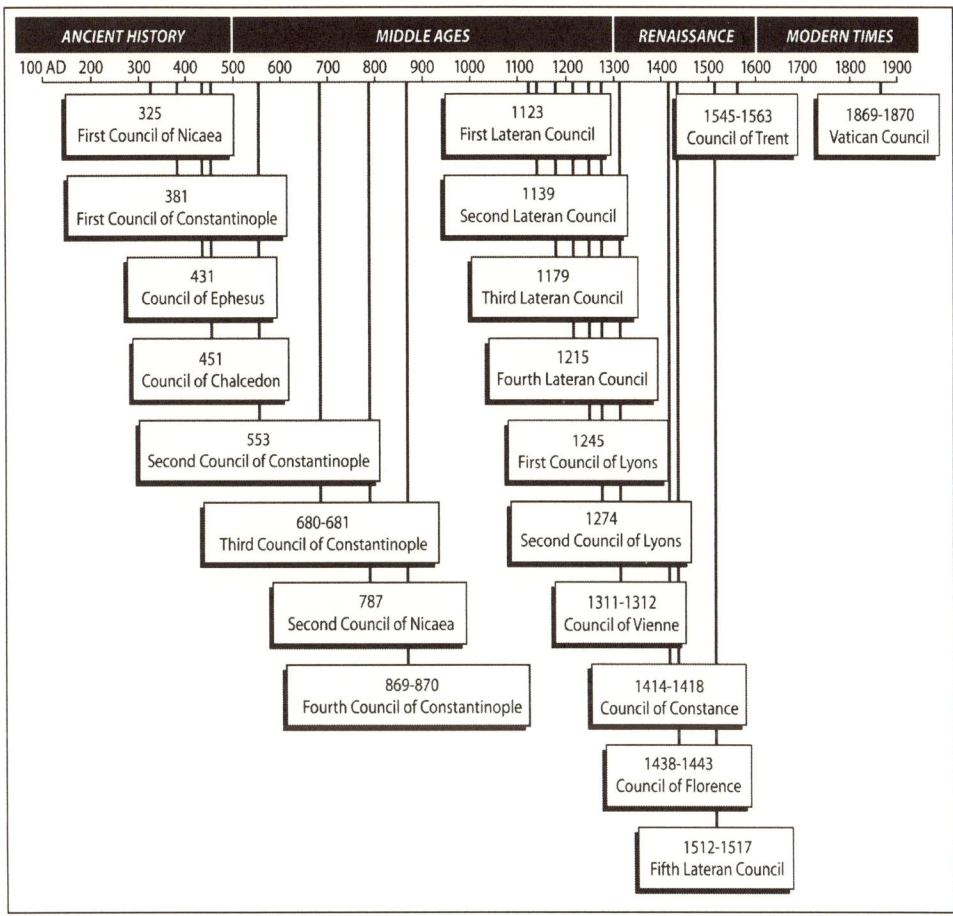

Chart of the Founders of the Various Religions

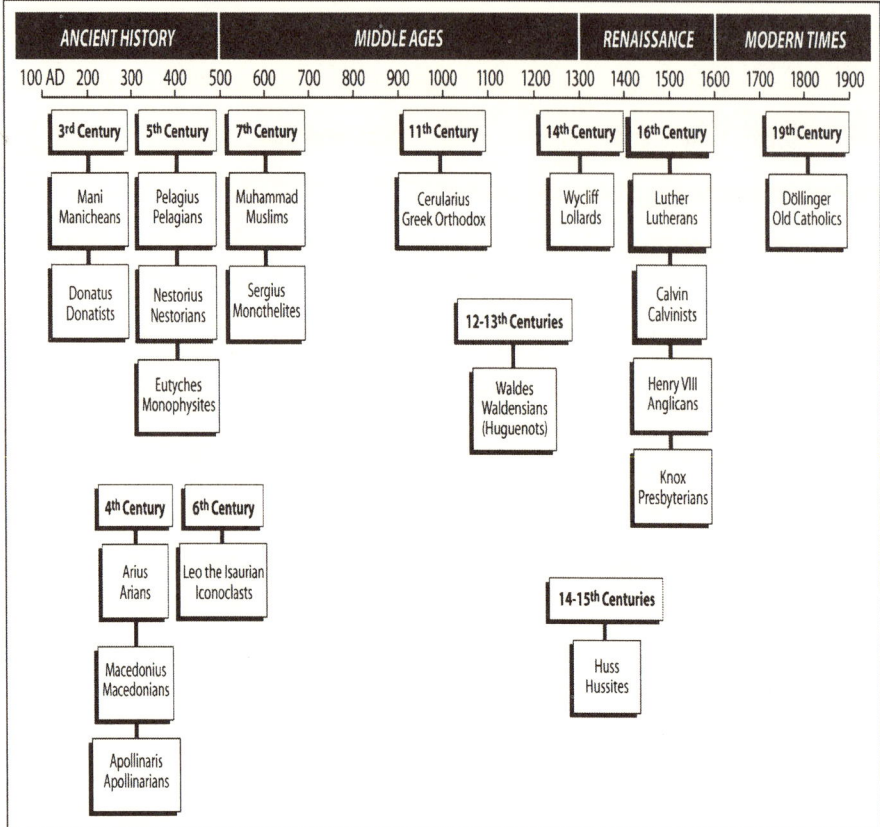

Heresies Combated by the General Councils

Albigenses—Constantine of Samosata

Believed in two deities—one good, the other evil—and denied the Trinity, Incarnation and Redemption. They rejected the Old Testament, infant baptism and claimed that marriage was sinful. Albigenses believed that everyone had the power to forgive sins, that penance was useless and that unworthy priests lost the power of consecrating the Holy Eucharist. They likewise taught that it is wrong to obey and support the clergy. The Third Lateran Council condemned the Albigensian heresy in 1179. (Chapter 12)

Arians—Arius (priest of Alexandria)

Denied the divinity of Christ and taught that God the Son was not eternal. They claimed that Christ was made the partaker of the divine nature as a reward for the work of the redemption. The Arian heresy was condemned at the First Council of Nicaea (325 AD) and the First Council of Constantinople (381 AD). (Chapters 1 & 2)

Donatists—Donatus the Great (African bishop)

Believed in predestination and declared that baptism was invalid unless it was conferred by a Donatist. Donatists believed that the sacraments conferred by unworthy priests were invalid. The Donatist heresy was condemned at the First Council of Nicaea in 325 AD. (Chapter 1)

Greek Orthodox—Michael Cerularius (patriarch of Constantinople)

Although several attempts were made to end the schism (the Second Council of Lyons 1274—Chapter 14, and the Council of Florence 1438-1443—Chapter 17) the rift from the West still remains. The Greek Orthodox Church denies the supremacy of the pope and teaches that the Holy Ghost proceeds from the Father alone. "The Roman Catholic Church believes in the Immaculate Conception of the Virgin, a doctrine which Eastern Orthodoxy does not accept. The Orthodox hold that only Christ was conceived and born without original sin, that the Virgin

Mary was cleansed of it on Annunciation Day."[2] The Eastern Orthodox do not believe in the physical assumption of Mary into heaven. (Chapter 8)

Iconoclasts—Leo the Isaurian (Byzantine Emperor)

Held that the veneration of sacred images was idolatry. Iconoclasm was condemned by the Second Council of Nicaea in the year 787 AD. (Chapter 7)

Jacobites—James Baradai (Monophysite bishop of Edessa)

Denied that Christ has a true human nature. (Chapters 4 & 17)

Macedonians—Macedonius (bishop of Constantinople)

Denied the divinity of the Holy Ghost in 341 AD. Condemned at the First Council of Constantinople in 381 AD. (Chapter 2)

Modernists—Modernist errors include dogmatic relativism, agnosticism, vital immanence, subjection of faith to science and the rejection of the historical institution of the Church by Christ. It is a contemporary synthesis of heresies aimed at the fundamental principles of theology. The Modernist heresy was condemned by Pope St. Pius X. (Part II)

Monophysites—Eutyches (abbot of a monastery near Constantinople)

Denied that Christ had a true human nature. The Council of Chalcedon in 451 AD condemned the teachings of the Monophysites. (Chapter 4)

Monothelites—Sergius (patriarch of Constantinople)

Denied that Christ had a true human will. Monotheletism was condemned at the Third Council of Constantinople in 680 AD. (Chapter 6)

Nestorians—Nestorius (bishop of Constantinople)

Believed that there were two separate persons in Christ—one was divine and the other was human. Nestorians denied that the Blessed Virgin Mary was the Mother of God. The heretical teachings of the Nestorians were condemned at the Council of Ephesus in 431 AD. (Chapter 3)

---

[2] Leo Rosten, *Religions in America*, p. 83. "What is Greek Orthodox?," by Arthur Douropulos.

Novatians—Novatus (Roman priest and antipope)

They believed that idolatry was an unforgivable sin, denied the Sacrament of Confirmation, held that mortal sins committed after Baptism could not be forgiven and refused to allow second marriages after the death of a spouse. The First Council of Nicaea in 325 AD condemned the Novatian heresy. (Chapter 1)

Old Catholics—Ignaz von Döllinger (priest historian)

Reject papal infallibility, the dogma of the Immaculate Conception, celibate clergy and in some instances the *Filioque* clause of the Nicene-Constantinopolitan Creed. (Chapter 20)

Pelagians—Pelagius (English monk)

Denied the need for God's grace in our sanctification and taught that natural goodness alone was sufficient. Pelagians believed that Adam's sin injured himself alone, not the human race and that baptism was not necessary for salvation. The heretical teachings of Pelagius were condemned at the Council of Ephesus in 431 AD. (Chapter 3)

Protestants—Various founders

Many Protestant sects have developed from Lutheranism which was founded by the German priest, Martin Luther, in 1517. Luther denied free will, the Papacy, praying to the saints, Purgatory, Tradition, Transubstantiation and the Holy Sacrifice of the Mass. Luther replaced the Mass with a memorial service commemorating the Last Supper. All the sacraments except Baptism and the Holy Eucharist were rejected. Luther held that after the fall of Adam, man cannot produce any good works.

Other Protestant churches were founded by John Calvin, by the former priests John Huss, John Knox, John Wycliff, Ulrich Zwingli and by King Henry VIII. Thousands of Protestant churches have been established since the Reformation. The Council of Trent condemned the beliefs of the Lutherans and other Protestant religions. As the name implies, Protestants protested against the authority, beliefs and worship of the Catholic Church. (Chapter 19)

List of the Illegitimate Councils

Antioch (341 AD)

Arles (353 AD)

Basel (1061) (1438)

Ephesus (John of Antioch) (431 AD)

Ephesus (Latrocinium) (449 AD)

Hieria (753 AD)

Mainz and Brixen (1080)

Milan (355 AD)

Parma (1063)

Philippopolis (343 AD)

Pisa (1409)

Pisa, Milan and Lyons (1511-1512)

Rimini (359 AD)

Rome (1084) (1089) (1098) (1412)

Seleucia (359 AD)

Second Council of Simirium (357 AD)

Synod of Photius (879-880 AD)

List of the Legitimate Popes

St. Peter, Apostle	d. 67	St. Gelasius I	492-496
St. Linus	67-76	St. Anastasius II	496-498
St. Cletus	76-88	St. Symmachus	498-514
St. Clement I	88-97	St. Hormisdas	514-523
St. Evaristus	97-105	St. John I	523-526
St. Alexander I	105-115	St. Felix IV	526-530
St. Sixtus I	115-125	Boniface II	530-532
St. Telesphorus	125-136	John II	533-535
St. Hyginus	136-140	St. Agapitus	535-536
St. Pius I	140-155	St. Silverius	536-537
St. Anicetus	155-166	Vigilius	537-555
St. Soter	166-175	Pelagius I	556-561
St. Eleutherius	175-189	John III	561-574
St. Victor I	189-199	Benedict I	575-579
St. Zephyrinus	199-217	Pelagius II	579-590
St. Calixtus I	217-222	St. Gregory I	590-604
St. Urban I	222-230	Sabinianus	604-606
St. Pontian	230-235	Boniface III	607-607
St. Anterus	236-236	St. Boniface IV	608-615
St. Fabian	236-250	St. Adeodatus I	615-618
St. Cornelius	251-253	Boniface V	619-625
St. Lucius I	253-254	Honorius I	625-638
St. Stephen I	254-257	Severinus	640-640
St. Sixtus II	257-258	John IV	640-642
St. Dionysius	259-268	Theodorus I	642-649
St. Felix I	269-274	St. Martin I	649-655
St. Eutychian	275-283	St. Eugenius I	655-657
St. Caius	283-296	St. Vitalian	657-672
St. Marcellinus	296-304	Adeodatus II	672-676
St. Marcellus I	308-309	Donus I	676-678
St. Eusebius	309-309	St. Agatho	678-681
St. Mechiades	311-314	St. Leo II	682-683
*St. Sylvester I	314-335	St. Benedict II	684-685
St. Marcus	336-336	John V	685-686
St. Julius I	337-352	Conon	686-687
Liberius	352-366	St. Sergius I	687-701
*St. Damasus I	366-384	John VI	701-705
St. Siricius	384-399	John VII	705-707
St. Anastasius I	399-401	Sisinnius	708-708
St. Innocent I	401-417	Constantine	708-715
St. Zozimus	417-418	St. Gregory II	715-731
St. Boniface I	418-422	St. Gregory III	731-741
*St. Celestine I	422-432	St. Zacharias	741-752
St. Sixtus III	432-440	Stephen II	752-757
*St. Leo I	440-461	St. Paul I	757-767
St. Hilary	461-468	Stephen III	768-772
St. Simplicius	468-483	Hadrian I	772-795
St. Felix III	483-492	St. Leo III	795-816

Stephen V	816-817	Clement II	1046-1047
St. Paschal I	817-824	Benedict IX	1047-1048
Eugenius II	824-827	Damasus II	1048-1048
Valentine	827-827	St. Leo IX	1049-1054
Gregory IV	827-844	Victor II	1055-1057
Sergius II	844-847	Stephen IX	1057-1058
St. Leo IV	847-855	Nicholas II	1059-1061
Benedict III	855-858	Alexander II	1061-1073
St. Nicholas I	858-867	St. Gregory VII	1073-1085
*Hadrian II	867-872	Bl. Victor III	1087-1087
John VIII	872-882	Bl. Urban II	1088-1099
Marinus I	882-884	Paschal II	1099-1118
Hadrian III	884-885	Gelasius II	1118-1119
Stephen V	885-891	*Calixtus II	1119-1124
Formosus	891-896	Honorius II	1124-1130
Boniface VI	896-896	Innocent II	1130-1143
Stephen VII	896-897	Celestine II	1143-1144
Romanus	897-897	Lucius II	1144-1145
Theodorus	897-897	Bl. Eugenius III	1145-1153
John IX	898-900	Anastasius IV	1153-1154
Benedict IV	900-903	Hadrian IV	1154-1159
Leo V	903-903	*Alexander III	1159-1181
Sergius III	904-911	Lucius III	1181-1185
Anastasius III	911-913	Urban III	1185-1187
Landus	913-914	Gregory VIII	1187-1187
John X	914-928	Clement III	1187-1191
Leo VI	928-928	Celestine III	1191-1198
Stephen VIII	928-931	*Innocent III	1198-1216
John XI	931-935	Honorius III	1216-1227
Leo VII	936-939	Gregory IX	1227-1241
Stephen IX	939-942	Celestine IV	1241-1241
Marinus II	942-946	*Innocent IV	1243-1254
Agapitus II	946-955	Alexander IV	1254-1261
John XII	955-964	Urban IV	1261-1264
Leo VIII	963-965	Clement IV	1265-1268
Benedict V	964-964	*Bl. Gregory X	1271-1276
John XIII	965-972	Bl. Innocent V	1276-1276
Benedict VI	973-974	Hadrian V	1276-1276
Benedict VII	974-983	John XXI	1276-1277
John XIV	983-984	Nicholas III	1277-1280
John XV	985-996	Martin IV	1281-1285
Gregory V	996-999	Honorius IV	1285-1287
Sylvester II	999-1003	Nicholas IV	1288-1292
John XVII	1003-1003	St. Celestine V	1294-1294
John XVIII	1003-1009	Boniface VIII	1294-1303
Sergius IV	1009-1012	Bl. Benedict XI	1303-1304
Benedict VIII	1012-1024	*Clement V	1305-1314
John XVIII	1024-1032	John XXII	1316-1334
Benedict IX	1032-1044	Benedict XII	1334-1342
Sylvester III	1045-1045	Clement VI	1342-1352
Benedict IX	1045-1045	Innocent VI	1352-1362
Gregory VI	1045-1046	Bl. Urban V	1362-1370

Gregory XI	1370-1378	Clement VIII	1592-1605
Urban VI	1378-1389	Leo XI	1605-1605
Boniface IX	1389-1404	Paul V	1605-1621
Innocent VII	1404-1406	Gregory XV	1621-1623
Gregory XII	1406-1415	Urban VIII	1623-1644
*Martin V	1417-1431	Innocent X	1644-1655
*Eugenius IV	1431-1447	Alexander VII	1655-1667
Nicholas V	1447-1455	Clement IX	1667-1669
Calixtus III	1455-1458	Clement X	1670-1676
Pius II	1458-1464	Innocent XI	1676-1689
Paul II	1464-1471	Alexander VIII	1689-1691
Sixtus IV	1471-1484	Innocent XII	1691-1700
Innocent VIII	1484-1492	Clement XI	1700-1721
Alexander VI	1492-1503	Innocent XIII	1721-1724
Pius III	1503-1503	Benedict XIII	1724-1730
*Julius II	1503-1513	Clement XII	1730-1740
*Leo X	1513-1521	Benedict XIV	1740-1758
Hadrian VI	1522-1523	Clement XIII	1758-1769
Clement VII	1523-1534	Clement XIV	1769-1774
*Paul III	1534-1549	Pius VI	1775-1799
*Julius III	1550-1555	Pius VII	1800-1823
Marcellus II	1555-1555	Leo XII	1823-1829
Paul IV	1555-1559	Pius VIII	1829-1830
*Pius IV	1559-1565	Gregory XVI	1831-1846
St. Pius V	1566-1572	*Pius IX	1846-1878
Gregory XIII	1572-1585	Leo XIII	1878-1903
Sixtus V	1585-1590	St. Pius X	1903-1914
Urban VII	1590-1590	Benedict XV	1914-1922
Gregory XIV	1590-1591	Pius XI	1922-1939
Innocent IX	1591-1591	Pius XII	1939-1958[3]

*Popes who ruled during the General Councils of the Catholic Church.

[3] See *Pontificio Annuario.*

List of the 41 Antipopes

Hippolytus	217-236	Clement III	1084-1100
Novatian	251-258	Theodoric	1100-1102
Felix II	355-365	Albert	1102
Ursinus	366-384	Sylvester IV	1105-1111
Eulalius	418-419	Gregory VIII	1118-1121
Laurentius	498-505	Celestine II	1124
Dioscorus	530	Anacletus II	1130-1138
Severinus	640	Victor IV	1138
Theodore	687	Victor IV	1159-1164
Paschal	687-692	Paschal III	1164-1168
Stephen II	752	Calixtus III	1168-1179
Constantine II	767-768	Innocent III	1179-1180
Philip	768	Nicholas V	1328-1330
John	844	Clement VII	1378-1394
Anastasius	855	Benedict XIII	1394-1424
Christopher	903-904	Alexander V	1409-1410
Boniface VII	974	John XXIII	1410-1415
John XVI	997-998	Clement VIII	1424-1429
Gregory	1012	Benedict XIV	1424
Benedict X	1058-1059	Felix V	1439-1449[4]
Honorius II	1061-1072		

---

[4] Felician Foy, OFM, *1967 National Catholic Almanac*, pp. 182-183.

Crusades to the Holy Land

Crusade	Date	Leaders	Results
First	1096-99	Godfrey de Bouillon Raymond of Toulouse Robert of Normandy Bohemund of Taranto Baldwin of Flanders	Capture of Jerusalem (1099) Establishment of Crusader States
Second	1147-49	Louis VII of France Emperor Conrad III	Unsuccessful siege of Damascus
Third	1188-92	Emperor Frederick Barbarossa Richard I of England Philip Augustus of France	Recapture of the Palestine coast and Cyprus
Fourth	1202-04	William of Montferrata Baldwin of Hainault	Constantinople sacked (1204)
Fifth	1217-21	Andrew of Hungary Cardinal Pelagius John of Jerusalem Hugh of Cyprus	Capture of Damietta (1219)
Sixth	1228-29	Emperor Frederick II	Gain of Jerusalem (1229)
Seventh	1248-54	[St.] Louis IX of France	Capture of Damietta (1249)
Eighth	1270-72	[St.] Louis IX of France	Unsuccessful attack on Tunis (1270)[5]

---

[5] John Haywood, *Historical Atlas of the Medieval World AD 600-1492*, p. 3.32.

15 Promises of Mary to Christians Who Recite the Rosary

If you are not yet convinced of the great benefits attached to praying the Rosary, consider the 15 promises which Our Blessed Mother has graciously attached to its recitation:

1) Whoever will faithfully serve me by the recitation of the Rosary will receive signal graces.

2) I promise my special protection and greatest graces to those who will recite my Rosary.

3) The Rosary shall be a powerful armor against Hell: it shall destroy vice, decrease sin, and defeat heresy.

4) I will cause virtue and good works to flourish; it shall obtain for souls the abundant mercy of God; it shall withdraw the hearts of men from the love of the world and its vanities and shall lift them to the desire of eternal things. Oh, that souls would sanctify themselves by this means!

5) The soul that recommends itself to me by the meditation of the Rosary shall not perish.

6) Whoever will recite the Rosary devoutly, applying himself to the consideration of its sacred mysteries, shall never be conquered by misfortune. God will not chastise him in His justice; he shall not perish by an unprovided death; if he shall be just he shall remain in the grace of God and become worthy of eternal life.

7) Whoever will have a true devotion for the Rosary shall not die without the sacraments of the Church.

8) Those who faithfully recite the Rosary shall have during their life and at their death the light of God and the plentitude of His graces; at the moment of death they shall participate in the merits of the saints in paradise.

9) I will deliver from purgatory those who have been devoted to the Rosary.

10) The faithful children of the Rosary shall merit a high degree of glory in heaven.

11) You shall obtain all that you ask of me by the recitation of the Rosary.

12) All those who propagate the holy Rosary shall be aided by me in their necessities.

13) I have obtained from my Divine Son that all the advocates of the Rosary shall have for intercessors the entire celestial court during their life and at the hour of death.

14) All who recite the Rosary are my sons, and brothers of my only Son, Jesus Christ.

15) Devotion to the Rosary is a great sign of predestination.[6]

---

[6] John Johnson, *The Rosary in Action*, p. 33.

Exorcism Prayer
Against Satan and the Apostate Angels

Pope Leo XIII's Prayer to St. Michael the Archangel

Most glorious prince of the heavenly hosts, Archangel St. Michael, defend us in the battle and in the tremendous struggle we carry on against the Principalities and Powers, against the rulers of the world of darkness and all evil spirits. Come to the help of man, whom God created immortal, fashioned to His own image and likeness, and rescued at a great price from the tyranny of the devil. With the great army of the holy angels fight today the battle of the Lord as thou didst of old fight against Lucifer, the leader of the proud, and his apostate angels, who were powerless against thee, and they had no longer a place in heaven; and that monster, the old serpent who is called the devil and Satan, that seduces the whole world, was cast into hell with his angels. But now that first enemy and homicide has regained his insolent boldness. Taking on the appearance of an angel of light, he has invaded the earth, and, with his whole train of evil spirits, he is prowling about among men, striving to blot out the name of God and of His Christ, to capture, to destroy, to drag to eternal perdition the souls destined to the crown of eternal glory. That malignant dragon is pouring abroad, like a foul stream, into the souls of men of ruined intellect and corrupt heart the poison of his wickedness, the spirit of lying, of impiety and blasphemy, the pestilent breath of impurity and of all vice and iniquity. Most cunning enemies have filled with bitterness and drenched with gall the Church, the Spouse of the Lamb without spot, and have lifted impious hands against all that is most sacred in it. Even in the holy place where the See of Blessed Peter and the chair of truth was set up to enlighten the world, they have raised the abominable throne of their impiety with the iniquitous hope that the Shepherd may be stricken and the flock scattered abroad. Arise, then, unconquerable Prince, defend the people of God against the assaults of the reprobate spirits, and give them the victory. Holy Church reveres thee as its guardian and patron; it glories in thee as its defender against the malignant powers of hell; to thee God has committed the souls that are to be conveyed to the seats of the Blessed in eternal happiness. Pray, then, to the God of peace, that He may put Satan under our feet, so completely vanquished that he may no longer be able to hold men in bondage and work harm to the Church. Offer up our prayers before the Most High, so that the mercies of the Lord may prevent us, and lay hold of the dragon, the old serpent, who is the devil and Satan, and hurl him bound in chains into the abyss where he may no longer seduce the souls of men. Amen.

> V. Behold the Cross of the Lord, fly ye hostile ranks.
>
> R. The Lion of the tribe of Juda, the Root of David, has conquered.
>
> V. May Thy mercies, O Lord, be fulfilled in us.
>
> R. As we have hoped in Thee.
>
> V. Lord, hear my prayer.
>
> R. And let my cry come unto Thee.

Let us pray.

O God, and the Father of our Lord Jesus Christ, we call upon Thy Holy Name and humbly beseech Thy clemency, that, through the intercession of the ever immaculate Virgin and our Mother Mary, and of the glorious Archangel Saint Michael, Thou wouldst vouchsafe to help us against Satan and all the other unclean spirits that are prowling about the world to the great peril of the human race and the loss of souls. Amen.

Pope Leo XIII, *Motu Proprio*, September 25, 1888, granted to the faithful who recite the above prayer an indulgence of three hundred days, once a day.

Raccolta, 1898, pp. 364-366.

Bibliography

Abbo, S.T.L., J.C.D., John and Jerome Hannan, A.M., S.T.D., J.C.D. *The Sacred Canons, Vol. I.* St. Louis: Herder Book Co., 1952.

——. *The Sacred Canons, Vol. II.* St. Louis: Herder Book Co., 1952.

Abbott, S.J., Walter. *Documents of Vatican II.* New York: Guild Press, 1966.

Ackroyd, Peter. *The Life of Thomas More.* New York: Anchor Books, 1998.

Acton, Lord. *Cambridge Modern History, Vol. I: The Renaissance.* Cambridge, England: University Press, 1934.

——. *Cambridge Modern History, Vol. II: The Reformation.* Cambridge: University Press, 1934.

——. *Cambridge Modern History, Vol. III: The Wars of Religion.* Cambridge: University Press, 1934.

——. *Cambridge Modern History, Vol. VII: The United States.* Cambridge: University Press, 1934.

——. *Cambridge Modern History, Vol. X: The Restoration.* Cambridge: University Press, 1934.

——. *Cambridge Modern History, Vol. XI: The Growth of Nationalities.* Cambridge: University Press, 1934.

——. *Cambridge Modern History, Vol. XII: The Latest Age.* Cambridge: University Press, 1934.

Addis, William and Thomas Arnold, M.A. *A Catholic Dictionary.* St. Louis: Herder Book Co., 1960.

Adoremus Bulletin. November 2000, Vol. VI, No. 8.

Adoremus Bulletin. September 2002, Vol. VIII, No. 6.

Adoremus Bulletin. March 2003, Vol. IX, No. 1.

Adrian, Bishop William. "The Threat to the Church in the U.S." *Wanderer.* 20 Feb. 1969.

Alexander, Fr. Anthony. *College Apologetics.* Rockford: Tan Books and Publishers, Inc., 1994.

Allen, Jr., John. "Vatican May Simplify Annulment Rules." *National Catholic Reporter.* 26 Apr. 2002.

——. "Chaotic Vatican summit produces flawed document." *National Catholic Reporter.* 10 May 2002.

——. "Twenty-Five Years." *National Catholic Reporter.* 10 Oct. 2003.

American Ecclesiastical Review Vol. 115. July-December, 1946.

American Ecclesiastical Review Vol. 122. April, 1950.

American Ecclesiastical Review Vol. 123. October, 1950.

American Ecclesiastical Review Vol. 128. January 1953.

Amerio, Romano. *Iota Unum—A Study of the Changes in the Catholic Church in the XXth Century*. Fr. John Parsons, trans. Kansas City, MO: Sarto House, 1997.

*Amiot, Francois. *The History of the Mass*. New York: Hawthorn, 1958.

Anderson, Floyd. *Council Daybook: Vatican II, Session 1, Oct. 11 to Dec. 8, 1962*. Washington, D.C.: National Catholic Welfare Conference, 1965.

——. *Council Daybook Vatican II: Session 2, Sept. 29 to Dec. 4, 1963*. Washington, D.C.: National Catholic Welfare Conference, 1965.

——. *Council Daybook Vatican II: Session 3*. Washington, D.C.: National Catholic Welfare Conference, 1965.

Anton, Mike and William Lobdell. "Hold the Fire and Brimstone." *Los Angeles Times*. 19 Jun. 2002.

——. "Today, hell hath no fury—at all." *News Tribune*. 6 Jul. 2002.

Approaches May 30, 1969, Nos. 56-57, July 1977, London.

Aquinas, St. Thomas. *Summa Theologica, Vol. II*. New York: Benziger Bros., 1947.

——. *Summa Theologica, Vol. III*. New York: Benziger Bros., 1948.

——. *Summa Theologiae Tertia Pars*. Ottawa, Canada: Commisio Piano, 1941.

Armento, Beverly, et al. *Across the Centuries*. Boston: Houghton Mifflin Co., 1991.

*Astons, A. *Communism: the Unpunished Crime* Islington, Ontario: Prelude Publications, 1985.

Atlanta Constitution. February 28, 1976.

**Atlas of World History*. Chicago: Rand McNally & Company, 1981.

*Attwater, Donald. *Catholic Dictionary*. New York: MacMillan Company, 1961.

*——. *Eastern Catholic Worship*. New York: Devin-Adair Co., 1945.

*——. *Martyrs from St. Stephen to John Tung*. New York: Sheed & Ward, 1957.

Aubert, Roger, et al. *Church in a Secularised Society*. London: Darton, Longman and Todd, 1978.

Ayrinhac, S.S., D.D., D.C.L., Fr. H. *Penal Legislation in the New Code of Canon Law*. New York: Benziger Bros., 1920.

Barbernitz, Patricia. *RCIA: What It Is, How It Works*. Liguori, MO: Liguori, 1983.

*Barnard, Leslie. *Council of Serdica 343 AD*. Sophia, Bulgaria: Synodal, 1983.

Barnes, Timothy. *Athanasius and Constantius: Theology and Politics in the Constantinian Empire*. Cambridge, MA: Harvard University Press, 1993.

Barraclough, Geoffrey. *Medieval Papacy*. New York: Harcourt Brace & World Inc., 1968.

*——. *Times Atlas of World History.* Maplewood, NJ: Hammond, 1978.

*Barron, Fr. Robert. *Heaven in Stone and Glass: Experiencing the Spirituality of the Great Cathedrals.* New York: Crossroad Publishing Co., 2000.

Barry, O.S.B., Colman. *Readings in Church History.* Westminster, MD: Newman, 1960.

Bartley, Robert. "Religious Crossfire Hits the President." *Wall Street Journal.* 21 Apr. 2003.

Barton, John. *Penance and Absolution.* New York: Hawthorn Books, 1961.

Bausch, William. *A New Look at the Sacraments.* Mystic, CT: Twenty-Third Publ., 1983.

——. *Brave New Church—From Turmoil to Trust.* Mystic, CT: Twenty-Third Publ., 2001.

Bayles, Fred. "Alleged abuse victims ready to settle." *USA Today.* 10 Dec. 2002.

——. "Alleged abuse victims ready to settle." *USA Today.* 13 Dec. 2002.

Bebow, John. "Celibacy Tests Catholic Church." *Detroit News.* 21 Apr. 2002.

Bellarmine, St. Robert. *Opera Omnia Tomus Secundus.* Edited by Cardinal Xisto Riario Sforza, Naples, Italy: C. Pedone Lauriel, 1872.

*Belloc, Hilaire. *Characters of the Reformation.* Garden City, NY: Image Books, 1958.

*——. *Crusades.* Milwaukee: Bruce Publishing Company, 1937.

*——. *Great Heresies.* Rockford, IL: Tan Books and Publishers, 1991.

*——. *How the Reformation Happened.* London: Jonathan Cape, 1928.

Belt, Don, ed. *The World of Islam.* Washington, D.C.: National Geographic, 2001.

Benedictines of St. John's Abbey. *Worship Vol. 39.* January 1965. Collegeville, MN: Liturgical Press.

*Benedictine Monks of Solesmes. *Papal Teachings on Our Lady.* Boston: Daughters of St. Paul, 1961.

——. *Papal Teachings: The Liturgy.* Boston: Daughters of St. Paul, 1962.

Benigni, Mario and Goffredo Zanchi. *John XXIII: The Official Biography.* Boston: Pauline Books and Media, 2001.

Bennett, Rod. *Four Witnesses: The Early Church in Her Own Words.* San Francisco: Ignatius Press, 2002.

Bergendoff, Conrad. *The Church of the Lutheran Reformation: A Historical Survey of Lutheranism.* St. Louis: Concordia, 1967.

Bergin, Robert. "Was John XXIII really a Pope?" Yarra Junction, Victoria, Australia: *Catholic.* June 1994.

Bergounioux, O.F.M., F. and Joseph Goetz, S.J. *Primitive and Prehistoric Religions.* New York: Hawthorn Books, 1966.

Bermejo, S.J., Luis. *Infallibility on Trial.* Westminster, MD: Christian Classics, Inc., 1992.

Bermúdez, Alejandro. " 'Catholic radicals' on rise in Brazilian government." *Our Sunday Visitor.* 20 Apr. 2003.

Bernier, SSS, Paul. *Eucharist: Celebrating Its Rhythm in Our Lives.* Notre Dame: Ave Maria Press, 1993.

Bernstein Carl and Marco Politi. *His Holiness: John Paul II and the Hidden History of Our Time.* New York: Doubleday, 1996.

Berry, Thomas. *Buddhism.* New York: Hawthorn Books, 1966.

Biallas, Len. "Turkey richly rewards search for the sacred." *National Catholic Reporter.* 11 Apr. 2003.

Binns, Elliott. *Decline and Fall of the Medieval Papacy.* New York: Barnes & Noble, 1995.

*Birkhaeuser, Fr. J. *History of the Church from Its First Establishment to Our Own Times.* New York: Fr. Pustet, 1891.

Bishop, Morris. *Horizon Book of the Middle Ages.* New York: American Heritage Publishing Co., Inc., 1968.

*Biskupek, S.V.D., A. *Ordinations: A Translation and Explanation of the Rite of Ordination.* Techny, IL: Mission Press, S.V.D., 1928.

——. *Ordination to the Holy Priesthood.* Techny, IL: Mission Press, S.V.D.

*Blake, Everett and Anna Edmonds. *Biblical Sites in Turkey.* Istanbul, Turkey: Redhouse Press, 1977.

*Bokenkotter, Thomas. *Concise History of the Catholic Church.* Garden City: Image, 1979.

Bolettieri, Stephen. *Fatima, the Shroud and John Paul II: Is There a Connection?* Santa Ana, CA: Agnus Dei Publishing, 2001.

*Bonaventure, St. *Life of St. Francis.* Rockford: Tan Books and Publishers, 1988.

Bonnot, Ph.D., Rev. Bob. *Pope John XXIII: Model and Mentor for Leaders.* Staten Island: St. Paul's, 2003.

Boston College Magazine Fall 2000.

Boucher, Arline and John Tehan. *Prince of Democracy: James Cardinal Gibbons.* Garden City: Hanover House, 1962.

Bouscaren, S.J., LL.B., S.T.D., T. and Adam Ellis., S.J., M.A., J.C.D. *Canon Law: A Text and Commentary.* Milwaukee: Bruce Publishing Co., 1946.

——. *Canon Law Digest, Vol. I.* Milwaukee: Bruce Publishing Co., 1934.

——. *Canon Law Digest, Vol. III.* Milwaukee: Bruce Publishing Co., 1934.

Bouscaren, S.J., LL.B., S.T.D., T. and James O'Connor, S.J., A.M., S.T.L., J.C.D. *Canon Law Digest, Vol. V.* Milwaukee: Bruce Publishing Co., 1963.

*Bouyer, Louis. *The Decomposition of Catholicism.* Chicago: Franciscan Herald, 1969.

*——. *Life and Liturgy.* New York: Sheed & Ward, 1956.

Boyer, S.J., Charles. *Christian Unity*. New York: Hawthorn Books, 1962.

*Brabbs, Derry. *Abbeys and Monasteries*. London: Weidenfeld & Nicolson, 1999.

*Brennan, A.M., LL.D., Fr. Richard. *History of the Catholic Church*. New York: Benziger Bros., 1881.

——. *Popular Life of Pope Pius the Ninth*. New York: Benziger Bros., 1877.

*Brodrick, S.J., James. *Robert Bellarmine*. Westminster: Newman Press, 1961.

Broderick, M.A., Robert. *Catholic Concise Encyclopedia*. St. Paul: Catechetical Guild Educational Society, 1956.

*Browne, Jane. *Mind Alive Encyclopedia—Early Civilization*. London: Chartwell, 1968.

Brucker, Gene. *Renaissance Florence*. New York: John Wiley and Sons, 1969.

Brueck, Dr. Heinrich. *History of the Catholic Church, Vol. II*. New York: Benziger, 1885.

Brusher, S.J., Joseph. *Popes Through the Ages*. Princeton: D. Van Nostrand, 1959.

Buchanan, Pat. *Conservative Focus: Church & State*. 18 Dec. 2002.

Bugnini, Annibale. *Reform of the Liturgy 1948-1975*. Collegeville: Liturgical Press, 1990.

*Bulfinch Press Co. ed. *One Hundred Saints*. Boston: Little, Brown & Co., 1993.

*Bungener, L. *History of the Council of Trent*. Edinburgh, Scotland: Thomas Constable and Co., 1853.

Bunson, Matthew. *Our Sunday Visitor's Encyclopedia of Catholic History*. Huntington, IN: Our Sunday Visitor Publishing Division, 1995.

——. *2002 Our Sunday Visitor's Catholic Almanac*. Huntington: Our Sunday Visitor Publishing Division, 2001.

——. *2003 Our Sunday Visitor's Catholic Almanac*. Huntington: Our Sunday Visitor Publishing Division, 2002.

——. *2004 Our Sunday Visitor's Catholic Almanac*. Huntington: Our Sunday Visitor Publishing Division, 2003.

Burckhardt, Jacob. *The Civilization of the Renaissance in Italy, Vol. I*. New York: Harper Torchbooks, 1958.

Burger, John. "No-Kneeling Rule Sparks Widespread Outcry." *National Catholic Register*. 29 Sept. 2002.

——. "A College Readjusts to No-Kneeling Rule." *National Catholic Register*. 26 Jan. 2003.

Burns, Chris, CNN Bureau Chief. "What the Berlin Wall still stands for." 8 Nov. 1999.

Bury, M.A., F.B.A., J. *Cambridge Medieval History, Vol. II: Foundation of the Western Empire*. Cambridge, England: University Press, 1967.

——. *Cambridge Medieval History, Vol. V: Contest of Empire and Papacy*. Cambridge, England: University Press, 1968.

Bury, D. Litt., LL.D., J. *History of the Papacy in the 19th Century.* London: Macmillan, 1930.

*Butler, Dom B. C. *Church and Infallibility.* New York: Sheed & Ward, 1954.

*Butler, Dom Cuthbert. *Vatican Council 1869-1870.* Westminster: Newman Press, 1962.

*——. *Vatican Council: The Story Told from Inside in Bishop Ullathornes's Letters, Vol. I.* London: Longmans, Green and Co., 1930.

*——. *Vatican Council: The Story Told from Inside in Bishop Ullathornes's Letters, Vol. II.* London: Longmans, Green and Co., 1930.

*Butler, Fr. Alban. *Butler's Lives of the Fathers, Martyrs and Other Saints, Vols. I, II, III & IV.* London: Virtue & Co. Ltd.

*——. *Little Pictorial Lives of the Saints.* New York: Benziger Bros., 1925.

*——. *Lives of the Saints.* New York: Benziger Bros., 1894.

Cahill, S.J., Fr. E. *Freemasonry and the Anti-Christian Movement.* Dublin: M. H. Gill and Son, Ltd., 1959.

Cahill, Thomas. *Pope John XXIII.* New York: Penguin Group, 2002.

Campion, S.J., Donald, et al. *The 2nd Vatican Council.* New York: America Press, 1962.

Campion, Msgr. Owen. "Confronting sin face to face." *Our Sunday Visitor.* 2 Jun. 2002.

Cannon, Angie. "Is There Any End in Sight?" *U.S. News & World Report* 22 Apr. 2002.

*Carey, Ann. *Sisters in Crisis: The Tragic Unraveling of Women's Religious Communities.* Huntington: Our Sunday Visitor Publishing Division, 1997.

——. "Pope seeks to correct misuse of general absolution." *Our Sunday Visitor.* 19 May 2002.

——. "New norms aim for fewer Mass surprises." *Our Sunday Visitor.* 29 Dec. 2002.

——. "Training for the leap of faith." *Our Sunday Visitor.* 2 Mar. 2003.

*Carlen, IHM, Claudia. *The Papal Encyclicals 1740-1878.* Pierian Press, 1981.

*——. *The Papal Encyclicals 1878-1903.* Pierian Press, 1981.

*——. *The Papal Encyclicals 1903-1939.* Pierian Press, 1981.

*——. *The Papal Encyclicals 1939-1958.* Pierian Press, 1981.

Carlozo, Lou. "Scandals draw attention to obscure condition: Ephebophilia." *Chicago Tribune.* 3 Jun. 2003.

Caro y Rodriguez, Cardinal Jose. *The Mystery of Freemasonry Unveiled.* Hawthorne, CA: Christian Book Club of America, 1980.

*Carre, Marie. *AA-1025 Memoirs of an Anti-Apostle.* Sherbrooke, Que., Canada: Editions Saint-Raphael, 1973.

*Carroll, Anne. *Christ the King: Lord of History.* Manassas: Trinity Communications, 1986.

Casini, Tito. *Torn Tunic.* Hawthorne: Christian Book Club of America, 1967.

Catalyst. July-August 2001, New York: Catholic League.

Catalyst. May 2002, New York: Catholic League.

Catalyst. September 2002, New York: Catholic League.

Catholic. January / February 1998.

Catholic. April 2000.

Catholic. May 2000.

Catholic. October 2001, Orkney Isles, Scotland.

Catholic. March 2003, Orkney Isles, Scotland.

Catholic. April 2003, Orkney Isles, Scotland.

Catholic. May 2003, "25 Catholic Bishops in search of Enlightenment."

Catholic Bulletin. Vol. 68, No. 40, October 4, 1978, St. Paul.

Catholic Bulletin. Vol. 68, No. 42, October 20, 1978, St. Paul.

Catholic Church in Crisis. "Bless Me Father For I Have Sinned." ABC News Special, Peter Jennings, April 3, 2002.

Catholic Family News. March 2000.

Catholic Family News. August 2001.

Catholic Family News. February 2002.

Catholic Family News. April 2002.

Catholic Family News. October 2002.

Catholic Herald. October 21, 1985.

Catholic News Service: http://www.catholicnews.com/data/briefs/cns/20021111.htm Catholic World News—News Brief—8/23/02.

http://www.cwnews.com/news/getstory.cfm?recnum=18797

http://www.cwnews.com/Browse/2002/08/18797.htm

Catholic World Report August 1992.

Catholic World Report September / October 1992.

Catholic World Report June 2001.

Catholic World Report November 2001.

Catholic World Report December 2001.

Catholic World Report January 2002.

Catholic World Report February 2002.

Catholic World Report March 2002.

Catholic World Report April 2002.

Catholic World Report July 2002.

Catholic World Report August / September 2002.

Catholic World Report December 2002.

Catholic World Report March 2003.

Catholic World Report October 2003.

Catholic World Report November 2003.

Cavallari, Alberto. *Changing Vatican.* Garden City: Doubleday, 1967.

*Cekada, Fr. Anthony. *Welcome to the Traditional Latin Mass.* Cincinnati: St. Gertrude the Great Catholic Church, 1995.

Chamberlain, Lesley. "The Mysteries of Latin—how a dead language continues to live." *Los Angeles Times.* 21 Jul. 2002.

*Chambre, S.J., Henri. *Christianity and Communism.* Hawthorn Books, 1960.

*Chapin, John. *Book of Catholic Quotations.* New York: Farrar, Stauss and Cudahy, 1956.

Chapman, O.S.B., Dom John. *First Eight General Councils and Papal Infallibility.* London: Catholic Truth Society, 1906.

Cheetham, Nicholas. *Keepers of the Keys.* New York: Charles Scribner's Sons, 1982.

Cherry, Sheila. "Crusaders or Opportunists." *Insight on the News* 29 Jul. 2002.

Chiffolo, Anthony. *Pope John Paul II In My Own Words.* Liguori: Liguori, 1998.

———. *Pope John XXIII In My Own Words.* Liguori: Liguori, 1999.

*Chinigo, Michael. *The Pope Speaks: The Teachings of Pope Pius XII.* New York: Pantheon, 1957.

*Chisholm, Fr. D. *Catechism in Examples, Vol. V—Virtues and Vices.* Ft. Collins, CO: Roman Catholic Books, original copyright 1919.

http://www.christianitytoday.com/ct/2002/103/13.0.html

*Christianson, Gerald. *Cesarini: the Conciliar Cardinal, The Basel Years, 1431-1438.* St. Ottilien, Germany: Eos Verlag Der Erzabtei, 1979.

Cicognani, Archbishop Amleto. *Canon Law.* Westminster: Newman Bookshop, 1934.

Clark, Edie. *Yankee Magazine* "Miracle at St. Joseph's." p. 90. Vol. 57, No. 11, Dublin, NH: November 1993.

*Clarkson, S.J., John, et al. *Church Teaches: Documents of the Church in English Translation.* St. Louis: Herder Book Co., 1955.

Clynes, O.F.M. Raphael. *Liturgy and Christian Life.* Paterson, NJ: St. Anthony Guild Press, 1960.

*Cobbett, William. *History of the Protestant Reformation in England and Ireland.* New York: Benziger Bros., 1824.

Coday, Dennis. "World Briefs." *National Catholic Reporter.* 7 Nov. 2003.

Code of Canon Law in English Translation. London: Collins Liturgical Publications, 1983.

Cogley, John. "Paul, poor fellow, has no friends." *Life* 20 Mar. 1970.

Coleman, J.C.L., Fr. John. *The Minister of Confirmation.* Washington, D.C.: Catholic University of America Press, 1941.

Collier. 1972 Collier's Encyclopedia Yearbook. Crowell-Collier Educational Corp., 1971.

Columbus Dispatch. October 26, 1986.

*Compilation of the writings of eminent prelates and priests of the Catholic Church in America and Europe. *Cabinet of Catholic Information.* New York: Murphy and McCarthy, 1911.

*Connell, C.SS.R. S.T.D., Fr. Francis. *Baltimore Catechism No. 3.* New York: Benziger, 1949.

——. *Fr. Connell Answers Moral Questions.* Washington, D.C.: Catholic University of America Press, 1959.

*Conway, Msgr. J. *Times of Decision: Story of the Councils.* Notre Dame: Fides, 1962.

Cooke, Bernard. *Christian Community: Response to Reality.* New York: Holt, Rinehart and Winston, 1970.

——. *The Future of Eucharist: How a new self-awareness among Catholics is changing the way they believe and worship.* New York: Paulist Press, 1997.

*Coomaraswamy, M.D., Rama. *Problems with the New Mass.* Rockford: Tan Books, 1990.

*——. *The Problems with the new post-Conciliar Sacraments.* Tours, France: Fortes in Fide, 1992.

Coriden, James, Thomas Green and Donald Heintschel. *Code of Canon Law: A Text and Commentary.* New York: Paulist Press, 1985.

Cornwell, John. *A Thief in the Night: The Mysterious Death of Pope John Paul I.* New York: Simon & Schuster, 1989.

*Corrigan, S.J., Ph.D., Raymond. *Church and the Nineteenth Century.* Milwaukee: Bruce Publishing Company, 1938.

Corte, Nicolas. *Who is the Devil?* New York: Hawthorn Books, 1956.

Coughlin, Fr. Charles. *Bishops Versus Pope.* Bloomfield Hills, MI: Helmet and Sword, 1969.

*Coulson, John. *Saints: A Concise Biographical Dictionary.* New York: Hawthorn, 1958.

Coulton, G. *Art and the Reformation.* New York: Alfred Knopf, 1928.

——. *Papal Infallibility.* London: Faith Press Ltd., 1932.

Cox, Fr. Thomas. *The Pillar and Ground of the Truth—A Series of Lenten Lectures.* Chicago: J. S. Hyland, 1900.

*Cozens, M. *Handbook of Heresies.* New York: Sheed & Ward, 1928.

Crane, S.J., Fr. Paul. *Christian Order.* November 1989, London.

Crary, David. "Annulment common but unpopular with conservatives and liberals." *Detroit News.* 8 Nov. 2003.

———. "Church split over ending of marriages." *Detroit News.* 9 Nov. 2003.

Creighton, M. *History of the Papacy, Vol. V: From the Great Schism to the Sack of Rome.* London: Longmans, Green and Co., 1911.

Crisis—Politics, Culture and the Church June 2001.

Crisis—Politics, Culture and the Church April 2002.

Crisis—Politics, Culture and the Church June 2002.

Crisis—Politics, Culture and the Church January 2003.

Crisis—Politics, Culture and the Church April 2003. "Letters to the Editor." by Alice von Hildebrand.

*Cristiani, Msgr. Leon. *Heretics and Heresies.* New York: Hawthorn Books, 1959.

*———. *Revolt Against the Church.* New York: Hawthorn, 1962.

*Crock, Fr. Clement. *Grace and the Sacraments.* New York: Joseph Wagner Inc., 1940.

*———. *Discourses on the Apostles' Creed.* New York: Joseph Wagner Inc., 1938.

Crosby, Alan. "Many question pope's ability to travel after his latest trip." *USA Today.* 15 Sept. 2003.

Crowder, C. *Unity, Heresy and Reform, 1378-1460.* New York: St. Martin's Press, 1977.

Curry, Bishop Thomas. *The Tidings.* November 1, 2002.

Daily News (Los Angeles). August 9, 1985.

Daily News (Los Angeles). April 6, 1991.

Daily News (Los Angeles). February 5, 1993.

Daily News (Los Angeles). November 5, 2002.

Dalmais, O.P., Irenée-Henri. *Eastern Liturgies.* New York: Hawthorne Books Inc., 1960.

*Daniel-Rops, H. *Catholic Reformation.* London: J. Dent and Sons Ltd., 1962.

*———. *Church in an Age of Revolution 1789-1870.* London: J. M. Dent, 1965.

*———. *Church in the Dark Ages.* London: J. M. Dent and Sons, 1959.

*Darras, Abbe J. *General History of the Catholic Church, Vol. III.* New York: P. J. Kenedy, 1897.

*———. *General History of the Catholic Church, Vol. IV.* New York: P. J. Kenedy, 1898.

Davidson, James. "How many young adults leave the church and why?" *The Tidings.* 12 Jul. 2002.

——. "Dramatic changes in Catholic school totals." *The Tidings.* 16 Aug. 2002.

Davies, Michael. *Second Vatican Council and Religious Liberty.* Long Prairie, MN: Newman Press, 1992.

——. *Una Voce—Buffalo, NY.* Feb. 2003, "The Church in Collapse."

Davis, Charles. *Liturgy and Doctrine: The Doctrinal Basis of the Liturgical Movement.* New York: Sheed & Ward, 1963.

Davis, S.J., Henry. *Moral & Pastoral Theology (Summary).* New York: Sheed & Ward, 1952.

——. *Moral & Pastoral Theology, Vol. II.* New York: Sheed & Ward, 1952.

——. *Moral & Pastoral Theology, Vol. III.* New York: Sheed & Ward, 1952.

Davis, S.J., Leo. *First Seven Ecumenical Councils (325-787): Their History and Theology.* Collegeville: Liturgical Press, 1983.

Deferrari, Roy, trans. *Enchiridion Symbolorum* of Henry Denzinger. *Sources of Catholic Dogma.* St. Louis: B. Herder Book Co., 1957.

*Deharbe, S.J., Fr. Joseph. *Deharbe's Catechism.* Christian Book Club of America, 1912.

*——. *History of Religion.* London: Burns and Oates, 1881.

*De Labriolle, P. *St. Ambrose.* Herbert Wilson, trans. St. Louis: B. Herder Book Co., 1928.

*Delaney, John. *Dictionary of Saints.* New York: Doubleday, 1980.

Delaporte, Fr. *The Devil: Does He Exist and What Does He Do?* South Bend: reprinted by Marian Publications, 1978.

De La Trinite, O.C.D., Philippe. *What is Redemption?* New York: Hawthorn, 1961.

*de la Sainte Trinite, Frere Michel. *The Whole Truth About Fatima: The Third Secret.* Buffalo: Immaculate Heart, 1985.

della Cava, Marco. "Pedaling furiously from the past." *USA Today.* 24 Jul. 2002.

DeLigney, S.J., Fr. Francis. *Teachings of the Holy Catholic Church.* New York: Office of Catholic Publications, 1886.

*De Marchi, IMC., John. *Mother of Christ Crusade.* 1947.

*——. *Our Lady of Fatima.* Catechetical Guild Educational Society, 1952.

*De Montfort, St. Louis. *Secret of the Rosary.* Bay Shore, NY: Montfort Publishing, 1954.

De Montor, Artaud. *Lives and Times of the Popes.* New York: Catholic Publication Society of America, 1911.

*Denzinger, Henry. *Enchiridion Symbolorum.* Barcelona, Spain: Herder Book Co., 1965.

*DePiante, James. "Shedding Light on the Mysterious Mysteries of the Rosary." *Catholic Voice.* Mar. 2003.

*——."Shedding More Light on the Mysterious Mysteries-Part II." *Catholic Voice.* Sept. 2003.

De Poncins, Vicomte Léon. *Freemasonry and the Vatican.* London: Britons Publishing Company, 1968.

*De Sales, St. Francis. *An Introduction to the Devout Life.* Rockford: Tan Books and Publishers, 1994.

Detroit Free Press. November 20, 1998.

Detroit News. "Protestants helped Revamp Catholic Mass, Priest Says." 27 Jun. 1967.

Detroit News. April 28, 2002.

Detroit News. May 4, 2002.

Detroit News. October 27, 2002.

*Devine, S. J., E. *Jesuit Martyrs of Canada Together With the Martyrs Slain in the Mohawk Valley.* Toronto: The Canadian Messenger, 1925.

*Dibble, S.D.S., S.T.L., Fr. Romuald. *John Henry Newman: The Concept of Infallible Doctrinal Authority.* Washington, D.C.: The Catholic University of America Press, 1955.

Dickens, A. *Counter Reformation.* New York: W. W. Norton, 1968.

——. *Reformation and Society in Sixteenth-Century Europe.* London: Thames and Hudson, 1966.

Diekmann, O.S.B., Godfrey. "Altar and Tabernacle." *Worship Vol. XL.* January 1966.

Dietzen, John. *New Question Box: Catholic Life in the 80's.* Peoria: Guildhall, 1986.

Dillenberger, John. *Martin Luther, Selections From His Writings.* Garden City: Anchor Books, 1961.

Dillon, Msgr. *Grand Orient Freemasonry Unmasked.* Dublin: Gill, 1885.

*Dodridge, D.D., Fr. Henry, et al. *Catholic Church Alone the One True Church of Christ.* New York: Catholic Educational Co., 1905.

**Dogmatic Decrees and Canons.* New York: Devin-Adaire Co., 1912.

*Dolan, Fr. Thomas. *Papacy & the First Councils of the Church.* St. Louis: B. Herder Book Co., 1910.

*Donovan, Fr. C. *Our Faith and the Facts.* Chicago: Patrick Baine, 1922.

Donovan, Gill. "Records further damage Boston church's Credibility." *National Catholic Reporter.* 13 Dec. 2002.

*Dorcy, O.P., Sister Mary Jean. *St. Dominic.* St. Louis: B. Herder Book Co., 1959.

Dorling Kindersley Multimedia. *Cartopedia: The Ultimate World Reference Atlas.* New York, 1995.

*D'Ormesson, Wladimir. *The Papacy.* New York: Hawthorn Books, 1959.

Dougherty, Fr. John. *Unto the Altar of God—A Spiritual Commentary on the Pontifical.* New York: Exposition Press, 1966.

*Douillet, Jacques. *What is a Saint?* New York: Hawthorn Books, 1958.

*Doyle, Charles. *Life of Pope Pius XII.* New York: Didier, 1945.

Doyle, Dennis. *The Church Emerging From Vatican II—A Popular Approach to Contemporary Catholicism.* Mystic, CT: Twenty-Third Publications, 2002.

*Doyle, S.J., Fr. Francis. *Defense of the Catholic Church.* New York: Benziger Bros., 1927.

Drake, Tim. "Catholic Universities Push Abortion to Students on Internet Web Sites." *National Catholic Register.* 22 Dec. 2002.

——. "Notre Dame to Parents: We Won't Tell." *National Catholic Register.* 6 Jul. 2003.

——. "John Paul the Saint-Maker." *National Catholic Register.* 12 Oct. 2003.

Draugas. May 6, 1970, "Communists used the Orthodox Church for their Goals." Chicago.

Dreher, Rod. "The Pope Has Let Us Down." *Wall Street Journal.* 20 Aug. 2002.

*Drinkwater, Fr. F. *Catechism Stories.* Westminster: Newman Press, 1948.

Dubois, J. Abbe. *Hindu Manners, Customs and Ceremonies.* Henry Beauchamp, trans. C.I.E. Oxford, England: Clarendon Press, 1897.

Dudley, Lavinia. *Americana Annual 1961.* New York: Americana Corporation, 1961.

Duffy, Eamon. *Saints & Sinners: A History of the Popes.* Yale University Press in association with S4C (Wales), 1997.

Dujardin, Richard. "How the clergy views eternal damnation." *Sacramento Union.* 9 Mar. 1985.

Dunn, Julia. "Americans Keep Faith, Lose Religion." *Insight on the News* 27 May 2002.

*Dunney, Fr. Joseph. *Church History in the Light of the Saints.* New York: MacMillan Company, 1944.

Duquoc, Christian, O.P. *Opportunities for Belief and Behavior.* New York: Paulist, 1967.

Durant, Will. *Caesar and Christ.* New York: Simon and Schuster, 1944.

——. *Reformation.* New York: Simon and Schuster, 1957.

——. *Renaissance: A History of Civilization in Italy from 1304-1576 A.D.* New York: Simon and Schuster, 1953.

——. *Story of Civilization: Our Oriental Heritage.* New York: Simon and Schuster, 1954.

*Dvornik, Francis. *Ecumenical Councils.* New York: Hawthorn Books, 1961.

Edwards, Patrick. *Pope John Paul II.* New York: Gramercy Books, 1995.

Elliott, Lawrence. *I Will Be Called John: A Biography of Pope John XXIII.* New York: Berkley Publishing Corp., 1973.

Elliott, Msgr. Peter. *Ceremonies of the Modern Roman Rite.* San Francisco: Ignatius Publishing Corp., 1995.

*Elmer, Fr. Vida. *Monograph No. 66.* Glenmont, NY: St. Michael's Chapel, May 1983.

——. *The Smoke of Antichrist.* Glenmont, NY: St. Michael's Chapel, 1983.

El Nasser, Haya. "Megachurches clash with critics next door." *USA Today.* 23 Sept. 2002.

Empie, Paul, T. Murphy. *Papal Primacy and the Universal Church.* Minneapolis: Augsburg Publishing House, 1974.

*Englebert, Omer. *Lives of the Saints.* New York: David McKay Co. Inc., 1951.

*Eppstein, John. *Has the Catholic Church Gone Mad?* New Rochelle, NY: Arlington House, 1971.

*——. *The Cult of Revolution in the Church.* New Rochelle: Arlington House Publishers, 1974.

Eric, M.A., F. R. Hist. S., John. *Popes.* New York: Hawthorn Books, Inc., 1964.

Ernster, Barb. "Married—and Happy?" *National Catholic Register.* 11 May 2003.

Estep Jr., W. *John XXIII and the Papacy.* Fort Worth: Deering Publications, 1959.

*Eudes, St. John. *The Priest: His Dignity and Obligations.* New York: Kenedy & Sons, 1947.

http://www.ewtn.com/library/CURIA/CDFEXORC.htm

Ex Decreto Ss. Concilii Tridenti Restitutum Summorum Pontificum Cura Recognitum. *Breviarum Romanum Pars Aestiva.* Mechlin, Belgium: H. Dessain, 1955.

——. *Breviarum Romanum Pars Autumnalis.* Mechlin, Belgium: H. Dessain, 1955.

——. *Breviarum Romanum Pars Hiemalis.* Mechlin, Belgium: H. Dessain, 1955.

——. *Breviarum Romanum Pars Verna.* Mechlin, Belgium: H. Dessain, 1955.

——. *Missale Romanum.* New York: Benziger Bros., 1956.

*Faber, Fr. Frederick. *Notes on Doctrinal and Spiritual Subjects, Vol. II.* Baltimore: John Murphy Co., 1866.

Farrow, Christopher. *Sacraments Today.* Liguori: Liguori, 1978.

*Farrow, John. *Pageant of the Popes.* St. Paul: Catechetical Guild, 1950.

*Fenton, STL, Fr. Francis. *An Open Letter to Priests.* November 15, 1977.

——. "Report! An Angry Priest Speaks Out." *Review of the News.* 16 Oct. 1968.

——. *The Athanasian.* 1 Jun. 1985.

——. "To Prove That John Paul II Is Not A True Pope—How Many Examples Are Required?" *The Athanasian.* 5 Jul. 1990.

——. *The Treason of the Churches.* Belmont, MA: American Opinion, 1972.

Ferm, Vergilius. *Encyclopedia of Religion.* New York: Philosophical Library Inc., 1945.

Ferrisi. Sabrina Arena. "Once Family-Oriented, Italians Choosing to Have Fewer Babies." *National Catholic Register.* 15 Dec. 2002.

Fesquet, Henri. *Has Rome Converted?* New York: James Heineman, Inc., 1966.

Feuerherd, Joe. "Just how bad is it? Priest shortage worse than experts predicted; laity, foreign priests filling in the gap." *National Catholic Reporter.* 17 Oct. 2003.

Fichtenau, Heinrich. *Heretics and Scholars in the High Middle Ages 1000-1200.* University Park, PA: The Pennsylvania University Press, 1992.

Fiji Times. "Letters to the Editor." Suva, Fiji Islands, 28 Jun. 2003.

Fiji Times. "Letters to the Editor." Suva, Fiji Islands, 2 Jul. 2003.

Fiji Times. "Letters to the Editor." Suva, Fiji Islands, 3 Jul. 2003.

Fischer, Mary. "A New Look at Life." *Readers Digest* Oct. 2003.

*Finn, S.J., Edward. *A Brief History of the Eastern Rites.* Collegeville, MN: Liturgical Press, 1961.

www.fiu.edu/~mirandas/bios-c.htm

Flannery, O.P., Austin. *Vatican Council II: The Conciliar and Post Conciliar Documents.* Collegeville: Liturgical Press, 1987.

http://www.flcpa.org/education/augsburg.html

*Forbes, F. A. *St. Athanasius.* Rockford: Tan Books and Publishers, Inc., 1998.

Formicola, Jo Renee. *Pope John Paul II: Prophetic Politician.* Washington, D.C.: Georgetown University Press, 2002.

Four Popes. March 1979 Issue, New York: Ideal.

*Fox, Fr. Robert. *Catechism of Church History.* Alexandria, SD: Fatima Family Apostolate, 1991.

Fox News Network: Reuters, March 29, 2003.

Fox, Thomas. "What they knew in 1985." *National Catholic Reporter.* 17 May 2002.

Foy, O.F.M., Felician. *1961 National Catholic Almanac.* Paterson: St. Anthony Guild, 1960.

——. *1963 National Catholic Almanac.* Paterson: St. Anthony Guild, 1962.

——. *1967 National Catholic Almanac.* Paterson: St. Anthony Guild, 1966.

——. *1970 National Catholic Almanac.* Paterson: St. Anthony Guild, 1969.

——. *1990 National Catholic Almanac.* Paterson: St. Anthony Guild, 1989.

*Francis, Joseph. *Laws of Holy Mass.* New York: Sheed & Ward, 1949.

*Fremantle, Anne. *Papal Encyclicals in Their Historical Context.* New York: G. Putnam's Sons, 1956.

Frost, LL.D., John. *Pictorial History of the World.* Hartford: O. D. Case & Co., 1855.

*Funk, Francis. *A Manual of Church History, Vol. I.* London: Burns, Oates & Washbourne, 1941.

*———. *A Manual of Church History, Vol. II.* London: Burns, Oates & Washbourne, 1941.

*Gamber, Msgr. Klaus. *The Reform of the Roman Liturgy: Its Problems and Background.* San Juan Capistrano: Una Voce Press, 1993.

*Gassner, Fr. Jerome. *The Canon of the Mass.* St. Louis: Herder Book Co., 1949.

*Gavin, S.J., Fr. M. *The Sacrifice of the Mass.* London: Burns and Oates Limited, 1903.

*Geanakoplos, Deno. *Byzantine East and Latin West: Two Worlds of Christendom in Middle Ages and Renaissance.* Oxford: Basil Blackwell Ltd., 1966.

*Gearon, O.Carm., D.D., B.A., Fr. Patrick. *The Rosary.* Tokyo, Japan: Dai Nippon Printing Co. Ltd., 1959.

Gibbs, Marion and Jane Lang. *Bishops and Reform.* Oxford: Oxford University Press, 1936.

Gibson, David. "Fewer Catholics than ever attend church, poll finds." *Jackson Citizen Patriot.* 26 Dec. 2002.

———. *The Coming Catholic Church: How the Faithful are Shaping a New American Catholicism.* New York: HarperSanFrancisco, 2003.

Gilchrist, Michael. "General absolutions continue." *Catholic World Report* May 2002.

Gilles, Anthony. *People of the Creed: The Story Behind the Early Church.* Cincinnati: St. Anthony Messenger Press, 1985.

*Gilson, Etienne. *The Church Speaks to the Modern World.* Garden City: Image, 1954.

Giordani, Igino. *Saint Catherine of Siena.* Thomas Tobin, trans. Boston: St. Paul's Editions, 1980.

*Glasfurd, Alec. *Antipope (Peter de Luna, 1342-1423) A Study in Obstinacy.* London: Barrie & Rockliff, 1965.

Glazier, Michael and Monika Hellwig. *Modern Catholic Encyclopedia.* Collegeville: Liturgical Press, 1994.

*Glenn, Ph.D., S.T.D., Msgr. Paul. *Apologetics.* St. Louis: B. Herder Book Co., 1952.

*———. *Ethics.* St. Louis: B. Herder Book Co., 1953.

Globe and Mail. " 'Countercultural' Pope wins hearts, loses minds." Toronto, Ontario. 12 Oct. 1998.

*Godrycz, D.D., Ph.D. UTR, JUR. D., J. *Doctrine of Modernism and Its Refutation.* Philadelphia: John McVey, 1908.

*Goffine, Leonard. *Goffine's Devout Instructions.* New York: Benziger Bros., 1896. Original publication 1690.

Goldberg, Vicki. "The Secret Photographs." *Readers Digest* Oct. 2003.

Gonzalez, Fr. J. *The Sixteen Documents of Vatican II.* Boston: Daughters of St. Paul, 1966.

Goode, Stephen. "Predicting the West's Decline." *Insight on the News* 4 Mar. 2002.

Gooden, Herman. "Pope may be man of century." *London Free Press.* 7 Mar. 1998.

*Gottfried, Robert. *Black Death: Natural and Human Disaster in Medieval Europe.* New York: The Free Press, 1983.

*Graber, Bishop Dr. Rudolph. *Athanasius and the Church of our Time.* Susan Johnson. trans. Christian Book Club of America, 1974.

*Grant, Dorothy. *So! You Want to Get Married!* Milwaukee: Bruce Publishing Co., 1947.

Grant, Michael. *Dawn of the Middle Ages.* New York: McGraw-Hill, 1981.

Gray, Patrick. *Studies in the History of Christian Thought, Volume XX: The Defense of Chalcedon in the East (451-553).* Leiden, The Netherlands: E. J. Brill, 1979.

greekorthodoxchurch.org—Greek Orthodox Church.

http://www.goarch.org/access/orthodoxfaith/sacraments.html.

*Graham, Msgr. Henry. *Where We Got The Bible: Our Debt to the Catholic Church.* Hawthorne: Christian Book Club of America, 1977.

Griffith, Fr. Paul. *Priest's New Ritual.* New York: Kenedy, 1947.

Grimm, Harold. *Reformation Era 1500-1650.* New York: Macmillan, 1973.

Grossman, Cathy. "John Paul at 83: 'Ministry of presence.' "*USA Today.* 12 May 2003.

——. " 'Papabili': The handicappers' pick for pope—31 become cardinals today." *USA Today.* 21 Oct. 2003.

*Grun, Bernard. *Timetables of History: A Horizontal Linkage of People and Events.* New York: Simon & Schuster, 1975.

Grundmann, Herbert. *Religious Movements in the Middle Ages.* Notre Dame: University of Notre Dame Press, 1995.

*Gueranger, O.S.B., Abbot. *Liturgical Year, Vol. I.* London: Britons Catholic Library, 1983.

*——. *Liturgical Year, Vol. VII.* London: Britons Catholic Library, 1983.

*Guggenberg, S.J., A. *A General History of the Christian Era, Vol. II: The Protestant Reformation.* St. Louis: B. Herder Book Co., 1901.

*——. *A General History of the Christian Era, Vol. III: The Social Revolution.* St. Louis: B. Herder Book Co., 1913.

*Guitton, Jean. *Great Heresies and Church Councils.* New York: Harper & Row, 1965.

*Guizot, M. *Popular History of France from the Earliest Times, Vol. I.* Boston: Estes and Lauriat, 1869.

*Gussoni, Lino and Aristede Brunello. *The Silent Church: Facts and Documents Concerning Religious Persecution Behind the Iron Curtain.* New York: Veritas, 1954.

Hagia Sophia—One of the Greatest Architectures in the World. Gilbert Tai-tsong Chen. http://www.newschool.edu/infotech/va2/va2s99/gilbert/HagiaSophia.html.

Hales, E. *Catholic Church in the Modern World: A Survey From the French Revolution to the Present.* Garden City: Hanover House, 1958.

———. *First Vatican Council.* Houston: University of Saint Thomas, 1962.

———. *Pope John and His Revolution.* Garden City: Doubleday & Co. Inc., 1962.

*Hallett, Litt. D., Paul. *Ecumenical Councils.* Wichita: Catholic Bookshop, 1959.

Halligan, O.P., Nicholas. *Administration of the Sacraments.* New York: Alba House, 1963.

Hanahoe, S.A., Edward. *Indifference in Religion.* Peekskill, NY: Graymoor Press, 1951.

*Hannan, Ph.D. J.C.D., Fr. Jerome, et al. *Story of the Church.* New York: Benziger Bros., Inc., 1935.

Hardin, S.J., Fr. John. *Protestant Churches of America.* Garden City: Image Books, 1969.

*Harney, S.J., Martin. *Magnificent Witness: 40 English and Welsh Martyrs.* Boston: St. Paul's Editions, 1970.

*Harrison, O.P., Martin. *Credo: A Practical Guide to the Catholic Faith.* Chicago: Henry Regnery Company, 1954.

*———. *Everyday Catholic: A Guide to Steady Growth in Holiness.* Harrison, NY: Roman Catholic Books, 1947.

Hatch, Alden. *A Man Named John.* New York: Hawthorn, 1963.

Hawkins, D. *Sketch of Mediaeval Philosophy.* New York: Greenwood Press, 1968.

Hebblethwaite, Peter. *Pope John XXIII, Shepherd of the Modern World.* New York: Doubleday, 1965.

———. *The Next Pope.* HarperSanFrancisco, 1995.

———. *The Year of Three Popes.* Glasgow: Collins, 1978.

Hefele, D.D., Right Rev. Charles Clark. *History of the Councils of the Church, Vols. I-IV.* Edinburgh, Scotland: 1876.

Heffernan, Virginia. *Outlines of the 16 Documents of Vatican II.* New York: America, 1965.

Heimbicher, Craig. "Did a Freemason Almost Become Pope?" *Catholic Family News.* August 2003.

Hendra, Tony. "Mass Appeal: A Latin lover laments the loss of magic and mystery in the liturgy of today's Catholic Church." *AARP* September & October 2003.

Hennesey, S.J., James. *First Council of the Vatican: The American Experience.* New York: Herder and Herder, 1963.

Henze, Anton. *Pope and the World: An Illustrated History of the Ecumenical Councils.* New York: Viking Press, 1965.

*Herbermann, Ph.D., LL.D., Charles. *Catholic Encyclopedia Vols. 1-15.* New York: The Encyclopedia Press, 1908.

Heresy in the Later Middle Ages: The Relation of Heterodoxy to Dissent: c. 1250-1450, Vol. 1. New York: Manchester University Press, 1967.

Herder and Herder. *Pope Paul VI in the Holy Land.* New York: 1964.

*Hergenröther, Dr. *Anti-Janus: An Historico-Theological Criticism of the Work, entitled "The Pope and the Council" by Janus.* Dublin: W. B. Kelly, 1870.

*Herrera, Angel Cardinal. *Preacher's Encyclopedia, Vol. II.* London: Burns and Oates Ltd., 1965.

*———. *Preacher's Encyclopedia, Vol. III.* London: Burns and Oates Ltd., 1965.

*———. *Preacher's Encyclopedia, Vol. IV.* London: Burns and Oates Ltd., 1965.

*Heston, C.S.C., Ph.D., S.T.D., J.C.D., Edward. *The Holy See at Work.* Milwaukee: Bruce Publishing Co., 1950.

Hillsdale Daily News, "Terror alert raised to 'high risk' orange, based on Muslim holy days." Washington (AP) 8 Feb. 2003.

Hitchcock, James. *Catholicism and Modernity.* New York: Seabury Press, 1979.

———. *The Pope and the Jesuits: John Paul II and the New Order in the Society of Jesus.* New York: National Committee of Catholic Laymen, 1984.

*———. *What is Secular Humanism?* Harrison: Roman Catholic Books, 1982.

*Hoever, S.O. Cist., Ph.D., Fr. Hugo. *Lives of the Saints.* New York: Catholic Book Publishing Co., 1955.

*Hogan, Richard. *Dissent From the Creed: Heresies Past and Present.* Huntington: Our Sunday Visitor Publishing Division, 2001.

Hollis, Christopher. *The Achievements of Vatican II.* New York: Hawthorn Books, 1967.

Holmes, George. *Oxford History of Medieval Europe.* Oxford: Oxford Press, 1992.

Holmes, Tara. "Grim Future Prospects." *Catholic World Report.* April 2002.

**Holy Bible.* New York: P. J. Kenedy & Sons, 1950.

**Holy Bible.* Chicago: Catholic Press, Inc., 1951.

*Hopkins, Andrea. *Knights.* London: Chancellor Press, 1990.

*Horn, Aloysius. *Christmas Chronicle.* Long Prairie, MN: Neumann Press, 2001.

Horton, Douglas. *Vatican Diary 1962: A Protestant Observes the First Session of Vatican Council II.* Philadelphia: United Church Press, 1964.

Houghton, Bryan. *Mitre and Crook.* Harrison, NY: Roman Catholic Books, 1979.

*Howe, Very Rev. Canon. *Stories from the Catechist.* Rockford: Tan Books, 1989.

Hughes, John. *Pontiffs: Popes Who Shaped History.* Huntington: Our Sunday Visitor Publishing Division, 1994.

*Hughes, Msgr. Philip. *Church in Crisis: A History of the General Councils, 325-1870.* New York: Hanover House, 1961.

*———. *Popular History of the Catholic Church.* New York: Macmillan, 1947.

*———. *Popular History of the Reformation.* Garden City: Hanover House, 1956.

*———. *Reformation in England.* New York: Macmillan Press, 1950.

Hull, S.J., Fr. Robert. *Medieval Theories of the Papacy.* London: Burns, Oates & Washbourne Ltd., 1934.

*Hurley, C.S.P., Fr. Wilfred. *The Pope is Infallible.* New York: Paulist Press, 1934.

*Husslein, S.J., Joseph. *The Mass of the Apostles.* New York: Kenedy, 1929.

In Search of History: The Knights Templar. A & E Home Video, The History Channel, Produced by Steven Talley, Film Roos Inc., 1997.

In Search of History: Secret Brotherhood of Freemasons. A & E Home Video, The History Channel, Produced by Tom Weidlinger, Film Roos Inc., 1998.

Inside the Vatican. January 2003.

Insight on the News August 26, 2002.

Insight on the News October 15, 2002.

Inter-Lutheran Commission on Worship. *Lutheran Book of Worship.* Minneapolis: Augsburg Publishing House, 1978.

International Commission on English in the Liturgy. *The Rites of the Catholic Church as Revised by the Second Vatican Ecumenical Council, Volume One.* Collegeville: Liturgical Press, 1991.

———. *The Rites of the Catholic Church as Revised by the Second Vatican Ecumenical Council, Volume Two.* Collegeville: Liturgical Press, 1991.

———. *Roman Pontifical.* 1978.

Investigative Staff of the *Boston Globe. Betrayal: The Crisis in the Catholic Church.* Boston: Little, Brown and Company, 2002.

*Iriarte De Aspurz, Fr. Lazaro. *Franciscan History: The Three Orders of St. Francis.* Chicago: Franciscan Herald Press, 1982.

*Jacobs, Jay. *Horizon Book of Great Cathedrals.* Boston: American Heritage, 1968.

*Janelle, Pierre. *Catholic Reformation.* Milwaukee: Bruce Publishing Co., 1949.

*Jedin, Hubert. *Ecumenical Councils of the Catholic Church.* New York: Deus Books, 1960.

*———. *History of the Council of Trent, Volume I: The Struggle for the Council.* Edinburgh, Scotland: Thomas Nelson and Sons Ltd., 1957.

*———. *History of the Council of Trent, Volume II: The First Sessions at Trent 1545-47.* Edinburgh, Scotland: Thomas Nelson and Sons Ltd., 1961.

Jessup, John. "An Open Plot to Rule the World." *Life* 20 Oct. 1961.

———. "The Key to Khruschev: Terror and Manipulation." *Life* 27 Oct. 1961.

———. "What We Must Do to Defeat Communism." *Life* 10 Nov. 1961.

———. "Pope Paul's Magnificent Risk." *Life* 15 Oct. 1965.

www.jesuites.com/histoire/lubac.htm

Johansen, Rev. Robert. "What's Wrong With Our Seminaries? An Insider Speaks Out." *Crisis* May 2003.

John Paul II. *Redemptor Hominis.* Washington, D.C.: United States Catholic Conference, 4 Mar. 1979.

John Paul II. *Ut Unum Sint.* Libreria Editrice Vatican, 25 May 1995.

http://www.vatican.va/holy_father/john_paul_ii/apost_constitutions/documents/hf_jp-ii_ 10/7/2003. *Universi Dominici Gregis* February 22, 1996.

John XXIII. *Journal of a Soul.* Dorothy White, trans. New York: Mc-Graw Hill Book Company, 1964.

*Johnson, John. *The Rosary in Action.* St. Louis: B. Herder Book Co., 1954.

Johnson, Paul. *Papacy.* New York: Barnes & Noble Books, 1997.

Jone, O.F.M., Rev. Heribert. *Moral Theology.* Westminster: Newman, 1945.

Jones, Arthur. "Poll of priests indicates signs of future church." *National Catholic Reporter.* 1 Nov. 2002.

Jones, Kenneth. *Index of Leading Catholic Indicators: The Church Since Vatican II.* St. Louis: Oriens Publishing Company, 2003.

Jones, Martin. *Counter Reformation, Religion and Society in Early Modern Europe.* Cambridge, England: Cambridge University Press, 1995.

Jurgens, William. *Faith of the Early Fathers Vols. 1-3.* Collegeville: Liturgical Press, 1979.

Kasindorf, Martin et al. "Boston church scandal starts chain reaction." *USA Today.* 19 Dec. 2002.

Keeley, N. *Oxford Dictionary of the Popes.* Oxford: Oxford University, 1986.

Keenshaw, Stanley and Kathryn Kost. *Abortion Patients in 1994-1995: Characteristics and Contraceptive Use.* New York: The Alan Guttmacher Institute, www.Guttmacher.org.

*Kelley, D.D., LL.D., Msgr. Francis. *Dominus Vobiscum.* Chicago: Matre & Company, 1922.

Kelly, Msgr. George. *Battle for the American Church Revisited.* San Francisco: Ignatius Press, 1995.

*Kempis, Thomas à. *My Imitation of Christ.* Brooklyn: Precious Blood Confraternity, 1954.

*Kennedy, John. *Light on the Mountain: The Story of La Salette.* New York: McMullen Books, 1953.

*Kenny, Anthony. *Thomas More.* Oxford: Oxford University Press, 1983.

Kestens, O.F.M. Cap. Adolf. *Spiritual Guidance: Fundamentals of Ascetical Theology.* Adapted from the Latin by Elmer Stoffel, O.F.M. Cap., Paterson: St. Anthony Guild Press, 1962.

Kilmartin, S.J., Edward. *The Eucharist in the West: History and Theology.* Collegeville: The Liturgical Press, 1998.

King, S.J., James. *Liturgy and the Laity.* Westminster: Newman Press, 1963.

Kirk, Andrea. "Rome: Catholic pols must be 'morally coherent.' " *Our Sunday Visitor.* 2 Feb. 2003.

*Kittler, Glenn. *Papal Princes.* New York: Funk & Wagnalls, 1960.

*Kitts, Eustace. *Pope John XXIII and Master John Hus of Bohemia.* London: Constable & Company Limited, 1910.

*Knights of Columbus. *The Reformation: Was it Reform or Revolt?* St. Louis: 1954.

———. *Vicar of Christ, Paul VI.* St. Louis: 1965.

*Kondor, SVD., Fr. Louis. Ed. *Fatima in Lucia's Own Words.* Fatima, Portugal: Postulation Centre, 1963.

Korson, Gerald. "Why Catholic politicos feel no shame." *Our Sunday Visitor.* 2 Feb. 2003.

Küng, Hans. *The Catholic Church.* New York: Modern Library, 2001.

———. *The Church.* New York: Sheed & Ward, 1967.

———. *Council, Reform and Reunion.* New York: Sheed & Ward, 1961.

Küng, Hans, et al. *The Church and Ecumenism.* New York: Paulist Press, 1965.

Kwasniewski, Peter. *Catholic Faith.* September / October 2001, Gaming, Austria.

Lambert, Fr. L. *Thesaurus Biblicus.* Waterloo: Observer Book Publication Co., 1880.

Lambert, Malcolm. *Medieval Heresy, Popular Movements from the Gregorian Reform to the Reformation.* New York: Barnes & Noble Books, 1977.

Landis, Benson. *Roman Catholic Church in the United States.* New York: Dutton, 1966.

*Landon, M.A., Rev. Edward. *Manual of Councils of the Holy Catholic Church, Vol. I & II.* Edinburgh, Scotland: Grant, 1909.

Langer, William. *Encyclopedia of World History.* Boston: Houghton, Mifflin Co.

*LaRavoire, S.T.D., Most Rev. Louis. *My Catholic Faith.* Kenosha: My Mission House, 1949.

*Laun, Fr. F. *The Chief Points of Difference.* New York: Joseph Wagner, 1915.

*Laux, M.A., Fr. John. *Church History.* New York: Benziger Bros., 1930.

*———. *Catholic Morality.* New York: Benziger Bros., 1934.

*———. *Mass and the Sacraments.* Rockford, IL: Tan Books and Publishers, Inc., 1990.

*———. *Catholic Apologetics.* Rockford, IL: Tan Books and Publishers, Inc., 1990.

Lawton, Michael. "Historical first: Catholics join in German church assembly." *National Catholic Reporter.* 20 Jun. 2003.

Lecler, S.J., Joseph, et al. *Religious Freedom.* New York: Paulist Press, 1966.

Leeming, S.J., Bernard. *Principles of Sacramental Theology.* London: Longmans, 1956.

*Lees-Milne, James. *Saint Peter's: The Story of Saint Peter's Basilica in Rome.* Boston: Little, Brown and Company, 1967.

Legrand, Catherine and Jacques. *John Paul II.* London: Dorling Kindersley, 2000.

*Leo XIII, Pope. *Apostolicae Curae.* New York: Paulist, 1949.

*——. *On the Unity of the Church.* Boston: Daughters of St. Paul, Promulgated: June 20, 1896.

Lemaître, Solange. *Hinduism.* New York: Hawthorn Books, 1959.

Lépicier, ORD. SERV. B.M.V., Fr. Alexio. *Tractus De Baptismo et de Confirmatione.* Rome, Italy: Pontificia In Instituto Pii IX, 1923.

*LeRoux, Abbé Daniel. *Peter, Lovest Thou Me?* Gladysdale, Australia: Instauratio, 1989.

**Letter of St. Athanasius to His Flock.* Spokane: Mary Immaculate Queen Center, 1993.

L'Huillier, Archbishop Peter. *Church of the Ancient Councils, The Disciplinary Work of the First Four Ecumenical Councils.* Crestwood, NY: St. Vladimir's Seminary Press, 1996.

Libreria Editrice Vaticana. *Catechism of the Catholic Church.* New York: Catholic Book Publishing Co., 1994.

Life December 26, 1955.

Life October 8, 1956.

Life June 7, 1963.

Life June 14, 1963.

Life January 17, 1964.

Life December 17, 1965.

Life December 26, 1969.

Liguori, St. Alphonsus. *Dignities and Duties of the Priesthood.* Brooklyn: Redemptorist Fathers, 1927.

*——. *Holy Eucharist.* Brooklyn: Redemptorist Fathers, 1934.

*——. *Great Means of Salvation and of Perfection.* Brooklyn: Redemptorist Fathers, 1927.

——. *Theologia Moralis, Vol. I.* A. Konnings, C.SS.R., trans. New York: Benziger Bros. 1881.

*——. *Victories of the Martyrs.* Brooklyn: Redemptorist Fathers, 1954.

Likoudis, Paul. "Religious Scandals Top News Stories." *The Wanderer.* 2 Jan. 2003.

Lilly, William. *Characteristics From the Writings of John Henry Newman.* London: Kegan Paul, Trench, Trübner & Co., Ltd., 1901.

Lindsay, D.D., LL.D. Thomas. *A History of the Reformation, Vol. II.* Edinburgh: T. & T. Clark, 1907.

Littell, Franklin. *Historical Atlas of Christianity.* Israel: Continuum, 1976.

Littlejohn, David. *Wall Street Journal,* September 11, 2002.

Lockwood, Robert. "Confessions of a Saturday Past." *Our Sunday Visitor.* 11 Mar. 2001.

Lopez, Kathryn. "Why Young Catholics Leave the Church." *Crisis* December 2002.

Lortz, Joseph. *How the Reformation Came.* New York: Herder and Herder, 1964.

Los Angeles Times. October 18, 1978.

Los Angeles Times. August 17, 1997.

Los Angeles Times. December 9, 2000.

Los Angeles Times. January 25, 2002.

Los Angeles Times. July 27, 2002.

Los Angeles Times. October 17, 2002.

L'Osservatore Romano. September 25, 1969, Vatican City.

L'Osservatore Romano. June 22, 1981, Vatican City.

L'Osservatore Romano. February 10, 1993, Vatican City.

L'Osservatore Romano. January 29, 2003, Vatican City.

Low, David. *Fodor's 97: Germany—The Complete Guide with the Best of the Cities, Medieval Villages and the Bavarian Alps.* New York: Fodor's Travel Publications, 1996.

*Loyola, O.P., Sister Mary. *Visualized Church History.* New York: Oxford Book Co., 1942.

Luxmoore, Jonathan. "Remembering Europe's Martyrs of Communism." *Our Sunday Visitor.* 14 Jul. 2002.

———. "Who'll minister to Ireland's Catholics?" *Our Sunday Visitor.* 29 Sept. 2002.

———. "East trumps West in Europe's seminaries." *Our Sunday Visitor.* 11 May 2003.

———." 'Eldest daughter' still desperately seeks faith." *Our Sunday Visitor.* 6 Jul. 2003.

———."How the future pope beat the Communists." *Our Sunday Visitor.* 12 Oct. 2003.

MacCaffrey, Fr. James. *History of the Catholic Church in the Nineteenth Century (1789-1908).* Dublin: M. H. Gill and Son, Ltd., 1910.

MacCarron, D.M.C. Daniel. *Great Schism.* Dublin: Universal Limited, 1982.

MacEoin, Gary. *What Happened at Rome?* New York: Holt, Rinehart and Winston, 1966.

Madges, William and Michael Daly. *Vatican II: Forty Personal Stories.* Mystic: Twenty-Third Publication, 2003.

Magri, Ed. "Pope Takes 40 Off Saints List." *Herald Examiner (Los Angeles)* 9 May 1969.

*Mandonnet, O.P., Pierre. *St. Dominic and His Work.* St. Louis: B. Herder Book Co., 1944.

Manhattan, Avro. *Vatican-Moscow Alliance.* New York: Ralston-Pilot Inc., 1977.

*Manning, Henry Cardinal. *The Vatican Council and its Definitions: Pastoral Letter to the Clergy.* New York: P. J. Kenedy & Sons, 1886.

Mannion, Msgr. M. "Pastoral Answers." *Our Sunday Visitor.* 16 Dec. 2001.

——. "Should there be absolution without confession?" *Our Sunday Visitor.* 16 Mar. 2003.

——. "Have the precepts of the Church changed?" *Our Sunday Visitor.* 23 Mar. 2003.

——. "What is the 'Cosmic Christ'?" *Our Sunday Visitor.* 20 Apr. 2003.

*Manton, C.SS.R., Fr. Joseph. *Straws From the Crib.* Boston: St. Paul Editions, 1964.

Marius, Richard. *Thomas More.* New York: Alfred Knopf, 1984.

*Markoe, S.J., Fr. John. *Triumph of the Church.* Bronx: Scafati Printing Co. Inc., 1960.

Marlin, George, Richard Rabatin and John Swan, eds. *The Quotable Fulton Sheen: A Topical Compilation of the Wit, Wisdom, and Satire of Archbishop Fulton J. Sheen.* New York: Doubleday, 1989.

*Martin, Charles. *Catholic Religion.* St. Louis: B. Herder Book Co., 1918.

Martin Luther's Works, *Liturgy and Hymns, Vol. 53.* Philadelphia: Fortress, 1965.

*Martin, Malachi. *The Keys of This Blood: The Struggle For World Domination Between Pope John Paul II, Mikhail Gorbachev and the Capitalist West.* New York: Simon and Schuster, 1990.

*Martindale, S.J., C. *The Sacramental System.* New York: Macmillan Co., 1928.

Martinelli, Giuseppe. *World of Renaissance Florence.* New York: G. Putnam's Sons, 1968.

Martos, Joseph. *The Church's Sacraments: Anointing of the Sick.* Liguori: Liguori Publications, 1991.

——. *The Church's Sacraments: Confirmation.* Liguori: Liguori Publications, 1991.

——. *The Church's Sacraments: Eucharist.* Liguori: Liguori Publications, 1991.

——. *The Church's Sacraments: Holy Orders.* Liguori: Liguori Publications, 1991.

Mascetti, Manuela Dunn. *Saints: The Chosen Few.* New York: Ballantine Books, 1990.

*Mathieu, Melanie. *Apparition of the Blessed Virgin on the Mountain of La Salette.* Lecce, Italy 1879, reprinted in Quebec: St. Raphael's Publications, 1984.

*Matimore, S.T.D., Fr. P. *Heroes of God's Church.* Long Prairie, MN: Newman Press, 1931.

Maurice, Fr. *A Grain of Wheat,* Vol. 1, No. 8, November, 2002.

Maxwell-Stuart, P. *Chronicles of the Popes.* London: Thames & Hudson Ltd., 1997.

Mayer, Peter. "Pope John Paul II's Legacy: Growing Flock, Widening Rifts." *Wall Street Journal.* 17 Oct. 2003.

McAleavy, Tony. *Life in a Medieval Abbey.* London: English Heritage, 1996.

McAuliffe, S.J., Clarence. *Sacramental Theology: A Textbook for Advanced Students.* St. Louis: B. Herder Book Co., 1958.

McBrien, Richard. *Lives of the Popes: The Pontiffs from St. Peter to John Paul II.* San Francisco: Harper 1997.

———. "Cardinal chronicles impact of Vatican II." *National Catholic Reporter.* 7 Mar. 2003.

*McDonald, Msgr. William. *The General Council.* Washington, D.C.: Catholic University of America Press, 1962.

*McEvedy, Colin. *New Penguin Atlas of Medieval History.* Singapore: Imago Production Ltd., 1992.

*———. *Penguin Atlas of Ancient History.* Hong Kong: Wah Tong, 1967.

*———. *Penguin Atlas of Medieval History.* Hong Kong: Wah Tong, 1961.

*———. *Penguin Atlas of Modern History (to 1815).* Hong Kong: Wah Tong, 1972.

*———. *Penguin Atlas of Recent History (Europe Since 1815).* Frong, England: Butler & Tanner Ltd., 1982.

McGeary, Hanna. "Can the Church be Saved?" *Time* 1 Apr. 2002.

*McGolrick, Fr. Edward. *The Unchangeable Church: Her Heroes, Her Martyrs, Her Trials and Her Triumphs, Vol. I.* New York: John Duffy, Publisher, 1907.

McGurk, M.A., M. LITT., Francis. *Papal Letters to Scotland of Benedict XIII of Avignon, 1394-1419.* Edinburgh, Scotland: Scottish Historical Society, 1976.

McInerny, Ralph. *What Went Wrong With Vatican II: The Catholic Crisis Explained.* Manchester, NH: Sophia Institute Press, 1998.

*McHugh, O.P., S.T.M., LITT.D. John and Charles Callan, O.P., S.T.M., LITT.D. *Catechism of the Council of Trent for Parish Priests.* New York: Joseph Wagner, Inc., 1958.

*McKenna, C.SS.R., Stephen. *Brief History of the Church.* New York: Paulist, 1946.

*McKenna, O.P., Bishop Robert. *Catholics Forever.* March 2000.

*McLaughlin, Fr. John, et al. *Half-Hours with the Servants of God.* New York: Murphy and McCarthy, 1889.

*McNaspy, C. *A Guide to Christian Europe.* New York: Hawthorn Books, Inc., 1963.

McNeill, William. *Plagues and Peoples.* New York: Doubleday, 1976.

McNeill, William and Schuyler Houser. *Medieval Europe.* New York: Oxford University Press, 1971.

*McSorley, Joseph. *Outline History of the Church.* St. Louis: Herder Book Co., 1943.

Mead, Frank. *Handbook of Denominations in the United States.* Nashville: Abingdon Press, 1990.

*Meadows, Denis. *Short History of the Catholic Church.* New York: Guild Press, 1959.

*Meagher, D.D., Fr. James. *Protestant Churches: Their Founders, Histories and Developments: How the Reformation Spread.* New York: Christian Press Assoc., 1914.

Menninger, Karl. *Whatever Became of Sin?* New York: Hawthorn Books, 1973.

*Metz, René. *What is Canon Law?* New York: Hawthorn Books, 1960.

Miami Herald. February 19, 1984.

Miceli, Fr. Vincent. *Freemasonry and the Church.* Cassette lecture, Montvale, NJ: Keep the Faith Inc.

Miesel, Sandra. "A Quiet Death in Rome: Was John Paul I Murdered?" *Crisis* July / August 2003.

Miller, C.S.C., S.T.D., John. *Vatican II: An Interfaith Appraisal.* Notre Dame: University of Notre Dame Press, 1966.

———. *Yearbook of Liturgical Studies, Vol 3.* Notre Dame: Fides, 1962.

*Mindszenty, József Cardinal. *Memoirs.* New York: Macmillan Publishing Co. Inc., 1974.

*Mioni, Jr., Anthony. *Popes Against Modern Errors: 16 Papal Documents.* Rockford: Tan Books and Publishers, Inc., 1999.

**Missal in Latin and English.* Westminster: Newman Press, 1962.

*Mollat, G. *Popes at Avignon, 1305-1378.* New York: Harper Torchbooks, 1963.

Montague, D.D., Gerard. *Problems in the Liturgy.* Westminster: Newman Press, 1958.

Morrison, Pat. "A Council Primer." *National Catholic Reporter.* 4 Oct. 2002.

*Morrison, Fr. M. *Official Catholic Directory of Traditional Latin Masses and Resource Book 2003.* Veritas: Santa Monica, CA: 2003.

Most Holy Family Monastery. *Communist Infiltration of the Roman Catholic Clergy.* Berlin, NJ: Gregorian Press.

*Mozley, M.A., Fr. Thomas. *Letters From Rome on the Occasion of the Oecumenical Council, 1869-1870, Vol. I.* London: Longmans, Green and Co., 1891.

*———. *Letters From Rome on the Occasion of the Oecumenical Council, 1869-1870, Vol. II.* London: Longmans, Green and Co., 1891.

*Mroz, O.F.M. Conv., Fr. Victor. *Ecumenism Leads to Apostasy.* ORCM Reprint No. 19.

MSN Learning & Research Plus—Dalai Lama from Encarta.

Mueller, John. *The Lutheran Confessions.* St. Louis: Concordia, 1953.

Muller, Herbert. *Religious Freedom in the Modern World.* Chicago: University of Chicago Press, 1963.

Müller, C.SS.R., Fr. Michael. *The Holy Eucharist: Our Greatest Treasure.* Rockford: Tan Books and Publishers, 1973. (Original publication-1868.)

Mulrine, Anna. "Risky Business." *U.S. News & World Report* 27 May 2002.

———. "Echoes of a Scandal." *U.S. News & World Report* 5 May 2003.

*Murphy, John. *General Councils of the Church.* Milwaukee: Bruce Publishing Co., 1960.

*Murphy, D.D., Ph.D., John. *Sacrament of Baptism.* New York: Macmillan, 1929.

National Catholic News Service. *Nights of Sorrow, Days of Joy.* Washington, D.C: N C News Service, 1978.

National Catholic Register. September 16, 1994.

National Catholic Register. November 15, 1998.

National Catholic Register. August 1, 1999.

National Catholic Register. May 20, 2000.

National Catholic Register. October 1, 2000.

National Catholic Register. December 10, 2000.

National Catholic Register. September 1, 2001.

National Catholic Register. November 4, 2001.

National Catholic Register. December 16, 2001.

National Catholic Register. January 20, 2002.

National Catholic Register. February 3, 2002.

National Catholic Register. April 7, 2002.

National Catholic Register. April 21, 2002.

National Catholic Register. May 12, 2002.

National Catholic Register. June 9, 2002.

National Catholic Register. June 16, 2002.

National Catholic Register. June 23, 2002.

National Catholic Register. August 4, 2002.

National Catholic Register. August 11, 2002.

National Catholic Register. August 18, 2002.

National Catholic Register. September 29, 2002.

National Catholic Register. October 6, 2002.

National Catholic Register. October 20, 2002.

National Catholic Register. October 27, 2002.

National Catholic Register. November 10, 2002.

National Catholic Register. February 2, 2003.

National Catholic Register. February 23, 2003.

National Catholic Register. March 2, 2003.

National Catholic Register. March 9, 2003.

National Catholic Register. March 16, 2003.

National Catholic Register. March 30, 2003.

National Catholic Register. April 6, 2003.

National Catholic Register. April 13, 2003.

National Catholic Register. April 20, 2003.

National Catholic Register. June 8, 2003.

National Catholic Register. July 6, 2003.

National Catholic Register. July 20, 2003.

National Catholic Reporter. August 9, 1996.

National Catholic Reporter. January 17, 1997.

National Catholic Reporter. January 16, 1998.

National Catholic Reporter. March 27, 1998.

National Catholic Reporter. October 1, 2000.

National Catholic Reporter. July 13, 2001.

National Catholic Reporter. October 5, 2001.

National Catholic Reporter. November 9, 2001.

National Catholic Reporter. January 11, 2002.

National Catholic Reporter. February 22, 2002.

National Catholic Reporter. March 8, 2002.

National Catholic Reporter. April 19, 2002.

National Catholic Reporter. May 31, 2002.

National Catholic Reporter. August 16, 2002.

National Catholic Reporter. September 13, 2002.

National Catholic Reporter. November 22, 2002.

National Catholic Reporter. January 17, 2003.

National Catholic Reporter. February 28, 2003.

National Catholic Reporter. October 17, 2003.

National Geographic Magazine December, 1983, Vol. 164, No. 6.

National Geographic Magazine August, 1995, Vol. 188, No. 2.

National Geographic Magazine August, 2002.

National Right to Life News. January 2003.

Nault, William. ed. dir. *The 1980 World Book Year Book.* Chicago: Childcraft International Inc., 1980.

Navas, Marco. "Hunger, Physical and Moral." *Catholic World Report* April 2002.

New American December 2, 1985.

New American December 11, 2002.

Newman, Albert. *Manual of Church History, Vol. II.* Philadelphia: American Baptist Publication Society, 1902.

*Newman, John Cardinal. *Arians of the Fourth Century.* Gloucester, England: Gracewing, 2001.

http://www.newsday.com/news/nationworld/worlds/sns-ap-vatican-cardinals-list,0.7888979... 10/7/2003.

Newsweek "Has the Church Lost Its Soul?" 4 Oct. 1971.

Newsweek September 4, 1978.

Newsweek "The Vision of a Socialist Pope." 20 Jun. 1983.

Newsweek September 22, 1997.

**New Testament:* Confraternity Edition. Paterson: St. Anthony Guild Press, 1941.

**New Testament:* Douay Rheims Edition. Commentary by Fr. George Haydock, Monrovia, CA: Catholic Treasures, 1991.

New York Daily News. November 27, 1969.

New York Post. June 15, 1974.

New York Times. July 5, 1973.

Noldin, S.J. H. *De Sacramentis.* Austria: Pustet, 1936.

Noonan, Peggy. *Life, Liberty and the Pursuit of Happiness.* Holbrook, MA: Adams Publishing, 1994.

———. "The Pope Steps In." *Wall Street Journal.* 19 Apr. 2002.

———. "A Tough Roe." *Catholic World Report* March 2003.

*North, Eric. *Book of a Thousand Tongues.* London: United Bible Societies, 1939.

www.nowahuta//nh.pl/english/socrealism.htm.

Noxon, Christopher. "Is the Pope Catholic?" *New York Times Magazine* 9 Mar. 2003.

Oakland (CA) News. September 3, 2002.

Oakland (MI) Press. "Devil-stoning ritual starts stampede that kills 14." (AP) 12 Feb. 2003.

Oberman, Heiko. *Luther—Man Between God and the Devil.* Eileen Walliser-Schwarzbart, trans. New York: Image Books, 1982.

*O'Brien, A.M. Fr. John. *History of the Mass and Its Ceremonies in the Eastern and Western Church.* New York: Catholic Publication Society Co., 1879.

*O'Brien, Ph.D. Fr. John. *Is Papal Infallibility Reasonable?* Huntington: Our Sunday Visitor Press, 1949.

*——. *First Martyrs of North America: the Story of the Eight Jesuit Martyrs.* Notre Dame: University of Notre Dame Press, 1953.

O'Brien, T. *Corpus Dictionary of Western Churches.* Washington, DC: Corpus Instrumentorum Editorial Offices, 1970.

*O'Connell, J. *Celebration of Mass.* Milwaukee: Bruce Publishing Co., 1959.

——. *Simplifying the Rubrics of the Roman Breviary and Missal.* Milwaukee: Bruce Publishing Co., 1956.

*Office of Catholic Publications. *Catholic Faith, Its Teachings and Defenders.* New York: Office of Catholic Publications, 1910.

*O'Hare, LL.D., Msgr. Patrick. *Facts About Luther.* Rockford: Tan Books, 1987.

*ature *Old Testament.* Commentary by Fr. George Haydock, Monrovia, CA: Catholic Treasures, 1992.

*Olin, John. *Catholic Reformation.* New York: Fordham University Press, 1992.

——. *Catholic Reform from Cardinal Ximenes to the Council of Trent, 1495-1563.* New York: Fordham University Press, 1990.

O'Meara, Kelly. "Sins of a Father: 'Sauna Kids' Abuse." *Insight on the News* 16 May 2002.

*Omlor, Patrick Henry. *Has the Church the Right?* Canandaigua, NY: *The Voice.* Oct. 1969.

——. *Letter of September 21, 2003.* Perth, Australia.

*——. *Questioning the Validity of Masses Using the New, All-English Canon.* Reno: Athanasius, 1969.

*——. *Robber Church.* Stouffville, Ontario: Silvio Mattacchione Co., 1998.

——. *Sedevacantists and the Una Cum Problem.* Veradale, WA: Catholic Research Institute, 2002.

*——. *"Unpersoning" of St. Philomena.* Greenacres, WA: Catholic Research Institute, 2001.

*O'Rafferty, Fr. Nicholas. *Discourses on St. Joseph.* Bruce Publishing: Milwaukee, 1951.

*O'Reilly, M.S., James. *The Story of La Salette.* Techny: Divine Word Publications, 1953.

http://www.osb.org/liturgy/altarbread.html

Ostling, Richard. "Calls mount for Catholic reforms." *Detroit News.* 27 Jul. 2003.

O'Sullivan, John. "Is Europe Losing Its Faith?" *Insight on the News* 26 Aug. 2002.

*Ottaviani, Cardinal Alfredo, Cardinal Antonio Bacci and Roman Theologians. *The Ottaviani Intervention.* Rockford: Tan, 1992.

*Ott, Ludwig. *Fundamentals of Catholic Dogma.* Cork, Ireland: Mercier Press, 1952.

Our Sunday Visitor. May 14, 1996.

Our Sunday Visitor. November 16, 1997.

Our Sunday Visitor. August 9, 1998.

Our Sunday Visitor. December 12, 1999.

Our Sunday Visitor. September 3, 2000.

Our Sunday Visitor. September 16, 2001.

Our Sunday Visitor. November 18, 2001.

Our Sunday Visitor. April 21, 2002.

Our Sunday Visitor. July 28, 2002.

Our Sunday Visitor. August 4, 2002.

Our Sunday Visitor. August 11, 2002.

Our Sunday Visitor. September 1, 2002.

Our Sunday Visitor. October 6, 2002.

Our Sunday Visitor. November 3, 2002.

Our Sunday Visitor. December 1, 2002.

Our Sunday Visitor. February 16, 2003.

Our Sunday Visitor. March 2, 2003. Editorial: "Why RCIA process needs improvement."

Our Sunday Visitor. April 6, 2003.

Our Sunday Visitor. April 27, 2003. Nation: "Confession Regression."

Our Sunday Visitor. May 11, 2003. "East trumps West in Europe's seminaries."

Our Sunday Visitor. May 18, 2003. World Briefings: "Pope John Paul II moves into fourth place."

Our Sunday Visitor. July 6, 2003.

Our Sunday Visitor. September 21, 2003, "Russia: Where have all the babies gone?"

Outler, Albert. *Methodist Observer at Vatican II.* Westminster: Newman Press, 1967.

Oxfort, Ursula. *Pope John's Revolution.* Lake Worth, FL: Christian Counter Revolution, 1965.

Pabuskite ismiego. Lithuanian apostolate publication, 1979.

Paci, Stefano. "The Smoke of Satan in the House of the Lord." *30Days.* No. 6, 2001.

Panneton, Georges. *Heaven or Hell.* Westminster: Newman Press, 1960.

*Parente, Pietro. *Dictionary of Dogmatic Theology.* Milwaukee: Bruce, 1951.

Parishes of Abbas and Templecombe with Horsington: Church of St. Mary the Virgin, Abbas and Templecombe. http://web.ukonline.co.uk/parish/stm.htm.

*Parish Priests of Chicago. *Instructions For Non-Catholics.* Orland Park: United Book Service, 1954.

Parrinder, Geoffrey. *World Religions From Ancient History to the Present.* New York: Facts on File, 1985.

Parsch, Dr. Pius. *Liturgy of the Mass.* St. Louis: B. Herder Book Co., 1946.

Pastor, Dr. Ludwig. *History of the Popes, Vol. 11.* London: John Hodges, 1891.

*Patte, Richard. *The Case of Cardinal Aloysius Stepinac.* Milwaukee: Bruce, 1953.

Paul VI. *Apostolic Constitution on the Sacrament of Anointing of the Sick.* Westminster: Paulist, 1972.

——. *Apostolic Exhortation on Evangelization in the Modern World.* Boston: St. Paul Books & Media, 1975.

Pell, Archbishop George. "From Vatican II to Today." *Catholic World Report* July 2003.

Pennington, M. *The Eucharist: Yesterday and Today.* New York: Crossroad, 1984.

*Phelan, D.D., Msgr. *The Ceremony of Consecration of a Bishop.* Spokane: Mt. St. Michael.

Pictorial Atlas of the World. Italy: Ottenheimer Publishers Inc., 1993.

Pieper, Lori. "Celebrating 'the Smiling Pope.'" *Our Sunday Visitor.* 28 Sept. 2003.

Pilsner, Connie. "Lies of Abortion Meet Their Match." *National Catholic Reporter.* 23 Mar. 2003.

Pisani, J. "Her recently widowed grandpa was shacking up." *Our Sunday Visitor.* 2 Mar. 2003.

*Pius V, Pope St. *Catechism of the Council of Trent.* Fr. J. Donavan, trans. Hawthorne, CA: Christian Book Club of America, 1975.

*Pius IX, Pope. *Syllabus of Errors.* Spokane: Mary Immaculate Queen Center, 1995.

Pius X, Pope St. *Codex Juris Canonici.* Westminster: Newman Press, 1949.

*——. *Encyclical Letter on the Doctrine of the Modernists.* Rockford: Tan Books, 1907.

*Pius XI, Pope. *Encyclical Letter on Fostering True Christian Unity.* Boston: Paulist, 1964.

*Pius XII, Pope. *Encyclical Letter on the Mystical Body of Christ.* New York: Paulist, 1943.

*Pivarunas, CMRI, Bishop Mark. *Pro Grege* 29 Jun. 1994.

*——. *Pro Grege* Jul. 1994.

*——. *Pro Grege* 2 Feb. 1995.

*——. *Pro Grege* 3 Sept. 1995.

*——. "On the Vacancy of the Holy See." *Pro Grege* 28 Aug. 2002.

*Pohle, Msgr. Joseph. *Sacraments, Vol. I.* St. Louis: B. Herder Book Co., 1915.

*———. *Sacraments, Vol. IV.* St. Louis: B. Herder Book Co., 1920.

*Pohlschneider, Bishop Johannes. *Adsum, A Bishop Speaks to His Priests. (Ein Bischof Spricht Zu Zeinen Priestern.)* Bishop Henry Grimmelsman, trans. St. Louis: Herder Book Co., 1962.

Pollock, Robert. *The Everything® World's Religions Book.* Avon, MA: Adams Media Corporation, 2002.

Pontificale Romanum. Editio Iuxta Typicam. Marietti: Sanctae Sedis Apostolicae Et Sacrae Rituum Congregationis Typographi, 1962.

Pontificale Romanum. Dessain: Mechlin, Belgium, 1958.

Pope Speaks. Church Documents Bimonthly May / June 1999. Huntington: Our Sunday Visitor Publishing.

Pope Speaks. Church Documents Bimonthly January / February 2002. Huntington: Our Sunday Visitor Publishing.

Pope Speaks. Church Documents Bimonthly March / April 2002. Huntington: Our Sunday Visitor Publishing.

Pope Speaks. Church Documents Bimonthly July / August 2002. Huntington: Our Sunday Visitor Publishing.

Pope Speaks. Church Documents Bimonthly March / April 2003. Huntington: Our Sunday Visitor Publishing.

Pope Speaks. Church Documents Bimonthly May / June 2003. Huntington: Our Sunday Visitor Publishing.

Pope Speaks. Church Documents Bimonthly July / August 2003. Huntington: Our Sunday Visitor Publishing.

Pope Speaks. Church Documents Bimonthly September / October 2003. Huntington: Our Sunday Visitor Publishing.

Pope Speaks. Church Documents Bimonthly November / December 2003. Huntington: Our Sunday Visitor Publishing.

Potter, Mother Mary. *Path of Mary.* Chicago: Little Company of Mary, 1878.

*Poulet, Dom Charles. *History of the Catholic Church.* St. Louis: Herder Book Co., 1934.

Powell, Michael and Lois Romano. "Church gets tough on claims of abuse." *Detroit News.* 19 May 2002.

Preces Ante et Post Missam. Editio Decima Quinta. Ratisbon: Fredrick Pustet, 1955.

Priest Life. http://www.ABCNews.go.com/sections/us/DailyNews/priestlife020403.html.

Proud, Linda. *2000 Years of Christianity in England.* Andover, England: Pitkin Unichrone Ltd., 1999.

Prümmer, O.P. Dominic. *Handbook of Moral Theology.* Rev. Gerarld Shelton, S.T.L., trans. Cork: Mercier press Limited, 1955.

*Puskorius, CMRI, Fr. Casimir. "Letters to the Editor." *Reign of Mary* Vol. XXXIII, No. 110. Summer 2002, Spokane, WA.

*Raab, O.F.M., Fr. Clement. *Twenty Ecumenical Councils of the Catholic Church.* Westminster: Newman Press, 1959.

Rabinovich, Abraham. *Israel.* Ljubljana, Yugoslavia: Delo-Flint River Press Ltd., 1989.

*Radecki, CMRI, Frs. Francisco and Dominic. *What Has Happened to the Catholic Church?* Alymer, Ontario: Alymer Express Ltd., 1994.

Rahner, Karl. *I Remember.* New York: Crossroad, 1985.

Ramstein, S.T. Mag. J.U.D. O.F.M. Conv., Fr. Matthew. *Manual of Canon Law.* Hoboken: Terminal Printing and Publishing, 1947.

Read, Piers. *Templars.* Cambridge, MA: Da Capo Press, 1999.

Reader's Digest January 1963, "The Roman Catholic Church's Biggest Challenge."

Reader's Digest April 1963, "Pope John's Great Gift."

Reader's Digest October 1996, "John Paul II and the Hidden History of Our Time."

Reader's Digest March 2003, "Detective Work." Charles Cosma.

Redemptorist Pastoral Publication. *Handbook for Today's Catholic: Fully Indexed to the Catechism of the Catholic Church.* Liguori: Liguori, 1994.

Reedy, S.C.S., John and James Andrews. *The Perplexed Catholic: A Guide Through Confusion.* Notre Dame: Ave Maria Press, 1966.

Reeves, Thomas. *America's Bishop—The Life and Times of Fulton J. Sheen.* San Francisco: Encounter Books, 2001.

Regatillo, S.J., Eduardus. *Ius Sacramentarium.* Editio Secunda, Santander, Spain: Sal Terrae, 1949.

**Reign of Mary* Vol. XXVIII, No. 91. Fall 1997, Spokane, WA.

**Reign of Mary* Vol. XXXII No. 106. Summer 2001, Spokane, WA.

**Reign of Mary* Vol. XXXIII, No. 108. Winter 2002, Spokane, WA.

**Reign of Mary* Vol. XXXIII, No. 109. Spring 2003, Spokane, WA.

Reilly, Patrick. "Are Catholic Colleges Leading Students Astray?" *Catholic World Report* March 2003.

Remnant. April 30, 1990.

Rengers, O.F.M. Cap., Fr. Christopher. *The 33 Doctors of the Church.* Rockford: Tan, 2000.

Ricciotti, Abbot Giuseppe. *Julian the Apostate: Roman Emperor 361-363.* Rockford: Tan Books and Publishers, Inc., 1960.

Ripley, Francis. *The Last Gospel.* New York: Sheed & Ward, 1961.

Ripley, Canon Francis. *This is the Faith.* Rockford: Tan Books, 2002.

Rituale Romanum. Pauli V, Pontifici Maximi jussu editum. Rome: Desclee, Lefebvre & Soc., 1903.

Rituale Romanum. Editio Taurinensis quarta juta typicam. Turin: Marietta, 1952.

Roberts, J. *Penguin History of Europe.* London: Helicon Publishing Ltd., 1996.

Robinson, Ph.D., James. *Medieval and Modern Times.* Boston: Ginn and Company, 1902.

Roche, Aloysius. *Apologetics for the Pulpit.* London: Burns, Oates & Washbourne Ltd., 1935.

Roche, Douglas. *Catholic Revolution.* New York: David McKay Company, Inc., 1968.

Roguet, O.P., Fr. A. *Holy Mass: Approaches to the Mystery.* Collegeville: Liturgical Press, 1953.

*Rolfus, D.D., Fr. H. *Explanation of the Commandments.* New York: Benziger Bros., 1897.

Roman Missal—Revised by Decree of the Second Vatican Council and published by authority of Pope Paul VI. Collegeville: Liturgical Press, 1970.

Rome (NY) *Sentinel.* October 26, 1986.

Rome Sentinel. October 6, 1988.

Rose, Michael. "Bishops' Actions Expose More Corruption." *Wanderer.* 27 Jun. 2002.

———. *Goodbye! Good Men: How Catholic Seminaries Turned Away Two Generations of Vocations From the Priesthood.* Washington, D.C.: Regnery, 2002.

Rosten, Leo, ed. *Religions in America.* New York: Simon & Schuster, 1952.

Royal, Robert. *Catholic Martyrs of the Twentieth Century.* New York: Crossroad, 2000.

*Rumble, M.S.C., Fr., Dr. Leslie and Fr. Charles Carty. *Radio Replies Vol. 3.* Rockford: Tan Books and Publishers, Inc., 1979.

Russell, Jeffrey. *History of Medieval Christianity Prophesy and Order.* New York: Thomas Cromwell Company, 1968.

*Rynne, Xavier. (penname for Fr. Francis X. Murphy, C.SS.R.) *Letters From Vatican City: Vatican II (First Session): Background and Debates.* New York: Farrar, Straus & Company, 1963.

Sabetti, S.J., Aloysius. *Compendium Theologiae Moralis.* New York: Pustet, 1920.

Sacramentary. New York: Catholic Book Publishing Co., 1974.

Sacramento Bee. April 1, 1984.

Sacramento Bee. October 26, 1986.

Sacramento Union, August 9, 1985.

Sacred Congregation of Rites. *Sacred Music and the Sacred Liturgy.* September 3, 1958, Washington, D.C.: National Catholic Welfare Conference.

*Sáenz y Arriaga, Fr. Dr. Joaquín. *Sede Vacante.* Angel Urraza, Mexico: Editores Asociados, 1973.

Saint, Steven. *"'Luther' tries hard, but historically flawed." Our Sunday Visitor.* 12 Oct. 2003.

Sallah, Michael and David Yonke. "Shame, sins and secrets." *Toledo (Ohio) Blade.* 1 Dec. 2002.

*Sanborn, Bishop Donald. *Catholic Restoration.* Nov.-Dec. 2002.

*———. "O Sacrament Most Unholy—John Paul II Approves a Mass With No Consecration." January 9, 2002.

———. "The Role of Freemasonry in the Destruction of the Catholic Order."
Catholic Restoration Jul.-Aug. 2003.

Sander, Dr. Nicolas. *The Rise and Growth of the Anglican Schism.* Original printing 1585, republished in 1988 by Tan Books and Publishers, Inc.

*Sarday Salvany, Fr. Felix. *What is Liberalism?* Rockford: Tan Books and Publishers, 1979.

*Schiatti, Lamberto. *Shroud: A Guide to the Reading of an Image Full of Mystery.* Cinisello Balsamo, Italy: Edizioni San Paolo.

Schillebeeckx, O.P., Fr. Edward. *Christ: The Sacrament of the Encounter with God.* New York: Sheed & Ward, 1963.

Schneider, Herbert. *Religion in 20th Century America.* New York: Atheneum, 1964.

Schreiter, C.PP.S., Robert. *Ministry of Reconciliation, Spirituality & Strategies.* Maryknoll, NY: Orbis Books, 1999.

*Schroeder, O.P., Fr. H. *Canons and Decrees of the Council of Trent.* English Translation, Rockford: Tan Books and Publishers, Inc., 1978.

*———. *Disciplinary Decrees of the General Councils.* St. Louis: Herder Book Co., 1937.

Scully, Gerald. *Murder by the State.* September 1997, National Center for Policy Analysis.

Sealey, Geraldine. "The Preaching Life." ABC News.com, 4 Apr. 2002.

Secretariat for Promoting Christian Unity. *Cases When Other Christians May be Admitted to Eucharistic Communion in the Catholic Church.* May 25, 1972, Boston: St. Paul's Editions.

Severy, Merle. *Renaissance: Maker of Modern Man.* New York: National Geographic Book Service, 1970.

*Shadler, Fr. F. *Beauties of the Catholic Church.* New York: Pustet, 1881.

*Sharkey, Don. *Madonna in Tears: Story of Our Lady of La Salette.* Ipswich, MA: National Shrine of Our Lady of LaSalette, 1952.

Sharp, Deborah. "Senior suicides increase as U.S. ages." *USA Today.* 20 Feb. 2003.

Shaughnessy, Fr. Paul. "The Gay Priest Problem." *Catholic World Report* May 2002.

Shaw, Russell. "Cardinal Law stays, but so do questions." *Our Sunday Visitor.* 28 Apr. 2002.

———. "Why Europe is no longer 'the faith.'" *Our Sunday Visitor.* 25 Aug. 2002.

——. "It won't end soon." *Our Sunday Visitor.* 12 Jan. 2003.

——. "Ignoring the Obvious: The Unreality of American Catholicism." *Crisis* Mar. 2003.

——. "I am just poor dust." *Our Sunday Visitor.* 28 Sept. 2003.

——. "Why he's the pope of the 'new evangelization.' " *Our Sunday Visitor.* 12 Oct. 2003.

*Sheed, F. *Is It The Same Church?* Dayton: Pelaum, 1968.

——. *Nullity of Marriage.* New York: Sheed & Ward, 1959.

*Sheehan, D. D., Bishop M. *Apologetics and Catholic Doctrine.* Dublin: M. H. Gill, 1951.

*Sheen, Bishop Fulton J. *Treasures in Clay.* Garden City: Image Books, 1980.

*Sheen, Msgr. Fulton J. *Communism and the Conscience of the West.* Indianapolis: Bobbs Merrill Co., 1948.

Sheler, Jeffery. "Faith in America." *U.S. News & World Report* 6 May 2002.

——. "A fall from grace." *U.S. News & World Report* 23 Dec. 2002.

Sheppard, Lancelot. *The Liturgical Books.* New York: Hawthorn Books, 1962.

——. *The Mass in the West.* New York: Hawthorn Books, 1962.

Shores, Ph.D. Louis. *Collier's Encyclopedia 1962 Yearbook.* Collier Publishing Co., 1962.

Signal (Santa Clarita, CA). January 25, 2002.

*Simmons, Fr. Ernest. *Fathers and Doctors of the Church.* Milwaukee: Bruce, 1959.

*Skarga, S.J., Fr. Peter. *Eucharist.* Milwaukee: Bruce Publishing Co., 1939.

Slaughter, Frank. *Constantine: The Miracle of the Flaming Cross.* Garden City: Doubleday and Co., 1965.

Sloyan, Gerald. *Worship in a New Key—What the Council Teaches on the Liturgy.* Garden City: Echo, 1966.

Smith, Bill. "Nuns as sexual victims get little notice." *STL Today.com* 5 Jan. 2003.

Smith, John. *Great Schism, 1378.* New York: Weybright and Talley, 1970.

*Smith, Richard. *John Fisher and Thomas More: Two English Saints.* New York: Sheed & Ward Inc., 1935.

*Smyth, Fr. Hugh. *Reformation.* Chicago: Extension Press, 1919.

Soubrier, Antoine. "Sainthood Factory?" *Catholic World Report* January 2003.

South Florida Sun-Sentinel. May 6, 2002.

Spalding, D. D., Bishop M. *The History of the Protestant Reformation in Germany and Switzerland and in England, Ireland, Scotland, the Netherlands, France and Northern Europe.* Baltimore: John Murphy & Co., 1860.

The Spectator. Gerald Warner:

http://www.spectator.co.uk/article.php3?table=old&section=current&issue=2002-12-14&id=2604

Spiritual Diary: Selected Sayings and Examples of Saints. (No author given. Original publication—1775). Boston: St. Paul Editions, 1979.

Staff of *The Pope Speaks* Magazine. *Encyclicals and Other Messages of John XXIII.* Washington, D.C.: TPS Press, 1964.

Stammer, Larry. "Organized Religion Slips in Survey." *Los Angeles Times.* 11 Jan. 2003.

——. *Los Angeles Times.* "When Priests Don't Run the Parish." 18 May 2003.

Steinfels, Peter. *A People Adrift: The Crisis of the Roman Catholic Church in America.* New York: Simon and Schuster, 2003.

*Stépanich, O.F.M., Fr. Martin. *Letter to James Condit,* ed. *All These Things,* 25 May 1999.

——. *Letters of November 30, 2002 and March 25, 2003.*

Steward, Robert. *Illustrated Almanac of Historical Facts.* New York: Prentice Hall, 1992.

*Sticco, Maria. *Peace of St. Francis.* New York: Hawthorn Books, Inc., 1962.

Stieber, Joachim. *Studies in the History of Christian Thought, Volume XIII, Pope Eugenius IV the Council of Basel and the Secular and Ecclesiastical Authorities in the Empire.* Leiden, The Netherlands: E. J. Brill, 1978.

http://stltoday.com/stltoday/news/stories.nsf/ St. Louis Dispatch. 5 Jan. 2003.

Stoller, Michael. *Schism in the Reform Papacy: The Documents and Councils of the Antipopes, 1061-1121.* Ann Arbor, MI: University Microfilms International, 1985.

Stravinskas, Ph.D., S.T.D., Fr. Peter. *Catholic Dictionary* (Revised). Huntington: Our Sunday Visitor Publishing Division, 2002.

Strype, M.A., John. *Memorials of Thomas Cranmer, Vol. I.* Oxford: T. Combe, 1848.

Stump, Richard. *Studies in the History of Christian Thought, Volume LIII, The Reforms of the Council of Constance (1414-1418).* Köln, Germany: E. J. Brill, 1994.

*Sullivan, D.D., Fr. John. *Fundamentals of Catholic Belief.* New York: P. G. Kenedy, 1925.

*——. *Visible Church.* New York: Kenedy & Sons, 1920.

Sullivan, Robert. *Pope John Paul II Life a Tribute.* New York: Life Books, 1999.

Suprenant, Jr., Leon. "Standing Up (And Not Kneeling) For The Church."
National Catholic Register. 26 Jan. 2003.

Suzzallo, Henry. *National Encyclopedia, Vol. II.* New York: P. F. Collier Corp., 1932.

Svidercoschi, Gian. *Stories of Karol—The Unknown Life of John Paul II.* Peter Heinegg, trans. Liguori: Liguori/Triumph, 2003.

Szyszkiewicz, Thomas. "How one gay bishop makes ecumenical road rocky." *Our Sunday Visitor.* 2 Nov. 2003.

*Tanner, S.J., Norman. *Decrees of the Ecumenical Councils, Volume One.* New York: Sheed & Ward, 1990.

*———. *Decrees of the Ecumenical Councils, Volume Two.* New York: Sheed & Ward, 1990.

*Tanquerey, S.S., D.D., Very Rev. Adolfe. *Manual of Dogmatic Theology, Vol. II.* Tournai, Belgium: Desclée & Co., 1959.

*———. *Spiritual Life.* Tournai, Belgium: Desclée & Co., 1930.

———. *Synopsis Theologiae Dogmaticae Specialis ad Mentem S. Thomae Aquinatis Hodiernis Moribus Accommodata, Vol. II de Deo Sanctificante et Remuneratore.* New York: Benziger, 1911.

Tarjanyi, Judy. "Kneeling regaining favor but posture is not always well received." http://www.toledoblade.com/apps/pbcs.d11/article?date=20030111&Category=NEWS10 January 11, 2003.

Tavard, Georges. *Protestantism.* New York: Hawthorn, 1959.

The Pope's Visit. Time-Life Special Reports. New York: Time Inc., 1965.

The Tidings. July 9, 1954, Los Angeles, CA.

The Tidings. March 6, 1992, Los Angeles, CA.

The Tidings. December 9, 1994, Los Angeles, CA.

The Tidings. April 26, 1996, Los Angeles, CA.

The Tidings. July 19, 1996, Los Angeles, CA.

The Tidings. June 6, 1997, Los Angeles, CA.

The Tidings. July 25, 1997, Los Angeles, CA.

The Tidings. September 8, 2000, Los Angeles, CA.

The Tidings. January 12, 2001, Los Angeles, CA.

The Tidings. February 16, 2001, Los Angeles.

The Tidings. March 30, 2001, Los Angeles, CA.

The Tidings. January 25, 2002, Los Angeles, CA.

Thielen, Thoralf. *What is an Ecumenical Council?* Westminster: Newman Press, 1960.

Thorndike, Ph.D., Lynn. *History of Medieval Europe.* Cambridge, MA: Riverside, 1917.

*Thornton, Fr. Francis. *Our Lady of Chartres in France.* St. Paul: Catholic Digest, 1959.

*Thomas, Gordon and Max Morgan-Witts. *Pontiff.* New York: Signet, 1983.

Thornton, Fr. James, "Gramsci's Grand Plan." *The New American* 5 Jul. 1999.

Time September 25, 1964.

Time October 16, 1964.

Time May 16, 1969.

Time September 27, 1971.

Time October 9, 1978.

Time February 5, 1979.

Time June 11, 1979.

Time October 15, 1979.

Time June 7, 1982.

Time July 9, 1984.

Time April 1, 2002, "Can the Catholic Church Save Itself?"

Time ed. *Great People of the 20th Century.* New York: Time Books, 1996.

*Time-Life Books ed. *Voyages of Discovery, TimeFrame AD 1400-1500.* Alexandria, VA: Time-Life Books, 1989.

——. *World's Great Religions.* New York: Time Incorporated, 1957.

*Toal, D.D., M. *Sunday Sermons of the Great Fathers, Vol. II.* Chicago: Regnery, 1958.

*——. *Sunday Sermons of the Great Fathers, Vol. III.* Chicago: Regnery, 1963.

*——. *Sunday Sermons of the Great Fathers, Vol. IV.* Chicago: Regnery, 1963.

Tobin, Rev. Eamon. *The Sacrament of Penance: Its Past and Its Meaning for Today.* Liguori: Liguori Publications, 1983.

Todoroff, Susan. "Breaking Down the Walls." *Ann Arbor Observer* August, 2003.

Toronto Sun. June 11, 2002.

Toronto Sun. October 21, 2002.

*Touron, O.P., Fr. A. *First Disciples of St. Dominic.* Somerset, OH: Rosary Press, 1928.

*Treacy, S.J., Fr. Gerald. *Five Great Encyclicals.* New York: Paulist Press, 1939.

Trevor, Meriol. *Pope John.* Garden City: Doubleday, 1967.

**Trento.* Hermosillo, Sonora, Mexico: Ano 4, Numero 12, 2002.

www.d.umd.edu/mich0212/Mass/whatis.html "Tridentine Mass."

*Trochu, Abbé Francis. *The Curé D'Ars: St. Jean-Marie Baptiste Vianney.* London: Burns, Oates & Washbourne, 1927.

Tushnet, Eve. "Christianity from the Outside." *Crisis* May 2002.

*Ullathorne, Bishop. *The Holy Mountain of LaSalette.* Hartford, CT: Fathers of LaSalette, 1901.

Ullmann, Walter. *Medieval Papalism.* London: Methuen & Co., 1999.

——. *Short History of the Papacy in the Middle Ages.* London: Methuen & Co. Ltd., 1972.

Umberg, S.J. Ioannes. *Enchiridion Symbolorum: Definitionum et Declarationum de Rebus et Morum.* Friburg: Herder & Co., 1922.

Undreiner, Ph.D., George, trans. *Church and Culture in the Middle Ages, Vol. I.* Paterson: St. Anthony Guild Press, 1956.

UPI, "Pope Paul VI: First Visit to the Americas," Amy Records, 4 Oct. 1965.

Urban, Leonard. *Look What They've Done to My Church.* Chicago: Loyola, 1985.

Urtasun, Joseph. *What is a Bishop?* New York: Hawthorn Books, 1962.

U.S. News & World Report April 1, 2002. "Can the Church Save Its Soul?"

USA Today. October 28, 1986.

USA Today. March 7, 2002.

USA Today. March 29, 2002.

USA Today. April 2, 2002.

USA Today. April 15, 2002.

USA Today. April 29, 2002.

USA Today. September 13, 2002.

USA Today. October 3, 2002.

USA Today. March 11, 2003.

USA Today. May 19, 2003.

Utley, John. "Why Has Marxism Hooked Clergymen?" *The New American* 2 Dec. 1985.

Vacancy. Newhall, CA: St. Joseph's Media, 1994.

Vandenabeele, Janet. "Sikhs talk about faith—and fear." *Detroit News.* 30 Mar. 2003.

*Van de Putte, C.S.Sp., LL.D, Fr. Walter. *Saint Pius X Daily Missal.* New York: Catholic Book Publishing Co., 1956.

*Van Noort, S.T.D., Msgr. G. *Christ's Church Vol II.* Westminster: Newman Press, 1957.

*Vann, O.P. and P. Meagher, O.P. *The Temptations of Christ.* New York: Sheed & Ward, 1957.

http://www.vatican.va/cgi-bin/w3-msql/news_services/bulletin/news/10019.html.

http://www.vatican.va/news-services/liturgy/documents/ns_lit_doc_20020124-assisi-impegno_it.html.

*Vécuyer, C.S.Sp., Joseph. *What is a Priest?* New York: Hawthorn Books, 1959.

Vermeersch, Arthurus. *Theologiae Moralis Tomus III.* Rome: Università Gregoriana, 1927.

Vennari, John. *Permanent Instruction of the Alta Vendita.* Rockford: Tan Books and Publishers, Inc., 1999.

Vennari, Susan. "Feast of the Holy Relics of the Saints: Feast Day—November 5." *Catholic Family News,* November 2003.

*Von Cochem, O.S.F., Fr. Martin. *The Incredible Catholic Mass.* Rockford: Tan Books and Publishers, 1997. Originally published in Cologne, Germany in 1704 under the title *Die heilige Messe für die Weltleute*—"Holy Mass for Everyone."

Von Galli, Mario. *The Council and the Future.* New York: McGraw-Hill, 1966.

Von Matt, Leonard. *Councils.* Chicago: Henry Regnery Company, 1961.

Wall Street Journal. September 25, 2000.

Wall Street Journal. October 18, 2002.

Walsh, M.D., Ph.D., LL.D., Litt., D., James. *Thirteenth: Greatest of Centuries.* New York: Catholic Summer School Press, 1913.

Walsh, Michael. *Illustrated History of the Popes: St. Peter to John Paul II.* New York: St. Martin's Press, 1980.

*Walsh, William. *Our Lady of Fatima.* Garden City: Doubleday, 1954.

Wanderer. May 1, 1997.

Wanderer. April 17, 2000.

Wanderer. September 7, 2000.

Wanderer. February 7, 2002.

Wanderer. March 28, 2002.

Wanderer. April 11, 2002.

Wanderer. April 25, 2002.

Wanderer. May 23, 2002.

Wanderer. June 20, 2002.

Wanderer. August 22, 2002.

Wanderer. October 3, 2002.

Wanderer. October 24, 2002.

Wanderer. October 31, 2002.

*Ward, Maisie. *Saints Who Made History: The First Five Centuries.* New York: Sheed & Ward, Inc., 1959.

Warren, Dr. Neil. "The Cohabitation Epidemic." *Focus on the Family* June/ July 2003.

Watkin, E. *Church in Council.* London: Darton, Longman and Todd, 1960.
*Waugh, Evelyn. *Edmund Campion: Jesuit and Martyr.* Garden City: Image Books, 1946.

Webber, Jude. "Pope: Hell not a real place." *Detroit News.* 28 Jul. 1999.

*Weber, Fr. Francis. *His Eminence of Los Angeles: James Francis Cardinal McIntyre,*

Vol. II. Santa Barbara: Kimberly Press, 1997.

Weber, Fr. Gerard, Fr. James Killgallon and Fr. Michael O'Shaughnessy, O.P. *Baptism and the Family.* New York: Benziger Inc., 1971.

Weigel, George. *Witness to Hope—The Biography of Pope John Paul II.* New York: HarperCollins, 1999.

Weiskittel, John. "Who is John Paul II? Part 1." *The Athanasian* 1 Mar. 1984.

——. "Who is John Paul II? Part 2." *The Athanasian* 1 Apr. 1984.

Welborn, Amy. "Who's the weaker sex?" *Our Sunday Visitor.* 9 Feb. 2003.

Weninger, D.D., F. X. *On the Apostolical and Infallible Authority of the Pope.* New York: Sadlier, 1869.

Whalen, William. *Christianity and American Freemasonry.* Milwaukee: Bruce Publishing Co., 1958.

*——. *Separated Brethren.* Milwaukee: Bruce Publishing Co., 1958.

Wheatley, Dennis. *The Devil and All His Works.* New York: American Heritage, 1971.

White, James. *Introduction to Christian Worship.* Nashville: Abingdon Press, 1980.

Whitehead, Ken. "The Cost of Theological Dissent." *Catholic World Report* Jun. 2003.

Wiles, Maurice and Mark Santer, eds. *Documents in Early Christian Thought.* Cambridge: Cambridge University Press, 1975.

Wilhelm, Anthony. *Christ Among Us: A Modern Presentation of the Catholic Faith.* Boston: Paulist Press, 1967.

Williams, Fr. Thomas. *Textural Concordance of the Holy Scriptures.* New York: Benziger Bros., 1908.

Wilkinson, Philip. *Illustrated Dictionary of Religions.* Toledo, Spain: Artes Graficias, 1999.

Wills, Gary. *Why I am a Catholic.* New York: Houghton Mifflin Company, 2002.

*Wilmer, S.J., Fr. W. *Handbook of the Christian Religion.* New York: Benziger Bros., 1891.

*Wiltgen, SVD., Fr. Ralph. *The Rhine Flows into the Tiber.* New York: Hawthorn, 1978.

*Windeatt, Mary. *Children of La Salette.* St. Meinrad: Grail, 1951.

Winston, Richard. *Charlemagne.* New York: American Heritage Publishing Co. Inc., 1968.

Wojtyla, Karol. *Sources of Renewal: The Implementation of the Second Vatican Council.* San Francisco: Harper & Row, 1979.

Wolleh, Lothar. *The Council: The Second Vatican Council.* New York: Viking Press, 1966.

*Woods, Ralph. *Treasury of Catholic Thinking.* New York: Thomas Cromwell Co., 1953.

Woodward, Kenneth. "By Pope John Paul II." *Newsweek* 26 Mar. 1979.

World Book CD ROM disk 1. Macintosh Edition, 1998.

Worship Vol. XXVI. December 1951 to November 1952. Collegeville: Liturgical Press, 1952.

Worship Vol. XXXI. December 1956 to November 1957. Collegeville: Liturgical Press, 1957.

Worship Vol. XXXIII. December 1958 to November 1959. Collegeville: Liturgical Press, 1959.

Worship Vol. XXXIX. January 1965. Collegeville: Liturgical Press, 1965.

Worship Vol. XLI. January 1967. Collegeville: Liturgical Press, 1967.

Worship Vol. XLII. January 1968. Collegeville: Liturgical Press, 1968.

Worship Vol. XLIII. January 1969. Collegeville: Liturgical Press, 1969.

Woywood, O.F.M., LL.B., Fr. Stanislaus. *A Practical Commentary on the Code of Canon Law, Vol. I.* New York: Joseph Wagner, 1945.

——. *A Practical Commentary on the Code of Canon Law, Vol. II.* New York: Joseph Wagner, 1945.

Wuerl, Donald. *Fathers of the Church.* Huntington: Our Sunday Visitor, 1975.

*Wynn, Wilton. *Keeper of the Keys: John XXIII, Paul VI and John Paul II—Three Who Changed the Church.* New York: Random House, 1988.

*Yallop, David. *In God's Name: An Investigation into the Murder of Pope John Paul I.* New York: Bantam Books, 1984.

Yost, SCJ, STL, Rev. Charles. *In His Likeness: Homilies for Liturgies in Honor of the Saints.* Hales Corners, WI: Priests of the Sacred Heart.

Zangrando, Alessandro. "Roman Landscape." *The Latin Mass: A Journal of Catholic Culture* Fall 2002.

Zaratti, O.C.D., Alfonso. *The Work of the Catholic Church in the United States of America.* Rome, Italy: Nardini Publishing Co., 1956.

Zelizer, Gerald. "Clergy Shortage Requires Youth." *USA Today.* 20 Dec. 2001.

Zmirak, J. "Popes, Presidents and Power." *National Catholic Reporter.* 23 Mar. 2003.

30 Days. June 1989.

30 Days. April 1991.

30 Days. May 1993.

30 Days. June 2001.

Index

a' Kempis, Thomas 212
Abortion 431, 454, 455, 491, 496-500
Acacius of Constantinople, Patriarch 45, 80
Achillas, Bishop 5
Acton, Lord 236, 239, 257
Aetius of Antioch 19
Agagianian, Gregorio Cardinal 328
Agatha, St. 389
Aggiornamento 302, 303, 333
Agnostics 300, 363, 369, 545, 549
Alan Guttmacher Institute 454
Alaric II, King of the Visigoths 30, 32
Albigensian Heresy 103, 106-109, 114, 197, 581, 584, 585
Albrecht of Brandenburg, Archbishop 187
Alemany, Bishop 267
Alexander of Alexandria, St. 5, 13
Alexander of Constantinople, Bishop 17
Alexander the Great 21, 88
Alfrink, Bernard Cardinal 308, 327
Almaric of Bena 581
Alphonsus Liguori, St. 4, 402, 405, 406, 575
Alta Vendita 519, 520, 524
Amat, Bishop 267
Ambrose of Milan, St. 11, 16, 278, 349, 373, 378
Ambrosian, Rite of the Catholic Church 375, 378
Amorth, Fr. Gabrielle 443
Amphilochius of Iconium, St. 27
Amphion, St. 9
Anaphora of Addai and Mari 553
Anastasius, Emperor 30
Andrew of Hungary, King 593
Andrew, St. 378
Andronicus II, Emperor 126
Andropov, Yuri 541
Anglican Church 198, 200-202, 337, 453, 550-552
Anglican Orders 460, 461, 463, 464, 466, 468, 552
Animism 360, 361, 533, 546, 550
Annulments 453, 454, 493, 495
Anthony of Padua, St. 554
Antioch (341 AD), Pseudo Council of 20
Antipope xix, xx, 89, 301, 335, 525, 528, 564

Antipopes:
  Alexander V 147, 148, 154, 592
  Albert 89, 592
  Anacletus II 93-96, 592
  Anastasius 592
  Benedict X 592
  Benedict XIII 145, 147, 148, 156, 592
  Benedict XIV 159, 592
  Boniface VII 592
  Calixtus III 101, 592
  Celestine II 592
  Christopher 592
  Clement III 89, 592
  Clement VII 145, 148, 592
  Clement VIII 159, 592
  Constantine II 592
  Dioscorus 592
  Eulalius 31, 592
  Felix II 23, 592
  Felix V 165, 592
  Gregory 592
  Gregory VIII 89, 592
  St. Hippolytus xx, 377, 592
  Honorius 89, 592
  Honorius II 592
  Innocent III 101, 103, 592
  John 592
  John XVI 592
  John XXIII xx, 148-155, 157, 159, 160, 301, 592, 301
  Laurentius 592
  Nicholas V 142, 592
  Novatian 11, 587, 592
  Paschal 592
  Paschal III 101, 592
  Philip 592
  Severinus 592
  Stephen II 592
  Sylvester IV 89, 592
  Theoderic 89, 592
  Theodore 592
  Ursinus 23, 592
  Victor IV 93, 95, 101, 592
  Victor IV 592
Antoninus, St. 146
Antonius, St. 212
Apollinarian Heresy 19, 28, 584
Apollinaris of Laodicea 19, 584
Apostasy xviii, 314
Apostate xviii, 276
Apostolicae Curae 204, 461, 467, 476
Apostolic Tradition 218, 219, 251, 260, 262, 327, 565, 566, 587

Arian Heresy xvi, 4-9, 13, 17, 18,
  23, 27, 30, 251, 568, 581, 584, 585
Arius xvii, 5-9, 13, 14, 17-19, 32,
  33, 572, 580, 584, 585
Arles, Council of 11
Arles (353 AD), Pseudo Council of
  22
Armenian, Rite of the Catholic Church
  374, 375, 378, 399, 411
Arnold of Brescia 93, 96, 97,
  333, 581
Askidas, Thgeodore 51, 52
Assisi 550, 556
Assyrian Orthodox 38, 553, 554
Athanasius Creed 169, 271
Athanasius of Alexandria, St.
  13-16, 18, 20, 21, 169, 251, 561,
  572, 573
Atheism 296, 297, 298, 314,
  315, 318, 319, 350, 363, 364, 369
Atheists 305, 319, 321, 323,
  337-339, 346, 356
Athenagoras I of Constantinople
  337
Attila the Hun 39
Augustine of Canterbury, St.
  197
Augustine of Hippo, St.
  xii, 11, 29, 32, 60, 100, 218,
  500, 561, 575
Augustinians 190, 211, 216
Aurelius of Carthage, St. 11
Auriol, Vincent 299
Avignon Popes 130, 131, 142,
  146, 151
Bacci, Antonio Cardinal 396
Baha'I 546, 550
Baldwin of Flanders, King 593
Baldwin of Hainault, King 593
Baltimore Catechism
  430, 454, 477
Baptists 195, 305, 551
Baradai of Edessa, James 586
Barbara, St. 555
Barnabas, St. 389
Basel (1061) (1438),
  Pseudo Council of 89
Basil of Ancyra 19
Basil, St. 17, 25, 77, 378, 497
Baum, Gregory O.S.B. 309, 326
Bayazid II 178
Bayley, Bishop 267
Baziak, Archbishop 538
Bea, S.J. Augustin Cardinal 308
Beghards 138, 581
Beguines 138, 581
Belloc, Hillaire xvii, 186, 484
Beran, Josef Cardinal 319, 340

Berengarius of Tours 115
Berlin Wall 317
Bernard of Clairvaux, St.
  94-96, 131, 575
Bernardine of Siena, St.
  184, 212
Bernini, Giovanni 241
Bertano, Bishop of Fano 218
Bessarion of Nicaea, Bishop
  166
Billot, Cardinal 275
Birthrates 494, 497
Black Death 139, 140, 174
Blaise, St. 381
Blanchet, Bishop 267
Bohemund of Taranto, King
  593
Bonaventure, St. 124, 125
Book of Common Prayer
  199, 202
Borgias 162, 179
Bramante, Donato 180, 241
Brand, Eugene 396
Brey, Fr. Lawrence 409-410
Bridget, St. 146
Brioloth,
  Archbishop of Uppsala 335
Bucer, Martin 192, 193, 195, 200
Buddhism 107, 337, 361-363,
  533, 546, 550, 551
Bugnini, Archbishop
  396, 446, 447, 466
Burgundians 29
Byzantine, Rite of the Catholic Church
  375, 411, 449
Cajetan 560
Caliph Yezid II 68
Calvi, Robert 531, 532
Calvinist Heresy 197
Calvin, John 141, 186, 188, 197,
  199, 206, 307, 583
Camara, Archbishop Helder 340
Campion, Edmund xx
Canonization of Saints 554-556
Canon of the Mass 375, 377,
  386-389, 394, 398, 401
Capovilla, Msgr. Loris 300
Capuchins 211
Caraffa, Cardinal 209
Carey, Archbishop 552
Carlo Malatesta, King 149
Carlstadt, Andreas 194, 195
Carmelites 216
Caro y Rodriguez, Jose Cardinal
  523
Carré, Marie 290
Carthusians 201
Casaroli, Agostino Cardinal 544

Casimir of Brandenburg, King 194
Casper, Walter Cardinal 552
Castro, Fidel 285, 339
Catechism of the Catholic Church 430, 455, 513
Catechism of the Council of Trent 403, 404, 406, 444, 475, 513
Cathar Heresy 104, 106-108
Cathars 186
Cathedrals 392-394, 412
Catherine of Alexandria, St. 555
Catherine of Aragon, Queen 198
Catherine of Siena, St. 142, 146
Catholic Reformation 208-211, 218
Ceausescu 340
Cecilian of Carthage, Bishop 9
Cecil, Sir William 200, 201
Celtic, Rite of the Catholic Church 378
Cerularius, Michael 80, 81, 581, 584, 585
Cesarini, Cardinal 164, 166
Cesena, Michael of 151
Chair of Peter 562-564
Chalcedon-General Council 1, 28, 39-46, 48, 54-56, 77, 169, 171, 580, 583, 586
Chaldean, Rite of the Catholic Church 38, 411, 553
Chardin, S.J. Teilhard de 303, 307, 310, 425, 426
Charlemagne, Emperor 75, 76, 100
Charles Borromeo, St. 220, 221, 223, 228, 373
Charles IV, Emperor 149
Charles Martel, King 68
Charles of Anjou, King 124, 126
Charles V, Emperor 137, 184, 192, 194, 215, 218, 219
Charles V of France, King 144
Charles VII of France, King 163
Chenu, O.P. Marie Dominique 309, 310, 334
Chesterton, G. K. 285
Christopher, St. 555
Cicognani, Amleto Cardinal 319
Civil War 229
Clement of Alexandria, St. 500
Clerical Immorality 468-472
Clotilda, St. 30
Clovis of Franks, King 30
Code of Canon Law 511, 512
Cody, Cardinal John 531
Coelestius 32
College of Cardinals 103, 145, 158, 159, 295, 302, 337
Collegiality 331-333

Colonna 127, 130, 158
Communicatio in Sacris 354-355
Communism 234, 239, 285-289, 291, 303, 314, 315, 317-321, 340, 519, 526, 535-540, 542, 544
Comte de Montalembert 232
Conditional Sacraments 426, 428, 452, 453, 461, 479
Confraternity of Christian Doctrine 228
Confucianism 551
Congar, O.P., Yves 309, 310, 334, 362 541
Conrad III, King 593
Conroy, Bishop 267
Consecration of Host and Wine 374, 388, 389, 394, 399, 402, 403-410
Constance-General Council xiii, 162, 237, 577, 580
Constans, Emperor 19, 20
Constans II, Emperor 62
Constantine Chlorus, Emperor 4
Constantine IV (Pogonatus), Emperor 63, 64
Constantine Monomachus, Emperor 81
Constantine of Samosata 581
Constantine the Great, Emperor 5, 8, 9, 13, 14, 19, 26, 49
Constantine V (Copronymus), Emperor 70, 71, 73, 84
Constantine VI, Emperor 74
Constantine XI, Emperor 173, 176
Constantius II, Emperor 14, 17-19, 22-24, 251
Constitution on Sacred Liturgy, Vatican II 358, 383, 384, 387, 391, 433, 445, 475
Constitution on the Church in the Modern World, Vatican II 329, 331, 539
Contarini, Cardinal 209
Coptic, Rite of the Catholic Church 374, 375, 377, 411
Cornelius, St. 556
Cornwell, John 532, 533
Cranmer, Thomas 185, 197-200, 203, 204, 317
Cromwell, Thomas 198, 199 204
Cuban Missal Crisis of 1962 319
Cullman, Dr. Oscar 312, 313, 353
Cum Ex Apostolatus 556
Curran, Fr. Charles 432
Cushing, Richard Cardinal 308
Cyprian, St. 561
Cyril of Alexandria, St. 7, 34-38, 40, 41, 47, 48, 52, 53, 169, 378
Cyril of Jerusalem, St. 27
d'Ailly, Peter, Cardinal 151, 158, 237

Dalai Lama 550
Danielou, S.J. Jean 309, 541
Darboy of Paris, Bishop 258, 269
Daru, Foreign Minister 245-247
De Defectibus 403, 404, 406, 410, 565
De Gaulle, Charles 298
de la Roche, Blessed Alan 507
De Lubac S.J., Henri 309, 310, 541
De Medicis 162
De Romano Pontifice 516
de' Medici, Cosimo 160
de Bruillard, Bishop 506
Decanonization of Saints 555, 556
Dechamps, Victor Cardinal 256
Decree on Ecumenism, Vatican II 331, 351, 353-56 359, 360, 363
Decree on Religious Freedom, Vatican II 332, 367-371
Decretals of Gratian 100
Decretals of Pope Gregory IX 122, 541
DeGoesbriand, Bishop 267
DeLai, Gaetano Cardinal 296, 297
Della Porta 241
DeMolay, Jacques 134
Deposit of Faith 249, 254, 255, 262, 273, 274, 555, 559
DeSmedt, Bishop Emile 308
de St. Omer, Geoffrey 131
Devil 285, 345, 381, 382, 393, 439-445, 474, 503 514, 516, 527
Diekmann, O.S.B. Godfrey 309, 387
Diocletian, Emperor 49
Dioscorus of Alexandria 41, 42, 44
Dismas, St. 556
Divine Office 10, 114, 189, 473
Divorce 431, 474, 493, 494, 496-498
Documents of Vatican II 284, 529, 565
Dodd, Bella 287
Dogmatic Constitution on the Church, Vatican II 364
Döllinger, Dr. 233, 235, 236, 239, 240, 258, 269, 270, 584, 587
Dominic, St. 107, 109-110, 113, 507
Dominicans 109-111, 140, 190, 211, 216, 218, 226, 299, 310
Dominus Jesus 529
Donatist Heresy 11, 584, 585
Donatus the Great 11, 584, 585
Donohue, William 493
Döpfner, Julius Cardinal 308, 328, 329
Dos Santos, Sr. Lucia 501, 502, 505, 507, 516
Doubtful Pope xix
Doxology 10
Druids 553
Dubuis, Bishop 267
Duke of Somerset 199, 204

Dulcinists 581
Dulles, Cardinal Avery 376
Duomo 168
Dupanloup of Orléans, Bishop 235, 258, 259, 261, 269
Eastern Rites of the Catholic Church 374, 387, 390, 392, 399, 411
Ecumenism 284, 289, 301, 304, 312, 343-345, 348-352, 357, 364, 370, 512, 529, 538, 549, 561, 565, 567
Edict of Milan 4
Edward VI, King 199, 204
Edwardine Ordinal 462, 468
Elder, Bishop 267
Elizabeth I of England, Queen xviii
Elizabeth of Hungary, St. 111
Encyclicals 271
Ephebophilia 469
Ephesus—General Council 31-39, 42, 46-48, 52, 169, 554, 580, 583, 586, 587
Ephesus (John of Antioch) (431 AD), Pseudo Council of 37, 588
Ephesus (Latrocinium) (449 AD), Pseudo Council of xx, 43, 588
Episcopalians 195, 398
Erasmus of Rotterdam 188
Ernest of Lüneberg 194
Ethiopic, Rite of the Catholic Church 411
Eugenius of Carthage, St. 8
Eulogius of Edessa, St. 27
European Alliance 307, 324, 327-329, 386
Eusebius of Caesaria, Bishop 8
Eusebius of Dorylaeum, Bishop 41
Eusebius of Nicomedia, Bishop 5, 8, 13, 18, 19
Eustace, St. 555
Eutyches xvii, 39-45, 48, 580, 582, 586
Evolution of Dogma 292
Ex Cathedra 237, 249, 263-265, 272
Excommunication 315
Exorcism, Rite of 425, 426, 443, 516
Faber, Fr. Frederick 381, 415
False Religious Liberty 367, 369, 370, 529, 541,
Fatima 440, 501, 504, 507
Ferdinand I, Emperor 222
Ferdinand II, Emperor 220
Fifth Lateran—General Council 100, 177-184 578, 580
Filioque 168, 169
First Constantinople—General Council xiii,13-30, 45, 46, 580, 583, 585
First Lateran—General Council 85-92, 581, 583

First Lyons—General Council
  117-122, 581, 583
First Nicaea—General Council
  3-12, 13, 19-21, 24, 27, 30, 44-36, 46,
  169, 187, 241, 465, 580, 583, 587
Fitzgerald, Bishop Edward 267
Flavian of Constantinople, St. 41-44
Florence—General Council 80, 126,
  161-176, 263, 314, 369, 403, 423,
  425, 474, 578, 580, 581, 584, 585
Forcade of Nevers, Bishop 246, 247
Fornari, Cardinal 504
Fourth Constantinople—General Council
  75-82, 580, 583
Fourth Crusade 105, 165, 593
Fourth Lateran—General Council
  105-116, 577, 580
Fra Angelico 162
Franciscans 110, 111, 114, 140,
  191, 201, 211
Francis de Sales, St. 379, 554
Francis of Assisi, St. 110-113,
  473, 554
Francis Xavier, St. 211
Franco-Prussian War 267, 269
Franks 30, 57, 84
Franz Joseph, Emperor 521
Fraticelli 581
Frederick I Barbarossa, Emperor
  100-102, 106, 117, 130, 581, 593
Frederick II, Emperor 113,
  117-120, 130, 581, 593
Frederick the Elector 191, 194
Freemasonry 285, 338,
  517-520, 522, 524
French Revolution 518, 520, 525
Friedrich, J. 269, 270
Friedrich of Austria, Duke
  154, 155
Frings, Joseph Cardinal
  308, 324, 327, 328
Fulda Conference 327-329
Gaito, Virgilio 522
Gallicanism 151, 152, 236-238
Gallican, Rite of the Catholic Church
  375, 378
Garibaldi, Giuseppe 231, 233
Gasser, Vincent Cardinal 257
Gelli, Licio 531
General Absolution
  433, 435-437
General Councils of the Church
  xiii, xiv, xix, xxi, 241, 249, 251,
  271, 272
Genseric of the Vandals 39
George, Raymond 396
George, St. 555
Germanus, St. 68, 69

Gerson, John 237
Gestapo 535
Ghibellines 121
Gibbons, James Cardinal
  247, 255, 267
Gierek, Edward 340
GIRM 415
Giraud, Maximin 504, 505
Gladstone, Prime Minister
  239, 240
Godfrey de Bouillon 593
Golden Spurs, Battle of 129
Gonzaga, Cardinal 220
Gratian 16
Gratian, Emperor 100
Greek Catholics 76, 172, 173
Greek Schism xviii, 77, 80,
  81, 165, 172
Greeley, Fr. Andrew 483
Gregory Nazianzen, St.
  17, 25, 26, 169
Gregory of Nyssa, St. 17, 27
Gromyko, Andrei 319
Guelfs 121
Hapsburgs 208
Häring, C.SS.R., Bernard
  309
Hattin, Battle of 132
Hefele of Rotterdam, Bishop
  238, 258
Heiss, Bishop 267
Helena, St. 4
Hell 438-441, 443, 444, 469
Henni, Bishop 267
Henry II of England, King 92
Henry III, Emperor 130
Henry IV, Emperor 88-90, 130
Henry V, Emperor 89, 90
Henry VI of England, King 163
Henry VIII of England, King
  197-199, 200, 204, 214, 301
Heraclius, Emperor 58, 62, 253
Heresy xvi, xvii, 312
Heretic xv, xvi, xvii,
  274-278, 349
Hergenröther, Cardinal 215
Hergenröther, Professor 258
Herrera, Bishop Angel 431
Hieria (753 AD),
  Pseudo Council of 71, 74, 588
Hilary of Poitiers, St. 17, 22, 251
Hilbert of Tours 115
Hinduism 337, 358, 360, 361, 533,
  546, 550, 551
Hitler, Adolf 316, 534
Hlond, Cardinal 536
Hohenstaufens 121
Holy Chrism 446-449, 453

Holy Office 297, 301, 302, 307, 308, 325, 334, 335, 356, 367
Holy Sacrifice of the Mass 373-383, 385, 386, 389, 432, 438, 459, 568, 577, 587
Holy Shroud of Turin 135
Holy Viaticum 10
Honorius, Emperor 32
Hosius, Cardinal 220
Hosius of Cordova, Bishop 5, 8, 9, 22, 24
Hospitallers, Knights (of Malta) 132, 137, 242
Hugh of Cyprus, King 593
Huguenots 186
Humiliati 110, 228
Hundred Years War 139
Huneric of the Vandals 29
Huns 31
Hussite Heresy 141, 584
Huss, John 141, 150, 157, 305, 584, 587
Ibas of Edessa, Bishop 44, 47, 48, 52, 53, 580
ICEL 387
Iconium, Battle of 102
Iconoclast Heresy 68, 70-74, 204-206, 580, 584, 586
Ignatius of Antioch, St. xv
Ignatius of Constantinople, St. 76, 78-80
Indulgences 121, 141, 187, 190, 191, 200, 204, 212, 225
Indult Mass 417-420
Interregnum 123
Irenaeus, St. 373
Irene, Empress 73, 74
Isabella II, Queen 229
Isidore of Kiev, Bishop 166
Isidore of Seville, St. xvi, 378
Islam 57-59, 68, 175, 337, 360, 361, 371, 529, 533, 554
Jacobite Heresy 171, 586
Jainism 361, 547, 550, 551
James della Marchia, St. 184
James I of Aragon, King 125
James of Nisibis, Bishop 9
James, St. 303, 474
Janissaries 174, 175
Januarius, St. 555
Jasper, Ronald 396
Jerome, St. 22, 100, 429, 561
Jesuits 114, 222, 234, 235, 249, 299, 309
Joachim of Floria, Abbot 115, 581
Joan of Arc, St. 554
John Bosco, St. 504

John Chrysostom, St. 378, 429, 575
John Damascene, St. 71
John Eudes, St. 469
John Fisher, St. 201
John of Antioch, Bishop 35-38
John of Burgundy, King 155
John of Capistrano, St. 184, 212
John of Jandun 236
John of Jerusalem, King 593
John of Saxony 194
John the Evangelist, St. xi, 34, 120, 444
John Vianney, St. 504
John VIII, Emperor 165, 167
Joseph II, Patriarch 167, 170
Judaism 305, 337, 398, 545, 547, 550, 551
Julian the Apostate, Emperor 15, 24, 25
Julius Caesar 88
Justina, Empress 16
Justinian, Emperor 48-55
Justin, St. 226, 375
Juvenal of Jerusalem 44
Kàdàr, Janos 340
Kamil, Sultan of Egypt 118
Katyn Forest Massacre 535
Kenrick of St. Louis, Bishop 258
KGB 287, 319, 544
Khwarazmi of Egypt 119
Kliszko, Zenon 538, 539
Kneeling for Communion 415-417
Knights Templar 130-138, 581
Know Nothing Party 233, 234
Knox, John 185, 197, 199, 206, 584, 587
König, Franz Cardinal 308, 327, 543
Korean War 316
Khruschev, Nikita 304
Küng, Hans 309, 311, 352, 558
Künneth, Friedrich 396
Lacordaire, Henri 232
Ladislaus of Naples 149, 150, 153
Lambruschini, Cardinal 506

Lamennais, Félicité de 232
Laodicea, Council of 349
La Salette, Secret of 504-506
Last Gospel 389, 390, 516
Last Sacraments 478
Lateran Treaty of 1929 545
Latin, Rite of the Catholic Church
  75-77, 374, 378, 384, 395, 411
Law, Cardinal Bernard 471
Lawrence, St. 473
Lay Investiture 86, 87, 90-92
Lectionary 398, 419
Lefebvre, Archbishop Marcel
  284
Léger, Paul Cardinal 308
Legnano, Battle of 102
Lenin, Nikolai 229
Leo III the Isaurian, Emperor
  67-71, 584, 586
Leonine Prayers 516, 517
Leo the Philosopher, Emperor
  79
Leo V, Emperor 73
Lercaro, Giocomo Cardinal
  308, 328, 329, 396
Liberalism
  229, 231, 232, 239, 524
Liberation Theology
  296, 322-334, 239
Licinius, Emperor 4
Liénart, Achille Cardinal
  308, 324, 325
Liturgy of St. James 374
Liturgy of St. Mark 374
Liturgy of St. Peter 374
Liutprand of Cremona 86
Loisy, Alfred 292
Lollard Heresy 186, 202
Lombard League 101, 102
Lombards 29, 57, 84
London, Council of 141
Longinus, St. 556
Lootens, Bishop 267
Lorenzo the Magnificent 180
Lorscheider, Aloisi Cardinal
  531
Los Angeles Times
  377, 533, 544
Loss of Faith 481-485, 498, 500
Loughlin, Bishop 267
Louis IV of Bavaria, King
  142, 151
Louis VII of France, King 593
Louis IX, St., King of France
  111, 119, 593
Louis XII of France, King 182
Louis Marie de Montfort, St.
  507, 509

Lucius of Adrianople 20
Lucy, St. 389, 555
Luminous Mysteries 509, 510
Lutheran Book of Worship 305
Lutheran Church
  xvi, xviii, 190-191, 195, 199, 202
  218, 398, 403, 545, 551, 587
Luther, Martin xviii, 101, 141,
  185, 186, 188-197, 204, 208,
  215, 218, 231, 235, 305, 325,
  332, 394, 396, 403, 410, 425,
  473, 526, 545, 570, 584, 587
Macarius of Jerusalem, St. 9
Macchi, Msgr. Paschale 341
Macedonian Heresy 28, 585, 586
Macedonius of Constantinople
  19, 20, 580, 584, 586
Machiavelli 179
Maderno 241
Magi 556
Magisterium 293
Mainz and Brixen (1080),
  Pseudo Council 89, 588
Major Orders 114, 457
Mani 32, 106-108, 584
Manichean Heresy 32, 106, 584
Manning, Henry Cardinal 190,
  250, 252, 254, 256, 259, 263
Mao Tse-Tung 339
Marcian, Emperor 43
Marcinkus, Bishop Paul 531
Maria-Teresa, Empress 173
Maris of Persia, Bishop 48
Maritain, Jacques 307, 333, 334
Mark of Ephesus, Bishop
  166, 170
Mark, St. 28
Maronite, Rite of the Catholic Church
  399, 411
Marsaudon, Yves 522
Marsilius of Padua 236
Martin of Paderborn, Bishop 250
Marto, Francisco 501
Marto, Jacinta 501
Marx, Karl 543, 544
Mary of Cleophas, St. 556
Mary Salome, St. 556
Masilius of Padua, 151, 152, 236
Mass Attendance
  438, 472, 482, 485
Mathieu, Melanie 504-506
Matthew, St. 378
Matthias, St. 389
Maurice of Saxony 219
Maxentius 4
Maximian, Emperor 4
Maximilian, Emperor 182
Maximos IV Saigh, Patriarch 308

Mayer, Bishop António de Castro 385
McBrien, Fr. Richard 549
McCloskey, Bishop John 267
McCloskey, Bishop William 267
McIntyre, James Cardinal 325, 384, 400
McManus, Frederick 309
Mehmet II 174-176
Melancthon, Philip 191, 193, 195
Melek-el-Kamil 111, 112
Meletius of Antioch, St. 27
Melitius of Lycopolis, Bishop 4, 5
Memnon of Ephesus, Bishop 35, 37, 38
Mennonites 551
Methodists 305, 551
Methodius of Constantinople, St. 74
Meyer, Albert Cardinal 308
Michael I, Emperor 76
Michael III (The Drunkard), Emperor 76, 77
Michael the Archangel, St. 517
Michael VIII Palaeologus, Emperor 124, 125
Michelangelo 162, 180, 184, 241
Miége, Bishop 267
Milan (355 AD), Pseudo Council of 22
Milvian Bridge, Battle of 4
Mindszenty, József Cardinal 314, 340, 341, 537
Minor Orders 457, 516
Missale Romanum 226, 377, 378, 403
Mixed Marriage 455
Modernist Heresy 271, 291-292, 513, 524, 541, 555, 584
Mohacs, Battle of 208
Mongols 133
Monophysite Heresy 39, 40, 42-45, 48, 49, 51, 53-55, 58, 59, 81, 171, 580, 586
Monothelite Heresy 58-66, 580, 586
Monti di Pietà 183, 184
Montini, Giovanni Cardinal (Paul VI) 298, 302, 311, 318, 326, 333
Moravians 551
Morone, Cardinal 220
Mozarabic, Rite of the Catholic Church 375, 378
Muhammad 54, 57, 59, 584
Muret, Battle of 107
Muret of Sura, Bishop 257
Murray, S.J. John Courtney 309, 310, 368
Napoleon Bonaparte, Emperor 88, 144
Napoleon III, Emperor 240, 245, 268
Nazis 534, 535, 537
Nectarius of Constantinople, Bishop 27
Nepotism 162, 177, 178
Nero, Emperor 3, 285
Nestorian Heresy xvi, 38, 171, 580, 584, 586
Nestorius of Constantinople xvi, xvii, 31-38, 40, 47, 48, 580, 584, 586
New Code of Canon Law 512, 513
Newman, John Cardinal 6, 15, 21, 23, 263, 274
New Mass—*Novus Ordo Missae* 384, 387, 389, 396-402, 405-407, 411-414, 416, 418-421, 565-567
Nicene Creed 10, 27, 36, 168, 270, 271, 576
Nicholas of Myra, St. 9, 555
Nietzsche, Friedrich 285
Nikodim, Patriarch Boris 318, 319
Ninety-Five Theses 189
Nogaret, William of 129-131, 134
Norbert, St. 94
Novatian Heresy 11, 587
Nowa Huta Ark Church 542, 543
Oath Against Modernism 294
Ockham, William of 151, 236
Offertory of Mass 374, 410
O'Connell, Bishop 267
O'Hara, Bishop 267
Old Catholics 233, 269, 570, 584, 587
Ollivier, Prime Minister 240, 245-247
Original Sin 425, 426
Orsini 127
Orthodox Churches 38, 44, 80-82, 172, 176, 258, 283, 297, 304, 312, 313, 337, 344, 346, 348, 361, 453, 545, 547, 551, 553, 554, 585, 586
Ostpolitik 544
Ostrogoths 31
Ottaviani, Alfredo Cardinal 311, 325, 330, 367, 386, 401, 502, 503
Ott, Dr. Ludwig 292, 446
Otto the Great, Emperor 86, 87, 130
Ottoman Turks 78, 165, 166, 174, 176, 208
Otto von Bismarck 233, 273
Outler, Albert 313, 330, 362
Palestrina, Giovanni 162

Papal Infallibility 23, 24, 236-240,
245-267, 269-274, 278, 279
Papal Primacy 160, 236, 237,
250, 251, 262, 263, 265
Papal States 84, 162, 164, 168,
230, 231, 235, 242, 268, 268
Paphnutius of Egypt, Bishop 9
Parker, Dr. Matthew 460
Parma (1063), Pseudo Council of
89, 588
Patrick, St. 484, 555
Paul of Constantinople, Patriarch
20
Paul of Neo Caesaria, Bishop
9
Paul, St. 28, 34, 189, 337, 389,
397, 444, 528, 563, 564, 575
Payns, Hugues 131
Pelagian Heresy 32, 583, 584
Pelagius 31, 32, 584, 587
Pelagius, Cardinal 593
Pelagius of Laodicea, St. 27
Pentecostals 551
People of God 362, 363, 540
Pepin 84
Periti 284, 302, 306, 309-311,
313, 328, 329
Persico, Bishop 267
Perugino 162
Peter Canisius, St. 226
Peter Chrysologus, St. 45
Peter of Alexandria, Bishop
4, 5, 26
Peter of Bruys 93, 98, 581
Peter of Luxemburg, Blessed
146
Peter of Sebaste, St. 27
Peter of Verona, St. 109
Peter Olivi 138, 581
Peter, St. 26, 28, 44, 46, 91,
169, 170, 178, 246, 248, 249,
255, 262, 263, 264, 272, 274,
275, 278, 329, 374, 378, 389,
397, 515, 525, 552, 565
Philip Augustus of France, King
593
Philip Benizi, St. 124
Philip Neri, St. 224
Philip of Hesse 193, 194
Philip of Macedonia, King 21
Philippopolis (c. 343 AD),
Pseudo Council 21
Philip the Fair (IV), King
128-131, 133-137
Philomena, St. 555
Photius of Constantinople
76-80
Photius (979-880 AD),

Pseudo Synod of 77, 80, 588
Piero 162
Pirates 102, 126, 153
Pisa, Milan and Lyons (1511-1512),
Pseudo Council of 182, 588
Pisa (1409), Pseudo Council of
xxi, 147, 148, 588
Plantegenets 214
Pole, Cardinal 209, 214, 217
Politburo 534
Polycarp of Smyrna, St. 120
Popes:
  Agapitus, St. 49-51
  Agatho, St. 57, 63, 65, 66, 580
  Alexander III 99-102, 554, 581
  Alexander VI 178, 179, 254
  Alexander VII 554
  Anastasius I, St. 24
  Benedict I 55
  Benedict VIII 27, 168
  Benedict IX 127, 254
  Benedict XI, Bl. 130
  Benedict XIV 519
  Benedict XV 290, 512, 516
  Boniface VIII 128-131, 152
  Boniface IX 145-148, 153
  Calixtus II 85, 90-91, 581
  Celestine I 31, 34-37, 580
  Celestine IV 119
  Celestine V, St. xix, 127, 128
  Clement I 378
  Clement IV 123
  Clement V 127, 128, 130, 131,
    135-138, 142, 581
  Clement VII 198
  Clement XII 518, 519
  Damasus I, St. 13, 23, 24, 26-28,
    580
  Eugene IV 161, 163-168, 172,
    582
  Eugenius I, St. 63
  Fabian 448
  Felix III, St. 45
  Gregory I, St. 28, 46, 69, 77, 197,
    378, 389
  Gregory II, St. 69, 71
  Gregory III, St. 71
  Gregory VII 87, 88, 152
  Gregory IX 118, 119, 122
  Gregory X, Bl. 115, 123, 124, 126, 581
  Gregory XI 142, 143
  Gregory XII 147, 148, 149, 153, 156,
    159, 581
  Gregory XVI 232, 233, 290, 291, 370,
    519, 520
  Hadrian I 67, 73, 74, 580
  Hadrian II 75, 79, 580
  Hadrian IV 97

Hadrian VI 208
Honorius I 60-62, 64-66, 251-254, 559
Honorius III 118
Innocent I, St. 32, 476
Innocent II 93-96, 133, 581
Innocent III 105, 108, 110, 112, 113, 115, 116, 152, 581
Innocent IV 117, 119, 120, 122, 577, 581
Innocent VII 146, 148
Innocent VIII 178, 254
Innocent XI 408
John II 253
John IV 62
John VIII 79
John XII 254
John XV 554
John XVIII 127
John XXII 138, 142, 236, 254, 366
Julius I, St. 20
Julius II 100, 177, 179, 180, 181, 182, 187, 582
Julius III 185, 216, 217, 219, 582
Leo I, St. 39-46, 77, 179, 378, 580
Leo II, St. 57, 61, 65, 580
Leo III, St. 75, 76
Leo IX, St. 81
Leo X 177, 180, 181, 183, 190, 254, 582
Leo XII 519
Leo XIII xvii, 204, 232, 234, 314, 338, 369, 370, 378, 380, 381, 460, 461, 463, 464, 466-468, 477, 504, 516, 517, 519, 523, 552
Liberius 21, 23, 24, 26, 251, 252, 254, 559
Lucius III 106
Marcellus II, St. 216, 217
Martin I, St. 62
Martin IV 126
Martin V 139, 158, 160, 581
Nicholas I, St. 76, 77
Nicholas II 87
Nicholas V 173
Paul III 185, 209, 216, 582
Paul IV 216, 222, 561, 562, 567
Paul V 443
Pelagius I 52, 55
Pelagius II 28
Pius IV 185, 216, 220, 222, 223, 225, 271, 512, 582
Pius V, St. 216, 225-227. 377, 378, 385, 389, 397, 406, 421, 430, 565
Pius VI 385, 519
Pius VII 519
Pius VIII 519
Pius IX 229-231, 234, 235, 240, 244-246, 248-250, 268, 269, 271, 273, 290, 353, 504, 506, 519, 520
Pius X, St. 100, 126, 271, 290, 291, 294, 295, 302, 334, 392, 425, 433, 510-512, 516 522
Pius XI 289, 314, 322, 345, 351, 353, 355, 356, 363, 509, 516, 544,
Pius XII 232, 271, 289, 290, 295, 298, 300, 314, 335, 341, 348, 350, 355, 369, 376, 379, 382, 383, 391, 502, 507, 519, 538, 560, 567
Pontian 127
Severinus 62
Silverius, St. 49, 50, 127
Sixtus IV 181
Stephen II 84
Sylvester I, St. 3, 8, 12, 580
Theodorus I 62
Urban IV 138
Urban V 142
Urban VI 143-146, 148, 254
Urban VIII 554
Vigilius 28, 47, 50-56, 254, 580
Postconciliar Popes:
   John XXIII 283, 284, 286, 295, 298, 299, 301-313, 318, 326, 332, 333, 335, 351, 384, 386, 389, 391, 418, 420, 502, 503, 522, 523, 529, 544, 561, 567
   Paul VI 298, 306-308, 310, 311, 318, 319, 328-330, 333, 334, 336-341, 351, 356, 357, 361, 365, 367, 384, 386, 396, 397, 400, 401, 405-407, 418, 419, 445-449, 456, 459, 460, 465, 476, 512, 527, 529, 542-544, 555, 567,
   John Paul I 306, 529-532, 543, 567
   John Paul II 305, 306, 308, 320, 321, 323, 325, 330, 338, 352, 359, 360, 361, 366, 384, 399, 415, 418, 419, 437, 439, 494, 509, 510, 513, 529, 533, 534, 539, 543-552, 554, 556-558, 566, 567
   Potamon of Egypt, Bishop 9
   Pothinus of Lyons, St. 120
Pope Leo XIII's Prayer to St. Michael 516, 579, 595, 596
Predestination 206
Presbyterians 398
Priest Shortage 486-489
Profession of Faith 13, 224, 225
Protestant Churches 186, 190, 192, 197-199, 207, 208, 216, 221, 258, 305, 312, 343, 345-348, 353, 357, 361, 362, 370, 371, 384, 385, 396-398, 406, 435, 482, 547, 550, 570, 572
Protestant Reformation 177, 184, 185, 186, 188, 207, 217, 307, 391, 570
Pulcheria, St. 43
Purcell of Cincinnati, Bishop 258
Purgatory 168, 170, 190, 215, 225, 438, 582, 587, 594
Puzyna, Cardinal of Krâkow 521
P-2 Lodge 531, 532,
Quakers 551

Quiroga, y Palacios, Fernando Cardinal 368
Quo Primum 227, 389, 397
Radini-Tedeschi, Bishop 295. 296
Rahner, S.J. Karl 309, 310, 327, 362
Rampolla Del Tindaro, Cardinal Mariano 521, 522
Raphael 162, 180, 241
Rappe, Bishop 267
Ratzinger, Joseph 309
Rauscher, Bishop Joseph 258
Raymond of Peñafort, St. 122
Raymond of Toulouse, King 593
Redemptorists 114, 249
Reformed Churches 551
Religious Indifferentism 250, 352, 561, 565
Religious Sisters 491,
Remigius of Rheims, St. 30
Renaissance 161, 162, 165, 171, 177, 184, 197, 208, 212, 241
Riccio, Bishop Luigi 267
Richard I of England, King 593
Richard II of England, King 141
Rimini (359 AD), Pseudo Council of 22, 588
Ritter, Joseph Cardinal 308
Robert Bellarmine, St. xiii, xix, 21, 249, 261, 275, 277, 560
Robert of Normandy, King 593
Roca, Canon 524. 525
Roman Curia 143, 181, 182, 187, 208, 212, 214, 222, 235, 240, 243, 283, 284, 324, 325, 327, 341, 384, 386
Roman Ritual 373
Rome (1084) (1089) (1098) (1412), Pseudo Councils of 88, 89,
Rosary 107, 109, 507-510
Ruffini, Ernesto Cardinal 325, 326
Runcie, Archbishop 552
Rupert, Emperor 149
Sacramentals 566, 576
Sacraments, Postconciliar:
  Anointing of the Sick 336, 364-366, 423, 474-477, 479
  Confirmation 446-449, 451, 453, 454, 478
  Holy Eucharist 478
  Holy Orders 467, 478
  Initiation (RCIA) 425, 427-430
  Ordination of Bishops 464-467
  Ordination of Priests 459-464
  Matrimony 454
  Reconciliation 339, 425, 435, 437
Sacraments, Traditional:
  Baptism 425, 427, 428, 430, 478
  Confirmation 445-453, 457, 468, 478, 479
  Extreme Unction 423, 474, 475, 476, 477, 478, 479
  Holy Eucharist 467, 478, 479
  Holy Orders 445, 450, 457-458, 460, 462, 463, 465, 467, 468, 479
    Consecration of Bishops 464, 465
    Ordination of Priests 457-459, 463
  Matrimony 453, 454,
  Penance 423, 429, 433, 434, 437, 438, 478
Saladin 132
Salvation Army 551
Satanism 369
Schillebeeckx, O.P., Edward 306, 309, 383
Schism xviii, xx, xxi, 312
Schismatic 233, 235, 241, 269, 276
Schmalkaldian League 219
Schwarzenberg, Bishop Friedrich 258
Second Constantinople—General Council 47-56, 580, 583
Second Council of Sirmium (357 AD), Pseudo Council 22, 588
Second Crusade 165, 593
Second Lateran—General Council 93-98, 333, 581, 583
Second Lyons—General Council 80, 123-126, 171, 312, 581, 583
Second Nicaea—General Council 67-74, 580, 583
Sede Vacante 123, 124, 127
Seleucia (359 AD), Pseudo Council of 22, 588
Seljuk Turks 131
Semi-Arian Heresy 17, 19, 22, 25
Serdica, Council of 20, 21
Sergius of Constantinople 58, 60-62, 64, 65, 253, 584
Seripando, Cardinal 220
Serra, Fr. Junipero 450
Servites 216
Shanahan, Bishop 267
Sheen, Archbishop Fulton 286, 287, 366, 372
Shepherd, Massey 396
Shintoism 360, 361, 547, 551
Sickingen, Franz von 192
Sigaud, Archbishop 319
Sigismund, Emperor 149, 150, 154-156, 163, 167
Sikhism 361, 547, 550, 551
Simeon, St. 556
Simon the Magician 86
Simony 86, 91, 92, 178, 180, 181, 222
Sin 424, 426, 429-441, 443-445, 448, 454, 459, 462, 469, 470, 474-477,
Sindona, Michele 531
Siri, Giuseppe Cardinal 325, 330
Sirmium, Council of 16, 22
Slipyi, Cardinal 320

Snake Worshippers 361
Social Gospel 288, 322, 334
Solzhenitsyn, Aleksandr 282
Sophronius of Jerusalem, St. 60
Spalding of Baltimore, Bishop
 250, 267
Spyridion of Cyprus, Bishop 9
St. Leo's *Tome* 42, 44
St. Palais, Bishop 267
St. Peter's Basilica 101,
 241-243, 266-268, 285, 554
Stalin, Joseph 287
Stephen, St. 473
Stépinac, Cardinal 314
Stritch, Samuel Cardinal 547
Strossmayer of Sirmio, Bishop
 258
Suarez, S.J. xix, 407
Suenens, Leo Cardinal 308, 326, 328, 329
Suhard, Emmanuel Cardinal 299
Suicide 500, 501
Suleiman the Magnificent 208
Syllabus of Errors 234-236, 259,
 290, 353, 368
Syrian, Rite of the Catholic Church
 375, 378, 411
Tanquerey, Fr. Adolfe 410
Taoism 361
Tarasius of Constantinople, St. 73
Tardini, Domenico Cardinal 283
Tartars 119
Tenrikyo 551
Tertullian 500
Testa, Gustavo Cardinal 336
Thant, U 338
Theatines 211
Theodehad of the Goths, King 49
Theodora, Empress 49, 50, 51
Theodore of Jerusalem, Patriach 71
Theodore of Mopsuestia 47, 48, 52, 580
Theodoret of Cyrrhus, Bishop 41, 43, 44,
 47, 48, 52, 53, 580
Theodosius I, Emperor 25-27
Theodosius II, Emperor 33, 35,
 37, 38, 40-43
Theophilus the Goth, Bishop 9
Thérèse of Lisieux, St. 554
Third Constantinople—General Council
 57-66, 545, 575, 580, 583
Third Lateran—General Council
 99-104, 581, 583
Third Secret of Fatima 501-504
Thomas à Becket, St. 92
Thomas Aquinas, St. 125, 226,
 378, 402, 404, 406, 408, 477
Thomas More, St. 201, 212, 554, 570-572
Three Chapters 48, 51-53, 580
Thurian, Max 396

Tisserant, Eugene Cardinal 318
Tito, Marshall 318, 339
Tlhagale, Archbishop 358
Toledo, Synod of 168
Tours, Council of 108
Trajan, Emperor 3
Transubstantiation 114, 115,
 141, 157, 225, 388, 402, 406, 587
Trent—General Council xiii,
 113, 150, 185-228, 240, 241,
 244, 249, 271, 307, 312, 325,
 326, 331, 367, 377, 378, 402,
 424, 429, 430, 457, 458, 474,
 475, 581, 583
Tridentine Latin Mass 375, 379, 402, 415,
 419, 422, 563
Troyes, Council of 131
Turrecremata, Cardinal 274
U.S. Catholic Schools 481,
 491-493, 500
Ulrich of Württemberg 194
Ulric, St. 554
Ultramontism 237, 238, 240, 255
Unam Sanctam 129
United Nations 338
Ursulines 211
Vaison, Council of 10
Valens, Emperor 15, 25
Valentine, St. 555
Valentinian II, Emperor 16
Vandals 29, 31
Vatican (1869-1870)—General Council
 229-279, 292, 293, 312, 323, 325,
 359, 578, 580
Vatican II 196, 200, 204,
 206, 241, 261, 279, 284, 285,
 287, 295, 302, 303, 306-311,
 314, 318, 322, 323, 334, 336,
 343, 344, 351-360, 362-364,
 371, 373, 376, 380, 381-390,
 392-393, 397, 398, 400, 403,
 406, 413-416, 419-421, 423-427,
 430-433, 435, 438, 439, 445,
 448, 451, 453, 455, 461, 462,
 466-468, 473-475, 477, 478,
 481, 484, 487, 489, 491, 494,
 497, 500, 509, 511-515, 525,
 526, 527, 529, 530, 540, 542,
 543, 548, 549, 559, 563-567
 569-572
 First Session 324-328
 Second Session 328-330
 Third Session 330-332
 Fourth Session 332
Vatican–Moscow Agreement 318
Venerius of Milan, Bishop 24
Victor Emmanuel II, King 231,
 233, 268, 269

Vienne-General Council
  127-138, 581, 583
Vietnam War 316, 339
Villot, Jean Cardinal 531
Vincent, St. 473
Vincent de Paul, St. 221
Vincent Ferrer, St. 146, 156
Vincent of Lerins, St. 279
Vinci, Leonardo da 162
Visigoths 29-31
Vitus, St. 555
Voltaire 343, 520
von Hildebrand, Alice 287, 290
von Kettler of Mainz, Bishop 258
von Senestrey of Ratisbon, Bishop 250
Voodooism 359-361, 533, 546, 550
Vouillé, Battle of 30
Vovk, Bishop Anton 321
Waldensian Heresy 103, 104,
  110, 114, 186, 197
Waldo, Peter 103, 104, 109
Wall Street Journal 304,
  323, 516, 550, 558
Walsh, Bishop 314
Weigel, Gustave 309, 541
Western Schism xviii, 131, 139,
  144-150, 156, 159, 160, 572, 581
Willebrands, Bishop Jan 308
William of Montferrata, King 593
Williams, Archbishop Rowan 551-553
Williams, Bishop 267
Wimmer, Abbot 267
Witchcraft 359, 369
Wojtyla, Archbishop Karol (John Paul II)
  308, 320, 321, 325, 534-543
Worker-Priest Movement 298,
  299, 309, 334
World Council of Churches 313,
  336, 338, 530, 551
World War I 316
World War II 299, 316
Wörms, Council of 88, 90, 92
Wright, Bishop Joseph 308
Wycliff, John 141, 156, 581, 587
Wyszynski, Stefan Cardinal
  320, 321, 538-540, 542
Ximenes, Cardinal 209
Yallop, David 531-533
Zakka, Patriarch Ignatius 545
Zoroastrianism 107, 361, 550, 551
Zwingli, Ulrich 185, 186,
  196, 197, 204, 205, 206, 208, 587
Zwinglian Heresy 197, 199, 205